Principles
of
Animal Cognition

William A. Roberts
University of Western Ontario

Boston, Massachusetts   Burr Ridge, Illinois   Dubuque, Iowa
Madison, Wisconsin   New York, New York   San Francisco, California   St. Louis, Missouri

McGraw-Hill

A Division of The McGraw·Hill Companies

PRINCIPLES OF ANIMAL COGNITION

This book is printed on acid-free paper.

1 2 3 4 5 6 7 8 9 0 DOC/DOC 9 0 9 8 7

ISBN 0-07-053138-2

Editorial director: *Jane Vaicunas*
Sponsoring editor: *Sharon Geary*
Marketing manager: *Jim Rozsa*
Project manager: *Margaret Rathke*
Production supervisor: *Heather D. Burbridge*
Senior designer: *Crispin Prebys*
Photo research coordinator: *Keri Johnson*
Compositor: *Shepherd Incorporated*
Typeface: *10/12 Palatino*
Printer: *R. R. Donnelley & Sons Company*

Library of Congress Cataloging-in-Publication Data

Roberts, William A. (William Albert), 1938–
    Principles of animal cognition / William A. Roberts.
      p.   cm.
    Includes index.
    ISBN 0-07-053138-2
      1. Cognition in animals.   I. Title.
    QL785.R495   1997
    591.5'1—dc21   97-5653

http://www.mhhe.com

*To Adrian and Verona,
Nancy and Doug, and
Jim and Suzanne*

Preface

The study of animal cognition has its roots in the 19th century and the theory of evolution proposed by Charles Darwin. As a natural extension of Darwin's theory, it was suggested that continuity of intellectual abilities should be found between humans and animals. Darwin and his colleague, Georges Romanes, pursued evidence of this continuity by amassing a large collection of stories or anecdotes about the intelligence of animals. Partly as a reaction to the excesses of this anecdotal approach to animal cognition, by the early years of the 20th century the study of animal psychology turned away from cognitive issues and toward a strong emphasis upon the study and control of behavior. The initial interest in a wide variety of cognitive processes narrowed to a concern with learning and motivational processes. Under the influence of the cognitive revolution in human psychology that arose in the 1960s, many scientists began to inquire again about the cognitive abilities of animals. However, investigators who now approached the study of animal cognition did so armed with powerful methodological tools for measurement and research design developed through behavioral investigations of learning. Over the past 25 years, vast strides have been made in our knowledge and understanding of animal cognition.

It is striking to me that, although a vast amount of research on animal cognition has been reported in books and journals over the past two decades, little of this information seems to have found its way into popular texts on psychology. For example, all introductory psychology textbooks have a chapter on learning that describes the details of classical and operant conditioning. The end of such chapters usually contains a section on "cognitive processes in learning." Typically, this section describes one or more of three studies: Kohler's studies of chimpanzee problem solving, the Tolman and Honzik latent learning study, and Harlow's discovery of learning-sets behavior in monkeys. Although all of these were important discoveries, they were all reported before 1950. The student might conclude that a few interesting instances of animal cognition were discovered in the first half of this century but that nothing of significance has been found since then. It is hoped that this book will help to correct this erroneous impression by disseminating the new, exciting findings being made in contemporary work on animal cognition.

In this text, I have tried to present current evidence about animal cognition in a systematic fashion. Although each chapter focuses primarily on recent developments, I have attempted to maintain an historical connection with earlier research by describing some of this formative work. The early chapters take a flow of information through the organism approach, by first discussing how animals perceive and attend to information, then how that information is held in working memory, and finally how information in working memory enters into learned associations that are stored in reference memory for later retrieval. The middle chapters deal with the processing of basic dimensions of human and animal experience: space, time, and number. The final chapters deal with what may be considered more advanced cognitive processes, under the headings of concept learning and primate cognition. The book has been written at a level that should be understandable to both advanced undergraduate university students and graduate students.

Thanks are owed to a number of people who helped in the production of this book. First, I want to thank my editor, Brian McKean, for taking an interest in the early chapters I sent to him and then seeing this project throught to the final text. Among the McGraw-Hill staff, I wish to thank Katy Redmond and Maggie Rathke for their tireless efforts to produce the book. I particularly want to thank the reviewers of earlier drafts of these chapters, each of whom helped to vastly improve them. My thanks to Jerry Cohen, Roger Mellgren, Sara Shettleworth, and Tom Zentall, and particularly to Russ Church and Vern Honig, both of whom provided detailed, page-by-page feedback. Thanks are also due to the reviewers of this title: Thomas Zentall, University of Kentucky; Russell M. Church, Brown University, Werner Honing, Dalhousie University; Jerome S. Cohen, University of Windsor; Roger L. Mellgren, University of Texas, Arlington; and Sara J. Shettleworth, University of Toronto. Finally, I wish to thank my wife, Nancy, who somehow remained patient during the endless hours during which I closeted myself to write this present volume.

William A. Roberts
London, Ontario, Canada

Brief Contents

Contents

8. Timing   241

9. Serial Learning and Memory   266

10. Numerical Processing

Introduction: History and Some Conceptual Issues

When asked, many people will render an opinion about animal cognition. Often, these opinions concern particular animals individuals have had prolonged contact with, usually pets. Claims for intelligence in dogs and cats range over a number of abilities, including the ability to learn, to remember, to feel emotion, to reason, to count, to dream, to understand spoken human language, and to communicate. People's willingness to ascribe such capacities to animals appears to vary with the perceived complexity of the ability. Rasmussen, Rajecki, and Craft (1993) found that university students rated some abilities as more reasonable to attribute to animals than others. Those capabilities rated most likely to be found in dogs and cats were the abilities to experience sensations and perceptions, experience pleasure and displeasure, have emotions, show gratitude, and play and imagine. Those capacities rated as less likely to be found in animals were conservation of quantity, enumeration and sorting, memory and foresight, formation of schemata or categories, morality, dreaming, and object permanence.

It may be argued that such attributions of mental life to animals are based on reasonable inferences from their behavior. My cat leaps on my bed early in the morning and proceeds to pace up and down purring until I rise and prepare her morning meal. Is it not reasonable to suggest that she understands that her activities will awaken me and that she can envision my rising and preparing her food? Many dogs seem to wait patiently at the door for the mailman to arrive and then bark ferociously until he leaves. The dog appears to anticipate the daily appearance of this unwanted intruder who must be driven off its property. During sleep, an animal may be seen to wince or to strike out with its limbs. Just as people are often seen to respond behaviorally to their dreams, the animal's behavior may reflect the internal experience of a fearful dream. These examples and many others suggest a rich depth of cognitive experience in animals.

The examples just described are examples of *anthropomorphism*, or reading human experience into animal behavior. From a reductionist point of view, we may need to make none of these assumptions about knowledge or foresight in

1

animals. We know that animals have nervous systems and that those nervous systems have innate reflexes and are capable of learning new associations. Nothing further is needed to explain animal behavior. My cat may leap on me in the morning not because she understands that this will awaken me and cause me to get her food but because the internal drive of hunger elicits a conditioned response of jumping on the bed, which is then reinforced by the delivery of food. Similarly, a dog may wait at the door and bark at the mailman because the internal state of its nervous system at that time of day has become conditioned to elicit an instinctual defensive response of barking when a foreign organism appears. Finally, animals may emit behaviors while sleeping not because they are dreaming but because random firings of neurons cause them to make involuntary responses.

These quite opposite points of view about animal behavior often are held dogmatically by both laymen and scientists as matters of fact. Although people also may express a variety of opinions about human nature, such opinions often can be confirmed or countered by reference to scientific studies reported in a psychology textbook. Discussions about the bases of human behavior often are informed by the fact that the discussants have taken at least an introductory course in human psychology. However, the same cannot be said for discussions of animal psychology. More often, these discussions are informed only by anecdotes and personal observations of a pet's behavior. However, many claims about animal abilities need not be so uninformed. The contents of this book will provide scientific evidence about cognitive processes in animals. Although much remains to be known about this topic, considerable evidence has accumulated in the past 25 years that takes a discussion of animal cognition far beyond arguments from anecdotes and personal observations.

Interestingly, the two polar points of view about animal cognition expressed earlier can be found to have been held by different philosophers and scientists for hundreds of years. Both the belief that animals have most of the cognitive abilities of humans and that animals are basically automata have been proposed by eminent scholars. The following section provides a brief historical review of these individuals and their positions.

A HISTORICAL REVIEW OF THE ANIMAL COGNITION QUESTION

In his classification of animals, Aristotle attributed both intelligence and morality to beasts:

> Men and mules are usually tame. The ox is gentle, the boar is violent. The serpent is crafty, the lion is noble and generous. Bears carry off their cubs at a sign of danger. Dolphins are to be commended for their extraordinary love of their young. Of all the animals Aristotle discussed, the lion and elephant are by far his favorites. The lion is described as gentle when not hungry, and never suspicious. The elephant is assigned the palm of wisdom, for he is a creature abounding in intellect, kindness, and fine memory (Vicchio, 1986, p. 193).

Although animals were thus praised in many ways by Aristotle, they were still viewed as not possessing the capacity for reason found in humans. In this respect, animals were only a pale imitation of people, although they were held to exceed humans in some of their sensory abilities (Pellegrin, 1986).

Over the ensuing centuries, various positions on animal cognition are found. The Roman Neoplatonic philosopher, Plotinus, stated that animals have souls and intelligence and should not be killed or eaten. Celsus, a Christian heretic, suggested also that animals had souls and could reason. He argued that animals appear different from people only from people's point of view; from a more objective external viewpoint, little difference would be seen. Notwithstanding these arguments of early philosophers, animals were seen within the Christian tradition as below men in the "Great Chain of Being." Animals were viewed as missing the rational element of the soul. Strangely, however, animals often were held accountable for moral transgressions. In the Middle Ages, cats, pigs, and even insects were put on trial for various crimes (Vicchio, 1986).

The philosopher Rene Descartes (1596–1650) presented an important theory of both the human mind and the difference between human and animal species. Descartes' position is often known as *mind-body dualism.* He held that much of human behavior is controlled by automatic response processes or reflexes. Thus, sensory stimulation may elicit *involuntary* reflexive responses. Other behavior may be *voluntary* or willed by the individual. Voluntary responses arise from the mind or the soul and give rise to a person's ability to respond flexibly in different situations. Conscious choice then arises from the mind, but the mind was held to be immaterial or noncorporeal. How does the mind then affect the body? Through his knowledge of anatomy, Descartes postulated that mind-body interaction took place in the pineal gland of the brain. At the pineal gland, or "conarium," voluntary thoughts arising in the mind were channeled into physical messages carried to the muscles.

Animals, on the other hand, were held to have no mind and thus to be incapable of thought and voluntary action. Animals were viewed as automata, capable only of fixed or reflexive responses to sensory stimulation. Furthermore, Descartes believed that humans, but not animals, were provided with certain universal truths as innate ideas. These included the ideas of God, self, and geometrical axioms and the conceptions of space, time, and motion (Boring, 1950).

Charles Darwin and the Descent of Man

Descartes' position regarding the absence of cognition in animals as compared with people was to hold sway until it was challenged in an important way by Charles Darwin (1809–1882). In his theory of evolution by natural selection, Darwin suggested that species evolved from other species as an adaptational process (Darwin, 1859). Variations in organisms that promoted their fitness or survival were passed to their offspring and thus spread through a population. Darwin found clear evidence for his theory in the morphological or structural characteristics of different species. The bone structure and organs of species living in close geographical proximity often were found to be highly similar or *homologous,* suggesting that these animals were descended as variants from a common ancestor.

Two further important implications followed from Darwin's theory. One was that we should find differences and similarities in behavior and psychological processes between species that parallel those found in morphological characteristics. In particular, if it is assumed that the nervous system is responsible for psychological processes, similar processes should be found in species with similar nervous systems. The second implication was that man himself was an animal that had been descended from other animals. In his day, Darwin was accused of suggesting that humans had descended from modern monkeys or apes. A more modern theory is that contemporary humans and apes descended from a common ancestor that lived some millions of years ago. (See Chapter 12 for a discussion of primate evolution and cognition.)

When these two ideas were combined, they led to a conclusion that is often referred to as the *continuity hypothesis*. This hypothesis suggests that we should be able to find psychological and behavioral continuity between humans and animals. As Darwin stated, " . . . differences in mind between man and the higher animals, great as it is, is certainly one of degree and not of kind" (Darwin, 1871, p. 105). If Homo sapiens evolved from an animal form, evidence for our continuity with animals should appear in the form of human-like psychological processes in animals. Darwin embarked upon a quest for evidence of continuity through a procedure that has been called the *anecdotal method*. This method involved collecting a number of anecdotes or stories about animal behavior from people who had considerable commerce with animals, such as pet owners, zoo keepers, and hunters.

Evidence for the continuity of intelligence between humans and animals was reported in a book written by Darwin in 1871, *The Descent of Man and Selection in Relation to Sex*. Numerous stories of intelligent behavior in animals were reported. It was claimed that this evidence showed that animals possessed most of the psychological faculties found in people, such as emotion, wonder, curiosity, imagination, reason, language, a sense of beauty, and a belief in God. As an example of reasoning, the case was reported of a New World monkey that was frequently given lumps of sugar wrapped in paper. The monkey avidly unwrapped these packages to obtain the sugar. However, on occasion, the monkey's trainer would substitute a wasp for the sugar. After being stung once by a hidden wasp, the monkey was reported to always hold the unopened package to its ear to listen for any sounds of movement before opening the wrapping. With regard to the possibility that animals might have a primitive conception of God, Darwin cited the case of a dog lying on a lawn near an open parasol. On occasion, the breeze would cause the parasol to move slightly, and this movement, in turn, caused the dog to growl and bark fiercely. Darwin suggested that the apparently spontaneous movement of the parasol may have caused the dog to reason unconsciously that some strange spiritual or living agent had invaded its territory.

George J. Romanes

A colleague and close friend of Darwin, George J. Romanes, also promoted the continuity argument. In his best-known book, *Animal Intelligence* (Romanes, 1882), he also presented the case for humanlike intelligence in animals. He suggested that for the evolutionist's theory, "there must be a psychological, no less than a physiological, continuity extending throughout the length and breadth of the animal kingdom" (p. 10). Romanes made a clear distinction between the *subjective* and *objective* analyses of mind. Subjective analysis refers to the fact that each person can analyze her mind through *introspection*, or examining the contents of her thoughts. When studying another person or an animal, however, we are limited to an objective analysis of that organism's behavior. The contents or activities of the organism's mind must be inferred from its activities. As Romanes put it, behavioral activity was the *ambassador of the mind.*

Much as Darwin had done in his book, Romanes presented anecdotal evidence for intelligent behavior in animals from protozoa to primates. For example, numerous stories of dog intelligence were presented. A dog not fed at its usual time was reported to go to the closet and fetch its food cup in its teeth and bring it to its mistress's feet. In another case, a man having fallen in a river was saved when his dog ran to a village and prevailed upon another man to follow it to the river by pulling on his coat. A report was made of a dog that was tied up at night for fear it might chase and/or slaughter sheep. When secretly observed, the dog was seen to slip its collar, and, after being absent for several hours chasing sheep, to return and slip into its collar in order to avoid suspicion.

Considerable social intelligence was attributed to primates, as indicated by the following report:

> A Cape baboon having taken off with some clothes from the barracks, I formed a party to recover them. With twenty men I made a circuit to cut them off from the caverns, to which they always fled for shelter. They observed my movements, and detaching about fifty to guard the entrance, the others kept their post. We could see them collecting large stones and other missiles. One old grey-headed one, who had often paid us a visit at the barracks, was seen distributing his orders, as if a general. We rushed on to the attack, when, at a scream from him, they rolled down enormous stones on us, so that we were forced to give up the contest (Romanes, 1882, p. 483).

Although these stories were seen as strong evidence in support of the continuity hypothesis by Romanes, they were to be seriously questioned as the basis for scientific conclusions by other investigators. What were the shortcomings of the anecdotal method? To begin with, the stories reported were often witnessed or reported by a single individual. The veracity of the individual's observations might then be questioned. Although Romanes attempted to obtain reports from reliable individuals, many of those who reported were not trained scientific observers. In addition, there is a tendency to embellish a good story. Details of the original observation may have been changed to enhance the apparent intelligence of the animal's behavior. Remember also that many of these reports were second- or third-hand by the time they reached Romanes. The psychology of rumor indicates that stories become progressively more exaggerated as they are told to successive individuals.

Suppose, however, that we could assume that such anecdotal reports were true. What could be made of them? In this case, we run into the problem of coincidence and a selection bias for unusual cases. Given a large number of animals of different species performing acts of behavior, it is perhaps not surprising that some of these acts will appear to be intelligent to a human observer. A complete accounting of all the animals performing in a given situation might show that 99 percent of the behaviors shown reflect stupidity or no evidence of intelligence, with only the remaining 1 percent appearing intelligent. A single case of behavior that appears to be highly intelligent might result from a single animal that is more intelligent than other members of its species, but it also might be a case of a behavior that just happened to look intelligent to a human but was not the consequence of an intelligent thought process. The social consequences of the remarkable and unremarkable observation are quite different. The infrequent observation of "intelligent behavior" becomes the circulating anecdote, while the frequent observation of unintelligent behavior is reported to no one because it does not violate people's expectations.

In Romanes' defense, it should be pointed out that he was not insensitive to the shortcomings of anecdotes. He wrote in his preface that "If the present work is read without reference to its ultimate object of supplying facts for the subsequent deduction of principles, it may well seem but a small improvement upon the works of the anecdote-mongers" (Romanes, 1882, p. vii). He pointed out that the use of anecdotes was the only method at his disposal and perhaps felt that the sheer weight of the evidence he presented would provide a synthesis in favor of the continuity position. Unfortunately for Romanes, history has judged his use of anecdotes harshly. Much of the subsequent theoretical and methodological work in the field of experimental animal behavior arose as a reaction against the anecdotal method.

C. Lloyd Morgan

Another well-known British psychologist, C. Lloyd Morgan, acted as an important counterweight to the excesses of interpretation Darwin and Romanes were led to by reliance on anecdotes (Wasserman, 1981, 1984). Morgan's position on questions concerning animal intelligence was presented in a volume entitled *An Introduction to Comparative Psychology* (Morgan, 1906). In this book, Morgan made clear the modern evolutionist's position of *monism*. In contrast to the dualist model advanced by Descartes, both mind and body were held to be a product of evolution. Psychological processes in all organisms were to be considered a product of the activities of the nervous system.

Much in the same vein as Romanes had discussed subjective and objective analyses of other minds, Morgan pointed out that inferences about the animal mind required a *double inductive process.* His diagram of this process, shown in Figure 1.1, required both objective induction and subjective induction. In Figure 1.1, the line from a to b represents a sequence of behaviors performed by another organism (animal) and perceived by the observer (objective induction). In addition, the psychologist responds to such objective observations with scientific hypotheses to account for the behavior; this sequence of ideas is represented as the line from c to d (subjective induction). The objective facts of behavior then are interpreted through hypotheses about the laws of mind as understood by the psychologist. Morgan fully realized that such a double inductive approach easily could lead to an interpretation of animal behavior as reflecting the most advanced psychological processes found in people. To curb

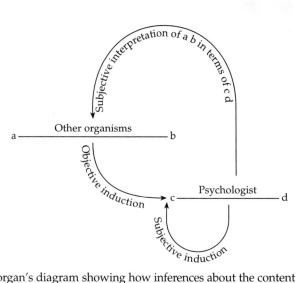

FIGURE 1.1. Morgan's diagram showing how inferences about the content and workings of the animal mind must involve a double inductive process, involving first objective induction and then subjective induction.
From Morgan, 1906.

this possibility, he introduced a basic principle for interpreting observed activity that has become known as *Morgan's Canon*. Morgan's canon states that "In no case may we interpret an action as the outcome of the exercise of a higher psychical faculty, if it can be interpreted as the outcome of the exercise of one which stands lower in the psychological scale" (Morgan, 1906, p. 53). This important principle often has been interpreted to mean that we should always exhaust simpler explanations of a phenomenon before turning to more elaborate interpretations. However, this is not exactly what Morgan intended in his famous canon (Burghardt, 1985). The canon was intended as a principle for interpreting animal behavior in terms of a hierarchy of mental processes, which varied in their degree of evolutionary advancement. If a less advanced process could explain an observed behavior, then a more advanced one should not be invoked.

In several tests of animal intelligence, Morgan applied his canon. He reported some experiments in which a Scotch terrier dog, which had been trained to retrieve sticks, was tested for its ability to go through a gap in a fence with a stick clutched in its mouth. The problem for the dog was that the stick was too wide for the gap and would hit the fence posts if carried at its middle. Even after many attempts, dogs often still grasped the stick at its center and blundered against the fence uprights. Morgan stated that he had no doubt dogs eventually would learn how to avoid this pitfall, but he suggested they would only acquire the solution by trial and error and not by reason. Morgan also observed how his fox terrier, Tony, learned to open the gate on his fence, thus allowing him to enter the road where cats could be chased and other dogs sniffed. Tony apparently by accident put his head between the gate and fence post and raised it, opening the latch and allowing the gate to swing open. Upon subsequent opportunities, Tony only gradually perfected the gate-opening technique, often going to other openings in the fence before finding the right one. Morgan suggested that the dog learned by trial and error, with no understanding of the relationship between the operation of the latch and the gate swinging open.

The contrast between Morgan's interpretation of the behaviors he observed in animals and the interpretation of anecdotes offered by Darwin and Romanes is striking. Morgan's application of his canon led him to conclude that there is scarce evidence of reasoning in animals. Yet, an examination of Morgan's canon does give rise to some concerns. The suggestion that behaviors should always be attributed to the lowest faculty or process on the psychological scale implies that there is such a scale that orders psychological abilities from lowest to highest. For Morgan, lower faculties were instincts or learned associations, and higher faculties were those used by humans to make inferences and form relationships. However, beyond such rough-and-ready assumptions, it is not at all clear that such a scale exists nor that one could be constructed. One possibility would be to use the evolutionary age of a process to establish a scale, with the oldest processes being the most primitive and the most recent processes being the most advanced. Another possibility might be to use neural circuitry, with processes that use a greater number of circuits being more advanced than those that use fewer circuits. Unfortunately, both of these possibilities run into the fact that we simply do not have sufficient information about either the evolutionary history or the neural apparatus underlying psychological processes to begin to establish a ranking.

An alternative possibility is to use the theoretical complexity of psychological processes to establish a scale. Processes that are theorized to require more stages of processing would be considered higher than those that require fewer stages of processing. The value of such an approach depends on how valid we feel our theoretical models are. At the current stage of psychological science, theories designed to explain a set of phenomena may conflict in their degree of complexity. A good example will be seen in Chapter 10 on numerical processing. With respect to the question of counting in animals, one theoretical position argues that counting is at the upper boundary of an animal's abilities. This theory would argue that counting should be placed near the top of the psychological scale. An alternative theory argues just the contrary—that counting is basic and occurs commonly and automatically in animals. This theory would place counting near the bottom of the psychological scale. If we are in disagreement about which processes are higher and lower on a psychological scale, the application of Morgan's canon becomes very difficult indeed.

A second concern with Morgan's canon is that it might lead to error in the explanation of animal behavior. With enough intellectual effort, virtually any behavior can be explained by what we may consider simpler processes. Too rigorous an application of Morgan's canon might then lead us to overlook a valid explanation in terms of a higher process.

Despite these criticisms of Morgan's canon, the general principle that we should consider alternative accounts of a phenomenon has served animal psychology well. As methods for experimental investigation developed with increasing sophistication, it became possible to test the hypothesis that a particular mechanism was responsible for a behavioral result. An experiment

FIGURE 1.2. A photograph taken of Clever Hans and Mr. von Osten. On the left side of the picture are a drawing board on which problems could be presented to Hans and an alphabet board that could be used to spell out answers to questions that required a written answer.
From Pfungst, 1965.

could be arranged that controlled or prevented the use of this mechanism. If the behavior occurred under these conditions, this mechanism could not have been responsible for it and could be ruled out. If the behavior did not occur, however, the hypothesis that the mechanism was responsible for the behavior was strengthened.

The Clever Hans Affair

A good example of the resolution of an issue in animal behavior by testing an alternative hypothesis is seen in the case of Clever Hans (Pfungst, 1965). Clever Hans was a Russian trotting horse owned by an elderly German former school teacher named von Osten. von Osten had trained several horses, but Hans appeared to show intellectual powers far beyond those other horses had revealed and far beyond human expectations for a horse. A picture of Clever Hans and Von Osten is shown in Figure 1.2, along with an alphabet table and a writing board on which Hans could be asked questions. When asked questions in several different areas, including mathematics, language, and music, Hans correctly answered by tapping his foot. Thus, asked to add, subtract, multiply, or divide a set of numbers, Hans would begin to tap on the ground and only stop tapping when he had completed the number of taps that corresponded to the correct answer. Hans could even solve fractions by first tapping out the

Method	Number Exposed	Number Tapped
Without knowledge	8	14
With knowledge	8	8
Without knowledge	4	8
With knowledge	4	4
Without knowledge	7	9
With knowledge	7	7
Without knowledge	10	17
With knowledge	10	10
Without knowledge	3	9
With knowledge	3	3 etc.

FIGURE 1.3. Some results from tests of Hans' ability to correctly tap out a number shown to him. With- and without-knowledge tests refer to trials when the tester could or could not see the number shown to Hans.
From Pfungst, 1965.

numerator and then the denominator. The horse also could read German and reply to questions with German words by using the alphabet table shown in Figure 1.2. Each letter of Hans' reply was indicated by tapping out the numbers of the row and column that contained a particular letter or diphthong. In the field of music, Hans could recognize notes played to him and could indicate which notes should be omitted or replaced to correct a dissonant phrase. Needless to say, Hans' fame grew as he became a major celebrity in the city of Berlin and became known worldwide as the famous horse that could write.

By 1904, Hans' popularity had grown to the point that a commission was appointed to investigate his abilities. Known as the September Commission, it contained both academics and several individuals who had worked as animal trainers (Candland, 1993). Members of the September Commission were quite sensitive to the possibility that Hans might be receiving signals from his trainer. However, the Commission concluded that there was no evidence that Hans was replying accurately to questions through trickery or secret cues. One point that was particularly convincing was the fact that Hans could answer correctly to questions posed by other trainers, in the absence of von Osten.

One member of the September Commission, Carl Stumpf, was not completely satisfied with the Commission's conclusion. Stumpf was a professor in Berlin and asked his student, Oskar Pfungst, to carry out a study of Clever Hans' behavior. Pfungst remained unconvinced that Hans was not responding to cues provided by his trainer. To test the cuing hypothesis, Pfungst carried out several experiments that controlled for the use of cues from a human source. In one critical test, Hans was asked to tap out a number shown to him on a card. On alternate trials, the card was shown with and without the knowledge of the tester; that is, the questioner saw the number before it was shown to Hans on with-knowledge trials but did not see the number on without-knowledge trials. The results of some of these tests are shown in Figure 1.3. It can be seen readily that Hans tapped out the precise number on with-knowledge trials and considerably overestimated the correct number on without-knowledge trials. In another set of tests, Hans was fitted with large blinders. On some tests, it was observed that these blinders clearly prevented Hans from seeing the tester, while on other trials he could see the tester. On tester-seen trials, Hans was correct on 89 percent of the tests, but on tester-not-seen trials, Hans responded correctly on only 6 percent of the tests. Pfungst concluded from his experiments that "Hans can neither read, count, nor make calculations. He knows nothing of coins or cards, calendars or clocks, nor can he respond, by tapping or otherwise, to a number spoken to him but a moment before. Finally, he has not a trace of musical ability" (Pfungst, 1965, p. 40).

How then did the tester convey the correct answer to Hans? Pfungst concluded that von Osten, and other questioners, signaled the appropriate time to start and stop tapping by slight changes in body posture:

> These signs are minimal movements of the head on the part of the experimenter. As soon as the experimenter had given a problem to the horse, he, involuntarily, bent his head and trunk slightly forward and the horse would then put the right foot forward and begin to tap, without, however, returning it each time to its original position. As soon as the desired number of taps was given, the questioner would make a slight upward jerk of the head. Thereupon the horse would immediately swing his foot in a wide circle, bringing it back to its original position (Pfungst, 1965, p. 47).

It should be emphasized that cues were not given to Hans intentionally. The experimenters were quite unaware that changes in their posture were acting as signals to the horse. We might say that Hans was reading the unintentional "body language" of the testers. A rather bizarre footnote to the Clever Hans affair indicates lack of complicity on von Osten's part in Hans' cuing. Upon the publication of Pfungst's book on Clever Hans, von Osten showed considerable upset, but not at his failure to understand the basis of Hans' performance. Rather, he directed his anger at Hans, who he felt had intentionally exploited and deceived him (Candland, 1993).

Two important points should be made about the Clever Hans episode. First, it occurred at a pivotal moment in the history of animal psychology. At the turn of the century, many were influenced by instances of humanlike intelligence in animals reported in anecdotes. In addition to Hans, there were several other animals in North America and Europe that were reported to be capable of amazing feats of intelligence (Candland, 1993). A dog could bark out the answers to questions, and a horse was capable of mind reading. Unlike the case of Hans, the behavior of some of these wondrous animals undoubtedly was the product of intentional tricks taught by a trainer. In any case, the discovery that Hans was not capable of human thought but was only responding to a simple cue acted as an important counteracting influence to unbridled speculation about the powers of the animal mind.

Secondly, the case of Clever Hans has had an important lasting influence on animal research throughout the 20th century. Most animal researchers are well aware of "Clever-Hans cues" and take pains to make sure they are eliminated through control procedures. Those who do not use controls for unintentional experimenter cues given to an animal subject have the need for such controls pointed out to them by their peers.

Edward L. Thorndike

Edward L. Thorndike is widely known as the first scientist to bring the problem of animal intelligence into the laboratory for experimental study. He clearly saw a need for objective tests of intelligent behavior in animals that would allow quantification and replication. Thorndike was scathing in his attack on the anecdotal method. In his famous report of his experiments, *Animal Intelligence* (Thorndike, 1911), he pointed out that "most of the books do not give us a psychology, but rather a *eulogy* of animals. They have all been about animal *intelligence,* never about animal *stupidity*" (p. 22). He saw the anecdotal method as totally failing to provide an analytical and objective depiction of animal intelligence. If other sciences proceeded in this manner, he argued, astronomers would satisfy themselves with marveling at how large the stars were, and bacteriologists would only want to describe how very little microbes were. He also satirized the selectivity of anecdotes:

> Dogs get lost hundreds of times and no one ever notices it or sends an account of it to a scientific magazine. But let one find his way from Brooklyn to Yonkers and the fact immediately becomes a circulating anecdote. Thousands of cats on thousands of occasions sit helplessly yowling and no one takes thought of it or writes to his friend, the professor; but let one cat claw at the knob of a door supposedly as a signal to be let out, and straightway this cat becomes the representative of the cat-mind in all the books (p. 24).

Thorndike pointed out that "The level-headed thinkers who might have won valuable results have contented themselves with arguing against the theories of the eulogists. They have not made investigations of their own" (p. 23). He set out to rectify this state of affairs by carrying out the first experimental studies of learning in animals. Thorndike's experiments testing cats in his problem boxes are described in Chapter 5 on associative learning. The important upshot of Thorndike's work was his conclusion that animals do not learn by insight or reason. Instead, he argued, the animals he studied learned by strengthening connections between sensory impressions and impulses to action. Furthermore, all animals, including humans, may learn in the same way. Thus, Thorndike arrived at a theoretical position of continuity between humans and animals, but it was a very different form of continuity from that envisioned by Darwin and Romanes. Where Darwin and Romanes saw reason in all species of animals, Thorndike saw the strengthing of stimulus-response bonds caused by repetition and reinforcement.

The Advent of Behaviorism

Throughout the second half of the 19th century and into the early 20th century, there was considerable interest in the animal mind. As we have seen, various forms of evidence were advanced that led to speculation about animal thoughts and about the intellectual abilities of animals. Lloyd Morgan discussed the "wave of consciousness" in humans and animals and suggested that animals associate ideas that simultaneously enter consciousness (Morgan, 1906). Even Thorndike entertained questions about the association of ideas in humans and animals (Thorndike, 1911). This concern with the animal mind was in keeping with the early experimental approach to study of the human mind. The psychology of structuralism began in Germany under Wilhelm Wundt and was further developed in America by his student, Edward Titchener. Structuralism emphasized an investigation of the sensory and associative structures of the human mind through the method of *introspection.* A trained human observer would introspect by looking within his mind and describing its contents. Because animals did not have language, they could not be trained to introspect. Thus, those interested in the animal mind could only speculate on its contents.

The pioneering research of Thorndike and others began a movement toward the use of carefully measured behavior to study questions about animal intelligence. This work was part of a general trend in North America toward the use of behavioral tests in psychological studies of animals and people. For example, preverbal infants, like animals, could not be asked to introspect, but their motor behavior still could be studied. Beyond the practical advantages of studying behavior, many North American psychologists saw theoretical advantages to making psychology the study of behavior. The problem seen with introspection was that only the person doing the introspecting could see the contents of her mind. How do we know those observations are valid or reliable? On the other hand, behavior could be observed and quantified by numerous observers. By carrying out experiments in which the experimenter varied the conditions of stimulation and observed their effects on behavior, laws relating performance to environment could be found, and these laws would form the basis for a new behavioral psychology.

These revolutionary currents in North American psychology were expressed clearly in the so-called behaviorist manifesto, issued by John B. Watson in 1913. In 1913, Watson published a paper entitled "Psychology as the Behaviorist Views It." In this article and in several books that followed, Watson argued that only behavior should be the subject matter of psychology. Mentalistic concepts such as consciousness, mind, and imagery had no place in an objective science since these events were available only to private experience. Watson emphasized the importance of learning in psychology and argued the empiricist position that both human and animal behavior could be substantially modified by the learning of new stimulus-response habits. This emphasis on learning was a natural extension of Thorndike's work with animals and his connectionist theory. Watson argued that even mentalistic terms might be reinterpreted as behavior. Thus, he theorized that thought may be nothing more than covert movements of the vocal musculature.

The effect of the behaviorist revolution on animal psychology was to rapidly funnel research toward an investigation of learned stimulus-response (S-R) associations. (The growth of the S-R psychology of learning and its discoveries is covered in Chapter 5 on associative learning.) The previous interest in the animal mind and in cognitive abilities of animals dwindled as interest in habit learning grew. It became a guiding belief of the new behaviorism that virtually all instances of intelligent behavior in animals would be explained on the basis of learned responses. In Europe, the development of the science of ethology had a similar effect on studies of animal cognition; many animal behavior researchers turned toward accounts of behavior in terms of innate response patterns released by sign stimuli (e.g., N. Tinbergen, 1960a).

The emphasis placed on behavior as the subject matter of psychology by Watson was carried even further in the theoretical approach of B. F. Skinner (Skinner, 1953, 1974). Although Watson had suggested that stimulus-response associations formed the basis for learning, Skinner eschewed any theorizing about internal processes, either cognitions or associations. Skinner's behaviorism focused on operant responses that were emitted by organisms and modified in strength by the consequences that followed them. Many of Skinner's ideas and contributions to research in animal learning are covered in Chapter 5. His approach has been particularly influential in the development of the applied psychology of behavior modification. The use of schedules of reinforcement to modify behavior is now common in many areas, including language acquisition, therapies applied to maladaptive behavior, and classroom teaching.

Among prominent learning theorists, the one individual who maintained a strong interest in cognitive processes in animals was Edward Tolman. In an important book, *Purposive Behavior in Animals and Men* (1932), and in numerous articles, Tolman developed a system of psychology in which animal behavior was understood as a product of such cognitive processes as *expectancies* and *cognitive maps.* Tolman's ideas were not a return to the 19th-century enterprise of speculating about the contents of the animal mind. He remained firmly within the behaviorist tradition of Thorndike and Watson by defining cognitive terms as *intervening variables,* which were operationally defined in terms of observable stimulus and response events (Tolman, 1938).

The Return of Interest in Animal Cognition

With the exception of Tolman, interest in animal cognition lay dormant until the late 1960s and early 1970s. As the renewed interest in memory, language, and thinking was defining the cognitive revolution in human psychology, the pendulum that had swung far away from the earlier interest in animal cognition, which had existed at the turn of the century, now began to swing in the opposite direction. Papers on language, memory, spatial cognition, timing, and other cognitive topics in animal behavior began to appear frequently in journals concerned with the experimental psychology of animal behavior, and several books containing chapters on animal cognition by prominent researchers served to promote the field (Honig & James, 1971; Hulse, Fowler, & Honig, 1978; Roitblat, Bever, & Terrace, 1984). This renaissance of interest in animal cognition has led to considerable new information and theory about how animals process information. Much of this new work is presented in the following chapters of this text. It should be emphasized that this new look at animal cognition is very different from the one found 100 years ago. Researchers interested in animal cognition have been steeped in the behaviorist tradition. Their research involves careful measurement of behavior using equipment, techniques, and control procedures that have been developed over decades of behavioral research on animals. Furthermore, theoretical models of cognitive processes in animals are based on closely reasoned inference from behavioral observations.

SOME CONCEPTUAL ISSUES
IN ANIMAL COGNITION

15

CHAPTER 1
Introduction:
History and Some
Conceptual Issues

The Question of Animal Consciousness

As the preceding section illustrated, concern with the conscious contents of the animal mind was common 100 years ago. Not only did Darwin and Romanes liberally attribute humanlike consciousness to animals, but critics of the anecdotal method, such as Morgan and Thorndike, discussed conscious ideas in animals. With the arrival of the behaviorist revolution, concern with consciousness in animals became virtually a taboo topic. If learned responses could explain everything, there was no need to appeal to a conscious mind. Even the new cognitive movement in animal psychology largely has not addressed the question of animal consciousness.

Cognitive Ethology

Outside the field of animal psychology, however, interest in animal consciousness has been renewed within the field of *cognitive ethology*. As the acknowledged leader of this field, Donald Griffin has argued strongly for recognition of animal minds in three books and several articles (Griffin, 1981, 1984, 1991, 1992). Much as Darwin did many years ago, Griffin has raised the possibility of continuity of mental life between humans and animals. This position was argued in several ways. First, humans are an evolved species, just as other animals are. Therefore, there are many similarities in the neurological structure of humans and animals. At the molecular level, we share the same form of communication by neurons, and, at the molar anatomical level, many animals, especially primates, have brain structures similar to humans. This similarity of neural mechanisms should then lead to similarity of information processing and awareness of the environment. A second argument involves the complexity of animal behavior. The fact that animals have been observed to perform complex behaviors involving communication, reasoning, and tool use appears to demand consciousness. How could animals plan and carry out such complex behaviors without being aware of them? A final argument concerns the functional value of consciousness. If consciousness has promoted human survival or fitness by allowing people to anticipate the consequences of their actions, then consciousness should similarly promote the survival of other species.

Griffin particularly opposes two alternative beliefs about consciousness, *epiphenomenalism* and *species solipsism*. Epiphenomenalism is the suggestion that, although conscious thoughts may exist in people and animals, they have no causal control over behavior. To the contrary, Griffin argues that conscious planning is an important causal component in many of the complex and novel behaviors seen in people and animals. Species solipsism is the belief that only humans, and no other species, have conscious awareness of the world. Such a position has obvious associations with Cartesian dualism and is strongly rejected by Griffin. To Griffin, all of the indicators point in the opposite direction—toward the existence of consciousness throughout the animal kingdom.

Consciousness and Animal Cognition

Griffin's views on the pervasiveness of consciousness among animals have sparked strong criticism from some psychologists working in the field of animal cognition (Yoerg, 1991; Yoerg & Kamil, 1991; Blumberg & Wasserman, 1995). These scientists point out that complexity in animal behavior in no way demands that animals are making conscious plans or are aware of their own activities. The argument that a conscious mind must be responsible for intelligent behavior in animals has been labeled *argument from design* by Blumberg and Wasserman (1995). They point out that the cognitive ethologist's argument for consciousness in animals is similar to the creationist's argument against evolution. This argument suggests that only an intelligent creator could have made something as complex as a human being. Yet evolutionary theory accounts for complexity by gradual change over eons of time (Dawkins, 1986). Similarly, argue Blumberg and Wasserman, complex behavior in an animal may be understood by a careful study of the animal's inherited behavioral tendencies and learned behaviors, without an appeal to conscious awareness. These critics also point to the fact that much of human behavior is controlled by factors of which the individual is not aware (Nisbett & Wilson, 1977). Consciousness then may be unnecessary for the performance of intelligent behavior.

The points of view expressed by Griffin and his critics represent extreme opposites with respect to the question of animal consciousness. Between these points of view, there may be some middle ground. In fact, questions about states of awareness in animals can be raised regarding some of the current theoretical ideas prevalent in animal cognition. One difficulty with a discussion of consciousness in animals is that consciousness, as discussed in the human literature, is not a single thing. There are several types or dimensions of consciousness. One form of consciousness is *sentience,* or the ability to experience sensations and perceptions. Most animal scientists would grant this level of awareness to animals. No one would want to perform surgery on an animal without an anesthetic because he assumed that the animal does not feel pain.

Given that animals, like humans, are exposed to environments that simultaneously provide a variety of different perceptions, is the animal equally aware of all sources of stimulation? This is the problem of *attention,* which is addressed in more detail in Chapter 2. However, several lines of evidence suggest that an animal's acquisition of information from a stimulus source varies depending on what other sources of stimulation are present. Evidence for attention in animals seems to imply different levels of awareness or sentience for different stimulus dimensions.

Another dimension of awareness frequently used in theories of human cognition is that between information in *working memory* and *reference memory.* A popular modern view of human working memory is that it is the retrieval of information from a reference memory or making that information conscious. That is, people are not constantly aware of all the information stored in their brain but can activate needed information when necessary (Spear & Riccio, 1994). As we will see in the chapters on memory in animals, the notion that information is retrieved from reference memory into working memory is commonly used in animal learning (Wagner, 1981) and memory (Lewis, 1979; Grant, 1981c). Numerous experiments have been carried out with animals in which some cue from a previous associative learning episode is presented to retrieve memory of that previous learning (Spear, 1981). In human cognition models, this retrieval of information is explicitly tied to a change in consciousness (Atkinson & Shiffrin, 1971). Does the adoption of such models by animal theorists suggest the recognition that information in animal brains also may change in state of awareness?

Still a further form of consciousness is self-reflective consciousness. Is an animal aware of itself as an independent being? Tulving (1985) raised the question of whether animals have *episodic memory* and *autonoetic* consciousness. To have autonoetic or self-consciousness, one must have episodic memory or memories for personal episodes that occurred in the past. Without episodic memory, an animal could still learn and function, but all of its memory would be of a general nature unrelated to itself. Although it may seem farfetched to think that an animal could be conscious and not have episodic memory, just such a state has been reported in a brain-damaged individual studied by Tulving (1989, 1993). This individual is aware of the present and is capable of learning some things, but he has no memory of a personal past and cannot conceive of a personal future. Could such a state be a model for the animal mind? On the other hand, Gallup (1970) has carried out mirror experiments with animals that have led him to conclude that at least some species of primates have self-awareness. In addition, D. Premack and Woodruff (1978b), Povinelli (1993), and Byrne and Whiten (1988) have suggested that some animals have a *theory of mind* or awareness of the existence of mind in other animals. All of this work is highly controversial and is discussed further in Chapters 3 and 12.

It should be apparent that some thorny questions about consciousness in animals can be addressed at several different levels. The question of animal consciousness will continue to be explored by some investigators, and eventually it may play a role in theories of animal cognition. However, it is not necessary to make assumptions about consciousness in order to have the science of animal cognition. For most researchers in the field of animal cognition, the bottom-line question is, *"How can we best predict and understand animal behavior?"* If, at some time in the future, a generally agreed upon physiological or behavioral measure of what an animal is aware of becomes available, and if such a measure can be causally related to an animal's behavior, then the study of animal consciousness undoubtedly will become more popular. For the time being, most animal cognition researchers find an animal's learning history—and the current stimuli it is exposed to—better predictors of its behavior than speculations about what it may or may not be aware of.

The field of animal cognition has grown over the past 25 years because a number of researchers have become convinced that animal behavior can best be predicted and understood if we assume that animals form *representations* about their environment and then *process information* (Honig, 1978; Terrace, 1984). In this book, a number of phenomena are discussed that appear to be best understood within the framework of these assumptions. Several theoretical models of information processing are presented that serve to organize, understand, and predict animal behavior. This discussion proceeds without a consideration of consciousness because we have no idea of the processes an animal might or might not be aware of and whether such awareness would be of any functional consequence.

The Comparative Dimension of Animal Cognition

The field of animal cognition often is called *comparative cognition.* The term "comparative" implies research with animals and also implies that cognition may be compared among species of animals. One purpose of comparing cognitive processes among species is to understand how these processes developed through evolution. To make comparisons that are meaningful within the framework of evolution, however, we must understand how the evolutionary process works. In an important article, Hodos and Campbell (1969) pointed out that an unfortunate misunderstanding about the relationship between different animals and human beings had developed over the centuries. The *scala naturae,* or Great Chain of Being, ranked types of animals from those considered most simple to those considered most complex. At the bottom of the chain were single-celled organisms followed by insects, fish, amphibia, reptiles, birds, and mammals graded up to humans at the top. The scale had religious overtones; some theologians saw God as being at the pinnacle of the scale, above man. In some cases, human races were placed along such a scale, suggesting that some people were closer to animals than others.

Hodos and Campbell argued that the notion of a *scala naturae* still persisted in the writings of many comparative psychologists as a *phylogenetic scale,* on which animals could be graded in terms of their recency of appearance in evolution and degree of structural and behavioral complexity. In the earlier comparative psychology literature, species of animals might be referred to as *subhuman, subprimate,* or *submammalian,* implying that the animal was lower on an evolutionary chain than a human, primate, or mammal, respectively.

To set the record straight, Hodos and Campbell reproduced several maps showing the probable course of evolution of different types of animals based on work in comparative morphology and paleontology. Two of these diagrams are shown in Figure 1.4. The upper diagram shows the probable evolution of mammals, including primates, and the lower diagram shows in more detail the probable evolution of primates. Both diagrams provide a time scale in millions of years and corresponding geological ages. The most important point to obtain from these diagrams is that evolution is treelike and not linear. The proper term to be used to describe these structures is a *phylogenetic tree.* Different forms of animals then evolve from common ancestors as successive branches along a tree, based on different adaptations to environmental demands.

Of particular importance is that many forms of animals found on the earth today did not evolve from one another but followed quite independent routes of evolution. Thus, it is completely wrong to refer to an elephant as subhuman or subprimate because elephants evolved along a separate branch of the phylogenetic tree from monkeys, apes, and people. In other words, elephants are not ancestral to human beings, and both species may be equally evolved in the sense of being adapted to their ancestral habitat. As the lower diagram shows, humans did not evolve from monkeys. The ancestors of contemporary New World and Old World monkeys began independent courses of evolution long before the ancestors of contemporary *Homo sapiens* appeared. Humans and great apes are presumed to have had a common ancestor, but these species also are the product of several million years of independent evolution.

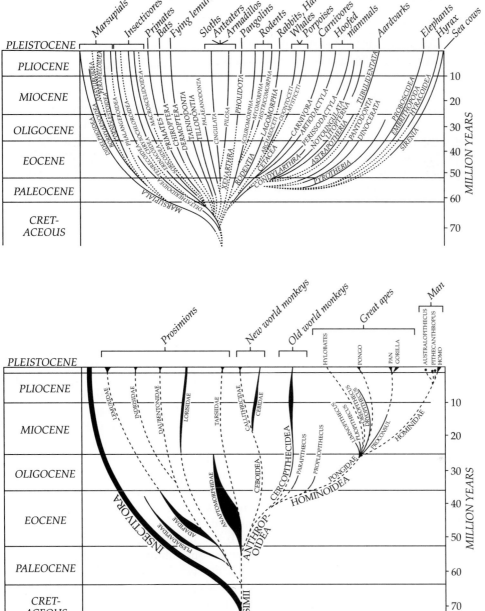

FIGURE 1.4. The upper diagram is a phylogenetic tree depicting the evolution of orders of mammals, and the lower diagram is a more detailed depiction of the evolution of the primate order. Both diagrams show probable age of origin in millions of years and geological age.

Making Comparisons among Species

Comparisons in Animal Learning Research

Common questions asked by people with a casual interest in animal intelligence include, "Which is smarter, a cat or a dog? A monkey or a chimpanzee? A fish or a rat?" In fact, animal psychologists have long been interested in such questions. An examination of the literature in comparative psychology in the first half of this century reveals a number of studies in which different species were tested on the same task and compared with one another. Two of these studies, comparison among species in the delayed-response problem and in the multiple-plate problem, will be discussed in Chapters 3 and 9, respectively. The comparisons made in these studies were *quantitative* in nature. Animals were compared in terms of how much time they could delay and still respond correctly in the delayed-response task or how many plates could be chosen in the correct order in the multiple-plate task. Different species were compared with a common metric and rank ordered in terms of their relative ability. One such set of comparisons (Warden, 1951) found that animals could be ranked from best to worst in this order: primates (monkeys and apes), carnivores (dogs and cats), ungulates (hoofed animals), birds, reptile, amphibians, and fish.

These quantitative differences among species of animals fit well with an approach to animal learning called the *general process approach.* Recall from the earlier historical discussion that Edward Thorndike concluded from his early experiments on animal learning that a common associative process could account for learning in all animals, including humans. This position became a cornerstone of much of the theoretical work in learning that followed Thorndike. Differences among species in the ease with which they could perform a particular task were explained as quantitative differences in the same process. Thus, if a monkey can learn a series of discrimination problems faster than a rat, it is because the monkey can form more associations or form associations faster than the rat. Both species are learning by the same process, but the process works faster or more efficiently in one species than in the other. One consequence of this general process approach to animal learning was that research on animals became focused upon a very limited number of species, mostly pigeons, monkeys, and especially rats (Beach, 1950; Munn, 1950).

In the 1960s, Bitterman (1965a, 1965b, 1975) challenged the notion that all differences in learning among species were quantitative. Different species of animals were tested on two problems—*habit reversal* and *probability learning.* In habit reversal, a discrimination first was learned between two stimuli. For example, an animal might be trained to prefer a white stimulus over a black stimulus because choice of white always yielded reward and choice of black always yielded nonreward. After this initial problem was well learned, the discrimination habit was reversed, and choice of black was rewarded while choice of white was nonrewarded. When this reversal of the discrimination was learned, the problem was reversed again and again over a number of reversals. Habit reversal experiments with rats showed that they eventually adjusted to these reversals by quickly reversing their stimulus preference when the reward contingencies were changed. Thus, the rat's rate of learning improved over successive reversals. When a very different animal, a goldfish, was tested, quite a different pattern of adjustment to successive reversals appeared. The fish learned successive reversal problems at the same rate, even when tested over a large number of habit reversals. Fish were unable to learn to quickly change their response tendencies in the way rats could.

Rats and goldfish also were tested on probability learning. In this task, an animal again was faced with discrimination between two stimuli. If a rat was required to choose between white and black stimuli, choice of one stimulus, say, white, might be rewarded on 70 percent of the trials, and the other black stimulus would be rewarded on the remaining 30 percent of the trials. Such a discrimination would be referred to as a 70:30 problem; other problems might be 80:20 or 60:40 problems. When confronted with a probabilistic reward of different stimuli, the rat's solution was to choose the majority stimulus on almost all of the trials. On the 70:30 problem just described, for instance, a rat would choose the 70 percent white stimulus nearly 100 percent of the time. This behavior was called *maximizing* because choice of the majority stimulus was maximized. By contrast, when goldfish were tested on probability learning, they showed a pattern of behavior called *matching*. The fish tended to choose each stimulus with about the same probability as it was rewarded. Thus, the 70 percent stimulus was chosen on 70 percent of the trials, and the 30 percent stimulus was chosen on 30 percent of the trials.

Bitterman argued that this pattern of findings suggested *qualitative* differences in learning processes among species. That is, the rat and fish may show these very different modes of adjustment to reversal and probabilistic reward because their nervous systems differ in some fundamental way. In further research using visual discrimination problems, it was found that monkeys and pigeons show progressive improvement in rate of habit reversal, as the rat does. Turtles, on the other hand, behaved like fish and showed no improvement in habit reversal. When tested on probability learning, monkeys maximized, as rats did, but pigeons and turtles tended to match, as fish did.

One important problem arises in doing experiments that compare different species. The differences found, whether they be quantitative or qualitative, could arise from differences between the experiments in *contextual variables*. Contextual variables refer to the conditions under which animals of a given species are tested and may include both factors in the external environment and the internal condition of the animals. One could argue, for example, that rats showed improvement in habit reversal and fish did not because the rats were hungrier than the fish or because the reward used with rats was more palatable to the rats than that used with fish was to them. One might attempt to control these variables by equating them. The problem with control by equation is that we have no idea of how many hours of food deprivation would lead to equal levels of hunger in rats and goldfish or what amounts or types of food would produce equal degrees of reinforcement in rats and fish. To circumvent this problem, Bitterman (1965a) proposed the method of *systematic variation* of contextual variables. If an investigator feels that the difference in habit reversal patterns between rats and fish is a consequence of differences in the hunger drive, experiments can be carried out in which the hunger drive variable is varied in both species. If hunger is the key factor responsible for the species difference, we would expect to find that rats would behave like fish at some drive level and that fish would behave like rats at some drive level. On the other hand, if rats continue to show improvement over reversals and fish continue to fail to improve over reversals at a wide variety of drive levels, we can rule out the hunger drive as a contextual variable responsible for the difference in habit reversal between the two species. The method of systematic variation has been used to control contextual variation in a number of experiments involving interspecies comparisons.

Bitterman's research in recent years has focused on an analysis of associative mechanisms in learning by honeybees (Bitterman, 1996). Surprisingly, many of his findings suggest that the same mechanisms of learning found in vertebrates may be found in bees.

Comparisons in Animal Cognition Research

Comparisons among species also have been popular in the recently emerging field of animal cognition. Two approaches to interspecies comparison, which Shettleworth (1993) has labeled the anthropocentric and ecological programs have become popular. The *anthropocentric program* involves comparisons between people and animals. Much of the work in this program undoubtedly arises from people's curiosity about their similarity to animals. As the historical introduction indicated, for centuries people have been interested in whether animals have the cognitive capacities to learn, remember, reason, use numbers, and use language. Research in animal cognition has important implications for human uniqueness. To the extent that certain cognitive abilities found in humans are also found in animals, we may have to conclude that we are not unique with respect to these abilities. In other areas of human cognitive abilities though, we may find that we are unique because nothing like those abilities is found in animals.

Research within an anthropocentric program may also be beneficial to theories of human cognition. As we shall see in the later chapters of this book, there is now evidence that animals form memories for serial lists, show a bowed serial-position curve, precisely keep track of intervals of time, have numerical competence, and form conceptual categories. Theories about human competence in these areas often rely on the use of language. Demonstrations that animals without language also have these abilities may lead human cognition theorists to consider alternative nonlanguage accounts of human performance.

Finally, the discovery of a common cognitive ability in humans and animals may provide neuroscientists with an opportunity to discover common brain structures associated with that ability. The study of cognitive neuroscience or the neural basis for cognitive abilities is a very popular and rapidly growing field. The study of brain mechanisms in people, however, is often limited to patients suffering brain damage; ethical concerns prohibit direct manipulation of the human nervous system. In animal research, it is often possible to create precise brain lesions, monitor the activity of specific parts of the brain, or administer drugs that selectively affect certain neurotransmitters. If certain cognitive processes are common to animals and humans, we may be able to study the neural basis of those processes in animals. Two examples will be mentioned: (1) Research with both rodents and birds has led to the development of sophisticated behavioral techniques for studying spatial memory, an ability undoubtedly shared by humans and animals. The examination of spatial memory in animals with selected brain lesions has led to the hypothesis that a brain structure called the hippocampus may be an important center for the storage of spatial information (O'Keefe & Nadel, 1978; Sherry, 1992; Sherry, Vaccarino, Buckenham, & Herz, 1989). (2) Both animals and humans are excellent time-keepers, and common mechanisms may be responsible for the ability to precisely measure intervals of time. The development of a sophisticated information processing model of timing (described in detail in Chapter 8) based on animal research now makes it possible to study the effects of drugs and nutrients on specific components of the timing process (Meck & Church, 1987a, 1987b).

The anthropocentric approach may be criticized on the grounds that it tells us nothing about the evolution of the processes being compared (Shettleworth, 1993; Riley & Langley, 1993). As can be seen in Figure 1.4, human evolution followed a very different course from that taken by many of the animals with which comparisons are made. Thus, a comparison of timing ability between a human and a rat (Church, 1993), for example, tells us nothing about when or how that ability appeared in either humans or rats or their ancestral relatives. Nevertheless, such a comparison can be of value in an *analysis of adaptation* (Hodos & Campbell, 1969). Dimensions such as space, time, and number are basic components of existence with which both humans and animals must cope. Studies of unrelated species may give us some ideas about what different forms of evolutionary response can be made to these dimensions. For example, it will be shown in Chapter 7 that bees and rodents code the location of objects in space very differently. In cases in which distant species show similar cognitive abilities, such as timing in humans and rats, a common adaptation to the same environmental problem may be shown. Such abilities are referred to as *analogous* because different species converged on the same process through independent evolutionary paths.

The alternative program for comparison among species, the *ecological program*, focuses on the evolution of cognitive processes that are essential to the survival of a species. This program also has been referred to as the *synthetic approach* because it emphasizes a synthesis between experimental animal psychology and evolutionary biology (Kamil, 1988). The term "ecology" means the study of the interrelationships between organisms and their environments. Thus, the ecological approach stresses the evolutionary adaptation of a species by the development of behaviors or cognitive processes that meet the environmental demands encountered by that species. The behaviors of an animal in its natural environment are studied carefully to determine what behaviors or abilities are most important for its survival and reproduction. The basis for these characteristics may then be examined through experimental studies carried out in either the field or the laboratory.

Often, species that are closely related to one another in evolutionary history are studied in the same experimental situation. Suppose that three species of birds are studied whose evolution is known to involve three recent branchings from a common ancestor. If all three species show the same behavioral trait, it could be hypothesized that the trait is *homologous*, meaning that it was passed on to all three species from the common ancestor. If the three species differed on this trait, there are two possible explanations: (1) Each species independently evolved its particular trait, and (2) all three species inherited the same trait from a common ancestor, but the trait underwent a secondary modification through the effects of different selection pressures each species encountered in its particular environment. Unraveling which of these possibilities underlies a pattern of findings is the job of the behavioral ecologist.

A good example of the ecological approach is found in recent studies of spatial memory in different corvid species of birds (Kamil, Balda, & Olson, 1994b; Olson, Kamil, Balda, & Nims, 1995). Observations of four species of related corvids (Clark's nutcracker, pinyon jays, scrub jays, and Mexican jays) indicated that all four hoarded food when it was plentiful and later recovered it. However, different species were observed to be differentially dependent upon cached food. From this observation, it was hypothesized that this differential dependence upon hoarding might have arisen from differences in the species' evolutionary ecology. That is, some species may have evolved in environments that demanded more food hoarding and spatial memory for hoarded food than other species. This hypothesis then was put to the test by measuring the spatial memory capacities of each species in several different spatial memory tasks. The findings of these interesting experiments are discussed in more detail in Chapter 7.

THE ETHICS OF RESEARCH IN ANIMAL COGNITION

Since the basic argument presented in this book is that animals have representations of their environment and use cognitive processes to combine and transform information, it is particularly appropriate that we consider the question of ethical treatment of animals. Much of the research on animals is medical or biological in nature. Research in animal psychology constitutes only about 1 percent of all research done with animals; furthermore, of all the animals used by people for different purposes, only 0.003 percent are used for psychological research (Domjan, 1993). Nevertheless, we should carefully consider the treatment animals receive in psychological experiments.

In the late 1970s and throughout the 1980s, several animal rights groups attacked the use of animals for research, with much of this attack directed at the use of animals in experimental psychology. Coile and Miller (1984) detailed the accusations against psychological research with animals made by a group called Mobilization for Animals. These accusations included the charges that animals were given electric shocks of extreme intensity, were left to die from food and water deprivation, were subjected to crushing forces that smashed their bones, were mutilated, and were made psychotic by subjection to extreme stress and pain. Coile and Miller then examined all of the articles involving animal research published in American Psychological Association journals over the five-year period from 1979 to 1983, in search of experiments that contained instances of these forms of animal mistreatment. Over the entire survey of 608 articles, no case of an animal being treated in any of the ways described by the

Mobilization for Animals organization was found. They concluded that attacks by animal rights activists upon animal research in psychology largely involved false and inflammatory suggestions about animal research, along with a suppression of the true facts.

N. E. Miller (1985) has detailed further many of the benefits that have arisen from animal research in the psychology laboratory. A number of benefits have accrued to animals, as well as people. For example, research on taste aversion conditioning in animals has been used to protect crops and livestock from predation without endangering predatory species. Knowledge of the imprinting process gained from animal research is being used to encourage breeding within endangered species. Principles of learning obtained from animal research have been used in numerous therapeutic applications with people, including treatments for enuresis, scoliosis, and chronic ruminative vomiting. Behavior therapies based on learning principles have been widely used to treat a variety of behavioral problems, including phobias, anxiety attacks, stuttering, and uncontrollable compulsive behaviors. Research with animals in behavioral medicine has contributed to a number of discoveries, such as the use of biofeedback as a treatment for headaches and other disorders, the effects of stress on hypertension and depression, the discovery of natural analgesics in the form of endogenous opiates, the role of Pavlovian conditioning in drug tolerance, and the effects of aging on learning and memory abilities.

In a recent comment, Herzog (1995) showed that the number of magazine and newspaper articles devoted to topics concerned with the treatment of animals and the animal rights movement rose steadily from 1975 to 1990 but has declined since 1990. There may be a good reason for this trend. A major effect of the animal rights movement and its influence on public concern with the treatment of animals was to mobilize both governments and animal research institutions to draw up enforced guidelines for the care and treatment of animals. Throughout the 1980s, federal and local regulations governing animal welfare and use in research were enacted. Virtually all universities, hospitals, and other institutions in North America where animal research is conducted now have animal care committees that must review and approve all research proposals before investigators can begin experimental work with animals. These committees are made up of both members of the institution and individuals from the local community and are charged with ensuring that animals are housed and used for research according to strict ethical regulations.

These regulations guarantee that animals are housed in comfortable cages, that they receive proper ventilation and climate control, and that they are fed a nutritional diet. Enrichment of captive animals' environment is encouraged, including social interactions with other members of their species. Guidelines for research insist that animals be subjected to no more stress or discomfort than is absolutely necessary. Surgery is carried out under anesthesia, and analgesics are given to recovering animals. In behavioral studies, animals may be deprived of food to motivate them to perform for food reward, but the degree of weight reduction rarely drops below 80 percent of an animal's body weight when given unlimited food. Since animals given unlimited food become obese and die sooner than weight-reduced animals, keeping experimental animals at a reduced body weight tends to maintain their health and longevity. In a small proportion of studies, investigators may use electric shock to study the effects of punishment on behavior and how animals learn to escape and avoid noxious stimulation. Although the level of shock used is sufficient to motivate animals to learn, it is not severe and causes no tissue damage. Furthermore, the level of shock that could be delivered to an animal is strictly regulated by an animal care committee.

It seems clear that the animal rights movement has had a considerable impact on research institutions using animals. With ethical guidelines for animal research and animal care committees in place, all research with animals is carefully scrutinized before it is performed, and procedures are often modified to agree with ethical requirements. Thus, the downturn in articles concerned with the treatment of animals since 1990 may reflect the fact that the concerns of most reasonable individuals concerned with animal welfare have been addressed.

SUMMARY

Claims about animal intelligence can be traced back as far as the ancient Greek philosophers, but Descartes' 17th-century theory marks the beginning of the modern debate on animal cognition. Descartes proposed that humans, but not animals, had minds; animals were conceived of as automata driven by reflexive responses to stimulation. Quite the opposite point of view emerged in the 19th century, based on Darwin's theory of evolution by natural selection. Darwin found evidence of continuity between different species of animals based on the similarity of structure of body parts. As an extension of his theory, he proposed that continuity between humans and animals should be found in the realm of psychological processes. The search for intellectual continuity between humans and animals led Darwin and Romanes to collect a vast number of anecdotes suggesting that various species of animals had demonstrated behaviors that clearly revealed humanlike abilities to reason, plan, and insightfully solve problems.

The use of anecdotes as evidence for animal intelligence was widely criticized. Lloyd Morgan and Edward Thorndike both warned against the excessive attribution of intellectual powers to animals based on anecdotes. Morgan suggested that animal behavior should be explained by the lowest process possible on a scale of ascending psychological processes. Thorndike brought the study of animal intelligence into the laboratory where it could be studied by repeated careful measurement of behavior. Based on his studies of animals learning to escape from a problem box for food reward, he concluded that all learning was a trial-and-error affair that involved connecting responses to stimuli through repetition and reinforcement. By the end of the first quarter of the 20th century, North American psychology had moved away from a concern with mental structures and processes and had adopted behaviorism as the favored approach. The study of animals focused on animal learning and the acquisition of behavioral habits.

With the exception of the research and theoretical work done by Edward Tolman, there was little interest in animal cognition until around 1970. With the emergence of a new interest in human cognition, investigators began to use the methods developed in the behavioral laboratory to once again address questions about information processing in animals. Over the past 25 years, several areas of cognitive processing in animals have been studied in depth. These include memory, attention, spatial cognition, serial learning, timing, numerical competence, language, reasoning, and tool use. The remaining chapters of this text review progress on these topics.

Considerable controversy surrounds the issue of consciousness in animals. Cognitive ethologists argue that field observations of apparently carefully planned and executed behavior in animals demand an acceptance of the functional importance of consciousness in animals. Some animal cognition experts reject these arguments and suggest that consciousness is an unnecessary construct; an animal's behavior can be understood through knowing its learning history, without recourse to assumptions about its awareness. Some models used in animal cognition, however, do seem to imply that state of awareness may be important in animals. Although state of consciousness is not a primary concern in most animal cognition research today, it might become a variable of more importance in the future if accepted neural or behavior techniques for its measurement become available.

The comparative dimension of animal cognition must be pursued with a clear understanding of the evolutionary paths different species of animals have followed. Evolution is best described as a phylogentic tree and not as a linear scale. Many modern-day animals evolved independently of one another and should not be described as above or below one another in an evolutionary hierarchy. Different species of animals may be compared with one another in terms of the behaviors and cognitive abilities they use to deal with environmental demands. The anthropocentric approach to comparative cognition emphasizes comparisons between people and animals and may reveal in what ways humans have similar and different cognitive processes from other species of animals. The ecological approach to comparative cognition focuses more on the evolution of behaviors within closely related species of animals. Field and laboratory investigations are aimed at determining the extent to which aspects of the behavior or cognition of different species are homologous with a common ancestor or have been modified by differential ecology.

Over the past 20 years, ethical guidelines for the care of animals used in research have been put in place throughout North America. Rules about animal care and procedures to be used in research are enforced by animal care committees in all universities, hospitals, and other animal research institutions. These rules guarantee that animals will be housed in comfort, fed a nutritious diet, and used in research in ways that minimize their stress and discomfort.

CHAPTER 2

Perception and Attention

Chapters 3 and 4 emphasize the coding and processing of information in animal working memory, and Chapter 5 addresses the formation of associations between different pieces of information. Before we get to those stages, however, this chapter considers how information to be remembered and entered into associations with other information initially gets into the nervous system. The focus is on problems of perception and attention in animals. The section on perception is concerned with how the visual system organizes patterns of retinal stimulation into meaningful, organized percepts. Beyond initial perception of information, we know that neither people nor animals process or react to all of the information received by their receptors. Information is selected for further processing and response, and the selection of this information is the problem of attention.

Most people interested in animals have asked a naive question: What does the world look like to a particular animal? Does a dog, cat, monkey, or bird see the same world that we do? This question gets us into phenomenology or private experience. In reality, we cannot know even whether the perceptual experiences of another person are exactly like our own because we have no way of plugging ourself into someone else's nervous system. We assume that people share common experiences because they have nervous systems that are similar in structure and function. In some cases, however, people do not share the same sensations. For example, a color-blind person does not see the same colors that a person with normal color vision sees. This difference may be traced to hereditary differences in the visual processing systems of normal and color-blind people. Since animals have evolved with sensory systems that sometimes differ radically from our own, is there any reason to think they share common experiences with humans? The answer is probably yes and no, and it undoubtedly varies with the species of animal being studied. We know that the capacity to sense certain physical dimensions by certain animals far exceeds our own. Dogs, for example, can hear sounds at far higher sound frequencies than we can. Many animals can detect odors to which we are not sensitive. Birds of prey have far better visual acuity from long distances than do humans.

Beyond differences in sensitivity to certain physical dimensions of stimulation, however, we may ask how similar whole patterns of perception are between humans and animals. Do some animals see the same complex three-dimensional patterns that we see? Although there is not a vast amount of information with which to answer this question for most animals, a number of recent studies of perceptual psychophysics, visual search, and perceptual transfer lead us to a qualified yes for one species of bird, the pigeon. This conclusion may seem surprising when it is considered that the visual system and brain of a pigeon are far different from our own. Human eyes are placed forward in the head so that they share a large overlapping binocular field. The pigeon's eyes, by contrast, are placed on the sides of its head, giving it excellent peripheral vision but a very restricted central field of binocular overlap (Emmerton, 1983). The human eye has a single central fovea, where cones are concentrated for detail vision, but the pigeon eye has two areas of increased cone density, one for frontal vision and another for peripheral vision. The pigeon's frontal field area is binocular and myopic, or nearsighted, and is used for locating and pecking at food on the ground; the peripheral field fovea, on the other hand, is farsighted and is used for scanning more distant scenes, including moving objects. The eyes and optic nervous system of a pigeon occupy a much larger proportion of the head than do those of a primate. Visual information from the eyes is transmitted to the cerebral cortex in humans, but pigeons have no cortex; thus, all information reaching the brain is processed by noncortical structures. Although there are clear structural differences in the pigeon and human visual systems, both eyes contain similar photoreceptor cells, or cones, which give rise to color vision. The pigeon eye contains cones with four or five different photopigments, whereas only three types of cones are found in the human eye (Waldvogel, 1990).

Clearly, humans and pigeons evolved independently and with visual systems that differ in structure. How could it be then that both systems give rise to similar perceptions? The answer may lie in the fact that both species evolved to perceive a common world. Through parallel evolution, different species may have developed similar visual mechanisms, which give rise to similar veridical perceptions of the environment. Veridical and accurate detailed visual representation of the world is necessary for the survival of species that must move over large areas in order to forage for food. Even though these visual systems may differ considerably in structure, they may share many common mechanisms and give rise to similar final experiences.

ANIMAL PSYCHOPHYSICS

Psychophysics refers to that field of perception that attempts to measure or quantify the sensitivity of perceptual systems to different dimensions of physical stimulation. The study of psychophysics was originated around 1850 by the German physicist, Gustav Fechner, who was interested in lawful relationships between physical dimensions and people's experiences of those dimensions. One important enterprise of psychophysics was determining sensory thresholds, or that amount of physical energy that a sensory system could barely

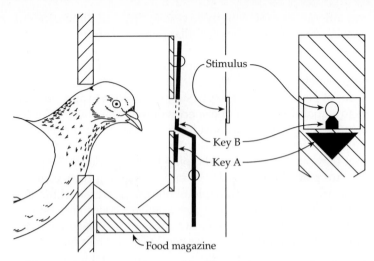

FIGURE 2.1. Diagram of the apparatus used by Blough to measure the pigeon's absolute threshold for light intensity. The panel on the right shows the stimulus patch and keys A and B as they would be seen by the pigeon.
From D. Blough, 1956.

detect. For example, an observer might be shown a small area illuminated with weak light and be asked to respond either "yes" for detection of the light or "no" for absence of any experience of light. By repeatedly raising and lowering the amount of light shown to the observer in gradual steps, a point could be established at which the observer would indicate the detection of light 50 percent of the time. This amount of light energy was defined as the *absolute threshold*.

Suppose that we wish to measure the absolute threshold for visual sensitivity in an animal. Since the animal cannot respond verbally to our presentations of light, how can we measure its threshold? The key to accomplishing such a task is to train an animal to respond in one way in order to say yes, or to indicate the detection of a stimulus, and to respond in another way to say no, or to indicate the absence of a stimulus. An elegant procedure developed by D. Blough (1958, 1961) shows how this was done with pigeons. Pigeons were tested in a darkened operant chamber. As shown in Figure 2.1, the pigeon was trained to put its head through an opening, behind which it could see a stimulus patch, and then respond to one of two keys. The stimulus patch was either lit or darkened. If it was lit, a response to key A was reinforced by the delivery of a grain reward, and a response to key B was not reinforced. If the stimulus patch was darkened, however, a response to key B was reinforced, and a response to key A was nonreinforced. It is important to note that pigeons were not reinforced for every correct response to keys A and B; reinforcement was delivered for correct responses to both keys only occasionally on variable ratio schedules. This point is important because the pigeon was not reinforced continuously for key responses during the testing procedure.

At the beginning of a test period, a pigeon was presented with a sufficiently intense light that it would respond to key A. The effect of each response to key

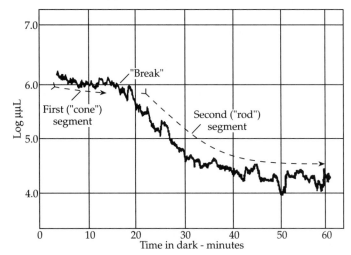

FIGURE 2.2. A dark-adaptation curve for the pigeon, showing the decrease in its absolute threshold for light intensity after different lengths of time in the dark. *From D. Blough, 1956.*

A was to reduce the intensity of the light by a fixed amount. Eventually, the stimulus patch would become so dim that the pigeon could no longer see it. For the pigeon, the light was no longer present, and it began to respond to key B. Since some light was still present, even if it was below the pigeon's threshold, responses to key B were not reinforced. Each response to key B raised the light intensity by a fixed degree. Of course, eventually the light then became visible to the pigeon, and it switched to pecking key A. This procedure is called *titration.* The stimulus intensity is driven repeatedly in small steps to points just above or just below the animal's absolute threshold. The bird's absolute threshold is estimated by taking the average of the stimulus intensities at which it switches from key A to key B and from key B to key A.

Psychophysical procedures such as the titration method can be used to compare the sensory sensitivity of animal perceptual systems with that of humans. Two examples are shown in Figures 2.2 and 2.3. We know from a common procedure carried out in the human psychophysical laboratory that the human eye adapts or becomes more sensitive to light over a period of confinement in the dark. Do animals also become more sensitive in darkness? Figure 2.2 shows the results of an experiment carried out by D. Blough (1956), in which a pigeon's absolute threshold was measured after it had spent different periods of time in the dark. The curve plots the absolute threshold in light energy units against minutes in the dark. The drop in the curve shows that the pigeon becomes more sensitive to light the longer it stays in the dark, just as a person does. The curve also shows a distinct break or sudden drop between 10 and 20 minutes. This well-known effect in human dark-adaptation curves is called the rod-cone break and represents the fact that the rods continue to become more sensitive after the cones have reached full sensitivity.

The human visual system is not equally sensitive to all wavelengths. We see light of certain colors better than that of others. If a person with normal

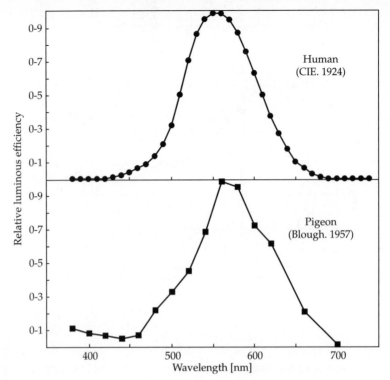

FIGURE 2.3. Curves showing relative spectral sensitivity for humans in the upper panel and for pigeons in the lower panel. The peaks of the curves represent greatest sensitivity or lowest threshold for detection of light.

vision has his absolute threshold measured for cone or photopic vision at different wavelengths along the visual spectrum, it will be found that the threshold is lowest around 550 nanometers (greenish-yellow light) and rises as the spectrum moves toward lower or higher wavelengths. Figure 2.3 shows relative sensitivity curves for humans and pigeons (D. Blough, 1957; A. Wright, 1972). Because sensitivity is the inverse of threshold, these curves peak at the point where threshold is lowest. Although the curves differ slightly, they tell us that pigeons, like people, have the best sensitivity in the middle range of the visible spectrum, with sensitivity declining at lower and higher wavelengths.

These experiments demonstrate how psychophysical methods originally developed to study human perception can be adapted for the study of animal perception by training animals to respond differently in the presence and absence of a stimulus. They begin to answer questions about similarities in the sensory experience of different species. We now know that pigeons become more sensitive to light in the dark and that pigeons, like people, are more sensitive to wavelengths in the middle of the visual spectrum than to those at the ends of the spectrum. Beyond these changes in visual sensitivity along continuous dimensions, how similar might the organization of complex patterns of stimulation be in a pigeon and a person? The next section addresses that question.

Human perception is typically described as being holistic. We see the world as made up of patterns that contain objects that stand out against a background. Gestalt psychologists (Koffka, 1935; Kohler, 1947) argued many years ago that mechanisms within the receptor systems and brain responded to certain properties of patterns of stimulation to yield organized perceptions. These mechanisms were held to operate according to principles or laws of perceptual organization. According to principles of *grouping,* perceptual elements that were in close spatial proximity or that looked similar in appearance would be seen as a grouping or *figure* that stood out against a *ground.* Points on a line appear to be part of the line because the line has *good continuation,* and closed-in structures appear to stand out from a background because of the principle of *closure.* In general, it was held that perceptual systems capitalize upon these properties of perceptual fields to yield the perception of *good form* or a simple symmetrical pattern.

An emphasis on perception being directed by information within the brain is referred to as a *top-down* approach. This approach stresses learned knowledge about the appearance of objects. Although the top-down approach helps to account for the immediate recognition of known objects, the initial elements of perception also must be considered. Perception begins with the activation of retinal receptors and low-level detection systems that are sensitive to basic physical dimensions of stimulation, such as the wavelength and intensity of light. Theories that emphasize the integration of these elements to form percepts are referred to as *bottom-up* approaches. Both the top-down and bottom-up approaches are needed for an understanding of perception.

Feature Integration Theory

In an influential bottom-up theory of perception, Treisman has suggested that percepts are formed through *feature integration* (Treisman & Schmidt, 1982; Treisman & Gelade, 1980; Treisman, Sykes, & Gelade, 1977). Features are defined as points on a dimension. For example, color and line orientation are dimensions, and blue and vertical are values on those dimensions. The theory suggests that processing mechanisms that deal with visual elements from the same dimension differ from those that involve *conjunctions* of features from different dimensions. When features come from the same dimension, perception is described as *automatic* and *preattentive,* and the processing of visual elements is held to take place simultaneously or *in parallel.* A blue dot placed among a field of red dots is immediately spotted, and a slanted line among a field of vertical lines is seen instantaneously. Further, the speed with which the blue dot or slanted line is seen is independent of the number of background red dots or vertical lines presented. The odd-appearing object is said to *pop out* immediately upon visual inspection.

Suppose that we now combine properties of the color and line orientation dimensions to form conjunctions. A display might be shown in which one has to spot a blue slanted line among a background of blue straight lines and red slanted lines. A subject now finds that it takes longer to find the odd item. In fact, the time it takes to visually locate the blue slanted line will increase linearly with the number of background lines presented in the display. According to Treisman and Gelade (1980), we have greater difficulty locating conjunctions of features because they must receive *attention* for their integration, and attention requires *serial* or element-by-element processing. It takes more time to perceive conjunctions of features as the number of background elements increases, and this difference reflects the larger number of potential targets that must be serially scanned by the attentional mechanism.

Texture Perception in the Pigeon

Although these processes of perception were discovered with human subjects, comparative psychologists have been interested in whether they also might be found in animals. A relatively new piece of apparatus in the animal cognition lab, the touchscreen, has made it possible to carry out highly sophisticated studies of pattern perception in animals. A computer monitor is used to present a very large number of different patterns to an animal. The animal responds by touching that region of the screen that contains a target stimulus. Sensors on or around the screen detect exactly where the subject responded and send this information to a computer for storage. Accurate responses are rewarded with food, and incorrect responses yield no reward.

Robert Cook recently carried out a number of studies to test Treisman's feature integration theory with pigeons (Cook, 1992a, 1992b, 1993a, 1993b). In Cook's experiments, pigeons were required to discriminate between the textures of a target area and a background area presented on the monitor screen. Examples of these displays are shown at the top of Figure 2.4. In the display on the left, the target consists of a rectangular area containing black circles and squares, and the surrounding background area contains white (unfilled) circles and squares. (In the actual displays shown to pigeons, the circles and squares would differ in color and not in brightness.) Notice how the target area appears to pop out against the background. According to feature integration theory, preattentive parallel processing of color features gives rise to the immediate impression of a rectangle. In the display on the right, elements are formed of conjunctions between different colors and shapes. A rectangle made up of unique color-shape combinations is located in exactly the same region as the rectangle in the left display; white circles and black squares form a rectangular area against the background of black circles and white squares. It should be obvious that this rectangle does not pop out. Rather, one has to search the display carefully to find it.

The graph in Figure 2.4 shows how accurately pigeons were able to find and peck at the target region over a testing period of 28 sessions. It should be pointed out that a number of different elements and colors were used in the experiment so that a pigeon saw a number of different displays. The results clearly indicate that pigeons were able to detect the target more accurately when a single feature defined a target area than when elements formed by conjunction formed a target area. Note that pigeons were able to detect the target substantially above chance accuracy with both feature and conjunctive targets. Thus, pigeons were able to detect the conjunctive targets, but less successfully than the feature targets. Humans given a similar task show almost

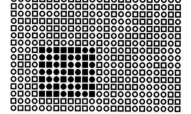

Feature – Color

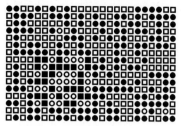

Conjunctive

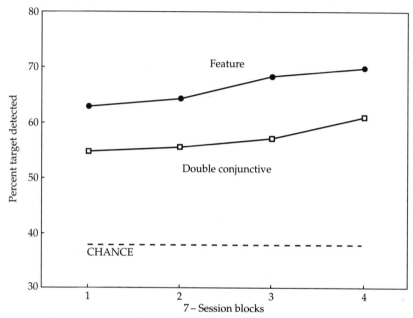

FIGURE 2.4. The top-left display shows an example of a pop-put figure created by using target and background elements that differ in color. In the top-right display, the target must be searched for when it is made up of color-shape conjunctions. Pigeons' ability to detect the target within such displays is shown in the lower graph.

perfect accuracy in locating both feature and conjunctive targets (Cook, 1992b). People take much longer to locate the conjunctive target, however, than to locate the feature target; reaction time was about 435 milliseconds for feature targets and about 1,150 milliseconds for conjunctive targets. Although pigeons showed a difference in accuracy, they showed no difference in reaction time, taking about 450 milliseconds to respond to both displays. These observations emphasize the importance of speed-accuracy trade-off in this task. The effects of display appearance will appear in one measure or the other. If accuracy is of primary importance, differences in ease of target location will be found in reaction time. If an organism stresses speed of response, as the pigeon did, display differences will appear in accuracy of target detection.

Odd-Item Detection in the Pigeon

Pigeons do not sacrifice accuracy for speed in all situations. In some cases, in fact, speed may be positively correlated with accuracy. In a task called *odd-item search* (D. Blough, 1989; D. Blough & Franklin, 1985), pigeons were shown a pattern on a computer screen that contained three, five, or eight black forms. One form was odd in appearance, and the remaining forms were identical to one another in any particular display. However, these "background" items differed among the various displays. An example is shown on the left side of Figure 2.5. Notice that the patterns differ not only in the number of forms shown but also in the basis for oddity. The odd item could differ from the background items in shape, orientation, and whether it was open or filled. If the pigeon pecked in the region of the odd item, it was rewarded, but pecks to incorrect regions ended the trial without reward.

The number of background forms affected both the accuracy of choice and the reaction time. These effects are shown in the graph on the right side of Figure 2.5, in which reaction time is plotted against the percentage of correct responses. The dots shown represent points for various combinations of forms.

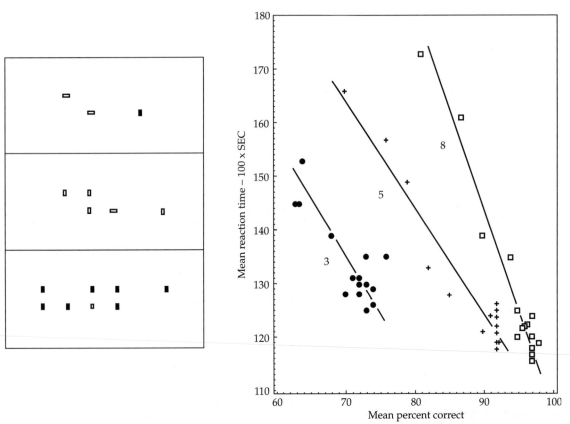

FIGURE 2.5. Three odd-item patterns containing different numbers of items are shown on the left. Reaction time is plotted against percent correct in the right graph for a number of odd-item displays containing three, five, or eight items. Easy-to-discriminate targets are represented by the points at the bottom of each display size best-fit line, and hard-to-discriminate targets are shown at the top of each line.

Best-fit lines are drawn through sets of dots that represent performance with three, five, or eight forms in a pattern. The lines fitted to increasing display size move to the right, which shows that pigeons became more accurate at finding the single target as the number of background forms increased. This observation suggests that the odd item stood out better against a background of many different items than against a background of just a few different items. The contrast can be increased by adding more homogeneous background forms, which causes the odd form to pop out more readily. The cluster of dots that appears at the bottom of each line represents odd item and background combinations of forms that were easily discriminated. Observe that the reaction time to respond to these items decreased as display size became larger. Pigeons not only could detect the odd item better in these cases but could also detect it more quickly. Finally, the few dots at the top of each line show performance with combinations in which the odd form and distractors were similar in appearance and discrimination was more difficult. The interesting finding here is that reaction time increased instead of decreased as number of background items increased. This rise in reaction time suggests that pigeons had to use a serial scan of the display to find the odd form. This rich set of data then indicates that pigeons were using preattentive parallel processing to detect highly discriminable odd items but were forced to use serial search to find odd items of low discriminability.

The findings of the Cook and D. Blough experiments suggest strong parallels between human and pigeon perception. Even though there are marked differences in the neural structures of vision between people and pigeons, both species detect targets and textures immediately under similar conditions, suggesting that they share an initial preattentive stage of visual processing. Both species take longer to detect conjunctions and targets that are difficult to discriminate. These findings suggest that a later attentional process that involves serial searching may also operate in both species.

Recognition by Components Theory

The memory for, and recognition of, the vast number of scenes and objects that a person encounters has long been a difficult theoretical problem for psychology. The Gestalt principles of organization emphasize the perception of forms as regular, simple, and symmetric. In reality, however, we readily recognize many objects that are complex in structure but that would not be called a good figure. In a recently developed theory called *recognition by components* (RBC), an attempt has been made to resolve this seeming paradox between the Gestalt principles and the reality of perception (Biederman, 1987). Biederman suggests that object perception is based on the recognition of component parts. These components are basic primitive structures that are processed before an object is recognized (bottom-up processing). These basic structures are called *geons.* Just as language generation and comprehension involves only about 40 basic sounds or phonemes, it is held that object perception involves no more than about 36 geons. Geons are simple three-dimensional solids made up of straight and curved lines with cross-sectional shapes of circles, ellipses, squares, and rectangles.

The properties of geons are described as *nonaccidental.* The visual system assumes that certain properties of two-dimensional images are true of three-dimensional objects because it is highly unlikely that a correspondence between the two would have occurred by an accidental alignment of viewpoint and object features. Properties of these patterns, such as straight lines, curved lines, parallel lines, and symmetry, are assumed to be properties of the three-dimensional objects that produce the images. It is highly unlikely, for example, that we would see the curved line of an object as a straight line because of an accidental point of view. Observe that these properties, which presumably make geons easily recognizable, are similar to the Gestalt laws. In fact, geons are basically simple figures that have the properties of good continuation, symmetry, and good form. The Gestalt principles of perception then nicely describe the properties of geons and offer an account of their early recognition in the process of object perception.

How does the RBC theory explain perception of the real world? The theory argues that complex objects seen in the real world are compounds of geons that articulate with one another at intersections. These intersections are referred to as cusps and often involve sharp angles that form concavities in the form being viewed. The theory suggests that people store memory of complex objects as patterns of geons and later recognize objects by matching the perceived pattern to memory (top-down processing). The points at which geons intersect in a pattern are critical for pattern recovery. If parts of the image of an object are deleted so that the cusps or intersections of geons are removed, pattern recognition is far more difficult than if midsegments of lines are deleted.

Pigeon Perception of Scrambled Objects

Experiments thus far discussed indicate that pigeons perceive textures and odd items against backgrounds in much the same way as humans. It is a big leap, however, to the perception of complex objects. If a pigeon is shown a two-dimensional picture of an object, does it see the same organized image of an object that we see? Some initial evidence suggested that pigeons do not see objects in pictures. In a well-known experiment, Cerella (1980; 1982) trained pigeons to peck when shown line drawings of the cartoon character Charlie Brown but not to peck when shown pictures of other characters from the Peanuts comic strip. As a test of pigeons' perception of the Charlie Brown picture, the picture was segmented into head, trunk, and legs, and scrambled pictures were shown. For example, a pigeon might see a picture with Charlie's feet at the top, his head in the middle, and his trunk on the bottom. Nevertheless, pigeons pecked as much when shown this scrambled Charlie Brown as they did when shown the intact Charlie. Cerella concluded that pigeons tend to segregate pictures into subpatterns without relating these subpatterns to one another to obtain the whole picture. Thus, when shown the scrambled Charlie Brown, pigeons responded strongly because all of the parts were there, and it did not matter what location they were in.

Both Cerella's theory and the RBC theory of Biederman suggest that perception begins with the recognition of subpatterns or components. The RBC theory holds, however, that recognition of components is only an initial stage and that matching the arrangement or pattern of those components to representations in memory is critical for the perception of whole objects. Imagine the geons of any object scrambled into a random arrangement; it

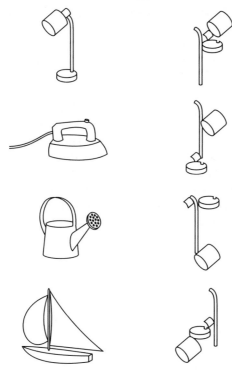

FIGURE 2.6. Pigeons first learned to discriminate between the four pictures shown on the left. Then they were tested with different scrambled versions of each picture. Four different pictures of scrambled lamp components are shown on the right.

would take you much longer to recognize these as the object than it would if they were arranged in the normal manner. According to Cerella's theory, on the other hand, scrambling should little disturb a pigeon's ability to identify these components as the original picture because pigeons process and remember the picture only as components. The theory clearly implies that pigeon and human perception of pictures of objects differ in a very fundamental way.

Wasserman, Kirkpatrick-Steger, Van Hamme, and Biederman (1993) performed an interesting test of these two theories. A group of pigeons was trained to discriminate between the four drawings of objects shown on the left side of Figure 2.6. These pictures were projected one at a time on a small screen in front of a pigeon. At the corners of the screen were four pecking keys. The pigeon was required to peck a particular key for reward each time a certain picture was shown. For instance, a pigeon might have to peck the upper right key when the lamp appeared, the upper left key when the iron appeared, the bottom left key when the watering can appeared, and the lower right key when the sailboat appeared. When pigeons had learned this discrimination to a high level of accuracy, they occasionally were tested with four scrambled versions of each object. The four scrambled versions of the lamp are shown on the right side of Figure 2.6. The critical question involved how accurately pigeons could classify the scrambled pictures. If only picture parts had been perceived and stored during discrimination learning, pigeons should classify the scrambled pictures well, since all of the parts are preserved in the test pictures. If the overall pattern is important, however, transfer to scrambled pictures should be poor. It was found that pigeons continued to discriminate among the original training pictures at a high level of accuracy; correct responses were made on 80.5 percent of the trials. When shown scrambled pictures, accuracy dropped to 52.3 percent. It should be recognized that a chance level of correct response was 1/4, or 25 percent. Pigeons then must have recognized components in scrambled pictures sufficiently well to choose the correct key substantially above random choice. Nevertheless, the drop in performance from the level of unscrambled training pictures suggests strongly that pigeons had also perceived the relations between the component geons in these pictures. The data suggest that pigeons do see patterns or emergent properties of pictures.

In a second experiment, Wasserman et al. (1993) trained pigeons to discriminate between the four scrambled versions of each picture. A pigeon was shown the four scrambled versions of the sailboat, for instance, and had to peck a different corner key for reward when each version was shown. If pigeons saw these pictures as only a collection of parts of an object, this task should be extremely difficult, if not impossible, because each picture contained the same parts. If pigeons perceived the different arrangements as different patterns, and not just as parts to be located, it would be possible to discriminate between them. Although acquisition of the discrimination was slow, showing that this was a difficult task, all of the pigeons tested learned to discriminate the four scrambled versions of each object. The data suggest again that pigeons, like people, have the ability to recognize different arrangements of components as different patterns.

Pigeon Perception of Contour-Deleted Images

As a more direct test of RBC theory with pigeons, Van Hamme, Wasserman and Biederman (1992) trained pigeons to discriminate the pictures of objects seen in Figure 2.7. Two pictures are shown of each of four objects—elephant, mushroom, chair, and telephone. The members of each pair of pictures are complements; if placed on top of one another, they would form a complete line drawing of the object. Part of the contour of each picture has been deleted at the midsegments of curved and straight lines. Importantly, vertexes or points of intersection between geons have been left intact in both complements. According to RBC theory, it should be possible to perceive the object from these contour-deleted images because the relationships between geons have been preserved.

Pigeons were required to discriminate between the four pictures in the left column by pecking a different corner key for each picture to obtain a reward. When pigeons had reached a high level of accuracy with these pictures, test trials were introduced in which the complementary pictures in the right

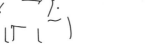

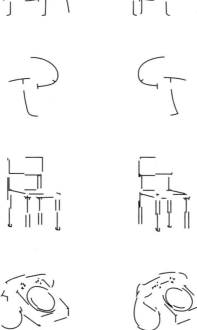

FIGURE 2.7. Complementary drawings of an elephant, mushroom, chair, and telephone. Pigeons first were trained to discriminate between the pictures in the left column and then were tested for transfer to the pictures in the right column.

column were periodically presented among the training pictures. If pigeons perceived these pictures as patterns of geons, then RBC theory suggests that there should be transfer between complementary pictures because relations between geons have been preserved. Quite a different prediction is made if one holds that pigeons learned these discriminations only as differences between collections of unrelated curved and straight lines. In this case, little transfer should occur because the lines contained in the complementary pictures are all different from those contained in the training pictures. Pigeons' level of accuracy on the original training pictures was 77 percent correct, and accuracy on the complementary pictures was 67 percent correct. Although there was a drop of 10 percentage points from training to complementary pictures, performance was far above the chance level of 25 percent on both classes of pictures. Pigeons evidently perceived some change in the pictures from original to complement, as would most people, and this would account for the slight drop in accuracy. The impressive aspect of this experiment, however, is the strong generalization between pictures. Pigeons responded in a way that suggests that they saw the same pattern of organization between geons in both sets of pictures.

We have seen that recent experiments on pigeon perception indicate strong similarities between pigeon and human visual experience. Experiments on target detection showed that textures or targets differing by a single dimensional feature appeared to pop out immediately for pigeons just as they do for people. However, textures and targets that formed conjunctions with background features, or that were highly similar in appearance, required serial search in pigeons, as they do in humans. Finally, perceptual transfer studies suggest that pigeons may perceive the same relationships among the parts of complex objects that people perceive. More specifically, evidence in support of RBC theory, or the perception of relationships among visual elements called geons, was found with both pigeons and people.

Since all of the research thus far described with pigeons has involved the presentation of patterns on two-dimensional surfaces, one might inquire how applicable these findings are to the perception of real three-dimensional objects. Some evidence from Cabe (1976; 1980) indicates that pigeons transfer readily between three-dimensional objects and two-dimensional depictions of objects. Pigeons were trained to discriminate among real objects and then were tested with black-and-white photographs of the same objects. When transferred to photographs, pigeons immediately pecked at photographs of previously rewarded objects and pecked little at photographs of previously nonrewarded objects.

In more recent research, Cole and Honig (1994) trained pigeons to discriminate between slide-projected pictures of two ends of a laboratory room. Pigeons learned to peck at the reinforced pictures of one end of the room and not to peck at the nonreinforced pictures of the other end of the room. The pigeons subsequently were placed in the actual room, with one subgroup of subjects required to find food in the end where reinforced pictures were taken (congruent-transfer group) and the other subgroup required to find food in the end where nonreinforced pictures were taken (incongruent-transfer group). The congruent-transfer group learned to choose the end of the room containing food significantly faster than the incongruent-transfer group, suggesting that the pigeons learned about the location of food in a three-dimensional environment from training with two-dimensional pictures.

THE ROLE OF LEARNING IN PERCEPTION

The top-down approach to perception stresses the importance of learned expectations in perception. People's perceptions of ambiguous figures may be biased by prior exposure to one alternative figure or the other (Leeper, 1935). The speed with which a word is recognized or a target is located in a field of objects may be increased through the use of preceding cues that provide relevant information. These cues often are called primes, and their facilitating effect on perception is called *priming*. We may inquire whether any evidence of such top-down influences on perception have been found with animals.

Based on observations of bird predation on insects, L. Tinbergen (1960) advanced a very influential theoretical idea. Tinbergen had observed that birds (great tits) foraging in the Dutch woods often seemed to specialize on certain species of insects, usually those that were most commonly available. Even though other species of insects might be available, the most abundant species was favored. To explain this finding, Tinbergen suggested that foraging animals form a *search image*. The search image could be a memory of the most abundant insect, which would guide an animal's search for food and tend to restrict its selection to items that matched the image. The search image acted as a perceptual filter that not only favored the abundant food type but tended to reduce the detection of other food types. The concept of a search image hypothesized that prior experience affected animal perception.

Laboratory Evidence for the Search Image

L. Tinbergen's hypothesis of a search image sparked a number of attempts to find confirming evidence for this idea in the laboratory. In experiments that used ecologically relevant stimuli, Pietrewicz and Kamil (1977, 1979) trained blue jays to peck at slide-projected pictures of moths upon which the blue jays preyed in their natural environment. Two species of moths, *C. relicta* and *C. retecta,* were photographed against the bark of trees that served as a natural camouflage for these insects. Pictures of both moths were described as *cryptic,* or difficult to perceive, because the moth tended to blend in with its background. Since the crypticity of the moths was an evolved defense against predation, the task should require perceptual effort on the part of blue jays, and moths would not always be detected. Blue jays were trained to peck at pictures that contained moths, for which they were given a food reward. Intermixed with the moth pictures were negative stimuli that consisted of pictures of tree bark without a moth; pecks to these pictures were nonrewarded.

As a test of the search image hypothesis, Pietrewicz and Kamil presented blue jays with two types of sequences of 16 slides. One sequence tested discrimination of only one species of moth. These sequences contained eight positive *C. relicta* slides and eight negative slides or eight positive *C. retecta* slides and eight negative slides. In the other type of sequence, mixed sequences containing both types of moths were presented along with negative slides containing no moth. The sequences containing only a single species of moth were referred to as *runs,* and the mixed sequences were referred to as *nonruns.* It was predicted that if a search image was formed for a frequently occurring prey, detection of the moth presented in a run should improve over the run. With nonruns, however, no search image could be formed for one moth or the other because both occurred equally often, and no improvement in detection should be found.

As seen in Figure 2.8, blue jays performed in agreement with predictions from the search image hypothesis. Correct responses were defined as pecks on the slides containing moths and omission of pecks on the slides without moths. In the left graph for slides with moths, correct responses were equivalent for run and nonrun conditions over the first four slides. On the last four slides, however, both moths in the run condition were detected at a higher level than the same moths in the nonrun condition. The same pattern appears in the right graph for correct responses defined as blue jays' withholding responses to negative slides. The data suggest that the consistent presentation of the same species of moth led to increased detection of both the presence and absence of the moth.

Guilford and Dawkins (1987) offered an alternative to the search-image hypothesis as an account of the Pietrewicz and Kamil data and related findings (Bond, 1983; Gendron, 1986; Gendron & Staddon, 1983). They argued that animals may come to better detect a consistent prey not because perception of that prey is improved but rather because animals adjust their search rate to be optimal for detection of that prey. If a particular prey is highly cryptic, the search rate may become very slow so that few prey will be missed; extra time will be taken to visually scan the environment for prey. For less cryptic prey, the time spent searching can be reduced, and most prey still will be detected. When prey are mixed, however, it may be difficult for an animal to adopt an optimal search rate, particularly if the prey differ in crypticity. A search rate appropriate for highly cryptic prey will be too slow for less cryptic prey, and a search rate appropriate for the less cryptic prey will be too fast for the more cryptic prey. In the latter case, in particular, a fast search rate will often lead the animal to miss the more cryptic prey.

One way in which the search image and search rate hypotheses can be tested against one another is to use two types of prey that have been shown to be *equally* cryptic. In this case, adjustment of the search rate to a speed appropriate for frequent detection of one prey should allow an animal to detect the other prey equally often. Under conditions of equal crypticity, animals should be equally successful at capturing prey either with an assortment of both prey items or with only one of the prey items. The search image hypothesis predicts, on the other hand, that animals should develop a search image for the most frequently occurring item and prefer it to the less frequently occurring item.

In a test of these different predictions, Reid and Shettleworth (1992) trained pigeons to search for grains of wheat placed upon a substrate of multicolored gravel. The grains of wheat were dyed either brown or green, and it

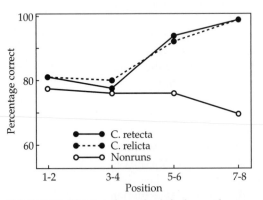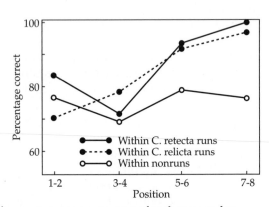

FIGURE 2.8. The graph on the left shows the percentage of correct responses to runs of each type and to nonruns containing a mixture of both types of moth. The graph on the right shows the percentage of correct responses to negative slides containing no moths.

was determined that both colors of grains were equally cryptic against the colored gravel. In an initial experiment, pigeons were allowed to forage or collect a number of grains of wheat under conditions that varied the proportion of each color. Over a number of foraging sessions, the percentage of each color of wheat was varied from 0 percent to 100 percent. On each session, a pigeon was stopped after it had eaten about half the grains available, and the number of green and brown grains consumed was determined. The graphs in Figure 2.9 indicate the proportion of green grains eaten as a function of the proportion of green grains available for each of four pigeons. The diagonal lines from the lower left corner to the upper right corner of each graph show the behavior predicted by the search rate hypothesis; that is, consumption should match availability. If a single search rate was used that was equally effective for finding brown and green grains, pigeons should have consumed, on the average, a proportion of green grains equal to the proportion available. The search image hypothesis predicts that as one color becomes more prevalent than the other, pigeons should develop a search image for that color of grain and show a preference for it. The data largely support this prediction. Although choice of green grains is near 50 percent when the mix of colors is 50:50, the curves tend to bow away from the diagonal as the mix moves toward more green than brown or more brown than green. Birds overselected the majority color, just as the search image hypothesis suggests.

In a further experiment, Reid and Shettleworth (1992) again used equally cryptic brown and green grains and required pigeons to make a choice between only two grains, one of each color, after a sequence of preceding opportunities to consume one type of grain or the other. A pigeon was required to peck a key in an operant chamber to advance a turntable containing seeds placed on a bed

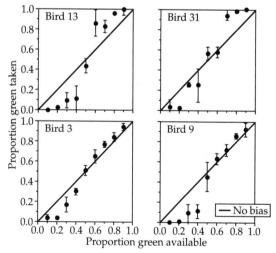

FIGURE 2.9. Proportion of green grains consumed as a function of the proportion of green grains in a distribution of green and brown grains of wheat. The diagonal lines show the behavior predicted from the search rate hypothesis.

of gravel (see Figure 2.10). The pigeon then could stick its head through an opening in the chamber wall and peck at seeds on the gravel. Within a daily session, a bird was given 30 trials or opportunities to peck at grains of wheat on different gravel beds. On the first 17 to 19 trials, the bird encountered one cryptic grain of the same color, either brown or green, on each trial. On the remaining trials, the bird was given a choice between two equally cryptic grains, brown and green. The graph on the right side of Figure 2.10 shows the proportion of green grains taken after initial runs of green and brown grains. The results are clear and favor the search image hypothesis. Pigeons preferred the grain that they had been consistently detecting and consuming in the preceding run. If only search rate were a factor in this experiment, no differential preference between grains should have appeared because the search rate established to find one color of grain should have been equally effective for finding the other color of grain.

Although it has been suggested that search images are important because they allow a foraging animal to locate cryptic food, is it important that the food is cryptic? Would the establishment of a search image be just as effective if the target food was not camouflaged? Recent research by Langley, Riley, Bond, and Goel (1996) answers this question. Pigeons were given runs in which they could consume a particular grain (red wheat or brown vetch) presented against a multicolored cryptic background or against a noncryptic gray background. On probe trials, trays containing equal numbers of both grains were presented; half the time, the probe was presented on the multicolored background, and half the time it was presented on the gray background. The experiment then was a 2×2 design, in which cryptic or noncryptic prey were presented during both the run and probe phases. The interesting finding revealed on the probe tests was that pigeons preferred the grain consumed during runs on which the background

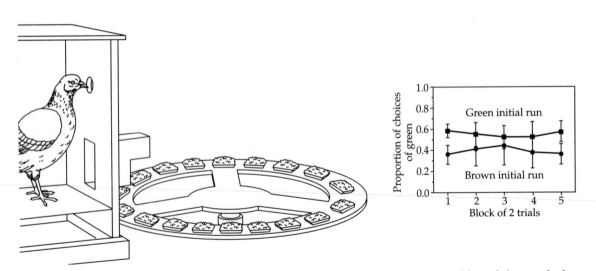

FIGURE 2.10. In the apparatus on the left, a pigeon pecked a key to advance the turntable and then pecked at wheat grains on beds of gravel. The graph on the right shows the proportion of green grains chosen after runs of green or brown grains.

was both multicolored and gray, but *only* if the probe background was multicolored. This finding indicates that a search image was activated by repeated capture of either cryptic or noncryptic food but that the use of the search image was maintained only if the pigeon continued to search for cryptic food.

Priming in Pigeons

The theoretical concepts of search image and priming are conceptually similar (P. Blough, 1991, 1992). The search image hypothesis suggests that the acquisition of a search image presets the perceptual system to be particularly sensitive to objects with defined characteristics. However, the search image idea was developed to explain foraging behavior in animals, and most tests of the search image hypothesis have used laboratory analogs of foraging. Other experiments with pigeons have used procedures more like those used in human target detection research and have yielded evidence of several types of priming effects. These experiments typically use the computer monitor and touchscreen methodology discussed earlier in this chapter and require pigeons to peck at target stimuli within a field containing a number of stimulus objects.

Sequential Priming

Demonstrations of sequential priming are very similar to the experimental designs used to demonstrate the search image. P. Blough (1991) rewarded pigeons for pecking at a single letter target presented among as many as 36 distractors made up of letters, numerals, and other standard characters. In a "blocked" condition, the same target object was presented over 20 successive trials. The control condition was one in which different target objects occurred in a mixed sequence. Because pigeons' accuracy at detecting targets typically was more than 90 percent, birds' ability to detect these targets was measured by their reaction time from the onset of the display to the initial peck. It was found that reaction times were lower when presentations of targets were blocked than when they were mixed. Reaction time increased as display size became larger, suggesting that the targets were sufficiently similar to distractors to require visual search. The advantage of blocked presentation was most apparent at the largest display size of 36 objects. There are several parallels between this finding and search image studies. In particular, the targets could be described as cryptic, and repeated presentation of a single target item enhanced speed of detection. In fact, P. Blough (1991) suggested that search images demonstrated in natural settings may be instances of the sequential priming process demonstrated by this experiment.

Cued Priming

In another experimental manipulation, P. Blough (1991) presented a cue just prior to the presentation of a target letter. These cues included patterns such as horizontal bars, grids, and checkerboards that varied in brightness. Each specific cue was mapped onto a particular target letter by always presenting the cue just before a display containing its associated target. These cues were called valid cues because they always predicted the appropriate target. As a control condition, an ambiguous cue was used; a white band containing three

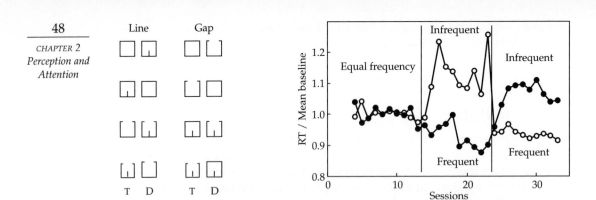

FIGURE 2.11. Target (T) and distractor (D) forms used in an odd-item detection experiment with pigeons are shown on the left. The graph on the right shows normalized reaction times (RT) when target-distractor pairs appeared equally often or when one pair appeared more frequently than the other.

vertical stripes was periodically presented and followed by displays containing any of the possible targets. The ambiguous cue provided virtually no information about which target would be presented. When either three or six different targets had to be detected during a session, reaction times were lower for targets cued by valid cues than for targets cued by ambiguous cues. Apparently, a cue that informed the subject about the nature of the target just an instant before display presentation speeded up target location.

Simultaneous Priming

Simultaneous priming refers to conditions in which distractor (nontarget) objects presented simultaneously with a target item serve to cue the presence of the target object. Target and distractor forms used in an experiment by D. Blough (1993) are shown on the left side of Figure 2.11. Note that these forms differ only by the presence of a line at the bottom of the box or a gap in the top of the box. Each display shown to pigeons contained 32 forms, 31 distractor forms, and 1 randomly placed target form. As in preceding experiments, a pigeon was rewarded only for pecking at the target. Pigeons were tested initially for 90 blocks of 16 trials within a session. Within each block of 16 trials, target and distractor pairs from the line and gap sets appeared equally often. After 16 sessions of this baseline testing, conditions were changed. Within successive blocks of 17 trials, pairs from the line set appeared on 16 trials (frequent pairs), while one pair from the gap set appeared on the remaining trial (infrequent pairs). After 10 sessions of testing under these conditions, another 10 sessions were carried out with the frequencies of the pairs reversed. That is, the gap pairs now were frequent, and the line pairs were infrequent. The curves shown in the graph on the right side of Figure 2.11 indicate that pigeons responded equally rapidly to line and gap targets when these pairs appeared with equal frequency. When sets of pairs differed in frequency, marked changes in reaction time appeared. Pigeons responded to targets found in frequent pairs considerably faster than to targets found in infrequent pairs. This was observed even when the frequencies were reversed.

Why did frequency of pairs have such a profound effect on reaction time? D. Blough argues that these results arise from priming or cuing effects of distractors. Since there were 31 distractors and only one target in each display, pigeons most often would first see a distractor when fixating the display. If a particular distractor occurs frequently with the same target, the distractors can activate information about the target that will aid in its search. Infrequent presentation of target distractor pairs would give pigeons little opportunity to practice quick retrieval of the target image.

In a second experiment, D. Blough (1993) showed that simultaneous priming could be extended to spatial position of the target form. In this experiment, targets paired with a particular distractor usually appeared on only one side of the screen, left or right. Thus, by first observing the distractor, a pigeon could restrict its visual search to only one side of the screen. On occasional probe trials, the target was presented on the opposite side of the screen. Reaction time data showed that pigeons pecked the target much faster when it appeared in its usual location than when it appeared on the opposite side of the screen.

An Overview of Priming and Search Image

An overview of this area of research suggests that experiments on priming and search image may be looking at largely the same phenomenon. Search image experiments may be classified as sequential priming studies and, as such, may be one type of priming among several. In addition to sequential priming brought about by repeated trials with the same target, we have seen that priming can be cued both by a preceding cue associated with the target and by simultaneously presented distractors consistently associated with the target. These distractors may cue both the form of the target and its spatial location.

It is not yet clear what aspects of the target stimulus get primed in priming experiments. The search image hypothesis implied that an actual image of the target prey or object is activated in working memory. Although an iconic representation of the target is certainly a possibility, other theorists have suggested that priming involves attention to features that identify the target (Reid & Shettleworth, 1992). Thus, a bird experiencing a series of green wheat grains may be primed to attend to the color feature of green and to the shape features that identify the wheat grain. A pigeon frequently seeing a target square with a small vertical line emerging from its base may be primed by distractor items to attend to the vertical line feature.

A recent experiment by Langley (1996) suggests that attention to cryptic prey may be complex. Langley presented runs of images of cryptic prey to pigeons, either wheat or beans, on a computer monitor framed by a touchscreen. After a run of either type of food, tests were given in which the color, shape, or both color and shape of the food were changed. The location of pecks on the test image were detected by the touchscreen and indicated how accurately the pigeon had located its search image. It was found that changing either the color or shape of beans led to a decrease in test accuracy relative to control tests in which no change in the image was made. However, only a change in the color of wheat produced a decline in the accuracy of detecting this food; shape change had no effect. This finding indicates that we cannot assume that an animal will form its search image by attending to particular features or dimensions of all prey objects; the features attended to may vary from prey to prey and may be determined by the animal's perceptual system and its foraging preferences.

ATTENTION

The concept of attention has been studied in two different ways in animal psychology. In studies of animal cognition carried out in recent years, attention in animals has been closely tied to questions of information processing capacity originally raised in human cognition research. In earlier literature, the concept of attention was prominent as a mechanism accounting for discrimination learning in animals. Although the focus of this section is on the information processing approach to attention, some discussion of the earlier use of the term is also provided.

Attention and Discrimination Learning

In the 1930s, a controversy began that raged for a number of years over the question of how animals learned to discriminate between stimuli that varied along a dimension, usually a visual dimension. For example, a rat might be trained to discriminate between a white arm and a black arm in a T-maze, with food always placed in the white arm and no food in the black arm. The positions of the white and black arms were randomly alternated between left and right, to ensure that the animal could not solve the problem by always going right or left. One theory of discrimination learning, referred to as *noncontinuity theory*, suggested that rats only gradually learned this discrimination because they focused attention on only one dimension at a time (Krechevsky, 1932; N. Sutherland & Mackintosh, 1971). Thus, a rat might begin by attending only to the spatial dimension of the problem and respond only on the basis of which side of the maze, left or right, was recently rewarded. When attention to spatial position did not yield consistent reward, the rat would switch its attention to brightness and eventually learn that white was the correct stimulus and black the incorrect stimulus. Importantly, the noncontinuity position assumed that the rat learned nothing about the relevance of the brightness dimension while it was responding to position.

Alternative approaches, called *continuity theories*, argued to the contrary that animals learned something about all of the stimuli present on each trial (Spence, 1936). If an animal turned right and went into the white goal box where it was rewarded, both the tendency to approach white and to turn right were strengthened. Over a number of trials, the rat always would be rewarded for approaching white and nonrewarded for approaching black, while rewards and nonrewards for going left and right would be equal. Eventually, the tendencies to go left and right would become equally strong and balance one another out, but the tendency to approach white would be much stronger than the tendency to approach black, leading the rat to consistently favor white over black.

Accounts of a number of discrimination learning phenomona were debated between these two positions. One example will be described. As suggested earlier, the noncontinuity or attentional account of discrimination learning suggested that as long as a rat showed no improvement in discriminating between black and white in a brightness discrimination, it was not attending to brightness and thus could learn nothing about the relevance of black and white cues. Suppose that the discrimination was reversed from white rewarded to black rewarded before the rat started to show any preference for white (the presolution period). According to the attentional account, this should have no effect on rate of learning the brightness discrimination since the animal had learned nothing about brightness prior to the reversal. Continuity theories, on the other hand, clearly predicted that initial training should retard subsequent reversal training because the tendency to approach white would have been strengthened to some extent by early training; this effect of differential reinforcement of black and white cues was masked during early training by initial differences in the strength of spatial responses or position habits. Although some early experiments did seem to favor the noncontinuity position (Krechevsky, 1938), other experiments showed clearly that some bias for the rewarded visual stimulus was learned even during an initial period of training when no behavioral preference for that stimulus was shown (Ehrenfreund, 1948; Spence, 1945).

Research on a number of other effects followed this same pattern. Findings that initially seemed to demand an attentional explanation could also be explained by continuity mechanisms that assumed no differential attention to multiple sources of stimulation (Riley & Leith, 1976). Although this research provided a great deal of information about discrimination learning in animals, it did not shed much light on possible attentional mechanisms. Let us now consider a more recent approach in which the focus is more narrowly directed at the question of attentional mechanisms in animals.

An Information Processing Approach to Attention

One form of attention can be found in tasks such as the odd-item visual search task previously described. In this case, attention referred to an animal's ability to scan its visual field and find a target stimulus. Target selection requires serial scanning that may involve peripheral eye movements or a more central search of the visual field. Still another form of attentional task is *analyzer selection* (Treisman, 1969). In this type of task, stimuli having values on two or more dimensions (analyzers) are presented at the same time, and the subject must register the values presented on each dimension. The stimuli usually occupy a considerable part of the perceptual field, and thus target selection is not a problem. For example, a human subject might briefly see a display that contains a line varying in size, color, and orientation. The line could be long or short, orange or blue, and vertical or horizontal. There are eight different combinations of displays that could be shown, and the subject might be asked to report on all three dimensions or only one randomly chosen dimension. Such experiments generally show that people's ability to detect the information from any one dimension declines as the number of other dimensions presented increases (Lindsay, 1970). Thus, it would not be too difficult for a person to remember that a line was orange if that was the only dimension to be reported. When the subject also must attend to the line's size and orientation, however, the task of detecting its color and remembering it becomes far more difficult.

Such an experiment is often referred to as a *divided-attention experiment*. When attention must be shared or divided among a number of dimensions, processing each single dimension suffers (Broadbent, 1958; Cherry, 1953). The input from each dimension is often conceived of as a *channel*; in the preceding example, information would be reaching the brain along three channels, one each for line color, size, and orientation. The difficulty for the central processing system is that it can only deal with one dimension at a time. As a consequence, processing must be switched back and forth between channels, and some information from each channel inevitably will be lost. Common analogies for this effect are the suggestion that a processing *bottleneck* is created or that the central processor becomes *overloaded* with incoming information.

Tests of Divided Attention in Pigeons

An interesting question for comparative cognition is whether animals faced with the need to process information from more than one dimension also suffer loss of information from divided attention. Evidence suggesting that they do has been accumulated in a series of studies carried out by Riley and his colleagues at the University of California (Riley & Leith, 1976; Riley & Roitblat, 1978). In these experiments, a procedure called "delayed matching-to-sample" was used. The delayed matching-to-sample procedure has been used extensively in the study of short-term or working memory in animals. Although its applications to memory research will be covered in detail in Chapters 3 and 4, its use for the study of divided attention is described here. The subject is once again a pigeon. The pigeon is initially trained to peck on each of three keys located in a horizontal row on the wall of an operant chamber. On matching-to-sample trials, the center key always presents the sample stimulus. The sample stimulus varies from trial to trial. If the pigeon is to match on the basis of color, the sample might be red on some trials and green on other trials. After the pigeon has seen the sample stimulus for a short period of time, it disappears, and two comparison stimuli appear, one each on the left- and right-side keys. The comparison stimuli are red and green; thus, one matches the sample, and the other does not. If the pigeon pecks the comparison stimulus that matches the sample, it is rewarded by several seconds of access to food. But, if it chooses the nonmatching comparison stimulus, the trial terminates without reward.

The delayed matching-to-sample procedure was used to study attention in the pigeon by presenting sample stimuli that varied in the amount of information they contained. Two kinds of sample stimuli were presented that contained either *element* or *compound* information. Tests using element sample stimuli are shown in Figure 2.12. Notice that each trial begins with the presentation of a white warning stimulus on the center key. The pigeon must peck this white key to introduce the sample stimulus; the requirement that the pigeon peck a warning stimulus guarantees that the pigeon will be looking at the sample stimulus when it appears. On the first trial shown, the sample is red, and its matching comparison stimulus is presented on the left key. A peck on the matching red

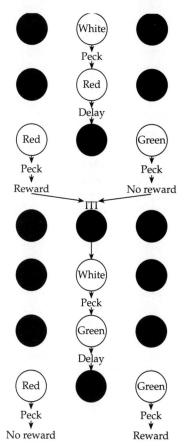

FIGURE 2.12. Stimuli and responses that would occur on two trials of delayed simultaneous matching-to-sample. The circles represent a row of three pecking keys a pigeon would see in an operant chamber. The filled circles represent darkened keys.

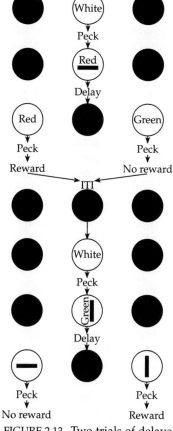

FIGURE 2.13. Two trials of delayed simultaneous matching-to-sample are shown using compound sample stimuli. On trial 1, a red horizontal line compound sample is presented, and memory for color is probed. On trial 2, a green vertical line compound is presented, and memory for line orientation is probed.

comparison key yields reward and introduces an intertrial interval (ITI) of several seconds spent in darkness. On the next trial, a peck on the white warning stimulus produces a green sample stimulus for a short period of time. A peck on the right-side green comparison stimulus now constitutes a matching response and is rewarded. Of course, the matching correct comparison stimulus appears equally often on the left and right following both red and green sample stimuli.

Trials in which compound sample stimuli are presented are shown in Figure 2.13. In the initial trial shown, the sample key contains a black horizontal line on a red background, and, on the second trial, the sample key contains a black vertical line on a green background. Thus, values on two dimensions, background color and line orientation, are contained in each compound stimulus. Not shown are the other two possible compound stimuli—a vertical line on a red background and a horizontal line on a green background. The other thing to note about the trials shown in Figure 2.13 is that memory for only one dimension of the sample stimulus is tested on each trial. On the first trial, only the color dimension is probed by presenting red and green comparison stimuli. On the second trial, only the line orientation dimension is tested by presenting vertical and horizontal lines as comparison stimuli. On other trials with these sample compounds, the alternate dimension would be tested by presenting the appropriate comparison stimuli. In a divided-attention experiment, pigeons are tested on both element and compound sample stimuli, which occur on different trials presented in a random order. The element sample trials tell us how well pigeons are able to match when they have to extract information about only one stimulus dimension, either color or line orientation. Performance on compound sample trials is compared with element sample trials to determine if having to extract information about two dimensions hinders information processing.

Consider an experiment carried out by Maki and Leith (1973), in which vertical and horizontal lines were superimposed on blue and red backgrounds as compound stimuli. On different tests, the sample stimulus was presented for different exposure durations, varying from a fraction of a second up to about 2.5 seconds. This exposure manipulation may be thought of as a variation in processing time or the time a pigeon is allowed to examine the sample stimulus. Processing time is a critical variable for a theory of divided attention. As more time is allowed for information to be transmitted along input channels, performance should improve on each channel. Furthermore, it should take a pigeon longer to process information from two dimensions than information from one dimension.

As can be seen in Figure 2.14, accuracy of matching grew as a function of duration of sample exposure on both compound and element tests. However, performance was higher at every duration on element tests than on compound tests. The filled and unfilled squares show the sample durations required for pigeons to match at a criterion of 80 percent correct choices. The duration required to achieve 80 percent correct was about twice as long for compound samples as it was for element samples. Just as the divided-attention model suggests, pigeons found it harder to match the correct dimension from a compound than from an element, and it took more time to process a compound stimulus than it did to process an element stimulus. These findings, and a number of others that replicated them (W. Roberts & Grant, 1978a; Santi, Grossi, & Gibson, 1982), have been used to argue that pigeons have a limited capacity for attending to multiple dimensions, just as people do (Langley & Riley, 1993; Leith & Maki, 1975; Maki & Leuin, 1972).

For human subjects, performance improves in a divided-attention experiment if they are cued about the test dimension before a compound stimulus is presented (Forbes, Taylor, & Lindsay, 1967). Knowing which channel is relevant to the test, the subject needs to attend only to that channel. Two types of studies

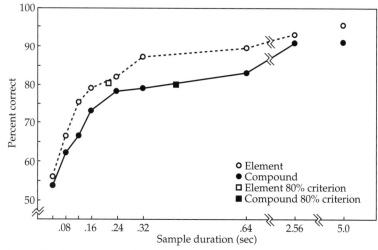

FIGURE 2.14. Matching-to-sample accuracy is plotted over sample durations for element and compound sample stimuli. The filled and unfilled boxes show the length of sample duration required to achieve a criterion of 80 percent correct.

carried out with pigeons suggest that they can also learn to selectively attend to a single channel, even though the sample stimulus may contain information from more than one dimension. Leith and Maki (1975) carried out a divided-attention experiment in which color and line orientation were presented in compound, and values on either dimension were tested randomly within a session containing a number of trials. The traditional divided-attention effect was found, with pigeons matching components of compound stimuli at a level below that found with color or line orientation stimuli presented separately as elements. Over some blocks of sessions, however, pigeons were consistently tested only on one dimension of compound stimuli. Each compound sample would be followed only by a color test for several sessions; on another block of sessions, each compound would be followed only by a line orientation test. With only one dimension tested, matching accuracy improved on compound tests, and the difference between compound and element tests declined. These data suggest that pigeons attended to only one dimension of a compound stimulus by learning that only that dimension would be tested.

Another way in which the information processing load imposed by a compound stimulus might be lowered is by telling the subject ahead of time which dimension is relevant. Lamb (1988) investigated this possibility by using a precue to inform pigeons about the dimension that would be tested on compound trials. Precuing was accomplished by presenting the element to be tested just before presentation of the compound sample stimulus. For example, a pigeon would see a red element stimulus on the center key followed by a horizontal line on a red background. Immediately following this compound sample, red and green comparison stimuli would appear on the side keys as a test for memory of the color dimension. On other trials, the precue would be a line on a neutral background, and the test would present a value from the line orientation dimension. On some probe trials, the precue would cue the dimension opposite to the one tested. After seeing a red element followed by a horizontal red compound, the pigeon would be tested with vertical and horizontal lines. The results were quite clear in showing that pigeons were able to match a value on the compound dimension far better when the cue indicated the dimension to be tested than when it indicated the irrelevant dimension. This finding implies that pigeons, like people, can selectively attend to one dimension of a complex stimulus if they have foreknowledge of the test dimension.

Challenges to the Divided-Attention Hypothesis

Although the findings just summarized suggest that pigeons show divided-attention effects similar to those found with people, other interpretations of some of these findings have been offered that have little to do with attention. In addition to divided attention, generalization decrement and coding decrement must be considered as possible causes of the difference in performance with element and compound sample stimuli.

Review the relationship between sample and compound stimuli presented earlier in Figure 2.13. The sample stimulus always consists of a line and a color, but the comparison stimuli presented only contain a line or a color. In other words, the comparison stimuli look somewhat different from the sample stimulus. This difference could lead to a drop in performance through *generalization decrement* (Cox & D'Amato, 1982; Maki, Riley, & Leith, 1976; Roberts & Grant, 1978a; Santi et al., 1982). Generalization refers to the tendency for a response trained to one stimulus to be made to other stimuli that have an appearance similar to the original training stimulus. Responses do generalize to other stimuli but usually with some loss in response strength. The less the new stimulus looks like the old stimulus, the more response strength will be lost, and this loss of responding is called a generalization decrement. In the case of divided-attention experiments, the lower performance seen with compound sample stimuli may arise from a generalization decrement caused by the difference in appearance of the sample and comparison stimuli. On element control trials, of course, the sample and comparison stimuli are identical, and no generalization decrement should occur.

The generalization decrement account of differences between compound and element matching emphasizes perceptual differences between these stimuli. In a somewhat different but related interpretation of this difference, Grant and MacDonald (1986) introduced the concept of *coding decrement*. They pointed out that in virtually all divided-attention experiments, animals were trained initially with element sample stimuli. Tests with compound stimuli were then introduced. Through extensive training with element stimuli, those stimuli come to elicit prospective response codes, such as "peck red" or "peck vertical line." (Prospective response codes are discussed in more detail in Chapter 4.) When compound stimuli are suddenly introduced, the difference in their appearance leads to coding decrement; that is, the response codes necessary for the correct choice between comparison stimuli are not produced as efficiently or as accurately as they were in element training, and a decline in performance on compound trials arises. One prediction from the coding decrement hypothesis is that pigeons initially given training with compound sample stimuli and then tested with element samples should show the same drop in performance on element samples previously seen with compound samples. The reason for this prediction is that the perceptual change, and hence the coding decrement, should be as great when element stimuli are substituted for compound stimuli as when compound stimuli are substituted for element stimuli. Grant and MacDonald carried out this experiment and found exactly that result. Their findings suggested that the divided-attention effect did not arise from divided attention at all but rather from coding decrement.

It should be emphasized that the generalization decrement and the coding decrement hypotheses both suggest that the compound element difference arises more from perceptual processes than from attentional processes. In fact, Grant and MacDonald argued that pigeons do not divide compounds into separate line orientation and color dimensions. Rather, compound sample stimuli are seen as a whole pattern or configuration. This configurational perception of compound samples contributes to the decrement in the coding response when animals are transferred from element to compound stimuli because removing one element of the compound changes the pattern that pigeons originally learned to match. The notion that animals process compound stimuli along separate dimensional channels then is ruled out by this perceptual hypothesis.

As often happens in psychological research, a finding that seemed to point clearly toward the operation of a particular process was also explainable by alternative processes. The difference in the ease with which pigeons could match element and compound sample stimuli could not only be explained as a difference in attention but also as an effect of generalization decrement or coding decrement.

New Evidence for Divided Attention in Pigeons

Fortunately for the divided-attention hypothesis, new findings have emerged to give it new life. Since generalization decrement and coding decrement may both be processes that contribute to the difference found between element and compound matching, these factors need to be controlled experimentally. If a difference between element and compound sample stimuli still appears after these decremental processes have been eliminated, we can attribute it to divided attention (Langley & Riley, 1993).

One way to control or eliminate the problem of generalization decrement is to use a procedure called *symbolic matching-to-sample*. The matching-to-sample procedure depicted in Figure 2.12 may be called *identity matching-to-sample* because the sample and correct comparison stimulus are visually identical to one another. In symbolic matching-to-sample, the samples and comparison stimuli bear no resemblance to one another. In fact, they may come from different dimensions. Thus, the samples might be red and green colors, and the comparison stimuli might be vertical and horizontal lines. Nevertheless, a pigeon can be taught to relate stimuli from these different dimensions to one another. For example, a pigeon may be trained to choose the vertical line when red is the sample and to choose the horizontal line when green is the sample.

The theoretical importance of symbolic matching-to-sample is discussed in Chapter 4. The important point here is that the use of this procedure controls for differences in generalization decrement between element and compound samples tests. If the sample and comparison stimuli look completely different from one another in both cases, then there can be no differential generalization decrement between sample and comparison stimuli.

The possibility that a difference in coding decrement causes the difference in matching between element and compound sample tests also may be eliminated. This is accomplished by training pigeons from the outset of an experiment with both element and compound sample stimuli; that is, trials in which animals have to match comparison stimuli to both element and compound sample stimuli would occur within the same session. Under these circumstances, codes for responding to both element and compound stimuli should be learned, and neither type of stimulus would be at a disadvantage relative to the other in terms of the availability of a response code.

Langley and Riley (1993) employed these controls in an experiment that used shape and color as sample dimensions. The design of their experiment can be seen in Table 2.1. Notice that the compound sample stimuli were circle or

TABLE 2.1 Design of the Experiment Carried Out by Langley and Riley (1993) to Compare Matching to Element and Compound Sample Stimuli
(Both generalization and coding decrement controlled)

Sample Stimulus	Comparison Stimuli	Response Outcome
ELEMENT SAMPLE STIMULUS TESTS		
Color tests		
Blue square	Top half key dark	Reward
	Bottom half key dark	No reward
Green square	Top half key dark	No reward
	Bottom half key dark	Reward
Shape tests		
White triangle	Thick horizontal lines	Reward
	Thin vertical lines	No reward
White circle	Thick horizontal lines	No reward
	Thin vertical lines	Reward
COMPOUND SAMPLE STIMULUS TESTS		
Color tests		
Blue triangle or	Top half key dark	Reward
blue square	Bottom half key dark	No reward
Green triangle or	Top half key dark	No reward
green square	Bottom half key dark	Reward
Shape tests		
Blue triangle or	Thick horizontal lines	Reward
green triangle	Thin vertical lines	No reward
Blue circle or	Thick horizontal lines	No reward
green circle	Thin vertical lines	Reward

triangle shapes drawn with blue or green lines. These compounds are referred to as *unified* stimuli and further control for the possibility that a decrement in compound matching could arise from peripheral receptor orientation. In other words, a pigeon cannot fixate shape separately from color; if it gazes at the form, it must also see the color. The results shown in Figure 2.15 clearly indicate that fewer correct responses were made when compound sample stimuli were presented than when element sample stimuli were presented. This difference appeared when the stimuli were presented for about 0.3 second and became larger as sample duration approached 6 seconds. The effect appeared when both color and shape dimensions were tested. This important experiment shows that when generalization decrement and coding decrement are both controlled, a clear difference between element and compound matching still emerges. Pigeons appear to show divided attention between color and shape dimensions.

A nagging problem with the divided-attention effects seen in both Figures 2.14 and 2.15 concerns the continued separation of these curves as sample duration grows longer. It has been argued that the deficit shown on tests with compound sample stimuli should disappear at longer durations (M. Brown & Morrison, 1990; Roberts & Grant, 1978a; Santi et al., 1982). With sufficient time to process both dimensions of a compound sample, a pigeon should show complete coding of both dimensions and equally accurate matching to both dimensions. In other words, all the information should get through the attentional bottleneck, given enough time. This prediction may not hold, however, if one considers in detail the attentional and memory processes active during the processing of a compound sample stimulus. If a pigeon cannot attend simultaneously to channels carrying color and shape information, it must switch back and forth between them. Each time it switches to one channel or the other, it will strengthen the memory code for the information coming in on that channel. However, at the same time, the memory code for the unattended channel may suffer some forgetting. Each dimension of a compound may then be strengthened when it is switched in and to some degree forgotten when it is switched out. The strengthening effect will lead to the rise in compound sample matching

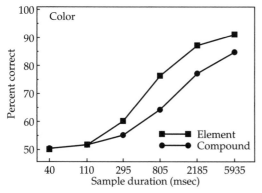
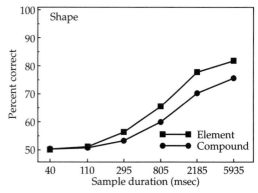

FIGURE 2.15. Results of the Langley and Riley experiment showing that pigeons matched element samples better than compound samples both on color and shape tests.

over increasing sample duration seen in Figures 2.14 and 2.15, but the forgetting effect will cause compound stimuli to be matched at a lower level of accuracy than element stimuli even at long sample durations.

Attention to Stimuli from Different Sensory Modalities

You have undoubtedly noticed that all of the experiments on attention thus far discussed have involved the presentation of information on a small key. Attention presumably should encompass a broader range of stimuli. For example, would a pigeon show differential attention to stimuli that are more ambient or that seem to come from several different locations in the environment? Kraemer and Roberts (1985) carried out a quite different attentional study in which the sample stimuli were light and noise. Both types of stimuli were *ambient* in the sense that they pervaded the entire chamber. Overhead diffuse light sources bathed the operant chamber in either red or green light. A speaker presented either a high tone of 3000 Hz or a low tone of 300 Hz. Both the red and green lights and the high and low tones were symbolically mapped onto comparison stimuli presented on the right- and left-side keys. Thus, following the red or green sample light, pigeons had to choose between vertical and horizontal lines; after a red sample, the vertical line would have to be chosen for reward, but, after a green sample, the horizontal line would have to be chosen for reward. Similarly, the high and low tone samples were followed by yellow and blue comparison stimuli; after the high tone, choice of yellow would be rewarded, and, after the low tone, choice of blue would be rewarded. Pigeons learned to match these element sample stimuli accurately, although it took them much longer to learn to match tone samples than color samples. On test sessions, element samples continued to be tested, but occasional tests with light-tone compounds also were performed. On a compound test, a pigeon might see the chamber bathed in green light and at the same time hear a low-pitched 300-Hz tone. Following such compound samples, either the horizontal and vertical lines or the yellow and blue side keys would be presented to test the pigeon's memory for either color or pitch.

The results of this experiment, presented in Figure 2.16, show a striking difference between light and tone tests. The bars on the left of the graph indicate that pigeons were able to match the light samples equally well as elements (L) or as light-tone (L*T) compounds. The bars on the right side of the graph show that although pigeons achieved about 80 percent matching accuracy when tone element stimuli (T) were presented, tone matching dropped to near the chance level of 50 percent when a light-tone compound (LT*) was presented. It appears that the ability of pigeons to attend to light was not interfered with at all by the presence of the tone, but their ability to attend to the tone was virtually eliminated by the presence of the light. The same results were obtained even when the light-tone compound was left on *during* the presentation of the comparison stimuli. Putting these results in a verbal metaphor, pigeons presented with compound stimuli were able to reply correctly when asked, "What do you see?" but were completely at a loss to

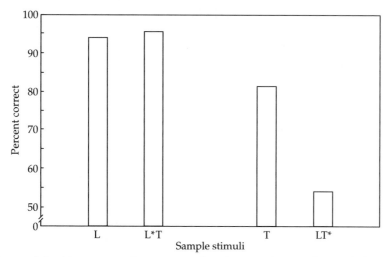

FIGURE 2.16. Matching-to-sample accuracy when the sample stimuli were light (L) or tone (T) elements or light-tone compounds. The asterisk indicates which member of the compound was tested, light (L*T) or tone (LT*).

answer the question, "What do you hear?"—even though they were quite capable of hearing the tone.

Divided-attention experiments in which line orientation or shape cues were presented on red or green keys generally showed equivalent losses of information for both color and form dimensions. Quite in contrast, the light-tone experiment produced an *asymmetrical* deficit in which light prevented processing of tone but tone had no effect on light processing. Kraemer and Roberts (1987) suggested that this effect should be referred to not as divided attention but as *restricted attention*. The data suggest that the presentation of a light-tone compound completely restricted processing to the visual modality. Rather than switching back and forth between analyzers or modalities, all of the subject's attention was devoted to the visual stimulus. Similar results have been found with people. Mowbray (1953) asked people to read and to listen to different prose passages presented simultaneously. When subjects were subsequently given a true-false test to measure their knowledge of these passages, they typically answered correctly for one passage and at chance for the other. Further, subjects were often significantly more knowledgeable about the visual passage than about the auditory passage. Such findings in people and pigeons may be attributed to *visual dominance* (Posner, Nissen & Klein, 1976), or a tendency to give visual input high priority over stimulation coming in other sensory channels. We know that pigeons have highly sensitive visual processing systems. In an animal for whom foraging and escape from predators is largely dependent upon visual information, it is not surprising that attention to visual input would dominate when visual information is placed in compound with information from other modalities.

Although there are clear differences between the human and pigeon visual systems in structure and function, various investigations suggest that the visual experiences of the two species may be similar. In psychophysical experiments, pigeons show dark adaptation and spectral sensitivity functions very similar to those found with people. Through the use of computers and touchscreens, it has been possible to examine pigeons' perception of complex images. Pigeons respond to texture patterns in much the same way people do. When a textured area differs from its background by only a single dimensional feature, such as color or line slant, pigeons detect the target area quickly and with little error, suggesting that the target "pops out" for pigeons as it does for people. Perception of such targets appears to be based on preattentive parallel processing. When common target and background features are placed in different conjunctions, both people and pigeons find it harder to locate the target. Targets difficult to discriminate require attentive serial search, as shown by increased reaction time to find such targets as the number of background stimuli increases. Both human and pigeon perception, then, seem well described by a two-stage model that involves an initial, quick pop-out of features and a secondary serial search.

Beyond the perception of features and simple objects, other research indicates that pigeons may perceive whole patterns the same as humans do. Tests of the recognition by components theory with pigeons suggest that they discriminate between different patterns of basic perceptual units or geons. Pictures of objects were not readily recognized when the arrangement of geons was changed. Pigeons learned to discriminate between pictures containing the same geons placed in different configurations. These findings suggest that pattern perception is emergent in both people and pigeons. Both species see complex patterns of features and geons as whole objects and not as collections of unrelated parts.

A review of research on search image and priming suggests that prior experience biases pigeon perception toward faster detection of particular targets. Sequential priming studies show that a block of trials devoted to detection of a single odd item enhances the speed with which that item is detected. In a similar fashion, search image research in foraging experiments suggests that continued capture of a prevalent prey item leads to faster detection and hence overselection of that prey item. Other types of priming seen in pigeons are cued priming and simultaneous priming. Through learning, both cues presented just before a display and distractors within a display can facilitate target detection by providing information about the features of the target.

Studies of attention in pigeons lead to the conclusion that they suffer from divided attention between information from different dimensions in much the same way that people do. As the number of dimensions seen in a visual display increases, both humans and pigeons show a decrease in the information acquired about any single dimension. Thus, pigeons given a delayed-matching test with compound shape-color sample stimuli match either the shape or color at a lower level of accuracy than is the case when these stimuli are presented as element samples. Further, it has been shown that attention may be biased toward one dimension within a compound by testing only that dimension over a number of sessions or by precuing the dimension to be tested. Although generalization decrement and coding decrement may contribute to the drop in matching found with compound samples, recent experiments controlling these factors indicate that pigeons still show a divided-attention effect. The divided-attention effect suggests that pigeons' attention switches back and forth between the visual dimensions presented in a compound stimulus. As exposure duration increases, each dimension provides more information and shows improved matching; forgetting during switches to the alternate dimension explains the fact that compound matching remains inferior to element matching even at long sample exposure durations.

When pigeons' ability to match visual and auditory stimuli placed in compound was tested, very different results from those found with compound visual stimuli were revealed. Although a tone presented with an ambient light stimulus had no effect on the pigeon's ability to match the light, the light stimulus virtually eliminated the pigeon's ability to match the tone. This finding suggests that visual stimuli restrict or dominate processing of auditory stimuli when they are placed in a compound. Although attention may be divided or shared between visual cues on a sample key, quite different attentional effects may be found when compounds are made up of cues from different sensory modalities.

Working Memory: Early Research and Contemporary Procedures and Findings

During the first half of the 20th century, research on human memory was largely focused on what came to be called *long-term memory*. In a tradition started by the ground-breaking research of Ebbinghaus (1885), people were asked to memorize by rote long lists of words or meaningless strings of three letters called nonsense syllables. Subjects would proceed through such a list repeatedly, each time trying to recite the items in their correct order. Once a list was mastered, memory for the items would then be tested minutes, hours, days, or, in some cases, even months later. A great deal of information about human long-term memory was discovered by many experiments carried out with these procedures. For example, the classic forgetting curve was revealed, in which it was shown that forgetting proceeds most rapidly immediately after learning and more slowly as the retention interval becomes longer. In keeping with the associationist theoretical approach to learning that dominated research at that time, emphasis was placed on *associations* between verbal items as the unit of memory analysis. Forgetting was explained by *interference theory*. According to this theory, people failed to remember verbal associations because other associations interfered with their recall in one fashion or another. This interference could be either proactive or retroactive. In the case of *proactive interference*, associations established by earlier learning would reduce the recall of more recent learning. *Retroactive interference* referred to the loss of associations formed earlier by interference from subsequently learned associations.

Against this background, long-term memory was thought to require many repetitions to be established and long periods of time to be forgotten. Reports of *short-term memory* came as a startling revelation. Almost simultaneous reports by J. Brown (1958) and L. Peterson and M. Peterson (1959) revealed that humans could form memories upon a single exposure to verbal material and forget them almost as quickly, over a period of only a few seconds. A verbal stimulus was presented for a few seconds, such as several words or a random assortment of letters. The retention interval typically varied between 1 and 30 seconds. At the end of the interval, the subject was asked to recall the items. An important feature of this procedure was the requirement that the subject engage in some task that prevented rehearsal during the retention interval, such as solving simple arithmetic problems or counting backward by threes from an arbitrarily designated number. Data from this type of experiment, obtained from tests with many subjects, are typically presented as a plot of percentage of correct responses as a function of retention interval. Although the opportunity for forgetting was short, such curves showed the traditional negatively accelerated form, with faster forgetting immediately after removal of the to-be-remembered items. By 20 to 30 seconds, as much as 80 percent of the material had been forgotten.

65

CHAPTER 3
Working Memory:
Early Research and
Contemporary
Procedures and
Findings

The distinction between short-term and long-term memory has given rise to some debate in the human memory literature, with some theorists arguing that they are only different aspects of a single processing system (Craik & Lockhart, 1972; Melton, 1963; Spear & Riccio, 1994; Tulving, 1968) and others arguing that they represent separate memory systems with different properties (Atkinson & Shiffrin, 1968; Baddeley, 1978; Waugh & Norman, 1965). In two-store theories, the long-term memory is thought of as the repository of past learning, whereas short-term memory represents immediate consciousness or the workbench for those thoughts or memories we are currently processing. Thus, the term *working memory* has been used as a metaphor that better describes the functional purpose of short-term memory (Baddeley, 1981).

TYPES OF ANIMAL MEMORY EXPERIMENTS AND MEMORY SYSTEMS

Influenced undoubtedly by the Brown and L. and M. Peterson demonstrations, and by the flurry of theory and research in human memory they stimulated, psychologists interested in animal learning and behavior became intrigued with the possibility of studying short-term memory in animals. A number of techniques have been developed for the study of short-term memory in animals. These techniques have in common the presentation of a stimulus (e.g., a visual pattern, a colored field, or a tone), the withdrawal of the stimulus for a delay or retention interval, and finally the presentation of one or more test stimuli, related to the initial stimulus, with the opportunity to make an operant response to these stimuli. The test stimuli might be two or more levers or lit keys, and the operant response would be pressing a lever or pecking a key. An operant response to the test stimulus that matched the initial stimulus yielded reward, whereas a response to one that did not match was nonrewarded. A number of trials would be carried out at several delay intervals, and the percentage of correct or rewarded responses (relative to chance expectancy) would be calculated. Choice of the matching or correct test stimulus significantly above chance indicated retention of the initial stimulus.

Although there are obvious similarities between procedures used to study short-term memory in animals and those used with human subjects, there are important differences. Typically, humans recall verbal items, but animals are usually given a recognition test for memory of a visual stimulus. Also, steps are not usually taken in animal experiments to prevent rehearsal since animals

66

CHAPTER 3
Working Memory:
Early Research and
Contemporary
Procedures and
Findings

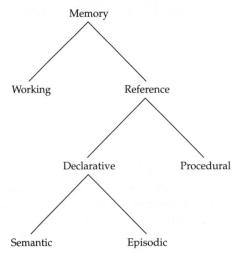

FIGURE 3.1. A tree diagram showing the hierarchical relationship between types of memory.

cannot use language to internally repeat encoded information. However, it is possible that animals could use a form of nonverbal rehearsal, and we shall see that the issue of rehearsal is important in animal studies. The term working memory has been borrowed from the human literature and is now used to describe most studies of short-term retention in animals (Honig, 1978). The term also emphasizes the fact that different memories must be responded to over repeated trials in animal experiments. Thus, the memory that was relevant on the previous trial may be irrelevant or even incorrect on the next trial, in which a new memory must form the basis for response.

Other types of memory experiments, which are examined in detail in Chapter 6, involve memory for behaviors based on associations that often require several trials or repetitions of a sequence of events to be acquired. Memory tests for these behaviors may be given hours or days after the original association was learned. There is an obvious similarity between these experiments and those already discussed that were performed to study human long-term memory. Honig (1978) has suggested that long-term memories for associations be called *reference memory*. Conceived of broadly, reference memory subsumes all of those associations an animal has acquired about its behavior, its environment, and relationships between its behavior and the environment.

Figure 3.1 presents a tree diagram that classifies types of memory. The distinctions made in this diagram are based on both methodological and theoretical grounds and offer a rough distinction between types of memory. The categories of semantic and episodic memory were developed to describe different forms of human memory, and their application to animal memory may be theoretically controversial. Nevertheless, the diagram provides an aid to understanding the types of memory discussed in this and later chapters.

The hierarchy of memory begins with a division of memory into working and reference memory, and some distinctions between working and reference memory tasks have already been described. The remainder of this chapter and Chapter 4 are concerned with working memory phenomena, while Chapters 5 and 6 deal with the formation of associations and reference memory for associations, respectively. Under the heading of reference memory, a distinction is made between declarative memory and procedural memory (Squire, 1987). With reference to human memory, *procedural memory* refers to memory for well-learned cognitive and motor skills that we perform relatively automatically. Examples would be riding a bicycle and playing a piano. *Declarative memory*, on the other hand, refers to cognitive information accumulated about our world. A further distinction is made between two forms of declarative memory: semantic memory and episodic memory (Tulving, 1972, 1983). *Semantic memory* is that memory we have that provides us with all the general cognitive information we need to function within our culture, such as vocabulary, numerical relations, and geographical maps about our immediate environment and the world at large. Much of this semantic memory would be shared in common among members of the same culture. *Episodic memory*, on the other hand, is a much more personal memory system that refers to memory for specific episodes that have occurred at particular times in the past history of an individual. Memory of the birthday party given to celebrate your 21st birthday or memory of what you ate for lunch yesterday are examples of episodic memory.

One item of evidence that dramatically demonstrates the separation of semantic and episodic memory systems is the case of the brain-damaged patient studied by Tulving that was briefly described in Chapter 1. This man, identified as K.C., suffered extensive brain lesions to the parietal and occipital parts of his cortex. As a consequence, K.C. showed complete loss of episodic memory (Tulving, 1989, 1993). He could not remember a single episode from his past. Further, he could not formulate a plan for any activity he would carry out in the future. His ability to conceive of personal episodes was completely lost. Nevertheless, he had a normal IQ, his language ability was intact, and he remembered a good deal of impersonal, general information about the world. His startling inability to maintain personal memories suggests that the damage sustained by his brain had destroyed those areas needed for episodic memory but spared those needed for semantic memory.

Distinctions among different reference memory systems are more difficult to make in the field of animal memory. Most people would agree that animal memory must include a number of virtually automatic motor routines used for various survival purposes (Aldridge, Berridge, Herman, & Zimmer, 1993) and that these memories would be classified as procedural memory. With behaviors based on learned associations, however, classification may be more difficult. For example, are classically conditioned responses a form of declarative or procedural memory (Squire, 1987)? If classically conditioned responses are conceived of as automatic stimulus-response associations, then it would seem reasonable to classify them as procedural memories. As we shall see in Chapter 5, however, a more contemporary view of classical conditioning suggests that it involves flexible cognitive associations between representations of conditioned and unconditioned stimuli (Rescorla, 1988). In this case, we may wish to classify the memories of at least some classically conditioned behaviors as declarative memories. Chapter 7 on spatial cognition makes the case for

67

CHAPTER 3
Working Memory:
Early Research and
Contemporary
Procedures and
Findings

68

CHAPTER 3
Working Memory:
Early Research and
Contemporary
Procedures and
Findings

animals forming cognitive maps or complex representations of their environments, which include the relationships between landmarks and important locations. These representations allow animals to take novel paths or shortcuts between one place and another. Cognitive maps would seem to be best classified as declarative memories.

Can the further division of declarative memory into semantic and episodic memory be made for animals? This question is controversial. Tulving (1985) has argued that episodic, semantic, and procedural memory are associated with different levels of consciousness that he refers to as autonoetic, noetic, and anoetic, respectively. *Anoetic consciousness* is the absence of awareness that would be associated with automatically performing an instinctual or highly learned motor sequence. *Noetic consciousness* is awareness of general, abstract knowledge about one's world. Finally, *autonoetic consciousness* refers to personal knowledge or memory of events one has participated in as an individual. Although animals may well have anoetic and noetic consciousness, corresponding to procedural and semantic memory, it is more difficult to leap to the assumption that they possess autonoetic consciousness and episodic memory. As pointed out with respect to the question of animal consciousness in Chapter 1, the question is whether an animal remembers past events it experienced as events that occurred to it as an individual. Patients who have suffered hippocampal damage can often acquire new semantic and procedural memories while being totally unable to remember any of the instances during which they learned new information or skills. Does an animal that learns to press a bar for reward or to turn right in a maze for food remember only that bar presses and right turns yield reward, or does it remember specific instances on which it pressed the bar or made the right turn and obtained the reward? This is not an easy question to answer, and there appears to be little evidence to guide us. To a certain extent, the issue is related to the question of self-awareness in animals, which is considered in Chapter 12.

It should be emphasized that working memory experiments with animals involve the interaction of both working memory and reference memory (Honig, 1978). Many studies of working memory in animals make use of the delayed matching-to-sample procedure introduced in Chapter 2. To perform accurately and to show evidence of working memory, an animal must first learn several if → then rules about the task. For example, a subject might have to learn, "If the sample was a green light → then choose the triangle stimulus to obtain reward;" but, "If the sample was a red light → then choose the circle stimulus to obtain reward." These rules give rise to accurate performance only after a number of repetitions or experiences with these relationships. The rules and their behavioral execution now reside in reference memory. However, the specific sample stimulus presented on each trial of a session varies unpredictably and gives rise to working memories that then may activate rules stored in reference memory. Most tasks of any complexity then involve an interchange of information between working and reference memory. Information about rules needed for the appropriate response to a presented stimulus or to a trace residing in working memory need to be retrieved into working memory from reference memory. New information just acquired and temporarily residing in working memory can then be incorporated into reference memory to update the rules governing the task.

In this chapter, some contemporary techniques for studying working memory in animals are described, the extent of retention in working memory is examined, and selected variables and processes that appear to affect retention and forgetting are discussed. Before an examination of contemporary research, it should be pointed out that a large number of experiments were carried out in the first half of the 20th century that could be described as studies of working memory in animals, although the study of memory processes was not usually the intent of these studies. An overview of these early studies is an important preface to the study of contemporary work.

69

CHAPTER 3
*Working Memory:
Early Research and
Contemporary
Procedures and
Findings*

EARLY STUDIES OF DELAYED RESPONSE

Hunter's Experiments

It is generally agreed that serious laboratory investigations of the delayed-response problem began with W. Hunter's classical studies (W. Hunter, 1913). Hunter approached his task from the point of view of the tough-minded new behaviorism, which had arisen as a reaction to the anecdotal approach to animal psychology of the late 19th century and the anthropomorphic interpretations of behavior it had spawned. He wished to explore the possibility of ideation in animals, but he rejected instances of conditioning in which an animal might show evidence of recognizing stimuli previously associated with food as cases of "sensory recognition." In other words, Hunter felt that responses to stimuli presented by an experimenter failed to show any ability on an animal's part to maintain a representation of a preceding event in the absence of external stimulation. A situation was needed in which only an internal representation of a previously presented stimulus could control behavior. If an animal could respond accurately in such a situation, the behavior would have to be attributed to higher order symbolic activity, or what Hunter referred to as an "intraorganic cue."

W. Hunter invented an apparatus to study this problem that consisted of a delay chamber, into which the animal was placed, and a choice chamber, which contained three different doorways. Food was placed in another chamber behind one of the doorways, and a light in front of the correct doorway was turned on to signal the location of food. Hungry animals were trained to run from the starting chamber to the illuminated exit to obtain food. The light then was extinguished midway through an animal's approach to the exit and eventually even before the animal left the delay chamber. Because the animal could see only the light and not the food from the delay chamber, Hunter referred to this procedure as the ""indirect method." In the "direct method", an already motivationally significant stimulus—food for a hungry animal or a toy for a child—was hidden within one of several locations while the subject watched, with the subject allowed to choose one of the locations after a delay.

Rats, dogs, and raccoons were tested in this situation. Once an animal could accurately approach the exit that had been lighted, the animal was required to observe the light from the chamber and then wait for a brief time after the light's termination before responding. The delay was lengthened progressively until a point was reached at which an animal could no longer

70

CHAPTER 3
Working Memory:
Early Research and
Contemporary
Procedures and
Findings

choose accurately. All of the animals tested showed some ability to make the correct response after delay, but the limits of delay varied among species. The maximum delay for rats was 10 seconds, whereas raccoons could delay for 25 seconds and dogs for as long at 5 minutes. In further work with children, W. Hunter (1917) used the direct method, in which a child was allowed to directly view the reward. Hunter found that his 13-month-old daughter could delay response successfully for 24 seconds, and older children showed successful delays as long as 20 minutes.

With regard to the question of symbolic processes in animals, W. Hunter concluded from his experiments that a form of "sensory thought" was used by raccoons and children. He reasoned that the ability of these subjects to choose the correct alternative must depend on an internal representation of the light or reward since these stimuli were absent at the end of the delay. Hunter's conceptualization of this memory process was surprisingly contemporary. It was theorized that an intraorganic cue (sensory thought) was aroused by the lighting of an exit but waned during the delay and was rearoused at the time of release, acting to guide the correct response. This theory bears a strong resemblance to the modern concept of memory retrieval.

In the case of rats and dogs, W. Hunter felt that no evidence of sensory thought had been revealed. Although these animals responded accurately after delays, their success appeared to be completely dependent upon the maintenance of a positional orientation toward the correct exit during the delay interval. By pointing at the correct doorway, these animals had solved the problem without the necessity for memory. Although Hunter concluded that sensory thought was absent in these animals, it should be pointed out that dogs and rats could have retained memories of the lighted exit but relied more heavily on the pointing strategy. In other words, the absence of evidence for sensory thought did not prove that this process was absent in animals.

W. Hunter's work had a significant impact on the study of animal behavior. Subsequent researchers were particularly impressed with the possibility of using delayed response as a means of distinguishing the intellectual capacities of different species of animals. This would be accomplished by examining two aspects of behavior in the delayed response problem. The first was the necessity of an animal to maintain orientation toward a cue in order to respond accurately. Orientation may be thought of as a form of behavior that mediates between stimulus and response and can allow the animal to make the correct response in the absence of memory of the stimulus. Presumably, species that did not require orientation possessed symbolic capacities. Those that did require orientation to make accurate choices would be weak or lacking in sensory thought. Second, among animals that could respond accurately after delays without pointing at the correct alternative, the ability to use symbolic thought could be graded in terms of the maximal delay an animal could tolerate and still respond accurately. Thus, species could be ranked in terms of their delay times, providing a phylogenetic hierarchy of the evolution of symbolic processes.

The Necessity for Orientation

W. Hunter therefore concluded that only certain animals were capable of symbolic thought and that others must depend on orientation. This led subsequent

71

CHAPTER 3
Working Memory:
Early Research and
Contemporary
Procedures and
Findings

researchers to pay close attention to animals' behavior during the delay interval. Research with primates (Harlow, Uehling & Maslow, 1932; Tinklepaugh, 1928; Yerkes, 1927) showed no need for postural positioning during delay; this result was not too surprising, however, since a capacity for symbolic thought was expected in monkeys and apes. More damaging to Hunter's thesis was the finding that even the cat (D. Adams, 1929; Cowan, 1923) and the rat (Cowles, 1940; MacCorquodale, 1947; McCord, 1939) could respond correctly after considerable turning and moving about during the delay interval.

Experiments in which the experimenter actually prevented orientation toward the correct choice provided even more convincing evidence that orientation was not necessary for memory. In some experiments, animals were first shown the correct cue and then removed from the delay chamber during the delay to prevent orientation. Upon return to the apparatus, monkeys, cats, and rats all showed memory of the cued choice (D. Adams, 1929; MacCorquodale, 1947; Maier, 1929; Tinklepaugh, 1928). Another method was to disrupt any possible orientation by rotating the delay chamber at the beginning of the delay. Walton (1915) rotated a dog 90 degrees and distracted the animal during the delay by calling to it and displaying a piece of meat; the dog still responded quite accurately to the original cue at delays as long as 5 minutes.

In other experiments, still more drastic measures were taken to prevent orientation toward the correct stimulus. In one experiment, R. Hunter (1941) rotated the delay chamber around horizontal and vertical axes at such high speeds that a rat was thrown to one end of the chamber and pinned there during the delay by centrifugal force! Still, rats responded at about 90 percent accuracy after a 20-second delay. Finally, Loucks (1931) and Ladieu (1944) anesthetized rats during the delay interval and found that they responded accurately after recovering from the anesthesia.

Faced with overwhelming evidence that animals could delay response successfully in a number of situations in which orientational cues were ruled out, most investigators came to the conclusion that all of the species studied could bridge the delay through the use of a centrally stored memory trace. That animals possessed representational processes did not mean, however, that orientation was never used as a basis for delayed response. Experiments by Cowles (1940) and by Fletcher and Davis (1965) showed that although performance was significantly above chance without orientation, it was enhanced still further if orientation was maintained. This finding suggests that, in some cases, animals use both orientation cues and memory to guide responding. The degree to which orientation plays a role in delayed response may be determined situationally. Most of the experiments that yielded evidence for the use of orientation were performed with homogeneous stimuli that were placed close to one another. If all of the stimulus alternatives look alike and are close to one another, it may be difficult to remember which one was cued without actually pointing toward it (Maier, 1929). As stimuli are made more distinctive and separated spatially, the need for orientation may diminish.

Interspecies Comparisons of the Limits of Delay

W. Hunter's suggestion that certain animals were limited in the length of time they could hold a sensory thought served as a challenge to many researchers to

72

CHAPTER 3
Working Memory:
Early Research and
Contemporary
Procedures and
Findings

find conditions under which longer delays could be obtained. Taking the rat as an example, Hunter had concluded that rats could respond accurately at delays no longer than 10 seconds. In a striking demonstration, Maier (1929) placed three ringstands at different locations within the laboratory and trained rats to climb a ladder on each ringstand and follow an elevated pathway to a table containing food. In memory tests, an animal was allowed to follow only one pathway to food for several trials and then was retained in its cage for the delay interval. On subsequent free choice tests, rats chose the previously rewarded pathway more often than chance expectancy after delays as long as 24 hours.

Similar findings were discovered with other species of animals. D. Adams (1929) found that cats could tolerate delays as long as 16 hours, and experiments with monkeys and apes revealed maximal delay times up to 20 hours. The implications of these findings gradually became apparent: Any attempt to rank species on the basis of length of delay in delayed-response experiments was futile. None of the species studied could be characterized as being able to delay for some fixed interval of time. The conditions under which animals were tested were far more important than the species. For any given animal, short and long delay times could be found, depending on the testing conditions. In general, conditions in which the stimuli used were made visually distinctive and were placed far apart in space led to higher delays than conditions in which visually homogeneous stimuli were placed close to one another (W. Roberts, 1972c).

CONTEMPORARY METHODS FOR THE STUDY OF WORKING MEMORY

The concern of most delayed-response studies was with questions of postural orientation and species differences in delay times. Researchers mentioned occasionally that memory was involved in delayed response, but no sophisticated analyses of this problem in terms of memory mechanisms were carried out (Spear, 1978; Winograd, 1971). Only more recently have procedures similar to the delayed-response problem been developed for the explicit study of problems in animal memory.

Delayed Simultaneous Matching-to-Sample

Since the problem of animals orienting toward the correct stimulus during a delay period was a major concern with the delayed-response procedure, modern studies of animal working memory have eliminated that problem by using delayed matching-to-sample procedures. In the simultaneous matching-to-sample procedure, spatial position is made irrelevant by randomizing the positions of the test stimuli. The paradigm for delayed simultaneous matching is shown in Figure 2.12 and described in Chapter 2. To review briefly, a pigeon is enclosed in an operant chamber, with the only sources of illumination being those presented at various locations by the experimenter.

A trial is initiated by a warning or alerting stimulus, which is a white light on the center key, with the left- and right-side keys remaining darkened. A single peck on the center key causes the white stimulus to change to a *sample stimulus*, a red key. The red key remains lit for a fixed period of time, usually a few seconds, or the subject is required to complete a certain number of pecks on the key, a fixed ratio. Upon completion of the time or fixed ratio, the red key is darkened for some delay period, and the two side keys then are illuminated, one with red light and the other with green light. A peck on the red key, which matches the sample key, yields immediate reward; some pigeon food appears in a hopper directly below the keys. Choice of the nonmatching green key, on the other hand, simply darkens the keys and produces no reward. After either a correct response and reward or an incorrect response and nonreward, the pigeon encounters an intertrial interval (ITI), during which all keys are turned off. At the end of the ITI, a new trial is initiated by presentation of the white center key.

Some important features of this procedure should be pointed out. First, the delay between the sample stimulus and the side key stimuli serves as a memory or retention interval, over which the subject must remember the sample stimulus in order to be able to choose accurately between the test stimuli. This interval can be varied to examine the progress of forgetting as the delay is lengthened. Another important aspect of simultaneous delayed matching is that the positions of the cues presented on the test side keys, often called the *comparison stimuli*, are varied randomly between trials. This aspect of the procedure ensures that a subject cannot simply point toward one key and always peck it for a correct choice because the position of the correct comparison key is unknown during the delay interval. A number of trials are normally given within a daily session, and the percentage of correct responses over a number of trials is used as an estimate of a subject's memory under a given set of conditions. With only two comparison stimuli, the probability of correct choice by chance alone is 0.5 or 50 percent. If more than two comparison stimuli are used, the level of accuracy expected by chance will be 1 divided by the number of comparison stimuli. Evidence of memory for the sample stimulus would always be indicated by a performance level better than chance. Finally, although keys varying in hue are used in this example, a variety of stimuli can be used as sample and comparison stimuli, including geometric patterns or even pictures of real objects. Thus, memory for different kinds of visual material may be studied in pigeons and other animals.

Data from a simultaneous matching-to-sample experiment carried out by W. Roberts (1972b) are shown in Figure 3.2. Pigeons were presented with colored sample stimuli on a center key and required to peck the key for fixed ratios (FRs) of 1, 5, or 15 pecks. The sample stimulus then disappeared, and the pigeon remained in darkness for a delay of 0, 1, 3, or 5 seconds. At the end of the delay, the comparison stimuli were presented, and the pigeon made its choice between a stimulus that matched the sample and one that did not. Notice that all three retention curves drop as the delay becomes longer and that the level of the curves rises as the FR increases.

73

CHAPTER 3
*Working Memory:
Early Research and
Contemporary
Procedures and
Findings*

74

CHAPTER 3
Working Memory:
Early Research and
Contemporary
Procedures and
Findings

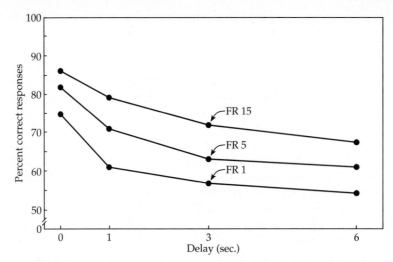

FIGURE 3.2. Working memory retention curves for pigeons in delayed simultaneous matching-to-sample. The curves show retention after pigeons pecked the sample key 1, 5, or 15 times.

Delayed Successive Matching-to-Sample

This procedure involves the successive presentation of two stimuli, which are either matching or nonmatching (Konorski, 1959; Nelson & Wasserman, 1978). As shown in Figure 3.3, only a single pecking key is used and is illuminated with either red or green light. An initial sample stimulus, a red or green key, is presented for a fixed period of time, say, 5 seconds. Pigeons tend to peck at this sample, and the first peck after 5 seconds terminates the sample stimulus and introduces a delay spent in darkness. At the end of the delay, a comparison stimulus is presented on the same key. The relationship between the sample and comparison stimuli is either matching (red-red or green-green) or nonmatching (red-green or green-red). On matching trials, the first response to the comparison stimulus after it has been presented for 5 seconds leads to reward delivery. On nonmatching trials, the trial simply ends without reward after the comparison stimulus has been presented for 5 seconds. Thus, the subject is rewarded on all matching trials and nonrewarded on all nonmatching trials.

To train a pigeon to perform the successive matching task, the sample and comparison stimuli are presented in immediate succession on initial learning trials. On half the trials, the comparison stimulus matches the sample stimulus, but on the other half of the trials, the sample and comparison stimuli do not match. The order of matching and nonmatching trials is random or unpredictable. Acquisition of successive matching is shown when the response rate (e.g., pecks per 5 seconds) to the comparison stimulus increases on matching trials and decreases on nonmatching trials. These two response rates then may be combined into a single measure of performance called the discrimination

75

CHAPTER 3
*Working Memory:
Early Research and
Contemporary
Procedures and
Findings*

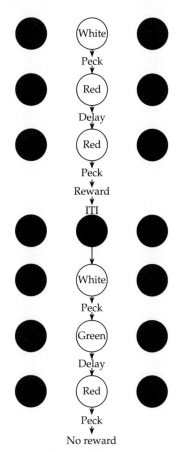

FIGURE 3.3. Stimuli and responses that would occur on two trials of delayed successive matching-to-sample. Notice that only the center key is used to present matching and nonmatching stimuli; the side keys remain dark.

ratio (DR). The formula for the DR is as follows: DR = (response rate on matching trials)/(response rate on matching trials + response rate on nonmatching trials). A DR of 0.50 indicates chance performance or equal pecking on matching and nonmatching trials, but as the DR approaches 1.00, an increasing majority of the responses shift toward the matching comparison stimulus. Since pigeons generally have a strong tendency to peck at stimuli associated with food, they tend to acquire successive matching by learning to inhibit responses to the nonmatching comparison stimulus.

As was the case with delayed simultaneous matching, delayed successive matching involves working memory because the subject must remember the sample stimulus to make a correct decision about pecking or not pecking the comparison stimulus. Once a pigeon has acquired successive matching, working memory may be studied at different retention intervals by varying the delay between the end of the sample stimulus and the beginning of the comparison stimulus. Retention curves from a delayed successive matching-to-sample

76

CHAPTER 3
*Working Memory:
Early Research and
Contemporary
Procedures and
Findings*

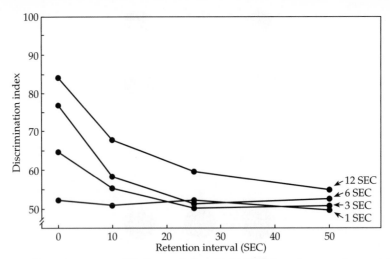

FIGURE 3.4. Retention curves from a study in which the delayed successive matching-to-sample procedure was used, and sample stimuli (red or green keys) were presented for 1, 3, 6, or 12 seconds.

experiment are shown in Figure 3.4. In this experiment, Nelson and Wasserman (1978) presented pigeons with sample red or green keys for 1, 3, 6, or 12 seconds. The chamber then was darkened for retention intervals (delays) of 1, 10, 25, or 50 seconds, at the end of which a matching or nonmatching red or green key appeared for the retention test. Observe that the discrimination index (DR × 100) drops as the retention interval becomes longer for all of the curves except the 1-second sample duration curve. The fact that the 1-second sample duration curve is near a discrimination index of 50 at all retention intervals suggests that pigeons may not have been able to sufficiently form a memory of a sample presented for only 1 second.

Delayed Yes-No Matching-to-Sample

This procedure is similar to yet different from both of the preceding methods. As in successive matching-to-sample, matching and nonmatching sample and comparison stimuli are presented successively on a center key. However, instead of using peck rate to the comparison stimulus as an index of memory, the subject is required to peck the left or right key to indicate that the comparison stimulus matches (yes response) or does not match (no response) the sample stimulus. As shown in Figure 3.5, the sample and comparison stimuli are red and green lights presented on the center key. When the comparison stimulus is presented, white lights also appear on the left and right keys. On red-red and green-green matching trials, the pigeon must peck the right, or yes, key to be rewarded; on red-green and green-red nonmatching trials, the pigeon must peck the left, or no, key to be rewarded. As was the case with simultaneous matching-to-sample, performance is measured over a number

77

CHAPTER 3
Working Memory:
Early Research and
Contemporary
Procedures and
Findings

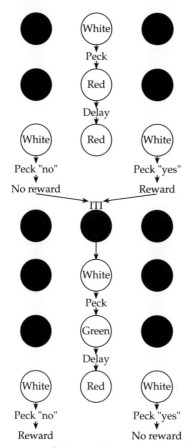

FIGURE 3.5. Stimuli and responses that would occur on two trials of delayed yes-no matching-to-sample. Matching and nonmatching samples are presented on the center key, and yes-no decisions are made by pecking the left (no) and right (yes) keys.

of trials with chance accuracy being 50 percent and perfect performance being 100 percent.

A particularly interesting adaptation of this procedure was carried out with a dolphin by R. Thompson and Herman (1977). They presented a bottlenosed dolphin with lists containing one to six sounds, emitted from a central speaker. Memory for one sound on the list was probed by playing the same sound from one of two peripherally placed speakers. If the dolphin judged the sound to be the same as one on the list, it swam to the left or right speaker that had emitted the sound and pressed a paddle adjacent to it (yes response). On half the trials, new sounds not heard on the list were presented, and the appropriate response was to press the paddle adjacent to the silent peripheral speaker (no response). Choice of the correct speaker was rewarded with a thrown fish, and response to the incorrect speaker yielded no fish. Such a procedure allowed the researchers to test the dolphin's memory for all six positions in the list of sounds and to generate what is called a *serial position*

78

CHAPTER 3
*Working Memory:
Early Research and
Contemporary
Procedures and
Findings*

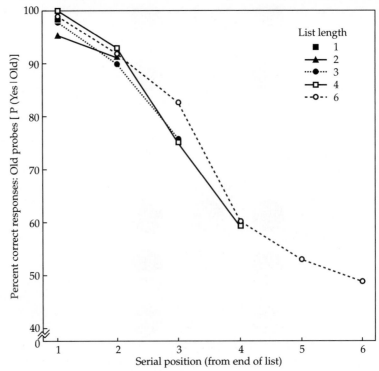

FIGURE 3.6. A serial position curve for a dolphin that was tested on lists of six sounds. The curve plots the probability of a yes response when a sound was from one of the six positions in a list. Serial position 1 was the last sound in a list, and serial position 6 was the first sound in a list.

curve. The serial position curve plots the percentage of correct (yes) responses for tests of the stimuli presented at each position in the list. The dolphin curve shown in Figure 3.6 indicates that accuracy on this task was between 95 percent and 100 percent for the final sound of a list but declined steeply at earlier positions within the list. Memory was best for the most recently presented sounds, and this finding is referred to as a *recency effect*. Recency effects in list memory have been widely interpreted as indicating recall of final items from a highly accessible working memory buffer.

RETENTION IN WORKING MEMORY

The curves seen in Figures 3.2 and 3.4 are typical of retention curves for pigeons in delayed matching-to-sample experiments. In both simultaneous and successive delayed matching, retention declines as the retention interval grows longer. Both sets of curves show also that the height of the retention curves improves the longer the pigeon was exposed to the sample stimulus. These curves are similar to working memory curves found in human experiments and suggest rapid forgetting of briefly presented visual information.

79

CHAPTER 3
Working Memory:
Early Research and
Contemporary
Procedures and
Findings

Other evidence suggests that forgetting in animal working memory experiments is not always so rapid and that retention may be influenced by practice. D'Amato (1973) tested a capuchin monkey (Roscoe) over a period of 6 years. After 4,500 trials of testing on delayed simultaneous matching-to-sample, forgetting was quite rapid, just as in the pigeon curves shown in Figure 2.4. After 30,000 trials of practice, however, Roscoe showed dramatic improvement. He now showed little forgetting over delays of several minutes and was correct about 70 percent of the time at a delay of 9 minutes.

The effects of practice are not limited to monkeys. Grant (1976) found accurate long-delay simultaneous matching-to-sample in four pigeons, each of whom had accumulated about 16,000 trials of training. Although performance still dropped as the delay interval was lengthened, pigeons matched color samples with about 70 percent accuracy after a 60-second delay. Since the chance level of accuracy was 50 percent, pigeons retained information well over a 1-minute interval. Both the D'Amato and Grant studies suggest that animals are not limited to the brief periods of accurate retention shown in the initial stages of delayed matching. These data suggest a "learning-to-remember" process. That is, through practice, animals, like people, may learn efficient ways to code information for retention over relatively long intervals. Further, these findings echo the earlier conclusion of delayed-response experiments that there is no universal retention function for a given species of animal in working memory experiments.

FACTORS AFFECTING RETENTION AND FORGETTING

A theoretical analysis of animal working memory must proceed from a database that indicates the variables that affect remembering and its complement, forgetting. We have already seen that the delay interval has a major effect on retention, with accuracy dropping as delay becomes longer. The effects of some other prominent variables on animal working memory are reviewed. It is interesting to note that many of the effects observed with animals have their counterparts in human memory research.

Exposure to the Sample Stimulus

Exposure to a stimulus may be increased either by presenting it repeatedly or by increasing the length of time it is shown on a single occasion. Both manipulations increase level of retention in human memory experiments, when memory is measured by recall tests (Hellyer, 1962; W. Roberts, 1972a) and by recognition tests (Potter & Levy, 1969; Shaffer & Shiffrin, 1972).

The data shown in Figures 3.2 and 3.4 indicate a similar effect in pigeon working memory; the more times a pigeon was required to peck the sample key or the longer the pigeon observed the sample key, the higher the matching scores. When exposure duration to the sample stimulus is varied, parallel

80

CHAPTER 3
Working Memory:
Early Research and
Contemporary
Procedures and
Findings

forgetting curves for the different exposure periods are often seen over limited delay periods. The curves shown in Figure 3.2 show that presentation time affected level of performance throughout the 6-second retention interval but did not affect the rate of forgetting. If the retention interval becomes sufficiently long, however, retention curves for different exposure durations will converge at chance performance, as seen for the retention curves shown in Figure 3.4.

Similar effects of sample exposure time have been reported with rats (W. Roberts, 1974) and with monkeys (Herzog, Grant, & Roberts, 1977; Jarrard & Moise, 1971). In an interesting contrast to these studies, D'Amato and Worsham (1972) studied working memory in capuchin monkeys and varied sample presentation time between values of 0.075 and 0.45 second. They found that retention was equally good at all presentation times when measured at delays ranging from 2 to 240 seconds. D'Amato and Worsham's monkeys had been tested extensively on delayed matching. Primates given thousands of tests with the same set of sample stimuli may well acquire the ability to encode these stimuli very rapidly, thereby making prolonged exposure unnecessary for a high level of retention.

Behavior During the Retention Interval

In one of the first studies of delayed matching in pigeons, Blough (1959) carefully observed birds' behavior during the retention interval. The study is notable for the differences in behavior he observed both within and among birds. Two of the birds developed different stereotyped behaviors following the sample stimuli, which were steady and flickering bars of light. One bird waved its head back and forth following the flickering light and pecked at the darkened key after a steady bar of light had been shown. The retention function for this bird was completely flat; a 90 percent accuracy level for choice of the correct comparison key was maintained over delays varying from 0 to 10 seconds. That the animal's behavior was mediating its choice was indicated when the bird occasionally adopted the inappropriate behavior. Following a flickering sample, the bird sometimes would drift from head waving to pecking. In this case, the comparison key chosen was the incorrect steady light. Two other pigeons tested never developed delay interval responses with different topography, and retention curves for these birds yielded forgetting functions similar to those seen in Figure 3.2.

Although Blough's birds appeared to adopt differential responses to the sample stimuli spontaneously, subsequent experiments showed that choice of comparison stimuli could be brought under the control of different patterns of responses trained to sample stimuli (Cohen, Looney, Brady & Aucella, 1976; Urcuioli & Honig, 1980; Zentall, Hogan, Howard & Moore, 1978). For example, a pigeon might be initially trained to peck at a red key and not to peck at a green key. The pigeon then would learn to match-to-sample with the red and green keys as sample stimuli. Since the pigeon had been trained to peck at the red and not to peck at the green, these behaviors would continue as responses to the sample stimuli and would be followed by choice between red and green comparison stimuli. Now suppose the pigeon was trained through reward and nonreward to peck a vertical line stimulus and not to peck a horizontal line stimulus. Eventually, the red and green comparison stimuli would be presented following both the vertical line and the horizontal line, and the pigeon then would choose red after the vertical line and green after the horizontal line. Since the pigeon had never been taught to match red and green comparison stimuli to vertical and horizontal lines as sample stimuli, vertical and horizontal lines are not controlling its choice behavior. Rather, the mediating response behavior of pecking or not pecking controls its choice of comparison stimuli. The original training established associations between pecking and choice of red and between not pecking and choice of green.

There is little doubt that pigeons that use mediating behaviors can associate them with comparison stimuli and thereby perform very accurately over long delays. In most experiments in which differential responses have not been trained, however, experimenters do not report the kinds of mediating behaviors observed by Blough. Animals choose accurately over short delays, and accuracy declines as the delay is lengthened, which suggests that pigeons use memory in delayed matching and that memories are forgotten over the delay period.

Interference with Working Memory

One of the most important causes of forgetting in human memory is interference from other learned information. In the case of proactive interference (PI), information acquired prior to the formation of a target memory leads to forgetting of that memory. Retroactive interference (RI) occurs when information presented after the formation of a target memory causes the memory of prior events to be forgotten. Both types of interference have been observed in animal memory. The importance of PI and RI on long-term or reference memory is reviewed in Chapter 6, but some examples of these forms of interference may be found in working memory.

Proactive Interference

Two sources of PI have been identified in pigeon working memory experiments, interference within a single trial, or *intratrial interference,* and interference between trials, or *intertrial interference.* An experimental design for the study of intratrial PI is shown in Figure 3.7. In the example shown, delayed simultaneous matching-to-sample is used, with the sample being a green center key and the comparison stimuli being red and green side keys. The additional factor that makes this a PI experiment is the presentation of a red center key just before presentation of the green sample key. Performance under this condition is compared with memory on control trials when only the sample stimulus is presented. Of course, on half of the PI trials, the sample stimulus will be red, and the prior interfering stimulus will be green.

81

CHAPTER 3
Working Memory:
Early Research and
Contemporary
Procedures and
Findings

82

CHAPTER 3
Working Memory:
Early Research and
Contemporary
Procedures and
Findings

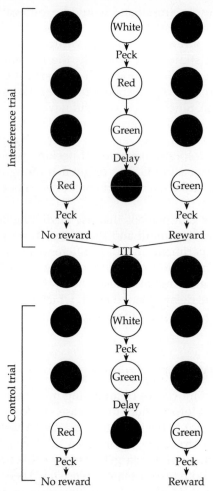

FIGURE 3.7. Sequences of stimuli and responses occurring on interference and control trials in an intratrial PI experiment.

In Figure 3.8, memory curves are shown from an intratrial PI experiment carried out by Grant and Roberts (1973). The control condition showed higher retention of the sample than the experimental (interference) condition at all delays, and the retention curves are parallel, suggesting that interference was equal at all of the retention intervals tested.

Since the interfering stimulus in this experiment was always the same color as the incorrect comparison stimulus, one straightforward way to account for this PI effect is by memory competition (W. Roberts & Grant, 1976). We may assume that both the interfering stimulus and the sample stimulus established memories and that each memory should direct test responses toward the comparison key matching that memory. Because the pigeon can

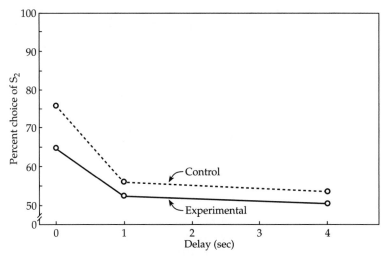

83

CHAPTER 3
Working Memory:
Early Research and
Contemporary
Procedures and
Findings

FIGURE 3.8. Retention curves from an intratrial PI experiment with pigeons. In the experimental condition, the incorrect comparison stimulus was presented first on the center key, followed by the correct sample stimulus. Only the correct sample stimulus was presented in the control condition.

only peck one comparison stimulus, the memories indicate conflicting responses. Note that there is a longer delay between presentation of the interfering stimulus and choice than between the sample stimulus and choice. If we assume that forgetting is a continuous process, memory for the interfering stimulus should be weaker than memory for the sample stimulus, and choice of the comparison matching the sample stimulus should win the majority of the time and lead to performance above a chance level. Memory of the interfering stimulus will win this competition on some occasions, however, thus leading to lower accuracy than found on control trials in which there is no competition.

A direct test of this explanation of intratrial PI was carried out by experimental manipulations that would weaken or strengthen memory of the interfering stimulus. In order to strengthen the memory, Grant and Roberts (1973) increased the duration of the interfering stimulus. To weaken its memory, they increased the interval between the interfering stimulus and the sample stimulus. Both manipulations had the predicted effect. Matching accuracy dropped steadily as duration of the interfering stimulus was increased, indicating a rise in PI. When the interstimulus interval was increased, matching accuracy increased, indicating a decrease in PI. The competition model was clearly supported.

A bit of reflection should suggest that if an interfering stimulus can cause PI within trials, PI should also arise among different trials. After the initial trial in a typical delayed matching test session, each further trial

84

CHAPTER 3
Working Memory:
Early Research and
Contemporary
Procedures and
Findings

occurs against a background of memories from preceding trials. These preceding trials have established memories of samples and of rewarded responses to comparison stimuli that could serve as sources of interference with memory for the sample stimulus on a current trial (Grant, 1975). The importance of intertrial PI is strongly supported by the observation that accuracy over trials within a session of memory tests is better when the interval between trials (ITI) is long than when it is short. This finding has been reported with several species of animals, including pigeons, rats, monkeys, and dolphins (Grant, 1981b; Herman, 1975; Jarrard & Moise, 1971; W. Roberts, 1980).

Further evidence of intertrial PI comes from a study by Worsham (1975), in which he rigged "easy" and "hard" sequences of delayed matching trials for monkeys. In easy sequences, the incorrect comparison stimulus of a trial had not appeared as a sample stimulus in the immediately preceding trials; in hard sequences, the incorrect comparison stimulus had been the sample on the immediately preceding trial. Performance was consistently better on easy sequences than on hard sequences. If memories of preceding trials exert an interfering effect on retention in subsequent trials, PI would be reduced or eliminated if different stimuli are used on each trial. If lingering memories from previous trials bear little similarity to a memory needed for correct choice on the current trial, little competition should arise. This prediction has been supported by several monkey studies in which memory improved substantially with increasing numbers of different stimuli in the procedure (M. Mason & Wilson, 1974; Mishkin & Delacour, 1975; Sands & Wright, 1980b).

Retroactive Interference

Although some forgetting in human working memory can be attributed to decay (Reitman, 1974), considerable additional forgetting is obtained when subjects are required to process additional information during the retention interval. In various studies, people have been asked to remember a prior verbal item while encoding further items, carrying out arithmetic, or counting backwards from an arbitrary number. The degree of forgetting produced by these tasks appears to be directly related to the difficulty or attentional demand of the interpolated task (Posner & Konick, 1966; Posner & Rossman, 1965) and to the degree of similarity between the items to be remembered and the material presented during the retention interval (Deutsch, 1970; Wickelgren, 1965).

In studies of RI in animals, a sample stimulus is to be remembered while other information is presented during the delay, which may interfere with memory of the sample. Performance on interference trials is compared with performance on control trials in which no new information is presented during the delay. In some experiments with pigeons, Grant and Roberts (1976) presented a sample stimulus on the center key and then presented other stimuli on the center key that varied in degree of information complexity and similarity to the sample stimulus. Although presentation of these interpolated stimuli caused RI, their information content appeared to be of little importance. Eventually, it was discovered that a single variable nicely accounts for the degree of RI found in delayed matching, namely, the sheer amount of light to which a pigeon is exposed. In the left graph shown in Figure 3.9, delayed matching accuracy drops progressively below the control level as a delay filled with an overhead houselight increases (Roberts & Grant, 1978b). In the right graph, light was kept on during a constant 5-second delay, but the intensity of the light was manipulated by varying the resistance in the light circuit (Grant & Roberts, 1976). Matching performance dropped consistently as light intensity increased.

Monkeys have provided similar findings of RI produced by light interpolated between sample and comparison stimuli (D'Amato & O'Neill, 1971; Etkin, 1972). Because animals are typically kept in a darkened operant chamber during delays, the presentation of light during a delay is a substantial change in illumination. Some investigators have argued that the change in illumination rather than the presence of light is the cause of RI (Cook, 1980; Tranberg & Rilling, 1980). Although change in illumination may be important, some studies indicate that change is not the whole story and that light alone does interfere with retention (Grant, 1988; Salmon & D'Amato, 1981).

Why light should produce such profound RI in delayed matching experiments is not completely clear. One possibility is that it acts directly to erase memories in some way. A more likely possibility is that stimuli illuminated by light during the delay become a focus of attention and thus interfere with rehearsal processes used by an animal to guide its choice of comparison stimuli.

85

CHAPTER 3
*Working Memory:
Early Research and
Contemporary
Procedures and
Findings*

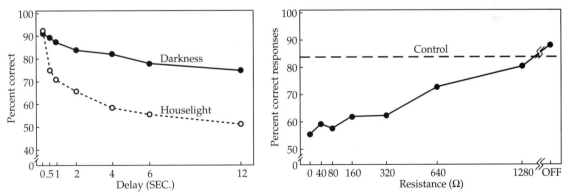

FIGURE 3.9. The effect of houselight presented during the delay interval on delayed simultaneous matching performance in pigeons. The left graph shows retention after different lengths of delay in darkness or houselight. The right graph shows the effect on matching accuracy of increasing the houselight brightness (decreasing resistance) during a 5-second delay.

86

CHAPTER 3
Working Memory:
Early Research and
Contemporary
Procedures and
Findings

A COMPARISON OF HUMAN
AND ANIMAL WORKING MEMORY

It is of considerable interest to note the similarities between working memory phenomena found with humans and animals. Although much of the animal data comes from delayed matching-to-sample experiments with pigeons, they show that pigeons, like people, quickly forget information presented just a few seconds earlier. The retention curves take similar shapes, with the most rapid forgetting taking place immediately after information has been encoded. Increased exposure or repetition of information improves working memory in both pigeons and people. Other experiments show that pigeons and monkeys, like humans, experience considerable interference in working memory. Information presented both before and after a target memory is encoded may cause that memory to be forgotten more rapidly than it would in the absence of the interfering information.

These similarities are even more striking when one considers the differences between procedures. Human subjects typically remember verbal material that they recall and must be prevented from rehearsing by some task that occupies their attention during the retention interval. Pigeons take recognition tests for colors or black-and-white patterns, and no steps are taken to prevent rehearsal. The interesting comparative question arising from these observations is whether similar processes of remembering and forgetting are responsible for similar memory phenomena. Are the neural representations of memories in animals and people affected in the same ways by exposure duration, retention interval, and other sources of information? We explore the ways in which animals encode and process information in working memory in Chapter 4. The information presented there will help us to further answer the question of how similar human and animal working memory may be.

SUMMARY

Two types of memory have been described—working memory and reference memory. Reference memory refers to long-term storage of associations acquired through experience that take the form of automatic responses, procedural memory, and factual information about the structure of the world, declarative memory. Working memory, by contrast, is usually short-term and contains information needed for immediate purposes but that then may be forgotten. Human multiple-store theories of memory assume that information processing involves constant transmission of information in both directions between working memory and reference memory. Working memory is shown in people by asking a person to remember verbal materials over short periods of time during which rehearsal is prevented.

A number of early delayed-response studies dealt with what we now refer to as working memory in animals. Although the focus of these experiments was not on memory processes, they established clearly that animals could remember events that signaled the location of food over substantial delay intervals. It was shown also that animals could remember for long periods of time without having to orient toward the correct response alternative. Attempts to use maximal delay interval as a measure of species intelligence proved futile because any given species of animal could be shown to remember during either short or long delay intervals, depending on the conditions of testing. In general, animals remembered longer when visually differentiated stimuli were used and placed far apart in space.

Modern methods for studying working memory in animals include several variations of delayed matching-to-sample. After exposure to a sample stimulus, a retention test may involve a choice between two or more comparison stimuli (delayed simultaneous matching), an opportunity to respond to a matching or nonmatching stimulus (delayed successive matching), or making a yes or no response by choosing different stimuli (delayed yes-no matching). All of these procedures yield retention curves that tend to drop from a high level of correct performance toward chance accuracy as the delay becomes longer. The level of these forgetting curves can be raised by increasing exposure to the sample stimulus and by giving animals considerable practice on delayed matching tests. As in human working and reference memory studies, PI and RI are found in animal working memory research. Animals show lower levels of retention on delayed matching tests when a conflicting stimulus has been presented previously (PI), either just before the sample stimulus on the same trial (intratrial PI) or on a just preceding trial (between-trial PI). A very strong source of RI is the introduction of any source of illumination during the delay interval on delayed matching tests. The brighter the light or the longer the light stays on, the more memory of the sample stimulus will be reduced.

87

CHAPTER 3
Working Memory:
Early Research and
Contemporary
Procedures and
Findings

Working Memory: Theoretical Approaches

EARLY MODELS OF ANIMAL WORKING MEMORY

As modern research on animal working memory has intensified over the past 20 years or so, theory has kept pace. Theoretical concepts have changed considerably over this period, and, to a certain extent, these changes reflect a similar evolution of theory in human memory. The dimension of theoretical modification might be described as a transition from passive to active models of working memory (Grant, 1981c). Early theories of human memory explained retention and forgetting by decay processes and stimulus-response associations, but more recent cognitive approaches stress encoding strategies, rehearsal, depth of processing, and retrieval mechanisms. In the case of animals, initial theory suggested that retention was under the control of a fading memory trace. More recent theories suggest that, as with humans, animal retention will vary with differences in encoding and the extent and kind of processing performed during a retention interval. This processing will be controlled by the conditions of training and the particular information received on any given trial. We turn now to a brief examination of two early models.

Trace Strength and Decay Theory

Based on early findings in pigeon working memory experiments using delayed simultaneous matching, W. Roberts and Grant (1976) developed a theory in which the critical processes were growth and decay of trace strength. The initial impetus for this theory was observations of the effects of presentation time and delay on retention. As reviewed in Chapter 3, accuracy of delayed matching increases as exposure to the sample stimulus increases and decreases as the delay becomes longer. Retention curves for sample stimuli presented for different durations are shown in Figures 3.2 and 3.4. As a parsimonious interpretation of these observations, W. Roberts and Grant suggested that trace strength grew progressively with exposure to a sample stimulus and decayed in the absence of the sample stimulus.

This account of working memory may be simply understood as a *hole-in-the-bucket model.* The analogy is envisioned as a bucket filling with water as a sample stimulus is presented—the longer the sample is presented, the higher the water level becomes. Terminating the sample and starting the delay is analogous to pulling a stopper from a hole in the bottom of the bucket and letting the water pour out. The longer the delay (the length of time the stopper is out), the more water will empty from the bucket. Finally, the accuracy of choice between comparison stimuli will be directly determined by the level of the water in the bucket. If the bucket was filled to a high level by a long exposure to the sample and only a little water was allowed to leak out by a short delay, performance should be very high. If water is allowed to pour out over a long delay, however, the water level and the retention level will be much lower. If all the water is allowed to leak out of the bucket after it has been filled to different heights, all of the retention curves will fall to chance accuracy at sufficiently long delays, as shown in Figure 3.4.

The trace strength model was bolstered further by the effects of spaced repetition of the sample stimulus on delayed matching. W. Roberts (1972b) and W. Roberts and Grant (1974) presented pigeons with the sample stimulus at the beginning of a trial; it was then turned off, and the chamber was darkened for some period of time (interstimulus interval). The sample stimulus was then presented again and followed by the usual delay and test. The variable of particular interest was the length of the interstimulus interval. Repetition of a sample stimulus led to higher performance than a single presentation, but the effect declined as the interstimulus interval became longer. If it is assumed that trace strengths established by repetitions of a sample stimulus are additive, total trace strength will become progressively weaker the longer the trace of the initial presentation is allowed to decay. In terms of the hole-in-the-bucket analogy, if the bucket is partially filled with water and then some is allowed to leak out through the hole before more is poured in, the bucket will end up with less total water than if none had been allowed to leak out between fillings.

Another area in which the trace strength theory had some success was in providing an explanation for proactive interference (PI) effects. In the case of intratrial PI, it was suggested that the successive presentation of conflicting sample stimuli established independent but competing memory traces (Grant & W. Roberts, 1973). If a red sample was presented first and a green sample was presented second, separate traces of red and green would be established. When red and green were then presented as comparison stimuli, with green correct, the green trace would be stronger than the red trace since red had longer to decay than green. Green then would be favored and would be chosen on a majority of trials. The distributions of the trace strengths of red and green (over many trials) would overlap, however, and the strength of red would exceed that of green on some trials. Interference would be created by choice of red on these trials, and overall accuracy would be lower than on control trials, when only a single sample stimulus was presented. Furthermore, just as the trace strength theory would predict, Grant and W. Roberts found that increasing the interstimulus interval between the interfering and correct sample stimuli reduced the degree of PI.

Although trace strength theory exhibited considerable success, there were some problems. One such problem was that the observation that increases in chamber illumination would produce retroactive interference (RI) was not immediately explainable by trace strength theory. Although it could be posited that light accelerated the rate of trace decay, there was no known behavioral or physiological mechanism that supported such an assumption. Grant and

W. Roberts (1976) and W. Roberts and Grant (1978b) acknowledged that changes in illumination could cause RI by disrupting a rehearsal process, an assumption not very compatible with that of trace strength.

Another problem was the accumulating evidence that the extent of retention varied considerably with conditions of training. As already described in Chapter 3, the level of retention in working memory experiments with birds and monkeys was boosted considerably by practice. Mechanisms other than trace strength would seem to be needed to account for the effects of practice.

The Temporal Discrimination Hypothesis

All events for an animal occur at a specific time, and time markers may be associated with memories of events. D'Amato (1973) and Worsham (1975) developed a theory of temporal discrimination, in which retention and forgetting in animal working memory were dependent upon how well an animal could discriminate the temporal recency of several memories. Memories of events were assumed to become more discriminable if the events were further apart in time. For example, an animal might take part in a delayed simultaneous matching session in which circle and triangle patterns were used alternately as sample and incorrect comparison stimuli. Suppose that the circle served as the sample stimulus on Trial 1 and that the triangle served as the sample stimulus on Trial 2. An animal faced with a choice between circle and triangle comparison stimuli on Trial 2 would choose the correct triangle pattern to the extent that it could discriminate memory of the triangle sample stimulus as an event that had occurred more recently than the circle sample stimulus. The temporal discrimination hypothesis then emphasized the importance of relationships between lengths of time and not the passage of absolute lengths of time, as the decay theory did.

The quality of the discrimination could be roughly indexed by the ratio of time elapsed since the more distant event to time elapsed since the more recent event. If the circle sample had been presented 2 minutes previously in the first trial, and the triangle sample had been presented 1 minute previously, the ratio would be 2:1. If an additional 4-minute intertrial interval were introduced, however, the circle would have occurred 6 minutes ago, and the ratio would become 6:1. Temporal discrimination and matching accuracy clearly should be better in the latter case.

Temporal discrimination accounts for a number of phenomena. The basic observation that retention declines as the retention interval is lengthened may be explained as a decline in the discrimination ratio. In the preceding example of a 2:1 ratio, if 1 minute is added to the retention interval in Trial 2, the ratio becomes 3:2. Discrimination of the most recent sample should become more difficult, and matching accuracy should go down. Inter- and intratrial PI effects are explained nicely as failures of a recency discrimination between memories of events occurring in close temporal succession. The well-known observation that delayed matching performance improves as the intertrial interval becomes longer follows directly from the temporal discrimination hypothesis since, as demonstrated earlier, increasing the intertrial interval also raises the discrimination ratio.

A number of experiments have shown that delayed matching improves as the number of different stimuli used within a session increases, and this is exactly what would be expected on the basis of the temporal discrimination hypothesis. Taking the most extreme case, if different samples and incorrect comparison stimuli are used on every trial, it should be easy to discriminate the memory of the sample stimulus as a recent event since only memory of the sample stimulus will contain a recent temporal marker.

Undoubtedly, temporal discrimination between memories plays a role in working memory. The limitation of the temporal discrimination hypothesis is that it identifies only one of several processes that are probably important in working memory. For instance, the hypothesis says nothing about the encoding, storage, and retrieval of memories. In experiments to be described in more detail later in this chapter, Sands and Wright (1980a, 1980b) tested monkeys' working memory for lists of slide-projected pictures, with different pictures presented on each trial. The temporal discrimination hypothesis suggests that retention should be uniformly high for all items on a list since recency discrimination should be easily accomplished on all tests. Yet, serial position curves were found with central items retained more poorly than initial and terminal items. This type of finding suggests that other processes in addition to temporal discrimination must be involved in working memory.

ACTIVE PROCESSES IN WORKING MEMORY

Although there is little doubt that sensory traces of sample stimuli and temporal discrimination play some role in working memory, evidence eventually began to accumulate to suggest that these theories did not adequately describe the processes involved in animal working memory. Although these theories were not necessarily wrong, they provided an incomplete description of working memory. Trace strength theory and the temporal discrimination hypothesis suggest relatively passive processes of memory. New evidence has suggested that animals process information more actively, and manipulations that stimulate or interfere with processing have strong effects on retention. Through innovative experiments, it became apparent that animals use a variety of codes to remember sample information and that retention involves an active rehearsal process.

Evidence of Coding in Working Memory

The term *matching-to-sample* implies that the correct comparison stimulus in this task is identical to the sample stimulus and that animals have learned to choose the comparison stimulus that looks like the sample stimulus. Some early transfer experiments brought this latter assumption into question (Cumming & Berryman, 1965). A pigeon learned to match-to-sample to a high level of accuracy with red, green, and blue sample and comparison stimuli. If the pigeon had learned the rule, "Peck the comparison stimulus that looks like the sample stimulus," we would expect the pigeon to transfer easily to a matching-to-sample problem containing new stimuli. The pigeon then was tested with a yellow sample stimulus and a choice between comparison stimuli that consisted of yellow and either red, green, or blue. On tests with the yellow sample, the pigeon's performance dropped to chance, suggesting that it had not learned a rule to pick the comparison that looked the same as the sample.

This important observation, along with others, led to the hypothesis that instead of learning a general matching principle, pigeons may be learning very specific types of "if–then" rules in working memory experiments (Carter & Eckerman, 1975; Carter & Werner, 1978; Cumming & Berryman, 1965). A pigeon may have learned two rules when red and green stimuli were used to train it to match-to-sample: "If red sample, then peck red comparison," and "If green sample, then peck green comparison." Note that these rules tell the pigeon nothing about what to do if it is confronted with a yellow sample and a choice between yellow and red or green comparison stimuli.

If animals learn if–then rules that map sample and comparison stimuli onto one another, this suggests that sample and comparison stimuli do not need to be identical for matching to take place. An alternate form of matching design now used as commonly as identity matching is *symbolic matching-to-sample.* An example of this procedure is shown in Figure 4.1. Note that the sample stimuli

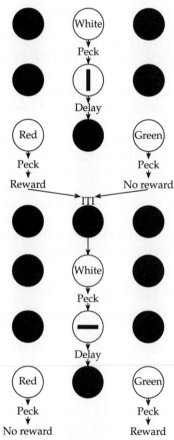

FIGURE 4.1 Stimulus and response sequences for two delayed symbolic matching-to-sample trials. The vertical bar is a sample stimulus mapped onto the red comparison stimulus, and the horizontal bar is a sample stimulus mapped onto the green comparison stimulus.

in this example are keys with horizontal and vertical bars projected on them, but the comparison stimuli are illuminated with red and green lights. Carter and Eckerman (1975) showed that pigeons learn to match-to-sample as rapidly with symbolic relationships of this nature between sample and comparison stimuli as they do with identical sample and comparison stimuli. In this example, then, pigeons would learn the rules, "If vertical bar sample, then peck red comparison," and "If horizontal bar sample, then peck green comparison," and these rules would be no different in principle from those specified earlier for identical sample and comparison stimuli.

It should be pointed out that although these findings suggest pigeons adopt if–then rules in matching-to-sample experiments, they do not prove that pigeons are incapable of learning the concepts of sameness and difference. Research discussed in Chapter 11 indicates that, with the proper kind of training, pigeons can learn to transfer matching readily to novel stimuli.

These discoveries have important implications for theory and research. On a theoretical level, they suggest that animals may be doing considerably more than simply responding to decaying traces in working memory experiments. Animals may be formulating rules and using these rules to help them remember. This outlook suggests a far more active model of working memory than that suggested by trace strength and decay theory. On a more practical level, the use of symbolic matching procedures makes it possible to study animals' memories for a wide variety of information. Although comparison stimuli may be a pair of response keys or levers, sample stimuli may be a wide variety of geometric patterns or even pictures of natural objects. It is also possible to use sample stimuli from other modalities, such as sounds or an animal's own behavior. Finally, it is possible to map more than one set of sample stimuli onto a single set of comparison stimuli. It will be shown later that many-to-one mapping has important theoretical value.

Evidence of Rehearsal in Working Memory

The idea of rehearsal in animal working memory seems far removed from the theory of trace decay suggested by Roberts and Grant (1976). From our own experience, we know that people remember information in working memory by silently rehearsing it or thinking about it repeatedly. Usually, such rehearsal involves language. In fact, it was exactly to prevent such silent rehearsal that subjects in working memory experiments were required to perform distracting tasks such as counting backward. Is it possible that a nonverbal organism can rehearse? Rehearsal would have to take some nonverbal form, such as visual images. Since people can rehearse in nonverbal modes, such as imagery, there appears to be no reason in principle why animals could not rehearse or recirculate information in memory. Several lines of evidence now suggest that animals may use rehearsal to maintain information in working memory.

The Effect of Surprise on Working Memory

Although our discussion of working memory in animals has dealt mostly with delayed matching and related paradigms, research in classical conditioning also provides evidence bearing on working memory processes in animals.

Wagner (1976; 1978) developed a model of memory processing that provides an interesting fusion of his own experiments in classical conditioning and the two-store model of human verbal memory (Atkinson & Shiffrin, 1968). He suggested that an animal's reference memory consisted of a network of inactive information from which environmental cues may directly activate their own representations or serve as retrieval cues to activate other representations. Representations thus activated are rehearsed or recirculated within a working memory buffer and will be available to direct behavior until they return to an inactive state, either through decay or through displacement by activation of new information (Wagner, 1981).

A critical aspect of this theory is that events vary in the degree to which they stimulate the process of rehearsal. Events that stimulate strong and prolonged rehearsal of their associated representations tend to have a definite advantage in retention. Prolonged rehearsal of a representation of course increases its time in working memory and thereby increases its probability of being available after a short delay. Also, the model holds that enhanced rehearsal increases the transfer of information from working memory to reference memory. The effects of rehearsal then may be found on a retention test given a day or more after initial learning.

What characteristic of information controls rehearsal? Wagner (1976) argued that it is the degree to which an event is surprising or unexpected. Representations activated by surprising events are allocated a larger share of the rehearsal capacity of working memory than those activated by expected events. This argument makes some intuitive sense. If we reflect on our own rehearsal activities, it is those occurrences that are novel or unexpected that we think about or rehearse the most. From an evolutionary standpoint, such a mechanism also makes sense. To a wild animal, surprising events may be the most important ones because they are most likely to signal danger or some important change in the environment. Such events should then be given disproportionate cognitive attention to be learned quickly.

Because working memory is held to be a limited capacity system, exclusive rehearsal of the representations of one set of surprising events should prevent the rehearsal and learning of representations set off by other events occurring nearby in time. It was this theoretical assumption that formed the basis for a set of experiments by Wagner, Rudy, and Whitlow (1973) using eyelid conditioning in rabbits. The design of the Wagner et al. experiment is shown in Table 4.1. In Phase 1, rabbits discriminated between a positive conditioned stimulus (CS+) and a negative conditioned stimulus (CS–). The CS+ was a train of auditory clicks and was associated with a weak shock to the area around the subject's eye, causing it to blink. On CS– trials, a vibrotactual stimulus was administered to the surface of the body, but no shock was delivered. After about 100 trials, rabbits responded immediately after the CS+ and made very few blinks after the CS–.

Phase 2 of the experiment involved conditioning the eyelid response to a new CS, a flashing light, by following it with shock. The critical manipulation involved the presentation of either surprising or expected episodes immediately after the light CS during each trial. The rabbits were divided into three groups for this Phase 2 conditioning. One group always had trials with the light

TABLE 4.1 Design of an Eyelid Conditioning Experiment Carried Out by Wagner, Rudy, and Whitlow (1973) with Rabbits to Study the Effects of Surprise on Memory

PHASE 1
Discriminative conditioning   Auditory clicks (CS+) → Shock (US)   Vibrotactual stimulus (CS–) → No Shock

PHASE 2
Surprise group   Light (CS) → Shock (US) → Auditory clicks → No shock   *No surprise group*   Light (CS) → Shock (US) → Vibrotactual stimulus → No shock   *Control group*   Light (CS) → Shock (US)

CS-shock pairing followed by a surprising posttrial episode; the CS+ from Phase 1, the auditory clicks, was presented but followed by omission of shock. Because the animals had been conditioned to expect shock after the noise CS over many trials, this sudden reversal in the sequence of events should have been surprising. In a second group, the posttrial episode was not surprising because the sequence of events was the same one the rabbits had learned to expect in Phase 1; these rabbits were presented with the vibrotactual CS– from Phase 1, and no shock was administered. A third control group received no posttrial episodes. The results yielded a finding of major interest. In Phase 2, fewer conditioned responses were made to the light CS when it was followed by the surprising episode than when it was followed by the nonsurprising episode or by no episode in the control group.

Wagner et al. (1973) explained this finding by suggesting that the surprising episode occupied more time in the rehearsal buffer than the expected episode; hence, it reduced the rehearsal time of the preceding trial (light CS and shock). This interpretation was supported in a further experiment in which the time interval between the conditioning trial and the surprising posttrial episode was varied between 3 and 300 seconds. As this interval increased, the strength of conditioning rose steadily. This finding also follows directly from the rehearsal model since increasing the posttrial interval before the surprising episode should allow longer rehearsal of representations of the prior light CS and shock.

These experiments provided support for rehearsal in animals in an indirect fashion by showing the effect of rehearsal on the acquisition of another learned association. Would it be possible to show directly that a surprising event was remembered better than a nonsurprising event? Based on the design of a rabbit conditioning experiment performed by Terry and Wagner (1975), Maki (1979) addressed this question using delayed simultaneous matching-to-sample with pigeons. Maki's experiment required three phases, as shown in Table 4.2. In Phase 1, pigeons were trained on a delayed symbolic matching task in which

TABLE 4.2 Design of Maki's (1979) Experiment Showing the Effect of Surprise on Working Memory for Food and No-Food Sample Stimuli in Pigeons
(Note that the response outcomes of Phase 2 (food and no food) become sample stimuli for a delayed matching-to-sample test in Phase 3)

PHASE 1		
Sample Stimulus	Comparison Stimuli	Choice Outcome
Food	Green	No reward
	Red	Reward
No food	Green	Reward
	Red	No reward

PHASE 2	
Stimulus	Response Outcome
Vertical line	Food
Horizontal line	No food

PHASE 3		
Stimulus	Response Outcome (Sample Stimulus)	Comparison Stimuli
Surprising trials		
Vertical line	No food	Red (incorrect)
		Green (correct)
Horizontal line	Food	Red (correct)
		Green (incorrect)
Nonsurprising trials		
Vertical line	Food	Red (correct)
		Green (incorrect)
Horizontal line	No food	Red (incorrect)
		Green (correct)

the samples were presentations of food or no food. Thus, following the delivery of grain from the food hopper, red and green comparison keys were presented, and the pigeon had to peck the red key to receive a reward, which was another delivery of grain. On other trials, the food hopper light came on but no food was delivered (no-food sample); following no food, the green comparison key had to be pecked for reward. After pigeons had learned to match at a high degree of accuracy, a relatively simple successive discrimination problem was given as Phase 2 training. On some trials, birds were presented with a vertical line on the center key, and a peck on this key produced food reward. On other trials, a horizontal line appeared, and a peck to it yielded no food reward.

In Phase 3, the tasks acquired in Phases 1 and 2 were cleverly combined to examine the effect of surprise on memory. Half the trials now began with the presentation of the vertical stripe and the other half with presentation of the horizontal stripe. On nonsurprising trials, a peck to the vertical stripe provided food, and a peck to the horizontal stripe provided no food, just as had occurred during Stage 2 training. On surprising trials, however, pecks to the vertical and horizontal stripes produced the opposite, and unexpected, outcomes of no food and food, respectively. Because pigeons had learned previously to match stimuli to food and no food when these stimuli were presented as samples in Stage 1, it was now possible to test pigeons' memory for these samples when they were surprising or nonsurprising by introducing a delay before the red and green comparison stimuli were presented. Pigeons matched more accurately following surprising samples than following nonsurprising samples. The important theoretical implication of this finding was that pigeons rehearsed surprising food or no-food samples longer than they rehearsed nonsurprising samples.

Directed Forgetting in Animals

A hallmark of models of human cognition is the concept of controlled processing. Encoding, maintenance, and retrieval of information may be controlled by the efforts of the individual, and controlled processing may be initiated either by external instruction or internal volition. Of course, we cannot study volitional control in animals, but it may be possible to exert stimulus control over cognitive processing. The experiments just reviewed on surprise suggested that rehearsal of information sustained it in working memory. Would it be possible to control this rehearsal process? To turn it off and turn it on?

One area of research in which control over memory processing was shown in people was *directed forgetting.* Bjork (1972) introduced a paradigm for studying an apparently simple question: Can people voluntarily forget something they have just learned? To answer this question, subjects were presented with word stimuli, with some words followed by a cue instructing them to remember the word (R-cue), and some words followed by a cue instructing them to forget the word (F-cue). On a series of retention tests, subjects were asked to recall only the R-cued words. The experiment involved some deception, however, because eventually subjects were given a list containing R- and F-cued words and were asked to recall both types of words. It was found in a number of experiments that people remembered R-cued words better than F-cued words. Research suggests that F-cued words were not erased from memory since greater memory for F-cued words could be shown on more sensitive recognition memory tests than on recall tests (Block, 1971; Epstein, Massaro, & Wilder, 1972). F-cued words then may reside in memory but may not be as easily retrieved as R-cued words because they are not given the postperceptual processing or rehearsal given to R-cued items (Epstein, 1972).

It seemed quite possible to psychologists interested in animal memory that directed forgetting through controlled processing could be studied in animals. In fact, a number of articles announced the discovery of directed forgetting in pigeons in the early 1980s (Grant, 1981a; Maki & Hegvik, 1980; Stonebraker & Rilling, 1981). The design of Grant's study is shown in Figure 4.2, as a delayed successive matching-to-sample procedure. Red and green fields illuminated the center key as sample and comparison stimuli, and information regarding retention was provided by a vertical bar (R-cue) and a horizontal bar (F-cue) presented on the same key. On half the training trials, the R-cue followed the sample stimulus after 0.5 second and lasted for 1 second; after another 1.5

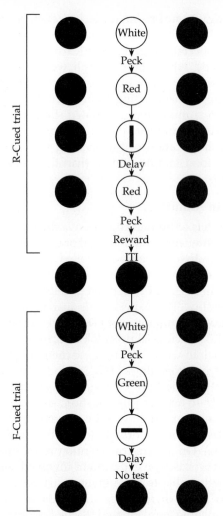

FIGURE 4.2 Design of Grant's directed-forgetting experiment. The vertical bar (R-cue) indicates a memory test, and the horizontal bar (F-cue) indicates test omission.

seconds spent in darkness (total delay = 3 seconds), the matching or non-matching comparison stimulus was presented. On the other half of the trials, the F-cue followed the sample, but no comparison stimulus was presented. The test chamber remained darkened throughout an intertrial interval until the next trial was initiated with a sample stimulus. This procedure is referred to as *comparison omission.* The F-cue may be thought of as a signal that tells the animal that the remainder of the trial is cancelled and that retention of memory of the sample stimulus is unnecessary.

Ultimately, the pigeons were "deceived," and a comparison stimulus was presented following the F-cue to determine how much was remembered about the sample stimulus. These tests of retention following F-cues occurred only on a few probe trials on each session. Over a number of sessions, sufficient observations were accumulated to allow a comparison with performance on R-cued trials. Grant's (1981a) data, and those from a number of other experiments using the comparison omission procedure, indicated that pigeons matched at a far lower level of accuracy on F-cued trials than on R-cued trials. Evidence of directed forgetting was also eventually found in rats (Grant, 1982) and in monkeys (W. Roberts, Mazmanian, & Kraemer, 1984).

Perhaps the most straightforward interpretation of the directed-forgetting phenomenon in animals is the suggestion that the R-cue initiates a rehearsal process that maintains a memory necessary to match accurately when the comparison stimuli are presented. Through experience with comparison omission on F-cued trials, an animal learns not to rehearse or maintain a sample-initiated memory in working memory. Further experimentation has suggested that R-cues are probably not necessary to initiate rehearsal of sample memories. When noncued trials have been compared with R-cued trials, subjects show equally good retention on both types of trials (Santi, 1989; Santi & Savich, 1985). Because delayed matching training begins without R-cues, rehearsal may always be initiated whenever a sample has been presented (Grant, 1981a). Although the presentation of an R-cue adds no further processing, the presentation of an F-cue inhibits rehearsal.

As an alternative account of directed forgetting, Rilling, Kendrick, and Stonebraker (1984) have argued that retention in delayed matching involves retrieval of memory encoded at sample presentation by the stimulus context present at the time of the test. Interestingly, this suggestion is very reminiscent of the theory originally suggested by Hunter (1913) to account for animals' performance in the delayed response problem. According to the Rilling et al. theory, pigeons come to behave differently following an R-cue and an F-cue. Only the behavior occurring after presentation of the R-cue establishes a context that facilitates retrieval of sample memories by the comparison stimuli. The omission of comparison stimuli on F-cued trials leads to a poor behavioral context for the retrieval of memory of the sample stimulus.

An important test of the retrieval explanation involves the manipulation of the point in the delay interval at which an F-cue is presented (Roper & Zentall, 1993). According to rehearsal theory, rehearsal should be initiated by the sample stimulus and persist until either an F-cue is presented or the comparison stimuli are presented for a test. Furthermore, the longer an animal is allowed to rehearse a memory during the delay, the better should be its chances of having a representation in working memory that it can use for accurate performance at the time of test. Therefore, rehearsal theory predicts that performance should improve or be less inhibited by an F-cue the later in the delay the F-cue is presented. Just the opposite prediction follows from the retrieval theory. If F-cues establish a context that prevents retrieval of sample memories, presentation of an F-cue at the end of a delay should interfere with retention far more than presentation of an F-cue at the beginning of a delay. The results of an experiment by Grant (1981a) clearly favored rehearsal theory. Retention increased in pigeon delayed matching as the F-cue was moved toward the end of the delay interval.

In still another account of directed forgetting, Roper and Zentall (1993) suggested that the phenomenon may be caused by factors that have little to do with memory. They suggest that it is the omission of reward in the omission procedure that is critical because it conditions a frustration response to the F-cue. The consequence of frustration elicited by the F-cue is to cause the animal to attend to cues that are incompatible with an efficient response to comparison stimuli. They also suggest that a surprise reaction to the presentation of unexpected comparison stimuli on probe test trials might interfere in some way with efficient performance. Although the possibility is interesting that frustration or surprise might be factors influencing directed forgetting, the exact mechanisms have not been worked out, and the theory is largely untested.

Although it is clear that comparison omission after an F-cue leads to directed forgetting, it may be asked what exactly it is about the omission procedure that causes a drop in performance on probe trials. Is it the omission of the entire test part of the trial, or could it be some component of the test procedure? For example, is the critical factor the omission of the comparison stimuli themselves, the omission of reward, or is it possibly the omission of the opportunity to make a response decision? A number of experiments have been carried out to answer this question using a variety of *comparison substitution* procedures. In these experiments, some aspect of the test portion of R-cued trials is presented on F-cued trials to determine the extent to which it may alleviate the normal forgetting caused by the F-cue. Thus, following the F-cue, animals might receive the reward alone, an opportunity to peck a key for the reward, or a choice between two stimuli unrelated to the sample stimulus, one of which may deliver the reward. The outcome of these experiments is complex (see Grant & Barnet, 1991, or Roper & Zentall, 1993, for reviews), and they will not be discussed in detail here. It is sufficient to say that, in some experiments, F-cue directed forgetting is reduced by such manipulations, but in other experiments it is not, and the reasons for these differences are far from fully understood. Aside from the specifics of these findings, one general possibility seems to be that presenting stimuli and rewards after the F-cue may simply serve to make it difficult for animals to evaluate the meaning of the F-cue. That is, the message that the F-cue will not be followed by a memory test and hence that retention of the sample memory is unnecessary may best be conveyed by the omission procedure.

Although directed-forgetting experiments with animals have been described as analogous to those performed with people, an important difference can be found. Most human directed-forgetting experiments allow subjects to differentially allocate processing time to R-cued and F-cued items. If a subject is receiving both kinds of items in succession, the presentation of F-cues after some items allows the subject to disregard memory of those items and rehearse only the items followed by R-cues. Since only one sample stimulus was presented on a trial in the animal experiments, the presentation of R-cues and F-cues provided no opportunity for differential allocation of processing time.

Roper, Kaiser, & Zentall (1995) performed a recent comparison substitution experiment that provided an opportunity for pigeons to use R-cues and F-cues as signals for differential allocation of processing time. Figure 4.3 shows training trials with remember and forget cues and ultimate probe trials in which memory tests were given for F-cued items. Red and green sample stimuli were presented at the beginning of a trial. On R-cued trials, the key turned either

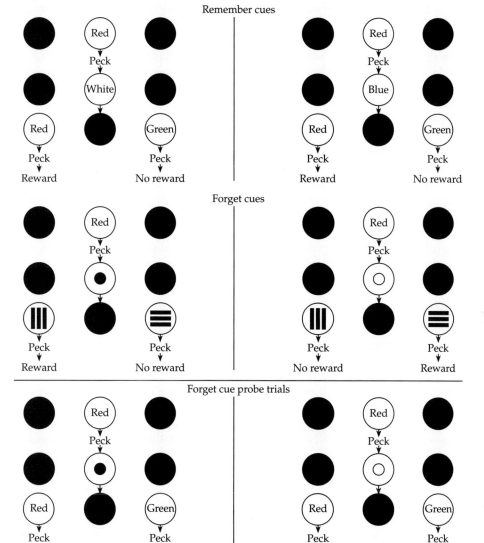

FIGURE 4.3 Design of an experiment that studied directed forgetting by requiring pigeons to reallocate memory processing to forget cues.
Adapted from Roper, Kaiser, & Zentall, 1995.

blue or white and remained on for a 4-second delay. At the end of the delay, red and green comparison stimuli were presented on side keys for the delayed matching test of memory. On half the trials, however, a circle or a dot appeared on the center key during the delay and served as the F-cue. An important feature of the experiment is that the circle and dot did not *just* serve as F-cues that told the pigeon it would not be tested on memory for red or green; the circle and dot also served as new sample stimuli, memory for which was tested by presentation of a choice between vertical- and horizontal-striped patterns on the side keys. In other words, the F-cues and the choice between stripe patterns that followed them formed a 0-second delayed symbolic matching-to-sample test of memory. Notice how this design forced the pigeon to differentially allocate processing time to sample stimuli. If an R-cue occurred, then the pigeon could devote its processing time exclusively to memory of the red or green sample stimulus. If an F-cue occurred, however, the pigeon had to switch its processing from memory of red or green to the circle or dot pattern to ensure a successful match on the forthcoming test.

Eventually, the pigeons were tested for memory of samples they had been instructed to forget, as shown in the lower trials depicted in Figure 4.3. The findings revealed a strong directed-forgetting effect, with pigeons making 86.4 percent correct responses on R-cued trials and 73.0 percent correct responses on F-cued trials. Thus, a clear directed-forgetting effect was found with a stimulus substitution procedure when it was made clear to pigeons that the substituted comparison stimuli were a test for memory of the F-cues. The important effect of this procedure was to ensure that pigeons did not rehearse memories of the red and green sample stimuli during the delay on F-cued trials. Rehearsal time was reallocated to the F-cues.

Serial Position Effects

Suppose that a person was presented with more than one piece of information to remember. She might be presented with a list of stimuli, and her memory could be tested for any stimulus in the list. How well would she remember items at the beginning, middle, and end of the list? Would her memory vary among these regions of the list? In fact, testing memory for lists of verbal items has been a popular procedure for many years in the field of human memory. A person was presented with a list of words, and her memory then was tested for some or all of the words on the list. When retention was examined at each of the successive positions in the list (serial position), a serial position effect was revealed in which items at the beginning and the end of the list were remembered better than those in the middle. Superior retention of initial items (primacy effect) and terminal items (recency effect) has been found in a wide variety of human memory tasks, including serial anticipation learning (McCrary & Hunter, 1953), free recall, and recognition memory tests for lists of words (Murdock, 1962; 1968).

It is of theoretical interest to ask whether an animal would also show a bowed serial position curve with primacy and recency effects. Finding the serial position effect in animals would suggest common processes used by people and animals to encode and retrieve memory of a list of items. In several early investigations, the procedures discussed in the preceding chapter were used to examine memory for lists of stimuli in animals. It is important to realize, however, that studies of list memory require that an animal be presented with a number of different stimuli. The examples shown in Chapter 3 depicted working memory procedures in which animals were tested alternately for memory of only two stimuli, such as red and green keys. In list memory experiments, a list of different stimuli was presented to an animal, and memory for only one of the stimuli then was tested. The stimulus would appear with an item not on the list as an incorrect comparison stimulus on delayed simultaneous matching tests, or a single item that either was on the list or was not on the list was presented on a delayed yes-no matching-to-sample test. Memory for each position within a list of a fixed length was probed a number of times over many trials, and percentage of correct choices was plotted as a function of serial position. Early experiments of this sort were performed with pigeons (MacPhail, 1980; Shimp, 1976; Shimp & Moffitt, 1974), rats (W. Roberts & Smythe, 1979), monkeys (R. Davis & Fitts, 1976; D. Gaffan, 1977), and a dolphin (R. Thompson & Herman, 1977). All of these initial experiments revealed recency effects but no evidence of a primacy effect.

Animals, like people, showed better memory for items at the end of a list than for those earlier in the list. This effect could be readily explained by assuming that memories of final items had a higher probability of being in the working memory at the time of test. On the basis of these initial findings, however, it appeared that only humans showed a primacy effect in serial memory. In a popular account of memory for serial lists in people, the primacy effect is explained as an effect of differential rehearsal of early and middle list items (Atkinson & Shiffrin, 1968; Rundus, 1971). Since early items on a list are presented with few items preceding them, they have ample opportunity to be rehearsed. As the middle of the list is approached, however, the backlog of items to be rehearsed increases, and each new item is given less rehearsal. The extra rehearsal given initial items is thought to transmit more information about these items from working memory to long-term or reference memory, from which they can later be successfully retrieved on a recall test. The important theoretical point here for animal memory is that the failure to find a primacy effect with animals might be caused by animals' inability to rehearse stimuli. If animals do not possess the ability to rehearse, then of course they would not differentially rehearse the early stimuli on a list and would not show a primacy effect.

As is often the case, initial assumptions about animal memory proved to be false. Through the 1980s, a number of experiments appeared showing primacy effects in animals. In a particularly impressive demonstration, Sands and Wright (1980a; 1980b) trained a rhesus monkey to make yes or no recognition responses to slide stimuli from serial lists as long as 10 or 20 items. The monkey sat in a primate chair and viewed a list of slides of various objects and scenes projected on a small screen. After this, a slide either from the list or not from the list was shown on an adjacent screen, and the monkey was required to move a lever to the right for a "yes" response or to the left for a "no" response. The monkey saw a different slide at each position in a list, and the slides changed between trials since they were drawn from a large pool of 211 pictures. Data from an experiment using a 10-item list are shown in Figure 4.4. Both a monkey subject and a human subject were tested for comparative purposes. Although the human showed a higher level of recognition than the monkey, the important point is that both curves show primacy and recency effects. These data suggest clearly that the primacy effect is not limited to human subjects.

Subsequent studies of serial memory in monkeys have confirmed the Sands and Wright observations, indicating primacy effects in memory for lists of travel slides (Wright, Santiago, Sands, Kendrick, & Cook, 1985), geometric patterns (W. Roberts & Kraemer, 1981), and computer-generated pictures

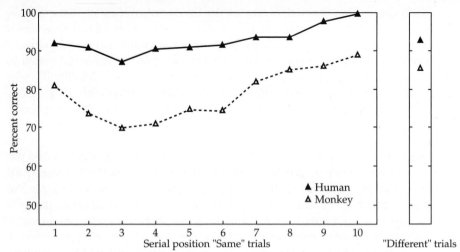

FIGURE 4.4 Serial position curves showing memory for 10-item lists of pictures in a human subject and a rhesus monkey.

(Castro & Larsen, 1992). In addition, Wright et al. (1985) found evidence for a primacy effect in pigeons, when a four-item list of pictures was used and the retention test was delayed for 1 or 2 seconds.

Memory for serial lists of spatial events was studied in rats with a piece of equipment called the *radial maze*. The maze consists of a central platform with eight or more arms branching from it, like the spokes of a wheel. Rats placed on the maze learn to enter these arms for a food reward. Rats may be trained either to avoid an arm previously visited for the food reward (win-shift strategy) or to return to an arm previously visited (win-stay strategy). In serial list experiments, a rat was allowed to enter several of these arms in a controlled order, and its memory then was tested for different arms in the list by giving it a choice between an entered arm and one it had not previously entered. If it had been trained to win-shift, it should prefer the unentered arm, but, if it had been trained to win-stay, it should prefer the previously entered arm. Although surrounded by some methodological controversy (E. Gaffan, 1992; Kesner, Chiba, & Jackson-Smith, 1994; Reed, 1994), a number of studies now have reported primacy and recency effects in rat memory for lists of arms entered on a radial maze (Bolhuis & Van Kampen, 1988; DiMattia & Kesner, 1984; Harper, McLean, & Dalrymple-Alford, 1993; Kesner & Novak, 1982). Other important findings in spatial memory made with the radial maze are discussed in Chapter 7.

The array of evidence now suggests that primacy effects in memory for serial lists of stimuli may be quite commonplace across many species of animals. If this observation is correct, and if we hold to the rehearsal interpretation of primacy offered to account for human primacy effects, the argument can be made that primacy reflects rehearsal in animals. In addition to the effect of surprise on working memory and the directed-forgetting effect, the primacy effect then may be used as a third piece of converging evidence in favor of a rehearsal process in animals.

Unfortunately, not all of the evidence from serial memory studies converges on the conclusion that animals rehearse. A number of studies suggest that humans rehearse visual information postperceptually. Suppose people are shown a list of pictures to remember, with each picture presented for 1 second. In one group of subjects, the pictures are presented massed together in time with each picture immediately following the preceding one. For another group of subjects, the pictures are spaced in time with a blank interval of 5 seconds following each picture. People show far better memory for the spaced list than for the massed list, and it is suggested that this difference arises from the opportunity for subjects given the spaced list to rehearse the image of the picture just seen (Intraub, 1980; Tversky & Sherman, 1975; G. Weaver, 1974; G. Weaver & Stanny, 1978). Monkeys clearly show improved memory for lists of pictures the longer they are exposed to each picture on a list (W. Roberts & Kraemer, 1984). Given the benefits of extended exposure to pictures and the suggestion that monkeys rehearse, one might fully expect that blank time after brief presentation of a picture would be beneficial to monkey memory, just as it is to human memory. This prediction was not supported in investigations by Roberts and Kraemer (1984) and Cook, Wright and Sands (1991). Introducing a blank interstimulus interval between picture presentations either had no effect on memory or slightly lowered retention.

This striking incongruity between the effects of spaced presentation on human and monkey picture memory creates somewhat of a theoretical puzzle. If we assume that humans and monkeys show a primacy effect because both rehearse early items in a list more than later items, then why don't both show rehearsal of spaced pictures? Several explanations are possible. One account is that, for some reason, monkeys differentially rehearse items on a serial list but do not take advantage of blank time to rehearse. Why this would be the case is not at all clear. Another possibility that has important implications for the primacy effect in human subjects is that primacy does not arise from differential rehearsal. As support for this possibility, A. Wright, Cook, Rivera, Shyan, Neiworth, and Jitsumori (1990) found a primacy effect in human memory for lists of kaleidoscopic pictures, even when subjects reported no rehearsal of these stimuli. Some process common to animals and people other than rehearsal might be responsible for the primacy effect. For example, some theorists have suggested that the serial position effect may be caused by the perceptual gestalt properties of lists (Asch, Hay, & Diamond, 1960; Glanzer & Dolinsky, 1965). Initial and final items seem to stand out because nothing precedes or follows them, whereas middle items are crowded among earlier and later items. If perceptually distinct stimuli are better encoded for memory retrieval, the serial position effect would be the result. Such a perceptual account of the serial position effect might easily anticipate the effect appearing in both humans and animals that share common processes of perceptual organization (see Chapter 2). Still a third alternative is that different processes might be responsible for primacy in humans and animals. Rehearsal might be responsible for primacy in people but not for primacy in animals.

Although the importance of rehearsal as an account of primacy in animals remains unclear, the evidence from experiments on surprise and directed forgetting, combined with the primacy effect, argues that we should continue to entertain the strong possibility that animal memory is improved by rehearsal. Research on rehearsal has clearly moved the field of animal working memory away from passive decay conceptions toward a more dynamic, controlled working memory.

PROSPECTIVE AND RETROSPECTIVE MEMORY

It was suggested earlier in this chapter that animals may learn rules about delayed matching tasks. In a symbolic delayed matching experiment, for example, a pigeon might learn, "If vertical line sample, then peck red comparison," and "If horizontal line sample, then peck green comparison." Through repetition of the same sequences of samples and comparison choices leading to reward and nonreward, these rules would be learned or stored in reference memory. They can then be quickly retrieved from reference memory to guide matching behavior. Since the sample stimuli are alternated in a random order in a typical experiment, working memory must be used to retain information over the delay that will allow the correct rule to be used for accurate choice between comparison stimuli. There must be an interplay between the perceptual information presented by the sample stimulus, retrieval of rules from the reference memory, and working memory remembered over a delay interval.

A bit of reflection suggests that successful delayed matching could be accomplished in two ways. A pigeon presented with a vertical line as a sample stimulus might encode the vertical line as a working memory and rehearse it throughout the delay. When the red and green comparison stimuli are presented, memory of the vertical line would retrieve the appropriate rule from reference memory, "If vertical line sample, then peck red comparison," and the correct response would be made. This process is referred to as *retrospective memory*. Representation of an event that occurred in the past is maintained in working memory, and instructions for use of that memory are retrieved when needed at the test. Another possibility is that retrieval of response instructions takes place earlier in a trial, at the time the sample stimulus is presented. Because the sample is seen to be a vertical line, and because the response rule indicates "peck the red comparison," the bird can know before the delay begins which response it will need to make to obtain the reward. In this case, the easiest thing for the subject to do is to forget the sample stimulus and simply remember the instruction to peck the red key. This process is referred to as *prospective memory*. In this case, working memory is said to be *instructional* in nature. As a descriptive metaphor for these two types of memory, we can describe retrospective memory as looking backward or asking, "What happened?" and prospective memory as looking forward and anticipating, "What should be done?"

In the early theories of animal working memory, it was assumed that memory was retrospective in nature. The very notion of a trace suggests an iconic representation of the sample stimulus that fades over time. The theory of temporal discrimination indicated that animals retrospectively remembered sample events and their associated time markers. In the 1980s, a series of theoretical papers by Honig and his associates (Honig, 1981; Honig & Thompson, 1982; Honig & Dodd, 1986), and a number of experimental papers, provided solid support for the idea that animals often use prospective memory. It then became of interest to know under what conditions working memory would be prospective and/or retrospective. As a consequence of the considerable research done on this question, we now have methods for inferring retrospective and prospective memory codes. Furthermore, manipulations are now available that allow us to bias coding in working memory experiments toward prospection or retrospection.

Evidence of Prospective Working Memory

Simple versus Conditional Delayed Discriminations

Consider two learning and memory tasks studied by Honig and Wasserman (1981). One group of pigeons was trained to perform a *delayed conditional discrimination* (DCD). The DCD task is another name for the delayed successive matching-to-sample task introduced in Chapter 3. Each trial began with a red or a green sample stimulus on a single key. Pecks on this key then led to a delay followed by a comparison stimulus, either a horizontal line or a vertical line. The conditional relationship between the sample and comparison stimuli was symbolic. Thus, following a red sample, pecking on the vertical line comparison stimulus was rewarded, but pecking on the horizontal line comparison stimulus led to nonreward. Conversely, following a green sample, pecking on the horizontal line stimulus led to reward, and pecking on the vertical line stimulus led to nonreward.

The other group of pigeons was trained to perform a *delayed simple discrimination* (DSD). Exactly the same sequences of sample, delay, and comparison stimulus events occurred on DSD trials, but the reward contingencies were different. If a trial began with a red sample stimulus, pecking on the comparison stimulus *always* produced reward, regardless of whether the comparison stimulus was a vertical line or a horizontal line. Trials beginning with a green sample stimulus *always* led to nonreward for pecks on the comparison stimulus. Note that a pigeon performing the DSD task only needed to know the color of the sample stimulus to determine whether it would or would not be rewarded and hence, whether it should or should not peck the comparison stimulus. A pigeon performing the DCD task, on the other hand, could not determine the correct response until it had seen both the sample and the comparison stimuli.

Pigeons learned to respond accurately much faster on the DSD problem than on the DCD problem. After learning these delayed discriminations to a high level of accuracy, both groups were given memory tests at several delays. The retention curves, shown in Figure 4.5, indicate far better retention in the DSD group than in the DCD group. Of particular importance, note that memory is equally good at a 1-second delay; thereafter, the DSD group showed no forgetting, while the DCD group showed substantial forgetting. These data suggest that both groups had sufficient memory information to respond quite accurately immediately after the sample had been presented. Information then was lost very rapidly by DCD pigeons but not by DSD pigeons.

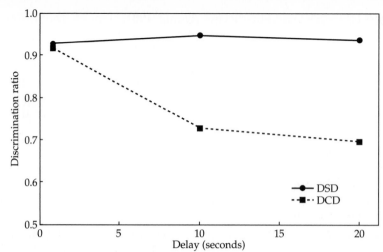

FIGURE 4.5 Retention curves for two groups of pigeons, one group trained to perform a delayed simple discrimination (DSD) and the other group trained to perform a delayed conditional discrimination (DCD).

Consider the rules pigeons had to learn in each group. Pigeons in Group DSD only had to learn "If red sample, then peck," and "If green sample, then don't peck." Pigeons in Group DCD had to learn the more complex rules, "If red sample, peck if vertical line comparison, but don't peck if horizontal line comparison," and "If green sample, peck if horizontal line comparison, but don't peck if vertical line comparison." Now consider the use of these rules when memory is retrospective or prospective. If retrospective memory was used, both groups would remember the red or green sample. When presented with a comparison stimulus, each group would retrieve the appropriate response rules. Since DCD pigeons had more complex response rules, one might expect errors in the retrieval of the rules or the implementation of the rules to occur more often in this group, but the level of errors should be constant at all delays. Instead, the retention curves indicate that Group DCD found it progressively more difficult to remember as the delay became longer.

If both groups used prospective memory, however, the observed differences in retention would be expected. Pigeons in Group DSD could simply encode the sample as an instruction to "peck" or "don't peck," but pigeons in Group DCD would have to remember more information, such as, "Peck if the comparison is a vertical line, but don't peck if the comparison is a horizontal line." Virtually all theories of working memory suggest that the more information that must be held in this short-term buffer, the greater will be the loss of information or forgetting. Pigeons forced to rehearse complex response rules over long delays in Group DCD should have a much greater chance of losing that information over the delay than pigeons required to remember a simple go or no-go response rule in Group DSD. These data then suggest that both groups of pigeons were using prospective memory coding, one far more successfully than the other.

The Differential Outcomes Effect

109

CHAPTER 4
Working Memory:
Theoretical
Approaches

The observant student may have noted that pigeons in group DSD in the Honig and Wasserman (1981) experiment not only could use the sample stimulus to anticipate which way to respond but also to anticipate the outcome of the trials—reward or nonreward. Other experiments suggest that, in fact, expectations of reward and nonreward elicited by sample stimuli play a key role as memory mediators. It may then be these prospective expectations that are remembered during the delay and used to guide responses to comparison stimuli. An important role for reward expectations should not be too surprising. Although events such as sample stimuli, delays, and comparison stimuli may be important to the human experimenter, the attention of a hungry pigeon is focused on food events, and it may always reduce a task to coding in terms of food whenever possible.

A series of experiments carried out by Peterson and his associates showed the importance of reward-outcome coding in pigeon working memory (Brodigan & G. Peterson, 1976; G. Peterson, Wheeler, & Armstrong, 1978; G. Peterson, Wheeler, & Trapold, 1980). A typical differential outcomes experiment using delayed simultaneous matching-to-sample is diagrammed in Figure 4.6. In the traditional delayed simultaneous procedure, both sample stimuli and their matching comparison stimuli yield the same reward outcome if the correct response is made. In the differential outcomes procedure, each sample and its matching comparison stimulus lead to different outcomes. These outcomes have been labeled A and B in Figure 4.6. In actual experiments, the differential outcomes may be food and water, different kinds of grain, food and no food, or a low versus high probability of reward. The results have been the same with all of these types of differential outcomes: Pigeons learn the problem very rapidly and show very high levels of retention over long memory delays. When compared with performance under the traditional procedure, in which both sample-comparison sequences are rewarded with the same outcome, differential outcomes lead to far faster learning and higher retention. This result is called the *differential outcomes effect,* or DOE.

As already suggested, the favored theoretical account of the DOE is based on differential expectations conditioned to sample stimuli. If a pigeon has learned, "If red sample, expect food," and "If green sample, expect no food," these expectations may then guide a choice between comparison stimuli. For example, an expectancy of food may be a prospective code for pecking a comparison key with a triangle, and the expectancy of no food may be a prospective code for pecking a comparison key with a circle. This is an interesting speculation, but how could we test this theoretical idea? Fortunately, a type of experimental design called *transfer of control* allows us to test the importance of reward expectancy codes (Edwards, Jagielo, Zentall, & Hogan, 1982; G. Peterson & Trapold, 1980; Urcuioli & Zentall, 1992).

The design of a revealing experiment performed by Urcuioli and Zentall (1992) is outlined in Table 4.3. The experiment required three phases and two groups of pigeons, the *consistent outcomes group* and the *reversed outcomes group.* Both groups were given identical training throughout Phases 1 and 2. In Phase 1, both groups were trained on a delayed simple discrimination in which red

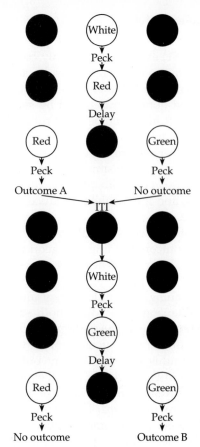

FIGURE 4.6 Design of trials from a delayed simultaneous matching-to-sample experiment with differential outcomes. A correct match to the red sample stimulus always produces Outcome A, and a correct match to the green sample stimulus always produces Outcome B.

and green samples were both followed by vertical line and horizontal line comparison stimuli, with pecking on the comparison key always leading to food after the red sample and always leading to no food after the green sample. Delayed simultaneous matching-to-sample training was carried out in Phase 2. A triangle or three dots were the sample stimuli, and blue and white fields were the comparison stimuli. Differential outcomes were delivered, such that the triangle sample followed by choice of the blue comparison always yielded food reward, and the dots sample followed by choice of the white comparison always led to no food. When the dots sample was followed by choice of the blue comparison, the outcome was also no food. What differentiated these choices was the use of a correction procedure that led to a repeat of the trial whenever the blue comparison was chosen. Thus, the pigeon always had to choose the white comparison to advance to the next trial. Notice that the sample and comparison stimuli used in Phases 1 and 2 were all different stimuli.

TABLE 4.3 Design of Experiment by Urcuioli and Zentall (1992) Showing Transfer of Stimulus Control from One Set of Sample Stimuli to Another through Use of Common Mediating Outcome Expectancies

	PHASE 1 (DELAYED SIMPLE DISCRIMINATION)	
Sample Stimulus	Comparison Stimulus	Response Outcome
Red	Vertical line	Food
Red	Horizontal line	Food
Green	Vertical line	No food
Green	Horizontal line	No food

	PHASE 2 (DELAYED SIMULTANEOUS MATCHING)	
Sample Stimulus	Correct Comparison Stimulus	Response Outcome
Triangle	Blue	Food
Dots	White	No food

	PHASE 3 (DELAYED SIMULTANEOUS MATCHING)	
Sample Stimulus	Correct Comparison Stimulus	Response Outcome
Consistent outcomes group		
Red	Blue	Food
Green	White	No food
Reversed outcomes group		
Red	Blue	No food
Green	White	Food

In Phase 3, the pigeons of both groups were given a new delayed simultaneous matching problem that combined the sample stimuli from Phase 1 and the comparison stimuli from Phase 2. Thus, the blue comparison was the correct comparison choice after a red sample, and the white comparison was the correct choice after a green sample. This mapping of sample and comparison stimuli ensured that the comparison followed by food in Phase 2 was matched with the sample followed by food in Phase 1; similarly, comparison and sample stimuli followed by no food were matched. No direct associations existed between the sample and comparison stimuli used in Phase 3, however, because the pigeons had never encountered these stimuli together before. The final important manipulation in the experiment was the use of different trial outcomes between the two groups. In the consistent outcomes group, food and no food followed correct comparison choices in agreement with the outcomes of Phases 1 and 2. For the reversed outcomes group, food now followed the sample and comparison stimuli that had been followed by no food in Phases 1 and 2, and no food followed the sample and comparison stimuli that had been followed by food.

Percentage choice of the correct or matching stimulus over 10 sessions of training in Phase 3 is shown in Figure 4.7. The curve from the consistent outcomes group shows that these pigeons began matching on the first session at greater than 80 percent correct and showed further improvement on subsequent sessions to near-perfect matching. On the basis of any direct associations between the sample and comparison stimuli, choice accuracy should have been near chance or 50 percent on the initial sessions. Why did these birds behave as if they had already learned the discrimination, even though they had never before encountered this combination of sample and comparison stimuli? A ready explanation follows from the theory of control by outcome expectancies. According to this theory, pigeons learned two different expectancies in Phase 1: to expect food following a red sample and to expect no food following a green sample. In Phase 2, two important things were learned: An expectancy of food was conditioned to the triangle sample, and an expectancy of no food was conditioned to the dots sample. Furthermore, pigeons learned that a food expectancy was a cue for pecking the blue comparison stimulus and that a no-food expectancy was a cue for pecking the white comparison stimulus. The positive transfer seen in Phase 3 then follows directly from the combined use of this prior learning. The red sample elicited an expectancy of food based on Phase 1 training, and the food expectancy elicited a response to the blue comparison stimulus based on Phase 2 training. Similarly, the green stimulus elicited an expectancy of no food, which guided choice toward the white comparison stimulus.

Now examine the curve in Figure 4.7 for the reversed outcomes group. This very interesting acquisition curve is nonmonotonic, meaning that it is initially above chance (about 70 percent) on the first session, drops slightly below chance on Sessions 2 and 3, and then progressively rises over subsequent sessions. If we examine the pigeons' use of expectations in Phase 3, this curve

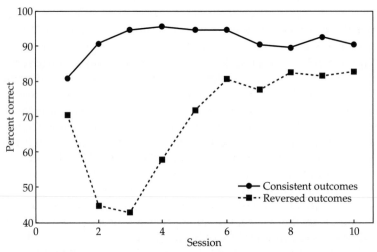

FIGURE 4.7 Curves showing the acquisition of delayed simultaneous matching-to-sample in Phase 3 of the transfer-of-control experiment diagrammed in Table 4.3. The trial outcomes (food or no food) are consistent with Phase 1 and 2 outcomes in the consistent outcomes group but inconsistent with Phase 1 and 2 outcomes in the reversed outcomes group.

begins to make sense. Pigeons in the reversed outcomes group begin Phase 3 with the same expectations as pigeons in the consistent outcomes group, and they also show initial evidence of positive transfer by above-chance correct matching. The pigeons soon learn, however, that the actual outcomes do not match their expectations, and this disconfirmation of their expectancies leads to confusion and inaccurate choice. Eventually, these pigeons begin to learn a new set of expectations: that red predicts no food and green predicts food. These new expectations then come to control the choice between blue and white comparison stimuli. The reversed outcomes group curve indicates that the relearning process is slow; even after 10 sessions, these pigeons have not caught up with the level of performance shown by pigeons in the consistent outcomes group. This slow acquisition seems reasonable, however, when one realizes that the reversed outcome birds must acquire both new expectations to sample stimuli and new associations between expectations and comparison stimuli.

Evidence of Retrospective Working Memory

The findings just described, along with others, seem to establish the existence of prospective working memory in animals. Could it be argued that all working memory in animals is prospective? Since virtually all working memory experiments involve trials that end with comparison stimuli and responses followed by reward or nonreward, it might be argued that animals will always code memory prospectively in terms of end-of-trial events. This does not appear to be the case, however, because there is solid evidence of situations in which animals retain retrospective memory of a preceding sample event. Recent evidence suggests that certain memory tasks lead to retrospective memory and that others lead to prospective memory. One area in which clear evidence of retrospection has been found is memory for time durations.

As mentioned earlier, a major advantage of symbolic delayed matching procedures is that memory for virtually any dimension of an animal's experience can be studied by mapping values on that dimension onto different comparison stimuli. In working memory experiments for time duration, two events lasting different lengths of time are used as sample stimuli. In a procedure developed by Spetch and Wilkie (1982; 1983), a trial always began with the onset of a houselight (a small light bulb mounted on the wall of the operant chamber) that lit up the entire chamber. The houselight would stay on for a period of 2 or 10 seconds. Immediately after the houselight went off, two side keys were illuminated—one with a red light and the other with a green light. If the houselight had lasted for the short 2-second duration, a peck on the green key produced a food reward, and a peck on the red key led to nonreward and the intertrial interval. Following the longer 10-second duration of the houselight, just the opposite contingencies were in effect, with a peck to red rewarded and a peck to green nonrewarded.

Pigeons quickly learned to match the correct comparison stimulus to its temporal sample stimulus under these conditions. It might well be argued that pigeons had learned two prospective codes. Whenever the sample was short, a pigeon could simply remember, "Peck the green key," and, whenever the sample was long, the pigeon could remember the code, "Peck the red key." When pigeons were tested for their memory of these time durations over several seconds, however, something very interesting happened that discouraged the prospective explanation. The retention curves for short and long duration samples shown in Figure 4.8 indicate quite different rates of forgetting for short and long samples. Although there is very little forgetting of the short sample, the long-sample memory curve plummets to points below 50 percent at 5- and 10-second delays. This difference in rates of forgetting for short and long samples has been observed in a number of temporal memory experiments and is referred to as the *choose-short effect*. As the delay increases, pigeons come to prefer the comparison stimulus associated with the short-sample stimulus, even on trials that began with a long-sample stimulus.

Spetch and Wilkie (1983) suggested that the choose-short effect could be explained by a process of *temporal shortening*. The suggestion is that a remembered duration of time begins to shrink or shorten with time spent in the delay. Thus, the time duration remembered after a 5- or 10-second delay is much shorter than the time remembered immediately after the sample duration was presented. Memory of the long sample, in particular, will shorten to a duration close to the 2-second sample. Based on rules learned during training at a 0-second delay and stored in reference memory, the long comparison key should be chosen only when the pigeon remembers a 10-second sample. This occurs at the 0-second delay, but, at the longer delays, the long sample will be remembered as short, and the correct response remembered from reference memory will be a peck on the short comparison stimulus. Data collected from other types of experiments converge on temporal shortening as the correct

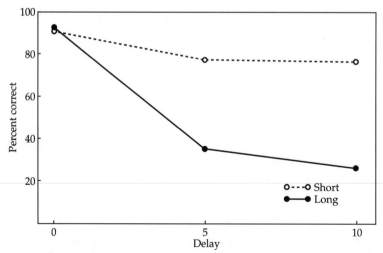

FIGURE 4.8 The choose-short effect is shown by the sharp drop in the long-sample stimulus retention curve while the short-sample stimulus curve drops very little. These curves show that pigeons develop a preference for the comparison stimulus associated with the short sample as the delay progresses.

For memory of time duration to shorten over a delay period, time must be remembered retrospectively. If time durations had been coded into response instructions that were remembered over the delay, no choose-short effect should have been found, because the instructions "peck red" and "peck green" are equivalent forms of information and should be forgotten at the same rate. Although such instructional codes are prospective and *categorical,* it appears that memory for time duration was retrospective and *analogical.* This means that the memory for time duration could take on many lengths as it shortened over a delay interval. How animals represent time is discussed later in Chapter 8.

BIASING MEMORY CODING TOWARD RETROSPECTION OR PROSPECTION

Recently, methods have been developed that allow experimenters to directly manipulate the kind of coding an animal may use. The evidence just reviewed suggests that pigeons normally code memory for time duration retrospectively and analogically. That is, pigeons remember the actual length of time that a sample stimulus was presented, 2 or 10 seconds. Would it be possible to change this code from a retrospective one of time duration to a prospective or instructional code, such as, "Peck the red key"? Grant & Spetch (1993) recently provided evidence suggesting that the pigeon's memory for time can be biased toward retrospective or prospective coding. This demonstration rests on the assumption that the choose-short effect is an indicator of restrospective memory. Remember that the explanation of the choose-short effect holds that pigeons have encoded a memory of time duration that shortens over a retention interval. If the memory code could be changed from an analogical representation of time duration to a prospective code, then retention curves for short and long samples should not differ. In other words, the choose-short effect should disappear under prospective coding.

Grant and Spetch (1993) employed a procedure called many-to-one (MTO) mapping. Two pair of sample stimuli were associated with one pair of comparison stimuli. Pigeons in the MTO group began the experiment by learning a standard delayed symbolic simultaneous matching-to-sample problem. If a vertical line appeared as the sample stimulus, a red comparison stimulus had to be chosen to yield a reward; if the sample was a horizontal line, then the green comparison stimulus had to be pecked for a reward. Once pigeons had learned this problem, a new pair of sample stimuli was introduced, namely, short (2 seconds) and long (10 seconds) presentations of houselight. Following the short houselight, pigeons had to learn to peck the green comparison key for the reward, whereas a peck on the red comparison key was required for a reward following the long houselight. Pigeons eventually learned to match the red and green comparison stimuli to houselight durations. The pigeons then had learned MTO matching: Two sets of sample stimuli (many)—lines and durations—could be matched by choosing between the members of one set of comparison stimuli—red and green. The delay interval was always 0 seconds throughout this training; that is, the comparison stimuli always followed immediately after the termination of the sample stimulus.

Retention testing then was carried out at several delays, and retention curves for each houselight duration can be seen in Figure 4.9. A control group also was trained with only houselight duration sample stimuli mapped onto red and green comparison stimuli. The retention curves for the control and MTO groups show a striking difference. The control group curves demonstrate the usual choose-short effect, with far less of a drop in accuracy for the short-sample stimulus than for the long-sample stimulus. By contrast, the curves for the MTO group are almost identical and indicate no difference in the rate of forgetting for short- and long-sample stimuli.

Based on these findings, Grant and Spetch (1993) argued that pigeons in the control group retained retrospective and analogical memories of time duration that led to the choose-short effect through subjective shortening of memory for the long-sample stimulus. Pigeons in the MTO group, however, formed prospective memories, such as "peck red" or "peck green," which were equivalent in information value and thus were forgotten at the same rate. Why would the MTO manipulation produce prospective coding of time? Note that the task given MTO pigeons was more difficult than that given control pigeons. Animals in the MTO group had to associate four sample stimuli with the appropriate comparison stimuli, whereas control animals only had to associate two sample stimuli with comparison stimuli. If retrospective memory were used by the MTO group, four sample stimulus memories would have to be remembered during delays—two houselight durations and two line orientations. If prospective memory were used, however, only two response codes would have to be remembered during delays, "peck red" or "peck green."

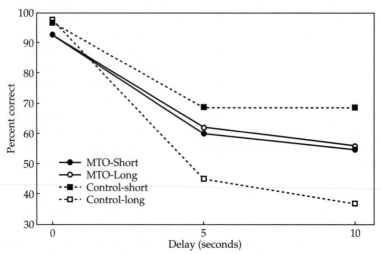

FIGURE 4.9
Retention curves for short- and long-sample stimuli in an MTO mapping group and in a control group that learned to match only temporal sample stimuli. The curves for the control group show a choose-short effect, but the curves for the MTO group do not.

Thus, it was simpler or more economical for birds to use prospective coding rather than retrospective coding to deal with MTO mapping. A general principle of animal cognition experiments is that animals will find the easiest or most parsimonious solution to a problem. The use of a common prospective code in MTO matching may be an example of that principle.

These findings are of considerable significance because they highlight the dynamic flexibility of animal memory. Although pigeons' normal proclivity may be to remember time durations retrospectively as an analog of duration, time memory can be completely reversed to a prospective categorical code when experimental demands make it more economical to do so.

THE COMMON CODE

The suggestion that pigeons in an MTO experiment represent different sample stimuli as a single code is referred to as *common coding theory.* Although prospective coding has thus far been presented as taking the form of either an outcome expectancy or a response instruction, we do not know for certain what common code animals might be using. One possibility that has been suggested is that the common code is a representation of one of the sample stimuli used in an MTO design (Zentall, Steirn, Sherburne, & Urcuioli, 1991). If red and vertical line sample stimuli are mapped onto a common comparison stimulus, for example, both the red sample and the vertical sample might elicit a representation of red as a common code. In this case, red would be favored as the common code because pigeons find colors more salient than black-and-white patterns. Another alternative that has been suggested is that animals might use intermediate codes for which we have no ready analogy. In the absence of strong evidence about the nature of common codes, theorists have suggested that we might simply refer to them as Code A and Code B (Urcuioli, Zentall, Jackson-Smith, & Steirn, 1989; Zentall et al., 1991; Zentall, Sherburne, & Steirn, 1993). Thus, in the Grant and Spetch (1993) experiment, pigeons in the MTO group might have coded horizontal line and short houselight as Code A and vertical line and long houselight as Code B. When the red and green comparison stimuli were presented, Code A would be decoded as an instruction to peck green, and Code B would be decoded as an instruction to peck red.

The Grant and Spetch (1993) experiment provided indirect evidence of common coding through the absence of a choose-short effect in the MTO group. There is more direct evidence of common coding, however, found in an experiment performed by Urcuioli et al. (1989). Two groups of pigeons were referred to as a consistent group and an inconsistent group. As shown in Table 4.4, both groups were trained in identical ways in Phases 1 and 2. In Phase 1, MTO delayed matching training involved two pairs of sample stimuli—red and green fields and horizontal and vertical lines—matched to one pair of comparison stimuli—horizontal and vertical lines. Since the vertical line comparison stimulus was correct after both the red sample and the vertical line sample, a common code should be elicited by these two sample stimuli according to common coding theory. Similarly, the green sample stimulus and the horizontal line should have a common code. In Phase 2, both groups were trained on a

TABLE 4.4 Design of Experiment by Urcuioli, Zentall, Jackson-Smith, and Steirn (1989) to Test the Theory of Common Coding

PHASE 1 (MANY-TO-ONE MATCHING)	
Sample Stimulus	Correct Comparison Stimulus
Red	Vertical line
Green	Horizontal line
Vertical line	Vertical line
Horizontal line	Horizontal line
PHASE 2 (ONE-TO-ONE DELAYED MATCHING)	
Sample Stimulus	Correct Comparison Stimulus
Red	Circle
Green	Dot
PHASE 3 (ONE-TO-ONE DELAYED MATCHING)	
Sample Stimulus	Correct Comparison Stimulus
Consistent group	
Vertical line	Circle
Horizontal line	Dot
Inconsistent group	
Vertical line	Dot
Horizontal line	Circle

second delayed matching problem using the red and green sample stimuli from Phase 1 and new comparison stimuli—circle and dot. Training in Phase 2 was one-to-one (OTO) because only one sample was matched to each comparison stimulus. Notice that the common codes learned in Phase 1 should transfer to Phase 2. Red should elicit a common code that becomes associated with the response of pecking the circle comparison stimulus, and green should elicit a common code that directs pecking toward the dot comparison stimulus.

As a test of these theoretics, the groups were transferred to different Phase 3 problems. Both groups now encountered a delayed matching problem in which the sample vertical and horizontal line stimuli from Phase 1 were paired with the circle and dot comparison stimuli from Phase 2. Neither group of birds had ever encountered this combination of stimuli. The pairing of sample and comparison stimuli in the consistent group was designed to promote positive transfer according to the common coding theory. By pairing the vertical line sample stimulus with the circle comparison stimulus and the horizontal line sample stimulus with the dot comparison stimulus, the common codes learned in Phase 1—and transferred to Phase 2—should promote correct matching responses. Just the opposite should be true for the inconsistent group, in which mediation by the common code should lead to incorrect responses.

Figure 4.10 shows the percentage of correct responses made on the first 16 trials of Phase 3 training for each bird in the consistent and inconsistent groups. The results were strikingly in agreement with common coding theory

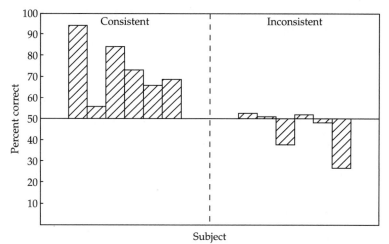

FIGURE 4.10 Mean percentage of correct choices made by pigeons in the consistent and inconsistent groups in Phase 3 of the common coding experiment diagrammed in Table 4.4. Strong positive transfer is seen when the sample comparison contingencies are consistent with a common code but not when they are inconsistent with a common code.

predictions. Whereas most of the birds in the consistent group were correct above the chance level of 50%, two of the birds in the inconsistent group scored below chance, and four responded at the chance level.

With regard to the nature of the common code, pigeons could have learned to use response instructional codes in Phase 1. The transfer of these instructional codes to Phase 2 might have created some confusion, however, because the comparison stimuli were now a circle and a dot, and the old response instructions would have been inappropriate. To maintain the common code learned in Phase 1, birds would have had to use the response instructions learned in Phase 1 as a mediator for those used in Phase 2. That is, it might be difficult to learn that the instruction "peck vertical line" had to be encoded into a different instructional code, "peck circle." The idea of an intermediate code that is noninstructional seems less theoretically awkward. If the common codes A and B were representations of the sample colors from Phase 1, for example, pigeons would have learned in Phase 2 to choose the circle when the red code occurred and to peck the dot when the green code appeared. In Phase 3, pigeons in the consistent group would readily show above-chance matching because the vertical line sample would elicit the red code and choice of the dot, and the horizontal line would elicit the green code and choice of the circle.

SUMMARY

We have seen that major theoretical developments have taken place in our understanding of animal working memory over the past 20 years or so. Although early theory suggested that animals simply remembered sensory images of sample stimuli that varied in strength and faded with the passage of a delay, more recent theory stresses active memory processes, that include rehearsal and alternative coding strategies. Findings from experiments on surprise, directed-forgetting, and serial position effects all suggest that animals may rehearse memory of preceding events. Rehearsal may be enhanced by presenting surprising or unexpected events, and rehearsal may be damped or inhibited by "forget" cues, which indicate that memory will not be tested on specific trials. A number of species show a primacy effect in memory for serial lists, which suggests that early items in a list may be rehearsed more than later items, in both humans and animals. However, serial memory in monkeys does not benefit from extended interstimulus intervals. This raises some doubts about an explanation of the primacy effect in terms of rehearsal because long interstimulus intervals substantially improve human list memory through extra time for rehearsal.

Although animal working memory initially was conceived of as retrospective in nature, we know now that it can be either prospective or retrospective. Further, the conditions of an experiment can bias coding toward retrospection or prospection. For example, memory for time duration is normally retrospective, as shown by the choose-short effect, but time durations may be transformed into prospective codes if additional sample stimuli are mapped onto a single pair of comparison stimuli in a many-to-one design. Differential reward outcomes are a powerful source of prospective codes in working memory. If different sample stimuli are consistently correlated with differential reward outcomes, the sample stimuli will come to control choice between comparison stimuli through expectations of the reward outcomes. The efficacy of reward outcome codes is shown by the fact that they accelerate learning and raise the level of retention above that found with common outcome procedures.

Recent evidence suggests that animals may use common codes to mediate between sample and comparison stimuli in many-to-one paradigms. Sample and comparison stimuli never encountered together may be matched above a chance level of accuracy if previous training has established a common code that can link those stimuli. The exact nature of common codes is yet to be identified.

CHAPTER 5

Associative Learning

The preceding three chapters dealt with perception, attention, and working memory. These topics encompass the means by which cognitive processing systems represent and initially store and maintain information. Beyond these early stages of processing, information may be combined, transformed, and stored in reference memory. Associations refer to combined units of knowledge that tell an organism how things go together in either space or time. Thus, associations may be formed by conjoining stimuli that appear contiguously in space. In Chapter 7, a theory of cognitive mapping is considered in which an animal's cognitive map of its entire environment is formed by associating views of space seen from different positions. For example, if you are in a familiar setting now, you can form a cognitive image of the area behind your head, even though you can see only that area in front of your head. Your front view of space allows you to retrieve an image of the space behind you because you represent them as contiguous or going together. Animals and people learn what events follow one another and the order in which they follow one another by forming sequential associations. The formation and storage of extended sequences is examined in Chapter 9. This chapter deals with the basics of associative learning, or how relatively simple structures of two or three units may be formed.

If associations are defined as combinations of stimuli, we must address the question of what a stimulus is. It has long been recognized that this is a fundamental question in the field of psychology. In highly controlled laboratory research, a stimulus is often defined as a localized event, such as the onset of a light on a key or the presentation of a tone from a single speaker. In Chapter 2, however, evidence was discussed that suggested that animals and people view complex, whole images of the world. In animal learning research, theorists often speak of the entire environment in which learning takes place as providing a *contextual stimulus*. In nature, the contextual stimuli for an animal may be as varied as whether it is night or day, whether the animal is in a wooded area or on a plain, or whether the air around it contains molecules secreted from prey, a predator, or a potential mate.

The term *stimulus* also may refer to afferent feedback from an animal's own behavior. When an animal or human moves through space, it continually monitors its own movements both visually and through kinesthetic feedback from receptors in the muscles, tendons, and joints. Movements also change the external environment, providing new or changed views or perhaps the sudden onset of some new event. These changes in stimulation produced by response are often referred to as *outcomes*. The notion of differential outcomes for responses to different stimuli was discussed with respect to delayed matching-to-sample experiments in Chapter 4. The examples discussed there, and others that are presented in this chapter, indicate that associations include sequences of stimuli arising from an initial external stimulus, stimulation from an animal's own response, and some final outcome stimulation arising from a change in the external environment.

The term *stimulus* is used here to refer both to discrete, localized events and to more pervasive aspects of the environment. Associative units may involve combinations of stimuli that vary in extent. For example, the idea of an *occasion setter*, discussed later in this chapter, suggests that contextual stimuli may form *hierarchical associations* with localized stimuli that allow an animal to predict differential outcomes to behavior performed in different contexts.

Although associations are presented here as one form of information controlling animal behavior, the student should realize that the contemporary study of animal cognition grew out of the earlier study of associative learning (see Chapter 1). Many of the procedures originally used to study learning have been adopted and extended to study new cognitive phenomena in animals. A student then should have an understanding of Pavlovian and operant conditioning methods and findings to aid in examining recent work in animal cognition. In this chapter, important procedures and findings from conditioning experiments are described, and some important theoretical issues in associative learning are discussed. An understanding of the material in this chapter will allow you to easily follow the discussion in Chapter 6, which deals with reference memory for learned associations.

A BRIEF HISTORY OF ASSOCIATIONISM

The notion that associations form a basic unit of learned information can be traced back as far as the ancient Greek philosophers. In an essay on memory, Aristotle (384–322 B.C.) suggested that one experience may remind a person of another if these experiences had occurred *contiguously* (closely in time), were *similar* to one another, or *contrasted* with one another. For example, seeing one person might remind you of another person because you saw these two people together recently (contiguity), because the two people physically resemble one another (similarity), or because they have completely opposite personalities (contrast). Several centuries later, these conditions for the association of ideas, along with others, became known as the *laws of association*. The laws of association formed an integral part of the theory of mind proposed by a group of philosophers known as the *British empiricists*. Spanning a period from the 1600s through the 1800s, the British empiricists were a succession of philosophers that included Thomas Hobbes, John Locke, George Berkeley, David Hume, James Mill, and John Stuart Mill. The basic premise of *empiricism* was that all knowledge held by an individual was acquired through the senses. In a famous statement, John Locke (1632–1704) argued that the mind of an infant is a *tabula rasa*, or a blank slate, upon which experience will write all that the person will come to know. The empiricist approach contrasts with the nativist ideas of Immanuel Kant (1724–1804), who suggested that much of our understanding of the world is in-born.

According to the British empiricists, ideas were remnants or memories of directly experienced sensations. The perception of complex patterns and the formation of complex ideas required association. Our ability to recognize complex objects and to think in terms of complex representations then arose from the association of elemental sensations and ideas into more complex ones. The philosopher Thomas Brown (1778–1820) added a number of further secondary laws of association to those proposed by Aristotle; some of these laws suggested that associations would be stronger if they occurred *frequently*, if they had been formed *recently*, and if the sensations that formed the association were *vivid*. Although the importance of different laws of association were debated and revised, the basic notion that all complex thought arose from the association of elemental ideas became known as *mental chemistry*. Thus, complex ideas often formed a compound within which it was not easy to recognize the elementary components.

It was against this background of empiricist and associationist philosophy that the early investigations of experimental psychology began. In the school of psychology known as *structuralism*, Wilhelm Wundt (1832–1920) and his student, Edward Titchener (1867–1927), made mapping of human experience the initial investigation of scientific psychology. Through the use of a procedure called *introspection*, observers were trained to examine their own experience and to describe it in terms of its elementary ideas. In a sense, the mind was put under a microscope to discover its basic structure. The Gestalt psychologists would later challenge this approach to understanding experience by arguing that it was artificial and that perceptions and memories are formed by innate neural organizational processes.

Many psychologists, particularly North American psychologists, began to challenge the notion that psychology should be the study of the structure of the mind. A new emphasis upon the dynamic and functional capacities of mind and its control of behavior was emerging. Psychologists were branching out into new fields of investigation, including developmental psychology, mental testing, and animal learning. In the pioneering work of Thorndike (1911) and others, the learning abilities of animals were studied through changes in their behavior over repeated training trials. Although the goal of studies of animal intelligence was initially to study the nature of the animal mind, the focus of this work became progressively more behavioral. Watson (1914) eventually declared that behavior should be the primary subject matter of psychology because behavior, unlike ideas, could be directly observed and measured.

The importance of association persisted, however, in the new field of animal learning. The association of ideas was no longer seen as necessary to explain behavior. Rather, it was assumed that behavior became directly associated with sensory events. Thorndike (1911) concluded that animals learned by forming connections between sensory impressions and impulses to action. This approach eventually became known as stimulus-response, or S-R, learning theory. Two of the older laws of association were particularly important for S-R associations: A stimulus and response should occur in close contiguity and should be repeated frequently for their connection to be strengthened. Although some behaviorists, notably Watson (1914) and Guthrie (1935), felt that contiguity between stimulus and response was sufficient for the growth of an S-R association, Thorndike had introduced an influential new factor, the *law of effect*. In the law of effect, it was proposed that connections between contiguous sensory and motor events were strengthened or stamped in by satisfying or pleasant events that immediately followed a response. In other words, a food reward acted to strengthen the S-R activities that immediately preceded it. Thorndike also proposed that annoying or painful consequences would weaken or stamp out an S-R association, but the positive-effect principle was far more influential than the negative-effect principle. The law of effect eventually became known as the action of *reinforcement*, a term originally introduced by Pavlov to refer to the unconditioned stimulus (such as food) in classical conditioning.

The importance of reinforcement for S-R learning was formalized by Clark Hull. In a series of articles and a book entitled *The Principles of Behavior* (Hull, 1943), Hull presented a highly systematic and mathematical formulation of S-R theory. The growth in strength of S-R associations was called *habit strength* and resulted from repeated contiguous sequences of stimulus, response, and reinforcement. To get away from the more subjective definition of effect used by Thorndike, Hull defined reinforcement as *drive reduction*, or the reduction in a physiological need. Hull's model provided formulas that described how habit strength and other internal factors, such as drive state and inhibition, multiplied and added to one another to determine the strength of a final response. Three important principles assumed by this theory were *equipotentiality, continuity*, and *automatic effect of reinforcement*. Equipotentiality means that habit strength or an S-R association could be formed between any stimulus and response. Habit strength would grow continuously over repeated S-R pairings through the automatic strengthening effect of reinforcement that followed the response.

It should be clear that the thrust of S-R theory was to explain both animal and human behavior by direct associations between stimuli and behavior. Within this framework, there was no need for intervening cognitive representations or any other cognitive processes that transformed representations. Much of the attitude toward cognition was captured in Guthrie's famous phrase that animal cognition left a rat in a maze "buried in thought." (Guthrie, 1935, p. 143). The suggestion here was that cognition provided no link with behavior. S-R theory, on the other hand, had no such problem because it assumed that behavior was elicited directly by stimuli.

Among those who challenged the validity of the S-R theory, the most important animal behaviorist was Edward Tolman. In numerous articles and a volume entitled *Purposive Behavior in Animals and Men* (Tolman, 1932), Tolman argued for a more cognitive interpretation of behavior. He suggested that learning was based primarily upon the association of sensory events or the formation of stimulus-

S associations, but behavior was not directly elicited by stimuli. Furthermore, Tolman argued that reinforcement was not necessary for the formation of S-S associations. Rewards or reinforcers were learned about as the stimulus consequences of behavior. Because reinforcers were usually motivationally significant, their representation took on significant value, or *valence*, and could strongly direct behavior. Tolman suggested that animals could form complex representations of their environments through sensory experience; the nature of these representations was captured in such theoretical terms as *expectancies* and *cognitive maps.*

Although S-R theory exerted a strong influence on the field of psychology throughout the first half of the 20th century, its strength began to wane by the 1960s. There are several reasons for its decline from eminence among learning theories. An initial concern was the challenge presented by findings from some traditional learning procedures that did not conform well to S-R predictions. Evidence from latent learning and sensory preconditioning experiments indicated that reinforcement was not necessary for learning to occur. In reinforcer contrast experiments, sudden switches in the quantity or quality of reinforcement led to dramatic changes in behavior that were not predicted by S-R theory. All of these phenomena could be better understood within a cognitive framework.

As a second problem, a number of new phenomena were discovered, many of which are discussed later in this chapter, that S-R theory could not easily explain (Bolles, 1975). Findings from taste-aversion conditioning experiments suggested that neither S-R contiguity nor the gradual accumulation of habit strength was necessary for a strong conditioned response to be learned. As investigators came to study the acquisition of a wider variety of behaviors, it became clear that all stimuli, responses, and reinforcers were not equipotential for learning. Based on evolutionary biological constraints, some behaviors appeared to be prepared for rapid association with certain stimuli and reinforcers, whereas other responses were unprepared or contraprepared for learning (Seligman, 1970).

Finally, the study of the human mind was undergoing what has been labeled the *cognitive revolution*. Influenced greatly by the emergence of computer technology, the study of human memory began to break away from its traditional concerns with rote learning phenomena. Models of information processing which contained multiple memory systems and mechanisms for the transformation of coded information, became increasingly popular. The new cognitive movement in human psychology had a substantial impact on those interested in animal psychology. As outlined in Chapter 1, many researchers turned away from traditional concerns about animal conditioning and began to address questions about animals that were of a more cognitive nature.

THE NATURE OF ASSOCIATIONS

If associations are linked representations of stimuli that allow an animal to know how events or objects go together in time or space, what mechanisms link these representations together? What is the glue that allows one sensory event or idea to elicit another one? Exactly what the format of associative representations should be is not clear, but some possibilities can be suggested (Roitblat, 1982; Roitblat & von Fersen, 1992). Associations that contain relational information may form *propositions* (Anderson, 1980). In the analysis of human language, a proposition is the smallest unit of information that can be judged true or false and expresses the *relation* among a set of *arguments*. For example, in the phrase, "The cat is under the chair," "the cat" and "the chair" are the arguments, and "is under" is the relation. In the case of animal cognition, propositional associations might be particularly useful for representing spatial relationships. Poucet (1993) has argued that animals understand topological relationships between objects or places in space, which constitutes a form of spatial propositional information. Poucet's theory is discussed in more detail in Chapter 7.

When associations between the environment and an animal's behavior are considered, representational units such as *expectancies* and *if–then* rules have been invoked. In an extension of his theory of S-S learning, Tolman suggested that animals learn S_1RS_2 expectancies (Tolman, 1959). An S_1RS_2 expectancy means that an animal had learned that when exposed to stimulus S_1, if the animal made the response R, it would experience stimulus S_2. Thus, a pigeon might learn that being in the presence of a lit key (S_1), the response (R) of pecking the key would lead to a new stimulus (S_2) of grain reward delivery.

When a learning situation is made more complex by introducing conditional relationships between events, more complex expectancies may be learned. It was suggested in Chapter 4 that pigeons may form if–then rules between sample and comparison stimuli in matching-to-sample experiments. Multiple if–then rules are needed to represent the fact that different sample stimuli signal that different responses are required for reinforcement. For example, a pigeon might learn, "If green sample stimulus, then peck horizontal lines comparison stimulus for food reward," and "If red sample stimulus, then peck vertical lines comparison stimulus for food reward." Notice that each of these rules has four components: a sample, a comparison stimulus, a response, and a reward outcome. Complex conditional associative chains are expressed by these if–then rules. Some evidence for the formation of such complex hierarchical associations by rats in instrumental learning are discussed later in this chapter.

Propositions, expectancies, and if–then rules begin to capture the relational and conditional nature of associative knowledge animals appear to acquire in learning experiments. The higher-order nature of associative units needed to account for animal behavior are pointed out at further points in this chapter and are examined as well in Chapter 9.

PAVLOVIAN CONDITIONING

Two basic forms of conditioning have been traditionally studied in the animal learning laboratory: operant or instrumental conditioning and classical or Pavlovian conditioning. Pavlov actually discovered conditioning somewhat late in his career. He had already become an eminent physiologist and had won the Nobel Prize for his studies of the digestive system. Rather serendipitously, he and his colleagues observed that the events preceding the daily feeding of his canine subjects often seemed to cause the dogs to salivate before food was actually given to them. It appeared that events such as an attendant entering the housing room and preparing food signaled the delivery of food to a dog and yielded the digestive response of salivation. When the importance of this observation was realized, more formal studies of signaling were performed (Pavlov, 1927).

The procedure commonly used in Pavlov's laboratory involved placing a dog in a harness with a fistula inserted into a salivary gland and leading to a container (see Figure 5.1). Each time the dog salivated, the flow could be measured in drops of saliva. The dog could be made to salivate at any time through the delivery of food, which was referred to as the *unconditioned stimulus* (US). The reflexive salivation that occurred whenever the US was presented was called the *unconditioned response* (UR). A few moments prior to the delivery of the US, a *conditioned stimulus* (CS) was presented. A common CS was a light or a tone, a stimulus that was *neutral* with respect to the UR. Although the dog might make an investigatory response of turning its head to look at the light or pricking up its ears to hear the tone, these stimuli produced no salivation. After several presentations of the CS with the US, however, the dog began to salivate when the CS alone was presented, and this response became stronger over successive pairings of the CS and US. The properties of the CS had changed; although it was initially neutral, it now yielded a new response. This new response to the CS was called the *conditioned response* (CR). In other experiments, it was shown that a variety of CSs could be used, including numerous sounds and visual cues and tactile stimulation applied to the surface of the body.

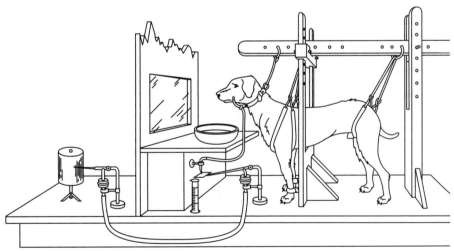

FIGURE 5.1 Drawing of a dog being trained in the salivary conditioning apparatus used by Pavlov.
From Yerkes & Morgulis, 1909.

Types of Conditioned Responses

Reflex Responses

Since Pavlov's classic experiment, numerous other conditioned responses have been studied. All of these cases have in common the delivery of a CS followed by a US, which elicits a UR. The reflexive nature of URs usually led to the choice of either internal smooth muscle responses or simple skeletal reflexes. For example, the *knee-jerk reflex* has been studied by presenting a tone CS and following it with a hammer strike to the patellar tendon as the US (Schlosberg, 1928). After several pairings of the CS and US, a subject would respond with movement of the knee (CR) to the sound of the tone. The *eyeblink reflex* has been conditioned in a number of experiments with human subjects and in animal experiments with rabbits. While the subject's head is immobilized, the US is delivered as either a puff of air on the cornea or a weak electric current to the skin below the eye. A tone CS presented just before the US comes to elicit the eyeblink as a CR either before the US is delivered or on test trials when the US is omitted. An electronic recording device attached to the eyelid measures the extent to which the eyelid closes on each blink. A common measure of performance both for the knee-jerk and eyeblink CRs is the *probability of response,* or the percentage of trials within a block of trials in which a CR was made.

Emotional Responses

The classical or Pavlovian conditioning of emotional responses of the sympathetic branch of the autonomic nervous system has been a popular area of research. With human subjects, the *galvanic skin response (GSR)* is easily measured as a change in the resistance of the skin to the conductance of an electrical current between two electrodes attached to the skin. A light or tone CS is followed by a shock US delivered to the arm. Over repeated deliveries of this CS–US pair, a progressively stronger GSR is elicited by the CS. The GSR response was assumed to reflect the conditioning of fear or emotional arousal to the CS.

Since it is not easy to measure the GSR in animals, an indirect means of measuring the conditioning of a *conditioned emotional response (CER)* is used. Rats are initially trained to press a bar for a food reward on a schedule that maintains a consistently high rate of responding. In a separate conditioning phase, a CS—a light—is presented and followed by the delivery of the US of shock to the rat's feet through the metal grid on which the rat is standing. In this procedure, the rat's overt response to the shock US is not used as a measure or the CR. Rather, it is assumed that the shock also elicits an internal emotional response of fear. To determine the extent to which the CS has become conditioned to elicit fear or the CER, the rat is returned to the bar-pressing task. Occasionally, while the rat is pressing the bar, the light CS is turned on. The effect of this presentation of the CS is to suppress bar pressing; that is, the rate of bar pressing drops, presumably because ongoing behavior is inhibited by fear.

The strength of the CER is measured by the *suppression ratio.* This ratio expresses responses during the CS as a proportion of the total responses made during the CS and during an equivalent period of time prior to CS presentation. If a rat made 50 bar presses during the 1-minute period before the CS was presented and then made only 10 responses during a subsequent 1-minute period during which the CS was presented, the suppression ratio would be $10/(10 + 50) = 0.17$. In a control group of rats that did not have the CS and US paired, presentation of the light caused no drop in responding, and the suppression ratio was $50/(50 + 50) = 0.50$. Thus, the suppression ratio varies between 0.50 (showing no conditioning) to near 0.00 (showing nearly complete suppression of bar pressing.)

Conditioned Taste Aversion

Taste aversion learning was first observed in the 1950s (Garcia, Kimeldorf, & Koelling, 1955) but was not clearly established as a form of conditioning until the late 1960s (Revusky, 1968). Considerable skepticism initially surrounded this form of conditioning because it appeared to defy long-held principles of association. Animals, typically rats, were allowed to ingest a substance with a distinct taste, often the sweet taste of saccharine or sucrose. Given a choice between a bottle containing sweetened water and a bottle containing plain water, rats preferred to drink the sweetened water about 90 percent of the time. On a conditioning day, rats were allowed to drink only the sweetened water for a period of time; four hours later, the subjects were made ill, either by exposure to X-irradiation or by being injected with a chemical that induced internal malaise and nausea. A day or so later, after they had recovered from the induced illness, the rats were given another preference test between sweetened and plain water. Preference for the sweetened water had disappeared, with rats now drinking it only about 20 percent of the time. An aversion to a particular taste had been conditioned by following that taste by illness, even though the substance consumed did not cause the illness.

The associative laws of contiguity and frequency both failed to predict this robust taste aversion conditioning. If taste was the CS and illness the US, learning occurred with a 4-hour interval between the CS and US. Prior to the discovery of taste aversion conditioning, it was thought that associative learning required short intervals on the order of seconds or minutes between stimuli. In addition, taste aversion conditioning did not require repeated CS–US pairings for a strong aversion to develop. Only a single taste-illness experience was needed to produce a strong aversion to the CS. Of course, the claim that this was a form of conditioning required the use of appropriate controls. These included groups of animals that were given the taste CS only or were exposed to the illness-inducing treatment without prior exposure to the CS. Subjects in such control procedures continued to show a strong preference for the taste of the CS, indicating that it was the pairing of the CS and US that was necessary for learning to occur.

Taste aversion conditioning is of particular interest because it is a phenomenon with which many people are familiar. When questioned, a number of individuals will describe food aversions that arose from prior experiences of becoming ill after eating a new or unusual tasting food. In the author's case, an aversion to shellfish was conditioned by becoming sick shortly after eating shrimp creole in the eighth-grade cafeteria. In the real world of animals, taste aversion conditioning is an important survival mechanism. If an animal becomes ill after eating a new food, the food may be poisonous and should not be consumed.

Autoshaping

The Pavlovian conditioned responses thus far discussed have been based on URs that generally could be described as reflexive and involuntary responses to a US. In fact, it was thought for a number of years that Pavlovian conditioning only involved these types of responses. Interestingly, a new form of classical conditioning was discovered by P. Brown and Jenkins (1968), which involved the complex skeletal response of key pecking by pigeons. This conditioning was initially reported as a means for shaping pigeons to peck a key without the experimenter observing the subject and controlling the delivery of the reward. Pigeons simply were left in an operant chamber with a key light programmed to come on periodically for 8 seconds; as the key light went off, the grain hopper delivered reinforcement. It is of importance to note that pecking the key did not cause food delivery. The key light and food simply were paired together, regardless of what behavior the pigeon performed. Nevertheless, pigeons came to peck at the lighted key repeatedly. Since this key-pecking had been shaped without the influence of a trainer, it was called *autoshaping*.

The discovery of autoshaping quickly became more than a convenient way to shape an operant behavior. The fact that key pecking arose simply from pairing the key light and food suggested that a complex CR (key pecking) had been conditioned by pairing the CS of the key light and the US of food. Further experiments showed that the autoshaped CR did not extinguish, even though key pecking was not reinforced during Pavlovian pairings (Gamzu & Schwartz, 1973). In an experiment performed by D. Williams and H. Williams (1969), an omission contingency was introduced. If the pigeon pecked the key while it was lit, the reinforcer scheduled at the end of the trial was omitted. Although this procedure weakened key-pecking behavior, it did not eliminate it; pigeons continued to peck at the key on about 30 percent of the trials.

In the photographs shown in Figure 5.2, the effects of using food and water as USs in autoshaping are shown. In the left panel, with water as the US, the beak is more closed, as in a drinking response. In the right panel, with grain as the US, the beak is more open and suggests a grain-eating response. In other words, birds responded to the lit key in much the same way as they did to the reinforcer the key predicted.

Conditioning Procedures

Among the numerous discoveries made by Pavlov was the fact that the extent to which a new CR could be established depended on the temporal relationship between the CS and US. In general, it was found that the best conditioning occurs when the onset of the CS precedes the onset of the US. This occurs in three of the procedures shown in Figure 5.3. In two of these procedures, *short-* and *long-delay conditioning,* the CS is introduced before the US but remains on throughout the presentation of the US, with the two stimuli terminating simultaneously. In short-delay conditioning, the interval between CS and US onset may be only a fraction of a second or a few seconds but may last up to 1 minute.

FIGURE 5.2 Photographs of autoshaped pecking responses made to a key. The four pictures shown in the left column depict pecking when the reinforcer is water, and the four pictures shown in the right column depict pecking when the reinforcer is grain. *From Jenkins & Moore, 1973.*

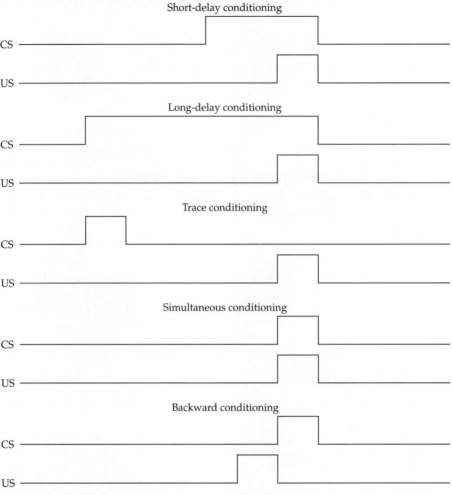

FIGURE 5.3 Procedures used in Pavlovian conditioning. The horizontal lines show the onset and offset of the CS and US at different points in time.

In long-delay conditioning, the interval may last several minutes. The short-delay procedure is most commonly used in Pavlovian conditioning experiments and typically yields the most rapid learning. The CS also begins before the US in *trace conditioning,* but there is a time interval between the end of the CS and the start of the US. Thus, a trace or memory of the CS must be maintained over this interval in order for an association between the CS and US to be learned. The finding that conditioning is weaker as the trace interval becomes longer (Ellison, 1964) may arise from forgetting the CS over the interval.

Relatively poor learning occurs when *simultaneous conditioning* and *backward conditioning* procedures are used. As seen in Figure 5.3, the CS and US are contiguous in both of these procedures; thus, contiguity alone predicts effective conditioning. However, an important aspect of the delay and trace conditioning procedures is missing: the predictive nature of the CS. In delay and trace conditioning, the initial presentation of the CS acts as a signal or predictor of the US—the event of most motivational concern to the animal in the episode. In simultaneous and backward conditioning, the CS provides no helpful information about the US because the US has either already occurred or is occurring at the same time as the CS. The CS must have warning or predictive value to rapidly condition a strong CR.

Conditioned Inhibition

In classical conditioning experiments in which the CS is followed by a US, other trials may be given in which a modified or different CS is followed by the absence of the US. Pavlov carried out such experiments and found that this procedure created *conditioned inhibition.* In a conditioned inhibition procedure, a dog might be presented with the CS of a light followed by food on some trials and the compound stimulus of a light plus a tone followed by no food on other trials. As trials proceed, the dog learns to salivate when the light alone occurs but inhibits salivation when the light-tone compound is presented. If the tone alone is presented, the dog withholds salivation; the tone has become a *conditioned inhibitor.*

In a somewhat different procedure, called *differential inhibition,* one stimulus is consistently reinforced with the US (CS+) on half the trials, and another stimulus is consistently nonreinforced by omission of the US (CS–) on the other half of the trials. The acquisition curves from such an experiment reveal increasing strength of the CR to the CS+ over repeated trials. Although some response to the CS– may occur on the initial trials of conditioning, the strength of response to the CS– drops to zero. The CS– has become a conditioned inhibitor.

As another instance of conditioned inhibition, Pavlov noted that, during long delays in delayed conditioning, the CR was weak or nonexistent during the early period of the delay but became pronounced during the later part of the delay. He suggested that a dog learned to inhibit salivation during the early part of the delay, when the US was absent, and to respond only as the moment for food delivery approached. This form of inhibitory conditioning was referred to as *inhibition of delay.* Temporal cues present during the early part of the CS–US delay had become conditioned inhibitors.

The discovery of conditioned inhibition suggests that animals learn associations between stimuli and the absence of the US as well as between stimuli and the presence of the US. Conditioned inhibition was not extensively studied by North American investigators, however, until a seminal article published by Robert Rescorla appeared in 1969 (Rescorla, 1969). Part of the reason learning psychologists had not pursued the topic of inhibition was the absence of procedures for measuring the relative strength of inhibition conditioned to a CS. Rescorla introduced two important tests for the measurement of conditioned inhibition: the *summation test* and the *retardation test.* In the summation test, an animal was trained with two stimuli, one as a conditioned inhibitor (CS–) and the other as a conditioned excitor (CS+). Tests then were given in which a compound consisting of both stimuli (CS+/CS–) was presented to the animal. The extent to which the summated effect of the excitor and the inhibitor reduced the strength of the CR below response to CS+ alone provided a measure of the strength of conditioned inhibition. In a retardation test, the conditioned inhibitor became a CS+, which was followed by the US in a new conditioning phase. The extent to which its previously conditioned inhibitory properties retarded its acquisition of the CR relative to a neutral CS that had not undergone conditioned inhibition indicated the strength of conditioned inhibition.

The phenomenon of conditioned inhibition may be related to the procedures for excitatory conditioning previously described. The fact that a strong CR is not conditioned to the CS in simultaneous and backward conditioning procedures does not necessarily mean that no association has been learned. An animal might still learn that the CS and US occur at the same time or that the US is followed by the CS. In backward fear-conditioning experiments, it has been suggested that the CS may become a conditioned inhibitor of fear. Suppose that an animal repeatedly receives the onset of shock (US) followed thereafter by a tone (CS) as the shock goes off and then a long shock-free intertrial interval after the tone. The offset of the shock may elicit a state of relaxation or relief that is coincident with the tone and that becomes associated with it (Denny, 1971). Also, the tone is followed by an extended period of no shock; the tone CS may become a *safety signal* for the absence of shock if it becomes associated with a shock-free period. The conditioned inhibition of fear by a CS from backward fear conditioning has been shown when that CS was superimposed on avoidance conditioning (Moscovitch & LoLordo, 1968). Since it was assumed that fear forms a basis for avoidance responses, a fear inhibitor should reduce avoidance responding, which is exactly what Moscovitch and LoLordo found.

Higher-Order Conditioning

In one experiment performed in Pavlov's laboratory, a dog was conditioned to salivate whenever it heard the sound of a metronome. When this CR was well established, a second CS, the sight of a black square form, was shown to the dog for 10 seconds, followed 15 seconds later by the presentation of the primary CS, the metronome. After several presentations of this sequence of events, the dog began to salivate at the presentation of the black square. Pavlov described this new CR to the black square as a *secondary conditioned reflex*. In this case, the primary CR to the metronome functioned as a UR, allowing the secondary CS to become conditioned, even though it was never paired with the primary reinforcement of food. It was found that higher-order conditioning could not be extended beyond the second order when food was used as the US. That is, a new CS, such as a touch on the leg, could not then be paired with the black square to obtain a third-order conditioned response. However, third-order conditioned responses were obtained when the initial US was a shock to the skin.

Second-order conditioning is important because it shows that the primary CS takes on some of the properties of the US. The CS may now function as a *conditioned reinforcer* in Pavlovian experiments. A CS that predicted food in a Pavlovian procedure may also act as a reward for instrumental behavior.

In Pavlovian conditioning, the US or reinforcer is contingent upon presentation of the CS. In *instrumental* or *operant* conditioning, the *reinforcer* is contingent upon an organism's response; a response must be made before a reinforcer will occur. The term *reinforcement* was first used by Pavlov (1927) to mean the US used to condition reflexes. Today, the term "reinforcement," or "positive reinforcement" is more commonly used to describe the process of delivering a reward or desirable consequence contingent upon a response. The "reinforcer" is the specific reward given, and the operation of delivering the reinforcer and its strengthening effect on the response is reinforcement. The terms "instrumental" and "operant" are interchangeable and mean that the response is instrumental in causing a reinforcer to appear or that it operates on the environment to yield the reinforcer. In a sense, the subject is responsible for reinforcement in operant conditioning, whereas the experimenter is responsible for reinforcement in Pavlovian conditioning.

As another distinction between Pavlovian and instrumental conditioning, CRs usually have zero strength initially, but instrumental responses often have some initial probability of occurrence. Although a dog does not salivate to a tone before conditioning, a rat will walk down a runway (a common operant response) before it is ever reinforced for doing so. Some component of a Pavlovian CR is *elicited* or caused to be made by the US. The elicited UR is based on innate or previously learned reflexes. In operant learning, the learned response is initially *emitted* by the organism. Emitted responses are already part of the subject's behavioral repertoire, and their causal precursors are unknown. An emitted operant response initially may be weak or have a low *baseline* rate of emission. This means that the response occurs infrequently and may be made only slowly when it does occur. If a positive reinforcer is delivered immediately after the operant response, each time it is emitted the response will grow in strength. It will be performed more often and will occur with greater strength and speed when it is performed. This growth in the strength of an operant response is operant conditioning or learning and may be measured by an increase in *response probability, speed of response,* or *strength of response,* or by a decrease in the *latency of the response,* which is the time taken to make the response when an opportunity to do so is presented.

Shaping Operant Responses

Trained animals are often seen to perform complex instrumental behaviors. These behaviors were not initially performed by an animal but were trained through a process of *shaping* or *successive approximations.* Initial behaviors that only approximated the final target behavior first were strengthened and then used to build the final complex behavior. For example, suppose you wished to teach your dog to roll over. You would wait until the dog made the response of lying down and then give it a food reward. Once the dog began to lie down frequently, reward would be withheld for that response and delivered only when the dog rolled over on its side. After this response was strengthened, reward would then be given contingent successively for the dog rolling still further, on its back, on its other side, and finally only for a complete roll. Shaping or reinforcement of successive approximations is commonly used to train complex operant behaviors in the learning laboratory, such as training a rat to press a bar or a pigeon to peck a key.

Discrete Trials and Free-Operant Responses

Discrete Trials

In *discrete trials* operant conditioning, the subject is allowed to make the instrumental response only on successive opportunities or trials provided by the experimenter. The first experimental studies of instrumental learning were carried out by Thorndike, using a discrete trials procedure. He carried out a number of experiments on cats, dogs, and chicks to study their associative processes and published his results in the volume *Animal Intelligence* (Thorndike, 1911). His best known experiments involved training cats to perform an instrumental response that would release them from a *puzzle box*. As the drawing of this apparatus in Figure 5.4 shows, the puzzle box was an enclosure containing a door. In different experiments, Thorndike designed the puzzle box so that the door could be opened by operating different manipulanda. Thus, pulling a string, turning a wooden button, or stepping on a platform could open the door and release the animal in different experiments. A trial began by placing a hungry cat in the locked enclosure, with food available outside the puzzle box. A cat typically scrambled about in the box, clawed at different parts of the box, and only by chance apparently operated the mechanism that opened the door and allowed the cat to escape and consume its food reward. On later trials or placements in the box, similar behavior was observed, but gradually the cat began to eliminate irrelevant behaviors and learned to operate the mechanism that released it from the enclosure.

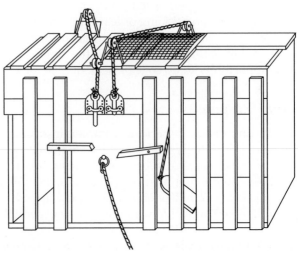

FIGURE 5.4 Drawing of a puzzle box used by Thorndike to study learning in cats. *From Thorndike, 1911.*

The curve shown in Figure 5.5 depicts the performance of one of Thorndike's cats. The dependent variable is the amount of time that elapsed between the moment the animal was placed in the puzzle box and the moment at which the animal escaped from the box. Escape time, or latency to make the operant response, is plotted across successive trials and drops slowly from an initially high value to times of only a few seconds required to operate the release mechanism. This type of curve has become known as a *learning curve.* Learning curves typically show some measure of response strength plotted over successive trials. Note that the curve drops rapidly over the initial trials of testing but changes more slowly on later trials. This pattern of change is typical of learning curves, and the shape of the curve is referred to as *negatively accelerated.* Learning curves then usually show rapid initial growth in performance followed by slower growth toward an *asymptote* or limit of performance.

Free-Operant Responses

Although the discrete trials procedure has the advantage of allowing the experimenter to test a subject's learning at specified points in time, it may seem somewhat artificial since organisms in the real world may perform operant responses repeatedly without intervening pauses or time-outs. In an apparatus devised by Skinner (1938; 1956), a subject was allowed to respond continuously or to perform a free operant response. The *Skinner box,* or *Operant chamber,* is a sealed enclosure that contains three important items: *sources of stimulation,* such as lights or speakers; a *manipulandum,* which the subject operates as the instrumental response; and a *reward delivery system,* typically a chute or hopper for food delivery. These situations often involve a rat pressing a bar repeatedly, as shown in Figure 5.6. Periodically, bar pressing is reinforced with a food pellet, according to a schedule of reinforcement. Since subjects respond continuously in a free operant situation, the strength of individual

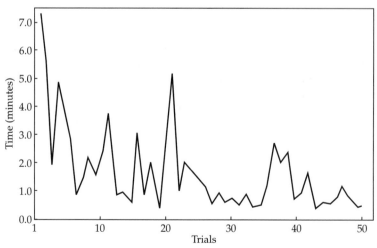

FIGURE 5.5 A learning curve showing one of Thorndike's cats learning to escape from a puzzle box.
Adapted from Thorndike, 1911.

FIGURE 5.6 A rat presses a bar for a food reinforcer in an operant chamber.
From Gray, 1991.

responses usually is not measured. A common measure of free-operant behavior is *rate of response*. In many free-operant experiments, a device called a *cumulative recorder* is used to measure performance. An ink pen rests on a continuously moving roll of paper. Each time a response is made, the pen moves upward a small distance. The effect of continuous response is to produce a curve that moves upward on the sheet of paper; the rate of response is directly related to the steepness of the curve.

Other Operant Responses

Although operant conditioning has been discussed here largely with respect to animals operating manipulanda in a Skinner box, it should be recognized that a wide variety of behaviors can be considered operant or instrumental responses. Basically, any behavior that is emitted and modified by its consequences is an operant or instrumental response. Thus, a child that has learned to cry or to bang a rattle to get the attention of her parents has learned an operant response. Learning to press different keys on a word processor to make different symbols appear on the monitor is a form of instrumental learning. In Chapter 7, we see that much of the operant behavior studied by scientists interested in spatial cognition involves movement over extended spatial terrain.

Learning with Aversive Outcomes

Operant conditioning with rewards or positive consequences has been discussed thus far. However, learning also may arise from aversive or painful stimulation that may precede or follow an operant response. Three forms of operant learning with aversive stimuli are *escape learning, avoidance learning,* and *punishment.*

Escape Learning

The *shuttle box* (see Figure 5.7) is an apparatus frequently used to study conditioning with aversive stimuli. It consists of an elongated, enclosed chamber with two compartments, often separated by a narrow opening or a barrier. Each side of the shuttle box has a grid floor through which a painful but not dangerous electric shock can be delivered. At the beginning of a training session, a rat would be placed on one side of the shuttle box, and the grid on that side would then be electrified. The rat's initial response to shock is to jump and run about the chamber in an agitated manner. Eventually, the rat crosses to the other side, where no shock is delivered. The rat has escaped from the painful shock. However, this situation is only temporary since the shock is delivered on the new side on the next trial, and the rat must now cross to the other side to escape. After several trials of such escape behavior, the time it takes the rat to cross the box after the shock is first introduced begins to drop. Eventually, the rat adroitly crosses to the safe side in only a second or two each time the shock is delivered. The drop in latency to escape over trials shows the acquisition of escape learning. Each escape response is reinforced by the termination of the aversive stimulus of shock. Reinforcement that strengthens an instrumental response by the termination of a painful stimulus is called *negative reinforcement.*

Avoidance Learning

Avoidance learning can be studied through a slight modification of the escape procedure. A warning stimulus is presented at a fixed interval of time

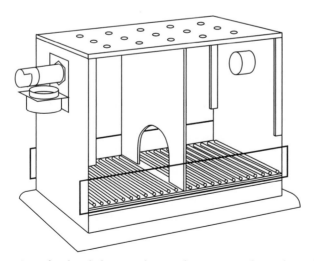

FIGURE 5.7 Drawing of a shuttle box used to study escape and avoidance learning. Shock may be delivered through the grid on either side of the box causing a subject to cross to the other side.

before the shock is initiated. A tone or a light is turned on 5 seconds before the shock is scheduled to occur. Initially, the rat continues to escape the shock by crossing the barrier, but eventually the subject begins to cross to the other side during the warning stimulus and before the shock is administered. This behavior is then rapidly acquired, and the rat crosses to the safe side without shock on almost every trial. When this occurs, the animal has shown the acquisition of *avoidance learning*. Instead of initially experiencing the noxious stimulus before responding, the animal now totally avoids any experience with it.

The discovery of avoidance learning created a major theoretical problem. What reinforced avoidance behavior? Since the avoidance response did not terminate a noxious stimulus, it was not clear why animals would repeatedly cross from one side of a shuttle box to the other for no consequence. One popular resolution of this apparent paradox was the *two-factor theory of avoidance learning* (N. Miller, 1948; Mowrer, 1947). The two factors proposed were Pavlovian conditioning of fear and operant conditioning of an escape response from fear. The presentation of a warning stimulus followed by a shock in the early stages of avoidance training is similar to Pavlovian conditioning. It was argued that these pairings involved Pavlovian conditioning of a fear response in which the warning signal was the CS and the shock was the US. Once the CS or warning stimulus could elicit a response of fear, the subject was motivated to perform an instrumental act that would remove it from the fear-provoking stimulus. By crossing to the other side of the shuttle box, the animal terminated the CS and the fear it elicited. From the point of view of the two-factor theory, both escape and avoidance learning were motivated by negative reinforcement. In escape learning, it was the termination of shock, a primary source of pain, that reinforced the operant response. In avoidance learning, it was the termination of the warning stimulus that reinforced the operant response through fear reduction.

A number of problems arose, however, with the two-process theory of avoidance learning. For one, investigators were not able to find any objective indicators of conditioned fear that mirrored the development of avoidance responding. Physiological indicators of autonomic nervous system arousal did not correlate with avoidance training (Rescorla & Solomon, 1967). When the CS from shock avoidance training was presented during bar pressing for food, Kamin, Brimer, and Black (1963) found that conditioned suppression of bar pressing increased after a few avoidance responses but then declined as animals became proficient at shock avoidance. This finding suggested that well-trained dogs and rats did not repeatedly cross the shuttle box because they were scared. In fact, observations of animals indicated that they performed the avoidance response in a routine fashion with no external show of emotion. Still another major problem was the fact that it was very difficult to extinguish avoidance learning. If shock US was no longer delivered for failure to make a crossing response in a shuttle box, animals often continued to make the avoidance response for hundreds of trials, showing no evidence of extinction (Solomon, Kamin, & Wynne, 1953). According to the two-factor theory, the absence of shock should have led to the extinction of the conditioned fear response. As the fear response weakened, animals should have progressively failed to make the avoidance response.

Although numerous attempts have been made to shore up these difficulties within the framework of the two-process theory, Seligman and Johnston (1973) suggested a more cognitive explanation of avoidance learning. Although they agreed that animals learned conditioned fear to the CS followed by shock in a shuttle box, they suggested that this fear was extinguished early in avoidance training and that avoidance behavior was maintained by two learned response–outcome expectancies. One expectancy was that failure to make the instrumental response would lead to shock, and the other expectancy was that making the instrumental response would lead to the absence of shock. Importantly, expectancies should only be changed if they are repeatedly violated. Thus, an animal in a shuttle box continues to cross to the opposite side when the CS is presented because it expects that no response will lead to shock and response will lead to the absence of shock. Since it continually responds on the basis of these expectancies, it has no opportunity to disconfirm the expectancy that failure to respond will lead to shock. Only if it fails to respond can it learn that shock no longer follows the absence of responding. In keeping with this cognitive explanation, it has been found that the most effective way to extinguish avoidance learning is to block an animal's opportunity to make the avoidance response and thus force it to learn that failure of response no longer leads to shock (Carlson & Black, 1960; Schiff, Smith, & Prochaska, 1972).

Punishment

The effect of both positive and negative reinforcement is to strengthen or increase the performance of an instrumental response. *Punishment* has the opposite effect of weakening or decreasing the performance of an instrumental response. The response usually has a fairly high frequency of occurrence, either through previous reinforcement or through a naturally high baseline rate of emission. As a laboratory example, a hungry rat may have been trained to press a bar at a rapid rate for food delivery. If bar pressing now is followed by a shock to the feet instead of food on several trials, the rate of bar pressing will begin to slow down, and, eventually, the rat will not press the bar at all. A decrease in the rate of an operant response, or cessation of the response, caused by the delivery of an aversive stimulus contingent on the response constitutes the process of punishment.

SOME BASIC PHENOMENA
OF ASSOCIATIVE LEARNING

Stimulus Generalization, Stimulus Control, and Discrimination Learning

Stimulus Generalization

In any learning situation that involves repeated trials or opportunities to make a response, the stimulus changes somewhat from one opportunity to the next. The stimulus itself may change somewhat in brightness or hue, and the state of the subject's receptors and angle of view may change. The Pavlovian or operant response continues to be made, however, regardless of changes in the stimuli presented. The readiness of an organism to respond to altered stimuli is called *stimulus generalization*. Although small changes in the stimulus lead to little change in responding, stimulus generalization is affected by larger changes in the stimulus.

The process of stimulus generalization has been studied systematically by training a subject to respond to a stimulus of a particular value along a dimension and then testing the strength of response to other points closer to and farther away from the training value. In a classic experiment, Guttman and Kalish (1956) trained pigeons to peck at a yellow key light with a wavelength of 580 nanometers. Once pigeons were pecking at a high rate for reinforcement, a series of tests was introduced with key lights that varied from 520 to 640 nanometers, including the training value of 580 nanometers. Each stimulus was presented for 30 seconds on several occasions, and responding was not reinforced during these test periods. In Figure 5.8, the number of responses to each stimulus is plotted as a function of wavelength of the testing stimulus. The *generalization gradient* generated shows that pigeons responded most to the yellow training stimulus and to stimuli close to it, greenish yellow and orange-yellow. As hues moved into the blue and red regions, rate of pecking progressively dropped to a low level.

Generalization gradients have been found along a number of sensory dimensions, using both operant and Pavlovian conditioning. For example, Pavlov (1927) conditioned a dog to salivate to the CS of a touch on the leg. On subsequent tests, he measured the degree of salivation elicited by touches to points at varying distances from the training point. He found that the number of drops of saliva produced dropped systematically the greater the distance of the test stim-

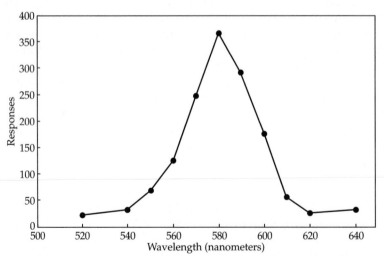

FIGURE 5.8 A generalization gradient based on operant responding by pigeons. Pigeons were reinforced for pecking at a key containing a light of 580 nanometers and were tested with lights varying from 520 to 640 nanometers.
Adapted from Guttman & Kalish, 1956.

ulus from the training stimulus. In this case, the CS was a tactile stimulus, and the generalization gradient was found over the spatial dimension of distance along the surface of the skin.

Pavlov (1927) accounted for the phenomenon of stimulus generalization by a process of irradiation or spread of excitation across the surface of the cerebral cortex. Excitation would be strongest at the point activated by the CS but would automatically spread with decreasing strength to adjacent points, yielding the tendency for adjacent points along a stimulus dimension to elicit the CR. Pavlov's theory was disputed by Lashley and Wade (1946), who argued that stimulus generalization is not determined by an innate spread of excitation but instead by the degree of experience an organism has with different points along a stimulus dimension. They suggested that a subject who had never been exposed to any value along a dimension but the training value would show a completely flat generalization gradient. As experience with varying points along a dimension increased, the generalization gradient should decline more steeply. A clearly testable hypothesis generated by the Lashley and Wade position was that discrimination training along a stimulus dimension should reduce generalization and increase the slope of the generalization gradient.

Stimulus Control

Generalization gradients are an indicator of the degree of *stimulus control* a training stimulus has on a learned response. A steep gradient indicates strong stimulus control because more of a response is made to the training stimulus than to nearby stimuli on the dimension, but a flat gradient indicates poor stimulus control because the degree of response to the training stimulus is little different from that to other stimuli on the dimension.

Sources of stimulation built into a Skinner box may be used in conjunction with the delivery of the reinforcer to establish stimulus control of operant responding. Suppose that the key upon which a pigeon has learned to peck is lit with red light. After the pigeon learned to peck the key at a steady rate for reinforcement, a series of stimulus presentations are delivered in which the key light is alternately lit with red light for 1 minute and with green light for 1 minute. When the red light is on, pecks on the key deliver a reinforcer, but, when the green light is on, pecks on the key deliver no reinforcer. Responding now comes under the stimulus control of the red key light in comparison to the green light; the pigeon learns to peck during the red light but to withhold pecking during the green light. Other sources of stimulation also might be used to gain stimulus control, such as the color of an overhead houselight or the pitch of a tone played through a speaker.

Discrimination Learning

The process of establishing stimulus control over behavior often involves *discrimination learning*. In the preceding example, the pigeon was required to learn to discriminate between the red light and the green light. The ease of discrimination learning depends on the similarity between the controlling stimuli. Although a pigeon rapidly learns to discriminate between red and green lights, discrimination learning proceeds more slowly if the stimuli were closer together in hue, for example, a green-blue versus a blue-green.

Requiring a pigeon to discriminate between alternately presented red and green keys involves the *successive presentation* of stimuli. Discrimination learning is also frequently studied using discrete trials procedures in which the subject makes a choice between *simultaneously presented* stimuli. In a simultaneous procedure, a pigeon is shown a red key and a green key at the same time, one on the left and other on the right, and has to choose between them by pecking one and not the other. If the red key, but not the green key, always yielded reward when chosen, the pigeon learns to choose the red key over the green key. The positions of the red and green lights alternate randomly between the left and right keys, making this problem a *visual discrimination* because the spatial positions of the keys cannot be used as a basis for discrimination. In *spatial discriminations,* choice is made on the basis of spatial position. For example, a rat may be trained in a *T-maze,* an apparatus in which a start alley leads to a choice between right-angle turns into an alley on the right or an alley on the left. If food is always placed in the goal box at the end of the left alley but never in the goal box at the end of the right alley, the rat will learn to always turn left at the choice point.

Recall that the Lashley and Wade (1946) theory of stimulus generalization argued that a stimulus generalization gradient should become increasingly steep as an animal had opportunities to discriminate among points along the stimulus dimension. Several experimental tests of this prediction have been carried out. H. Jenkins and Harrison (1960; 1962) trained pigeons to peck at a white key for reinforcement while a 1000-Hz tone was played in the operant chamber. The 1000-Hz tone alternated with the presentation of a 950-Hz tone, during which pecking was not reinforced. Pigeons learned to discriminate between these tones by pecking at a higher rate in the presence of the 1000-Hz tone than in the presence of the 950-Hz tone. Generalization tests were then carried out by measuring the rate of pecking obtained when tones varying from 300 Hz to 3500 Hz were presented. Subjects showed a very steep gradient, with strong response at 1000 Hz and little response at adjacent frequencies. By contrast, a control group of pigeons trained to discriminate between the presence of the 1000-Hz tone and its absence showed greater stimulus generalization, and another group of pigeons trained only to peck in the presence of the 1000-Hz tone produced a completely flat generalization curve. These findings indicated clearly that discrimination training along a dimension weakens stimulus generalization and increases stimulus control by the reinforced stimulus.

Giving an animal discrimination training between two points on a dimension also has an important effect on the point at which the strongest response occurs along the dimension. This phenomenon, called the *peak-shift effect,* can be seen in an experiment by Hanson (1959), depicted in Figure 5.9. Pigeons in control and discrimination groups were trained to peck at a key lit with a 550-nanometer light for food reinforcement (the S+). Although the control group was not trained with any other stimulus, the discrimination group also was presented with a 555-nanometer light, and pecks at this stimulus were nonreinforced (the S–). Both groups were then given generalization tests at a number of points along the wavelength dimension. Figure 5.9 shows that the control curve peaks at exactly the S+ value of 550 nanometers, but the discrimination group's curve peaks at 530 and 540 nanometers. The effect of

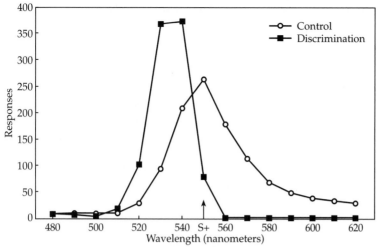

FIGURE 5.9 Generalization gradients showing the peak-shift effect. Pigeons in the control group were reinforced only for pecking at a key illuminated with 550 nanometers. Pigeons in the discrimination group were reinforced for pecking at a key illuminated with 550 nanometers and nonreinforced for pecking at a key illuminated with 555 nanometers. Both groups were then given extinction tests over a range of wavelengths.
Adapted from Hanson, 1959.

discrimination training was to shift the peak of response to the side of the S+ opposite that on which the S– occurred. The peak-shift effect has been observed in a number of experiments. We return to a theoretical account of the peak-shift effect later in this chapter.

Extinction

Pavlov found that after conditioning a strong CR by repeatedly pairing a CS and US, it was possible to gradually eliminate the CR by repeatedly presenting the CS and withholding the US. He referred to this process as the *experimental extinction of conditioned reflexes*. Since Pavlov's demonstration, the phenomenon of extinction has been observed on numerous occasions in both Pavlovian and operant learning. In operant conditioning, extinction is achieved by allowing the subject to make the instrumental response without delivery of the reinforcer. Over repeated trials in a discrete trials experiment, the response is made with greater latency and lower probability as extinction progresses. In free-operant responding, the rate of response declines over time, leading to a flattening of the cumulative record.

From a practical point of view, for example, in behavior modification, extinction is a valuable tool for eliminating unwanted behavior. From a theoretical point of view, however, extinction is seen as a phenomenon to be explained. One account of extinction is that the loss of a response in the absence of reinforcement represents unlearning, or the elimination of the original learning that gave rise to the learned response. Pavlov rejected this interpretation, in part based on a further important observation, *spontaneous recovery*. Following the complete extinction of a salivary CR, a dog was returned to its quarters and not tested for a day. On the next day, the dog was returned to the conditioning apparatus and presented with the CS. Surprisingly, the dog now salivated when the CS was presented. Apparently, the CR had spontaneously recovered simply through the passage of time. This finding, among others, convinced Pavlov that conditioning and extinction were caused by different processes. The acquisition of a CR reflected the growth of *excitation,* or a connection between the brain centers activated by the CS and US. The process of excitation was not weakened by extinction. Rather, extinction led to the growth of another cortical process, *internal inhibition,* which gradually overrode or blocked the process of excitation. It was suggested further that the inhibitory process was more labile or temporary than the excitatory process. Thus, over a 24-hour interval following extinction, inhibition would wane while excitation remained stable. The greater relative strength of excitation after 24 hours then resulted in the renewed expression of the CR or spontaneous recovery.

Although the physiological aspects of Pavlov's theory of extinction are no longer seen as valid, the notion that extinction represents new learning and not the cancellation of a learned response remains an important theoretical idea. According to one recent account (Kraemer & Spear, 1993), the events of acquisition and extinction are stored as different memories. Although memory of extinction is dominant at the end of extinction training, memory of acquisition becomes more accessible over time, thus yielding spontaneous recovery of the conditioned response. This memory retrieval account of extinction is discussed more fully in Chapter 6.

Overshadowing

In yet another type of experiment originally performed by Pavlov (1927), subjects are conditioned to respond to a compound CS consisting of two stimuli presented simultaneously. One stimulus is more noticeable or salient than the other, for example, a loud tone and a dim light. When a CR has been fully conditioned to the compound, the strength of response to each of the components is measured by presenting it alone and measuring the CR. The typical finding is that the more salient stimulus, the loud tone, elicits a strong CR, but the weaker stimulus, the dim light, yields only a weak response. As a control condition, a separate group of subjects is conditioned with only the light as the CS. The CR conditioned to the light in isolation is found to be substantially stronger than that conditioned to the light presented in combination with the tone. In some way, the stronger tone stimulus *overshadows* or prevents the weaker light stimulus from eliciting the CR it produces when used as a CS by itself.

Blocking

In a set of experiments that were to have an important impact on associative learning, Kamin (1968, 1969) established a conditioned fear response in rats using light and tone CSs and shock as the US. Strength of conditioning was measured by the suppression of bar pressing. An experimental group of rats was initially conditioned by pairing one CS, in this instance, the tone, with shock for a number of trials until presentation of the tone completely suppressed bar pressing. In a second phase of the procedure, the tone and light were presented simultaneously as a CS that was again followed by the US of shock for a number of trials. Subsequently, the tone and the light were presented alone to determine the strength of response to each. The interesting finding discovered was that rats strongly suppressed bar pressing when the tone was presented but showed little suppression when the light was presented. A control group was also trained with pairings of the tone and light combination with shock but without previous conditioning of the tone by itself. When tested with the tone and light alone, the control group suppressed bar pressing to both stimuli. The term *blocking* then refers to the finding that a new stimulus placed in combination with a stimulus that already has been conditioned shows little evidence of conditioning after repeated pairing with a US.

The blocking effect led theorists to question the importance of contiguity for conditioning. Contiguous presentation of a CS with a US did not guarantee that the CS would elicit a CR. The informative value of the CS appeared to be of more importance. If a new CS added no new information beyond the original CS about the delivery of the US, then the new CS failed to become conditioned. Kamin suggested that the problem lay in the fact the US in the second phase of the experiment was no longer surprising. Since the original CS perfectly predicted the US, there was no surprise in Phase 2 when the US occurred. If surprise was necessary for a new association to be learned, its absence prevented the new CS from becoming associated with the US.

Both overshadowing and blocking have traditionally been accounted for as a failure of association. A stronger stimulus or a previously conditioned stimulus prevents another stimulus from being associated with the US through competition for attention or association strength. In Chapter 6, an alternative account of these phenomena in terms of retrieval failure is discussed.

REINFORCEMENT

Since the process of reinforcement is critical for building and maintaining Pavlovian and operant conditioned responses, it is not surprising that the nature of reinforcers and how they are delivered has been a continuing focus of interest in the study of learning. Some prominent topics addressed in the area of reinforcement are the temporal relationship between the response and the reinforcer, the effects on behavior of different schedules of reinforcement, and the effects on response of variation in the quantity and quality of reinforcers.

Delay of Reinforcement

Just as the law of contiguity between stimulus and response was long held to be vital for association, it was also long believed that contiguity between response and reinforcer was essential for instrumental conditioning. For example, a key factor in shaping operant behavior is delivering the reinforcer immediately after the response to be shaped has been made. Early studies clearly supported the importance of response-reinforcer contiguity. In an early study by Grice (1948), different groups of rats were trained to discriminate between black and white boxes, with delays of 0, 0.5, 1.2, 2, 5, and 10 seconds spent in a neutral gray box between the choice response and access to the food reinforcer. Although rats given a 0-second delay learned the task quickly, learning ability declined rapidly in the other groups. The group that experienced a 5-second delay took hundreds of trials to learn the discrimination, and the group required to delay for 10 seconds failed to learn the problem after more than 1,000 trials. The curve relating rate of learning to delay of reinforcement then falls steeply within a few seconds. This curve is called the *delay-of-reinforcement gradient* (Kimble, 1961).

In an interesting set of more recent experiments, Lieberman and G. Thomas and their colleagues found that it is possible to obtain discrimination learning with a delay of reinforcement as long as 60 seconds, provided the correct response is *marked* each time it occurs (Lieberman, McIntosh, & G. Thomas, 1979; G. Thomas, Lieberman, McIntosh, & Ronaldson, 1983; Lieberman, Davidson, & G. Thomas, 1985). In these experiments, a rat was trained to make either a spatial discrimination between left and right alleys in a T-maze or to choose between white and black compartments in a visual discrimination apparatus. After making a response, a rat was confined in a delay box for 60 seconds before entering a goal box to find food after a correct choice and no food after an incorrect choice. Under these standard delay-of-reinforcement conditions, little learning was found, as we would expect from the delay-of-reinforcement gradient. However, groups of rats were also trained that were briefly handled by the experimenter after making each response. These animals showed clear learning of the discrimination over 60 trials of training. In other experiments, it was found that presenting a brief tone or light immediately after each choice response also led to significant learning with a long delay of reinforcement. These investigators suggested that marking each response by following it with a salient or surprising event somehow mediates the temporal gap between the response and reinforcer. An animal's memory for the response seems to be a particularly important factor in the marking effect. Marking a response may make it stand out in memory some seconds later and thus facilitate its association with the trial outcome. If this is the case, contiguity may still be important. However, it is the contiguity of the memory of a response and the reinforcer that causes an association to be learned.

Schedules of Reinforcement

In free-operant conditioning, every response made by a subject can be reinforced. Such a schedule of reinforcement is called *continuous reinforcement.* However, there are two disadvantages to the use of a continuous reinforcement schedule. For one, it is difficult to obtain a high rate of response because the subject pauses to consume a reinforcer after each response. Second, subjects may become rapidly satiated by continuous reinforcers and lose motivation for performing the operant response. In practice, it is more common for reinforcement to be delivered on an *intermittent schedule.* In intermittent schedules, only an occasional response is reinforced. The rules by which occasional responses

are reinforced are varied and determine a number of different schedules of reinforcement. The most frequently used types of schedules of reinforcement are
interval and *ratio* schedules, and each of these may be programmed to deliver
reinforcers on a *fixed* or *variable* basis (Ferster & Skinner, 1957).

Interval schedules are based on time, specifically the amount of time that
has elapsed since the last reinforcer was delivered. In a *fixed-interval* (FI) schedule, each reinforcer is delivered for the first response that is made a fixed period
of time since the last reinforcer occurred. For example, a subject responding
under an FI 30-second schedule could always earn a food pellet for responding
30 seconds or more after the last food pellet was delivered; responses made
before the 30 seconds had elapsed would have no consequence. On a *variable-
interval* (VI) schedule, the opportunity to earn a reinforcer also depends on time
since the last reinforcer, but the time interval varies from one reinforcer to the
next. In a VI 40-second schedule, the time from one reinforcer to the next might
be 20 seconds, then 65 seconds, then 33 seconds, and so on, with the average of
these intervals being 40 seconds.

The defining characteristic of ratio schedules is that the delivery of reinforcement depends on the number of responses made. On *fixed-ratio* (FR)
schedules, a reinforcer is delivered only after a fixed number of bar presses or
key pecks have been made. A bird working on an FR 25 schedule would always
have to complete 25 pecks on the key since the last reinforcement before the
food hopper would operate again. *Variable-ratio* (VR) schedules obey a number-
of-responses rule also, but the number of responses required varies unpredictably from one reinforcement to the next. On a VR 25 schedule, a rat might
have to press a bar 50 times to get its first reinforcer, 25 times to get the next
one, and perhaps only 10 times to get the next one, as long as the average ratio
over many reinforcers was 25.

Some examples of the cumulative records generated by these four types of
schedules are shown in Figure 5.10. Notice that both the VI and VR schedules

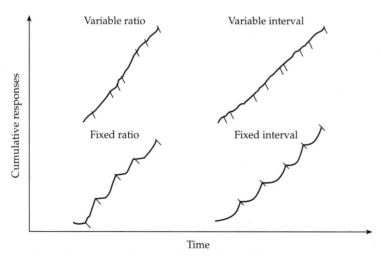

FIGURE 5.10 Cumulative records obtained with four different operant schedules of
reinforcement.

yield consistent, high rates of response. The major property of these schedules from an information processing point of view is that one cannot predict precisely when a reinforcer is going to occur, based on time or amount of work performed. The next response made on either schedule may result in reinforcement since the VI or VR criterion for that reinforcer may have just been achieved. Under these schedules, an organism should respond at a high rate to maintain a high rate of reinforcement.

Just as the reinforcer is unpredictable in VI and VR schedules, it is highly predictable based on time in FI schedules and based on number of responses in FR schedules. The cumulative records for FI and FR schedules in Figure 5.10 show regular variations in rate of response at times following and preceding reinforcement. The FR schedule yields a flat region after each reinforcement during which little responding occurs. This period is called the *postreinforcement pause* and is followed by a period of rapid acceleration of response, called the *ratio run*. The FI schedule produces what is called an *FI scallop* pattern of response, which consists of a slow rate of response through the first half of the FI, followed by a higher rate of response during the last half of the FI.

These patterns of response suggest that animals are sensitive to number of responses on FR schedules and to the time elapsing between reinforcements on FI schedules. The increase in rate of response toward the end of FI schedules appears to be a reasonable strategy for a subject that is timing the interval. That is, little response should occur during the early part of the interval, when it is certain a response will yield no reinforcer. As the end of the interval approaches, response rate should increase to ensure that the reinforcer is obtained as soon as it becomes available. The use of FI schedules to study timing processes and FR schedules to study numerical processing is discussed in Chapters 8 and 10.

The Partial Reinforcement Effect

It is possible to deliver reinforcement on different schedules during discrete trials training as well as during free-operant training. Consistent reinforcement consists of delivering a reinforcer on every trial, and intermittent or partial reinforcement is achieved by reinforcing a response on some trials and withholding reinforcement on other trials. Suppose that two groups of rats have been trained to run down a runway to a goal box, with one group consistently reinforced and the other partially reinforced on a randomly chosen 50 percent of the trials. After a number of trials of training to the point at which animals in both groups are running swiftly to the goal box, extinction is introduced by withholding reinforcement on every trial for both groups. An examination of the course of extinction as shown by running speed over successive trials reveals that the consistently reinforced group extinguishes much faster than the partially reinforced group (see Figure 5.11). Put another way, the partially reinforced rats show greater resistance to extinction than the consistently reinforced group. This finding is referred to as the *partial reinforcement effect*.

When the partial reinforcement effect was initially discovered, it was seen as paradoxical. The paradox lay in the fact that resistance to extinction was viewed as a measure of strength of conditioning, and strength of conditioning was assumed to be directly related to the consistency of reinforcement. There-

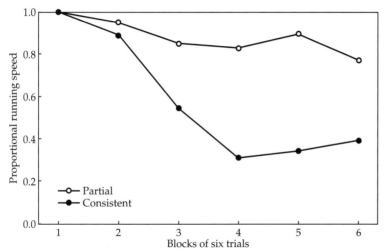

FIGURE 5.11 Extinction curves following training with partial and consistent reinforcement in a runway. Performance is shown as the proportion of running speed during the final trials of acquisition.

fore, consistent reinforcement should have led to greater resistance to extinction than partial reinforcement, while just the opposite had been discovered. As is often the case in science, this paradoxical or counterintuitive finding led to a vast amount of research and theory directed toward its understanding. Although a number of theories have been proposed to explain the partial reinforcement effect, two prominent contemporary accounts are offered by the *frustration theory* (Amsel, 1962; 1967) and the *sequential theory* (Capaldi, 1966; 1967; 1971).

Frustration Theory

According to frustration theory, consistently reinforced animals develop a strong expectancy of reinforcement because they experience nothing but reinforced responses during learning. When extinction is introduced, these animals suffer massive frustration as their expectancy is violated. The strong emotional frustrative response interferes with the instrumental response and causes it to rapidly extinguish. Partially reinforced animals also experience frustration, based on initial reinforcements followed by nonreinforcement. However, the frustration experienced at the outset of learning is sufficiently weak so as to not totally block responding, and animals make further responses, some of which are reinforced. This process of experiencing frustration followed by reinforced responding has the effect of training animals to run while experiencing frustrational cues. In other words, animals are taught to continue responding in the face of frustration. When extinction then is introduced, animals that have been partially reinforced continue to respond longer than consistently reinforced animals because they have learned to respond to the very cues of frustration produced by extinction.

Sequential Theory

The sequential theory also assumes that differential associative learning is occurring during acquisition in consistently and partially reinforced subjects, but this difference is not related to the animal's emotional reaction to nonreinforcement. Instead, this theory focuses on different associations animals learn by being exposed to different sequences of reinforced and nonreinforced trials. According to sequential theory, animals remember the outcomes of preceding trials and associate these with rewarded response on subsequent trials. When an animal is consistently reinforced, all of its memories are of reinforcement, and response is conditioned to these memories. The association learned under consistent reinforcement is symbolized as $S_R \rightarrow R$, meaning that an animal has learned to respond while remembering the stimulus of reinforcement, S_R, that occurred on preceding trials. When extinction is introduced, all of the trial outcomes are nonreinforcement and establish memories of the stimulus of nonreinforcement, S_N. Since the animal has learned no association between S_N and the instrumental response, it has no basis for continued responding, and extinction takes place rapidly.

During partial reinforcement, sequences of trials occur in which reinforced responses follow both reinforcement and nonreinforcement. Thus, both $S_R \rightarrow R$ and $S_N \rightarrow R$ associations are learned. In other words, an animal learns to respond while remembering both prior reinforcement and prior nonreinforcement. During extinction, memories of S_N become prominent, but the $S_N \rightarrow R$ association continues to support response and yields resistance to extinction. Eventually, the number of nonreinforcements experienced in extinction becomes far greater than anything experienced in acquisition, and the response is extinguished. One prediction from this theory is that resistance to extinction should be increased by training animals with long runs of nonreinforcement followed by reinforcement. This training should establish associations between S_N memories of long periods of nonreinforcement and the instrumental response. In fact, such training does increase resistance to extinction (Gonzalez & Bitterman, 1964).

Switching Reinforcers: Contrast Effects

It is well known that reinforcers that vary in quantity or quality produce different levels of operant response. Typically, animals respond at higher rates or run faster to obtain larger or more desirable reinforcers than to obtain smaller or less desirable reinforcers. According to the classic S-R theory of Hull (1943), reinforcers exerted these effects on behavior because magnitude of reinforcement determined the strength of S-R associations. However, this position was brought into question by experiments that suggested that reinforcers were stimulus events that animals learned to expect as consequences of response. Furthermore, this research indicated that switches in the nature of a reinforcer that violated an animal's learned expectation could lead to rapid changes in instrumental behavior based on emotional reactions.

Tinklepaugh (1928) carried out an experiment to study the role of quality of reward on delayed-response performance by rhesus monkeys. After a monkey was shown that a reward was placed in one of two containers, its view of the containers was blocked for several minutes before it was allowed to choose between the containers. If it chose correctly, the monkey was allowed to consume the reward placed in the container. Two rewards were used—a piece of lettuce and a piece of banana. Given a choice, monkeys strongly preferred the banana over lettuce. However, monkeys performed the task readily and consumed either lettuce or banana after choosing the correct container. The experimenter then introduced the *substitution procedure.* On a substitution trial, a monkey was shown that a piece of banana was hidden in one of the containers. During the delay period, while out of the monkey's view, the experimenter substituted lettuce for the banana. The monkey then chose the correct container, but, upon seeing the lettuce, refused to pick it up. It then began to search around the area, emitted a shriek, and went off to look out a window. The monkey's reaction to lettuce when it expected lettuce was always to eat it. When its expectation was for a piece of banana, however, it showed signs of emotional upset and refused to eat the lettuce.

In a similar experiment performed with rats, Crespi (1942) trained rats to run down an alley for rewards in the goal box of 1, 4, 16, 64, and 256 units of food. Rats reinforced with 16 units were kept at this amount of reward throughout the experiment as a baseline level of running speed. After establishing a stable speed of running, rats at each of the other levels of reinforcement were shifted to 16 units of food. The upshifted groups, 1–16 and 4–16, showed a rapid rise in running speed to levels that clearly exceeded that shown by the rats reinforced with 16 units from the beginning. The downshifted groups, 256–16 and 64–16, rapidly slowed down, with their running speeds dropping below that of the 16-unit baseline curve.

The clear effect of switching quantity of reward was to produce a sudden increase or decrease in speed of response that overshot the baseline control level established with the new reinforcer. The effect of an upward shift in quantity of reward usually is referred to as a *positive contrast effect,* and the effect of a downward shift is referred to as a *negative contrast effect.* In general, they have been interpreted as the behavioral consequences of emotional reactions to a reward outcome different from that expected. These reactions were captured in Crespi's original suggestion that the effect of a downshift in reward on behavior was to cause depression, and the effect of an upshift in reward was to cause elation.

SOME THEORETICAL ISSUES IN ASSOCIATIVE LEARNING

In this final section, four theoretical issues are discussed concerning the nature of associative learning. An initial question is, What is learned in associative learning? What kinds of events or forms of representation get associated within the organism when learning takes place? A second issue concerns the conditions that are necessary for association to take place. A third issue is the nature of the stimulus in discrimination learning. The final issue discussed is stimulus and response relevance. Are some types of associations learned faster than others because of genetic predisposition?

What Is Learned in Associative Learning?

During a period extending from around 1930 through the early 1960s, there was considerable debate about what kind of associations were learned by animals. As mentioned earlier in this chapter, many behavioral learning theorists felt that all learning could be reduced to S-R connections. This idea was challenged by Tolman (1932) and his followers, who argued that animals often formed S-S associations by experiencing sensory events in close contiguity. Today, most theorists agree that animals learn both S-S and S-R associations. Exploration of a novel environment or exposure to a series of events in temporal succession leads to the formation of a number of S-S associations. On the other hand, animals, like people, learn to perform highly practiced responses automatically at the presentation of a stimulus, and this behavior may be based on S-R associations. However, in many learning situations, careful experiments have to be performed to determine the nature of the associations that are learned.

Associations in Pavlovian Conditioning

Pavlov argued that conditioned reflexes were based on associations between brain centers. The center activated by the US automatically activated a UR center, as a consequence of an inherited reflex. The major question was how the center activated by the CS came to elicit the CR. There were two possibilities: A pathway could be established directly between the CS center and the UR center (S-R association), or a pathway could be established between the CS center and the US center (S-S association). In the latter case, CRs would be elicited by the CS because the CS would activate the US center, which, in turn, would activate the UR center. Pavlov favored the S-S alternative, and this model of conditioning came to be called *stimulus substitution*. The basic assumption of stimulus substitution was that the CS became a substitute for the US and would basically elicit the same response as the US elicited.

It was recognized early that there were problems with the notion of stimulus substitution. Often, the CR did not match the UR. For example, Zener (1937) observed that a dog that was delivered food in a food tray lowered its head to the tray and made chewing and swallowing movements in addition to salivating. Although the dog also salivated at the presentation of a bell CS, its other responses were different from those to the food; instead of chewing and swallowing, it often looked at the bell and actually tried to move closer to it. In more contemporary research, we can find examples in which the responses to the CS and US are actually opposite one another. In fear conditioning measured by response suppression, the response to the US of shock is increased activity, but the response to the CS is reduced activity (Rescorla, 1988). In studies of conditioned drug reactions, the CR is often a *compensatory response* opposite in nature to the UR. For instance, Crowell, Hinson, and Siegel (1981) found that the UR in rats to ethanol injection was a reduction in body temperature, but the CR to predrug cues was an increase in body temperature.

It appears then that a CS does not simply activate those neural structures that respond to the US, as the stimulus substitution principle suggests. A more contemporary view of the effect of pairing a CS and US is that the CS comes to elicit a representation of the US and its effect on the organism (Domjan, 1993; Hall, 1996). The subject's reaction to this representation is then a response that is most appropriate or adaptive. In some cases, the most appropriate response may be one that mimics the UR, but, in other cases, it may be a response that is different from or even opposite that of the UR.

The US-Devaluation Procedure

A particularly convincing piece of evidence for the representational approach is the findings of *US-devaluation experiments.* If presentations of a CS–US pair cause the CS to elicit a representation of the US, what happens if the value of the US representation is changed in the absence of the CS? If the CS now elicits a changed representation of the US, the organism should change its CR in accord with the new representation. In an experiment carried out by Holland and Rescorla (1975b), rats were initially exposed to repeated presentations of a tone followed by food. This procedure conditioned a CR of general activity to the tone CS. Following this conditioning, one group of rats was allowed to eat some of the food US and was then subjected to high-speed rotation. A control group was not subjected to rotation. The effect of rotation was to devalue the food; rats subjected to rotation came to eat far less of the food than control rats not subjected to rotation. Both groups were then tested for degree of response to the CS. The experimental group subjected to rotation responded significantly less to the CS than did the control group. When the experimental animals were then allowed to eat food without rotation until their consumption level returned to normal, their response to the CS also rose to the control level. This finding, along with other demonstrations of US-devaluation effects, suggests that the value of a US representation can be changed independently of the CS–US association.

Evidence for S-R Associations

The Holland and Rescorla (1975b) experiment also contained groups of rats given second-order conditioning. After experiencing a light CS paired with food, a tone CS was presented and followed by the light. Activity elicited by the tone showed that second-order conditioning had occurred. The US now was devalued by the rotation procedure. Interestingly, subsequent presentations of the tone CS showed no effect of devaluation on the CR. It appears that US devaluation strongly affects first-order conditioned responses but not second-order conditioned responses. This pattern of results suggests that first-order conditioning is based on an S-S association between the CS and a representation of the US but that second-order conditioning is based on S-R association between the CS and CR. That is, if devaluing the US has no effect on the CR in second-order conditioning, it may be because the US representation is bypassed by a direct link between the CS and the CR.

Another source of support for S-R associations in second-order conditioning experiments comes from studies in which it is shown that extinguishing the CR to the first-stage CS has no effect on the strength of the CR made to the second-stage CS (Holland & Rescorla, 1975a; Rizley & Rescorla, 1972). On the other hand, other studies found effects in support of S-S associations in second-order conditioning (Rashotte, Griffin, & Sisk, 1977; Rescorla, 1982).

The Rescorla-Wagner Theory

Most contemporary theories of Pavlovian conditioning conceive of the subject learning an association between the CS and a representation of the US. Furthermore, it is assumed that the strength of this association grows over repeated conditioning trials and that the strength of the association is reflected in the strength of the CR. Theories differ in what aspects of the conditioning situation and what processes are responsible for association growth (see Domjan, 1993, for a review of several theories). The most influential theory of Pavlovian conditioning has been the Rescorla-Wagner theory (Rescorla & Wagner, 1972). This theory suggests that conditioning proceeds to the extent that the US is unexpected or surprising to the subject. If the subject has no expectation the US will occur, its presentation leads to considerable associative learning. As the US becomes more and more expected, growth in the CS–US association becomes less and less on each successive trial until the US is completely expected and no further learning can take place. A US that is particularly salient and draws a good deal of attention leads to a stronger association than one that is less salient. Mathematically, the growth in the CS–US association is calculated as a constant proportion of the difference between the current level of association and the maximal level of association the US will support.

The Rescorla-Wagner theory accounts for a number of phenomena. One particularly good example is the blocking effect described earlier. Recall that this effect might involve initially pairing a tone with shock until the tone reliably showed conditioned suppression. The tone was then presented simultaneously with a light, and both were followed by shock for several trials. A subsequent test for the strength of conditioning established to each stimulus showed that the tone strongly suppressed bar pressing, but the light had almost no effect. The presence of the previously conditioned tone CS blocked conditioning of the light CS. According to the Rescorla-Wagner theory, the initial pairings of tone and shock established a strong association between the tone and a representation of shock. The tone now elicited a strong expectation of shock, and the actual arrival of shock caused little surprise. Thus, when the light was combined with the tone and both were followed by shock, the tone completely predicted the arrival of shock. Since there was no discrepancy between what the subject expected and what happened, no surprise occurred; thus the light gained no associative strength. To put it another way, if the tone already told the subject about the arrival of shock, then the light could acquire no new information and thus could not be associated with shock.

Hierarchical Associations

Subjects associate discrete events in learning experiments, such as a CS and US in Pavlovian conditioning or a bar press and food reward in instrumental conditioning. In addition to these events, however, learning takes place against a background field of stimulation, or a *context*. The context may consist of the room or the chamber within which conditioning takes place. Contexts often provide an ambient source of stimulation and involve a number of multidimensional attributes (Spear & Riccio, 1994). Furthermore, contexts may serve as stimuli for a *conditional discrimination*. In a conditional discrimination, the US that follows a CS or the reward that follows an operant response is conditional upon some other cue present throughout the trial. For example, a rat might be trained in a situation in which a bar press delivers a food pellet if a houselight is on during the trial, but a bar press delivers no food if a noise is on during the trial. The rat might then learn to press the bar when the light is on and to withhold bar pressing when the noise is on.

The question of interest is how the contextual stimulus controls behavior. One possibility is that separate associations are formed between the contextual stimulus and the trial outcome (S-O association) and between the instrumental response and the trial outcome (R-O association). The S-O association then exerts a motivational effect on the subject's tendency to make the operant response. In the preceding example, the houselight signals food and might encourage bar pressing by eliciting a positive emotional response. Conversely, the noise that signals no food might elicit a negative emotional response, which would inhibit bar pressing.

An alternative account of conditional responding controlled by context is that context serves as an *occasion setter*. The occasion setter is a hierarchical cue that sets the occasion for a particular relationship between response and outcome. Instead of depicting what is learned as separate S-O and R-O associations, the hierarchical account suggests that an S(R-O) association is learned. One way to think of this approach is to conceive of a subject learning conditional sets of if–then rules. In the bar pressing example, a subject might learn the rules, "If light then (if bar press then food)," and "If noise then (if bar press then no food)."

A particularly clever experiment carried out by Colwill and Rescorla (1990) provided support for such hierarchical structures in instrumental learning. Rats were trained to make two instrumental responses—chain pulling and bar pressing—and the outcomes of these responses could be either of two rewards—food pellets or liquid sucrose. Which response yielded which reward depended on a contextual stimulus. In one condition, chain pulling was followed by pellets and bar pressing by sucrose if a light was on in the operant chamber. However, if a noise was played in the chamber, then chain pulling yielded sucrose and bar pressing yielded pellets. After a number of sessions of training under these contingencies, one of the reinforcers was devalued by following its ingestion with an injection of lithium chloride. The effect of lithium chloride is to make animals temporarily ill and to condition an aversion to the taste that preceded it. After the rats had fully recovered from the illness, they were placed back in the operant chamber and tested in the presence of both the light and noise contextual cues. Suppose that food pellets had been devalued by taste aversion conditioning. It was then found that rats preferred to press the bar instead of pull the chain when the light was on but to pull the chain instead of press the bar when the noise was played. Just the opposite pattern of preferences was found if sucrose was devalued instead of pellets. Rats preferred to make the response that yielded the nondevalued reinforcer.

Notice that in this experiment both of the contextual stimuli and both of the responses were associated equally often with each reinforcer. Therefore, S-O and R-O associations could not yield the behavior observed. Only hierarchical S(R-O) associations between the contextual stimuli and the responses and reinforcers could have allowed the rats to choose accurately the response that led to the nondevalued reinforcer.

Evidence for occasion setting is also found in conditioned inhibition studies (Holland, 1985). Recall that in a conditioned inhibition experiment, an animal might receive a tone CS+ followed by a shock US on some trials but also experience the tone plus a light followed by the absence of shock on other trials. Subsequent summation tests showed that the tone became a conditioned excitor of fear but that the light became a conditioned inhibitor of fear. Holland and Lamarre (1984) introduced a slight modification to this procedure by presenting the light and tone serially instead of simultaneously. Thus, the light appeared first and was followed by the tone on nonreinforced trials. Although rats learned not to show fear when the light was followed by the tone, a summation test showed that the light did not act as a conditioned inhibitor as it did when presented simultaneously with the tone. Why did response to the light differ so much when it preceded the tone? Holland (1985) argued that the light became directly associated with the absence of shock when simultaneously paired with the tone and thus acted as a conditioned inhibitor. When light preceded the tone, however, it became a higher-order stimulus, or occasion setter, that indicated this was a trial in which the tone predicted the absence of shock. In its role as an occasion setter, the light was not directly associated with the trial outcome and thus did not acquire the properties of a conditioned inhibitor.

What Conditions Are Necessary for Association?

Returning again to the principles of associative learning established by theorists such as Thorndike and Hull, it was held that two conditions absolutely necessary for association were *contiguity* and *reinforcement.* A stimulus had to be followed closely in time by a response, and reinforcement had to follow immediately after the response for the S-R bond to be formed. Several experimental findings challenged these ideas.

Sensory Preconditioning

In a study carried out by Brogden (1939), dogs were given an initial stage of training in which they were repeatedly exposed to the simultaneous presentation of a light and buzzer. The dogs then were given standard foot-withdrawal conditioning by pairing a CS with shock to the foot. The CS used in foot-withdrawal conditioning was the light for half the dogs and the buzzer for the other half of the dogs. When these subjects were reliably withdrawing the foot upon CS presentation, tests were carried out in which the other stimulus from Stage 1 was presented. Thus, a dog conditioned to withdraw its foot when light came on now was tested with the buzzer, and a dog conditioned to withdraw its foot when the buzzer came on was tested with the light. The CR of foot withdrawal was found to be frequently elicited by the Stage 1 stimulus that had never been paired with shock. Control dogs that had been conditioned to withdraw their feet to the light or tone CS but had been given no prior light-buzzer pairings made few foot withdrawals when tested with the nontrained light or buzzer stimulus. Since this initial experiment, the phenomenon of *sensory preconditioning* has been replicated a number of times under different conditions and with human as well as animal subjects.

The important implication of the sensory preconditioning effect was that animals could learn associations between sensory stimuli just by being exposed to these stimuli simultaneously. This was an embarrassing conclusion for S-R reinforcement theory. First of all, it appeared that two events could be associated even when there was no response made to either stimulus. Stage 1 of sensory preconditioning could best be described as S-S learning. Second, this association was learned without reinforcement. Sheer sensory experience in the absence of any need reduction could lead to associative learning.

Latent Learning

Similar findings were discovered in instrumental learning experiments carried out in Tolman's laboratory (Blodgett, 1929; Tolman & Honzik, 1930b). Rats were allowed to explore a complex multichoice maze for a number of daily trials. Importantly, no food reinforcer was present in the maze during these exploration trials. The experimenter kept track of the number of errors or blind alleys rats entered on the maze and of the time taken to go from the start box to the goal box. As might be expected, the subjects maintained a high level of error and took long periods of time to complete the maze during these trials. After several of these nonrewarded runs during which rats showed little evidence of improvement, reward was introduced in the goal box for a series of test trials. As shown in Figure 5.12, the effect of this sudden introduction of reward was to cause an immediate drop in the level of errors animals made as they traveled through the maze; time scores showed a similar dramatic decrease. In fact, performance rapidly reached the level of that of animals that had been reinforced with food on all of the preceding trials of the experiment.

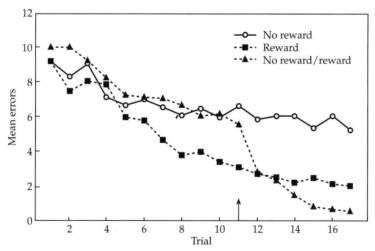

FIGURE 5.12 Learning curves for three groups of rats given daily trials in a multiple-choice maze. One group was nonrewarded on every trial (no reward), a second group was rewarded on every trial (reward), and a third group was nonrewarded on trials 1 through 10 but rewarded on trials 11 through 17 (no reward/reward). Latent learning is shown by the sudden drop in errors made by the no reward/reward group after Trial 11.
Adapted from Tolman & Honzik, 1939b.

This discovery led to an important distinction between learning and performance. Tolman argued that while rats appeared to wander through the maze without learning, they were in fact learning about the layout of the maze by forming a cognitive map. This learning remained latent, however, until some form of incentive was introduced to motivate animals to reveal what they had learned. Once the goal box became a valuable source of food reward within an animal's cognitive map, the animal quickly revealed what it had learned by its sudden improvement in performance. Latent learning was subsequently shown in a number of different types of experiments (Thistlethwaite, 1951). As was the case with sensory preconditioning, latent learning indicated that animals did not need to be reinforced to learn. The experience of wandering through a maze was sufficient for animals to learn associations between one place and another.

Is Contiguity Necessary or Sufficient for Learning?

One phenomenon already discussed, taste aversion conditioning, indicates that contiguity is not always necessary for associative learning to take place. Animals can learn to associate a taste with illness, even though these events may be separated by several hours. However, in more conventional Pavlovian conditioning procedures, such as pairing a light with food or a tone with shock, contiguity may be of greater importance. Most experiments that involve appetitive or fear conditioning present the CS and US in fairly close proximity, using the delayed or trace conditioning procedures outlined earlier in this chapter. Is contiguity of these stimuli then sufficient for learning to occur? Can we be assured that an association will always occur if a US follows a CS closely in time?

The answer to this question is no. In an important series of experiments carried out by Rescorla (1966; 1968), it was discovered that the acquisition of an association between a contiguous CS and US is critically dependent upon the other events occurring within the conditioning session. To understand Rescorla's findings, consider two conditional probabilities: the probability that the US will occur during the CS, P(US/CS) and the probability that the US will occur in the absence of the CS, P(US/no CS). In many conditioning procedures, P(US/CS) = 1.0, and P(US/no CS) = 0.0. If each time a tone is heard a shock is delivered, and shock never occurs in the absence of the tone, the tone is a perfect predictor of the shock, and a strong fear response is conditioned to the tone CS. However, suppose that P(US/CS) = P(US/no CS) = 0.5. In this case, half of the occasions in which the shock US occurs the tone also occurs, but, on the other half of the occasions in which the shock occurs, the tone is absent. The tone is an imperfect predictor of shock; tone only predicts half the shocks that occur.

When Rescorla studied fear conditioning in rats, he found that conditioned suppression of bar pressing increased as the P(US/CS) increased during fear conditioning but dropped continuously as the P(US/no CS) increased. If a fixed number of tone/shock pairings were given during training, suppression was very high if no other shocks were given. When an equal number of shocks were delivered in the absence of the CS, suppression was negligible. This finding clearly shows that contiguity of CS and US alone is not sufficient for association to take place. The predictive value of the CS/US relationship within the total context of events determines the level of conditioning (Rescorla, 1988).

Absolute versus Relational Perception in Discrimination Learning

Recall the difference in the way Pavlov (1927) explained the generalization curve and the way in which Lashley and Wade (1946) explained it. Pavlov held that generalization arose automatically from the irradiation of excitation around an activated cerebral center, whereas Lashley and Wade argued that it arose from an inadequate opportunity to compare relationships between stimuli. Although later learning theories did not accept Pavlov's ideas about cortical irradiation, the notion that processes of excitation and inhibition became conditioned to single points on a stimulus dimension and then generalized automatically to neighboring points along the dimension formed the basis for discrimination learning theories that emphasized the *absolute properties* of stimuli (Spence, 1936). Other theorists opposed the absolute view and stressed the importance of *perceptual relationships* in discrimination learning (Kohler, 1925; Krechevsky, 1932; Lashley, 1942).

The nature of this debate was captured particularly well in a discrimination learning effect called *transposition*. Assume a stimulus dimension of size along which stimuli get bigger from the smallest size of 1 to the largest size of 10. An animal is given simultaneous discrimination training between Stimuli 4 and 5, with Stimulus 4 as the S– and Stimulus 5 as the S+. After the animal learned to always choose 5 over 4, we may ask what the animal learned. Has it learned to always approach the absolute size 5 and avoid the absolute size 4, or, has it learned the relationship of always choosing the larger of the two stimuli? On a transposition test, the animal is given a choice between the previously reinforced Stimulus 5 and a new stimulus, Stimulus 6. Which should it choose? It appears that an absolute theory predicts the animal should choose Stimulus 5 since it was always reinforced for choosing 5 and has never been reinforced for choosing 6. A relational theory, on the other hand, suggests the animal should choose Stimulus 6. If the animal has encoded the discrimination as "choose the larger stimulus," then it should choose the larger 6 over the smaller 5. In fact, animals typically show transposition of the discrimination by choosing 6 over 5.

On the surface, transposition of discrimination learning appeared to be a clear victory for the relational learning position. This proved not to be the case, however, as shown by Spence's (1937) derivation of the transposition effect from absolute learning principles. Spence's theory, shown in Figure 5.13, depicts the generalization of excitation around the S+ stimulus and the generalization of inhibition around the S– stimulus. Preferences between stimuli are based on the *net generalization curve,* which is obtained by subtracting the inhibition curve from the excitation curve. The net curve is actually higher at Stimulus 6 than it is at Stimulus 5 and thus predicts that an animal should choose 6 over 5. This rather startling derivation of the transposition effect from absolute learning principles has long been considered one of the most elegant theoretical accomplishments in psychology.

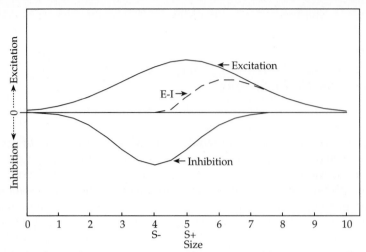

FIGURE 5.13 Curves for the generalization of excitation and inhibition based on Spence's theory of discrimination learning. The curve for net excitation (E-I) determines which stimulus should be chosen on a test. Note that net excitation is greater at Stimulus 6 than at Stimulus 5 after training with Stimulus 5 as an S+ and Stimulus 4 as an S–.

Note another important prediction from Spence's theory. The peak of the net generalization curve shown in Figure 5.13 is shifted away from the S+ stimulus in the direction opposite from the S– stimulus. In other words, Spence's theory clearly predicts the peak-shift effect shown in Figure 5.9. Remember, however, that Spence published his theory in 1937, and the peak-shift effect was not reported until 1959!

Although Spence's theory demonstrated that the transposition effect did not provide crucial evidence for relational learning in animals, other evidence accumulated that did suggest that animals learned relationships between stimuli. Lawrence and DeRivera (1954) trained rats to make a conditional spatial discrimination between stimulus cards that presented different shades of gray on the top and bottom. There were seven shades of gray that ranged from the lightest gray of 1 to the darkest gray of 7. The middle gray number 4 was always placed on the lower half of the card during training, with grays numbering 1, 2, 3, 5, 6, and 7 on top. If the top half of the card was lighter than the bottom half (1/4, 2/4, and 3/4), rats were reinforced for jumping to the right on a Lashley jumping stand; if the top half of the card was darker than the bottom half (5/4, 6/4, and 7/4), the correct response was a jump to the left. After learning this discrimination, rats were trained with a number of combinations of grays they had not encountered before. In virtually all of these tests, the rats responded on the basis of the relationship between the top and bottom halves of the cards. Of particular interest were tests in which gray 4 was placed on top of the card (4/1, 4/2, 4/3, 4/5, 4/6, and 4/7). Predictions from absolute theory were clear. Since gray 4 had been equally paired with jumps to the left and right in training, while grays 1, 2, and 3 had been paired with jumps to the right and grays 5, 6, and 7 had been paired with jumps to the left, stimuli 4/1, 4/2, and

4/3 should elicit a jump to the right, and stimuli 4/5, 4/6, and 4/7 should elicit a jump to the left. In fact, the results were just the opposite; on 74 percent of these trials, rats jumped to the left when presented with 4/1, 4/2, and 4/3 and jumped to the right when presented with 4/5, 4/6, and 4/7. These responses, of course, were in agreement with the original relational training to go left when the top is darker than the bottom and to go right when the top is lighter than the bottom.

Still another relationship between stimuli is intermediacy, or the middle item. In the *intermediate-size discrimination,* an animal was trained to discriminate between three stimuli. Suppose stimuli of sizes 4, 5, and 6 are presented in different arrangements over repeated trials, with choice of Stimulus 5 always rewarded and choice of Stimulus 4 or 6 nonrewarded. Once again, this problem can be learned on the basis of absolute stimulus properties or by the relationship between the stimuli. The animal might learn to always choose the stimulus of size 5, or it might learn to "choose the stimulus of middle size." As you may have anticipated, we can next give the animal a transposition test by shifting to stimuli larger or smaller than the training stimuli. Suppose we now give the animal a choice between 5, 6, and 7. It is important to realize that Spence's absolute theory does not predict transposition of the intermediate-size discrimination, as it did for the two-stimulus problem discussed earlier. According to his theory, an excitatory gradient should have developed around Stimulus 5, and inhibitory gradients should have developed around Stimuli 4 and 6. If an animal learns to approach 5 instead of 6 on training with 4, 5, and 6, it must continue to prefer 5 over 6 when presented with a choice between 5, 6, and 7. In fact, Spence (1942) tested chimpanzees on the intermediate-size discrimination and found no evidence of transposition, just as his theory predicted. Later research by Gonzalez, Gentry, and Bitterman (1954), however, did reveal clear evidence of transposition of intermediate size in chimpanzees. They did find some evidence of absolute stimulus preferences, as well as relational choice. These findings indicate that animals can learn associations based on both the absolute and relational properties of stimuli.

Stimulus and Response Relevance in Associative Learning

In a well-known experiment carried out by Garcia and Koelling (1966), rats were given Pavlovian conditioning with a compound CS and two forms of US. All animals were presented with a CS that consisted of an audiovisual component—a flashing light and a clicking relay—and a flavor component—the taste of saccharin. When rats licked a tube, it yielded saccharin-flavored water at the same time as the light and clicking sound occurred. Although all rats were exposed to this compound CS, one subgroup of subjects received shock as the US immediately after each lick. The other subgroup of rats was made ill through exposure to X-ray treatment after licking the tube a number of times. Subsequently, animals in both groups were tested for the amount of drinking they would perform (1) when the tube contained saccharin flavored water but the audiovisual stimulus was absent and (2) when the tube contained unflavored water but each lick produced the audiovisual stimulus.

The important finding of this experiment was that the association of a CS and US depended on the nature of the stimuli (see Figure 5.14). Rats exposed to X-ray as a US drank bright noisy water readily but reduced intake of saccharin-flavored water. Rats that received shock as the US did just the opposite, drinking the saccharin-flavored water but avoiding the plain water presented with the audiovisual stimulus. It was argued that rats were biologically prepared to associate the taste of a substance with illness but not with the delivery of shock. However, shock could be easily associated with visual and auditory stimuli but not with taste.

Other research suggested that stimulus and response relevance for association varied between species. Wilcoxon, Dragoin, and Kral (1971) showed that quail made ill after drinking blue, sour water subsequently showed an aversion to both the blue color and the sour taste, whereas rats learned an aversion only to the sour taste. This interaction between species in the associability of taste and visual cues could be related to the fact that quail had better vision than rats and commonly used vision to search for food during the daytime.

In the 1970s, a number of other instances of stimulus and response relevance were demonstrated in both Pavlovian and operant conditioning. In the case of avoidance conditioning, it was suggested that animals were biologically prepared to make *species-specific defense reactions* (SSDR) to painful or fear provoking stimuli (Bolles, 1970). Thus, rats could be easily trained to run down an alley or to cross a shuttle box to avoid shock because the response of fleeing is an SSDR. Training a rat to press a bar to avoid shock is very difficult, however, because bar pressing is not an SSDR made to painful stimulation. Pigeons readily learn to peck keys for food through shaping by a trainer or through autoshaping. The pecking response for food appears to readily transfer to pecking a circumscribed stimulus when that response causes food to appear or the stimulus predicts the

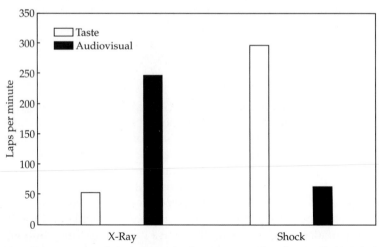

FIGURE 5.14 Rats consumed tasty water in the presence of audiovisual stimulation and were either shocked or given an X-ray treatment. The bars show the amount of drinking rats performed in each type of US condition when tested in the presence of either the audiovisual CS or the taste CS.

occurrence of food. When a pigeon is required to peck a key to avoid shock, once again the process of learning is slow and difficult. Thorndike (1911) observed early that cats learned more easily to escape from the puzzle box with some responses than others. Cats learned relatively quickly how to escape if they had to claw at a loop of wire or push a button. If a cat was required to lick or scratch itself, however, the response was learned more slowly and would often deteriorate into "a mere vestige of lick or scratch." (p. 48). One interpretation of this observation is that the evolutionary adaptive purposes of licking and scratching made these responses difficult to learn because they are irrelevant to the task of escaping from a puzzle box.

These examples of stimulus and response relevance are contrary to the principle of equipotentiality—all stimuli, responses, and reinforcers should be equally associable. Some theorists suggested that such observations brought a general-process theory of learning into question (Lockard, 1971; Seligman, 1970). Perhaps general principles of learning would have to be scrapped, and different principles of association would have to be worked out for each learning situation and species. In response to this challenge to general-process theory, some theorists more recently have come to believe that examples of relevance between associated events may be readily incorporated into a general approach to associative learning (Domjan, 1983; Domjan & Galef, 1983; Mazur, 1994). Animals indeed may have inherited predispositions to acquire some associations faster than others. Nevertheless, these differences may only be quantitative in nature; difficult associations may still be learnable. Rats can learn to press a bar to avoid shock (Feldman & Bremner, 1963; Keehn & Webster, 1968) and can associate taste with shock (Krane & Wagner, 1975). Taste aversion learning occurs over CS–US periods far in excess of the intervals originally thought to be necessary for conditioning. However, taste aversion conditioning still weakens as the CS–US interval lengthens, just as in more traditional learning procedures (Logue, 1979). The law of contiguity then holds for taste aversion learning, only over a longer time scale than seen when light and tone CSs are paired with food and shock USs. In general, a contemporary view of associative learning holds that phenomena of biological preparedness or stimulus and response relevance do not require a major restructuring of the principles of associative learning. Instead, those principles need to be expanded to incorporate differences between the conditions under which associations take place, based on evolutionary adaptive considerations.

SUMMARY

Associations are basic units of information acquired by people and animals that are critical for understanding the environment and how it works. Associations link together stimulus events that occur contiguously in time and space and allow organisms to predict where things will be relative to one another in space and what will happen next in time. Most topics in the field of animal cognition involve the use of associative learning procedures and the study of memory for associations of one type or another.

The study of the conditions under which association occurs can be traced back to the ancient Greek philosophers and was a major concern of a group of philosophers known as the British empiricists. When behaviorism emerged in the early 1900s as the dominant approach to experimental psychology, the laws of association were adopted and modified to account for early research on animal learning. Thorndike's early experiments on animals learning to escape from puzzle boxes were the first experimental studies of instrumental or operant learning. Based on his observations, Thorndike concluded that animals learned by the gradual strengthening of associations between sensory impressions and impulses to action. According to his law of effect, these associations were strengthened by the delivery of a reward or some other event that had pleasant consequences. Thorndike's ideas were expanded by a number of other behaviorists and became the basis for S-R learning theory, the idea that all learning involved the association of stimuli directly with responses through the strengthening action of reinforcement. A great deal of research was devoted to developing the principles of this theory through the study of instrumental learning in runways, mazes, and operant chambers.

In Russia, another type of learning was discovered by Pavlov. It was found that repeated pairings of a neutral CS with a US that reflexively elicited a UR led to the emergence of a new CR made to the CS in the absence of the US. In salivary conditioning, the delivery of a food US shortly after the presentation of a tone CS caused a dog to begin to salivate simply to the occurrence of the tone. Pavlov reasoned that the brain center activated by the CS developed an association with the brain center activated by the US. The CS then eventually became a substitute for the US and elicited the same response as the US.

Pavlovian conditioning became widely accepted as a second major form of learning, and instrumental and classical (Pavlovian) conditioning became the cornerstones of the study of animal learning. These two forms of learning shared a number of common phenomena. (1) Both showed stimulus generalization, or a tendency for a response conditioned to one stimulus to be made strongly to similar stimuli and less strongly to dissimilar stimuli. (2) The degree of stimulus control could be modified in both cases by discrimination training, or the differential reinforcement of stimuli along a dimension. Discrimination learning had the effect of sharpening stimulus control by the reinforced stimulus by decreasing the extent of stimulus generalization. (3) Both types of learning were susceptible to extinction. If the US or the operant reinforcer was omitted over a number of trials or responses, the learned response gradually weakened to a low level of occurrence. (4) It was also seen that these two types of learning might interact to produce new learned behavior in certain situations. In the case of avoidance conditioning with aversive stimulation, an animal learns to respond to a warning signal in order to avoid the delivery of a painful shock. The two-factor theory of avoidance learning held that initial pairings of the warning stimulus (CS) and the delivery of shock led to the Pavlovian conditioning of a fear response to the warning stimulus. Animals then learned to make an instrumental response of crossing to the other side of a shuttle box to escape from the fear elicited by this CS.

New findings in the field of animal learning gradually eroded many of the earlier principles of learning. Although it was initially thought that reinforcement was necessary for all learning, findings such as sensory preconditioning and latent learning suggested that animals could learn just through sensory experience, without the occurrence of reinforcement. Tolman argued that reinforcers were stimuli animals learned to expect and that behavior could be motivated through the valence or value of these reinforcers to an organism. Other research on reinforcer contrast effects led to similar conclusions and indicated that switches in the quantity or quality of reinforcers led to sudden changes in behavior, apparently caused by emotional reactions to a violation of the animal's expectancy of a particular reinforcer.

Still more recent discoveries questioned some of the very basic laws of association. The discovery of blocking in Pavlovian conditioning indicated that simply pairing a new CS with a US did not guarantee the formation of an association. Rescorla's studies of contiguity in fear conditioning showed that contiguity between a CS and US led to learning only if the CS was a good predictor of the US. If the US occurred only when the CS was presented, strong fear conditioning was observed by conditioned suppression of bar pressing. However, if the US appeared on a number of occasions when the CS was not present, the CS no longer effectively predicted the US, and little fear of the CS was conditioned. These discoveries led to new theories of conditioning, which hold that animals learn about the informative or predictive properties of the CS or of controlling stimuli in instrumental learning. Based on the relationships between a number of events occurring within a learning situation, animals learn to expect certain events to follow a CS or their own response. According to the Rescorla-Wagner theory of conditioning, growth in association depends on the extent to which delivery of a US is surprising or unexpected.

The adequacy of the traditional laws of association was also questioned by the discovery of a number of examples of stimulus and response relevance. For example, it was found that taste aversions can be learned between a novel taste and toxicosis, even though these events occurred only once and there was an interval of several hours between the taste experience and illness. This finding seems to question the principles of both temporal contiguity and frequency. On the other hand, taste is difficult to associate with shock, and lights and sounds are difficult to associate with toxicosis. Such findings have prompted a realization that all associations are not equipotential. Evolved adaptive mechanisms influence the ease or difficulty of different S-S and S-R associations, and the relevance of certain events for association may vary between species of animals. In general, however, most of these adaptive specializations for learning tend to follow traditional laws of association when parametric variations in the conditions for learning are examined. For example, taste aversion associations become weaker as the taste-toxicosis interval in made longer. Such observations suggest that biologically prepared or contraprepared learning may be incorporated into a general-process theory of learning.

CHAPTER 6

Reference Memory

It was suggested in Chapter 3 that long-term memories in animals fall into the categories of procedural and declarative memory (see Figure 3.1). Memory for highly learned motor routines is part of procedural memory. On the other hand, learning information about the environment and the various ways it must be responded to involves the formation of declarative memory. All of the spatial information an animal may store about its habitat is declarative memory. Learning that a conditioned stimulus (CS) is followed by an unconditioned stimulus (US) in Pavlovian conditioning or learning that a particular behavior is followed by food or pain in instrumental conditioning both involve the formation of declarative memories. In animal research, declarative memory is usually called *reference memory* (Honig, 1978).

Two factors generally distinguish reference memory from working memory. First, reference memory typically involves learning over repeated trials. As we have seen, most working memory tests involve a single presentation of a sample stimulus. Although reference memory is usually memory for Pavlovian or instrumental behaviors learned over multiple trials, we see some instances of reference memory formed on one trial. One-trial reference memory may be found when the stimulus events producing the learning are highly intense or salient. The second important characteristic of reference memory is that memory typically persists over relatively long time intervals. In working memory experiments, memory for sample stimuli is measured over intervals little longer than a few seconds. Reference memory typically persists for minutes, hours, or days. Reference memory was integral to the study of working memory in the studies discussed in Chapters 3 and 4. To respond accurately to sample stimuli, memory codes stored in reference memory have to be drawn on to indicate the appropriate choice between comparison stimuli. These reference memory codes persist from day to day and are formed by many repetitive trials that teach the relationships between sample and comparison stimuli. Reference memory for complex spatial relationships is discussed in Chapter 7.

Most people can relate a story of outstanding memory in some animal. Tales of dogs and cats that were lost but eventually found their way home months or even years later are not uncommon. Folklore suggests that an elephant never forgets. How accurate is this common wisdom about the goodness of animal memory? In fact, there are several laboratory studies that support the notion that animals remember well over long periods of time.

Wendt (1937) used Pavlovian conditioning to train a dog to flex its leg. A tone was followed repeatedly by a shock to the leg until the dog made the CR of leg flexion whenever the tone was presented. Two-and-one-half years later, retention was measured by presenting the tone 20 times. The dog exhibited a conditioned flexion response on 16 of these 20 trials. In another experiment involving Pavlovian conditioning, Hoffman, Fleshler, and Jensen (1963) trained pigeons to peck a key for food reward on a variable-interval (VI) 2-minute schedule. Once key pecking was established at a high stable rate, the experimenters presented a 1000-Hz tone that terminated with the delivery of a shock. The effect of presenting the tone followed by shock was to establish a conditioned emotional response (CER) of fear to the tone CS. As described in Chapter 5, the strength of the CER was measured by presenting the tone during key pecking. During presentation of the tone, key pecking was completely suppressed. Tests were also made with tones that varied in frequency from 300 to 3400 Hz. A generalization gradient was found; key pecking increased as a function of how distant the test tone was from the 1000-Hz training CS. This gradient showed *stimulus control* by the dimension of tone frequency. Hoffman et al. then returned their subjects to the loft for about 2 1/2 years. At the end of this period, the pigeons were retrained to key peck, and tones between 300 and 3400 Hz were presented during key pecking. Immediate stimulus control equivalent to that established by original conditioning was shown. A further test given 1 1/2 years later also showed no loss of memory (Hoffman, Selekman, & Fleshler, 1966).

A well-known example of long-term retention of an instrumental response is found in a study by Skinner (1950). Pigeons were trained to peck a spot on an illuminated key for a food reward and were not tested again for 4 years. When exposed to the illuminated key after this 4-year interval, pigeons immediately pecked the key and continued to respond for an extended period, although no reward was given. Ehrenfreund and Allen (1964) trained rats to run down a runway for a food reward. After 17 days of training, rats ran down the runway at a high stable or asymptotic speed. The rats were returned to home cages for a 27-day period and then retested in the runway. The rats ran at the same high asymptotic speeds seen before the retention period.

In experiments comparable to studies of human memory for lists of verbal material, it has been shown that animals remember multiple discrimination problems over long intervals. Rensch (1957) trained an elephant to choose between two wooden boxes containing different visual patterns, with food under the correct box. The elephant was tested with a number of different pair of visual patterns and came to learn them progressively faster, taking 330 trials to learn the first problem but only 10 trials to learn the fourth problem. In all,

20 such problems were learned by the elephant. After about a year, the animal was tested on 13 of these problems and demonstrated 70 percent to 100 percent accuracy on individual discriminations. In a similar study with rhesus monkeys, Strong (1959) trained monkeys to discriminate between the rewarded and nonrewarded members of 72 pair of stereotaxic objects, stimuli that varied in form, size and color. Retention tests that involved a single presentation of each stimulus pair were carried out 30, 60, 90, 120, and 210 days after completion of original training. The results were impressive, in that retention was close to 90 percent correct at each retention interval.

Some of these experiments may be criticized. In many cases, only a single retention test was given at a long retention interval so that the memory function could not be studied. Although the investigator was impressed with performance at the long interval, it may still have been poorer than it would have been at a shorter retention interval. For example, Skinner reported that although his pigeons pecked immediately and continued to peck after a 4-year delay, their rate of pecking was only one-fourth to one-half that of other pigeons tested soon after training. Rensch's elephant scored as low as 70 percent on some problems; perhaps performance closer to 100 percent would have been seen on these problems if retention tests had been given only a few days after learning. Nevertheless, these studies, and others, clearly tell us that animals are capable of maintaining reference memory over long time intervals.

EVIDENCE OF FORGETTING IN ANIMALS

Given that animals sometimes remember very well, there is no difficulty finding examples in the literature of long-term forgetting. Early studies of retention often used multiple-unit mazes. Over a number of training trials, rats learned to make correct left or right turns at a dozen or more choice points. Retention of complex maze learning dropped progressively over periods of weeks and months (Brockbank, 1919; Bunch, 1941; Tsai, 1924). Contrary to the findings of Ehrenfreund and Allen (1964), forgetting of runway performance has been demonstrated by Gagne (1941) and by Gleitman and Steinman (1963).

Gleitman and Bernheim (1963) and Gleitman, Steinman and Bernheim (1965) examined retention of bar pressing learned under a fixed-interval (FI) 1-minute schedule of reward. Rats learned to make very few responses during the first 30 seconds of the FI and to make almost all of their responses during the second 30 seconds of the FI. A group of rats tested 1 day after FI training continued to show this pattern of responding. However, rats tested after 24 days made significantly more responses during the first 30 seconds of the FI than the rats tested after 1 day. As is demonstrated in Chapter 8, the FI task requires animals to time the interval between rewards accurately to emit responses at the appropriate time. Apparently, rats forgot the time periods in which responses should be withheld or emitted.

Evidence that animals may forget magnitude of reward was reported by Gleitman and Steinman (1964). Recall from Chapter 5 that rats that are trained to run down an alley for a large amount of reward and then are shifted to a small reward show a negative contrast effect. They typically run even more slowly than control animals trained throughout with the small reward. A frustration response to this sudden decline in fortune may interfere with the alley running response. Gleitman and Steinman found a clear negative contrast effect in rats if the shift in magnitude of reward occurred 1 day after initial training, but this effect was completely absent if the same shift occurred 68 days after initial training. The emotional reaction of frustration would not be expected if an animal could not remember how much food it had received 68 days earlier.

Conditions That Produce Forgetting

Clear evidence of marked forgetting in animals is found under certain conditions. Two of these conditions are described briefly here: age and interference.

Infantile Amnesia

Most if not all people experience infantile amnesia. Try to remember your experiences during your first year or two of life. If you are like most people, you find this period to be blank in your memory; earliest memories of childhood typically begin after this early period. Although it would be of considerable interest to study this phenomenon in people, practical considerations make it difficult to do so. For one thing, it is difficult to know exactly the actual experiences from childhood of an individual tested as an adult. Accurate study of this problem would require expensive longitudinal studies of people, and years would have to pass before experimental questions could be answered. Finally, ethical prohibitions limit manipulations one might wish to perform on infants to improve memory for early experiences.

Researchers interested in infantile amnesia have turned to animals as subjects. Rodents have the advantage that they mature faster than people and thus allow memory for early experiences to be tested over relatively short intervals of time. A number of studies of retention of behaviors learned by immature rats have revealed steep forgetting curves (Campbell, Jaynes, & Misanin, 1968; Feigley & Spear, 1970). These curves appear to reveal infantile amnesia in rats because control retention curves taken with adult rats show far less forgetting. An example of this phenonmenon is shown in Figure 6.1. These curves show retention of a light-dark discrimination by young rats trained at 23 to 26 days of age and adult rats trained at 98 to 102 days of age (Campbell et al., 1968). After training subjects to press a bar in an operant chamber during periods of darkness (VI 15-second schedule of reward) but not during periods of light (extinction), retention was measured by extinction tests 0, 1, 38, 75, and 150 days later. Retention was measured by the percentage of total responses made during the dark (rewarded) periods; the adult curve shows almost no loss, whereas performance by young subjects approached chance by 75 days.

Interference

As was the case in working memory, major losses in reference memory arise from both proactive interference (PI) and retroactive interference (RI). The reversal of a previously learned discriminative response has often been studied

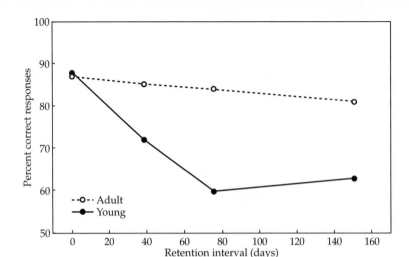

FIGURE 6.1. Retention curves of young and adult rats for a light-dark discrimination.

as a source of interference. As an example, Kraemer (1984) used a successive or go/no-go procedure to train pigeons to discriminate between patterns containing two and three green dots. One group of pigeons was trained with three dots as the positive stimulus and two dots as the negative stimulus. On half the trials within a session, three dots appeared on the pecking key, and pecks on the key yielded a food reward. On the other half of the trials, the key with two dots appeared, and pecks on the key were nonrewarded. After pigeons learned to peck only when the key displayed three dots, half of the pigeons were trained on a reversal of the first discrimination; these pigeons now had to learn to peck when the key contained two dots and to withhold pecks to the key when three dots appeared. The other half of the pigeons were not trained on the reversed discrimination. As a retention test, both groups of pigeons were retrained to criterion on the most recently learned problem; relearning took place at two retention intervals—1 day and 20 days.

The findings are displayed in Figure 6.2 as the mean responses to the negative stimulus (S–) during retraining to criterion. Pigeons have a strong tendency to peck at both positive and negative lit keys, and learning to discriminate largely involves the withholding of pecks to the nonrewarded stimulus. Thus, responses to S– are a good measure of rate of relearning and retention; forgetting would be greatest for the condition in which the most S– responses were made. The curves show that forgetting was minimal after 1 day for birds that had to remember both reversed and nonreversed discriminations. After 20 days, however, pigeons that had to remember the reversed discrimination showed far more forgetting than those that had to remember the nonreversed discrimination. These findings suggest that memory of the original discrimination learned before reversal learning acted as a strong source of PI, which became more pronounced at a longer retention interval.

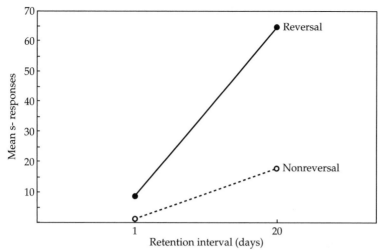

FIGURE 6.2. Retention of a go/no-go discrimination by pigeons between two-dot and three-dot patterns. The reversal group was retrained on the reversed discrimination after 1 and 20 days, and the nonreversed group was retrained on the original discrimination after 1 and 20 days.

Retention of Different Kinds of Information

In most memory experiments, the investigator trains animals to perform a particular behavior and then measures retention of that target behavior. It may be asked, however, whether animals retain more than just that aspect of training in which the experimenter is interested. Theories of memory in both humans and animals have stressed the idea that memories consist of a number of attributes encoded during learning (Bower, 1967; Kraemer & Spear, 1993; Spear, 1971, 1978; Spear & Riccio, 1994). Given this assumption, it seems possible that different attributes or kinds of information might be forgotten at different rates. Evidence from some animal experiments supports this idea.

The notion that animals might differentially retain different types of information was raised some years ago by Bunch (1939; 1941). Bunch first trained a large number of rats to turn left in a T-maze. He then divided them into five subgroups and required each group to learn the reversed discrimination (turn right) after a certain retention interval of time had passed. One group learned the reversal immediately after the original learning, and the other groups learned after 2, 7, 14, or 28 days. Learning the reversed discrimination may be seen as a test of retention; the better animals remembered the original discrimination, the more this memory should interfere with their acquisition of the reversed discrimination. Marked negative transfer or difficulty in learning was observed in rats tested immediately after learning to turn left. These animals made more errors than a control group of rats that had been trained only on the right-turn problem. Rats that learned the reversal after 2 and 7 days required about the same number of trials to learn as the control group.

The surprising finding was that rats tested 14 and 28 days after learning to turn left showed positive transfer; they required fewer trials to learn the right turn than control subjects. Bunch suggested that this shift in transfer effects over the retention interval could be explained by assuming memory for two kinds of information: the left-turn response originally rewarded and more general information about how to learn in the maze. On the immediate test, strong retention of the rewarded response made learning of the opposite response difficult. With the passage of the retention interval, memory of the left-turn response diminished, and interference with learning the right-turn response was reduced. Bunch further assumed that memory of learning strategies in the maze was forgotten more slowly and thus was available to animals at all retention intervals. Thus, animals tested after 14 or 28 days could benefit from this maze know-how while at the same time suffering little interference from memory of the left-turn response.

Further evidence that memories acquired in the same situation may be forgotten at different rates comes from tests of stimulus generalization made at different retention intervals. Perkins and Weyant (1958) and Steinman (1967) trained rats to run down a runway of a particular color (black or white) and then measured retention of this running response at short and long retention intervals in either the original training runway or in one of the opposite color. Perkins and Weyant used retention intervals of 1 minute and 1 week, whereas Steinman used intervals of 1 and 66 days, but the results of both experiments were the same. At the short interval, animals showed generalization decrement and ran considerably slower on the runway of a different color than on the runway on which they had been trained. At the long retention interval, however, rats actually ran faster on the novel runway than they had on the short-interval test, and no difference in speed of running was seen between the same-color and changed-color conditions. The implication of these findings is that rats remembered well the runway response and the consequent reward but forgot incidental information about the specific color of the runway in which they had been trained (Riccio, Rabinowitz, & Axelrod, 1994).

THEORIES OF LONG-TERM FORGETTING

Since animals, like people, tend to forget information in reference memory with the passage of time, theoretical accounts of forgetting in animals must be considered. By and large, theories of forgetting in animals arose from theoretical attempts to explain forgetting in people. With the vast accumulation of data on animal memory now available, theoretical efforts are often directed specifically at animal findings. In earlier years, however, researchers often turned to animals as a convenient means of testing theories originally developed to explain human forgetting. Three major theoretical accounts of forgetting are reviewed.

Decay Theory

A decay theory of forgetting in working memory was discussed in Chapter 4, and it was shown that more active views of working memory have replaced this relatively passive conceptualization. In working memory, decay was presented as a rapid loss of trace strength over a period of seconds. When applied to reference memory, the notion of decay has usually referred to the gradual erosion of some biological substrate of memory, such as a change in biochemistry or the elimination of synaptic connections. Such a theory suggests that a rat, having learned to traverse a complex maze, forgets how to respond in the maze over a period of days because the neural basis for maze memory is being constantly modified.

Decay has not been a generally popular explanation for human forgetting, and its lack of popularity can be traced to McGeoch's (1932) attack on the law of disuse. McGeoch argued that to attribute forgetting to the passage of time did little more than describe the forgetting function and was vacuous as an explanatory concept. Of course, decay is meant to refer to not just the passage of time but to physiological processes correlated with time. To find evidence for a decay theory, one must first identify the relevant biological processes responsible for decay and then demonstrate that speeding up or slowing down those processes affects memory. This is a daunting task because one would have to know what biological processes code memory. On the other hand, McGeoch and other members of the functionalist school demonstrated that very rapid forgetting could be produced by introducing new learning, which generates interference. A person learning a list of verbal items could be made to forget a great deal over a 24-hour retention interval simply by requiring the subject to learn other verbal materials either prior to the target list, causing PI, or after the target list, causing RI. Furthermore, laws based on generalization and competition were worked out to account for variations in interference. Given these powerful effects of interference on forgetting, it is no wonder that behavioral psychology turned away from decay in favor of interference.

Some theorists have still entertained decay as a process responsible for forgetting in both people (Wickelgren, 1972) and animals (Gleitman, 1971). There is some evidence that reducing body temperature, and presumably physiological activity, during a retention interval slows down the process of forgetting. Most of this work has been done with cold-blooded animals. French (1942) trained goldfish to swim through a maze to escape from strong illumination and join the company of other goldfish. After goldfish learned to swim through the maze with few errors, different groups of fish were maintained for 24 hours at temperatures of 4°C, 16°C, and 28°C. When retention was measured, the 4°C group was consistently superior to the 16°C group, which, in turn, was better than the 28°C group. Alloway (1969) trained grain beetles to turn right or left in a T-maze and then kept animals at cold or warm temperatures during retention intervals of 2 or 10 days. Animals kept in the warm temperature showed loss of performance between 2 and 10 days, but animals kept in cold actually showed improvement in performance between 2 and 10 days. Finally, McNamara and Riedesel (1973) exposed ground squirrels to temperatures ranging from 7°C to 10°C after the squirrels learned to choose either a black or a white alley to escape from water. During retention intervals lasting up to 21 days, some squirrels entered a state of hibernation, while others did not. Retention tests showed that those squirrels that hibernated retained the correct response better than those that did not hibernate.

These findings are interesting, but it is difficult to use them as evidence of a memory decay process. Although a decay theorist might argue that lowering body temperature or entering a state of hibernation slows the biological processes responsible for erosion of the memory trace, theorists of other persuasions have alternative accounts. Interference from other behaviors could be reduced by low temperatures or hibernation, which limits activity, whereas warm temperatures do not have this effect. Therefore, animals kept under warm conditions during the retention interval may acquire interfering responses, while animals kept in the cold do not. Theorists who feel that forgetting is primarily caused by retrieval failure may argue that memory stays intact over the retention interval regardless of temperature but that normal growth processes are inhibited by cold but not warmth. To the extent that these growth processes have taken place, internal retrieval cues that were present during learning have changed, thus leading to retrieval failure. Animals kept in the cold may have more access to original retrieval cues and thus show a higher level of retention. Studies of the effects of temperature on retention are theoretically ambiguous and do not therefore provide strong support for a decay process.

Interference Theory

Interference theory refers to a set of mechanisms that were designed to explain forgetting found in human verbal learning experiments. Typically, a person was asked to memorize by rote a list of words or nonsense materials and was given a retention test at some later time. Retention was studied as a function of such variables as the number of lists learned before or after the target list, the length of the retention interval, and the similarity of materials on the target list to those on interfering lists. Some of the mechanisms postulated to account for interference effects were response competition, unlearning, spontaneous recovery of unlearned associations, and list differentiation. These mechanisms received varying degrees of emphasis as the theory evolved between the 1930s and 1960s. Around 1960, a major effort was made to extend interference theory as an account of everyday forgetting by showing that previously learned language habits act as a source of PI for recent verbal learning. This extension of interference theory proved to be largely unsuccessful (Postman, 1961; Underwood & Postman, 1960).

Although interference theory was applied to animal retention, either to test mechanisms of forgetting suggested by studies with human subjects or as an explanation of animal forgetting, its success was rather limited. As Spear (1978) pointed out, there are certain difficulties with the extension of interference theory to animal research. A major factor is the obvious fact that animals do not possess spoken language. Interference theory was developed as a means of accounting for the transfer and forgetting of verbal learning, and structural and semantic similarities between verbal items were important variables. The extension of a language-based theory to animals may be inappropriate. In animal conditioning experiments, the important attributes of a target memory are the nature of the CS, the US, discriminative cues, response, reward, and the context in which learning occurs. The extension of theoretical laws developed with verbal materials to these types of stimuli used with animals is not necessarily appropriate. Another problem created by the language barrier is that we cannot instruct animals as easily as we can people. After learning several lists of items, a person can be instructed to recall the first, middle, or final list. With animals, we must rely on the animal's tendency to perform the most recently learned behavior, or we must use elaborate conditional cuing techniques to probe memory of earlier behavior.

Although the application of interference theory to long-term retention in animals is problematic, there is no doubt that experimentally programmed interference can produce substantial drops in performance. In particular, animals learning successive competing responses often show dramatic PI over extended retention intervals. The Kraemer (1984) data on PI in pigeon memory shown in Figure 6.2 are a good example. However, more recent developments in theories about animal reference memory emphasize the role of interference as a secondary factor producing forgetting. A previously learned response may interfere with the performance of a more recently learned conflicting response to the extent that the first response is remembered. Proactive interference will arise from retention of the competing response, but the extent to which the competing response is remembered is held to be determined by the number of appropriate cues provided for its retrieval. This approach suggests that the fundamental processes of retention and forgetting are retrieval and its failure, and interference is a consequence of these more fundamental mechanisms.

Retrieval Failure

The activities of learning and remembering information often are divided into three component parts: encoding, storage, and retrieval. Both decay and interference theory emphasize storage as the critical stage for forgetting. According to decay theory, traces erode while in storage. Interference theory proposes that associations are unlearned and then spontaneously recovered while in storage. A theory that emphasizes retrieval failure, on the other hand, deemphasizes changes in stored information. Although memories remain *available* in an unaltered state, it is their *accessibility* or retrievability that determines retention (Spear, 1973; Tulving & Pearlstone, 1966). A failure to *express* what is stored in memory is emphasized as being responsible for forgetting (R. Miller & Grahame, 1991; Spear, 1981; Spear, Miller & Jagielo, 1990; Spear & Riccio, 1994). Whether a memory will be retrieved or not critically depends on an interaction between cues encoded and cues present on a retention test. This interaction is best understood by the principle of *encoding specificity* (Tulving, 1983; Tulving & Thompson, 1973). The principle suggests that the encoding of any event into memory includes a number of attributes or cues associated with the event. Retrieval of memory of that event at some later time is facilitated to the extent that the context of the retention test provides cues that are identical to those originally encoded.

In a number of articles and a book, Spear (1971; 1973; 1976; 1978; 1981) emphasizes the importance of retrieval and encoding specificity for reference memory in animals. He suggests that the attributes stored in conjunction with the target memory are multidimensional and are representations of both environmental stimuli and internal physiological stimuli. In a learning experiment, the environmental stimuli include those events directly involved with the procedure, such as the discriminative stimuli, the response, and reward or aversive stimulation. In addition to these specific events, attributes of the context in which learning takes place may be encoded. These might include the shape of the apparatus, the color of its walls, and the presence of any ambient stimuli, such as a houselight or a constant sound. Attributes provided by internal states of an organism may include motivational cues (hunger, thirst, pain), hormonally induced states, and drug states.

The principle of encoding specificity holds that the more these external and internal cues can reinstate the cognitive conditions present at the time a memory was encoded, the better the memory is and the more the memory is expressed in the animal's behavior. Environmental cues may be reproduced fairly easily; an animal is put back in the conditioning chamber, and the stimuli used in conditioning may be presented. Internal states may be manipulated but may be more difficult to reinstate with precision, and disparities between the internally coded attributes and those present on a retention test may be an important source of forgetting. For example, it may be impossible to reproduce the exact degree of hunger, thirst, sexual arousal, amount of hormones in the blood stream, etc., that existed at the time an animal learned to perform some behavior. Deviations from those training conditions may increase with time after training and lead to increasingly severe retrieval failure. So-called normal forgetting, or progressive loss of retention with the passage of time, may be explained within a retrieval failure framework by progressive modification of internal states. However, an important implication of retrieval theory is that there is no fixed curve of forgetting for a particular animal or a particular task. Degree of retention primarily depends on the effectiveness of retrieval cues presented on a retention test and not on the passage of time.

In a sense, the foregoing discussion may seem trivial. Any student of animal learning knows that animals are most likely to perform what they have learned in the past when the conditions used in training are reintroduced. The principle of stimulus generalization covered in Chapter 5 tells us that animals suffer progressive decrement in performance as the testing stimuli are made more dissimilar to the training stimuli. These observations are often described as changes in stimulus control. The concept of stimulus control has been at the heart of learning theories and is a basic reason such theories have seen little need for the process of memory. If it is assumed that in some way stimuli serve to directly produce behavior, then losses in performance with changes in external and internal stimuli may represent loss of stimulus control over behavior, with no need for an intermediate concept of memory.

The problem with attributing retention or loss of behavior to stimulus control is that predictable changes in performance can be found in the absence of changes in the "controlling" stimuli. It can be shown that exposing animals to some aspect of a previous training situation (*reactivation*) before a retention test leads to better retention than that observed in a control group not given a reactivation treatment. Reactivation treatments may consist of exposure to the CS or the US alone or simply of placement in the conditioning context for a few minutes. A number of examples of reactivation effects are presented in the remainder of this chapter.

A final point concerns the scope of the theoretical framework that emphasizes a process of retrieval. Although this section dealt with retrieval failure as a theory of forgetting, it should be clear that retrieval is concerned with the causes of both remembering and forgetting in animals. By contrast, decay and interference theories mainly emphasized the question of forgetting. By stressing the importance of encoding and its interaction with the retrieval context, retrieval-based models seem to address a broader range of questions about memory.

DIRECT REACTIVATION OF MEMORY

Direct reactivation experiments usually involve the presentation of some aspect of the original learning situation during the retention interval. Performance on a retention test is compared with that of a control group not given the reactivation treatment. Superior performance by the reactivated group is taken as evidence that memory of original learning was retrieved.

In a well-controlled reactivation experiment, Spear and Parsons (1976) placed rats in a white compartment and presented a 7-second flashing light 30 times, each time delivering a footshock during the final 2 seconds. This procedure should be recognized as Pavlovian fear conditioning with the flashing light as the CS and the shock as the US. After a 28-day retention interval passed, memory of fear conditioning was measured using an active avoidance procedure. Rats were placed in the white chamber with only a hurdle separating this chamber from a black one. The light CS, but not the US, was presented, and the speed with which a rat crossed from the white side to the black side was measured; we can assume that the faster an animal crossed to the black side the better it remembered the original fear conditioning. Three groups of rats were tested, one being a control group that was simply trained and tested 28 days later. A reactivation group was given a single presentation of the footshock US in a separate apparatus 24 hours before the retention test. A second control group was never given the original Pavlovian conditioning but was given the US reactivation treatment and tested for avoidance 24 hours later.

In Figure 6.3, the findings of this experiment are shown as reciprocal latency, or speed of response, so that higher scores reflect better retention. The data show quite clearly that the animals that were trained and reactivated crossed the hurdle into the "safe" white compartment very rapidly after the first five trials of testing. The two control groups showed little evidence of retention throughout testing. Since reactivation consisted of a single footshock given 24 hours before testing in another apparatus, the possibility that new learning could account for the reactivation effect is virtually nil. Furthermore, because the footshock was administered 24 hours before testing, any immediate effect of aversive stimulation on behavior should have had time to dissipate. The possibility that unconditioned effects of the US could persist over 24 hours and perhaps produce a fast response through hyperactivity is further

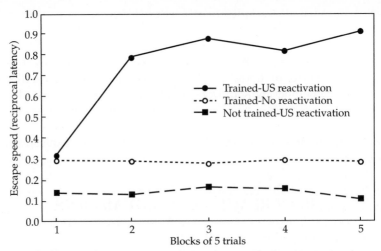

FIGURE 6.3. Speed of escape from a white chamber in which rats previously experienced a flashing light CS and a footshock US. The reactivation treatment was delivery of footshock in a different chamber 24 hours prior to testing.

ruled out by the control group given the US with no prior training. The findings suggest that the footshock given 24 hours before testing served as a potent reactivation cue that retrieved memory of the earlier fear conditioning and thus promoted speedy escape behavior on the avoidance test.

Although most reactivation effects have been seen in tasks in which aversive stimulation and avoidance behavior were employed, reactivation of choice behavior with food reinforcers has been shown. Hamberg and Spear (1978) trained rats to enter the bright or dark arm of a T-maze to escape from shock and tested retention 28 days later. A reactivation group was given shocks alone in a neutral chamber on the 27th day of the retention interval and subsequently showed stronger avoidance of the shocked side of the T-maze than animals not given the reactivation treatment. In a second experiment, Hamberg and Spear trained rats to enter the left or right compartment of a two-choice discrimination apparatus in order to obtain food reward. On Day 27 of the retention interval, one group of rats was given a reactivation treatment that consisted of running down a central alley in the discrimination apparatus for food, but with no choice allowed. Retention tests on Day 28 showed significantly better performance in reactivated animals than in nonreactivated controls. In one other example, DeWeer, Sara, and Hars (1980) trained rats to run accurately through a multiple-choice maze for a food reward and then tested retention 31 days later. As a reactivation treatment, some animals were placed beside the maze, in a wire cage, for 90 seconds before the retention test. These animals showed better retention of the correct maze pathway than control rats not given reactivation. It should be noted than none of the reactivation treatments used in these experiments allowed animals to perform the originally learned choice behaviors; nevertheless, memory of original learning was clearly reactivated in each case.

Table 6.1 shows the distinction made here between memory and its expression. The columns of this 2×2 table indicate the cue condition under which learning took place, Cue A or Cue B. The rows indicate the cue condition present at testing. The cells of the table tell us that retention is good only when the cues at learning and testing match one another. If these cues mismatch, then retention is poor. The table stresses the importance of encoding specificity or that cues encoded at the time of a memory's formation serve best to retrieve the memory. It also makes an important distinction between learning and performance. Animals in both cells of the Cue A column and both cells of the Cue B column learned the same thing or stored the same memory after training. However, what was learned or stored in memory is only expressed if matching cues are present that can retrieve the appropriate memory.

Interestingly, a number of standard findings from the animal learning laboratory underwent reinterpretation recently. Variation in behavior as a consequence of training or exposure to stimuli was traditionally explained as a product of differences in associative strength. Stronger performance reflected stronger association, and weaker performance reflected weaker association. New findings suggest that, in many cases, differences in learned behavior reflect more the expression or retrieval of what was learned rather than differences in degree of learning. The following are some examples that support the importance of retrieval for understanding learning phenomena.

Warmup Decrement

The phenomenon of warmup has been observed for years in both people and animals. It refers to the observation that performance at the beginning of a training session is often worse than it was at the end of the preceding session but improves rapidly after the initial trials or responses of the session. The initial loss of performance is referred to as *warmup decrement*. The effect has been found with human subjects both in studies of rote verbal learning (Irion, 1949; Irion & Wham, 1951) and in studies of motor learning (Adams, 1961; Ammons, 1947).

Warmup decrement was also noted in a number of experiments with animals. Pavlovian conditioned responses were weak or absent on the initial trials

TABLE 6.1 Design of Memory Experiments that Show the Importance of Encoding Specificity

| | | Learning Cues | |
		Cue A	Cue B
Testing Cues	Cue A	Good retention	Poor retention
	Cue B	Poor retention	Good retention

of a session, but they were stronger as trials progressed both in acquisition (Schlosberg, 1934; 1936) and extinction (Hilgard & Marquis, 1935). Instrumental responses for food rewards showed warmup effects; improvement in performance over the initial trials of extinction were found with rats using both a bar-press response (Ellson, 1938) and runway running (Finger, 1942). Dramatic warmup effects were seen in avoidance conditioning experiments with rats. Nakamura and Anderson (1962) trained rats to avoid shock by turning a wheel within 5 seconds after the onset of a tone CS. Frequency of avoidance responses increased within sessions from less than 20 percent on initial CS presentations to more than 40 percent on later CS presentations.

The term "warmup" was borrowed from the field of athletics and suggests loosening muscles, taking practice throws, etc. Theories of warmup in human motor learning suggest that improvement within a session arises from the extinction of competing responses (Adams, 1961) or from the subject learning to set himself for the task by making adjustments in attention, receptor orientation, and posture or position of the muscles (Irion, 1948). In animals, it is suggested that warmup effects in avoidance conditioning arise from the growth of fear during a conditioning session (Nakamura & Anderson, 1962; Hoffman, Fleshler, & Chorny, 1961). To account for warmup in appetitive reward situations, we need to assume the growth of incentive motivation over the early trials of a session. A troublesome problem with these accounts is that warmup effects have been observed during successive extinction sessions when no reinforcers are delivered to induce motivational states (Ellson, 1938; Finger, 1942; Hilgard & Marquis, 1935).

Spear (1973; 1978) argued in favor of a retrieval interpretation of warmup. He suggested that the decrement found on the early trials of a session represents a brief lapse in the memory of previous training. Initial trials provide exposure to the apparatus, training stimuli, and reinforcer and thereby serve to retrieve memories that improve performance. One implication of this theoretical analysis is that reactivation treatments introduced just prior to a session should alleviate warmup decrement. In fact, Hoffman et al. (1961) demonstrated that initial delivery of unsignalled shocks eliminated warmup decrement in discriminated bar-press avoidance training. In a well-controlled study, Spear, Gordon, and Martin (1973) showed that a single footshock given in an apparatus separate from the avoidance training apparatus before testing eliminated the warmup decrement seen in animals that were not given a reactivation treatment.

If trials within an experimental session are widely spaced, it seems possible that forgetting might occur between trials and that warmup might occur on every trial. R. Miller (1982) trained rats over repeated trials to run a multiple-choice maze either to escape from footshock or to obtain sucrose solution in the goal box. The experiment continued for eight trials, with a 5-minute interval between trials. Three groups of rats were trained with escape from footshock as the reinforcer, and three groups were trained with sucrose as the reinforcer. Each group was given two identical treatments, one midway between Trials 3 and 4 and a second midway between Trials 4 and 5. Animals in each group were taken from the maze apparatus and placed in a different apparatus for 30 seconds. Control groups in the footshock (FS-H) and sucrose (S-H) reinforcer conditions were simply left in the treatment apparatus for 30 seconds and returned to the maze. Treatment groups were exposed to the reinforcers used in the maze for 30 seconds. Thus, animals reinforced with escape from footshock received footshock (FS-FS) or sucrose (FS-S), and animals reinforced with sucrose also received footshock (S-FS) or sucrose (S-S).

Learning curves for each group are shown in the two graphs in Figure 6.4. Note that beginning with Trial 4, Groups FS-FS and S-S show a drop in error rate, indicating faster learning than the other groups. The delivery of a reinforcer between trials enhanced rate of learning relative to the absence of a reinforcer (FS-H and S-H). However, the reinforcer was effective only if it was the

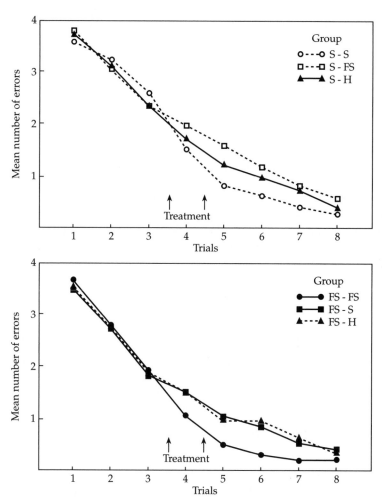

FIGURE 6.4. Learning curves for rats trained in a multiple-choice maze shown as a reduction in turning errors over eight trials. Groups in the upper graph were trained with a sucrose (S) reinforcer, and groups in the lower graph were trained with escape from footshock (FS) as a reinforcer. Memory reactivation treatments occurred between Trials 3 and 4 and between Trials 4 and 5.

same reinforcer as that used in the maze; Groups FS-S and S-FS showed no improvement in learning relative to the control groups. Miller argued that forgetting took place over 5-minute retention intervals and was reactivated by delivery of the relevant reinforcer. These findings may be viewed as the alleviation of a short-term warmup decrement that occurred over 5-minute intertrial intervals. The finding that only the relevant reinforcer alleviated warmup decrement further supports the idea that retrieval cues that match memory attributes of the learning task best retrieve forgotten memories.

Extinction and Spontaneous Recovery

Table 6.2 illustrates the designs for producing several of the learning phenomena discussed in Chapter 5. One of these, extinction of a Pavlovian CR, is produced by presenting the CS without the US, causing the CR to progressively weaken over extinction trials. Although it appears that the CR is lost when extinction is complete, the phenomenon of *spontaneous recovery* shows that the CR reappears after a time period of a day or more has elapsed. How can a response that has been unlearned or eliminated spontaneously recover? Within the framework of a retrieval theory (Spear, 1971; Kraemer & Spear, 1993), it is suggested that memory of the originally learned response is not unlearned by extinction. Rather, its retrievability is temporarily depressed by nonreinforcement. During a period of nonreinforced responding, a new memory is formed (the extinction memory), and retrieval of this memory is dominant immediately after extinction took place. However, with the passage of time, an animal's ability to retrieve memory of the conditioned response returns, and expression of that memory is seen in spontaneous recovery of the response.

Within a model of memory retrieval, Kraemer and Spear (1993) formalized these ideas by proposing that memories of learning and extinction have sepa-

TABLE 6.2 Experimental Designs Used to Produce Four Different Learning Phenomena

Group	Stage 1	Stage 2	Retention Test
		EXTINCTION AND SPONTANEOUS RECOVERY	
	CS→Reinforcer	CS alone	CS alone
		LATENT INHIBITION	
Experiment	CS alone	CS→Reinforcer	CS alone
Control	—	CS→Reinforcer	CS alone
		OVERSHADOWING	
Experiment	CS XY→Reinforcer	CS Y alone	
Control	CS Y→Reinforcer	CS Y alone	
		BLOCKING	
Experiment	CS X→Reinforcer	CS XY→Reinforcer	CS Y alone
Control	—	CS XY→Reinforcer	CS Y alone

rate activation thresholds. Sufficient attributes of either memory must be activated to exceed that memory's threshold, leading to remembering and performance of the behavior directed by that memory. Extinction training has the effect of lowering the activation threshold for memory of extinction while raising the activation threshold for memory of original learning. Once extinction is terminated, however, the activation threshold for memory of the conditioned response drops over time, leading to spontaneous recovery. Kraemer and Spear further suggest that memories of biologically significant events, such as reinforced responses, quickly regain ascendancy over memories of less biological significance, such as the absence of reinforcement.

If learning and memory establish separate memories that are independently retrievable, it should be possible to reinstate acquisition or extinction behaviors through the use of contextual cues. A test of this implication was carried out in a study of conditioned suppression by Bouton and King (1983). Two conditioning chambers labeled Contexts A and B differed in their visual appearance and smell. Three groups of rats were trained to press a bar for food pellets in Context A. Once animals pressed the bar at a high rate for the food reward, they were given Pavlovian fear conditioning by presenting a tone for 60 seconds and delivering a footshock during the final 0.5 second of the tone. After 15 tone shock pairings, subjects showed almost no bar pressing when the tone was presented. Conditioned fear of the tone suppressed the instrumental response of bar pressing. On subsequent sessions, the conditioned fear response was extinguished in two groups by presenting the tone 20 times without delivering the shock. One of these groups was extinguished in Context A (Ext A), and the other group was extinguished in Context B (Ext B). The third group was not extinguished (NE). The two curves on the left side of Figure 6.5 show the rise in the suppression ratios and indicate that Groups Ext A and Ext B extinguished at the same rate.

After the completion of extinction, all three groups were placed in Context A and given four presentations of the tone without shock. Response suppression

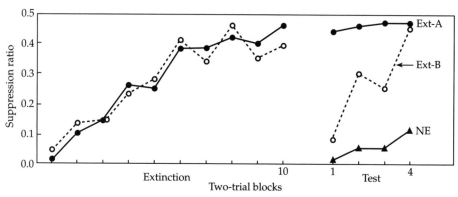

FIGURE 6.5. The curves on the left show the extinction of a Pavlovian conditioned fear response by the loss of its suppressive effect on bar pressing. The curves on the right show the renewal effect by the return of conditioned suppression in the Ext B group but not the Ext A group.

on these tone presentations is shown on the right side of Figure 6.5. Group NE animals, the control group, continued to show strong suppression, indicating no loss of conditioning without extinction. The Ext A subjects continued to bar press with little suppression, showing the effects of extinction. Group Ext B rats, however, strongly suppressed bar pressing on the initial tone presentation and only gradually increased bar pressing as further tones were presented in the absence of shock. Even though fear of the tone CS was virtually eliminated by extinction in Context B, fear of the CS immediately reappeared when the CS was presented in Context A. Bouton (1991) refers to this outcome as the *renewal effect*. Fear of an extinguished CS is renewed when the conditioning context is reinstated. He suggests that the CS–fear association forms a memory that is context specific. In Group Ext B, the B context retrieves memory of an extinguished or safe CS, but the A context retrieves memory of a fearful or dangerous CS. Quite independent memories of acquisition and extinction then can be retrieved by the appropriate contexts.

Latent Inhibition

Suppose the order of experimental stages used in a conditioning and extinction procedure is reversed as shown in the second procedure in Table 6.2. That is, an animal is first exposed to a nonreinforced CS and then is given presentations of the CS followed by a reinforcer. This operation may seem pointless because the CS has not acquired any conditioned properties before its initial presentation. Nevertheless, initial presentation of a CS alone acts to retard the subsequent acquisition of a CR when the CS is presented with a reinforcer. This fact has been established by comparing a group conditioned after preexposure to the CS with a control group that learns to perform the CR with no preexposure to the CS. The control group learns significantly faster than the preexposure group. The inhibitory effect of CS preexposure on subsequent conditioning has been labeled *latent inhibition* (Lubow, 1973; Lubow & Moore, 1959).

Initial explanations of latent inhibition suggested that preexposure to the CS acts to weaken associations with the CS formed on subsequent conditioning trials, either through competition from CS–context associations (Wagner, 1976) or through a loss of attention to the CS (Mackintosh, 1975). Once again, however, there is evidence to suggest that failure of retrieval rather than failure of learning may be responsible for latent inhibition. One such observation is the finding that latent inhibition may disappear when a retention interval is placed between the end of conditioning and some subsequent test. Several examples of this effect have been found in taste aversion conditioning experiments (Kraemer & Roberts, 1984; Kraemer & Spear, 1992). Rats allowed to drink a substance with a distinct flavor, such as saccharin, and then injected with a drug that makes them ill temporarily show aversion to the saccharin substance on a test given after recovery from the effects of the drug. If rats are preexposed to the CS or even to a different CS, such as apple juice, prior to conditioning, aversion to the CS is reduced relative to a control group given no CS preexposure. This latent inhibition effect appears on a test given 1 day after conditioning. On a test given 21 days after conditioning, however, the latent inhibition effect disappeared, because both the group preexposed to the CS and the control group consume the same amount of the saccharin solution. This effect, called *release from latent inhibition,* is seen clearly in Figure 6.6.

Suppose that the strong latent inhibition of conditioning to the CS seen after one day in the preexposed group were caused by a failure to form an association between the CS and sickness. The subsequent appearance of a strong aversion to the CS in the preexposed group after 21 days is then difficult to understand because associations presumably do not grow in strength over time. As an alternative account, we may assume that preexposure and conditioning established separate memories, with preexposure leading to the memory that nothing follows the CS (Bouton, 1991) and conditioning leading to the memory that illness follows the CS. Retrieval of the preexposure memory suggests to an animal that it is safe to consume the CS, and retrieval of the conditioning memory suggests that it is dangerous to consume the CS. Kraemer and Spear (1993) hold that at a 1-day retention test, the activation thresholds of both of these memories are low and that both will be retrieved. The effect will be that an animal perceives the CS as somewhat safe and somewhat dangerous and consumes more of the CS than a control animal that only retrieves the memory of conditioning. With the passage of a 21-day interval, the activation threshold of the more biologically significant memory of conditioning drops below that of the less significant memory of preexposure, and the consequence is that presentation of saccharin retrieves only memory of conditioning. Release from latent inhibition as seen in the equivalent aversions to saccharine after 21 days in Figure 6.6 is the result of this shift in retrievability of memories.

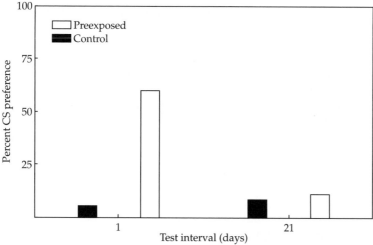

FIGURE 6.6. The two bars on the left show preference for the saccharin-flavored CS 1 day after conditioning. A strong latent inhibition effect is shown by the difference between the preexposed group and the control group. The bars on the right show that the latent inhibition effect has disappeared after 21 days; both groups show a strong aversion to saccharin.

There is also evidence that memory for a CR reduced by latent inhibition can be alleviated by a memory reactivation treatment given outside the conditioning context. Kasprow, Catterson, Schachtman, and Miller (1984) presented a white noise followed by footshock to rats. The white noise CS became a conditioned fear stimulus; even though the rats were thirsty, presentation of the white noise suppressed their water-licking behavior. If the white noise had been preexposed to rats before its pairing with footshock, however, the degree of conditioned suppression was reduced relative to a control group, showing latent inhibition. On a retention test, a group of rats that had gone through the preexposure followed by conditioning sequence was given a reactivation treatment of a single footshock in a different context. When they were returned to the conditioning context and presented with the CS, these subjects showed suppression equivalent to that seen in animals given no preexposure to the CS. In other words, the reactivation treatment eliminated the latent inhibition effect. Kasprow et al. concluded that latent inhibition arose primarily from a failure to completely retrieve the conditioning episode and not from a failure to completely learn the conditioning episode. A reactivation or reminder treatment serves to fully activate memory of conditioning events.

Overshadowing

As shown in the third procedure in Table 6.2 and described in Chapter 5, overshadowing refers to conditioning with a compound CS consisting of the simultaneous presentation of two stimuli, X and Y, with Stimulus X stronger or more salient to the animal than Stimulus Y. After conditioning to the compound is complete, X and Y are presented separately to determine how strong a CR is elicited by each stimulus. The typical finding is that Stimulus X elicits a strong response, and Stimulus Y elicits only a weak response. A control group conditioned with Stimulus Y alone shows a stronger response to Stimulus Y than do the animals trained with the compound.

One common account for overshadowing is to suggest that Stimuli X and Y compete for association with the US and that the stronger X stimulus wins out and obtains most of the associative strength. Therefore, little is learned about the relationship between Stimulus Y and the US. With this explanation of overshadowing in mind, the results of an experiment by Kasprow, Cacheiro, Balaz and Miller (1982) are surprising. Using a lick suppression procedure, Kasprow et al. showed that a tone presented in a light-tone combination CS overshadowed the light stimulus; as measured by lick suppression, rats showed little fear of the light and strong fear of the tone. Following conditioning with the combination, a group of animals was given a reminder treatment that consisted of the presentation of the overshadowed light CS in a chamber separate from the conditioning chamber. On a subsequent test, the reminded rats showed as much suppression to the light CS as did control animals trained with the light CS alone. This sudden disappearance of overshadowing caused by a reminder treatment argues that intact associations are formed during conditioning between the weaker member of a combination CS and the US. The weak response seen to the overshadowed CS may represent a retrieval failure that can be reversed by a reminder treatment.

Blocking

The blocking experiment described in Chapter 5 is shown as the fourth procedure in Table 6.2. Recall that blocking involves an experimental group and a control group. The experimental group is first conditioned by presenting Stimulus X as a CS paired with a reinforcer. In a second stage, the experimental group has Stimulus X put in combination with a new stimulus, Stimulus Y, and the XY compound is paired with the reinforcer. The control group is given only Stage 2 conditioning. When the strength of response to Stimulus Y is subsequently measured, the experimental group shows a far weaker response than the control group.

As the name "blocking" implies, it appears that this phenomenon arises from the association formed initially between Stimulus X and the US, which blocks the formation of a new association between Stimulus Y and the US. According to the Rescorla-Wagner (1972) theory described in Chapter 5, all of the associative strength or expectancy of the US is accumulated by Stimulus X, and none is left to condition it to Stimulus Y in Stage 2. In another explanation of blocking, Mackintosh (1975) suggests that subjects ignore or pay no attention to Stimulus Y and thus form no association between it and the US.

As was the case with overshadowing, recent experimental findings lead us to question the notion that little or no association was formed between Stimulus Y and the US. When conditioned lick suppression was used as a measure of fear conditioning, it was shown that initial conditioning with tone-footshock pairings blocks subsequent conditioning to a light CS when a light-tone compound is paired with footshock. However, the presentation of reminder treatments after compound conditioning led to *unblocking*; that is, on postreminder tests, rats showed strong suppression of licking when the light CS appeared, revealing a learned association between light and the US (Balaz, Gutsin, Cacheiro, & Miller, 1982; Schachtman, Gee, Kasprow, & Miller, 1983). Furthermore, a variety of reminder cues produced this effect; these included placement in the conditioning chamber, exposure to the light CS in a different chamber, and delivery of the shock US in a different chamber.

These findings from overshadowing and blocking experiments point out the importance of retrieval. Associations may be formed between both members of a compound stimulus and a US, but the stronger or previously conditioned member of the compound may act in some way to interfere with retrieval of the other member of the compound. This interference is not permanent, however, and can be reversed through the delivery of reminder cues.

STATE-DEPENDENT MEMORY

A friend of mine, who is an actor, recently told me a story about a theater company in which she once acted. In a production of *Hamlet,* a problem arose when the leading man found difficulty in remembering the lines to the soliloquies. This actor had no difficulties with the lines in rehearsals, but during actual performances, he might begin with, "To be or not to be," and then suffer an excruciating pause as he silently groped for the next line. This silence was an embarrassment to the company and to the audience since virtually everyone else in the house knew the next line. I was puzzled by this lapse of memory until my friend explained further that the actor had an attack of stage fright before each performance and had several drinks to calm his nerves. A possible explanation for his failure of retention then became apparent. He rehearsed the play in a sober state but then attempted to perform it in an inebriated state. He may have fallen victim to *state-dependent memory,* or an inability to remember in one state what was learned in a different state.

In a number of experiments, it has been observed that animals trained to perform a behavior in one state may show little or no retention of that behavior when tested in an alternate state. A subject's state is usually altered by the administration of a drug, and state change may involve going from a nondrug state to a drug state or from a drug state to a nondrug state. The design of many of these experiments is shown in Table 6.1, if we substitute Drug Condition for Cue A and Nondrug Condition for Cue B.

In an early study, Girden and Culler (1937) conditioned leg flexion in dogs in a nondrug state and subsequently found that the animals did not respond to the CS when they were tested under the influence of curare. A paralytic effect of curare might produce this effect, but dogs were still capable of responding to the US while drugged. More impressive was the further demonstration that dogs conditioned while drugged with curare showed no retention of conditioning when tested in a nondrugged state.

Overton (1964) carried out an interesting study of drug discrimination. Rats were placed in a T-maze and had to learn to enter the correct arm to escape from footshock. Two training trials were given on each day. On one trial, the rat was not drugged and had to turn right to escape shock. On the other trial, the rat was injected with sodium pentobarbital and had to turn left to escape shock. A nondrugged control group had to learn only to turn right, and a drugged control group learned only to turn left. In Figure 6.7, the upper curves for animals trained nondrugged and the lower curves for animals tested while drugged tell the same story; both the experimental and control animals learned the correct response at the same rate. If the experimental rats had remembered the right turn in the drugged state or the left turn in the nondrugged state, interference with learning should have occurred. Instead, these findings show complete dissociation between the drugged and nondrugged states. Experimental rats that learned to turn right in the nondrugged state showed no memory of this learning when trained to turn left in the drugged state, and vice versa.

One explanation of drug dissociation effects is that drugs alter perception of the environment, and different perceptions in drug and nondrug conditions gain control of behavior. Evidence seems to contradict this interpretation. Tests carried out with peripherally acting drugs that may alter peripheral receptors are generally ineffective in producing drug-dissociation effects. Drugs that pass the blood-brain barrier and affect the central nervous system are the most potent sources of dissociation effects. Anesthetics and addictive drugs produce state-dependent effects. Virtually all drugs abused by people have been shown experimentally to have strong dissociative properties.

These observations suggest that drugs produce distinctive central states that act as retrieval cues for memories (Eich, 1977, 1980; Spear, 1978). Highly discriminable states produced by drugs become attributes of memories

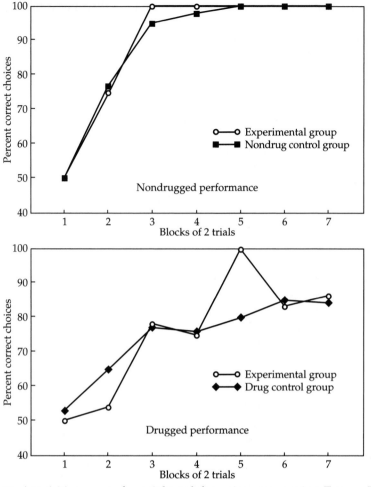

FIGURE 6.7. Acquisition curves for a right or left turning response in a T-maze. The experimental group learned different responses in drugged and nondrugged states, and the control groups learned only one response under either the drugged or nondrugged states.

acquired during the period the subject is under the influence of the drug. When the drug wears off, the current cues may overlap so little with attributes of memories stored in the drug state that retrieval is not possible. When the drug is reinstated, appropriate retrieval cues are available again, and the behavior based on the drug memory returns. Similarly, subjects trained in a nondrug state may have no access to memories acquired in that state when central cues are drastically changed by drug administration.

The Kamin Effect

Normal forgetting is seen in the traditional forgetting curve, in which retention drops monotonically or consistently as the retention interval becomes longer. It was then a considerable surprise when Leon Kamin discovered that rats' memory for avoidance conditioning followed a very different course (Kamin, 1957). Kamin used a shuttle box to condition rats to respond to a buzzer CS by crossing the box within 5 seconds to avoid shock from the grid floor. After 25 training trials, rats were returned to their home cages. Rats that had learned the avoidance response were divided into different groups for retention testing. These groups were returned to the apparatus for a relearning retention test either 0, 0.5, 1, 6, or 24 hours, or 19 days after original learning. Retention at these intervals can be seen in Figure 6.8, with the best retention shown by the highest number of avoidance responses made. This retention curve appears U-shaped; retention was best on an immediate test or after 19 days and was worst at intermediate intervals, particularly after 1 hour. This strange nonmonotonic retention curve, known as the *Kamin effect,* has been found in numerous laboratories, with the retention trough usually appearing between 1 and 4 hours after original conditioning.

Theoretical accounts of the Kamin effect fall into two general categories. One type of explanation suggests that animals become relatively immobilized or unable to cope with avoidance contingencies a few hours after learning. It was suggested that fear might grow or incubate over the first few hours after learning and lead to freezing behavior on a retention test (Denny & Ditchman, 1962). In another account, Anisman (1975) held that a depletion of brain neurotransmitters or catecholamines took place after learning and that the behavioral consequence of these changes was response inhibition and poor performance on avoidance retention tests at intermediate intervals. At longer intervals, both explanations assumed that an animal returns to its normal state and is able to show retention of the avoidance response.

As an alternative account of the Kamin effect, Klein and Spear (1969; 1970a; 1970b) emphasized the importance of memory retrieval mechanisms. For them,

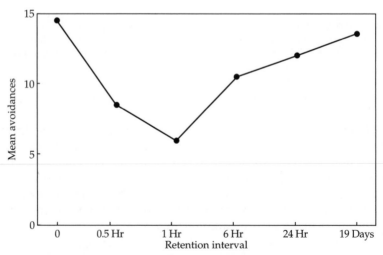

FIGURE 6.8. The Kamin effect is shown by the U-shaped retention curve for avoidance conditioning measured over retention intervals from 1 minute to 19 days. *Adapted from Kamin, 1957.*

the key to understanding the Kamin effect is the immediate physiological response of the subject to the stress of avoidance conditioning. They argue that fluctuations in hormones and neurotransmitters alter the internal cues, which were present at the time that avoidance was learned, to such a degree that little access to memory of original learning is possible at intermediate retention intervals. As the stress reaction wears off, internal cues similar to those present during learning return, and retrieval is again possible. This theory explains the Kamin effect as a form of state-dependent memory, with the state change arising from endogenous chemical change and not the injection of a drug.

There is evidence to support both of these theoretical explanations of the Kamin effect, suggesting that both retrieval failure and response inhibition may be responsible for the effect. Strong evidence supporting the importance of memory retrieval comes from experiments in which it was shown that memory at intermediate retention intervals could be reactivated. Klein and Spear (1970b) trained rats to avoid shock and then gave them shocks as reminder treatments in a separate apparatus 2.5 hours after conditioning. These subjects were given a retention test after the reminder treatment and showed the same level of retention as other animals tested after 10 minutes and 24 hours. In a further set of experiments, Klein (1972) tested the hypothesis that inhibition of adrenocorticortrophic hormone (ACTH) release by the action of corticoids on the central nervous system may be the basis for critical modification of internal states and retrieval failure. He found that electrical stimulation of the lateral anterior hypothalamus, which stimulates the output of ACTH, or the direct delivery of ACTH crystals into the hypothalamus via implanted cannulas alleviated the retention deficit otherwise seen 2.5 hours after avoidance conditioning. These findings suggest that either shocks or the reinstatement of ACTH in the brain provide retrieval cues for memory of traumatic avoidance conditioning that took place 2.5 hours earlier. Once memory was reactivated, animals showed retention equivalent to that seen at shorter and longer retention intervals.

Circadian Cues and Memory

Circadian rhythms refer to repetitive daily cycles of biological change, which can be observed in all organisms. Circadian variations in physiology include changes in the concentrations of hormones and neurotransmitters, protein synthesis, and degree of neural activity. Internal changes are accompanied by behavioral oscillations in activity level, including sleep and wakefulness.

Researchers working in animal learning laboratories are well aware of the effects of time of day on animal training and testing. Animals generally perform best when tested at the same time each day; marked variations in time of day of testing often lead to decrements in performance. Stroebel (1967) found that rats learned and extinguished a conditioned emotional response more slowly when tested at different randomly determined times each day than when they were tested at the same time each day.

Experiments by Holloway and Wansley (Holloway & Wansley, 1973a; Wansley & Holloway, 1976) provided striking evidence that retention mirrors or tracks circadian rhythms. In one study, rats were initially given passive avoidance training. Passive avoidance training is equivalent to the punishment procedure discussed in Chapter 5. A rat was placed in a lighted chamber and could step from this chamber into a darkened one. However, immediately upon stepping into the darkened chamber, the animal received a footshock. On a subsequent retention test, the animal was put in the lighted chamber, and the time it took it to step through the opening into the dark chamber was measured. Good retention was indicated by a long step-through latency, showing that the animal remembered being shocked and passively avoided the darkened chamber. Through the use of many groups of rats, retention was charted very precisely for six retention intervals within the first hour after conditioning and for 2-hour intervals thereafter, throughout a period of 36 hours. In Figure 6.9, retention at successive intervals is shown by step-through latency. Retention was minimal at 6, 18, and 30 hours after learning and maximal immediately after learning and at 12, 24, and 36 hours. Similar findings have been revealed for active avoidance learning (Holloway & Wansley, 1973b) and for one-trial appetitive learning (Wansley & Holloway, 1975).

These data may be interpreted in keeping with an emphasis on retrieval processes and state-dependent memory. When a response is trained, attributes associated with the biological state of the organism at the time of training become incorporated with memory of learning. If biological state cues then oscillate so that they are maximally changed at retention intervals of 6, 18, and 30 hours but are close to the state present at the time of learning at 12, 24, and 36 hours, retrieval should be best at the latter retention intervals and poor at the former. It might be objected that these fluctuations in avoidance behavior simply represent changes in activity level. Control experiments have been carried out in which animals were exposed to the training apparatus and components of the training situation but not to the full learning contingency. When these

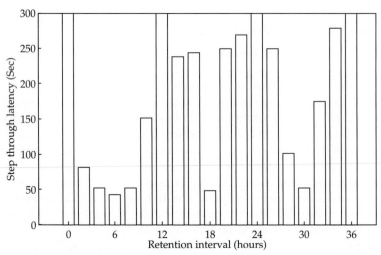

FIGURE 6.9. Retention of passive avoidance conditioning at retention intervals from immediately after learning to 36 hours. Good retention is shown by a high step-through latency, up to a limit of 300 seconds

animals were tested at periodic intervals, oscillations in behavior like those seen in Figure 6.9 were not found (Holloway & Wansley, 1973a; Wansley & Holloway, 1975; 1976). The retention data appear to be best interpreted as oscillations in the retrievability of training memory.

ELECTROCONVULSIVE SHOCK AND MEMORY

Electroshock applied to the brain causes massive firing of neurons and produces convulsions and unconsciousness. When used as a therapy for depression or certain psychotic disorders in human patients, electroconvulsive shock (ECS) may alleviate symptoms, but it also produces *retrograde amnesia;* that is, patients cannot remember events that immediately preceded the delivery of ECS. Although it would be difficult to carry out systematic studies of ECS-induced amnesia in people, such investigations have been carried out with animals.

The pioneering work in this field was carried out by Duncan (1949), who gave rats one active avoidance training trial per day for 18 days, with each trial followed by ECS. Duncan was particularly interested in the relationship between time of learning and time of ECS delivery, so different groups of animals had ECS delivered at intervals from 20 seconds to 14 hours after the learning trial. The results, shown in Figure 6.10, indicated very little learning when ECS came 20 seconds after a trial, with performance improving as a direct function of the trial–ECS interval. When ECS was delivered 1 to 14 hours after a trial, ECS seemed to have no effect on learning. The finding that amnesia was more severe with short trial–ECS intervals was in keeping with observations of human patients and has been replicated a number of times with animals.

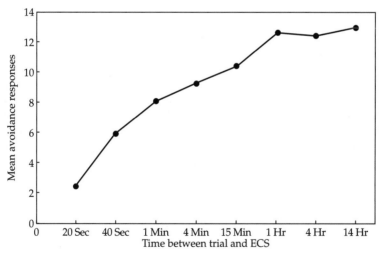

FIGURE 6.10. The effect of ECS delivery on the acquisition of an active avoidance response by rats. The successive times on the abscissa are the intervals between the end of a daily trial and the delivery of ECS.
Adapted from Duncan, 1949.

One problem with Duncan's procedure, later pointed out by Coons and Miller (1960), was that application of ECS shortly after each trial may have had a punishing effect on performance as well as an amnesic effect. That is, any aversiveness animals might have experienced from the ECS could have directly punished or weakened the tendency to make the avoidance response. Since punishment is most effective when it follows immediately after a response, the low performance seen in Figure 6.10 at the shorter intervals agrees with this interpretation. As a consequence of this insight, later investigators turned to the use of one-trial passive-avoidance learning followed by a single ECS. A single ECS had little punishing effect, and any punishment effect ECS might have biased performance against a demonstration of amnesia in passive avoidance. Typical procedures involved placing a rat or mouse in a compartment or on a raised pedestal and waiting for it to leave that position by either crossing to another compartment or stepping down off the pedestal. The animal then received a footshock in its new location, and ECS was delivered some time after the footshock. After a subsequent retention interval (often 24 hours), the subject was placed back in the original compartment or on the pedestal, and the latency for it to move from that position was measured. Long latencies indicated passive avoidance and good memory of the prior day's learning, and short latencies indicated amnesia. Experiments of this nature generally showed amnesia when the ECS was administered within 10 seconds of the footshock, with the effect disappearing at a training–ECS interval of between 10 and 30 seconds (R. Miller & Marlin, 1979).

Initial theoretical accounts of retrograde amnesia focused on a process of neural consolidation (Glickman, 1961; McGaugh, 1966). It was assumed that immediate memory of recent events took the form of an activity trace that provided short-term storage of information. Although it was assumed that it would ultimately decline, the active trace promoted the growth of a structural trace that was passive but provided long-term storage of the training information (Hebb, 1949). The building of the structural trace, based on the temporarily active trace, was the process of memory consolidation. A violent disruption of electrical activity in the brain, caused by ECS, terminated the active memory process but left the passive trace in its current state of development when the ECS was delivered. Thus, ECS delivered at a long interval after learning caused no amnesia because consolidation was completed.

Toward the middle 1960s and into the 1970s, evidence began to accumulate that led theorists to question the assumptions of consolidation theory. A finding of considerable significance was the *reminder effect.* In the reminder effect, it was shown that reactivation treatments, like those already discussed in this chapter, could restore memory of events that were followed by ECS. Koppenaal, Jagoda, and Cruce (1967) showed that a reminder footshock led to very high latencies of approaching and drinking from a waterspout in rats that were shocked while drinking 24 hours earlier and then immediately given ECS. Further, experiments by Lewis, Misanin, and R. Miller (1968) and R. Miller and Springer (1972) replicated this effect and showed that a reminder footshock was equally effective in restoring memory when administered at intervals ranging from 2 hours to 7 days after ECS delivery. Further, it was found that the effect of the reminder was relatively permanent since animals tested as long as 5 days after the delivery of the reminder showed excellent retention. Reminders were found to be specific to aversive or appetitive reinforcers used in learning. Footshock was an effective reactivation treatment for passive avoidance learning based on footshock (Springer & R. Miller, 1972) but was ineffective as a reminder for learning based on appetitive reinforcement (R. Miller, Ott, Berk, & Springer, 1974). R. Miller et al. did find that the appetitive memory was restored, however, when either drinking the sucrose reinforcer or placement in the training apparatus was used as a reminder treatment.

The reminder effect implied that ECS had not destroyed or prevented consolidation of reference memory but had made such memory difficult to retrieve. Lewis and R. Miller (Lewis, 1969; R. Miller & Springer, 1973; R. Miller & Marlin, 1979) suggested that memory consolidation or fixation is very rapid, perhaps equivalent to neural transmission from the receptors to the brain. It was held that the effect of ECS is not to alter the formation of memory but to alter cataloging operations that follow trace formation and promote retrieval. They argued that when ECS follows memory formation, this is analogous to shelving a new book in a library but failing to place its location in the library computer. The book has been stored, but it is inaccessible because the necessary retrieval information is not available. Lewis and R. Miller suggested further that ECS delivered immediately may prevent a subject from relating the training memory to contextual cues provided by the training environment. Retrieval cues may reinstate that environment sufficiently to make retrieval possible. In terms of the library analogy, retrieval cues may limit search for a book to only certain shelves, making it easily recoverable.

THE STATUS OF RETRIEVED MEMORIES

Throughout this chapter, the reactivation of stored memories through the action of retrieval cues has been emphasized. It was shown that retrieval cues lead to a behavioral expression of memories that otherwise remain forgotten. Beyond this demonstration of the retrieval of memories that are otherwise inaccessible, we may ask about the properties of retrieved memories. Do they have the same properties as memories originally formed, or are they more or less fragile than those original memories? Although there is not a great deal of information available on this question, some findings suggest that retrieved memories may be as robust or more so than initially encoded memories.

Retention of Retrieved Memory

In an extension of the techniques developed in the animal memory laboratory to the study of human infants, Rovee-Collier, Sullivan, Enright, Lucas, and Fagen (1980) reinforced footkicks by 3-month-old infants with movements of an overhead mobile. An infant lay in its crib with a ribbon attached to its ankle so that each footkick moved a mobile above the child connected to the other end of the ribbon. After children had learned to footkick frequently, retention was measured 2 weeks later. Infants given a reminder consisting of brief exposure to the moving mobile showed significant reactivation of memories relative to a control group given no reminder. After reactivation, retention of the reactivated memory was measured 3, 6, 9, and 15 days after reactivation. When the retention curve for reactivated memory was compared with a retention curve for memory of original training, both curves were found to decline at the same rates, suggesting that the forgetting of reactivated memory was equivalent to that of new memory.

Evidence from the animal laboratory suggests that retrieved memories may be even more memorable than original memories (J. Miller, Jagielo, & Spear, 1991; Spear, Hamburg, & Bryan, 1980). J. Miller et al. established fear conditioning to an odor stimulus in 18-day-old rats. In a discriminative Pavlovian conditioning procedure, the rats first were exposed to a lemon odor (CS–) with no US delivered and then were exposed to the odor of methyl salicylate (CS+) paired with the US of footshock. On a subsequent retention test, rats were given a choice between the methyl odor and an orange odor; a rat's head was placed along a midline between sources of the CS– and CS+ odors, and the length of time it spent with its head turned toward each odor was measured. Better retention was indicated by a short period of time spent in the presence of the CS+. An important aspect of this experiment was that rats forgot the original conditioning in 3 hours. The curves shown in the left panel of Figure 6.11 index the progress of forgetting by the rise in the paired or conditioned curve toward the unpaired control curve; by 3 hours, conditioned animals behaved like unconditioned control animals.

Even though it appeared that infant rats had totally forgotten the odor–footshock association, the delivery of reminder cues such as the US, the CS–, or the conditioning context, led to reinstatement of memory up to 24 hours after learning. Rats exposed to a reminder now avoided the CS+ odor. J. Miller et al. (1991) then examined retention of the reinstated memory by initially conditioning animals, reactivating memory 3 hours later, and finally testing different groups of reactivated rats at intervals extending up to 6 hours. The

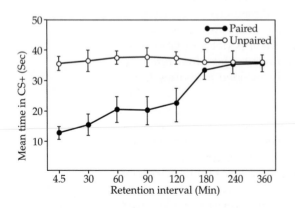
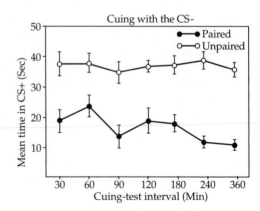

FIGURE 6.11. Retention of an odor-shock aversion in young rats shown by the rise in the paired condition curve relative to the unpaired control condition curve. The graph on the left shows retention of original conditioning, and the graph on the right shows retention of reactivated memory.

curves on the right side of Figure 6.11 show retention after rats were given exposure to the CS– (lemon odor) as a reminder. The curves remain parallel throughout all of the retention intervals, indicating that no forgetting of the reactivated memory took place over 6 hours. A further experiment showed that the reactivated memory was still retained 48 hours after reactivation. A comparison of the graphs on the left and right sides of Figure 6.11 shows clearly that the reactivated memory was remembered far better than the memory of original conditioning. These findings with rats, and those of Rovee-Collier et al. (1980) with human infants, suggest that retrieved memories are quite robust, being either as robust or even stronger than originally learned memories.

Amnesia for Retrieved Memory

A final question addressed is the susceptibility of retrieved memory to forgetting caused by amnesic agents. Misanin, R. Miller, and Lewis (1968) gave rats light-shock pairings and 24 hours later presented the light CS as a reminder cue. In one group of subjects, the reminder was now followed by ECS. A lick suppression retention test given 24 hours later revealed amnesia in this group but not in a control group given ECS 24 hours after training but without a preceding reminder. Schneider and Sherman (1968) found the same effect and showed that amnesia was produced if ECS followed the reminder by 0.5 second but not if it followed by 30 seconds. These findings suggest that both a retrieved memory and a just-formed memory are susceptible to amnesia caused by delivery of ECS. Further, both types of memory become more resilient to the amnesic effect of ECS as time passes before the ECS is delivered. The exciting possibility raised by these findings is that original and retrieved memories may be equivalent to one another. In other words, each time a memory is retrieved, the process of normal forgetting is reset to its starting point. Regular retrieval of information may prevent it from ever being forgotten.

SUMMARY

This review of reference memory in animals has shown that animals can remember past learning over long periods of time but that they also show normal forgetting with the passage of time. Certain conditions may accelerate forgetting, such as PI from learning acquired prior to the acquisition of a target memory. Age of the subjects is of considerable importance; immature rats forget much more rapidly than adult rats, suggesting that infantile amnesia may be found in both people and animals. Memory of learning episodes involves the storage of several attributes, and these attributes may be forgotten at different rates. Thus, a running response for reward may be well remembered over a long period of time although the color of the runway in which training took place is forgotten.

Early theories of forgetting in both people and animals emphasized processes of decay and interference. Little unequivocal evidence supports a decay process. Although interference between conflicting responses may cause a drop in the performance of a particular behavior, interference does not appear to be a direct cause of forgetting. Contemporary theory of forgetting emphasizes the importance of retrieval failure. That is, memories that appear to have been forgotten may still be in storage but may have become resistant to retrieval. Retrieval, or the expression of apparently forgotten memories, may become possible when retrieval cues are presented. Experimental manipulations that reinstate environmental cues, or endogenous physiological states that were present at the time a memory was formed, act as the most effective cues for retrieval.

The use of retrieval cues to reactivate memory has proven to be an invaluable tool for the understanding of a number of learning and memory phenomena. The effects of a number of treatments carried out in the learning laboratory were originally interpreted as instances of learning failure. The learning of one association was held to inhibit or block the formation of another. Recent experiments suggest that what appeared to be failures of learning were failures of retrieval. Associations that seemed to have been lost or blocked (by extinction, latent inhibition, overshadowing, or blocking) reappeared when relevant retrieval cues were presented.

State-dependent memory stresses the importance of the biological state of an organism as a memory retrieval cue. Drug dissociation experiments have shown that memories acquired under the influence of a centrally acting drug depend on the reinstatement of that drug for retrieval. Similarly, memories acquired while in a nondrug state may be inaccessible when an animal is placed in a drug state. The Kamin effect suggests that reaction to the stress of avoidance conditioning may so alter an animal's internal state as to make memory of conditioning inaccessible 1 to 4 hours after learning. Once again, memory may be reinstated by treatments that reestablish internal cues present during original learning. The experiments of Holloway and Wansley (1973a; 1973b) suggest that memories may become more or less retrievable throughout a day as circadian rhythms fluctuate in and out of phase with those present during a prior learning experience.

The delivery of ECS immediately after learning causes retrograde amnesia. Rats given a footshock after crossing from one side of an apparatus to the other show no passive avoidance when tested 24 hours later if ECS was delivered immediately after the footshock. Although ECS was initially viewed as a treatment that prevented consolidation of a neural memory trace, the discovery of the reminder effect suggested that ECS interfered with retrieval and not storage of the memory of footshock. Footshocks delivered outside the training apparatus shortly before the retention test reactivated passive avoidance behavior. The few experiments performed to examine the characteristics of retrieved memories suggest that they have the same properties as originally formed memories. Retrieved memories in infant children were forgotten at the same rate as original memories, and reactivated memory of odor aversion conditioning in young rats was actually more resistant to forgetting than the original memory of conditioning. Like initially formed memory, retrieved memory has been found susceptible to amnesia caused by the immediate delivery of ECS.

CHAPTER 7

Spatial Cognition

One of the most fundamental forms of information learned by both animals and people is position in space. The locations of foods, water, and home must be remembered so that they can be returned to, and the locations of poisonous objects and predators must be remembered so that they can be avoided. Equally as important as memory for the position of objects or places is memory for movement through space. For an organism located at Point A with the desire to reach Point B, memories of the environment encountered in previous travels between Points A and B is invaluable.

The topic of spatial cognition is concerned with the encoding and remembering of spatial information that allows successful orientation toward objects and movement through space. This chapter describes how animals retain both working memory and reference memory for spatial information. The chapters on working and reference memory emphasized that animals store information in a number of different formats. Thus, in working memory experiments, pigeons may encode information provided by the sample stimulus as either retrospective memory or prospective memory. Our review of reference memory research suggested that memory of conditioning was stored as a number of different attributes of the conditioning stimuli and environment. This theme is continued in this chapter, as we find that a number of different sources of information can serve as the basis for spatial cognition.

PATH INTEGRATION

Path Integration in People

Imagine that you were blindfolded and led about a room by an experimenter. The experimenter first takes you along a straight line for some distance. Then you are turned at an angle and led along another straight line for some distance. At this point, the experimenter releases you and asks you to travel back

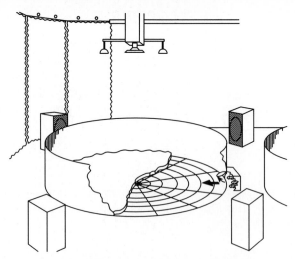

FIGURE 7.1. An arena used to study path integration in the golden hamster. The arena is surrounded by a wall, and its floor is covered with sawdust. An overhead video camera records the hamster's travels under infrared light.

to the starting point. If you are like most subjects tested on this task, you would be able to find your way to a position somewhere in the vicinity of the starting point, but you would show some error (Loomis, Klatzky, Golledge, Cicinelli, Pellegrino, & Fry, 1993). This task requires a subject to complete a triangle. In more complex tasks, the subject is led through more line segments and turns, and the degree of error involved in returning to the start increases.

The process by which a subject is able to keep track of her position relative to the start is called *path integration* or *dead reckoning*. Since the subject is blind-folded, visual cues can play no role in the acquisition of spatial information. However, other receptor systems still operate and make dead reckoning possible. Vestibular organs in the semicircular canals respond to the acceleration and speed of motion along a straight line and to the speed of rotation when a turn is made. Additional information is provided by kinesthetic feedback from our muscles when we locomote through space. Our ability to estimate time is also important; by knowing speed of motion and the time it took to move between two points, it is possible to estimate the distance traveled. Path integration is then possible by keeping track of distance traveled along a straight line and the angles at which turns are made. Since these calculations are estimates that involve error, the degree of error is compounded as more turns are made and longer distances are traveled.

Path Integration in Animals

Path integration is commonly used by animals. In particular, animals that travel in darkness, or that have limited sensory access to environmental stimuli, rely heavily on path integration. An interesting model for the study of path integration has been developed by Etienne (1992) using the golden hamster as a subject. The apparatus used, shown in Figure 7.1, is a circular arena, surrounded by a wall, with the floor covered with sawdust. The arena is further surrounded by a wall that allows the experimenter to control background stimulation. A camera over the arena is used to record a hamster's movements under infrared light, to which the hamster is insensitive. The hamster's nest box is placed next to the arena, and the hamster is released into the arena through a circular door operated by the experimenter. The experimenter placed a pile of hazelnuts in the center of the arena. With a bit of training, the hamster learns to go directly to the center, where it hoards hazelnuts by stuffing them in its cheek pouches. The behavior of primary interest is the efficiency with which the hamster now returns to its nest box with the hoarded nuts.

The hamster's travels were measured by examining videotape of its trip on a monitor containing an overlay of the arena broken into angular sections, as seen in Figure 7.1. The exact angular direction of the hamster's return trip was expressed as a vector or arrow showing how closely the direction of its return trip pointed toward the nest box. When hamsters were tested in total darkness, they went directly to the center of the arena, hoarded hazelnuts, and returned directly to a point very near the nest box. At this point, they searched for the nest box, which they found easily.

While loading their cheek pouches with nuts, hamsters had a tendency to circle the pile of food. These rotations did not interfere with accuracy of the return trip, however, indicating that hamsters were able to use self-generated cues to correct for rotation. The effects of rotation at the food site were investigated more systematically by Etienne, Maurer, and Saucy (1988). Hamsters were led from the nest box by a dimly illuminated spoon containing food. When a hamster in the control condition reached the center of the arena, it was immediately allowed to hoard hazelnuts and to return to the nest box. In the experimental condition, the hamster continued to be led by the baited spoon in circles that rotated the animal either clockwise or counterclockwise. In different experiments, hamsters were rotated through a full circle three, five, or eight times before being allowed to hoard food.

Accuracy of their return visits to the nest box is shown in Figure 7.2. The arrow vectors shown represent the return trip taken by several hamsters over several tests; the direction of the vector indicates the average direction taken, and the length of the vector indicates the extent of agreement among the directions taken on different tests. On the control tests (C) carried out in each experiment, hamsters returned directly to the position of the nest box. In the experimental conditions, hamsters tested after three rotations in either direction showed slight inaccuracy in their return direction but still returned to a point near the nest box. However, after five and eight rotations, the average direction of the return trip deviated more and more from the location of the nest box, and there was more variability in the direction of trips. Thus, hamsters were able to compute the location of the nest box fairly accurately after a few turns. As was suggested in the experiment with people, however, as the number of turns increased, the degree of error involved in path integration became magnified, and the return vector became highly inaccurate. Note that the errors made under rotation conditions were always in the direction of the rotation. Error apparently was caused by undercompensation for rotation. When hamsters were rotated in both clockwise and

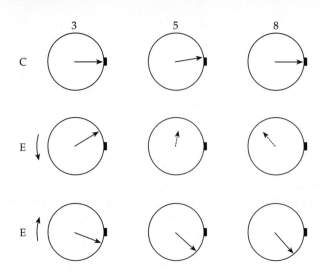

FIGURE 7.2. Arrow vectors show the accuracy with which golden hamsters traveled back to the nest box after hoarding food in the center of the arena. Hamsters made three, five, or eight rotations in the center under experimental (E) conditions but were led through no rotations in the control (C) condition.

counterclockwise directions on the same trial, directional errors did not occur more in one direction than the other.

Suppose hamsters are provided with a visual cue in the arena. Will they continue to use path integration, or will they depend on the visual cue? To examine this question, hamsters were tested with a dim spot of light placed at the periphery of the arena (Etienne, Teroni, Hurni, & Portenier, 1990). Over a number of foraging trials, the light always appeared at a position directly opposite the nest box; that is, the light was rotated 180 degrees around the periphery of the arena from the position of the nest. On test trials, a hamster was led to the center in darkness. As it began to hoard food, the spot of light appeared at a position rotated 90 degrees from the training position. On return trips, animals traveled in a direction opposite to the light source, which took them to a location on the periphery of the arena almost 90 degrees away from the nest box. It appears that hamsters learned to navigate by the light cue; their return strategy could be described as "travel in the direction opposite the direction of the light."

In another test, the light cue was rotated 180 degrees to a position directly in back of the nest box. Now hamsters tended to return along a vector almost directly in line with the nest box, although the use of the light cue should have directed them in just the opposite direction. It appears that if the light cue is shifted too far from its normal position, hamsters ignore it and fall back on the use of path integration. These are important findings because they indicate considerable flexibility in an animal's use of alternate sources of directional information.

Evidence from learning experiments further suggests the flexible use of internal and external directional information. Etienne, Lambert, Reverdin, and Teroni (1993) created a situation in which external visual cues and path integration cues demanded different return directions. Initially, animals strongly preferred the direction indicated by visual cues. Over a number of learning trials, hamsters were always rewarded by finding the nest box in the site indicated by path integration. Eventually, animals came to use path integration and to disregard visual cues.

It should be pointed out that exclusive use of either path integration or sources of stimulation external to an animal is probably rare in the real world. More often, these sources of directional information are used in conjunction with one another. For example, homing or migrating birds may fly accurately over long distances by using path integration with periodic corrections of error by the use of external cues from the sun or stars.

VISUAL CUES AND SPATIAL ORIENTATION

Both people and animals use visual cues to locate their position in space and to guide their travels. Visual cues may be distant background stimuli, such as mountains, trees, or a cityscape, or they may be nearby objects. Such nearby objects are often referred to as *landmarks* and may be used in isolation or in conjunction with background cues to determine spatial location. In the previous section, we saw that a visual cue could be put in conflict with path integration or could supplement path integration. Different kinds of memory are necessary for the use of path integration and the use of visual cues. An organism that uses path integration only has to keep track of the direction of home as it makes successive turns. Working memory may be updated as each turn is made to recompute the direction home; previous turns no longer need to be held in memory. When an animal uses visual cues, however, reference memory is usually involved. That is, the locations of stable landmarks relative to one another and to background cues must be retained over long periods of time. Although the use of visual cues for spatial cognition seems obvious to us, the ways in which visual cues are used varies considerably between organisms and situations.

Beacon Homing

Suppose that a hungry animal is placed in a darkened room with only a dim light bulb located at a fixed position. Adjacent to the light is a piece of food. Without actually doing this experiment, it can be predicted that the animal will learn quickly to find the food, even though it may be released from different points in the room on different occasions. The animal quickly learns to use the spot of light as a *beacon*. To find the food, it only needs to home on the beacon or to move toward the light until it reaches it. Although animals may sometimes have the good fortune to be able to locate important places in their environment by the use of a beacon, such locations often may be found where no significant landmark or beacon exists.

Locating Places in Empty Space

The Hoverfly

The hoverfly is a particularly interesting example. Hoverflies remain suspended in the air in a restricted location. The hoverfly may then suddenly depart from its hovering location to chase a passing fly. After flying some distance away and making several turns, the hoverfly then returns to the same area where it was initially hovering (Collett & Land, 1975). Some excursions and return trips of a hoverfly are shown in Figure 7.3. The numbered dots indicate the hovering locations the fly returned to after chasing another fly. These dots tend to cluster together in the same area, showing the fly's tendency to return to the same region after each flight. Studies of hoverfly chases and returns indicate further that the accuracy of the fly's return to its original position does not depend on the distance of the flight. Hoverflies find their original hovering position just as accurately after a long flight with many turns as after a short flight with few turns. This finding indicates that hoverflies are not using path integration to keep track of their original position. Recall that homing behavior based on path integration tends to deteriorate the longer and more tortuous the trip away from home. More and more error enters into the computation of the direction of home as the trip is prolonged. The fact that length

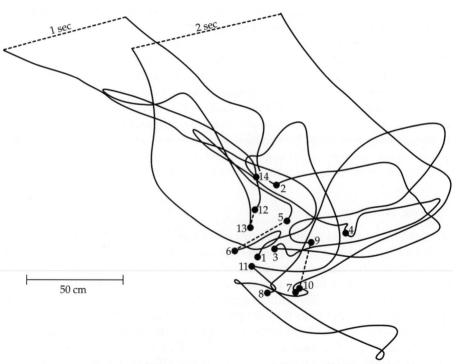

FIGURE 7.3. A diagram of the flight path of a hoverfly. The numbered dots indicate successive hovering positions to which the fly returns after chasing another fly.

of trip has no effect on the hoverfly's ability to return to its home in space indicates that it is not using path integration.

Rats in a Water Tank

In a clever procedure devised by Morris (1981), rats were tested in a circular tank filled with an opaque mixture of milk and water. When placed in the tank, rats were required to swim about until they located a submerged platform, upon which they could stand and receive relief from the exhaustion of swimming. Three groups of animals were trained with the platform located in the northeast quadrant of the pool and the starting position on the west side of the pool. After 15 escape training trials, all animals swam directly to the platform. On transfer tests, the procedure was changed for two groups of subjects. The same-place group now had the platform still in the northeast quadrant, but two rats were started from the north side of the tank, two from the east, and two from the south. Rats in the new-place group also started from different points, but the position of the platform also was moved; the angular location of the platform was always the same as it had been in training so that swimming in a leftward direction would lead to the platform. Finally, three control rats continued to swim from the west side of the tank to the platform in the northeast quadrant. The paths taken by animals in locating the platform are shown in Figure 7.4. Most of the new-place rats encountered considerable difficulty in finding the platform, as shown by the wandering lines that represent their travels in the tank; these rats tended to search in the area where the platform had been on training trials. By contrast, control and same-place rats swam directly to the platform. Although rats in the same-place group had never swum from the north, east, or south sides of the pool before, they located the point in space of the submerged platform from these positions and took very direct routes to it.

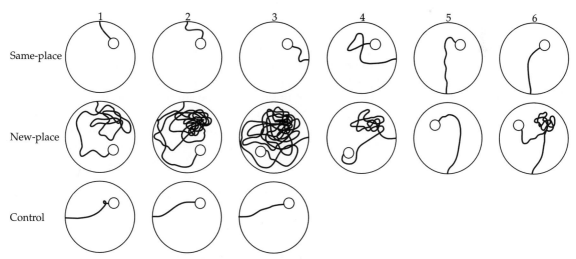

FIGURE 7.4. Diagrams of the paths taken by rats to find the submerged platform in the water tank. Rats in the same-place and control groups swam directly to the platform. Most of the rats in the new-place group searched in the area where the platform had been previously.

The behavior of both the hoverfly and rats in the water tank cannot be explained by either path integration or beacon homing. Both hoverflies and rats found their way to a point in space that was completely homogeneous with surrounding points in space. These animals must have used landmarks to locate the critical point in space. The use of multiple visual cues or landmarks to orient and direct spatial travels is called *piloting*. However, the types of landmarks and the way in which they are used may vary considerably between animals and locations.

PILOTING WITH LANDMARKS

Snapshots in Bees

In experiments carried out by Cartwright and Collett (1983), honeybees learned to fly into a laboratory room to find a sucrose solution placed in a small cup. The room was painted entirely white, but a black cylinder was placed at a fixed distance several centimeters from the sucrose cup. Bees returned repeatedly to the room to take sucrose from the cup. On tests of the bees' ability to locate the position of the sucrose or goal, the sucrose was removed, and the bees' searching behavior was videotaped. These tests revealed that bees came to search at or very near the location of the goal. If the cylinder was removed, bees failed to search near the goal, indicating that it was used as a landmark for sucrose. In further tests, the size of the cylinder was changed, being either smaller or larger than its standard or training size. When the landmark was larger, bees searched for sucrose at a greater distance from the landmark than its normal location. If the landmark was smaller than the standard, the bees searched at a position nearer to the landmark than the normal location of sucrose.

Cartwright and Collett suggested that bees used the *apparent size* of the landmark to locate the goal. Bees learned to associate a particular size of the landmark projected on their visual receptors with the location of food. This apparent size of the landmark was stored as a memory or *snapshot*. On subsequent visits to the room, a bee flew about successively observing the landmark until the perceptual image matched its snapshot, at which point it was at the goal. The effect of shrinking or enlarging the landmark was to make the landmark appear to be the appropriate apparent size when the bee was closer or farther away from the landmark than the actual distance of the goal. Thus, the bee could be made to err by searching either too close or too far from the landmark, simply by changing its size. Bees appeared not to appreciate the actual distance between goal and landmark; only the match between a percept and a two-dimensional memory was important. Essentially the same mechanism has been suggested to explain the hoverfly's use of a landmark to return repeatedly to the same area in space (Collett & Land, 1975).

In another set of experiments shown in Figure 7.5, bees were tested with three landmarks placed in a triangular relationship, with each landmark equidistant from the sucrose. As we would expect, tests showed that bees learned to use these landmarks to search precisely at the location of the goal. More interesting is the manner in which these multiple landmarks were used.

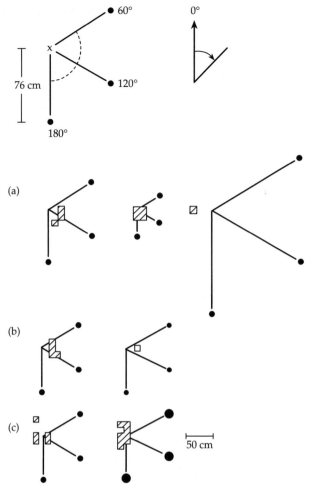

FIGURE 7.5. The top diagram shows the angular placements of the three landmarks relative to the goal (x). The lower diagrams show the effects of moving the landmarks closer together or farther apart than during training (a) and the effects of varying the size of the landmarks (b and c). Hatched areas indicate the locations where bees spent the most time searching.

Changes in the size of the three landmarks now had little effect on the location where bees searched, but changing the distance between the landmarks had a marked effect. When the three landmarks were moved close together, bees searched nearer to the landmarks than normal, and, when the landmarks were moved far apart, the bees searched farther away than normal. As the diagram at the top of Figure 7.5 shows, the landmarks were originally placed at successive 60-degree angles from the goal. The search locations chosen by bees when the distances between landmarks were changed allowed them to perceive the same compass directions between the landmarks as bees encountered at the goal with the landmarks in their original positions. In other words, a bee had taken a two-dimensional snapshot of the three landmarks spaced out evenly across its receptors. It then subsequently searched for sucrose at positions where its percept matched the positions of the landmarks to those of its snapshot memory. The bees were not affected by the distance of the landmark from the food source; their search behavior was governed by the angles between the cues.

Further research with bees suggests that their mechanisms for determining spatial location give more weight to landmarks near a goal than to those farther away (Cheng, Collett, Pickhard, & Wehner, 1987) and that the color of landmarks is important (Cheng, Collett, & Wehner, 1986). However, as we shall see, it appears that these processes used by bees and perhaps other insects may be very different from those used by vertebrates.

The Geometric Module

In a well known experiment, Cheng (1986) examined rats' spatial memory for buried food in a rectangular arena. The apparatus consisted of a rectangular box located in a darkened room, with only a weak light placed over its center. The two shorter end walls and one of the long walls were black, and the other long wall was white. Panels were placed in the corners of the box that contained different visual patterns; two of the panels were scented with different odors—anise and peppermint. Thus, the wall colors and the patterns and odors on the corner panels provided featural cues that could allow an animal to determine its position in the box.

With a bit of training, rats learned to dig in the bedding placed on the floor of the box to find hidden food. The food was buried at one corner location in the box. Although rats showed that they had learned the location of food by frequently digging at the location where it was hidden, they often made errors and dug in the wrong place. When an error was made, it was invariably found to be made by digging in the corner diagonally across from the one where the food was actually hidden. In other words, rats dug at a location 180 degrees displaced from the true location. Why did they dig there? Any of the featural cues should have told them not to dig there. The opposite corner had the wrong pattern and the wrong odor on its panel. If the rat had remembered the location of the food as being in the corner with the white wall on the left and the black wall on the right, the opposite corner would be incorrect because it contained black walls on both sides. Cheng concluded that rats paid little attention to any of these cues. What was important was the geometric framework of the box itself. He suggested that rats learned to dig in the corner with the long wall on the left and the short wall on the right. With the location of food coded in this way, it is not surprising that rats made errors by digging in the opposite corner, which had the same properties. Rats did dig more frequently in the correct corner than in the diagonal corner, suggesting that featural cues played some role. Nevertheless, the frequency and the precision of diagonal corner errors suggested that rats represented the box primarily as a *geometric module* or environmental frame.

The Gerbil's Use of Landmarks

Vertebrate animals may use a variety of landmarks in a variety of different ways to pilot in space. In Cheng's experiment, rats apparently found the geometric

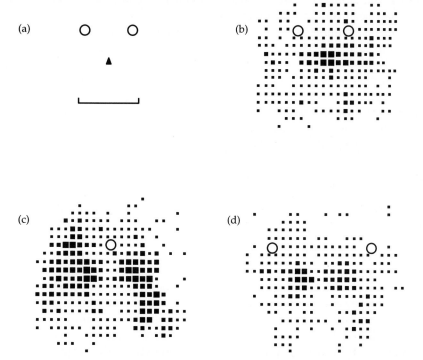

FIGURE 7.6. A sunflower seed (triangle) was buried south of and equidistant from two identical landmarks (circles) for a number of training trials (a). The size of the grid squares shows the density of search activity by gerbils on tests without a buried seed. Tests were carried out with the landmarks in the training positions (b), with a single landmark (c), and with the distance between landmarks doubled (d).

shape of the testing box the most salient landmark for the location of food. In experiments with another rodent, the Mongolian gerbil, Collett, Cartwright, and Smith (1986) found that landmarks placed on the floor of a circular arena controlled spatial behavior. Gerbils learned to dig for a sunflower seed buried in bedding, with a white cylinder landmark placed a fixed distance away. During tests, it was observed where the gerbil dug in the bedding when no sunflower seed was available. The gerbils' search behavior was highly accurate on these tests; they dug at or very near the location where the sunflower seed had been buried. Of particular interest was that when the size of the landmark was made smaller or larger than the training landmark, the location at which gerbils searched for food was little affected. Unlike bees, the apparent or retinal size of the landmark had little effect on their judgment of the location of the goal. This finding suggests that gerbils can judge the distance between the landmark and goal regardless of the landmark's size.

Gerbils also learned to find a buried sunflower seed accurately when an array of landmarks was placed in a fixed relationship to the location of the food. In Figure 7.6, Panel a shows the position of two landmarks (circles) and the buried sunflower seed (triangle) used to train gerbils. Panel b shows that digging behavior on test trials without food was concentrated in the area where seeds had been hidden during training. Panels c and d show two interesting transfer tests. In Panel c, a test with one of the landmarks removed is shown; the gerbils now dug at two locations, one southwest of the landmark and one southeast of the landmark. The landmark was treated as if it could have been either of the two training landmarks. Panel d shows what happened when the distance between the landmarks was doubled. Gerbils again dug in two locations, one southeast of the western landmark and the other southwest of the eastern landmark. These findings suggest something quite important about the gerbil's organization of space. It appears that gerbils computed the distance and the direction of food from each landmark independently. An alternative possibility would have been for gerbils to learn that the hidden seed was at a point equidistant from each landmark. In this case, they would have had no basis for locating the position of food when a single landmark was presented, and they should have dug at a single location equidistant between the landmarks when the distance between the landmarks was doubled. Rather, the data suggest that the location of food was coded relative to each landmark independently.

In other tests, Collett et al. turned off the room light as a gerbil was midway in its approach toward single or multiple landmarks. The remainder of the gerbil's journey and digging behavior were recorded under infrared light. Even though now in the dark, gerbils accurately traveled to the landmarks and dug at the location of the goal. Thus, gerbils were able to compute a trajectory to the goal before beginning a trip and to continue to execute this trajectory without the aid of visual cues. The finding suggests that the computed trajectory was based on information held in working memory about both the direction and distance of the goal. Without visual input, the gerbil presumably matched kinesthetic and vestibular feedback information to trajectory information in memory to find the correct location.

Pigeons, Landmarks, and the Vector Sum Model

Collett et al. (1986) suggested that gerbils' searching behavior could be explained by a vector summation model. This idea was developed and extended by Cheng (1988; 1989) in research on landmark use in pigeons. Pigeons' homing ability over long distances is well known and may be based on a variety of distal cues, including celestial cues, geographical terrain, and perhaps odors and magnetic stimulation. Once a pigeon has reached an area near its home loft, however, more local cues take over. Cheng's research may be related to the pigeon's use of local landmarks. Pigeons were tested in a large, square, walled-in arena, with bedding covering the floor. Birds were trained to peck at the bedding to dig for food pellets hidden in a food well. The hidden food was always located in the same place, a short fixed distance from the back wall of the arena. Placed on the back wall of the arena was a blue card, a landmark placed directly in line with the location of the goal. After several training trials, a pigeon learned to dig with its beak at or very near the location where the food was hidden.

Once pigeons learned the location of the hidden food, Cheng carried out tests in which he shifted the location of the landmark left or right along the

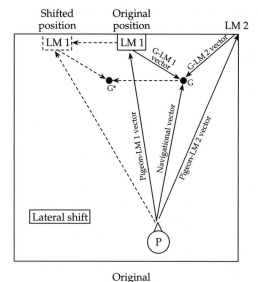

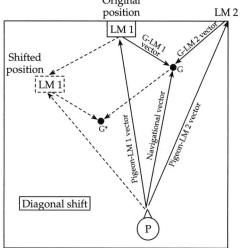

FIGURE 7.7. Diagrams showing the theoretical vectors formed between the location of buried food (G) and landmarks (LM). The vector sum model assumes that a pigeon (P) computes a navigational vector to G by adding the G-LM vectors in memory to perceived pigeon-LM vectors. The broken line vectors show new vectors used to locate food at G* when LM 1 is shifted. The upper diagram depicts a lateral shift, and the lower diagram depicts a diagonal shift. The model holds that pigeons should search at a point on the line between G and G*.

back wall of the arena distances of 10 cm or 20 cm. The landmark was moved to test specific predictions from a vector sum model. Predictions from this model are diagrammed in the upper and lower sections of Figure 7.7. The model assumes that pigeons learn specific vectors between the goal and various landmarks available in the environment. By viewing landmarks from the goal where food is found, the bird learns the specific direction and distance between the goal and each landmark. In Figure 7.7, these vectors containing direction and distance information are shown as arrows. In Figure 7.7, only two goal landmark (G-LM) vectors are shown, one for the experimentally manipulated landmark, the blue card (G-LM 1), and the other for the corner of the arena (G-LM 2). It may be assumed that there are a number of other landmarks available in the arena or the testing room that also form G-LM vectors. In addition to G-LM vectors stored in reference memory, a pigeon perceives vectors between its current position in space and landmarks. Two pigeon-LM vectors are shown in Figure 7.7, one for LM 1 and the other for LM 2. The final assumption of the vector sum model is that the pigeon will sum pigeon-LM vectors and G-LM vectors by adding the direction and distance of G-LM vectors to the direction and distance of pigeon-LM vectors. Addition of these vectors in Figure 7.7 is shown by connecting the point of the pigeon-LM vectors with the tails of the G-LM vectors. All such additions of vectors converge on the same point in space, Point G, the location of food. Thus, the addition of vectors based on several landmarks allows the pigeon to compute accurately a navigational vector or path that will take it directly to Point G.

Consider what happens within the model when LM 1 is shifted leftward to a new position, as shown in the upper section of Figure 7.7. A pigeon searching for food should now perceive a new vector between itself and LM 1 and should add to that vector the G-LM 1 vector. The consequence of this vector addition should tell the pigeon that food is at location G*. On the other hand, LM 2 has not moved, and it will continue to indicate that food is at location G. The model assumes that the pigeon will search at some point along a line between G and G*, based on a weighted average of the G-LM vectors. Since LM 1 was closer to the goal, it may have more weight than other landmarks. On the other hand, numerous other landmarks in the environment that may have formed G-LM vectors have not been moved and may exert a strong collective influence. Without knowing all the vectors and their relative weights, the best the model can predict is that the pigeon will search at a new location between G and G*. This is a fairly powerful prediction, however, because it requires that searches must be between G and G*, and it requires that searches must be at a fixed distance from the back wall of the arena.

Some findings of Cheng's experiments are shown in Figure 7.8. The data in the left panel show the effects on search behavior of shifting the landmark 10 cm or 20 cm to the right for one pigeon. The curves show the percentage of time the pigeon searched in the goal area on nonshifted control trials and the displacement of the pigeon's searching on shifted trials along the left-right axis. The curves clearly show that the bird shifted the peak of its search activity to an area directly in front of the landmark. The curves in the right panel of Figure 7.8 show the distributions of search time along the up-down axis on control and landmark shifted trials. The pigeon searched at the same fixed distance from the back wall of the arena on control and landmark shifted tests, just as Cheng's model predicted.

Not all of the pigeons tested were as influenced by the landmark shift as the bird whose data are shown in Figure 7.8. Other pigeons shifted their search efforts along the left-right axis to points between the original goal and the shifted landmark. Presumably, different birds gave different degrees of weight

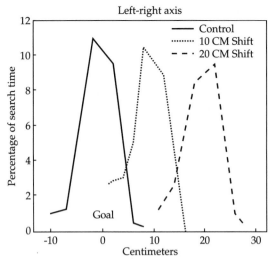

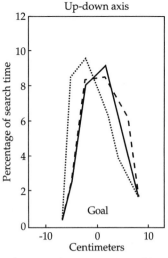

FIGURE 7.8. Curves show the distributions of search time for one pigeon on tests with the landmark placed at the goal or shifted either 10 cm or 20 cm to the right along the back wall of the arena. The left panel shows the distribution of search time along the left-right axis, and the right panel shows the distribution of search time along the up-down axis.

to the landmark shift. All of the birds tested, however, showed continued search at the fixed distance of the goal from the rear wall of the arena under all shift conditions.

In a further test of the vector sum model, the landmark was moved diagonally. The diagonal displacement of the landmark involves movement along both the left-right axis and the up-down axis, as shown in the bottom section of Figure 7.7. The pigeon should now search at some point on the diagonal line connecting G and G*; the search point should be displaced an equal distance along the left-right and up-down axes from the original goal location. When this experiment was carried out with both pigeons and chickadees, it was found that both species of birds shifted their search location more along the left-right axis than along the up-down axis (Cheng, 1990; Cheng & Sherry, 1992). An interesting confirmation of this finding was found with pigeons tested on a touch-screen monitor (Spetch, Cheng, & Mondloch, 1992). Pigeons were trained to peck at a location on the screen relative to a landmark presented on the screen. When this landmark was shifted diagonally, pigeons shifted their pecking location more in the horizontal direction than in the vertical direction.

The results of landmark experiments suggest several ways in which animals use landmarks to locate places in space. In the case of bees, it appears that matching apparent size and compass bearings between memory and percept is sufficient to locate a goal relative to nearby landmarks. More information appears to be used by the vertebrates that have been examined. Although only the geometric framework of an environment may be used when it is sufficient to locate food, the direction and distance of isolated landmarks can be encoded and used to compute trajectories to the location of hidden food. How animals determine distance and direction is still somewhat of a puzzle. The notion that animals determine a number of vectors between locations and landmarks was supported by Cheng's (1988; 1990) experiments with birds when a landmark was moved laterally but not when it was moved diagonally. Cheng and Sherry (1992) suggested that edges may be particularly salient landmarks for coding location in space. A particularly strong memory code for a goal placed a short distance from an edge may be its perpendicular distance from the edge. Vectors to other landmarks may be secondary. Thus, diagonal shifts of a landmark may lead to only minor shifts in search behavior along the up-down axis because the animals are reluctant to shift their search from points dictated by the previously encoded distance of the goal from the edge.

COGNITIVE MAPS

The preceding discussion has advanced ways in which an animal might learn the location of food goals relative to landmarks. Although learning about isolated goal locations undoubtedly takes place, it may form only part of a richer acquisition of knowledge about space. Animals also may learn about the environment in which goal locations are embedded and where different objects and locations are found relative to one another. Such knowledge may be put to use in travels through that environment that efficiently take the animal from one point to another. The proposal that animals, as well as people, form sophisticated representations of their environments was captured in the term *cognitive map,* introduced by Tolman. Tolman's theoretical ideas were based on experiments with rats in mazes, which suggested to him that "something like a field map of the environment gets established in the rat's brain" (Tolman, 1948, p. 192). Since Tolman introduced the idea of a cognitive map, various forms of evidence have been advanced to support it, and theories about the development and neural bases of cognitive maps have been introduced (Menzel, 1978; O'Keefe & Nadel, 1978; Poucet, 1993; W. Roberts, 1984).

In a recent article, Poucet (1993) advanced a theoretical framework for the development of cognitive maps in animals. He suggested that cognitive maps are not formed immediately and automatically upon an animal's first exposure to an environment. Rather, a cognitive map is built up gradually through extensive travel and exploration through an environment. Even a final cognitive map formed by an animal may not be a complete representation of its environment. On the other hand, cognitive maps allow an animal to forage efficiently and may form the basis for spatial reasoning or inference, as shown by shortcuts and detours through space. Two types of information are acquired about space: topological information and metric information. *Topological information* refers to knowledge of spatial relationships between objects, such as one object being in front, below, on top of, or behind another, or objects being connected or separated from one another in space. *Metric information* refers to more quantitative information about specific angular directions and distances of objects from one another. Goal-landmark vectors are one form of metric information. Poucet suggests that initial cognitive maps of an environment may take the form of crude topological maps, which then become refined by the acquisition of metric information through exploratory experience with the environment.

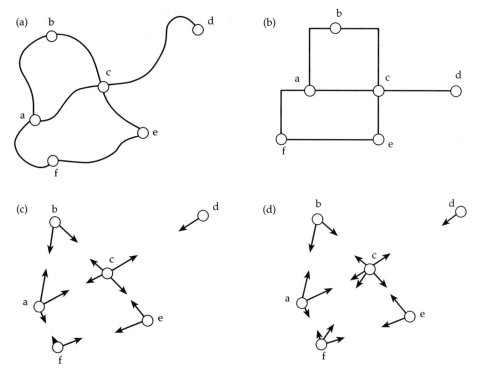

FIGURE 7.9. Hypothetical diagrams of location points between which an animal travels. The diagrams show actual travel routes (a), a transformed topological representation (b), a representation containing distance and direction vectors (c), and a representation containing additional computed vectors (d).

An animal begins to form a cognitive map of a region by forming *local charts,* which specify the relationships between places within one area. Poucet (1993) suggests that the integration of local views is important for learning about places. An animal may remain in one place and completely rotate its head and body through 360 degrees. Successive local views seen during rotation establish the continuity of space and are integrated into a complete representation of that place. A single local view perceived upon a subsequent visit to that area may reactivate an entire memory of the place. When animals travel between places, a map of what-leads-to-what is established. Initially, this map may take the form of limited strip maps (Tolman, 1948) or route maps that tell an animal only the direction from one point to another. This kind of representation is described as *location dependent.* Only at certain well-traveled locations may an animal be able to plot a trajectory to another location. Certain locations are privileged in the sense that more processing is done there than at other locations; the choice points in a maze are a good example of such locations. With further exploration, animals learn about more locations and routes, and a more complex map or local chart of an area is formed.

The development of a location-dependent framework is shown in Figure 7.9. Diagram a shows a number of locations linked together by paths an animal would take between them. A topological transformed representation of the relationships between these locations is shown in Diagram b, which might represent an initial map of this area in terms of relationships, such as "Point c is east of Point a," or "Point e is south of Point c." With further exploration of the region, vectorial metric information is developed, as shown in Diagram c. The animal learned the distances and directions of certain points from other points. Notice that vectors have not been established between all possible points; knowledge of how to get from Point c to Point f, for example, requires the animal to travel through either Point e or Point a. Additional vectors may be computed, expanding the map. In Diagram d, vectorial information has been increased at Points c and f, allowing the animal to travel directly from one of these points to the other without going through intermediate points. However, the map is still not complete; note that the animal cannot travel from Point d to other points without traveling through Point c.

Ultimately, an animal may form a more global or *location-independent* map of an area, in which it can determine the direction from any point to any other point. To do this, however, the animal must establish a *reference direction.* In reading human maps, our reference direction is taken from the cardinal compass points—north-south and east-west. An animal in the real world may use naturally occurring distant cues to establish a reference direction. Celestial cues from the sun, moon, or North Star may serve this purpose for some animals. Others may use geographical features of the environmental landscape, such as a mountain range or a line of trees. In the laboratory, the walls of the room or a door might provide a reference direction. Cheng's (1988) experiments with birds suggested that the back wall of the arena was a salient edge from which the distance of the goal was measured. If this edge formed a reference axis for birds, the goal-landmark vectors shown in Figure 7.7 may have been measured in angular deviation from the edge. Poucet (1993) suggested further that major axes of travel within an area may form reference directions. In Cheng's (1988) experiments, pigeons usually approached the goal along trajectories perpendicular to the rear wall of the arena. Thus, major reference axes for the pigeons tested may have been the edge of the rear wall and the orthogonal axis formed by the pigeons' route to the goal.

As a final process in the formation of an overall or global representation of an environment, local charts are linked together. Poucet (1993) suggested that one way this might be accomplished is through a common or *linking place.* A linking place lies on the common borders of two areas for which an animal has local charts. By knowing the directions and distances of places in each area from this common point, an animal may be able to integrate these charts into a single map. The other possible mechanism for combining local charts is through a general reference direction common to both areas by which different local charts can be oriented. For example, if an animal can orient two or more local charts with reference to a line of trees on one side and a mountain range running perpendicular to the trees, it may be able to determine the relative positions of the local charts and how to travel directly from a point in one local chart to a point in another local chart. This final stage in the formation of a global representation reemphasizes the point that cognitive maps are established gradually and hierarchically through travel and exploration. Topological and metric information are gradually woven together to form an increasingly sophisticated understanding of an animal's environment.

The Water Tank

The observation that rats can swim directly to a submerged platform although released from new locations (Morris, 1981) is often advanced as evidence for a cognitive map. Rats apparently use extramaze cues to determine a reference direction from which vectors to the hidden platform can be computed. Research by Sutherland and his colleagues (Sutherland & Dyck, 1984; Sutherland, Chew, Baker, & Linggard, 1987) indicates that, in keeping with Poucet's (1993) model, forming a sufficient map to locate the platform from novel directions requires varied experience. Sutherland et al. trained rats to swim within a circular tank that was divided down the middle into two sections, A and B, by a partition above the surface of the water; the hidden platform was always on Side A. For different groups of animals, the partition was either transparent or opaque. Two groups of rats were allowed to start from Side A and to swim on both the A and B sides of the pool to find the platform. For one group, the transparent partition allowed the rats to see Side A of the pool when swimming on Side B. In the other group, the opaque partition prevented animals from seeing Side A while swimming on Side B. Both groups learned to swim rapidly and directly to the platform over eight training trials.

On a transfer test, rats in both groups were released from Side B with the partition removed. Rats that learned to find the platform with the transparent partition swam directly to the platform, but rats that learned with the opaque partition separating Sides A and B spent considerable time searching for the platform before locating it. It appears that rats had to swim toward the platform from Side B and see the background cues from that direction in order to form a map that was complete enough to locate the platform when released from Side B. In keeping with Poucet's (1993) ideas, rats trained with the opaque partition may have learned only certain location-specific routes about getting to the platform from points on Side A but not from points on Side B. A more complete map showing vectors from Side B as well as Side A was learned by rats trained with the transparent partition.

Detours

One implication of the concept of a cognitive map is that an animal should be able to use detours through mapped areas. That is, given the knowledge that a barrier will block its normal path, it should be able to plot an alternate pathway around the barrier. The maze shown in Figure 7.10 is taken from a classic experiment carried out by Tolman and Honzik (1930a). There are three paths leading from the start box (S) to the food box, with Path 1 being a direct trip and Paths 2 and 3 being detours; Path 2 is a shorter detour than Path 3. The paths could be blocked at Points X, Y, and Z, and rats were trained to run down each of these paths to get to the goal by blocking off two of the paths. Rats adopted the strategy of running down Path 1 first. If they found Path 1 blocked, they returned to the intersection of paths and took Path 2 next. Only if Path 2 was blocked did they then take Path 3. In other words, rats' hierarchy of preferences for paths and detours was directly related to the length of the path to the goal.

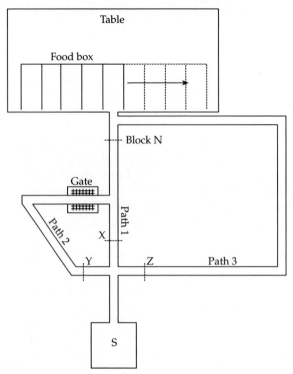

FIGURE 7.10. Drawing of the maze used to study detour behavior in rats. Paths 1, 2, and 3 could be blocked at Points X, Y, and Z, respectively. In addition, Path 1 could be blocked at Point N, nearer the food box goal.
From Tolman & Honzik, 1930a.

On a further test, rats ran down Path 1 and for the first time encountered a block not at Point X but at Point N. The critical aspect of placing the block at Point N is that it blocks access to the goal from both Paths 1 and 2 but not Path 3. Rats now returned to the intersection of paths and entered Path 3. These findings suggest not only the use of detours in rats but the use of *spatial reasoning* to demonstrate *innovative behavior* (Thinus-Blanc, 1988). The implication of this finding is that rats avoided their normal preference for Path 2 because they could represent this as a detour that would lead back into Path 1 at a point where their travel still would be impeded by Block N.

Shortcuts

If an animal forms a global cognitive map of an area that has been explored, it should be possible for it to compute new vectors between places, even though the animal has never traveled between those places. In particular, if such a route constitutes the shortest distance to a goal, the animal should take a *shortcut* to the goal. Chapuis and Varlet (1987) tested the ability of Alsatian dogs to use shortcuts. The dogs were first allowed to explore a meadow on a leash and to fetch pieces of meat that were thrown for them. The testing procedure is

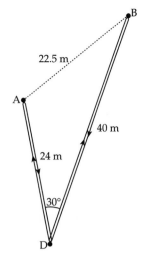

FIGURE 7.11. A map of the paths used to test shortcut behavior in dogs. A dog was walked successively along the Paths DA, AD, DB, and BD and shown pieces of hidden meat at Points A and B. It was then released at Point D. The broken line shows the direction and distance of a direct shortcut between Points A and B.

diagrammed in Figure 7.11. Trials always began at Point D, from which a dog was walked on a leash to Point A, where it was shown a piece of meat hidden in the grass. The dog then was walked back to Point D and then to Point B to be shown another piece of hidden meat and, finally, it was walked back to Point D. The leash was removed from the dog, and it was allowed to search freely for the meat. On almost all trials, dogs took the shortest distance to food and retraced Path DA to find and consume the meat at Point A. The observation of most importance was that dogs did not return to Point D to get to Point B but took a short cut to B from A on 96 percent of the trials. Shortcuts were taken repeatedly even though dogs were tested at many different locations and in two different meadows, one with sparse vegetation and one with numerous bushes, trails, and puddles. The possibility that dogs simply smelled the food and followed the scent was ruled out by control tests on which dogs' ability to find hidden meat was tested without initially being walked to the food sites; not a single dog found the hidden food. Dogs apparently computed new travel vectors quite readily when a delicious morsel of food was at stake.

A further example of shortcut behavior is found in experiments with non-human primates. Menzel (1973; 1978) tested six chimpanzees in an open outdoor field, which the chimps had explored on numerous previous occasions. On a test, a single chimp was taken from the enclosure where the group was housed. This animal was carried around the field by an experimenter, who periodically hid 18 pieces of fruit in randomly selected places. The subject then was returned to its enclosure. Two minutes later, the subject was released, along with the other five chimpanzees. These latter animals served as controls for the possible location of food through sight or odor. Over a number of trials, the subject shown the locations of food collected 12.5 pieces per trial, while the control animals combined found only 0.21 piece per trial.

Equally as impressive as the chimpanzee's ability to locate hidden food was the paths taken during food collection. Animals collected food according to a *least-distance traveled* principle. Regardless of the order in which food was hidden, the subject collected all of the food in one area before moving to another area. The data suggest that these chimpanzees formed a global cognitive map of the field and could use this map combined with their memory for the hiding places of food to compute successive shortcuts between food locations. More recently, similar findings have been reported for yellow-nosed monkeys (MacDonald & Wilkie, 1990).

SPATIAL MEMORY

The Radial Maze

Most of the experiments considered thus far involved spatial memory. Certainly, the concept of a cognitive map implies the storage of detailed information about space. We now turn to a consideration of the properties of spatial memory, such as its capacity and how spatial information is forgotten. This discussion focuses on the considerable literature developed by observing rats perform upon a particular apparatus, the *radial maze*. It has long been observed that rats tend to avoid returning to places that have recently been visited. Rats prefer to visit novel locations before returning to places previously explored. Given successive trials in a T-maze, rats spontaneously alternate the arms entered far above chance expectancy (Dember & Fowler, 1958). Similar behavior is observed if rats are tested with three alleys that branch out from a central place (N. R. F. Maier, 1932).

Although the tendency for rats to explore novel places may have evolved as an efficient foraging tactic, psychologists interested in memory note that such behavior implies that the rat is remembering places previously visited. Olton and Samuelson (1976) took advantage of these observations by testing rats on an eight-arm radial maze. The maze consisted of an octagonal central platform, with eight arms branching out from it at equal angles (see Figure 7.12). The maze was elevated and open, which means it was built on legs that raised it 50 cm above the floor, and the arms had no walls. A pellet of food was placed at the end of each arm, and hungry rats were trained to run down the arms for food. After this preliminary training, the rats were placed at the center of the maze and allowed to travel freely through the maze. After 10 to 20 days of practice, it was common for rats to enter all eight arms without repetition. Although rats did occasionally make errors by repeating arm entrances, the average number of different arms entered in the first eight choices was between 7.5 and 8.0. By chance alone, the number of different arms that should be entered in the first eight choices is 5.25. The conditions for this excellent performance were optimal; in addition to taking advantage of rats' natural tendency to explore new places, the behavior of visiting different arms maximized the rate of food collection.

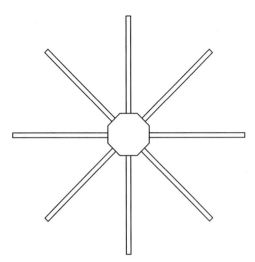

FIGURE 7.12. A top view of an eight-arm radial maze.

Is Radial Maze Performance Based on Memory?

Algorithms

Although rats' performance on the radial maze suggested spatial memory, alternative accounts had to be explored. One possibility was that rats were using an *algorithm* or a fixed pattern of searching alleys. The simplest and most efficient algorithm would be for rats to enter adjacent arms and go around the maze in a consistent clockwise or counterclockwise direction. Such a strategy would minimize demands on memory since only the most recently exited arm would have to be remembered. Olton and Samuelson (1976) observed that their animals sometimes tended to make successive 90-degree turns after leaving arms and to progress around the maze in a clockwise or counterclockwise direction; interestingly, rats made a correction after three such turns to avoid reentering the same four arms repeatedly. It was not necessary for rats to do this, however, to achieve an accurate score; even when rats used no discernable pattern, performance was highly accurate.

The most convincing evidence against the need for algorithms comes from experiments in which rats were forced to enter selected arms prior to a retention test. Animals were initially allowed to enter only a randomly selected subset of arms (three or four) and were then allowed to choose among all eight arms. Rats very accurately picked out those arms they had not previously visited, even though no algorithmic pattern could be used (Zoladek & W. Roberts, 1978; W. Roberts & Dale, 1981).

Odor cues

The use of odor cues provided another possible explanation of performance on the radial maze. Perhaps while traveling among arms, a rat left an odor trail on the maze. The rat might learn to avoid arms with an odor and only enter those which did not contain its odor. This possibility seems somewhat implausible to begin with since a number of rats typically are tested in succession on the maze. The maze would become so swamped with the odors of different rats that the detection of any one rat's odor on a particular arm would become very difficult.

Nevertheless, specific tests of the odor hypothesis have been carried out. One class of experiments attempted to directly interfere with rats' ability to detect odors. Olton and Samuelson (1976) and Maki, Brokofsky, and Berg (1979) saturated the radial maze with a strong foreign odor (aftershave lotion) and failed to find any interference with performance. Zoladek and W. Roberts (1978) made rats temporarily anosmic and found this condition to have no adverse effect on radial maze accuracy. Finally, Olton and Samuelson (1976) carried out an experiment in which rats were allowed to enter three arms, and the positions of these arms then were interchanged with those of arms not entered. When rats then were allowed to complete the maze, they ran down arms that carried them to places they had not yet visited, even though this meant traveling on arms just recently traversed. Clearly, this is not the behavior of animals avoiding their own odor trails.

Another version of the odor hypothesis, that animals enter arms on which they can smell food, has also been ruled out. Both Olton and Samuelson (1976) and W. Roberts (1979) rebaited arms after rats collected food on them and found that rats still avoid these arms in preference for arms not previously entered.

What Defines a Goal?

It appears that rats on a radial maze learn to visit novel locations in space which form food goals. Some experiments carried out by S. Brown and Mellgren (1994) suggest that goals may not always be separate locations in space. They constructed a four-arm radial maze on which rats climbed from ladders in a start box to the middle of each of the four arms. From there, a rat could either travel to a platform at the end of each arm or to a central platform located directly above the start box. One group of rats was rewarded in the normal fashion; each time it visited the platform at the end of a different arm, it received food. A second group was rewarded only on the central platform and only for taking a different path after each return to the start box. The group rewarded at the end of each arm took more novel routes (made fewer route repetitions) than the group rewarded on the central platform. These findings suggested that rats find paths that all lead to the same place less novel or distinctive than paths that lead to different places.

In a further experiment, S. Brown and Mellgren (1994) tested rats under the same conditions but with a slight change for the group that had to go to the central platform for food. The central platform was partitioned into four separate compartments so that a rat arriving along each arm path from the start box would eat its reward in a different compartment. These rats now chose as many novel routes to the central platform as rats that were rewarded on the ends of the arms. Rats apparently prefer novel routes defined by different goals, but different goals do not always have to be different locations in space. Simply

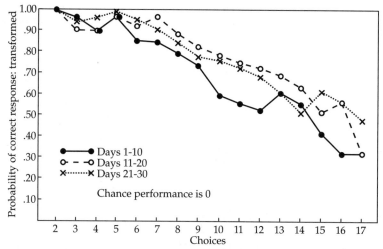

FIGURE 7.13. Probability of correct response plotted as a function of choices for rats on the 17-arm maze. Probability correct has been transformed so that zero is the level of chance performance at each choice. Different curves plot performance at different stages of training.

dividing a central location into different compartments where food was consumed created novel goals for the rats.

The Storage Capacity of Spatial Memory

It should be pointed out that the radial maze experiments described thus far are working memory experiments. Rats must remember the specific arms entered on the current trial to avoid errors. On the next trial, which might occur a few minutes or a day later, a different set of arms may be entered initially and have to be remembered during the trial. It is possible to study reference memory on the radial maze. Olton and Papas (1979) trained rats on a radial maze with food always placed on the same subset of arms. Over many days of training, animals learned to restrict their choices only to those arms. Although reference memory can be studied in this fashion, most research on the radial maze has been concerned with working memory.

The 17-Arm Maze

One question that has arisen is whether working memory storage capacity in the rat is limited. It has long been held that human verbal working memory is limited to about seven units of information (G. Miller, 1956). Perhaps the use of an eight-arm radial maze was fortuitous because it just encompassed the limit of spatial working memory in rats. If we take as an initial hypothesis the possibility that human verbal memory and rat spatial memory are both limited to about seven or so units of information, we expect rat performance to begin to decline sharply as the number of visits to be remembered exceeds the eight required on the eight-arm maze. The data shown in Figure 7.13 suggest that this is not the case. These data show the probability of a correct response over Choices 2 through 17 on a 17-arm radial maze (Olton, Collison, & Werz, 1977). Since the probability of attaining a correct choice by chance changes as choices are made, the probability of correct choice is corrected to set chance equal to zero at all choices. Performance remains high through the first five to eight choices and then declines gradually over subsequent choices. Since rats must remember the arms previously entered, the memory load increases as successive choices are made, and this increasing load may account for the gradual drop in the curves. Nowhere on the curves do we see a sudden drop in accuracy, which would suggest that a capacity limit has been reached. Furthermore, performance is still substantially better than chance at Choice 17; Olton et al. pointed out that an extrapolated curve would not reach chance until 25 to 30 choices had been made.

The Hierarchical Maze

In some experiments carried out by W. Roberts (1979), a radial maze was modified to form a hierarchical maze. This maze contained the usual eight primary arms extending from the central platform and appended as many as three secondary arms onto the end of each primary arm. In the initial experiment, different groups of rats were tested with one, two, or three secondary arms on each primary arm of the maze, each baited with a reward pellet. Within 10 to 20 trials of testing, animals in all groups were collecting all of the food pellets, with little repetition of entrances into either primary or secondary arms. In subsequent experiments, rats explored the maze with some of the secondary arms blocked off and the others open and baited with food. When all of the blocks were removed, rats very accurately entered the previously unentered secondary arms and avoided those previously visited. Accurate choice of primary arms was maintained throughout the test phase. In the case of rats that ran a maze with three secondary arms on the end of each primary arm, these animals were keeping track of visits to $8 \times 3 = 24$ secondary arms plus 8 primary arms. A total of 32 choices was being remembered.

These experiments with the 17-arm maze and the hierarchical maze suggest that rats can remember visits to far more places than would be expected within a limited capacity memory system modeled on those used in human verbal memory. These findings and others from the bird food storing literature to be discussed led W. Roberts (1984) to conclude that spatial memory capacity in animals is probably not limited by brain structure. The only limitation may be imposed by the number of discriminable spatial locations available in an environment.

Retention of Spatial Memory

Spatial working memory in rats is far more resistant to forgetting with the passage of time than the working memory in pigeons examined in delayed matching experiments and described in Chapters 3 and 4. In those experiments, birds showed substantial forgetting over periods of seconds, and at best they could remember the sample only for a few minutes. In experiments carried out by Beatty and Shavalia (1980a), rats were forced to enter four randomly chosen arms on an eight-arm radial maze. The rats then were returned to the home cage and only later brought back to the maze to make four more choices from among all eight arms. At a retention interval as long as 4 hours, rats showed virtually no forgetting by selecting the unentered arms with more than 90 percent accuracy. Although there was substantial forgetting after 24 hours, retention was still better than chance. Working memory for spatial locations in rats appears to be particularly resistant to forgetting over time.

Forgetting of Spatial Memory

Retroactive Interference

Not only is spatial working memory on the radial maze persistent over time, but it is highly resistant to retroactive interference (RI). Maki, Brokofsky, and Berg (1979) tested rats by first allowing them to enter four arms of an eight-arm maze for reward on each arm and then subjecting the rats to various forms of interpolated stimulation before returning them to the maze to test their memory for the unentered arms. In different experiments, the interpolated stimulation consisted of exposure to lights, sounds, a distinctive odor, feeding on the maze, and running a four-arm maze in a different room. None of these interpolated experiences reduced retention relative to control trials on which animals were exposed to no new stimulation during the retention interval. The finding that interpolated experience on another maze produced no RI is particularly impressive. Beatty and Shavalia (1980b) extended this experiment by requiring rats to enter four arms on a different eight-arm maze at various temporal points within a 4-hour retention interval. Still no evidence of RI was found. W. Roberts (1981) also repeated this experiment and found no evidence of RI when rats were tested on two interpolated radial mazes in different rooms. Only when the number of interpolated mazes was raised to three did W. Roberts find significant RI.

In some further experiments, W. Roberts (1981) attempted to establish RI with only one interpolated maze by placing the test maze and the interpolated maze within the same room. It was reasoned that arms on mazes placed close together within the same location would share many cues and should therefore provide greater confusion between spatial memories. In one experiment, the mazes were placed side by side, with corresponding arms of each maze pointing in the same compass directions. Only selected arms on the interpolated maze were open, and rats were rewarded for entering those arms; these arms pointed in exactly those directions that rats had not gone in the test maze. Even this procedure revealed no evidence of RI. In another experiment, the same experimental design was used, but the mazes were displaced vertically, instead of horizontally, by placing one maze on top of the other. This experiment also yielded equivalent performance in RI and control conditions. In a final experiment, only a single maze was used. After a rat had been forced to four arms on the maze, the interpolated condition consisted of placing the rat directly onto the end of each of the remaining four arms it had not entered and allowing it to eat a food pellet. The retention test now revealed significant RI because experimental animals often failed to choose the correct arms upon which they had been placed.

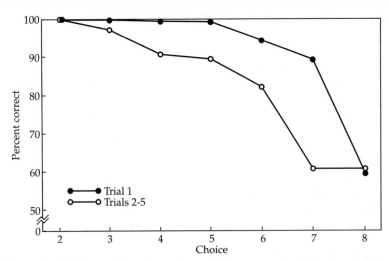

FIGURE 7.14. Curves show percentage of correct choices made on Choices 1 through 8 during five massed trials on an eight-arm radial maze. The higher curve shows performance on Trial 1, and the lower curve shows performance on Trials 2 through 5.

These findings suggest that rats can encode their position in space very precisely. Although arms on two mazes may point at the same cues, different locations are encoded as long as the rat can experience these cues from different perspectives, and memories of these locations are easily discriminated. However, RI was created when animals were placed at exactly the arm locations they had to choose to be correct on the retention test. The importance of this finding becomes more apparent in the subsequent discussion of proactive interference (PI).

Proactive Interference

In some radial maze experiments, rats were tested over massed trials. That is, after a rat collected all of the food on the arms of the maze on an initial trial, the rat was tested immediately on further trials by repeatedly rebaiting the arms of the maze. Data from such an experiment carried out by W. Roberts and Dale (1981) are shown in Figure 7.14. The percentage of correct responses is plotted over the first eight choices for the first trial on the maze and for the average of the last four trials, Trials 2 through 5. Two things are apparent from these data. First, performance is nearly perfect on Choices 2 and 3 in both curves. Second, as further choices are made, and as the memory load increases, level of accuracy drops, but it drops much faster for the remaining choices on Trials 2 through 5 than on Trial 1. W. Roberts and Dale argued that this pattern of results indicates a PI effect in spatial memory. In fact, these findings are exactly what one would expect to find, based on research on PI in human working memory (Keppel & Underwood, 1962). On the initial choices of a trial, the memory load is light, and the retention interval since the first choice or two is short. Retention then is easy, and little evidence of PI should be found. On the later choices of a trial, however, both the memory load and the retention interval have increased, and it seems to be under these conditions that interference from preceding trials becomes most pronounced.

It is important to recognize that PI was found in a situation in which a rat had to repeatedly choose among the same arms it had just entered on preceding trials. Similarly, RI was found by W. Roberts (1981) when rats had to return to arms on which they had just received interpolated placements. The problem created for an animal in these situations may be one of *temporal discrimination*. In the case of PI, animals may confuse early and late arm visits because they have difficulty discriminating the points in time at which they entered arms on the current trial and the immediately preceding trials. Similarly, in the experiment that produced RI, rats may have found it difficult to remember whether they had been on a particular arm on the initial forced choice or the interpolated direct placement.

How Is the Radial Maze Represented?

Based on the previous section on the cognitive map, we can hypothesize that as a rat explores the arms of a radial maze, it builds a cognitive map or representation of the maze and its surrounding environment. Arms on the maze are recognized by landmarks, such as doors, windows, pictures, and other objects in the experimental room. Of critical importance to the concept of a global map, arm locations are learned by their relationships to the full array of landmarks available; the entire configuration of cues is important. If the end of each arm is a goal, multiple goal-landmark vectors between the end of each arm and a number of landmarks in the experimental room allows the animal to locate each goal in space.

As an alternative account of radial maze memory, it has been suggested that rats may process only a limited set of cues at the end of each arm of the maze (Olton, 1978; M. Brown, 1992). Arms are remembered as a *list* of cues, each cue representing one arm of the maze. These cues are then checked off as arms are visited. A rat would not keep track of its travels over a map representation as it goes through the maze. Instead, it would peer down arms to compare the cue at the end of the arm with those on its list that have and have not been checked as entered. A match between an arm cue and an entered arm on the list would lead to avoidance of an arm, but a match between an arm cue and an unentered arm on the list would trigger a decision to enter the arm.

As a test of these alternative accounts of radial maze memory, Suzuki, Augerinos, and Black (1980) used a highly controlled environment—a cylindrical chamber placed around an eight-arm maze—with specific stimuli placed at the end of each arm. Prominent stimuli were used, such as Christmas tree lights, a fan with tinsel, and a wooden pyramid. On test trials, rats were given three forced choices and then confined to the center platform for 2.5 minutes before being allowed to choose freely among the eight arms. One of three different manipulations was carried out during the retention interval, as shown in Figure 7.15. In a control condition, the wall of the cylinder, on which the stimuli were mounted, was rotated varying distances but always returned to the original position of the cues. In the other two conditions, transpose and rotate, the positions of the stimuli were changed. In the rotate condition, the wall of

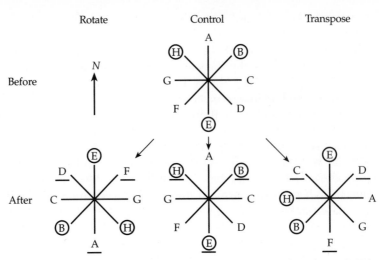

FIGURE 7.15. Diagrams show the positions of extramaze stimuli A through H before and after the stimuli were manipulated. The circled stimuli are those at the ends of arms a rat was forced to enter before the positions of the stimuli were changed for the retention test.

the cylinder was rotated 180 degrees; although the compass positions of the stimuli were changed, the pattern or relative positions of the cues was maintained. In the transpose condition, both the positions and the configuration of the cues were altered by randomly interchanging the stimuli.

Performance on the free-choice test was scored by the accuracy with which animals approached stimuli that had not been approached on the forced choices. The results showed clearly that rats performed very accurately on control and rotate tests but were very inaccurate on the transpose tests. As long as the configuration of stimuli was preserved, as in the control and rotate conditions, animals responded as if no change in cues had occurred. When the configuration was changed, however, animals behaved largely as if they were in an unfamiliar setting. Such results are exactly what we would expect if the environment no longer matched the map an animal had initially formed of it. A list theory, on the other hand, suggested that each arm should be coded just by the stimulus at the end of it; transposing the cues should not interfere more than rotation because the cues at the end of each arm remain intact.

FORAGING AND SPATIAL MEMORY

Now that the representation of spatial memory and its mechanisms have been considered, we turn to the question of the *functional* role of spatial memory. How is spatial memory beneficial to an organism? One important answer is that spatial memory promotes the *fitness* of organisms, or their ability to survive and pass their genes on to their offspring. Spatial memory in this regard may provide an advantage to an animal in foraging for food throughout its habitat. A number of models of foraging developed by biologists fall into a general theoretical category called *optimal foraging theory*. These models suggest that selective evolutionary pressures on animals have led to the development of behaviors that promote highly efficient or nearly optimal foraging. One definition of optimal foraging is behavior that maximizes the energy (E) obtained for the time (T) spent foraging. Thus, foraging behavior that maximizes the E/T ratio is optimal.

Optimal foraging theory suggests certain principles of animal foraging behavior. Animals should prefer large energy foods that can be consumed quickly to small energy foods that take longer to consume. Animals should prefer to consume food that is nearby or takes little time to reach over food that is more distant in space and time. In some cases, trade-offs must be made between competing needs. Although high-energy food may be preferred, it may be avoided if its consumption takes an animal into an area where predators may be waiting. All may be lost in terms of an animal's fitness if it becomes another animal's meal.

Spatial memory seems to be a critical form of spatial cognition for efficient foraging. If an animal is to travel through space to the best and nearest food sites while avoiding potential predators or competitors, it must have a memorial map of its habitat and of the locations of food, water, and predators within the habitat. The examples of shortcuts and least-distance-traveled routes already discussed suggest that a knowledgable forager uses spatial memory to plot efficient foraging trips. In some recent experiments, foraging on the radial maze has been studied in the laboratory. Two examples of this type of research are described.

Foraging for Different Amounts of Food

In the traditional radial maze experiment, a single piece of food is placed in a cup at the end of each arm of the maze. However, in some experiments, different amounts of food were placed on the arms of the maze. Hulse and O'Leary (1982) placed different numbers of food pellets on the arms of a four-arm radial maze, and W. Roberts (1992) placed cubes of cheese varying in size on the arms of a six-arm radial maze. The results were the same in both experiments. Rats initially entered the arms without regard to the food on the arm, but, after several trials on the maze, animals came to enter arms very precisely in decreasing order of food size. This result suggests that animals formed reference memory for the food contents of each arm. In running the maze, rats used working memory to remember which arms had been entered, but reference memory was used to direct choices of arms according to their content.

From the human experimenter's point of view, the rat's behavior may seem unnecessary. Why should a rat always go the largest food arm first, the second largest next, and so on, when the animal was allowed to collect all of the food on the maze on each trial? If the rat always gets all of the food, why should the animal prefer to enter arms in one order versus another? The key to the rat's behavior lies in evolved foraging strategies found in both the laboratory rat and its wild ancestors. In a natural setting, a forager may not always be allowed to complete a sequence of visits to different food sites. Its foraging activities may

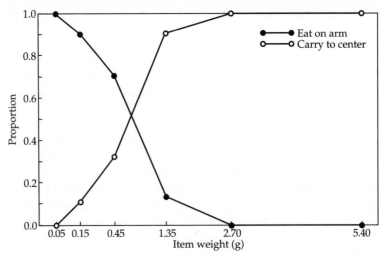

FIGURE 7.16. Central-place foraging on the radial maze by rats. Rats ate small pieces of food on the arms of the maze but increasingly carried food to the center to consume as food-item size increased.

be interrupted by the need to flee from a predator or a fight with a conspecific over food. In this environment, the most efficient strategy for maximizing food intake is to always go to the richest food sources first and the leanest ones last. If the animal is interrupted during its foraging activity, it has maximized its E/T ratio up to that point. On the radial maze, we are seeing rats execute an optimal foraging strategy that would promote their survival in the real world.

Central-Place Foraging

Many foraging animals are *central-place foragers*. A central-place forager often carries its food to its home, a nest or a burrow, to consume it. The reason for this behavior is fairly obvious; it allows the animal to consume its food in a safe place rather than risk eating it in the open where it might be attacked by a predator or conspecific. However, food is sometimes eaten at the place where it is found instead of being carried to the animal's home. The critical factor controlling carrying behavior is the size of the food. It has been suggested that animals adopt an optimal trade-off between the demand for foraging efficiency and the demand for minimal exposure to risk of predation (Lima & Valone, 1986). Thus, making constant trips back and forth between a central place and the site of food is costly in terms of time and energy spent traveling. On the other hand, spending too much time in the open consuming food could cost an animal the ultimate price of its life. As an optimal trade-off, animals tend to eat small food items at the food site; exposure to predation is minimal, and travel time is saved. When large food items are encountered, however, these items are carried home, where they may be eaten in relative safety.

It has been suggested that rats perform well on mazes because mazes mimic, to a certain extent, the natural ecology of wild rats. The radial maze, for example, is similar to a rat burrow system with a central chamber containing many tunnels that exit from it. Phelps and W. Roberts (1989) inquired whether rats might show central-place foraging on the radial maze if appropriate conditions were used. They tested rats on a four-arm radial maze, with different sizes of cheese placed on the arms of the maze. Just as suggested by the optimal trade-off model of central-place foraging, rats ate small pieces of food on the arms of the maze but tended to carry food back to the center to eat as the size of the food items increased (see data in Figure 7.16). In other experiments in which multiple pieces of food were put on the arms of the maze, rats showed multiple-item loading by stuffing two or three food items in their mouth to carry back in one trip (Ash & W. Roberts, 1992). Such behavior saved the animal the energy required by multiple trips.

Other findings supported the model by suggesting that rats perceived the arms of the maze as less safe than the center of the maze (Phelps & W. Roberts, 1989). When rats carried food, they sped back to the center of the maze in about 1 second, whereas they would return much more slowly, taking 4 to 7 seconds, if they had consumed food on the arm. This time difference suggested a strong imperative to carry food to the safety of the center as quickly as possible. Eating times further suggested that rats felt less safe on the arms of the maze than in the center. When rats ate on the arms of the maze, they ate faster than when they ate food at the center of the maze. Finally, it was possible to reduce central-place foraging in two ways. The work and travel time required to carry food items from the arms to the center of the maze was increased by requiring rats to climb over barriers placed at the entrance to each arm. Rats still carried food to the center but at a lower frequency than they did without the barriers. In one other experiment, another rat was placed at the center of the maze in a transparent box while the subject foraged. The tendency to carry food to the center was significantly reduced when the rat had to carry food to the vicinity of a conspecific.

Why should rats feel safer at the center of the radial maze than on the arms of the maze? One explanation is that the center provides more escape routes. That is, a rat at the center of the maze perceives the arms branching from it as potential escape routes to be used should a food competitor happen along. On the end of an arm, however, there is only one route available back to the center. To test this idea, W. Roberts, Phelps, and Schacter (1992) built a radial maze on which different numbers of escape routes or arms branched off the ends of arms containing food. In support of the escape-route hypothesis, central place foraging declined as the number of escape routes increased.

SPATIAL MEMORY IN FOOD-STORING BIRDS

Observations in Natural or Seminatural Settings

Although foragers typically consume food when it is found, an animal may sometimes encounter an abundance of food that is more than it can consume at the moment. One strategy used to deal with this situation is to hoard food or hide it in a safe place. As the need for food arises in the future, the animal is able to safely eat from its hoard. Food storing in birds is an example of hoarding that has been of particular interest to memory theorists. Some species of birds regularly store or hide food in different locations within their environment and later return to consume the food. Two families of birds that have been studied in some detail are the tits (*Paridae*) and corvids (*Corvidae*).

In Wytham Wood, near Oxford University, marsh tits have been observed to store pieces of food, such as seeds, nuts, and insects, in a variety of locations—under moss or the bark of a tree or in natural crevices formed by a hollow stem or the needles of a pine cone. Storage sites were not clustered together but tended to be evenly spaced apart. Within a few hours, marsh tits often returned to these locations to collect the hidden food items (Sherry, 1987). The questions that arise are, Do marsh tits use spatial memory to locate hidden food? Does the individual bird remember where it previously hid pieces of food? There are other possible explanations of marsh tits' ability to locate hidden food. Birds might have preferred hiding places for food and then preferentially search at those places at a later time, without memory of hiding food in those specific locations. To test this possibility, Cowie, Krebs, and Sherry (1981) offered marsh tits sunflower seeds that were radioactively labeled and then traced the hiding places of those seeds with a scintillation meter. These seeds were replaced with regular seeds, and control seeds were placed in a similar hiding place at distances of either 10 cm or 100 cm from the original hiding place. When these locations were inspected periodically, it was found that the average time it took seeds in the original hiding places to disappear was about 8 hours. The near-control seeds disappeared in an average of about 14 hours, and the far-control seeds disappeared in an average of about 20 hours. Marsh tits found the hidden-seed locations very effectively but apparently often passed up nearby seeds, suggesting that they were using spatial memory.

A well-known species of corvid, Clark's nutcracker, is found in the southwestern United States. Nutcrackers collect pine seeds in a sublingual pouch and carry them over distances of several kilometers to bury them in the ground on the higher southern slopes of mountains. With an abundant seed crop, a nutcracker hoards as many as 33,000 seeds; it must recover at least 2,500 seeds to survive the winter (Balda & Turek, 1984). Observations of the locations where nutcrackers dig in the snow and ground throughout the winter suggest that they are not searching randomly but dig at or near buried seed caches (Tomback, 1980). The question again arises as to whether this behavior is guided by memory or by some nonmemorial search strategy. Vander Wall (1982) kept nutcrackers in an outdoor aviary. Among four birds given an opportunity to hoard seeds in the sandy floor of the aviary, two birds hoarded seeds, and the other two did not. When all four birds were allowed to search for food, the hoarders found 70 percent of the caches, but the nonhoarders found only 10 percent. Memory may have given the hoarders a substantial advantage. On the other hand, the hoarding nutcrackers might have been hiding food and searching for it in favored locations, without using memory. If the favored locations differed between individual birds, the hoarders would still have an advantage.

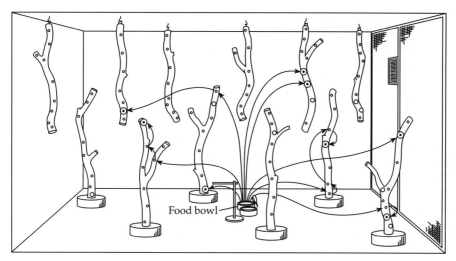

FIGURE 7.17. Drawing of the experimental room used to study food storing and retrieval in marsh tits and black capped chickadees. The subjects carried seeds from the food bowl on the floor to holes in tree branches that served as hiding places.

Laboratory Experiments

The observations of food-storing birds in natural or seminatural settings suggested that they were using spatial memory to find hidden food, but final proof of spatial memory awaited more controlled laboratory research. Figure 7.17 shows a laboratory test room used to study memory for stored food in marsh tits and another parid, the blackcapped chickadee (Shettleworth, 1983; Shettleworth & Krebs, 1982; 1986). The room contained a number of tree branches with 97 holes drilled in them as potential storage sites. A small piece of cloth covered each hole so that its contents could not be seen without pecking at the hole. Birds were released into this room with a bowl of seeds on the floor and were allowed to hide 12 seeds in the holes of the trees. After removal from the room, birds were returned 2 hours later for a retention test in which they could obtain seeds only by retrieving them from the covered locations. Birds flew about the room and retrieved stored seeds at a far higher level of accuracy than would be expected by chance or by a selective search strategy. To control for the possibility that birds were using some cue provided by the hidden seeds, tests were run in which the hidden seeds were moved to other sites between storage and test. Tits still searched at the original hiding locations above chance expectation.

Clark's nutcrackers have also been tested in an experimental room specifically designed to reveal their spatial memory ability (Kamil & Balda, 1983; 1990). The floor of the room contains 180 sand-filled holes, along with rocks and logs that may serve as landmarks. The advantage of this arrangement is that any of the holes in the room can be capped, allowing the experimenter to decide in which holes the nutcracker will store its seeds. In this way, birds cannot hide food in preferred locations. In fact, this apparatus and procedure are often described as an analog of the rat radial maze for testing birds. After nutcrackers were given caching sessions in which they stored pine seeds in the experimenter-chosen holes, they were allowed to search among all 180 holes on recovery sessions given 10 days later. Cache recovery was highly accurate on the initial session; about 50 percent of the holes visited contained cached seeds, whereas only about 15 percent of the holes visited should have contained seeds by chance alone. Although accuracy of cache recovery remained above chance throughout further sessions of testing, it dropped from the initial high level. It was suggested that nutcrackers may visit those sites for which they have the best memory first, leaving sites less well remembered for later. These findings leave little doubt that Clark's nutcrackers, like marsh tits and chickadees, use spatial memory to recover hoarded food.

Is Spatial Memory in Food-Storing Birds an Adaptive Specialization?

Not all birds, not even all parids and corvids, hide and recover food. What characteristics of marsh tits, chickadees, and Clark's nutcrackers lead them to use this mode of energy conservation? Beyond the functional advantage this behavior confers, one possibility is that these birds have evolved memory capacities that are specially designed for hoarding and recovering food (Sherry & Schacter, 1987). In one set of experiments, Shettleworth, Krebs, Healy, and Thomas (1990) investigated the possibility that food-storing tits might remember well only food items that they had hidden. If this were the case, it would suggest that any memory superiority food-storing birds might have over other birds is narrowly restricted to remembering hidden food items. Interestingly, Shettleworth et al. did not find that this was the case. An experiment was arranged in which chickadees hid seeds in trees but occasionally encountered holes that already contained seeds that were placed there by the experimenter. When the chickadees' memory was tested, their accuracy at recovering encountered seeds was equally as good as that for seeds they had hidden.

In some interesting experiments with Clark's nutcracker, evidence was found that memory performance may differ for stored and nonstored food. In one set of experiments (Olson, Kamil, & Balda, 1993), pine seeds were buried in four out of eight holes by the experimenter. Two groups of birds were allowed to dig in all eight holes until all of the seeds were consumed. The birds then returned to the aviary for a retention interval. The birds returned to the apparatus for a retention test at intervals that varied from 5 minutes to 24 hours. One group of birds was always tested with a stay contingency in effect; that is, the same holes that contained seeds before the retention interval contained seeds after the retention interval. The other group, the shift group, was always tested with seeds placed in the holes that were empty during the preretention phase. The data showed little difference between the two groups. Clark's nutcrackers were able to remember the locations of hidden seeds equally well regardless of whether they had to show their memory by going to previously baited or empty locations.

In subsequent experiments, Kamil, Balda, and Olson (1994a) again looked at nutcrackers' memory under stay and shift contingencies but with an important change in procedure. The birds now stored the seeds themselves instead of finding seeds hidden by the experimenter. During the retention interval, the experimenter ensured that seeds were placed in the holes where the bird had hidden them (stay group) or that seeds were placed only in the holes where the bird had not hidden them (shift group). The striking outcome of these experiments was that the stay group showed good memory for hidden seeds but the shift group showed no evidence of retention. Apparently, nutcrackers can only manifest memory for seeds they have hidden by returning to the same locations where they hid the food. If hidden food is encountered, however, they can learn equally well to return to the same or different locations on retention tests.

The possibility has been explored that food-storing birds have better spatial memory than nonstoring birds. Several recently discovered lines of evidence lend some support to this hypothesis. Olson (1991) studied spatial memory in three species of birds—nutcrackers, scrub jays, and pigeons—using a nonmatching test performed in an operant chamber. The memory test began with the illumination of a left or right key on the front panel of the chamber. The subject pecked this key several times until it darkened. After a delay, another key on the rear panel of the box was illuminated, and the bird had to peck this key to illuminate both the left and right keys on the front panel. A final peck on the nonmatching key (the one that had not been lit) was the correct response and yielded reward. Olson found that nutcrackers could remember the correct key on this task over substantially longer delays than could either scrub jays or pigeons. Pigeons, of course, do not store food. The scrub jay is a corvid relative of the nutcracker but spends far less time than the nutcracker storing and recovering food. Thus, a food-storing specialist showed superior memory to nonspecialists, even though it was tested on a memory task far removed from its natural food-storing activities. This finding was further confirmed in memory tests carried out in the open-room analog of the radial maze. Clark's nutcrackers showed faster acquisition and better retention of hidden seed locations than pinyon jays, scrub jays, and Mexican jays (Kamil, Balda, & Olson, 1994b).

Could it be that the superior spatial memory of Clark's nutcracker is the result of generally superior memory? Maybe these birds would perform better on any memory test. Olson, Kamil, Balda and Nims (1995) addressed this possibility by training four species of jays to perform a color nonmatching-to-sample task. This task was similar to the matching-to-sample procedure described in Chapters 3 and 4 except that birds had to choose the color that did not match the sample. Thus, a bird that had seen a red sample stimulus would have to choose the green stimulus for reward when given a retention test with red and green comparison stimuli. It is important to remember that this task is nonspatial in nature; because the matching and nonmatching colors are randomly alternated between left and right positions, only memory of color allows the bird to make the correct choice. On this task, no species differences in retention were found. In particular, Clark's nutcrackers were no better than the other three species of jays. When spatial memory was measured, however, nutcrackers again excelled over the other species. These data strongly suggest that the nutcracker, a bird that has evolved through a heavy dependence on spatial memory for hidden food caches, is a spatial memory specialist. However, its superior memory for space does not appear to extend to other forms of memory, at least visual memory for color. An important implication of this finding is that different neural systems may underlie memory for spatial and nonspatial features of the environment.

The Hippocampus and Spatial Memory

The *hippocampus* is a relatively large neural structure that resides in the limbic system beneath the cortex of the mammalian brain and has been implicated as a critical area for spatial memory (O'Keefe & Nadel, 1978). Lesions to this area in rats lead to a severe deterioration of working memory on the radial maze. Birds also possess a hippocampal complex of brain structures homologous to the mammalian hippocampus. Sherry and Vaccarino (1989) surgically removed the hippocampus in chickadees and then tested their ability to cache and retrieve food. Although chickadees continued to cache food at a high rate, their ability to subsequently retrieve food was seriously disrupted. Lesioned birds often flew to empty sites and repeatedly visited previously visited sites, whereas nonlesioned control birds efficiently collected food from cache sites without repetitive visits.

Having established that the hippocampus is essential for memory of stored food in chickadees, Sherry, Vaccarino, Buckenham, and Herz (1989) examined the size of the hippocampus relative to body weight and other brain structures in families of birds containing both food storers and nonfood storers. The data indicated that the relative size of the hippocampus is greater in food-storing birds than in birds that do not store food. Thus, lesion studies and comparative anatomical studies both suggest that the hippocampus is essential for accurate food retrieval in food-storing birds. Presumably, a larger hippocampus evolved in food-storing birds in response to the cognitive demands of storing and retrieving large numbers of food items (Sherry, 1992).

Converging evidence from behavioral and neural studies supports the notion that food-storing birds have evolved superior spatial memory as an adaptive specialization (Shettleworth, 1990; 1992). Although it is too early to reach a firm conclusion, existing data encourage the notion that food-storing birds may have superior spatial memory in a variety of tasks and that this superiority may arise from the selective evolution of a larger hippocampus.

SUMMARY

Spatial cognition refers to a variety of cognitive processes used by people and animals to encode and remember places in space, the contents of places, and the organism's travels through space. One form of spatial navigation without visual cues is path integration or dead reckoning. Through the use of vestibular and kinesthetic feedback from its own movements, an animal can keep track of the direction and distance of its starting point. However, path integration becomes progressively less accurate as more turns are added to a trip and more error is added to the computation of a return vector.

A number of species of animals can find hidden goals if those goals maintain a consistent relationship to landmarks. The ways in which the landmarks are used vary among species. Bees appear to record two-dimensional memories of landmarks and then locate goals by matching the apparent size and compass bearings of perceived landmarks with their memory. Rodents and birds, on the other hand, appear to encode the distance of landmarks from goals and to compute goal-landmark vectors. These vectors specify the distance and direction of a goal from a particular landmark. The addition of self-landmark vectors to goal-landmark vectors allows an animal to plot a course directly to the goal.

Vector information forms a part of cognitive maps that specify global relationships between locations within areas and between areas. Local charts of areas contain both topological information about the relative positions of places to one another and metric information about specific angles and distances. Through exploration and travel between places, increasingly sophisticated route maps are developed specifying vectors between different locations. The computation of metric information and the linking of local charts critically depends on an animal establishing reference directions. Reference directions may be based on distant cues or a frequently used axis of travel. Evidence for cognitive maps in animals comes from a number of experiments showing that animals take detours and shortcuts to goals and compute a least-distance-traveled path among multiple goals or food locations.

Considerable research with the radial maze has established that spatial memory in rats is robust. Spatial working memory is highly capacious; experiments with the 17-arm maze and the hierarchical maze indicate that rats can remember large numbers of visits to different arms of the maze. Spatial working memory is also resistant to normal forgetting from the passage of time; rats remembered perfectly arms they were forced to enter 4 hours earlier. When interpolated stimuli were presented during a retention interval between forced and free choices, rats did not suffer RI. Spatial memory appeared to be disturbed only in experiments in which rats had to return repeatedly to the same arms or locations in space. Proactive interference appeared when rats had to visit all of the arms on a radial maze in the course of repeated massed trials. Evidence of RI was found when correct retention depended on returning to arms upon which the rat had just been placed as an interpolated treatment. These instances of PI and RI can be attributed to temporal confusion or difficulty in discriminating how recently a particular arm was entered.

The functional value of spatial memory appears to lie in the advantages it confers on a foraging animal. By knowing the locations of different food sources, water, mates, and predators in its habitat, a forager can travel efficiently through the environment. Efficient or optimal foraging allows the forager to approach a maximum E/T ratio while avoiding competitors. Some demonstrations with the radial maze suggest that rats adopt optimal foraging strategies even in the laboratory. Thus, given different quantities of food on the arms of the maze, rats rapidly learn to visit arms in decreasing order of food magnitude. Central-place foraging is seen in the tendency of rats to carry larger food items to the center of the maze for consumption. Other experiments suggest that the center is perceived as the safest location on the maze because it contains multiple escape routes.

Recent natural and laboratory investigations of food-storing birds indicate that they recover hidden food by using spatial memory. Comparative experiments testing laboratory memory in a nonmatching spatial task suggest that a food-storing corvid, Clark's nutcracker, has generally superior spatial memory to birds that do not store food. Recent research indicates that differences in the size of the hippocampus underlie differences in spatial memory ability between storing and nonstoring birds. Anatomical data show that storing birds have a relatively larger hippocampus than birds that do not store food.

CHAPTER 8

Timing

Most organisms must learn and store information about space and time in order to survive. The preceding chapter dealt with spatial cognition, and this chapter discusses temporal cognition. Most people have made observations that suggest that animals have a sense of time. Cats howl at feeding time each day, and dogs seem to wait expectantly at the door at about the time the mailman arrives. Wild animals are often reported to hunt at the time of day when their prey is most likely to make an appearance. Beyond casual observation, however, there is extensive experimental evidence to support the impression that animals are indeed sensitive to time of day.

TIME-PLACE LEARNING

Time of Day

If wild animals seek food in different places at different times of day, it should be possible to test this ability in the laboratory. Biebach, Gordijn, and Krebs (1989) carried out just such an experiment with garden warblers. A bird was housed in an experimental chamber that consisted of a central living room and four feeding rooms, any one of which could be entered from the living room (see Figure 8.1). Although all four feeding rooms contained feeders, only one feeder could be opened at a given time. If a warbler went to the correct room, it was allowed to open the feeder and eat from it for 20 seconds. After visiting a feeding room, a bird always had to return to the living room and stay there for 280 seconds before it could enter another feeding room. Access to food was allowed in different rooms at different times of day. Food was available in Room 1 from 0600 to 0900 hours, in Room 2 from 0900 to 1200 hours, in Room 3 from 1200 to 1500 hours, and in Room 4 from 1500 to 1800 hours.

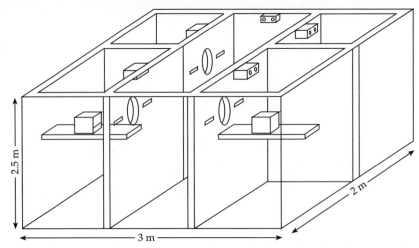

FIGURE 8.1. The experimental chamber used to study time-place learning in garden warblers. Birds could fly back and forth between a central living room and any one of four feeding rooms.

Within 10 days, all five birds trained learned to go to the rewarded room during the 3-hour period when food could be obtained in that room. These findings alone, however, do not prove that warblers associated food in a particular place with a particular time. Perhaps the birds initially sampled all four rooms until they found one that yielded food. They then stuck with this room until it failed to provide reward, at which time they sampled the other rooms until they found another one that contained food, and so on. Therefore, a critical test of time-place learning was carried out on two days on which all four rooms contained open feeders throughout the 12-hour period. As shown in Figure 8.2, birds made the majority of visits to each room during the time when that room had been rewarded during training. These data constitute an impressive demonstration of the effects of time-place training because the subjects could have obtained equal amounts of reward by going to the same room throughout the day or by visiting rooms randomly. Instead, the warblers regularly shifted from room to room at the time each room had been scheduled to yield food.

Circadian Time Cues

Changes in the environment provide salient circadian time cues both for people and animals. The change in illumination tells us when it is day and night, and the position of the sun in the sky acts as a clock during the day. In addition, internal or endogenous circadian cycles provide cues for time of day. For example, one's state of hunger may act as a rough indicator of time of day. It was suggested in Chapter 6 that the state of a circadian oscillator at the time of learning may act as a retrieval cue for memory of that learning. Endogenous oscillators refer to internal states of an organism that cycle through high and low states throughout the day. Examples are changes in rate of firing of neurons in the nervous system or changes in the concentrations of hormones in the blood stream.

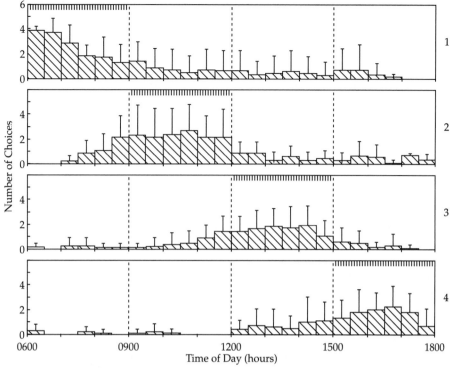

FIGURE 8.2. From top to bottom, the panels show the number of choices of feeding Rooms 1, 2, 3, and 4 over successive 3-hour periods from 0600 hours to 1800 hours. The vertical line above each bar is the standard deviation of five birds.

Oscillators affect behavior, such as changes in activity level, and state of consciousness, such as sleep and wakefulness. External circadian cues, particularly changes in illumination, act to *entrain* or maintain a regular oscillation of internal states. Such external modulators are called *zeitgebers* or "time givers."

Endogenous circadian cues would seem to be a prime candidate for explaining the time-place learning found in the Biebach et al. (1989) study. Birds may have learned to associate different internal states with the different locations of food. However, we cannot immediately rule out exogenous cues. Although the experiment was performed within an enclosed chamber, it is possible that warblers had access to environmental cues that might have controlled responding. A recent study by Saksida and Wilkie (1994) suggests such cues are not necessary. Saksida and Wilkie trained pigeons in an operant chamber that contained a pecking key on each of four walls. Birds were placed in this chamber for 17 minutes in the morning (about 0930 hours) and for 17 minutes in the afternoon (about 1600 hours). For the first minute of each session, no reward was delivered for key pecking. Thereafter, reward was delivered for key pecking, but Key 1 had to be pecked for reward in the morning, and Key 3 had to be pecked for reward in the afternoon. As warblers did in the Biebach et al. study, pigeons learned to peck Key 1 in the morning and Key 3 in the afternoon.

Of particular importance, these preferences appeared during the first minute of testing, when differential reward could not influence birds' choice of keys.

Saksida and Wilkie (1994) then carried out some control experiments to determine the basis for the pigeon's time-place learning. One possibility was that pigeons might have learned to alternate keys between sessions. In this case, a pigeon would remember only which key was rewarded during the previous session and then choose the alternate key; time of day would not be relevant. To test this hypothesis, pigeons were tested for blocks of days in which only the morning or the afternoon trial was given. If pigeons had learned to alternate, they should choose the correct key one day and the incorrect key the next day when tested only in the mornings or afternoons. Instead, birds continued to choose the correct key indicated by the time of day.

In another experiment, pigeons were *clock shifted.* The light in the room where the pigeons were housed normally came on at 0600 hours. On test days, it was shifted back 6 hours to 2400 hours. Although such a shift in daily light onset eventually entrains new endogenous rhythms, it should have little immediate effect on endogenous oscillators. If the state of these endogenous oscillators is providing time-of-day cues that control choice behavior, pigeons should continue to make correct choices on morning and afternoon tests. On the other hand, if pigeons were somehow timing the interval since daily light onset to determine which key was correct, errors should appear since the morning trial occurred at an interval after light onset that was equivalent to the interval that normally preceded the afternoon test in training. The results were very clear; pigeons continued to peck correct keys on both morning and afternoon tests. These findings suggest quite clearly that pigeons' place selection was controlled by the time of day as indicated by the state of endogenous circadian cues.

Interval Timing

Circadian timing is a mechanism by which an organism keeps track of the time of day. At specific temporal points within a 24-hour day, an animal may be affected by endogenous cues that establish a motivational state or retrieve a memory that prompts a particular behavioral act. In addition to this time-of-day timing, animals often need to keep track of short intervals of time that may elapse at any time of day. For example, foraging animals may pause in one location to search for prey for a fixed interval of time before moving to a new location. Each interval is timed to give the animal time to adequately search for potential food but also to keep it from becoming the target of a predator. Since the animal may forage at numerous times throughout the day, it must be able to time short intervals at any time. Some mechanism other than circadian cues is necessary to accomplish this interval timing.

To illustrate the phenomenon of interval timing, we examine some further experiments from Wilkie's laboratory that appear to be highly similar to the Saksida and Wilkie (1994) studies just discussed but that suggest a different timing process. In these experiments, all four of the keys mounted on different walls were used. Pigeons were placed in the apparatus for 60 minutes. During the first 15 minutes, pecking on Key 1 delivered reward; pecks on Key 2 produced reward during the next 15 minutes, and so on for Keys 3 and 4

(Wilkie & Willson, 1992). Pigeons learned to peck at each key during the time it yielded reward and then to switch to the next key near the end of 15 minutes. During test sessions, reward was omitted during the 5-minute periods preceding and following the points in time at which reward had been switched from one key to the next. Subjects continued to shift from one key to the next at approximately 15-minute intervals, showing time-place learning.

In other experiments, Wilkie, Saksida, Samson, and Lee (1994) examined the effects of introducing a timeout on time-place behavior. After pigeons completed 15 minutes of pecking on Key 1, the lights on all four keys were turned off for a 15-minute period during which no reward was delivered for any key pecks. The key lights then were turned back on, and the pigeons were given a nonrewarded 5-minute test during which they could peck any key. If pigeons used endogenous circadian cues to keep track of the time at which each key would deliver reward, they should have pecked Key 3 since two 15-minute periods had elapsed since the beginning of the session. Instead, pigeons pecked at Key 2. In another experiment, the same procedure was used, but the 15-minute timeout was spent in the pigeons' home cage. When they were returned to the apparatus, they pecked Key 1. In neither experiment did pigeons peck Key 3, the key that should have been indicated by endogenous cues.

When pigeons were trained to peck different keys in the morning and afternoon, the omission of opportunity to peck a key in either the morning or the afternoon had no effect on control of behavior by time-of-day cues. However, the omission of a 15-minute opportunity to peck a key when the rewarded key was shifted every 15 minutes led to very different behavior—either pecking the key that was appropriate at the beginning of the timeout or returning to the key that was correct at the beginning of the session. The difference between these phenomena is explained by the large difference in the lengths of the time periods during which keys deliver reward. When the location of reward stays fixed for periods of 3 hours, as in the Biebach et al. (1989) experiment, or during morning versus afternoon sessions, animals use endogenous circadian cues to determine time and the correct location of food. When the location of reward changes every 15 minutes, however, changes in endogenous circadian cues are not sufficient to allow such fine temporal discriminations. Yet, pigeons clearly were able to learn the different locations of correct keys that changed every 15 minutes. To do this, it appears that animals use a quite different timing system: *interval timing.* In interval timing, the subject keeps track of the amount of time that has elapsed since the beginning of an event, such as the beginning of a trial or a session. Thus, pigeons in the Wilkie and Willson (1992) and Wilkie et al. (1994) studies timed successive 15-minute intervals from the start of a session and switched keys at the appropriate times.

One theory of interval timing suggests that animals accomplish the timing of intervals by the use of an *internal clock* (Church, 1978). The theory suggests that the internal clock has many of the properties of a common stopwatch. Thus, it may be stopped at a particular value for a period of time and then restarted at that value, or it may be stopped and reset back to zero for timing a new interval. These properties may help us understand the effects found in the Wilkie et al. (1994) experiment. Pigeons given a 15-minute timeout in the apparatus after completing 15 minutes of pecking on Key 1 then pecked Key 2 when the keys were relit. If the internal clock was stopped for the 15-minute period and began to run again when the keys were relit, the time on the internal clock would indicate that the subject was in the second 15-minute period and should peck Key 2. On the other hand, removing the pigeon from the apparatus may have signaled that the session was completed and that the internal clock should be reset to zero. When the subject was returned to the apparatus 15 minutes later, it would begin timing the first 15-minute interval again, and Key 1 should be the appropriate key to peck.

Considerable data and theory on interval timing in animals has accumulated over the past 20 years, and a number of timing phenomena can be understood by theories of the internal clock. In the remainder of this chapter, these issues are discussed in some detail.

PROCEDURES FOR THE STUDY
OF TIMING IN ANIMALS

Methods for studying interval timing in animals usually consist of *discrimination procedures or production procedures. Discrimination procedures* require a subject to respond differentially to signals that vary in their length of presentation. In the case of *production procedures,* the subject actually tells the experimenter its estimate of a time interval through its behavior. As we shall see, the development of the *peak procedure* provided a particularly powerful production tool for determining behavioral estimates of time in animals.

Discrimination Procedures

In some early studies of time discrimination in rats, an animal was trained in an apparatus in which it could enter a left or right chamber after first being delayed for some period of time in a delay chamber. Cowles and Finan (1941) rewarded rats for choosing one door of a discrimination apparatus after a delay of 10 seconds and rewarded choice of another door after a delay of 30 seconds. Six out of nine rats were able to learn this problem to above a chance level of accuracy. In a similar experiment, Heron (1949) trained rats to discriminate between intervals of 5 and 45 seconds and then gradually reduced the length of the longer interval. The number of animals that could maintain this discrimination dropped progressively until only 1 of the 11 rats that learned the initial discrimination could discriminate between intervals of 5 and 10 seconds.

In a more modern version of this type of experiment, an operant chamber is used, and rats are presented with a signal—a houselight or a noise—that lasts for a "short" period of time or a "long" period of time (Meck, 1983; S. Roberts & Church, 1978). When the signal ends, two retractable levers emerge from the wall of the chamber. One lever is correct after the short signal, and the other lever is correct after the long signal. It should be realized that "short" and "long" are defined on a relative basis by the experimenter. Thus, 10 seconds is the long stimulus if 2 seconds is the short stimulus, but 10 seconds is the short stimulus if 50 seconds is the long stimulus.

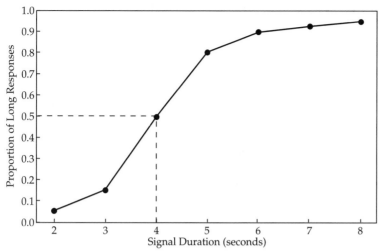

FIGURE 8.3. A psychophysical curve based on hypothetical data showing the proportion of choices of the "long" response following test stimuli varying from 2 to 8 seconds in duration. The broken lines show determination of the subjective midpoint.

As an example of such an experiment, suppose that rats are presented with two white noise signals that last for either 2 seconds or 8 seconds. The two durations of noise occur in a random order, and a response to the right or left lever is required after each noise signal. After the 2-second signal, the left (short) lever must be pressed for the rat to earn a food pellet. After the 8-second signal, food is delivered for a press on the right (long) lever. Rats acquire this discrimination readily and respond at 90 percent or greater accuracy after about 10 sessions of training. A typical psychophysical procedure followed once a discrimination between extreme durations has been formed is to test the subject's response to intermediate durations. While the original discrimination between 2 and 8 seconds is maintained, probe test trials are occasionally given at signal durations of 2, 3, 4, 5, 6, 7, and 8 seconds. No reward is given for response to either lever on these test trials, but the subject's choice of the short or long lever is recorded. After sufficient test trials have been carried out, a curve can be plotted that shows the proportion of responses to the long lever as a function of signal duration (see Figure 8.3). This curve is called a *psychophysical function,* and its shape is an *ogive;* it starts out with a flat portion, over which subjects usually choose the short lever, then rises rapidly, over durations in which judgments change from short to long responses, and flattens out at longer durations, in which subjects regularly choose the long lever.

An important property of the ogive shown in Figure 8.3 is that we can estimate the *subjective midpoint* of the curve. The subjective midpoint is that value on the test dimension at which the subject is equally likely to press the left (short) or the right (long) lever, thus indicating it is midway between the short and long training stimuli. We calculate the subjective midpoint as the test stimulus at which the subject shows indifference between the short and long keys.

A line is drawn parallel to the abscissa from the 50 percent point on the ordinate to the psychophysical curve. A vertical line is drawn from this point to the abscissa, and the point at which the curve hits the abscissa indicates the subjective midpoint. Notice that such an estimation of the subjective midpoint in Figure 8.3 yields a value of about 4 seconds. The subjective midpoint does not occur at the arithmetic mean between 2 and 8 seconds, which would be 5 seconds. In fact, rats judged that the duration of the noise signal was equidistant in time between 2 and 8 seconds when it had been on for about 4 seconds.

This finding has considerable generality. Church and Deluty (1977) trained rats in a lighted operant chamber and darkened the chamber to provide short and long signals. Rats were trained with short and long signals of 1 and 4 seconds, 2 and 8 seconds, 3 and 12 seconds, and 4 and 16 seconds. When accurate discrimination between these durations was achieved, signals of intermediate length were presented during nonrewarded probe test trials. The psychophysical curves produced by test trials yielded subjective midpoints of about 2 seconds between 1 and 4 seconds, 4 seconds between 2 and 8 seconds, 6 seconds between 3 and 12 seconds, and 8 seconds between 4 and 16 seconds. Notice that a pattern appears in these data that allows us to predict the subjective midpoint. The subjective midpoint has the same ratio to the short duration as the long duration has to the subjective midpoint. Thus the ratio of 4/2 is the same as the ratio 8/4. The subjective midpoint is the geometric mean of the short and long stimuli, as calculated by the square root of their product. Thus the square root of $2 \times 8 = 16$ is 4. Comparable data from pigeons similarly suggest that the subjective midpoint falls at the geometric mean of training durations (Gibbon, 1986; Platt & Davis, 1983; Stubbs, 1976).

Production Procedures

Fixed-Interval Responding

Some well-known conditioning experiments originally performed by Pavlov (1927) involved delay conditioning and temporal conditioning. In delay conditioning, the CS precedes the food by a constant interval of time; in temporal conditioning, no CS is presented, and the food US is delivered to the dog at regular time intervals. With both procedures, dogs typically inhibit salivating during the interval preceding the US but salivate copiously just before food delivery. This result is a form of inhibition of delay, as discussed in Chapter 5. One interpretation of this finding is that the dog learned to time the interval between the CS and US in delay conditioning or between food deliveries in temporal conditioning.

In operant conditioning, a similar example is found in the behavior generated by a fixed-interval (FI) schedule of reinforcement. In this schedule, a response yields reward only after a fixed interval of time has passed since the preceding reward. An animal well trained on an FI schedule shows the scalloped cumulative response curve found in Figure 8.4. Rate of response is very low during the initial part of the interval but accelerates during the latter part of the interval. This behavior maximizes the rate of reward collection but tends to minimize effort; an ability to time the FI should lead to little response at the beginning of the interval, when it is clearly too early to obtain food, and frequent response at the end of the interval so that the reward may be obtained as soon

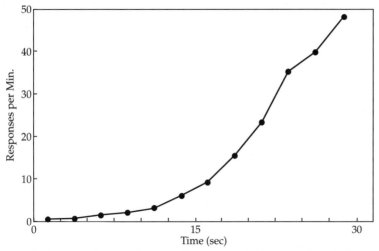

FIGURE 8.4. The increase in rate of responding over an FI 30-second period. The scallop is shown in the low rate of responding over the first 15 seconds and the rapid acceleration of responding over the last 15 seconds.

as it becomes available. The smooth curve shown in Figure 8.4 is produced by averaging data from a number of trials in which animals begin responding at different times around the midpoint of the FI. The importance of averaging data from trials with different start times is emphasized further in the theoretical section at the end of this chapter.

Similar behavior is seen when a form of temporal aversive conditioning is used. Free-operant avoidance conditioning involves schedules in which shock follows each response by a fixed interval of time, and shock can be delayed only by another response. If the response-shock interval is 20 seconds, rats learn to respond very little during the first 10 seconds after a response, but the probability of a response increases progressively as the last 10 seconds of the interval elapse (Gibbon, 1972; Libby & Church, 1974). In this way, both punishment and effort are minimized.

In a number of different interval timing situations involving production, the *proportionality result* has been found (Dews, 1970; Church, 1978; Gibbon, 1977). If animals are trained under different FI schedules for food reward, a family of scalloped curves can be plotted, with the period of low responding extending further into the interval the longer the FI. The proportionality principle tells us that curves obtained under different FIs can be transformed to duplicate one another by plotting response rate as a proportion of the terminal rate and time as a proportion of the length of the FI. An impressive example of proportionality is seen in Figure 8.5, taken from Dews (1970). Three curves are shown based on pigeons' behavior under FI schedules involving intervals between reinforcements of 30, 300, and 3,000 seconds. When a relative time scale is used, and when rate of response is based on proportion of terminal rate, the curves for the three FIs are virtually identical. Similar instances of proportionality are found in experiments in which aversive stimulation is delivered at regular intervals (LaBarbera & Church, 1974; Libby & Church, 1974).

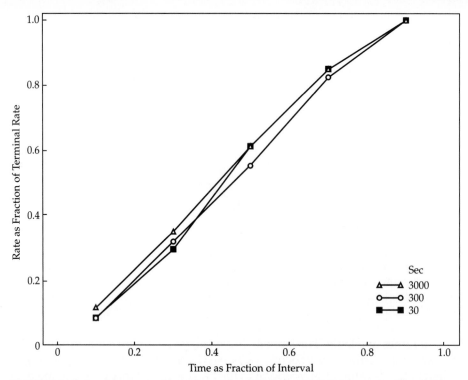

FIGURE 8.5. Rate of response throughout FIs of 30, 300, and 3,000 seconds. The abscissa plots time as a proportion of the total FI, and the ordinate plots rate of response as a proportion of the terminal rate of response under each FI.

An important theoretical implication that has been drawn from these repeated demonstrations of proportionality is that animal timing is based on a scalar process (Church & Gibbon, 1982; Gibbon, 1972; 1977; 1991; Gibbon & Church, 1981). Scalar timing suggests that animals use the fixed interval in effect during a particular phase of training as a base time or unit of measurement. A ratio is computed between the absolute time elapsing within an interval and the base time, and response decisions are determined by the ratio of times. Thus, after 20 seconds have elapsed in a 40-second FI, an animal responds at about the same rate as it would after 10 seconds have elapsed in a 20-second FI because the ratio between the base time and the time elapsed is 2:1 in both instances.

The Peak Procedure

Based on a procedure originally used by Catania (1970), Seth Roberts (1981) introduced an important new technique for studying timing in animals: the *peak procedure.* Rats were trained to time light and noise signals by rewarding responding according to different FI schedules in the presence of the two signals. During training of performance under FI schedules, occasional probe trials called *empty trials* were inserted among the FI trials. Either the light or the noise signal was presented, no reward was given, and the trial extended a

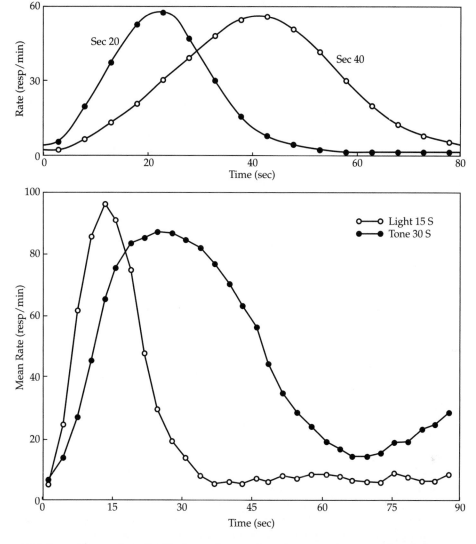

FIGURE 8.6. Data gathered with the peak procedure from rats (top graph) and pigeons (bottom graph). Rate of response is plotted as a function of time on empty trials for light and sound signals that correspond to FIs of different length.

considerable time beyond the length of the FI. Rate of response was observed throughout the empty trial. It peaked at a point very close to the value of the FI and then declined as the trial continued beyond this interval.

Some typical data from the peak procedure are shown in Figure 8.6. The upper graph shows data from rats trained with two signals that corresponded to FIs of 20 and 40 seconds (S. Roberts, 1981). Whenever a houselight came on, it signaled a 20-second FI; the first lever press after 20 seconds would yield reward. When a white noise signal was sounded, it signaled a 40-second FI, indicating that reward could be obtained for the first response after 40 seconds.

On empty trials, the houselight or white noise signals were presented for at least 80 seconds without reward. The curves show rate of lever pressing as a function of time over the first 80 seconds of empty trials. In the lower graph in Figure 8.6, data taken from pigeons using similar procedures are shown (W. Roberts, Cheng & Cohen, 1989). Pigeons were trained to respond to an FI 15-second schedule signaled by a houselight and to an FI 30-second schedule signaled by a tone. The curves show rate of pecking throughout 90-second light and tone empty trials.

Note that the curves for both rats and pigeons look like normal or Gaussian curves. All of the curves have an ascending limb rising from a low initial level of response to the peak and a descending limb that drops from the peak to a low level of response. These limbs are approximately symmetrical. However, in the pigeon data, the curves descend somewhat more slowly than they ascend, and there is a tail of continued response after the curves have reached the bottom of the descending limb. These data from rat and pigeon peak procedure experiments are remarkably similar and contain two important features: (1) The times at which the peak rates of these curves were reached (peak times) are very close to the FIs under which subjects were trained. In the case of rats, the peak times were calculated to be 22.0 seconds for the FI 20-second signal and 41.1 seconds for the FI 40-second signal. The peak times calculated for pigeons were 15.2 seconds for the FI 15-second signal and 30.3 seconds for the FI 30-second signal. Both rats and pigeons then were very accurate at estimating the length of the interval to reward on the basis of peak responding. (2) The spread of the curves is considerably greater for the signal corresponding to the longer FI than to the shorter FI. In fact, a calculation of the standard deviation of these curves shows that the variability of the higher FI curve is about twice as high as that of the lower FI curve for both rats and pigeons.

This same principle can be seen visually by observing the horizontal spread of the curves or the distance between the ascending and descending limbs of each curve at a rate of response midway between zero and the peak rate. The width of the line between the two limbs is about twice as long for the higher FI than for the lower FI. The general principle is that the spread or variability of the curves is proportional to the length of the interval to be timed. The principle of proportionality then extends to the variability of peak time curves. This observation may be recognized as an instance of *Weber's law.* When making estimates of the size of points along a dimension that increases in magnitude (such as time), the variability of estimation increases proportionally to the magnitude of the point estimated (Cheng & W. Roberts, 1991; Gibbon, 1977).

PROPERTIES OF THE INTERNAL CLOCK

Various fundamental questions about timing in animals have been addressed experimentally, and the answers generally suggest that the internal clock used for interval timing has many of the properties of a common stopwatch (S. Roberts & Church, 1978). Some of the well-known properties of a stopwatch are that it usually times up from zero to some finite amount of time, it can be stopped and either reset to zero or restarted at the time it was stopped, and it can time the lengths of many different events. We examine research on the internal clock to see to what extent it possesses these properties.

Direction of Timing

Although a stopwatch times up, many other timers time down. The countdown to a missile launch is down-timing. Turning over an hourglass and timing an interval by the loss of its contents is down-timing, and an oven clock that may be set at 50 minutes and then times down to zero is a down-timer. Although we know that the internal clock accurately times fixed intervals, this could be accomplished by either up- or down-timing. Some process in the nervous system could grow over time until a magnitude criterion is reached (up-timing), or a process of a fixed magnitude established by reinforcement could dwindle over time to zero (down-timing).

The direction of timing was examined in experiments that involved shifting rats midway through a trial from one FI schedule to another (S. Roberts, 1981; S. Roberts & Church, 1978). In S. Roberts' study, rats were trained to respond to two FIs, with one signal (light or noise) indicating FI 20 seconds and the other signal indicating FI 40 seconds. When clear patterns of FI scalloping appeared, empty trial tests were carried out, and peaks near the FIs were found. Test trials then were performed that always began with the 20-second signal; however, after 5, 10, or 15 seconds of the 20-second signal, an animal was shifted to the 40-second signal. Peak curves obtained under these shift conditions indicated when the animal expected to receive reinforcement.

Let us take the case in which 15 seconds have elapsed in the 20-second signal, at which time a rat is shifted to the 40-second signal. When the animal is shifted from the 20-second signal to the 40-second signal, it is presumed that the time accumulated during the 20-second signal is transferred to timing the 40-second signal. However, a new criterion dictated by the 40-second signal is now in effect. If a down timer was used, only 5 seconds should be left on the timer when the switch to 40 seconds occurs. It should seem to the animal that it has only 5 seconds left to reach the 40-second criterion, and it should respond appropriately. The peak of response then should appear 5 seconds after the 40-second signal started or 20 seconds from the start of the 20-second signal.

The use of an up timer leads to quite a different prediction. When switched to the 40-second signal, the internal clock should indicate that 15 seconds have gone by and that 25 seconds are left to reach the 40-second criterion. In this case, peak response should not appear until 25 seconds have gone by on the 40-second signal or until 40 seconds have elapsed since the beginning of the 20-second signal.

In Figure 8.7, response rate is plotted as a function of time both for the 20-second and 40-second signals. Note that response rate dropped when rats were shifted from the 20-second signal to the 40-second signal after 10 and 15 seconds, indicating that animals were adjusting their response rate downward for that amount of time into the 40-second signal. Of primary importance, peak response occurred at about 40 seconds regardless of whether the shift occurred at 5, 10, or 15 seconds. These findings suggest that rats timed up to 5, 10, or 15 seconds during the 20-second signal and then continued to time up when

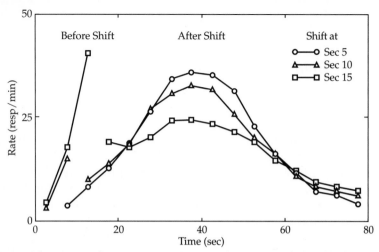

FIGURE 8.7. Mean rates of response over time on the 20-second signal before the shift and on the 40-second signal after the shift. Rats showed peak response at around 40 seconds after each shift, indicating that they were using an up timer.

shifted to the 40-second signal, having shifted the criterion time for reinforcement from 20 seconds to 40 seconds when the signals changed.

Note that the results of this experiment indicate that rats added time that passed in the presence of the second signal to time that had accumulated in the presence of the first signal. There are two important properties of the internal clock shown by this outcome. First, the continuity of timing indicates that the timer added the time from these two signals together. This was not the necessary outcome of the experiment; rats could have reset the internal clock back to zero when a signal in a new sensory modality was presented. Second, the fact that time continued to accumulate across a switch from noise to light or vice versa suggests that the internal clock is centrally located in the nervous system and is readily accessed by different sensory modalities. It also indicates that time is an abstract property that animals represent independently of other properties of a signal, such as whether the signal is a light or a noise (Meck & Church, 1982).

Timing through a Gap

Suppose you were asked to use a stopwatch to measure how much time a friend of yours took to run a mile. However, during the run, your friend stopped for several seconds to have a drink of water. You are faced with a decision: Should you keep the watch running during the water break and count this time as part of the run, or should you stop the stopwatch during the drink and restart it when your friend begins to run again, thus counting only the time your friend is actually running? Fortunately, most modern stopwatches give you the option between these two possibilities. It is possible either to keep the

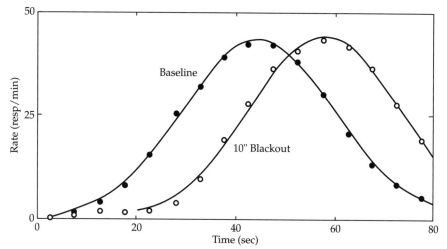

FIGURE 8.8. The mean response rate of bar pressing in rats over time on empty trials. The baseline curve comes from trials in which the houselight signal was presented without interruption. The 10-second blackout curve shows the effect of a 10-second timeout introduced 10 or 15 seconds after the houselight came on.

watch running or to stop the watch for a timeout and then to restart it at the point where it was stopped.

A question very similar to this one has been asked of the rat's internal clock. Once an animal begins to time a signal, what happens if a timeout is introduced in the middle of the signal? S. Roberts (1981) carried out an experiment in which the onset of a houselight initiated a trial, with food primed to be delivered at the first response made after 40 seconds (an FI 40-second schedule). On empty test trials, the houselight stayed on for at least 80 seconds, and no reward was delivered. On selected empty trials, gaps were introduced by blacking out the experimental chamber for 10 seconds after the light had been on for 10 or 15 seconds. The question of interest is how a rat responds to this gap or timeout in the light signal to be timed. One possibility is that it will continue to run the internal clock during the gap; in this case, its rate of responding should peak at 40 seconds after the signal began, and there should be no difference between response curves on empty trials with and without gaps. Another possibility is that a rat will stop the internal clock during the gap and restart it when the light comes back on; if it does this, the response curve for empty trials with a timeout should be shifted to the right of one for empty trials without a timeout. Still a third possibility is that the rat might reset the internal clock back to zero when the gap is introduced and start timing the signal all over again when the light is relit. If it reset the internal clock, the peak response rate should be shifted far beyond 40 seconds since the initial houselight time of 10 or 15 seconds and the timeout time of 10 seconds would be added to the regular signal time of 40 seconds before the peak would be reached.

The result of the experiment was quite clear, as can be seen in Figure 8.8. The curve for baseline or empty trials without a gap peaked at slightly over

40 seconds, and the curve for the 10-second gap was shifted to the right of the baseline curve by about 13 seconds. It appears that rats were able to stop and restart the internal clock during a gap, just as one might stop and restart a stopwatch during a timeout period. S. Roberts (1981) suggested that the extra 3 seconds the gap curve was shifted to the right might arise because it took longer to restart the internal clock than it did to stop it.

Resetting the Internal Clock

Both of the experiments just described suggest that the internal clock maintains time accumulated and continues to add time to it when either the modality of the signal is changed or a gap in the signal is introduced. Nevertheless, it must be possible to stop and reset the internal clock. The obvious piece of evidence that supports this conclusion is that animals can time accurately over multiple trials given within a daily session. The fact that animals time accurately trial after trial suggests that the clock is reset at the end of each trial. Presumably, salient signals for the end of a trial provide a resetting instruction. The most obvious signals are the delivery of reward and the introduction of the intertrial interval. If one of these signals is omitted, it should adversely affect timing on the next trial.

In fact, a phenomenon known as the *omission effect* suggests just such an outcome. If animals are trained to respond to an FI schedule over a series of trials, omission of reinforcement at the end of one trial leads to acceleration of responding on the next trial (Staddon & Innis, 1969). The omission effect may be explained as a failure to completely reset the internal clock between trials (S. Roberts, 1981; Staddon, 1974). If food delivery and the intertrial interval act as signals for resetting the internal clock, omission of food means the signal is incomplete, and the clock may be only partially reset. Since some time is then already on the clock at the beginning of the next trial, the FI seems to have timed out to the animal at a point that is short of the interval for food delivery on the experimenter's clock. The effect of this mismatch between internal and external clocks should be a shift of the response rate function to the left and an increased rate of responding early in the interval.

In an experiment carried out by S. Roberts (1981), the peak procedure was used to examine the omission effect. Reward was omitted on trials in which rats had to time an FI 40-second signal, and the effect of reward omission was observed during an empty test trial that followed the trial on which reward was omitted. It was found that rats responded sooner and reached a peak time earlier on empty trials following the omission of reward than on baseline empty control trials in which the reward was given on the preceding trial. Removing the reward at the end of an FI then appears to prevent the internal clock from completely resetting. It appears that reward, along with the intertrial interval, acts as a strong signal that normally resets the internal clock to zero and allows accurate timing trial after trial.

The modality switch experiment, the gap experiment, and the omission effect taken together suggest that the internal clock is quite flexible and has many of the properties of a common stopwatch. We have seen that it times up, that it can continuously time events signaled to different sensory modalities, and that it can hold a time setting over a timeout or gap in a signal and then continue timing after the signal resumes. Furthermore, it can be stopped and reset to zero by end-of-trial cues.

It should be noticed that the findings of Wilkie et al. (1994) discussed earlier can be understood in terms of these properties of the internal clock. Wilkie et al. found that pigeons reset the internal clock when removed from the testing apparatus for 15 minutes. However, when left in the apparatus for a 15-minute timeout, pigeons appeared to stop and restart the internal clock from where it left off. Although a timeout may only temporarily stop the clock, the more dramatic change in cues provided by a return to the home cage appears to reset the internal clock.

Although we have casually ascribed a number of properties to the internal clock, more formal theoretical development of the internal clock is needed to understand how it can accomplish the timing feats thus far described. In the following section, theoretical models of the internal clock are presented.

THEORIES OF INTERVAL TIMING

We usually keep track of time by noting changes in some physical indicator. The numbers on a digital clock or the positions of the hands on an analog clock tell us the time of day or measure elapsed time. Without these modern instruments, the position of the sun in the sky or the position its shadow casts upon a sundial may be used to measure time. In our discussion of time-place learning experiments, it was held that changes in the states of internal circadian oscillators are used to determine time of day. Theories about the ability of animals to time intervals precisely are based on an internal clock. These appeal to some dynamic or changing process within the organism that may form a basis for time detection. A popular conceptualization is that the internal clock is driven by a neural *pacemaker* that regularly emits pulses. Two well-known theories of animal timing are based on this premise: the *behavioral theory of timing* and the *scalar timing theory*.

Behavioral Theory of Timing

According to the behavioral theory of timing advanced by Killeen and Fetterman (1988; 1993), a pacemaker emits pulses at successive points in time according to a Poisson distribution with a fixed mean probability. The cumulation of several pulses then drives behavioral states of the organism, which give rise to different classes of overt behavior. These classes of behavior are referred to as *adjunctive behaviors*—common forms of behavior performed by an animal that do not result in reinforcement. For example, a pigeon might be driven by the cumulation of pulses first to enter a state in which it pecks a wall, then to advance to a state in which it bobs its head, and finally to advance to a state in which it flaps its wings. If key pecking is reinforced with food during any of these states, that state comes to control or act as a discriminative stimulus for key pecking. Suppose the pigeon is reinforced for key pecking while wing flapping. It learns to peck the key whenever the wing flapping class of response is made. On subsequent tests, the beginning of a timing signal initiates the pacemaker, and its successive pulses drive the subject through different behavioral states until it reaches wing flapping and the peck response is made. Because it takes the subject approximately the same amount of time to cycle through different behavioral states each trial, the subject's own behavioral state can act as an interval timing device.

Scalar Timing Theory

Scalar timing theory is also based on the activity of a pacemaker but suggests that timing is controlled by more central, computational processes. Because this theory is somewhat more developed and related to a number of empirical studies, it is presented and discussed in some detail. An information processing model of scalar timing is presented in Figure 8.9. Three different stages of the behavioral act of timing involve successively a clock process, a memory process, and a decision process. The clock process consists of a pacemaker that emits pulses at a constant average rate and an accumulator in which those pulses accumulate. Of critical importance, the flow of pulses from the pacemaker to the accumulator is controlled by an intermediate switch. Only when the switch is closed are pulses transmitted to the accumulator, and pulses cease to enter the accumulator when the switch is opened. Through learning, an external signal to be timed comes to control the switch, thereby closing the switch when it comes on and opening it when it goes off. The total pulses in the accumulator at the end of presentation of a signal are then correlated with the length of the signal and can be used to time the signal.

Information from the accumulator in the form of total pulses is then transmitted to working memory. Information in working memory may be transmitted to reference memory. The pulse total present in working memory when a response is rewarded is stored in reference memory. Finally, at the decision level, the current pulse count in working memory is transmitted to a comparator, as is a sampled value from the distribution of pulse totals in reference memory. The comparator process compares the working memory and reference memory totals. If the values match or are close to a match, a yes decision to respond is made; a rat begins to press a lever, or a pigeon starts to peck a key. If the values do not approach a match, a no decision is made, and responding is withheld.

The comparator process is carried out by calculating a ratio between the absolute value of the difference between the pulse total sampled from reference memory (RM) and the pulse total in working memory (WM) divided by the RM total. The decision ratio (DR) then is calculated as $DR = |RM - WM|/RM$. Note two things about this formula. First, by taking the absolute value of $RM - WM$, it makes no difference whether $RM > WM$ or $WM > RM$; only the absolute difference between them is used. Second, the numerator of the ratio, and hence the ratio, equals zero when $RM = WM$. Therefore, a decision that RM matches WM should occur as the DR approaches zero. The

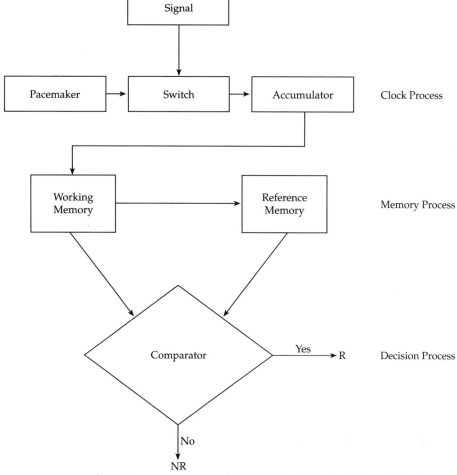

FIGURE 8.9. An information processing model for timing behavior that contains three processes: a clock process, a memory process, and a decision process.

model handles this decision by assuming that there is a threshold, *b*, above which no response occurs and below which the subject responds. Thus, when DR drops to *b* or less, the subject should begin to emit the operant response that indicates it is at or near the reinforced time interval.

The scalar timing model is now shown using a numerical example to help you better understand how it works. Two examples of timing on empty trials are shown in Table 8.1—one for timing after a subject has been trained with a signal that yields reward on an FI 20-second schedule and the other for timing a signal that indicates reward on an FI 40-second schedule. Let us assume that the pacemaker emits pulses at the rate of 5 per second. The successive seconds that accumulate on an empty trial are shown in the first row. The second row shows the pulse count that is transferred to working memory after

TABLE 8.1 Hypothetical Pulse Counts in Working Memory (WM) Shown at Successive Points in Empty Trials Based on the Assumption That Pulses Are Emitted from the Pacemaker at the Rate of 5/sec.

(Decision ratios (DR) are shown at each point based on the assumption that reference memory (RM) values of 100 and 200 pulses were sampled in the 20-second and 40-second conditions, respectively.)

				FI = 20 SECONDS				
Assume pulse count sampled from RM = 100 pulses								
Seconds 0	5	10	15	20	25	30	35	40
WM 0	25	50	75	100	125	150	175	200
DR 1.00	0.75	0.50	0.25	0.00	0.25	0.50	0.75	1.00
				FI = 40 SECONDS				
Assume pulse count sampled from RM = 200 pulses								
Seconds 0	10	20	30	40	50	60	70	80
WM 0	50	100	150	200	250	300	350	400
DR 1.00	0.75	0.50	0.25	0.00	0.25	0.50	0.75	1.00

each number of seconds, and the third row shows the DR calculated by the comparator at each point. Observe that the DR is zero when the time interval reaches the length of the FI, showing a perfect match between counts in WM and RM; the DR then rises symmetrically toward lower and higher pulse counts from the point where WM = RM. Thus, decisions about responding should be symmetrical about the FI.

Let us assume that the threshold, *b*, is equal to 0.50. The subject should begin responding when 10 seconds have elapsed on the 20-second signal and when 20 seconds have elapsed on the 40-second signal. Similarly, the subject should cease responding when 30 seconds have gone by on the 20-second signal and when 60 seconds have gone by on the 40-second signal. Notice that this example leads to the proportionality result. That is, response should begin when half of the length of the FI has elapsed in both signals, even though that time is 10 seconds in the 20-second signal and 20 seconds in the 40-second signal. In the cases of both signals, response begins prior to the FI and ends after the FI. However, the difference between the times of the start and the end of response are twice as great when FI = 40 seconds as when FI = 20 seconds. Thus, the model shows that the spread of time judgments should obey Weber's law and increase in proportion to the length of time estimated.

It should be pointed out that there are several sources of variance in the scalar timing theory (Gibbon & Church, 1984). Although a single criterion time retrieved from reference memory was used in the examples shown in Table 8.1, the theory holds that a distribution of criterion times are stored in reference memory; the peak time obtained from peak procedure curves is an estimate of the mean of that theoretical distribution. Variation in the times stored in reference memory arises from two sources of variation, variation in the rate of the pacemaker, and variation in the transmission of pulse totals from working memory to reference memory. Thus, the number of pulses in the accumulator when the reinforcer occurs may differ from one trial to another because the rate of the pacemaker (λ) changes between trials. The second source of memory variation is caused by variation in storage of working memory times in reference memory. A multiplicative constant, k^*, yields an exact transmission of the number of pulses in working memory to reference memory if $k^* = 1.0$. However, the value stored in reference memory may underestimate the value in working memory if $k^* < 1.0$ or may overestimate the value stored in working memory if $k^* > 1.0$.

A third source of variation in scalar timing theory is variation in the response threshold, b. Although a single constant threshold was assumed in Table 8.1, the theory actually assumes that momentary fluctuations in b cause a subject to begin responding early and to stop responding late if b is high or to begin responding late and stop responding early if b is low. The average times at which response begins and ends reflect the means of a distribution of b, from which trial to trial thresholds are sampled.

Break-Run-Break Response and Gaussian Curves

Although the numbers shown in Table 8.1 predict symmetry and proportionality, it is not clear how they could generate the Gaussian distributions of responding seen in Figure 8.6. Instead of gradually rising and descending curves, this numerical example suggests that an animal should fail to respond during the initial part of an empty trial, suddenly begin responding when DR drops below threshold, and continue responding until the threshold is exceeded, at which point response would stop altogether. In fact, exactly this pattern of response has been observed in both rats and pigeons (Cheng & Westwood, 1993; Cheng, Westwood & Crystal, 1993; Church, Meck & Gibbon, 1994; Gibbon & Church, 1990). Typically, a break-run-break pattern is seen in which the subject breaks into a high constant rate of response for an extended run and then breaks off response and returns to little or no response.

This pattern of response is shown in Figure 8.10, taken from Cheng and Westwood (1993). Cheng and Westwood trained pigeons to time a 12.5-second FI and then tested them on empty trials of several lengths. Performance was examined on individual trials; numbers of key pecks were counted in successive time bins of 1.25 seconds. Breaks from no response to response were identified when a bin with no responses was followed by responses in each of two successive bins. The zero point on the abscissa of the curve on the left side of Figure 8.10 represents the last bin before the break. Relative response frequency is plotted backward and forward from this point by averaging the number of responses in time bins before and after the break. The data were obtained over many trials given to three subjects. Similarly, the curve on the right side of Figure 8.10 is anchored at a zero point that represents the first of two bins in which no responses were made after a run of bins containing responses. The drop in the curve represents the break from the run phase to a no-response phase. Of particular importance, note that birds continued to respond at a high constant rate for a number of bins after the initial break and before the final break. These data look very much like what one would expect to see if the DR dropped below or rose above a threshold and changed the comparator's decision from no response to response or from response to no response.

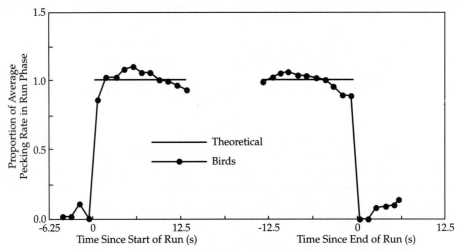

FIGURE 8.10. Break-run-break curves found in pigeons by averaging data from individual trials forward and backward from a zero time bin in which no response either preceded a run or ended a run.

Given that animals produce break-run-break patterns of response on individual trials, how are the smooth Gaussian curves seen in Figure 8.6 produced? Two factors explain this apparent inconsistency. First, variability in criterion times retrieved from reference memory and variation in response threshold occur between trials. As a consequence of variability in these trial parameters, break-run-break sequences do not show breaks at the same points in time on every trial. This point is shown in Figure 8.11. Considering just variability in the response threshold (*b*), the different rectangular break-run-break curves would be produced. If the threshold sampled on a given trial is low, the result is a narrow break-run-break function, as seen in Example b in Figure 8.11, because the accumulated pulses in WM have to be close to the total sampled from RM before the DR dips below threshold and triggers a response. By the same token, the animal stops responding at a high rate quickly because a relatively small increase in the WM total beyond the RM value takes the DR above threshold. On another trial, however, the threshold sampled is high, and a wide break-run-break curve, like that in Example c, occurs.

The second factor to consider is that the curves seen in Figure 8.6 represent averaged data from a number of trials and subjects. If a number of break-run-break curves varying in width are averaged together, the result is the smooth Gaussian curve shown at the top of Figure 8.11. Thus, average curves obtained on empty trials with the peak procedure are not inconsistent with the assumption that response to a signal is an all-or-none behavior, with the start of response triggered by the DR dropping below threshold and the end of response signaled by the DR rising above the threshold.

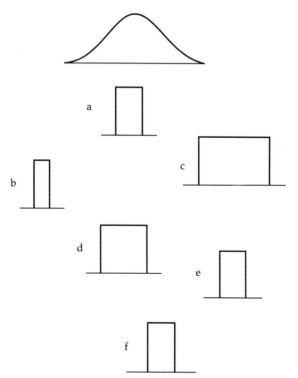

FIGURE 8.11. Variability in break-run-break functions is shown by the rectangular curves varying in width. These functions would arise on different trials if the threshold for response, *b*, in the scalar timing model varies from trial to trial. The smooth Gaussian curve at the top arises from averaging the separate break-run-break curves.

Point of Bisection

Recall the time discrimination experiment presented earlier in this chapter. Rats and pigeons are able to learn to make different responses to short and long time intervals. When then tested with times intermediate between the extreme values, animals produce a psychophysical curve with the subjective midpoint or the point of bisection of the curve lying at the geometric mean between short and long times.

One way in which this finding can be explained within the framework of the scalar timing theory is to assume that two distributions of reinforced or criterion times are stored in reference memory as pulse totals, one for the short signal and the other for the long signal. Whenever a test duration is presented, its similarity to both short and long criterion values is computed as a ratio between the shorter total and the longer total; choice of the manipulandum indicating short or long duration then is based on which ratio indicates closer similarity of its total to the test duration (Gibbon, 1981; 1986; Allan & Gibbon, 1991).

Assume again that pulses are emitted from the pacemaker at a rate of 5 per second and that an animal must discriminate between signals lasting 2 and

8 seconds. Following the 2-second signal, 10 pulses reside in working memory, and, following the 8-second signal, 40 pulses reside in working memory. Further, assume that the criterion totals sampled from reference memory also are 10 from the short-signal distribution and 40 from the long-signal distribution. When the short signal has been presented, a ratio of $10/10 = 1.00$ is computed for the short-signal criterion, and a ratio of $10/40 = 0.25$ arises for comparison with the long-signal criterion. The ratio nearest 1.00 indicates greater similarity to the criterion, and the short-signal response will be made. If the long signal has been presented, the corresponding ratios for the short and long criterion values are reversed, 1.00 for the long duration and 0.25 for the short duration, and the long-signal response is performed.

These ratios become closer and more similar as intermediate values are tested, making discriminations of relative similarity more difficult and yielding the ogive seen in Figure 8.3. When the geometric mean of 4 seconds is presented, 20 pulses should accumulate and be transmitted to working memory; the ratio of similarity to the short-signal criterion is $10/20 = 0.50$, and the ratio of similarity to the long-signal criterion is $20/40 = 0.50$. The 4-second duration should seem equally similar to the short and long durations, and the subject should make the short and long responses equally often. Thus, the assumption that subjects make similarity judgments based on ratios between pulse totals in working and reference memory accounts for the fact that the subjective midpoint usually falls at the geometric mean between short and long training durations.

Scalar timing theory provides an elegant and powerful model of the timing process that incorporates a number of empirical features of timing. By assuming that interval timing is accomplished by ratio comparisons between working and reference memory pulse totals, it accounts for the high degree of accuracy in animal timing and for phenomena such as proportionality, Weber's law, and bisection at the geometric mean.

SUMMARY

Like space, time is a fundamental dimension of animal and human experience, and it is therefore no surprise that animals are highly sensitive to time and able to judge it with considerable accuracy. Furthermore, it appears that animals judge time in two different ways. They are able to make gross discriminations between time of day, and they are able to make much finer judgments of short intervals of time. Experiments carried out with birds suggest that they can associate time of day with different spatial locations where food may be obtained. Time-place associations may be based on circadian cues, or daily cycles in an animal's endogenous state. When birds have learned stable time-place associations between widely separated times of day, control procedures that involve omission of test sessions or clock shifting show that birds depend on endogenous cues to determine the location of food.

Various experiments have shown that animals can also precisely time intervals in the range of seconds. Discrimination procedures are used to study fine discriminations between short and long signals that differ in length by only a few seconds, such as 1 and 4 seconds or 2 and 8 seconds. When tests are given at intermediate intervals, rats and pigeons show a psychophysical curve with the subjective midpoint lying at the geometric mean of the short and long durations.

The peak procedure provides a powerful method for obtaining a precise measure of an animal's estimate of the length of a time interval. Light and sound signals are associated with different time durations by reinforcing animals for responding to different FI schedules in the presence of these signals. When each signal is presented on empty or nonreinforced trials, plots of response rate as a function of time yield Gaussian curves for each signal that peak near the duration of the FI schedule associated with the signal. The time at which a curve peaks provides a measure of the time on the animal's internal clock between signal onset and reinforcement.

Research using FI training and the peak procedure has revealed a number of properties of the internal clock, which is the theoretical mechanism responsible for timing ability. Experiments with rats involving switching of modalities and the introduction of a gap into a signal suggest that the internal clock times up, that it times continuously across modality switches, and that it can be stopped and restarted without loss of time during the timeout period. Furthermore, the fact that animals can time accurately over successive trials within a session indicates that the internal clock can be stopped and reset to zero between trials. Reward and the intertrial interval serve as markers that signal the end of a trial and allow the internal clock to be reset.

Curves that show response rate as a function of time during FI and empty trials reveal scalar properties of the timing process. When curves that depict animals' timing of intervals of different lengths are plotted using relative time and response rate, they superimpose, showing proportionality. In accordance with Weber's law, the variability or spread in response curves increases in proportion to the length of the interval to be timed.

These observations have led to the development of the scalar timing theory. The theory suggests that animals time intervals as ratios between current elapsed time and memory for previous reinforced time intervals. An information processing model suggests that the entire process leading to timing behavior consists of a clock, a memory, and a comparator. External signals control a switch that allows pulses to be transmitted from a pacemaker to an accumulator. Elapsed time is recorded in working memory as the number of pulses sent to the accumulator. A ratio comparison is carried out in the comparator between the time or pulses in working memory and a criterion for reinforced time. This process provides a yes or no response decision.

An important implication of this model is that response during timing trials should take the form of a break-run-break pattern. The animal breaks from no response to a steady rate of response for a period of time, followed by a break from response and a return to no response. Examination of behavior on individual trials reveals that this pattern of response does indeed occur in both rats and pigeons. When the trial data are averaged, smooth Gaussian curves arise from variability in the times at which the start and stop breaks occur. Thus, scalar timing theory accounts for properties of average response curves, as well as behavior shown on individual trials.

CHAPTER 9

Serial Learning and Memory

Closely related to the estimation of time is the order in which we perceive events to occur. These events may be perceived as stimuli external to us or as responses that constitute our own behavior. Furthermore, we readily learn sequences of events and show our memory for them by reproducing them in the order they occurred. The most common human examples are in the area of language. Actors rehearsing a new play learn precisely the order in which words and sentences are to be spoken. In numerous studies of verbal learning that were carried out earlier in this century, subjects were asked to memorize lists of words, numbers, or nonsense syllables that were presented in an arbitrary order. With sufficient practice, people could repeat such lists from memory in the exact order in which they were presented. You may remember that the tradition for such experiments was begun by Ebbinghaus in the 19th century in his original studies of memory.

Serial learning and memory are, of course, also important in the area of motor learning. A musician must learn to play notes in a precise order on her instrument, and athletes in all sports learn sequences of movements that will be effective in such activities as running, kicking, and hitting. When learning to perform a motor sequence, the verbal utterances or behaviors involved form the items to be remembered and constitute *item information*. The order in which these elements must occur to perform an effective sequence is remembered as *order information*. In some cases, these two forms of information may be somewhat independent of one another. For instance, we may learn to reproduce all of the words on a list before we learn the precise order in which they should occur.

Early studies of serial learning required subjects to go through lists of items repeatedly until each item could be anticipated correctly from the item that preceded it. Thus, given the list A-B-C-D-E-F, a subject would have to respond with B when A appeared, respond with C when B appeared, and so on. It was assumed that sequences of associations were formed between successive items in the list. We now know that a variety of other processes may be used to learn such lists, in addition to sequential associations (Wickelgren, 1993). Ebbinghaus and many theorists who followed him argued that people learning lists also form *remote associations.* Thus, Item E in a list may not only be cued by Item D, but also by the preceding Items A, B, and C. One piece of evidence for remote associations is *anticipatory errors;* for example, given Item D, a subject might respond with Item F instead of the correct Item E. If Item D has some tendency to recall Item F, as well as Item E, such anticipatory errors would be expected. Still another source of serial information is the *ordinal position* of an item in the list (Young, 1968). Thus, A, B, C, D, and E might be remembered as the first, second, third, fourth, and fifth items in the list. Even if specific position numbers are not used, A and B might be remembered as early items, C as the middle item, and D and E as late items.

Within lists of things to be remembered, people may form *chunks* or sublists of items that form a coherent superordinate unit. Chunks may be formed by finding common perceptual attributes among items or by combining them based on their semantic properties. Words may be linked into a chunk by making a sentence out of them or forming a visual image that combines them. Thus, the words *elephant, trousers, baseball* might be chunked by remembering a bizarre image of an elephant wearing trousers and hitting a baseball. Lists of numbers may be remembered by relating groups of them to familiar number sequences, such as one's telephone number or license plate number (Ericsson, Chase, & Faloon, 1980).

In some cases, lists of items may occur in a nonrandom order because some rule is used to determine successive members of a list. In this case, subjects may find it easy to learn and remember the list if they can discover the rule that generates successive items in the list. Thus, the sequence 44554455 is generated by a double alternation rule. Once it is known that the responses are the numbers 4 and 5, the rule can be acquired that each number is stated twice in sequence and then alternated with two successive presentations of the other number. Once a person has learned the rules for string construction, the sequence can be generated indefinitely.

This brief review of research on serial learning and memory in people serves as a basis for an examination of similar topics in animal research. The following questions are addressed in this chapter: To what extent is animal behavior serially organized? Can animals learn arbitrary serial orders of stimulus events or of responses? If they can learn order information, what cognitive processes are involved? Is chunking found in animal cognition? Can an animal learn about rules that govern the production of a sequence of events?

SERIAL ORGANIZATION IN ANIMAL BEHAVIOR

The Kinesthetic-Machine Hypothesis

Serial organization in animal behavior can be observed at many levels, extending from the molecular level of muscle fiber twitches to the molar level of whole behavioral acts. Behaviors such as a rat running through a maze, a cat chasing its prey, or a bird pecking at a grain of food all involve precise sequences of muscle and limb activation. In the early part of this century, behavioral psychologists advanced an account of such behaviors, which Olton (1979) called the *kinesthetic-machine hypothesis*. It was argued that integrated motor activity could be understood as a chain of stimulus-response associations. Each movement produced feedback stimulation that then acted as a stimulus for the next movement in the sequence. Given an initial stimulus, S_1, the sequence $S_1 \rightarrow R_1 \rightarrow S_2 \rightarrow R_2 \rightarrow S_3 \rightarrow R_3$ would automatically follow, in which S_2 is the kinesthetic feedback from R_1 and serves to elicit R_2. Lashley (1951) challenged this doctrine on a number of grounds. One prominent criticism was his observation that sequences of movements performed by either people or animals occurred at such a rapid rate that there was not time for sensory feedback from the muscles to travel to the brain and trigger off a motor message that would then have to be transmitted back to the muscles. Lashley argued that instead the brain must contain programs that control whole sequences of organized motor responses. Today, it is thought that integrated behavioral sequences are the product of both central nervous system control programs and feedback servomechanisms (Gallistel, 1980; Roitblat, 1987).

Fixed-Action Patterns

At the level of more extended sequences of behavioral activities, evidence for serial organization is found in *fixed-action patterns*. Ethologists described fixed-action patterns as series of instinctive or genetically programmed behaviors that repeatedly follow the same course when an organism is exposed to the appropriate releasing stimulus (N. Tinbergen, 1951). A number of examples of such behavior are often cited. In one well-known observation made by Jean Henri Fabre (H. Wells, Huxley, & G. Wells, 1934, as cited in Ratner, 1980), a Sphex wasp was observed to leave its burrow and find a cricket, which it stung into paralysis. The wasp dragged the cricket back to the entrance to the burrow and left it there while the wasp went inside the burrow. When the wasp emerged from the burrow, it carried the cricket inside and deposited it with its eggs; the burrow was then sealed up, thus providing food for the young when they hatched. In observing this behavior, Fabre performed a simple experiment by moving the cricket a distance from the burrow while the wasp was inside it. The wasp reemerged from the burrow, found the cricket, dragged it back to the entrance to the burrow, and then entered the burrow. Over as many as 40 displacements of the cricket, the wasp performed the same behavioral sequence. Provisioning the burrow involved an invariant sequence of behaviors that was unaffected by previous experience.

Perhaps the most famous example of stereotyped instinctual behavior is the wagging dance found in honeybees (von Frisch, 1962). Upon finding a rich source of food, a honeybee flies back to its hive and communicates both the distance and direction of the food to its hivemates through the performance of a wagging dance. The wagging dance takes the form of a figure-eight, with the bee wagging its abdomen during the straight-line portion of the dance. Other bees in the hive are recruited to follow the dancer, and the dancer occasionally stops to share samples of the food it has brought back with its mates. Von Frisch observed that the direction of the wagging dance pointed toward the location of the discovered food source relative to the position of the sun. Furthermore, the vigor of the dance was correlated with the distance of the food from the hive. After following the dance for a period of time, other members of the hive fly to the location of the food.

Although sounds emitted by the dancer were initially thought to be of little importance, more recent research has shown that sound, as well as the movements of the dance, is a critical component of the bee's communication system (Kirchner & Towne, 1994). Honeybees hear sounds made by the dancer's wings through hearing organs located on their antennas, and these sounds help members of the hive track the movements of the dancer. Although the type of dance performed varies among species of bees, the dance performed by members of the same species is remarkably similar over repeated communication episodes, indicating a fixed-action pattern or serial behavior under the control of neural programs common to most members of the species.

In both insects and vertebrates, a number of fixed-action patterns have been observed that are performed in mating rituals (N. Tinbergen, 1952; 1960b) or in combat over mates or defense of territory (Eibl-Eibesfeldt, 1961). The reproductive behavior of the male stickleback fish, for example, involves a number of steps that occur in a fixed sequence (N. Tinbergen, 1952). In the early spring, the male stickleback establishes a territory and defends it against all intruders. Eventually, it digs a nest and covers it with algae to serve as a tunnel. During this period, the male begins to change color and eventually its ventral surface becomes a bright red. Upon the approach of a gravid female carrying a distended abdomen filled with eggs, the male performs a zigzag dance consisting of alternately darting toward the female and toward the nest. Eventually, the female is led to the nest, where she enters the prepared tunnel and lays her eggs. She then departs from the nest, and the male fertilizes the eggs. After inducing several females to lay their eggs in his nest, the male then ventilates the eggs until the fry are hatched and protects the young fish until they swim away to join other groups. The important point to note is that the behavior of the male stickleback follows the same serial sequence of actions on each mating encounter with a female.

LEARNED SERIAL BEHAVIOR

The behaviors just described all have a common feature: They occur in the same sequential order time after time in most members of the species when the appropriate stimulus is presented. Their basis is largely genetic, and typically they depend little upon learning. With respect to behaviors that may have a more cognitive origin, however, we may ask if animals can learn to place behaviors in serial orders that they have never performed before. The answer is a clear yes. However, the cognitive processes used to achieve serial performance may vary from one experimental situation to another.

Multiple-Choice Maze Learning

In a procedure that was commonly used to test rat intelligence in the early part of this century, rats were placed in a multiple-choice maze—a maze that led

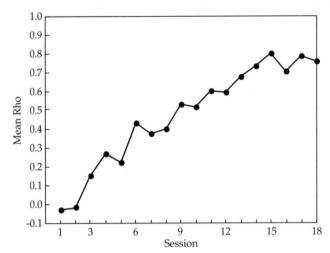

FIGURE 9.1. The curve shows the rise over trials in the mean correlation (rho) between the ranks of arm entries and the quantities of food on the arms. Rats increasingly visited arms in the order from most food to least food.

from a start box to a goal box containing food through a number of intervening choices. Incorrect choices led to a dead-end or blind alley. After several trials of training, rats learned to go from start to goal with almost no errors at the intervening choices. Although multiple-choice maze learning indicated rats were able to learn a series of new responses, each response was a left or right turn that could have been learned as a response to a new location in the maze.

Radial-Maze Performance

In a more contemporary experiment using the radial maze (see Figure 7.12 in Chapter 7), a more complex form of serial learning was obtained when rats had to make each response from the same central location, and a greater number of choices were available. As mentioned in Chapter 7, Hulse and O'Leary (1982) placed different quantities of food on each arm of a four-arm radial maze, either 0, 1, 6, or 18 food pellets. Rats were allowed to choose freely among the arms of the maze over successive trials, with each arm containing the same quantity of food from day to day. Within an average of 35 trials, rats reached a criterion of entering the arms in the order 18-6-1-0 on 8 out of 10 trials. Even when violations of this monotonic order were made, they were typically inversions of 18-6 or 1-0. Rats apparently divided the arms into the two with the larger quantity and the two with the smaller quantity and then made finer discriminations within these pairs. In a similar experiment (W. Roberts, 1992), a six-arm radial maze was used, and each arm contained a cube of cheese, with the cubes weighing 0, 0.05, 0.45, 0.90, 1.80, and 2.70 grams. Performance over daily sessions is shown in Figure 9.1. A correlation coefficient on the ranks of arm entries and amounts of food (rho) was used to measure performance. When rho = 0, there is no relationship between the order of arm choices and the amount of food on the arms; if rho = 1.0, this indicates that arms were entered in a perfect descending order from the arm with most cheese to the arm with no cheese. As the graph shows, the correlation between order of arm entry and amount of food on the arms rose from an initial value of around 0 to about 0.80 within 15 sessions.

Both the Hulse and O'Leary (1982) and the W. Roberts (1992) experiments indicate that rats learn about differential amounts of food on the radial maze and order their choices of arms to obtain the largest quantities first. Have rats memorized a serial sequence in which arms should be entered? Although this is one possible account of these findings, it is possible that rats have not learned a serial list of responses. Another possibility is that rats formed a cognitive map of arm locations and their food contents. Before each arm choice, the rat may scan this map and simply choose the unentered arm with the largest amount of food on it. By this process of elimination, the rat enters arms in descending order of food quantity. Thus, serial learning is not necessarily the basis of this serial behavior on the radial maze.

Learning Arbitrary Sequences of Responses

Training animals to produce long and seemingly complicated chains of responses is a popular activity for animal trainers. A trained dog may pull a cart from one end of a stage to the other, load the cart with objects, and then pull it to another designated spot and unload it. Elephants, long trained as beasts of burden in India, perform long sequences of lifting, carrying, and lowering responses to transport timber from one place to another (Rensch, 1957). To examine such training more analytically, psychologists devised experiments in which animals are required to complete a sequence of arbitrary responses in a given order to earn reward.

In an early form of this type of experiment, animals were tested in a box that contained three plates on the floor and a central food box (T. Jenkins, 1927). An animal's task was to enter the box and depress a number of plates in a pre-scribed sequence; if this requirement was completed accurately, the door to the food box opened, allowing the subject access to reward. The multiple-plate problem box was adopted by Warden (1951) as a means of comparing the intelligence of animals, in much the same way as the delayed-response problem discussed in Chapter 3. The limits of learning in various species of animals would be determined by the number of plates they could accurately learn to depress in sequence. The training procedure involved the gradual addition of sequential responses, contingent upon successful completion of the preceding sequence. An animal was initially required to depress only Plate 1 to be rewarded. When this response was learned, response to Plate 1 had to be followed by depression of Plate 2 for reward. Next, the sequence 1-2-3 was required for reward. Once an animal learned the 1-2-3 pattern, it was trained to double back to Plate 2 and then to Plate 1 to form a sequence of five responses. As training progressed, a subject could be trained to go back and forth across the plates in the order 1-2-3-2-1-2-3, and so forth. When an animal's ability to add still another plate to the sequence broke down, it was concluded that this number of plates marked the limit of that animal's learning ability.

Comparisons of different species indicated that the guinea pig could learn to depress only one plate and that the rat could learn only to depress two plates in series (Riess, 1934). Shuey (1931) found that kittens could do better since they learned to perform sequences of from three to seven plates. Monkeys were far better than the nonprimates studied, with the cebus monkey learning a sequence as long as 15 plates (Koch, 1935), and rhesus monkeys achieving a string of 22 plates (Fjeld, 1934). Although we may question the meaning of these findings for a comparative analysis of intelligence, the results do indicate that animals can learn to perform sequences of responses that involve at least three different responses. Although the results with monkeys seem impressive, it is possible that monkeys did not memorize sequences of responses as long as 15 or 22 plates. Another possibility is that monkeys learned a rule about pressing the plates in forward and reverse orders and then extrapolated that rule for a number of responses. Such a rule would dictate a subject depress Plates 1, 2, and 3 and then sweep back and forth across them. The fact that monkeys could extend the string of plates much further than the other animals tested suggests that primates are able to formulate a rule more easily than nonprimates.

In more modern studies of response-pattern learning, pigeons or monkeys were required to respond to stimulus keys in a predetermined sequence for reward. In a particularly interesting study, Hursh (1977) presented monkeys with a panel containing two rows of three keys, all colored yellow. Monkeys were required to learn to press a set of three keys in a particular order, with the designated keys and their order changed from day to day. Each time a correct key was pressed, a white spot of light appeared on the key; reward was delivered only after the third correct key was pressed. Two rhesus monkeys and one cynomologous monkey learned to make the correct sequences of responses within sessions, and their patterns of acquisition were of considerable interest. Acquisition was very sudden or steplike; subjects went rapidly from a period of no correct sequences to a period of consistently correct sequences. The fact that all three responses were learned simultaneously and equally well suggests that monkeys suddenly learned the pattern and not individual responses.

In some test sessions, Hursh (1977) omitted reward after correct sequence completion. This manipulation had little effect on performance since monkeys continued to rapidly acquire the correct sequence. In other sessions, the feedback light presented after correct presses was omitted. This change had a devastating effect on performance; the frequency of correct responses now dropped to little better than chance. Accurate responding reappeared only when the feedback light was restored. Monkeys learned patterns within sessions suddenly, but sensory feedback from each response was crucial for monkeys to recognize the correct sequence. The ability of monkeys to suddenly learn the correct pattern agrees with the observations from the older multiple-plate studies that monkeys could learn to repeat the same pattern of responses a number of times and thus achieve a high number of correct plates pressed.

Learning Arbitrary Stimulus Sequences

In all of the experiments thus far discussed, some internal or external stimulus changed each time a response was made that could have served as a cue for the next response. In multiple-choice mazes and in the multiple-plate problem, the subject traveled to different spatial locations to make each response, and these locations could provide differential cues for the next response in the sequence. Animals pressing different keys in a Skinner box received different muscular and visual feedback from each response that could become associated with the next behavior to be performed.

In an important series of experiments carried out by Terrace and his associates, pigeons were trained on a *simultaneous chaining* procedure that eliminated most of these sequential cues (Terrace, 1983). Pigeons were trained to peck keys containing different visual stimuli in a predetermined arbitrary sequence (Straub & Terrace, 1981). Suppose that four colors are displayed simultaneously on four keys, and a pigeon is to be taught to peck those keys in the order *red→yellow→blue→green.* Initially, the pigeon is taught to complete the *red→yellow* sequence; only red and yellow keys are presented, and only pecks in the order of red followed by yellow are rewarded. When the pigeon learns to peck these stimuli in the correct order at a high level of accuracy, the blue key is introduced, and only pecks in the order *red→yellow→blue* are rewarded. When the three-stimulus chain is accurately performed, the green key is introduced, and the full four-stimulus chain must be completed in the correct order for reward.

Of considerable importance is the fact that the configurations or patterns of the stimuli change from one trial to the next, as shown at the top of Figure 9.2. Thus, pigeons cannot learn the chain by responding to a sequence of spatial positions. Both spatial position and differential kinesthetic feedback are eliminated as potential cues for serial learning. Nevertheless, pigeons have learned to peck up to five stimuli in a predetermined order. The task is not easy for pigeons to acquire, and more than 100 daily sessions of training may be required to take a pigeon through all of the steps necessary to learn a five-item chain. Furthermore, accuracy on four- and five-item chains usually is not much better than successful completion of the correct chain on 70 percent of the trials. On the other hand, considering that the likelihood of completing a five-item chain by chance alone is 1 out of 120, 70 percent accuracy clearly indicates substantial serial learning on the part of the pigeon.

What did the pigeon learn that allows it to chain stimuli together? Although the simultaneous chaining procedure prohibits the possibility that pigeons are chaining stimuli and responses on the basis of spatial position or kinesthetic feedback, pigeons might have learned a series of associations between each visual cue and response to the next visual cue. Thus, as a pigeon pecks the blue key, its frontal visual field is filled with blue, and this color stimulation could act as a cue that triggers a response to the yellow key. According to this hypothesis, a pigeon learns only a series of stimulus-response associations that allow it to chain, but the pigeon has no overall representation of the sequence of stimuli in the chain.

Tests with Subsequences

Although such a process may be partly involved in acquiring the chains, tests carried out with only selected items of the chain suggest that it is not the whole story. Given a chain of four stimuli, ABCD, pigeons have been tested on

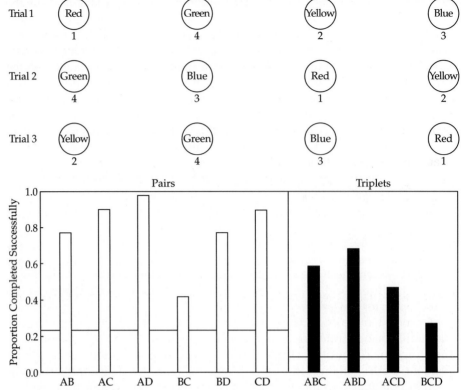

FIGURE 9.2. The upper diagram shows the simultaneous presentation of four keys containing different colors on three successive trials. A pigeon must peck the keys in the order *red*(A)→*yellow*(B)→*blue*(C)→*green*(D) on each trial for reward. The bar graph shows the proportion of subsequences successfully completed on tests with pairs and triplets taken from the ABCD chain. The horizontal lines show the chance levels of performance.

subsequences that consist of all possible pairs or triplets of stimuli in the chain (Straub & Terrace, 1981; Terrace, 1987; 1991). On pair tests, a pigeon is presented with only two stimuli—AB, AC, AD, BC, BD, and CD; tests of triplets presented sets of three cues—ABC, ABD, ACD, and BCD. Notice that some of these tests involve stimuli that were adjacent in the original chain, such as AB, BC, and BCD, but other tests involve nonadjacent stimuli, such as BD and ACD. According to the associative model, pigeons should peck adjacent stimuli in the correct order but have difficulty with nonadjacent stimuli. For example, the sequence ABC should be completed correctly because A cues response to B and B cues response to C. The sequence ABD should be difficult, however, because B cues a response to C and not to D. Stimulus B might cue a response to D through a remote association. However, since remote associations are held to be weaker than primary associations, we would expect sequences with nonadjacent stimuli to be ordered less accurately than those with adjacent stimuli.

The results of tests with subsequences, shown in the graph at the bottom of Figure 9.2, did not follow the pattern predicted by associative theory. On testing with pairs of stimuli, pigeons completed the sequence in the correct order at 80 percent or better accuracy whenever the pair contained either the A or the D stimulus. Pigeons were actually somewhat more accurate on AC and AD pairs than on AB pairs. Only the pair containing BC yielded a low level of accuracy near chance; pigeons pecked these stimuli in the order CB about as often as they pecked them in the order BC. On triplets, pigeons scored substantially above chance on tests containing ABC, ABD, and ACD, with lower accuracy seen on the BCD triplet. Once again, the absence of adjacent stimuli did not appear to be a critical factor in pigeons' ability to peck stimuli in the correct order.

Theory of Pigeon Serial Learning

These findings clearly suggest that something beyond a chain of associations is necessary to explain pigeons' acquisition of serial performance. The findings also indicate that pigeons do not have an adequate representation of the entire chain; they fail to respond with the correct order when certain subsets of stimuli are presented. As an account of these findings, Terrace (1991) suggests that pigeons actually learned some fairly simple rules that allow them to do well at this task. Three rules are important: (1) Always respond to Stimulus A first, (2) always respond to Stimulus D last, and (3) when neither of these first two rules applies, respond to other stimuli by default. Notice how the first two rules allow the pigeon to order pairs beginning with A or ending with D correctly. When triplets ABD or ACD occur, accurate responding should occur: The pigeon should apply the first rule and peck A first, then apply the third rule and peck B or C by default, and finally apply the second rule to peck D last. Problems arise, however, with the pair BC and the triplet BCD. If the pigeon responds by default to B and C, it has no basis for placing one of these stimuli before the other, and accuracy should approach chance.

Although the application of these three rules accounts for the results of tests with subsequences of pairs and triplets, one problem remains. How do pigeons accurately order the four stimuli into an ABCD sequence if they have no basis for placing B before C? After pecking A first, the rules specify no mechanism for choosing B before C. Even more problematic is how pigeons successfully complete the BCD sequence within the ABCDE chain. Given this paradoxical inconsistency between performance on whole chains and on chain subsequences, Terrace (1991) concluded that associations between stimuli must also be involved in serial learning. Thus, visual stimulation provided by response to A must serve as a cue for response to B, and cues provided by response to B must guide response to C. This assumption accounts for the high level of performance found with full chains but still predicts poor performance on the BC subsequence after learning the ABCD chain and poor performance on the BCD subsequence after learning the ABCDE chain. In both subsequences, the absence of an initial response to Stimulus A means that no cue is present to direct the initial response to Stimulus B, and performance should drop to near chance.

Terrace's (1991) research is a very nice example of how a complex cognitive process may be analyzed into several components. It appears that pigeons' completion of four- and five-stimulus chains is based on several factors. First, pigeons seem to learn rules about which stimuli are to be pecked first and last,

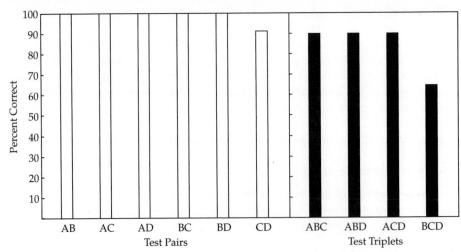

FIGURE 9.3. Percentage of sequences successfully completed on subsequence tests with pairs and triplets of stimuli taken from the ABCD chain initially learned by cebus monkeys.

as well as a default option when these rules do not apply. Superimposed on these rules are interstimulus associations governing sequential choices among internal items within the chain. By using these learned devices, the pigeon can show what appears to be highly sophisticated serial learning without having any representation of the entire sequence of stimuli in the chain.

Serial Learning in Monkeys

An interesting comparative analysis of serial memory in pigeons and monkeys was provided by experiments carried out by D'Amato and Colombo (1988). In their experiments, cebus monkeys were trained on the simultaneous chaining procedure. Monkeys were shown projected black-and-white geometric patterns, with the configuration of these stimuli changed from trial to trial. Just as pigeons were trained to peck keys, monkeys were trained to press on keys in front of these projectors for reward at the end of a chain of responses. Subjects learned ABCD and ABCDE chains of responses by starting with the AB sequence and adding one item at a time. After a monkey mastered the full sequence, tests were given on all possible two- and three-item subsequences. As shown in Figure 9.3, the pattern of results obtained after acquisition of the ABCD series was quite different from the pigeon data shown in Figure 9.2. In particular, notice that monkeys were able to correctly order all pairs of stimuli at near 100 percent accuracy. No drop in accuracy was found with the BC interior pair. Accuracy on the BCD triplet dropped to about 65 percent, but this value was far above the corresponding level of accuracy seen with pigeons on this test. Monkeys apparently had access to information that allowed them to correctly order all of the subsequences.

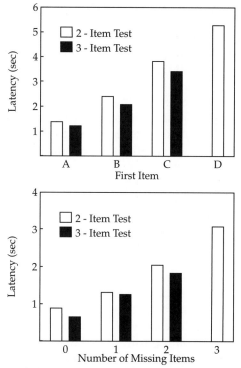

FIGURE 9.4. The top panel shows latency of responses to the first item in pairs or triplets that began with A, B, C, or D. The bottom panel shows latency of responses to the second item in pairs that were separated by 0, 1, 2, or 3 missing items.

Some insight into the monkeys' representation of lists was obtained when latencies of responses were examined for completion of subsequences. In the graph at the top of Figure 9.4, response latencies are shown to the first stimulus in two- or three-item tests that began with a response to the A, B, C, or D stimulus. Notice that latencies increased consistently the later in the list the starting item occurred. In the graph at the bottom of Figure 9.4, latencies are shown for the response to the second stimulus in pairs tests as a function of the number of missing items intervening between the two items tested. Latencies climb as the distance between items increases. For example, monkeys took progressively longer to respond to the second stimulus on AB, AC, AD, and AE tests.

In one model that nicely accounts for these data, the monkeys have access to a linear representation of the ABCDE sequence and scan that sequence in memory from beginning to end to find the item that should be chosen. Thus, when shown the pair DE, items A, B, and C are scanned before D is reached and triggers a response to Stimulus D. Since it takes time to mentally scan items, it will take longer to respond to DE than to AB, BC, or CD because more initial items must be scanned. To explain the data in the lower graph, it is assumed that monkeys scanned the missing intermediate items on pairs tests. Given the pairs AB, AC, AD, and AE, for example, a monkey would have to scan 0, 1, 2, and 3 intermediate items in memory, respectively, to reach the second item in the test. The latencies nicely reflect the number of intermediate items.

Further convincing evidence that monkeys used a linear representation of the entire sequence of stimuli was provided in a second set of experiments by D'Amato and Colombo (1989). Monkeys that were able to produce the ABCDE sequence correctly on 90 percent or more of their attempts were tested with wild cards. A wild card (W) consisted of a new stimulus pattern to which the monkeys had not been trained to respond. Different patterns of the stimuli ABCDE were presented with one stimulus missing and the wild card substituted. Thus, a monkey might see the configuration CBWAE, and the correct response would be to respond to these stimuli in the order ABCWE; the logical place to substitute the wild-card stimulus is in the position where the missing D stimulus normally would go. Over a number of wild-card tests, each of the five stimuli in the ABCDE string was replaced on different trials. Monkeys successfully completed these wild card tests with 60 percent accuracy, far better than the level of chance expectancy of 20 percent. In still further tests, two wild cards were placed in a display of stimuli. For example, a monkey would see DWAWC, and the correct response sequence would be AWCDW. The level of accuracy on these tests remained at about 60 percent, even though the probability of a correct sequence by chance dropped to 10 percent.

The monkeys' success on the wild-card tests is quite important because it cannot be explained by an associative chain. Since monkeys were not trained to respond to wild cards, there could be no learned associations between wild cards and the items in the training list. In the CBWAE example, C should have no more tendency to produce a response to W than any other stimulus in the list, and W should have no more tendency to yield a response to E than to any other stimulus in the list. In other words, there was no associative basis from prior learning for the choices the monkeys made.

These wild-card data, along with the findings of the subsequences tests and the latency data, strongly imply that monkeys used a representation of the entire list, within which each stimulus had a specific serial position. How could monkeys have such a representation? One possibility is that they counted the items in the list, Stimulus A being one, Stimulus B being two, and so forth. The topic of numerical processing and counting in animals is discussed in more detail in Chapter 10, but little current evidence suggests that monkeys are able to assign numerical symbols to successive items in a list. Still another possibility is that monkeys used a spatial representation (D'Amato & Colombo, 1989). Suppose that monkeys are able to image a length of space, either an imaginary line or a memory from some frequently viewed location. Suppose further that Stimulus A is placed at one end of the spatial dimension and Stimulus E at the other end, with Stimuli B, C, and D placed in order between them. Whenever, a monkey is presented with a set of stimuli, it scans this image from the A end to the E end and responds to stimuli as it encounters them in its memory image. Such a process then explains monkeys' ability to correctly complete all subsequences. Assuming it takes time to scan this image, the increases in latency seen in Figure 9.4 follow from the extra time taken to scan more and more locations. Finally, the placement of wild cards at correct positions in lists may represent a kind of default option; if all the stimuli from the training list have been matched to locations on the image, wild cards can only be placed in empty positions by default.

The data on serial list completion are most interesting from a comparative point of view. Although both pigeons and monkeys can successfully learn to respond to up to five stimuli in order, the similarity of their performance is only superficial. When analytical tests are carried out, the data suggest important comparative differences. Monkeys apparently have access to an entire representation of the linear sequence of stimuli, but pigeons use rules and interitem associations that allow them to correctly produce the sequence but provide no cognitive appreciation of the entire list of stimuli.

A further prediction from this comparative account of the differences between pigeons and monkeys is that pigeons should do poorly when tested with wild cards. The rules and interitem associations hypothesized to be used by pigeons provide no basis for responding to wild cards. After training different groups of pigeons to order three-, four-, and five-item lists accurately, Terrace, Chen, and Newman (1995) tested each group's ability to correctly place a wild card at the position of an omitted stimulus. Unlike monkeys, all three groups of pigeons responded to wild cards at about chance level on the initial sessions of testing. After 27 sessions of training, the three-item group learned to place wild cards at the correct position at a 75 percent accuracy level; within a three-item list, it was possible for birds to learn specific associations between the wild card and the other three items. However, birds in the four-item and five-item groups never approached this level of accuracy after 90 sessions of training, their performance remaining below 40 percent correct. Unlike cebus monkeys, pigeons apparently do not have the cognitive tools to deal with wild cards in an extended sequence.

TRANSITIVE INFERENCE

In a popular test of reasoning in human cognition, a subject might be presented with the following statements, "Bob is smarter than Harry," and "Harry is smarter than Tom." The subject then is asked, "Who is smarter, Bob or Tom?" Although neither of the initial statements contained a direct comparison between Bob and Tom, it is possible for the subject to infer that Bob is smarter than Tom by comparing their relationships to Harry contained in the two statements provided. In this case, knowledge about the serial order of a set of stimuli is obtained through inference and not through direct experience with the stimuli in their serial order. A subject's ability to solve this problem is called *transitive inference,* and a popular account of transitive inference is that people reason deductively from the initial statements or premises to the conclusion, using verbal symbols. It was, therefore, a considerable surprise when evidence of transitive inference was found in animals.

Transitive inference in animals was demonstrated initially in nonhuman primates, first in squirrel monkeys (McGonigle & Chalmers, 1977) and then in a chimpanzee (Gillan, 1981; see Boysen, Berntson, Shreyer, & Quigley, 1993, for a more recent demonstration of transitive inference in chimpanzees). In these experiments, an animal was trained to make a number of discriminations between pairs of stimuli, such as two boxes that were painted different colors or contained different patterns. If these stimuli are designated by letters, the discriminations learned can be expressed as A+B–, B+C–, C+D–, and D+E–; within each discrimination problem, choice of the stimulus followed by a plus sign yields reward, and choice of the stimulus followed by a minus sign yields nonreward. These discriminations might be learned in sequence or concurrently, with each problem presented on different trials within a session. It is assumed that the subject is learning relative relationships between stimuli, such as Stimulus A is more valuable than Stimulus B, Stimulus B is more valuable than Stimulus C, and so on. When all of the discrimination problems have been learned to a criterion, two stimuli from the middle of the sequence that never were presented together now are shown simultaneously. For example, Stimuli B and D could be presented to see which of the two the subject prefers. Transitive inference is shown by a preference for Stimulus B. On tests of this nature, monkeys and chimpanzees chose Stimulus B significantly more often than Stimulus D.

How can we explain transitive inference in animals? Because monkeys and chimpanzees without language training have shown the phenomenon, we cannot attribute its presence to the use of verbal symbols. It might be argued that primates without language are still able to deduce the solution to transitive inference problems by using nonverbal symbols. More recent evidence makes this account of transitive inference in animals seem unlikely. Transitive inference has now been reported in experiments with pigeons (Fersen, Wynne, Delius, & Staddon, 1991) and with rats (Davis, 1992). The discovery of transitive inference in nonprimates suggests that we should look for a less sophisticated explanation than deductive reasoning.

Value Transfer Theory

Fersen et al. (1991) argued that the findings of their transitive inference experiments with pigeons can be explained by conditioning principles. That is, Stimulus B is favored over Stimulus D because Stimulus B has more associative strength than Stimulus D. The basis for this conclusion is a new theory of associative learning called *value transfer theory*. The important assumption made by this theory is that within a pair of stimuli, one of which is rewarded and the other of which is nonrewarded, the rewarded member transfers some of its associative strength or value to the nonrewarded member. In the series A+B–, B+C–, C+D–, and D+E–, Stimulus A transfers considerable value to Stimulus B in the A+B– discrimination because Stimulus A is always reinforced. In turn, Stimulus B transfers value to Stimulus C in the B+C– problem, but the degree of value transferred to Stimulus C from Stimulus B is not as great as that transferred from Stimulus A to Stimulus B because Stimulus B was nonreinforcement during half of the trials. The degree of value imparted from the rewarded member of a pair to the nonrewarded member becomes progressively less as we move from Pair A+B– to Pair D+E–. Thus, on a test between Stimuli B and D, Stimulus B has more transferred value than Stimulus D and is the preferred stimulus.

Although value transfer theory accounted for transitive inference in pigeons, there was little independent evidence for the process of value transfer itself. More recently, Zentall and Sherburne (1994) provided such evidence. Pigeons were trained to perform two discrimination problems, A+B– and C+/– D–. On Problem A+B–, choice of Stimulus A was always rewarded, but, on Problem C+/– D–, choice of Stimulus C was rewarded on half the trials and nonrewarded on the other half of the trials, while D was always nonrewarded. According to value transfer theory, more value should be transferred to nonrewarded Stimulus B from Stimulus A than to nonrewarded Stimulus D from Stimulus C. When pigeons were given a choice between Stimuli B and D, they chose Stimulus B about 65 percent of the time, a frequency significantly higher than the 50 percent expected by chance.

Although Fersen et al. (1991) used value transfer theory to explain transitive inference in pigeons, and although evidence of value transfer has been found independent of the conditions necessary for transitive inference (Steirn, Weaver, & Zentall, 1995; Zentall & Sherburne, 1994), the theory's account of transitive inference remains in doubt. Weaver, Steirn, & Zentall (1997) found transitive inference in pigeons even under conditions in which the degree of reward provided for stimuli within a series of problems did not promote transitive inference through value transfer. Pigeons were trained on the sequence of discriminations A+/– B–, B+C–, C+D–, and D+E+/–. By reinforcing Stimuli A and E on only half of the training trials on discriminations A+/–B– and D+E+/–, the value transferred to B is reduced, and the value transferred to D is increased. Even under these conditions, Weaver et al. found that pigeons chose B over D on 78 percent of the test trials. Value transfer may be one process contributing to the transitive inference phenomenon in animals, but other processes also may be responsible for this effect.

The Spatial Coding Hypothesis

Still another explanation of transitive inference relies on the spatial coding hypothesis already discussed with respect to D'Amato and Colombo's (1988; 1989) account of serial learning in monkeys. Suppose that a subject is able to place images of the stimuli encountered in a transitive inference experiment along a linear dimension, with Stimulus A at one end and Stimulus D at the other end. The relative value of each stimulus is indicated by its distance from the end of the continuum anchored at Stimulus A; the closer a stimulus lies to that end of the dimension, the more it is valued. In fact, evidence for the use of spatial codes in human transitive inference experiments is often reported (DeSoto, London, & Handel, 1965; Huttenlocher, 1968; Sternberg, 1980). Given the excellence of spatial cognition in animals reviewed in Chapter 7, it seems quite possible that animals use a spatial representation to code the relative values of stimuli in a transitive inference task.

In an experiment designed to reveal the memory structure established in a transitive inference experiment, W. Roberts and Phelps (1994) used procedures developed by H. Davis (1992) to train rats on five olfactory discrimination problems, A+B–, B+C–, C+D–, D+E–, and E+F–. Rats made choices between pairs of tunnels that were visually identical but had their doors painted with

Linear Arrangement

Circular Arrangement

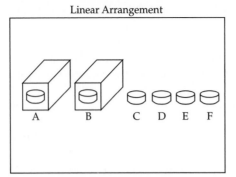
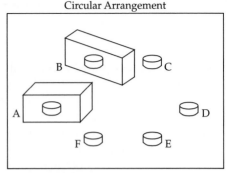

FIGURE 9.5. The diagrams show two arrangements of tunnels used in transitive inference experiments. The stimuli A, B, C, D, E, and F refer to different odors placed on the doors of the tunnels. The disks are food cups placed inside each tunnel.

different odors; the odors were coconut, orange, vanilla, cherry, banana, and almond. In an initial experiment, two groups of rats were trained, but the arrangement of the tunnels during training differed between the groups. In the linear arrangement group, the tunnels always were placed in the same spatial positions, according to the linear arrangement shown in the left diagram in Figure 9.5. Thus, Stimuli A and B always were placed adjacent to one another at one end of a table in the A+B– problem, and Stimuli E and F always were placed adjacent to one another at the other end of the table in the E+F– problem. For animals in a random arrangement group, each pair of stimuli was placed in all of the possible adjacent positions along the table. Thus, animals in the linear arrangement group could form a stable representation of stimuli located at different positions along a linear dimension, but animals in the random arrangement group could not.

After animals in both groups learned all five problems to a criterion of learning, a choice test between Stimuli B and D was carried out in a different testing room from that used in training. Thus, animals could not use any of the visual cues present during training to choose between Stimuli B and D. However, if animals could retrieve a *memory* of the location of those stimuli relative to the spatial cues present in the training room, then subjects in the linear arrangement group but not the random arrangement group could base their choice on the proximity of each stimulus to the more valued end of the linear dimension. It was found that rats in the linear arrangement group chose Stimulus B on 74 percent of the trials, but rats in the random arrangement group chose Stimulus B on only 48 percent of the trials.

In a further test of the spatial coding hypothesis, W. Roberts and Phelps (1994) trained rats on the circular arrangement of tunnels shown in the right diagram in Figure 9.5. Notice that now the initial and final stimuli in the sequence of problems, Stimulus A and Stimulus F, no longer have distinct spatial anchors at opposite ends of a table. In fact, Stimuli A and F are as close to one another as any other pair of stimuli. Under these conditions, the spatial coding hypothesis predicts little evidence of transitive inference since the spatial code provides little basis for valuing one stimulus over the other. Under these conditions, rats chose Stimulus B over Stimulus D on only 52 percent of the trials.

It is clear from the evidence reviewed that animals show the transitive inference phenomenon. Formal deductive reasoning appears to be ruled out since few investigators would want to accord these processes to rats and pigeons. A clear alternative account of transitive inference in animals has not emerged, but recent research suggests that conditioning mechanisms such as value transfer or a process of spatial coding may eventually help to form the basis for a complete understanding of this effect.

CHUNKING IN SERIAL MEMORY

Some years ago, an experiment was performed by Wishner, Shipley, and Hurvich (1957) in which human subjects memorized lists of nonsense syllables by the serial anticipation procedure. A subject was shown a list of 18 nonsense syllables, one at a time for 2 seconds, on a memory drum. On subsequent trials, the subject was asked to recall the item that followed the one currently seen in the window of the memory drum. It takes subjects a number of trials to learn a list of items by this method. The positions of items in the list affect the speed at which they are learned, as shown by a serial position curve that plots the number of correct anticipations made at each serial position. Typically, a bowed serial position curve is found, in which early and final items are learned most rapidly and middle items take longer to memorize.

Wishner et al. (1957) introduced an interesting variation to the traditional procedure. Although lists of items are typically homogeneous in appearance, Wishner et al. presented nonsense syllables that varied in color; the first six items were printed in green capital letters, the second six in black lowercase letters, and the last six in red capital letters. The consequence of this manipulation was a serial position curve in which each sublist of colored nonsense syllables showed its own bowed curve. Thus, curves that rose and fell appeared at Positions 1–6, 7–12, and 13–18. It appears that subjects treated each set of colored nonsense syllables as a separate list or chunk of information to be learned. One consequence of being able to chunk items into sublists was that the overall list was learned faster than a control list of all black nonsense syllables; although it took an average of 31.4 trials for subjects to memorize the control list, subjects took only 20 trials to learn the chunked list. Visual chunking led to both faster learning and to a different organization of the material for learning within the list.

Chunking in Pigeon Serial Learning

The process of chunking is not restricted to people. Recent evidence suggests that animals may also be able to combine similar kinds of information into hierarchically organized chunks for memory processing. In an experiment reminiscent of the Wishner et al. (1957) experiment with people, Terrace (1987; 1991) used the simultaneous chaining procedure to train pigeons to peck sequences of keys that varied in their visual appearance. Five keys were illuminated with either black-and-white patterns or colored fields. In chunked conditions, the sequence in which these keys had to be pecked placed stimuli of similar appearance in blocks. For example, in the list A→B→C→D'→E', A→B→C was a block of three colors, and D'→E' was a block of two black-and-white patterns. In control lists, all of the stimuli were of the same appearance, or stimuli of different appearance had to be pecked in a nonblocked order, such as A→B'→C→D'→E. Striking differences in the ease with which these lists could be learned to criterion was found (Terrace, 1987). Whereas the control lists required 120 or more sessions to learn, the blocked lists were learned in 70 or fewer sessions.

Other pieces of evidence also suggested that pigeons dealt more easily with chunked sequences than with control sequences. When the time required to complete a sequence of responses to all five stimuli was measured, it was found that birds completed the chunked A→B→C→D'→E' list in 5.42 mean seconds but required more than 7 mean seconds to complete control sequences (Terrace, 1991). To examine this time difference more closely, latencies of response to each member of a sequence were measured. The latency was defined as the time from the last peck to the preceding stimulus to the first peck at the current stimulus. The latency to each item in the A→B→C→D'→E' sequence was lower than that to corresponding items in control sequences. Apparently, pigeons were accessing information necessary for placing items in a serial order more rapidly with chunked lists than with nonchunked lists.

Tests with pairs of subsequences were carried out with items from the chunked list and the control lists (Terrace, 1987). On the homogeneous control list, A→B→C→D→E, the results were the same as those already discussed; subjects accurately ordered all but the interior pairs, B→C, B→D, and C→D, which suffered near chance accuracy. On the chunked list, A→B→C→D'→E', however, subjects maintained a high level of accuracy on all pairs, including the interior pairs, B→C, B→D', and C→D'. This striking difference in pigeons' ability to order subsequences suggests that birds' performance on chunked lists was guided by quite a different memory organization from that which guided performance on the control list.

Suppose that pigeons segregated rules for ordering the chunked list into two different sets stored in reference memory—rules for pecking colors and rules for pecking black-and-white forms. An initial superordinate rule would be to retrieve the rules for color stimuli, ABC, first. These rules then would follow the familiar form discussed earlier: Peck A first, Peck C last, and Peck B by default if neither of the other rules apply. Having pecked C, rules for pecking black-and-white forms, D'E', would be retrieved. Here, only two rules are necessary: Peck D' first, and Peck E' last. These rules should then generate correct ordering of interior pairs. The rules for the ABC color stimuli lead to production of the correct B→C subsequence. The subsequences B→D' and C→D' should be produced because initial retrieval of the color rules should lead to choice of B by the default rule and choice of C by the "last" rule; when the rules for black-and-white forms are retrieved, choice of D' follows from the "first" rule. Note that according to this hypothesis, pigeons taught the chunked list would not have to learn any interstimulus associations, as do pigeons taught the homogeneous control list. Possibly the extra sessions taken to learn the nonchunked lists were required to learn these interstimulus associations. Furthermore, the time differences in latency and overall list completion could arise from a greater amount of information control pigeons needed to retrieve in order to peck the stimuli in the correct sequence.

Terrace (1991) also measured a second time component. As pigeons pecked their way through a list, they often pecked several times on a given stimulus before proceeding to the next stimulus in the list. The time spent in repetitive pecking on a key was defined as the *dwell time.* In general, dwell time was lower on items in the chunked list than on items in control lists. There was one notable exception to this rule; pigeons' dwell time increased substantially on the last item of a chunk. Thus, in the chunked list A→B→C→D'→E', dwell times were low on all four of the first four stimuli, with the exception of Stimulus C, which had a dwell time that was about twice as high as those for the other stimuli. One explanation of this interesting pause is that it reflects the time required for the pigeon to retrieve the set of rules needed to deal with the next set of stimuli in the list.

Chunking in Rats

Terrace's (1987; 1991) experiments suggest that pigeons, like people, find serial lists easier to learn if the material in the list is presented in a chunked organization. However, suppose that material to be memorized is not presented in a segregated or chunked organization. In a free-recall experiment, a subject is presented with a list of words and asked to recall as many words from the list as possible, *in any order.* In such experiments, the order in which items are recalled becomes an important dependent variable that tells us a great deal about the way people organize their memory. In a classic experiment, Bousfield (1953) read subjects a list of 60 words that contained items from different conceptual categories. The list contained 15 words each from the following categories: animals, men's first names, professions, and vegetables. These words were presented in a random order when read to subjects; a typical list could begin with the sequence, "muskrat, blacksmith, panther, baker, wildcat, Howard, radish, Jason, printer, mushroom, chemist . . . ." When subjects recalled words from the list, however, they tended to recall them in category clusters. That is, words were recalled in groups of animals, names, professions, and vegetables. Subjects reorganized the input lists into conceptual chunks, based on the conceptual similarity of the words. Further, it seems that conceptual reorganization of material promoted more efficient retention of material; subjects recalled more words from lists in which they put words into meaningful chunks than they did from lists of words that did not fall into common conceptual categories.

Two interesting questions are, "Do animals also show structured output on a memory test?" and "Does such structure improve retention?" Dallal and Meck (1990) devised an experiment with rats, which is analogous in several respects to the Bousfield (1953) study. They used a 12-arm radial maze to study the acquisition of spatial memory in rats. Rats collected food on the arms of the maze over a number of daily trials until they seldom made an error by reentering an arm already visited. Three types of food were made available on the arms of the maze: sunflower seeds, rice puffs, and standard reward pellets. In an experimental group of rats, each food type was assigned to four different arms of the

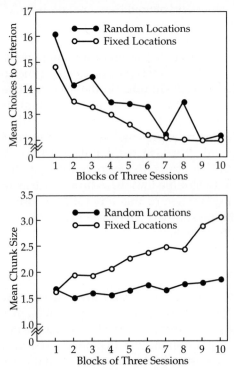

FIGURE 9.6. The upper graph shows how accurately rats in fixed and random location groups could enter all 12 arms on the maze without errors. The lower graph shows the growth of mean chunk size over sessions in each group.

maze, and rats always found the same foods on the same arms throughout training. One control group found the same food on all arms of the maze. Another control group had the three foods placed on different arms of the maze on each trial but had the arm positions of the foods changed randomly from one trial to the next. Thus, control animals could not learn fixed locations for different foods. Two important findings came out of the experiment: (1) Experimental rats learned to run the maze without errors faster than the control rats, and (2) experimental rats clustered their visits to arms of the maze according to the food the arms contained. They tended to enter arms containing sunflower seeds first, arms containing reward pellets second, and arms containing rice puffs third.

Macuda and W. Roberts (1995) repeated the Dallal and Meck (1990) experiment, also using a 12-arm radial maze and placing three different foods on the arms—pieces of cheese, pieces of a chocolate-flavored breakfast cereal, and reward pellets. In the fixed location group, each of the three foods were placed on four different arms of the maze, and these arm assignments remained constant throughout training. Rats in a random location group served as a control and had the locations of the three foods changed randomly from one session to the next. The findings of the experiment are displayed in the two graphs shown in Figure 9.6. The upper graph shows accuracy on the maze by the number of arm choices rats had to make in order to enter all 12 arms of the maze; a perfect score of 12 indicates an errorless session with no repeats. Although both groups approached perfect performance over sessions, the fixed location group consistently demonstrated superior spatial memory to the random location group.

Rats generally came to enter arms that contained cheese first, then chocolate cereal arms, and finally reward pellet arms. Suppose that a rat entered the 12 arms containing different foods in the order *cheese, cheese, chocolate, cheese, cheese, chocolate, chocolate, pellets, pellets, chocolate, pellets, pellets.* Mean chunk size was calculated by segregating strings of arm visits by common foods. The numbers of arms in each string were added together and divided by the number of strings to obtain a mean string or chunk size. In the preceding example, the mean chunk size would be calculated to be $(2+1+2+2+2+1+2)/7 = 12/7 = 1.71$ arms per chunk. In a perfectly chunked sequence, an animal might enter the arms in the order *cheese, cheese, cheese, cheese, chocolate, chocolate, chocolate, chocolate, pellets, pellets, pellets, pellets,* and the mean chunk size would be $(4+4+4)/3 = 12/3 = 4.0$. The lower graph in Figure 9.7 shows that rats in the fixed location groups increasingly chunked their visits to arms over sessions, whereas rats in the random location group showed little change in chunking over sessions.

These findings suggest the interesting possibility that rats' improved memory for spatial locations under the fixed location condition arises from a chunked hierarchical representation of the maze. Following the ideas of Dallal and Meck (1990), Macuda and W. Roberts (1995) suggested that rats in fixed location conditions may remember location on the maze according to the organizational structure shown in Figure 9.7. The figure describes a hierarchical memory system in which the radial maze retrieves memory nodes corresponding to each of three different food types, A, B, and C. Each food node retrieves a memory chunk that contains the locations of four arms where that particular food may be found.

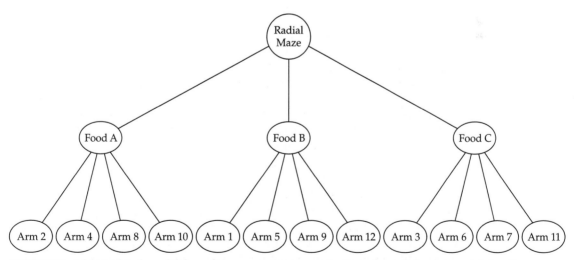

FIGURE 9.7. A hierarchical model for reference memory organization of a radial maze containing three different types of food, A, B, and C, on different arms of the maze. The ovals containing foods represent higher-order nodes in memory, and the sets of ovals containing arms represent chunks.

Consider a rat keeping track of arms as it visits them on the maze. It may use retrospective memory and remember the arms previously visited. By the time the rat reached the final arm, it would have to remember 11 previously entered arms in working memory. Or, the rat might use prospective memory and remember the arms it has not yet visited. In this case, the rat encounters a large memory load at the beginning of its travels; after the first arm visited, it must remember 11 arms not yet visited. Cook, Brown, and Riley (1985) suggested that rats may use both retrospective and prospective memory on a 12-arm maze, switching from the former to the latter after half the arms have been visited. Thus, a rat might start off remembering the arms it has visited, but, after it has visited six arms, it would switch to remembering the arms not yet visited. In this way, the maximum load an animal would have to keep in working memory is six arms.

If a rat could use the memory structure shown in Figure 9.7, however, it could further reduce the load on working memory. By accessing different chunks of arms in reference memory through their food nodes, only four arms have to be held in working memory at one time. Successively accessing these food-tree maps and visiting the arms in each map or chunk leads, of course, to a clustering of visits to maze arms by food type. Therefore, the hierarchical model accounts for both the superior memory and the growth in mean chunk size seen in the fixed location group, compared to the random location group.

In a further test of the model shown in Figure 9.7, Macuda and W. Roberts (1995) asked what would happen if rats were required to reorganize their reference memory for food locations on the radial maze. Rats trained in the fixed location group in the previous experiment were divided into two new groups: the chunk maintained group and the chunk compromised group. Both groups encountered completely new food locations on the maze; each arm now contained a different type of food from the one it contained on the preceding session. However, the way in which foods were rearranged differed between the two groups. For rats in the chunk maintained group, foods were exchanged between arms in chunks. For example, the four arms that had contained cheese now contained the chocolate cereal, the four arms that contained the chocolate cereal now contained food pellets, and the four arms that contained food pellets now contained cheese. In the case of the chunk compromised group, each set of four arms that previously contained one type of food now contained two different food types. Thus, two of the arms that had contained cheese now contained chocolate cereal, and the other two now contained reward pellets. Similarly, the arms that had contained chocolate cereal now contained cheese and reward pellets, and the arms that had contained reward pellets now contained cheese and chocolate cereal.

Figure 9.7 can be used to clarify what the restructuring of memory would require for rats in each group in order to deal with these new food locations. In the case of the chunk maintained group, the chunks or groups of arms containing a common food were maintained, but the food nodes were interchanged. Rats would have to rearrange the cheese, chocolate cereal, and reward pellets nodes, but the chunks can remain intact. The memory reorganization task is not as easy for rats in the chunk compromised group. Since arms that previously contained the same food now contain two different foods, rats in this group

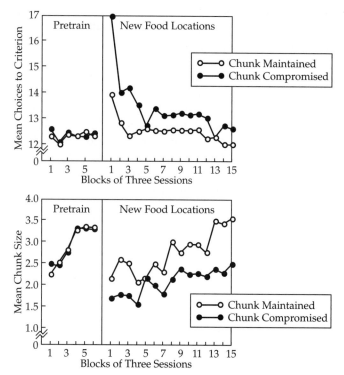

FIGURE 9.8. The upper graph shows how accurately rats in the chunk maintained and chunk compromised groups entered all 12 arms without errors before and after foods were placed at new locations. The lower graph shows the growth of mean chunk size in both groups before and after new food locations were introduced.

must construct entirely new chunks or sets of arm locations that correspond to cheese, chocolate cereal, and reward pellet nodes in reference memory. The model then predicts that rats in the chunk compromised group should show greater disruption, both of memory accuracy and of chunking on the maze, than the chunk maintained group.

Figure 9.8 shows the results of the memory reorganization study. The top graph shows maze accuracy during sessions before and after food locations were rearranged. Both groups entered arms on the maze with almost no errors prior to the introduction of new food locations. Choices to criterion rose in both groups when new food locations were introduced, but the disruption in performance was greater for the chunk compromised group than for the chunk maintained group throughout training. The bottom graph shows the effect of new food locations on mean chunk size. Both groups attained a high level of arm clustering before food locations were changed. With the introduction of new food locations, mean chunk size dropped considerably in both groups. However, animals in the chunk maintained group were able to reestablish a high level of chunking based on the new food locations, whereas animals in the chunk compromised group showed only a slight improvement in chunking over sessions.

The data from Dallal and Meck's (1990) radial maze experiments combined with those shown from Macuda and W. Roberts (1995) suggest that rats do not learn a radial maze containing different foods in fixed locations as a set of isolated arms. Rather, these findings suggest that rats form hierarchical memory structures in which arm locations are indexed as chunks of information under higher-order food nodes. Undoubtedly, these structures are based very much on motivational and foraging concerns. Rats visit arms containing different foods according to food preferences, much as they visit arms containing different amounts of food in decreasing quantities (see Figure 9.1). The formation of a highly organized memory system may then allow animals to forage in an optimal fashion by providing them with rapid and efficient access to the reference memory locations of the most preferred or valuable types of food. In support of this idea, Menzel (1973) reported that chimpanzees using spatial memory to find hidden food in a field collected all the pieces of fruit before searching for pieces of vegetables. Sherry (1987) reported that black-capped chicadees that had stored both sunflower and safflower seeds later retrieved the favored sunflower seeds before the less favored safflower seeds.

SERIAL PATTERN LEARNING

As mentioned earlier in this chapter, people may be asked to learn sequences of stimuli that follow a pattern or are rule governed. One example is the sequence EFEFEFEF, which involves a single alternation rule. In another repeating pattern, QQPPQQPP, the elements of the pattern show double alternation. Other rule-governed patterns may be based on monotonicity, such as 98765, a monotonically decreasing pattern that follows a minus-one rule, or 2468, a monotonically increasing pattern that follows a plus-two rule.

Single-Alternation Pattern Learning

Although such patterns are trivially easy for people to learn, they may pose a challenge to animals, and numerous experiments have been performed to assess the pattern learning abilities of animals. The *single-alternation pattern* has been used in a number of experiments both in runways and mazes. In a T-maze, a rat is reinforced on alternating trials for entering right (R) and left (L) arms in an RLRLRL pattern. Rats rapidly learn such a pattern, and part of their success arises from a species' predisposition to investigate novel locations or places not visited recently (Dember & Fowler, 1958). In a straight runway, rats have been trained to run from a start box down an alley to a goal box, with reward (R) and nonreward (N) alternated according to an RNRNRN pattern over multiple trials given within daily sessions. After several sessions of training in this manner, rats learn to run fast on the rewarded trials and to run slowly on the nonrewarded trials (Capaldi, 1958; Tyler, Wortz, & Bitterman, 1953). Rats appear to have learned the pattern and respond in an appropriate fashion.

Just what have the rats learned that allows them to correctly anticipate rewarded and nonrewarded trials? Although one interpretation of this finding is that rats learn the repetitive rule governing the single-alternation pattern

(Tyler et al., 1953), a more widely held account is that animals learned sequential associations (Capaldi, 1966; 1967). Capaldi's theory of sequential associations holds that each trial outcome serves as a stimulus that becomes associated with the rewarded or nonrewarded outcome of the next trial. Because rewarded trials always follow nonrewarded trials and nonrewarded trials always follow rewarded trials, animals learn to run fast after nonreward and to run slowly after reward. These associations require animals to retain memories of previous trial outcomes that then enter into associations with memories of subsequent trial outcomes (Capaldi, 1971). These two accounts of pattern learning—rule learning and sequential associations—provide alternate and sometimes conflicting explanations of a number of phenomena (Capaldi, Verry, & Davidson, 1980; Hulse, 1980).

Double-Alternation Pattern Learning

In addition to the contributions of W. Hunter (1913) to the study of the delayed-response problem (see Chapter 3), he also carried out a number of early studies of the double-alternation problem. In double alternation, an animal is required to learn to make two responses in one direction followed by two responses in the opposite direction. Thus, in a maze, an animal has to learn the patterns RRLL or LLRR. Whether animals could learn such sequences was viewed as having considerable theoretical importance. Acquisition of a single-alternation pattern was easily explained by the kinesthetic-machine hypothesis as sequential associations between feedback from one response and execution of the next. Kinesthetic feedback from a turn to the right triggers a turn to the left, and feedback from a turn to the left cues a turn to the right. The double-alternation problem intrigued W. Hunter (1929) because it could not be easily accounted for by kinesthetic chaining. A double-alternation pattern shows *branching;* that is, the R response precedes both R and L responses at different points in the pattern, as does the L response.

Solution of the double-alternation problem seemed impossible on the basis of associations to kinesthetic feedback from the immediately preceding response. W. Hunter reasoned that successful double-alternation pattern performance demanded symbolic representation or what he referred to as a "neural supplement" (W. Hunter, 1929). By neural supplement, he meant that the feedback from two or more responses accumulates to serve as a cue for later responses in the sequence. Thus, the feedback from one left turn cues another left turn, but the accumulated feedback from two left turns signals a right turn. In contemporary theoretical language, we can say that the animal remembered the sequence of preceding choices. In fact, the notion of a symbolic representation or memory of the response pattern cannot be divorced from such a process. It is hard to imagine how an animal could learn an LLRR pattern without having some continuing memory for the preceding choices in the series.

As the ultimate control for kinesthetic and other sensory cues, W. Hunter (1929) devised the *temporal maze.* An animal was required to run down a central alley from the entrance and to make either a right or left turn at the choice point. The subject then made a series of right or left turns that led it back down the central alley for another choice at the same choice point. The value of the temporal maze was that all choices were made at exactly the same point in the maze; therefore, differential auditory, olfactory, and tactile cues could not serve as bases for different responses. W. Hunter felt that a demonstration of double-alternation learning in the temporal maze would constitute strong evidence for some perseverative symbolic process in animals.

Although W. Hunter found that rats learned to perform single alternation on the temporal maze, the double-alternation problem proved to be exceedingly difficult (W. Hunter, 1918; 1920; W. Hunter & Hall, 1941; W. Hunter & Nagge, 1931). Individual animals seemed to master the sequence for a series of trials but then lost this behavior. In particular, a tendency to make single-alternation response patterns, RLRL or LRLR, interfered with learning RRLL and LLRR patterns. It may be that the choice of rats and the temporal maze was unfortunate; the innate tendency of rats to alternate successive responses made at the same choice point may have placed a boundary on the extent to which rats could perform double alternation.

Clear evidence of double alternation in rats was eventually demonstrated in the temporal maze. H. Gallup and Diamond (1960) and Diamond (1967) gradually trained rats to perform LLRR and RRLL sequences of turns at the choice point. An animal was first trained to go left for food reward. When this response was learned, two left responses were required for reward, then two lefts and a right, and finally two lefts followed by two rights. After 85 training trials, rats double alternated on test trials at a far higher level than either untrained control animals or animals that had been trained to perform the double-alternation pattern from the beginning of training. Gradually building the required sequence of responses appears to be a far better way to teach rats double alternation than demanding the entire pattern from the outset. Notice that this corresponds to the procedure Terrace (1983) used to teach four- and five-item simultaneous chains to pigeons.

Evidence of accurate double-alternation behavior was also found with a number of other species, including dogs (Karn & Malamud, 1939), cats (Karn, 1938; Karn & Patton, 1939; Livesey, 1965; Warren, 1967; Yamaguchi & Warren, 1961), rabbits (W. Livesey, 1964, 1965), raccoons (W. Hunter, 1928; Johnson, 1961), and monkeys (Gellerman, 1931a; 1931c; Leary, Harlow, Settlage, & Greenwood, 1952). The problem was not easy for animals to learn, and they typically needed many trials to show accurate performance. In some cases, animals showed emotional reactions to the problem, such as crying and urinating at the choice point.

Gellerman (1931b) had people walk through a temporal maze scaled to human size. People typically solved the double-alternation problem at the time they verbalized a solution such as "you go twice in one direction and then twice in the other direction." Did animals learn a similar double-alternation rule? One piece of evidence for this question comes from experiments in which the number of responses allowed was extended beyond that used in initial training. Animals were often trained to make RRLL and LLRR sequences of four responses; when this pattern was learned, they were allowed to make eight responses instead of four. If a general double-alternation rule was learned, we would expect subjects to be able to extrapolate the pattern and perform RRLLRRLL and LLRRLLRR. Animals generally did not show this extrapolation. Dogs (Karn & Malamud, 1939), cats (Yamaguchi & Warren, 1961), and raccoons (Johnson, 1961) all failed to extend the double-alternation pattern. A frequent observation was that an animal given an extended series of choices would respond RRLLLLLL or LLRRRRRR (W. Hunter, 1928; W. Hunter & Nagge, 1931; Johnson, 1961; Karn, 1938). This outcome suggests that the rule learned might be best paraphrased as "make two responses in one direction and all subsequent responses in the opposite direction."

As an important exception to this general failure to find extrapolation of the double-alternation pattern, Gellerman (1931c) did find extrapolation with rhesus monkeys. Monkeys were trained to lift the lids of left and right boxes for grape rewards. After learning to make eight responses in the sequence RRLLR-RLL, they were tested with 12 and 16 responses. The monkeys consistently continued to perform the double-alternation pattern beyond the initial eight responses. Monkeys, then, may be able to learn a more generalized double-alternation pattern than nonprimates. This finding also agrees with previously mentioned instances of superior serial learning in monkeys.

Learning a Monotonic Reward Pattern

In experiments carried out in a runway, Hulse (1978) and his colleagues examined rats' ability to track patterns of *monotonically* decreasing reward quantity. In such an experiment, a rat was allowed to run from the start box to the goal box over five trials given in immediate succession. The amount of food in the goal box decreased consistently or monotonically; the number of 0.045-gram food pellets given over successive trials was 14-7-3-1-0. The length of time it took a rat to run from the start box to the goal box was the measure of interest. If a rat could learn the monotonic structure of this pattern, it should begin to run more slowly as the amount of reward decreased. In particular, a rat that accurately tracked the sequence of rewards should run very slowly on the fifth trial, when 0 reward pellets were available. A control group of rats was trained with exactly the same quantities of reward, but the numbers of pellets were delivered in a *nonmonotonic* sequence. The nonmonotonic group received numbers of food pellets in the order 14-1-3-7-0.

After several sessions of training on these sequences, rats began to track the 0-element by running more slowly on the final nonrewarded trial than on the preceding rewarded trials. The upper graph in Figure 9.9 shows the time taken for rats to run down the runway to successive quantities of food pellets. Note that rats reached the food in 1 to 3 seconds on rewarded trials but took about 13 seconds to travel the runway on the fifth nonrewarded trial in the monotonic group. The rats in the nonmonotonic group slowed down on the fifth trial as well, but not as much as the rats trained with the monotonic pattern. Furthermore, rats given the monotonic pattern began tracking the 0-pellet element much sooner that those given the nonmonotonic pattern. It was argued that rats learned and used the structure of the monotonic pattern to anticipate the final nonrewarded element of the sequence (Hulse & Campbell, 1975; Hulse & Dorsky, 1977).

As a further test of the importance of pattern structure, Hulse and Dorsky (1977) examined rats' ability to track a strong monotonic pattern and a pattern

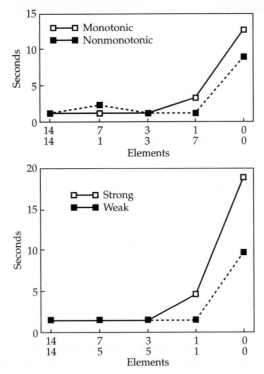

FIGURE 9.9. The upper graph shows pattern tracking of monotonic and nonmonotonic sequences of reward pellets, and the lower graph shows tracking of strong and weak monotonic sequences of reward pellets. The number of reward pellets given on each trial is shown on the abscissa.

that was only weakly monotonic. One group of rats was trained using the 14-7-3-1-0 sequence of rewards as the strong monotonic pattern, in which each succeeding reward was smaller than the preceding one. A second group of rats received a weak monotonic pattern consisting of the sequence 14-5-5-1-0. In the weak pattern, monotonicity is not as clearly defined because two successive elements are equal in quantity. Rats learned to track the strong sequence faster than the weak sequence. As can be seen in the bottom graph of Figure 9.9, rats' asymptotic running times show better tracking of the 0-pellet element in the strong pattern than in the weak pattern.

It should be pointed out that these findings are difficult to explain by alternatives to pattern tracking. For example, it might be argued that rats used time or number to track the final element of the monotonic pattern. That is, they learned to run slowly after a certain amount of time had passed since the beginning of the sequence of trials or they counted the trials in some way and ran slowly when they reached the fifth trial. If rats were using one of these cues for tracking, we would expect the nonmonotonic and weakly monotonic groups to track equally as well as the strong monotonic group since these groups also could use the same time and number cues. Another possibility is that rats used interelement associations, with each quantity of reward serving as a cue for memory of the next quantity. A problem with this account is that both the strong and weak monotonic patterns ended in the sequence 1-0. If animals were using interelement associations, the 1-pellet trial should have cued memory for the 0-pellet element equally well in both groups. Since rats in the groups trained with a strong monotonic pattern tracked better than rats that learned either nonmonotonic or weakly monotonic patterns, the data imply that rats learned about the rule structure of the entire monotonic pattern.

Chunking in Serial Pattern Learning

Chunking is often held to be of importance for pattern learning. For example, is it easier to detect and learn the pattern QRSGHITUVJKL or the pattern QRS GHI TUV JKL? Most people would find the second pattern far easier to detect and learn because it is *phrased* into meaningful subsequences that correspond to adjacent letters of the alphabet. We have seen in the experiment of Wishner et al. (1957) on human serial learning and the Terrace (1987; 1991) serial learning experiments with pigeons that dividing a list into different segments by color promotes learning through chunking. If a visual pattern is spaced into units that are recognized as having their own pattern, this also promotes serial pattern learning in people. Now consider the previous sequence of letters phrased as QRSG HITU VJKL. Notice how difficult it would be to detect the underlying pattern in this sequence because the pattern is *misphrased*. In this case, breaking the pattern visually at inappropriate locations makes it harder to learn than having no phrasing at all.

Chunking and Rule Learning in Rats

The importance of chunking and phrasing on pattern learning in rats was examined in experiments reported by Fountain, Henne, and Hulse (1984). In this experiment, rats were trained on sequences of 25 trials within a daily session that yielded the following pattern of reward pellets: 14-7-3-1-0-14-7-3-1-0-14-7-3-1-0-14-7-3-1-0-14-7-3-1-0. A nonphrased group encountered this sequence with only a few seconds between each trial and the next. In two other groups, however, phrasing was used, and the pattern learned was 14-7-3-1-0 14-7-3-1-0 14-7-3-1-0 14-7-3-1-0 14-7-3-1-0. In a temporal phrasing group, an interval of 10 to 15 minutes broke up successive repetitions of the monotonic sequence. In a spatial phrasing group, rats were given five trials of the sequence in one arm of a T-maze and then were transferred to the other arm of the T-maze for the next five-trial repetition of the sequence. Rats trained with either of these phrasing cues learned to track the 0-pellet element much more quickly than control rats run without phrasing cues.

In another experiment, Fountain et al. (1984) tested the effect of misphrasing on rat pattern learning. A misphrased group of rats was trained with the phrasing cue introduced in the middle of monotonic sequences; these animals learned the pattern 1-0-14-7-3 1-0-14-7-3 1-0-14-7-3 1-0-14-7-3 1-0-14-7-3. This phrasing produced very poor learning of pattern tracking as compared with conditions in which the phrasing cue was placed between monotonic sequences. The findings of Fountain et al. then suggest some striking parallels between the effects of phrasing on pattern learning in humans and animals. Taken in conjunction with the experiments discussed earlier on simultaneous chaining and the organization of radial maze behavior, these findings reinforce the importance of chunking in animal serial learning.

Chunking and Levels of Organization

From a somewhat different theoretical orientation, Capaldi (1992) emphasized the importance of chunking in behavioral organization and sequential pattern learning. Although Hulse and his colleagues emphasized the importance of chunking for the discovery of rules that govern pattern structure (Fountain et al., 1984), Capaldi argued that pattern learning is based on sequential associations. Through repeated experiences with a series of events, events earlier in the series retrieve memories of upcoming events, upon which animals act accordingly (Capaldi, 1966; 1967; 1971). It was mentioned earlier that Capaldi's sequential theory readily accounted for the learning of an RNRNRN single-alternation pattern, by assuming that reward signaled nonreward and nonreward signaled reward. In his more recent research and theoretical work, however, Capaldi (1992) maintained that sequential associations may be formed at different levels of organization; at the highest levels of organization, entire chunks of information may lead to the anticipation of other chunks of information.

Capaldi's model is hierarchical. At the most elemental level, individual behaviors become integrated to form *trial chunks*. Thus, a rat learning to run down a runway must learn to combine the initial steps of leaving the start box with repeated running movements in the runway and with slowing down at the goal box and eating the reward placed in the food cup. A trial chunk, and particularly its outcome (reward or nonreward), is stored in memory. If multiple trials are given, a series of trial chunk memories is formed. Through repetition of the series, a *series chunk* is formed; that is, a single memory containing multiple trials is stored as a single unit. Finally, Capaldi suggests that if multiple series of trials are repeated a number of times, animals may learn to integrate series together into *list chunk* memories.

The functional importance of these different levels of chunking is that they allow an animal to anticipate strings of events far in advance of their occurrence within a pattern. As an example, let us examine an experiment reported by Capaldi, Miller, Alptekin, and Barry (1990). Two groups of rats were trained to run down a runway for several trials each day. Rewarded and nonrewarded trials always occurred in either a two-trial sequence, RN, or a three-trial sequence, RRN. Rats in Group Separate always received six repetitions of the RN sequence or six repetitions of the RRN sequence on separate days, and the orders alternated randomly between days. Animals in Group Intermixed experienced three RN and three RRN sequences on each day, in random orders that changed from day to day. The behavior of interest was the speed with which rats ran down the runway on each trial of a sequence, reflecting their anticipation of reward or nonreward. After 26 days of training under these conditions, both groups were tested over 3 days. On the first test day, the RRN pattern was repeated six times, and, on the second and third test days, the RN pattern was repeated six times.

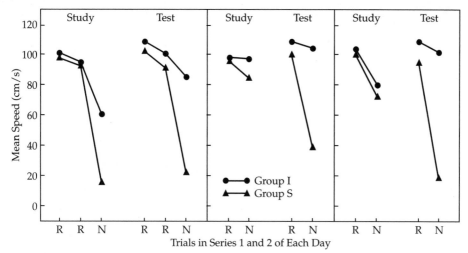

FIGURE 9.10. Running speed on study and test sequences of trials over three test days. Curves are shown for Group Intermixed (I) and Group Separate (S), and reward (R) and nonreward (N) sequences (RRN and RN) are shown on the abscissa.

Findings from these test days are shown in Figure 9.10; the study curves show performance on the first run through a pattern, and the test curves show performance on the second run. First, notice that running speed was equally high in the intermixed (I) and separate (S) groups on the first two trials of study sequences. Given an initial R trial, an animal in either group could not anticipate whether the next trial would be R or N and ran rapidly down the runway. On the third trial of the RRN pattern, both groups slowed down, although this effect was more pronounced in the separate group. The same pattern of results is seen for the RRN pattern on test trials. The most important aspect of these findings can be seen in running speeds on test trials with the RN pattern. Rats in both groups ran rapidly on the initial R trial, but a major difference appeared on the second N trial; Group Intermixed rats continued to run rapidly, while Group Separate rats slowed down. The implication of these results is that rats in the separate group anticipated the absence of reward on the second RN test trial.

To fully account for these findings, all three levels of Capaldi's hierarchical model must be invoked. Rats initially formed trial chunks by learning to run from the start box to the goal box for reward or nonreward. Since rats could anticipate the absence of reward on the third N trial in the study series, this suggests that rats formed series chunks. The RRN series chunk told the rat that two rewarded trials in a row must be followed by a nonrewarded trial. Performance on the test trials of RN sequences cannot be explained by a series chunk. On the basis of the initial R trial of a series, an animal could not know if it was beginning an RN series or an RRN series. However, rats in the separate group could predict that a nonrewarded trial would follow a rewarded trial based on the initial RN study sequence. If these animals learned that an initial RN series meant that all further series would be RN, they could then anticipate a nonrewarded trial after every subsequent rewarded trial. Performance of the separate group

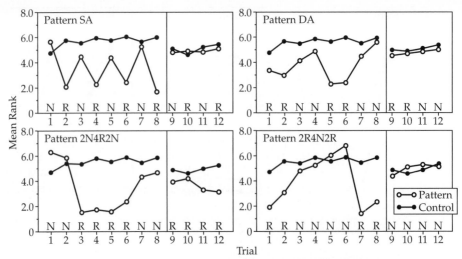

FIGURE 9.11. Mean rank of entry into rewarded (R) and nonrewarded (N) arms of the radial maze for four different patterns. The data on the left of each panel show performance over training Trials 1 through 8, and curves on the right of each panel show performance over extrapolation Trials 9 through 12.

on RN test trials then shows the formation of series chunks that allow an animal to anticipate the events of a future series based on the current series.

Multiple-Pattern Learning on the Radial Maze

In some experiments carried out by Phelps and W. Roberts (1991) and Wathen and W. Roberts (1994), rats were tested repeatedly on a radial maze over several trials within a daily session. The unique aspect of these experiments was that different patterns of reward and nonreward were assigned to different arms of the maze. Over eight trials, animals received reward (2 food pellets) or nonreward (0 food pellets) on a single-alternation pattern (NRNRNRNR), a double-alternation pattern (RRNNRRNN), a pattern that consisted of two nonrewards followed by four rewards followed by two more nonrewards (2N4R2N), and a pattern that contained two rewards followed by four nonrewards followed by two rewards (2R4N2R). The other four arms on the maze were designated control arms and contained one food pellet on every trial. Thus, on the first trial of a day, each of the four patterned arms contained the amount of reward indicated by the first element in its pattern, and each of the four control arms contained one food pellet. On the second trial, each patterned arm contained the second element of its pattern, while the control arms again contained one pellet, and so on until eight trials were completed.

The order in which a rat entered the arms of the maze was recorded on each trial, and the rank of arm entry was used to measure an animal's preference or aversion for particular arms on a given trial. Performance in this experiment is shown after 28 days of training in Figure 9.11. A separate graph is shown for each pattern, with the curves for eight daily trials shown on the left side of each panel. The curves plot mean rank of visit to the arm containing a particular pattern; the important finding to note is that the mean rank tracks each pattern accurately, dropping to a low rank (early arm entry) when a reward (R) is programmed and rising to a high rank (late arm entry) when a nonreward (N) is programmed. The control curves show that the mean rank of entry into control arms stayed fairly high on each trial.

The accuracy with which rats tracked each pattern suggests that they were able to learn four different patterns on the radial maze, a fairly prodigous cognitive feat for a rat. However, further evidence led Wathen and W. Roberts (1994) to question this interpretation. If rats learned the repeating single-alternation and double-alternation patterns by learning rules or sequential associations that governed the structure of these patterns, they should be able to extrapolate these patterns beyond the training trials. After 28 days of training with only eight trials of testing on each day, four further days of testing were given on which four further trials were added to the first eight. Reward and nonreward continued to be delivered on these extrapolation trials according to the pattern of delivery on the initial eight trials. The curves on the right side of each graph in Figure 9.11 show the mean rank of entry into arms on these four additional trials. The data show very clearly that rats did not continue to track the training patterns on the extrapolation trials.

The failure to find any evidence of pattern extrapolation suggests that rats may not have learned four different patterns during acquisition. Wathen and W. Roberts (1994) suggested a "trial-number hypothesis" as an account of these findings. If rats could have in some way kept track of the ordinal position or number of each trial, they may have learned that certain arms were the rewarded or "hot" arms that should be entered first on each trial. These arms would then have a low rank of entry, and other arms would take on a higher rank by default. It can be seen in Figure 9.11 that rats did not enter control arms containing one food pellet earlier than nonrewarded arms containing no food pellets. If rats remembered only the rewarded arms and had no memory of the contents of control and nonrewarded arms, they should enter rewarded arms first and then show no preference between control and nonrewarded arms. Finally, the absence of any pattern tracking on extrapolation trials makes sense from a trial-number hypothesis because rats would have no basis for preferring one arm over another after the eighth trial. In other words, rats had not been trained where the rewarded arms were on Trials 9 through 12.

SUMMARY

A number of instances of serial behavior in animals have been described. Although many of these behaviors involve genetically programmed fixed-action patterns, it has been shown that animals also can learn to complete a variety of arbitrary serial sequences. Learned sequences include visits to arms of a radial maze in decreasing order of quantity of food on the arms, pressing plates or keys in a particular order based on their spatial position, and responding to simultaneously presented visual stimuli in a fixed order. Animals also learn to track rule-generated patterns. These include repeating patterns, such as single alternation and double alternation, and patterns of monotonically decreasing reward quantity.

Two general principles seem to arise from a review of these studies. First, pattern learning is hierarchically organized. In particular, memories that give rise to organized sequential behavior are based on superordinate and subordinate chunks of information. Several examples were discussed. Terrace (1987, 1991) found evidence that pigeons segregated a set of simultaneously presented stimuli into a chunk of colors and a chunk of black-and-white patterns. Evidence was presented that rats organize visits to arms on the radial maze according to chunks or sets of arms that contain the same food. In studies of pattern tracking in animals, theorists emphasized the importance of chunking. Pattern learning takes place much faster when recognition of pattern structure is facilitated by phrasing sequences of trials into meaningful chunks. As a theoretical synthesis, Capaldi argued that chunking is found in animal behavior at a number of levels of organization. Animals organize individual responses into trial chunks. The events of one trial serve to cue memories of the events to occur on subsequent trials within series chunks. At the highest level of organization, the list chunk, one series chunk signals the events forthcoming in another series chunk.

The other important principle arising from the studies reviewed here is that serial learning in animals is accomplished by several different processes. People learn serial lists by memorizing sequential associations, ordinal associations, and mental images and by chunking and rule learning. It appears that animals also use a variety of mechanisms that vary with the species and the learning situation. Certainly, animals appear to learn sequential associations between items in a list. These may be simple item-to-item associations in some cases. For example, Terrace's (1991) pigeons needed A→B, B→C, C→D, and D→E associations to respond to five stimuli in the correct order 70 percent of the time. However, tests with subsequences indicated that pigeons also learned rules concerning first, last, and default responses to stimuli. Capaldi's rats tested in a runway appeared to be able to learn sequential associations between both trials and series of trials. The excellent ability of D'Amato and Colombo's monkeys to learn a serial sequence and then to correctly order all of the subsequences led to the hypothesis that these animals used spatial representation as an analog for serial order in time. In transitive inference experiments, animals and humans appear to learn the relative values of stimuli that are never directly compared in training. Wathen and W. Roberts found that rats could accurately track four patterns on a radial maze but could not extrapolate these patterns to new trials given beyond the number used in training. They suggested that rats used ordinal position of training trials to access memories of the rewarded arms on each trial. Chunking is often involved in animal pattern learning, particularly if the learning situation is structured to promote the formation of higher-order units in memory. It appears that serial learning provides a rich source of information about memory processes in animals. Future research in this area should inform us further about the representation of sequential information and about processes of association, imaging, and chunking.

CHAPTER 10

Numerical Processing

The possibility that animals understand number was raised in Chapter 9 concerning processing of serial learning. It was suggested, for example, that animals might keep track of how many times they were rewarded or nonrewarded in a double-alternation pattern or other patterns that involve sequential repetition of these events. Wathen and W. Roberts (1994) suggested that rats might track patterns on a radial maze by associating rewarded arms with the number of trials within a session. That is, rats learned which arms were rewarded on the first trial, which were rewarded on the second trial, and so on. Although this hypothesis assumes that rats can count trials, no independent evidence was provided about animals' ability to process numbers. From a human point of view, cognitive processing of number, along with time and space, constitutes one of our most fundamental and important abilities. In people, numerical processing is carried to a high level of abstraction; we are able to use numbers to count virtually any objects or activities. Furthermore, we perform operations such as addition, subtraction, multiplication, and division on numbers to transform them. In this chapter, we explore numerical processing in animals and examine how closely it approaches human numerical processing.

The initial experimental studies of numerical abilities in animals were carried out with two rhesus monkeys by A. J. Kinnaman at Clark University (Kinnaman, 1902). The following quotation from the introduction to Kinnaman's paper provides the flavor of the background that prompted his experiments:

> There has been considerable written but very little done toward a rigorous examination of the number notions of lower animals. Stories of their wonderful achievements in counting and comprehending numerical relations are abundant. For example, it is said that shepherd dogs count sheep. One drove sheep to the wash in groups of ten each. Bird dogs are said to count the number of birds that fall when the master fires. One dog counts the railway stations when on a train, and so knows where to get off. Another displayed "thorough proficiency in the first four rules of arithmetic," barking off the answers of the problems put to him. A mouse came nine times to carry away each time one of her young handed to her from a cup, and did not return after the last was taken. A Cincinnati mule counted fifty. A dog counted her six puppies and knew when one was missing. Leroy reports a crow that counted four. One of the nearest approaches to real counting appears with some insects. A species of wasps, the Eumenes, supplies for its prospective young five victims for each egg laid (p. 173).

301

It should be obvious from this quotation that people's beliefs about numerical abilities in animals at the beginning of the 20th century were largely based on anecdotes, many of which supported the idea that animals could count and manipulate numbers as well as people. The story of the barking dog actually presages the more famous episode of the horse Clever Hans, discussed in Chapter 1.

Objective experimental studies of numerical competence in animals were obviously needed. Kinnaman (1902) attacked the problem of counting in monkeys by constructing an apparatus that consisted of 21 uniform wide-mouthed bottles placed on a 10-foot-long board. The tops of these bottles were covered with white paper so that the contents of a bottle could only be seen by removing the paper. Food was placed in one of these bottles, and the monkey subject was allowed to choose one bottle and consume its contents if it chose the correct bottle. On different occasions, the food was placed repeatedly in the bottle located in Position 1, 2, 3, 4, 5, or 6 from the right end of the row. A monkey was given a number of opportunities to find the food in the rewarded location. It was reasoned that if the monkeys could count the bottles, they should soon learn to choose the correct bottle on every trial. Although both monkeys learned to restrict their choices to the general vicinity of the correct bottle, numerous errors were made by choosing bottles adjacent to the correct one. Kinnaman concluded, "They were able to do no real counting, but position in a series of objects was recognized by one as far as 3 and by the other as far as 6" (p. 211). The latter phrase suggests that Kinnaman recognized the confounded nature of this experiment. Monkeys did not need to count in order to locate the position or at least the approximate position of the correct bottle. They only needed to respond to a spatial position along the array of bottles to choose the correct bottle frequently (Honigmann, 1942).

Kinnaman's (1902) research is important because it raised theoretical questions and initiated an area of empirical research on number processing in animals that would be pursued sporadically by other researchers throughout the 20th century (Rilling, 1993). Were animals sensitive to number? If they were, could they count numbers? Our concepts and definitions of numerical processing, particularly counting, have become more refined over the years since Kinnaman's work. Kinnaman's study also pointed to the fact that elaborate controls were needed to study number processing in animals. In Kinnaman's experiment, spatial position was not controlled as a confounding variable. In most numerical experiments, variables other than number are correlated with variation in number and may serve as alternate cues for the correct response. Research on numerical processing has become increasingly sophisticated as these correlated variables have been controlled.

LEVELS OF NUMERICAL PROCESSING

Relative Numerousness Discrimination

Before discussing further research on numerical processing, let us examine different levels of competence at which organisms may respond to number. Perhaps the simplest level of responding is making a *relative numerousness discrimination* (H. Davis & Perusse, 1988). These are judgments of inequality that involve a more-or-less judgment. For example, an experimenter might hold out two hands to a child, one containing five beans and the other containing two beans. If the child chooses the hand containing two beans, he receives a candy reward, but no reward is given for choosing the hand containing five beans. On the next trial, one hand contains eight beans and the other hand seven beans, and choice of the hand with seven beans is rewarded. On the third trial, three and six beans are shown, with three beans being the correct choice, and so on. The rule to be learned is that the lesser quantity is to be chosen. No number of beans is always correct; four beans is the correct choice if the alternative is seven beans, but four beans is the incorrect choice if the alternative is three beans.

Absolute Number Discrimination

A more advanced level of numerical competence may be required to make an *absolute number discrimination.* Suppose that in the procedure just described, we show a child successive pairs of hands containing two and five beans, five and six beans, four and five beans, and five and nine beans. On each trial, the correct response is to choose the hand containing five beans. A more-or-less judgment no longer suffices to solve the problem since five beans is sometimes more and sometimes less than the alternative quantity. Choice must be based on the absolute number 5. Thus, an absolute number discrimination requires a specific response to a unique numerical value. As another form of absolute numerical discrimination, the experimenter could ask the child to give her 5 beans from a pile containing 20 beans. If the child repeatedly picks up just five beans and hands them to the experimenter, this behavior constitutes a further demonstration of absolute number discrimination.

It is clear that relative numerousness and absolute number discriminations can be accomplished by counting stimuli before responding, and counting is often used to deal with such problems by people. However, some years ago Kaufman, Lord, Reese, and Volkmann (1949) showed that people can accurately indicate the number of objects seen in a simultaneously presented visual array, even though the array was seen for only 200 milliseconds. Subjects responded accurately up to a limit of six items in an array. Since the exposure time was so brief, it was presumed that subjects could not count the items in the array before responding. Kaufman et al. called this ability to rapidly recognize arrays of up to six items *subitizing,* from the Latin verb *subitare,* meaning *to arrive suddenly.* Above six items in an array, subjects were able to indicate the correct number with less than perfect accuracy, and here it was suggested subjects used a process of *estimation.*

Exactly how subjects are able to subitize is not totally clear. It has been suggested that subjects learn to assign number labels to patterns without counting the items in the pattern (Davis & Perusse, 1988; Von Glasersfeld, 1982; 1993). Up to three objects, *canonical* patterns, or patterns that are highly familiar and easily recognized may be seen in an array. A single item forms a single point in space, two items must form the end points of a straight line, and three items usually form a triangle. With four, five, and six objects in an array, however, the number of different patterns possible becomes large, and it is not clear that easily recognized canonical patterns can be found. Although some theorists argue that subitizing up to six items is based on the recognition of patterns that constitute flexible templates or prototypes (Davis & Perusse, 1988; R. Thomas & Lorden, 1993), other theorists suggest that counting may be involved in subitizing. Mandler and Shebo (1982) concluded that recognition of familiar canonical patterns explained subitizing for arrays of one to three items but that a process of postperceptual counting from a representation of the array held in consciousness was necessary to explain subitizing for arrays of four to six items. Gelman and Gallistel (1978) theorized that subitizing may simply reflect a routinized, rapid counting process.

Although animals have not been tested with rapidly presented arrays, Davis and Perusse (1988) argued that processes of subitizing and estimating may be used by animals to solve relative numerousness and absolute number problems in which stimuli are presented for longer periods of time. They argue that, through practice, animals learn to recognize patterns made up of arrays of objects and to make differential responses to these patterns. Further, they extended this argument to the recognition of sequential patterns of intermittent stimulation. Relative or absolute discriminations between different numbers of sequentially presented light flashes or noise bursts are explained on the basis of *rhythm.* Just as we learn to recognize songs by the rhythm of their first few notes, it is suggested that people and animals attach number labels or other responses to well-learned patterns of sequential stimulation. The importance of Davis and Perusse's position is that it makes it possible to explain instances of relative and absolute numerical discrimination in animals without appealing to a counting process. Not all theorists agree on this point. For example, D. Miller (1993) argues that both simultaneous and sequential discrimination in animals may be more parsimoniously interpreted as instances of counting. This controversy raises the question of what exactly we mean by the process of counting.

Counting

Counting constitutes a still more advanced level of numerical competence for H. Davis & Perusse (1988). Counting is defined as a formal process of enumeration in which each item in an array must be given a unique tag (Gelman & Gallistel, 1978; Piaget, 1952). Counting must demonstrate the properties of *cardinality* and *ordinality.* Cardinality refers to the sequence of different number tags or labels used to count; we commonly use Arabic numerals as number tags, but Roman numerals or fingers on the hands could be used as number tags. Ordinality refers to the fact that these number tags must be used in a fixed order. Three basic principles of counting illustrate these properties. The *one-to-one principle* means that each number tag can be applied to only one item in an array being counted, and the *stable order principle* states that the tags must always be used in the same order. Thus, the numeral 2 can only be assigned to one object in an array that is being counted and must be assigned to the second item counted. The *cardinal principle* specifies that the last tag used when counting a set of things defines that set. If one counts fifty-three apples left in a barrel, the value 53 provides a numerical definition of the set of apples.

Two further principles are particularly characteristic of human counting and show its abstract properties. The *abstraction principle* refers to the use of number tags to count any set of items. People can count things (such as horses or airplanes), activities (such as the number of home runs hit in a baseball game), or more intangible things (such as the number of seconds needed to run 50 yards or the number of new ideas thought of in a single day). This principle may be particularly important for the question of counting in animals. To the extent that animals show the abstraction principle, they should show transfer of counting behavior learned in one training situation to a new training situation. A final counting principle is the *order irrelevance principle*. Although the stable order principle requires that number tags be used in a fixed order, the order irrelevance principle indicates that items counted may be counted in any order. If one wishes to count the spots on a leopard, one could begin with those on the head and count toward the tail, or one could begin with those on the tail and count toward the head. As long as number tags are assigned in a fixed order, one should end up with the same cardinal number, regardless of what order the tags are applied to items in the set counted.

Concept of Number

Beyond the ability to count, most people have a *concept of number*. They understand relationships among numbers, such as the fact that 10 is twice as much as 5 but half as much as 20. They can perform operations on numbers by adding, subtracting, multiplying, and dividing them, and these basic operations are carried to higher levels of abstraction in the science of mathematics.

Whether animals are capable of counting and applying operations to numbers is a contentious issue, which we examine. We begin, however, with an examination of relative numerousness and absolute number discriminations in animals.

EVIDENCE OF RELATIVE NUMEROUSNESS DISCRIMINATION

Some Earlier Research

The most intensive early work on numerical processing was carried out in the laboratory of a German ethologist named Otto Koehler (Koehler, 1951; Rilling, 1993). Using a variety of bird species as subjects, Koehler and his students and colleagues studied a variety of relative numerousness and absolute number discriminations. In a typical relative numerousness problem, a bird was confronted with containers covered with lids showing different numbers of pieces of grain glued to the lid. If the bird chose the correct lid by pecking at it, it was rewarded with food. Pecking at an incorrect lid led to punishment. A bird might be shooed away from the container verbally or by hand as a mild punishment; in the case of particularly recalcitrant subjects, a device called the "frightening springboard" was used, which threw the incorrect lid up in the air upon an incorrect choice (Honigmann, 1942).

In relative numerousness experiments, pigeons were trained to discriminate between two lids—one containing more grains than the other, with the lid containing the smaller number of grains correct. Easier discriminations were learned between nonconsecutive quantities, such as 7:4, 6:3, and 5:2. With the aid of punishment, pigeons learned to select the smaller number with above-chance accuracy in difficult discriminations between adjacent numbers, including 5:4 and 6:5. It should be pointed out that several cues other than number could be used to solve a relative numerousness discrimination. In a 7:2 discrimination, for example, an animal might learn to choose the stimulus containing 2 not because 2 is a smaller number than 7 but because the total area occupied by two grains is smaller than the total area occupied by seven grains. Another possibility is that the background areas of two stimuli are discriminated. In this case, the background area of the lid containing two grains would be larger than the background area of the lid containing seven grains. Another possibility is that the discrimination could be made on the basis of the patterns formed by two versus seven grains and not by relative numerosity. Although it seems that these potential confounds were recognized by these investigators, it is not clear that they were adequately controlled (Salman, 1943; R. Thomas & Lorden, 1993; Wesley, 1961).

Contemporary Experiments with Monkeys

Let us examine a more contemporary experiment that uses thorough controls. R. Thomas, Fowlkes, and Vickery (1980) studied relative numerousness discriminations in squirrel monkeys. In an apparatus called the Wisconsin General Test Apparatus, a monkey was allowed to choose between two cards placed in vertical cardholders. If the monkey displaced the holder containing the correct card, it was allowed to eat currants placed in a food well under the holder; choice of the incorrect card yielded an empty food well. On the stimulus cards, solid black circles were drawn, with the number of circles ranging from 1 to 10. Examples of the type of stimuli used are shown for a 3:4 discrimination in Figure 10.1. Note that the sizes of the circles varied within patterns, with the size of an individual circle varying between 19.6, 78.5, and 314.1 mm^2. Furthermore, the pattern or arrangement of the circles varied from card to card. In the actual experiment, 100 different patterns were used for each number of circles.

Two monkeys were trained on a sequence of relative numerousness discriminations, beginning with pairs of cards that differed by several numbers of circles, such as 2:7, 2:6, 3:7, 3:6, 4:7, and 4:6. On each discrimination, the rewarded alternative was the card with the smaller number of circles. Eventually, both monkeys were tested with pairs of cards that differed by only one circle. Both monkeys correctly chose the smaller number above the chance level of 50 percent on all problems up to an 8:9 discrimination. One monkey continued to choose accurately on a 9:10 discrimination. On some trials, pairs of cards were presented on which the black circles of the correct card occupied a greater surface area than the circles of the incorrect card. Both monkeys were equally as accurate on these trials as they were on those in which the card with the larger number had the greater blackened surface area. We can safely conclude that monkeys did not discriminate between patterns on the basis of the surface

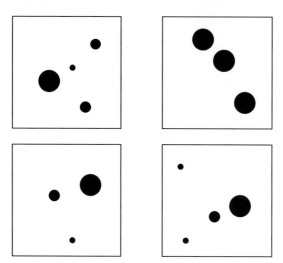

FIGURE 10.1. Examples of stimuli used in a relative numerousness discrimination. The problem shown is a 3:4 discrimination. Note in the top pair that the three stimulus occupies more surface area than the four stimulus.

area occupied by either the circles or the background. Furthermore, the large number of different patterns used guaranteed that monkeys did not learn to choose between cards based on simple differences in pattern. The findings convincingly showed that monkeys used differences in the number of circles to make accurate choices.

In a further experiment, R. Thomas and Chase (1980) showed that monkeys could respond to relative numerousness under the conditional control of an external stimulus. Three cards, containing different numbers of black circles, were shown to a monkey at the same time, with food reward placed in the well under only one of the cards. The cards used were chosen at random on each trial. Some examples of the cards displayed are 2:4:6, 3:5:7, 2:3:6, and 4:5:6. Keep in mind that the spatial positions of these cards was randomly determined from one trial to the next. In front of the monkey was a row of three lights that indicated which number should be chosen. If the middle light was turned on, the monkey was to choose the card with the fewest circles to be rewarded. Illumination of the left and right lights signaled rewarded choice of the intermediate number card, and illumination of all three lights indicated that the card with the most circles was correct. This was a difficult task for monkeys to acquire. Three squirrel monkeys were trained through a number of stages in which different aspects of the problem were gradually introduced. Two monkeys failed to complete all stages, but one monkey successfully completed all stages and showed accurate relative numerousness judgments based on light cues. It is important to realize that this experiment revealed a more sophisticated judgment than that of R. Thomas et al. (1980). In addition to making correct choices based on conditional light cues, the monkey showed it could distinguish between the most, least, and intermediate number of circles in a set of arrays.

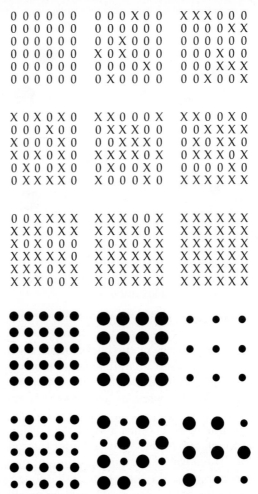

```
0 0 0 0 0 0    0 0 0 X 0 0    X X X 0 0 0
0 0 0 0 0 0    0 0 0 0 0 0    0 0 0 0 X X
0 0 0 0 0 0    0 0 X 0 0 0    0 0 0 0 0 0
0 0 0 0 0 0    X 0 X 0 0 0    0 0 0 X 0 0
0 0 0 0 0 0    0 0 0 0 X 0    0 0 0 X X X
0 0 0 0 0 0    0 X 0 0 0 0    0 0 X 0 0 X


X 0 X 0 X 0    X X 0 0 0 X    X X 0 0 X 0
0 0 0 X 0 0    0 X X X 0 0    0 0 X X X X
X 0 0 0 X 0    0 0 X X X 0    0 X 0 X X 0
X 0 X 0 X 0    X X X X 0 X    0 X X X 0 X
0 X 0 0 X 0    0 X 0 0 X 0    0 0 0 0 X 0
0 X X X X 0    X 0 0 0 X 0    X X X X X X


0 0 X X X X    X X X 0 0 X    X X X X X X
X X X 0 X X    X X X X 0 X    X X X X X X
X 0 X 0 0 0    X 0 X 0 X X    X X X X X X
X X X X X 0    X X X X X X    X X X X X X
X X X 0 X X    X X X X X X    X X X X X X
X X X 0 0 X    X 0 X X X X    X X X X X X
```

FIGURE 10.2. Examples of the arrays used to study relative numerosity discrimination in the pigeon. In different experiments, pigeons were required to discriminate between arrays of Xs and Os and between arrays of small and large circles.

Pigeon Experiments

In the experiments just presented, animals were confronted with arrays of items that varied in numerosity and were required to choose among them. In a different approach to the question of relative numerousness discrimination, Honig (1991; 1993; Honig & Stewart, 1989) presented pigeons with arrays that contained two visually differentiated sets of objects mixed together. Some examples of these arrays are shown in Figure 10.2. An image of an array was projected on a screen, and pigeons responded to an array by pecking at the screen. During initial training, homogeneous arrays were presented, such as the pattern of all Xs or all Os shown in Figure 10.2. Pigeons were allowed to peck at an array for 20 seconds. The first response after 20 seconds yielded food reward for a positive array. A negative array was presented for 20 seconds also

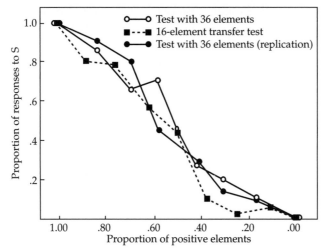

FIGURE 10.3. Proportion of responses made to test stimuli that contained different proportions of elements from the positive array.

but without reward. A pigeon was then rewarded for responding at the array of Xs and nonrewarded for pecking at the array of Os. When this discrimination was well learned to the point where almost all pecks were made to the positive array, tests were carried out with new arrays that contained randomly intermixed Xs and Os, as shown in Figure 10.2. These mixtures varied from predominantly Xs to a 50:50 mixture to predominantly Os.

The data of interest in this experiment are the proportions of responses to the positive array compared with arrays with different proportions of positive and negative elements. If pigeons are responding to relative numerosity, control by the proportion of positive elements should appear as a gradient that declines steadily as the proportion of positive elements decreases. The curves presented in Figure 10.3 show that pigeons' rate of pecking was strongly controlled by the proportion of positive elements. Note that in addition to tests with 36 elements, a curve for arrays of 16 elements is also presented and shows the same control by proportion of positive elements. This finding shows further that relative numerosity and not the absolute numbers of Xs or Os controlled pigeons' behavior. In other experiments, the stimuli used were arrays of red and blue dots, arrays of circles that varied in area, and arrays of small pictures of birds and flowers. All of these dimensions showed the same orderly gradients seen in Figure 10.3, suggesting that pigeons readily perceive relative numerousness among a wide variety of objects.

After training with arrays containing 36 red and 36 blue dots, transfer was tested with mixed arrays containing 36 or 64 dots. Both sizes of arrays showed similar relative numerosity gradients. After training with arrays of large and small circles, pigeons were tested with mixed arrays of both large and small circles and medium and small circles (see lower arrays in Figure 10.2). Equivalent relative numerosity gradients were found with both sizes of circles. Thus, even though the size of the larger circle in the array was changed, pigeons responded in an equivalent way to the mixture or proportion of circles of different sizes.

As in the monkey experiments discussed earlier, the area occupied by items appears to be of much less importance than their relative number. Furthermore, some of the items presented, Xs and Os and the pictures of birds and flowers, could not readily be summed in terms of their areas.

A Rat Experiment

In all of the experiments on relative numerousness discussed thus far, animals were required to respond to items that were presented *simultaneously* in separate or mixed arrays. It is possible also to study relative numerousness discrimination with *successively* presented stimuli. Fernandes and Church (1982) placed rats in an operant chamber containing two levers and presented sequences of either two sounds or four sounds. A rat was rewarded for pressing the right lever after hearing two bursts of white noise of 0.2 second each and was rewarded for pressing the left lever after hearing four such bursts of white noise. You may have recognized a potential confounding variable in this experiment. If it took longer to present four sounds than to present two sounds, a rat could discriminate between the two sequences based on a difference in time and not number. We know well from the material reviewed in Chapter 8 that a rat can easily learn such a temporal discrimination. Fernandes and Church controlled for this problem in several ways. During training, the bursts in the four-sound sequence always were separated by 0.8 second, but the bursts in the two-sound sequence were separated by 0.8 second half the time and by 2.8 seconds half the time. As a consequence, the two-sound sequence was sometimes shorter than the four-sound sequence (1.2 seconds) and sometimes equally as long as the four-sound sequence (3.2 seconds). Rats learned to press the left lever after four sounds and to press the right lever with equal accuracy after two sounds separated by a short or a long interval.

Fernandes and Church (1982) were also concerned that rats might learn to sum durations of the sound bursts; they could then form a temporal discrimination based on the total times of the sounds in the two-sound and four-sound sequences. To examine this possibility, they tested rats with sequences of four sounds, each sound lasting 0.1 second, and two sounds, each sound lasting 0.4 second. The two-sound sequence now had a longer sound-on period than the four-sound sequence (0.8 versus 0.4 second). This control procedure did not affect rats' choice behavior; they continued to respond to the right lever after two sounds and the left lever after four sounds, regardless of duration. As was the case in experiments with simultaneous arrays, controls for the use of alternate cues indicated that animals responded primarily on the basis of relative numerosity.

EVIDENCE OF ABSOLUTE NUMBER DISCRIMINATION

The evidence suggests that monkeys, rats, and birds can all learn to discriminate among numbers based on relative numerousness or proportionality. We now address the question of absolute number discrimination. Can animals learn to respond on the basis of a fixed number value?

In an experiment that bears a clear resemblance to the Fernandez and Church (1982) study, H. Davis and Albert (1986) added an additional stimulus sequence that transformed the design into an absolute number discrimination. Rats were presented with sequences of white noise bursts containing two, three, or four sounds. To control for the use of time cues, the length of each noise burst was varied between 0.2 and 0.5 second, and the interval between bursts was varied between 0.5 and 0.9 second. Of critical importance, rats were reinforced for pressing a lever only when the three-sound sequence was presented; all responses made during two-sound or four-sound sequences were nonrewarded. All three rats trained on this procedure learned to press the lever at a higher rate when three sounds were played than when two or four sounds were played.

In an experiment of similar design, H. Davis, MacKenzie, and Morrison (1989) used an unusual source of sensory stimulation, vibrissal touch. When a rat entered the information chamber of a Y-maze, it was immediately given a piece of popcorn to eat. While the rat consumed the popcorn, the experimenter brushed its vibrissae (whiskers) with a brush either two, three, or four times. The rat was then released to make a choice between left and right arms of the maze. If its vibrissae were stroked three times, it was rewarded with more popcorn for choosing the right arm, but, if its vibrissae were stroked two or four times, it was rewarded only for choosing the left arm. Although several phases of training were required, rats learned to choose the correct arm at slightly better than 70 percent accuracy, significantly better than the chance level of 50 percent. To control for the possibility that rats were discriminating the times taken to deliver the different numbers of vibrissal strokes, tests were carried out with short and long sequences of brushing the vibrissae two, three, or four times. Rats continued to discriminate number of brush strokes at all sequence durations.

Discrimination among Simultaneously Presented Arrays

Suppose an animal is presented with two or more arrays of items and can obtain reward only by choosing one that shows a fixed number of items. Koehler (1943) trained a raven named Jakob to choose among five pots. They were distinguished by different numbers of spots on their lids. Only the pot containing five spots yielded reward. It was reported that Jakob accurately learned to choose the five-spot lid and did so even when the absolute area of the spots on the lids was varied over a range of 1 to 50 units (Rilling, 1993).

H. Davis (1984) reported an experiment in which a raccoon named Rocky was trained to choose among clear plastic cubes containing different numbers of items. Rocky learned to open cubes to obtain a grape reward placed inside. Over a six-month training period, Rocky acquired the ability to choose the cube containing three grapes from among five cubes containing one, two, three, four, and five grapes; only the cube containing three grapes could be opened. Control for choice based on the total size of the grapes was introduced by testing Rocky with different sizes of grapes; he continued to choose three at

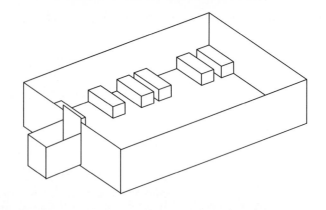

FIGURE 10.4. A drawing of the apparatus used to study absolute number discrimination in rats. A start box led into an arena containing six identical tunnels placed along the left wall. The lower photograph shows a rat entering one of the tunnels.

around 80 percent accuracy. Furthermore, Rocky continued to choose the container with three items when toy bells replaced the grapes. Reward in this case was social praise and an opportunity to play with the bells and wash them in a pail of water.

In an experiment reminiscent of Kinnaman's (1902) early tests with monkeys, H. Davis and Bradford (1986) trained rats to discriminate among a number of simultaneously presented tunnels. A drawing of their apparatus and a picture of a rat entering a tunnel are shown in Figure 10.4. Six identical tunnels were placed along the left side of an arena. All of these tunnels contained food, but the doors to five of the tunnels were locked so that a rat could obtain food only by pushing through the door of the correct tunnel. Three groups of rats were trained—one group to enter the third tunnel, another group to enter the fourth tunnel, and a third group to enter the fifth tunnel. Remember that a major criticism of the Kinnaman experiment was that monkeys could learn the correct spatial position of bottles without using number. H. Davis and Bradford controlled spatial position by changing the positions of the tunnels from one trial to the next but always rewarding choice of the third, fourth, or fifth tunnel from the start. Thus, a rat could not be consistently correct by entering a tunnel that was a fixed distance from the front or rear wall of the enclosure. Also, with all tunnels baited with food, rats could not solve the problem by olfactory cues. Nevertheless, rats in each group rapidly learned to enter the correct tunnel far above chance expectation. Even after a retention interval of one year, rats continued to choose the correctly numbered tunnel.

In a further experiment using the same procedure, H. Davis and Bradford (1987) showed that rats could perform two absolute number discriminations at the same time. Rats were required to enter the correctly numbered tunnel on three successive trials; after each tunnel entry and reward, the rat could return to the start box to initiate another trial. After the third trial, it could no longer reenter the start box, but it could leave the apparatus by climbing on a wood block placed along the right wall and from there to a chair containing its home cage. After some training, rats entered the correct tunnel three times in a row. After the third tunnel visit, they made no further effort to enter the start box but instead left the apparatus and returned to the home cage. Apparently, rats were capable of keeping track of tunnel number and trial number simultaneously.

As one further example of absolute number discrimination between simultaneously presented arrays, Hicks (1956) had rhesus monkeys discriminate between two or three cards containing one to five geometric shapes. Various shapes were used, such as triangles, circles, and squares, and the shapes varied in size, color, and their pattern of distribution. Monkeys were always rewarded for choosing the card containing three items. Although monkeys required considerable training on this task, Hicks reported that his monkeys eventually learned to choose the card containing three shapes, regardless of their size, color, or pattern. The results of this well-controlled study led Hicks to conclude that monkeys had learned a "concept of threeness."

Learning to Consume a Fixed Number of Food Items

To an extent, the simultaneous and successive presentation procedures involve passivity on the animal's part, in the sense that the animal must only choose among numbers of objects already prepared by the experimenter. In a more active procedure, the animal has to perform an action a fixed number of times in order to be rewarded. In fact, a variety of experiments of this nature were carried out by Koehler (1943) and his associates. Perhaps the best controlled of these experiments were studies of pigeons conducted by Arndt (1939). Arndt delivered peas successively to a pigeon and required the pigeon to eat only a fixed number of peas, for example, five. Two devices were used to control the rate or rhythm at which the peas were presented. One was a turntable, on which one pea was exposed at a time and the interval between deliveries of successive peas varied from 1 to 60 seconds. The other apparatus was a tube down which the experimenter could deliver peas from behind a screen; the interval between peas was varied between 1 and 20 seconds.

Pigeons were discouraged from taking more than the appropriate number of peas by mild punishment. If a pigeon was supposed to take only five peas, it was shooed away from the apparatus if it attempted to eat a sixth pea. A successful trial was one in which a pigeon ate five peas and then walked away from the turntable or chute without eating the sixth pea. The highest level of accuracy Arndt found with these tasks was about 65 percent (Wesley, 1961).

In still another variation of this procedure, Arndt (1939) presented pigeons with lid-covered boxes, one at a time on the turntable. In a task that required the pigeon to discriminate the number 2, the first two boxes each contained a pea, but the third box did not. One pigeon learned to open the first two boxes but not the third. The question arose as to whether the pigeon was discriminating peas or boxes. To answer this question, it was presented with four boxes in a row. The first and third boxes contained a pea, but the second and fourth boxes were empty. The pigeon now opened the first three boxes but not the fourth, suggesting that it was discriminating on the basis of the number of peas and not the number of boxes.

As impressive as these experiments are, Wesley (1961) criticized them on several grounds. For example, the experimenter might have unintentionally cued the animal after the criterion number of peas had been eaten by turning the turntable at an abnormal speed. In the box experiments, no controls were introduced for possible auditory cues generated by a pea bouncing around inside a box, and no controls for olfactory cues were used; these could differ since the box following the one containing the criterion number was always empty. For example, if three boxes each containing peas had been presented, would the pigeon still have stopped after opening two boxes?

Fortunately, a recent version of this experiment was performed with rats by H. Davis and Bradford (1991). Rats were allowed to walk from a starting platform along an elevated plank to a chair on which a number of small reward pellets were located. Different groups of rats were designated "three-eaters," "four-eaters," and "five-eaters." A rat was allowed to eat freely from a collection of pellets that varied in size from trial to trial. If the rat ate the correct number of pellets and then walked back over the plank to the start area, it was rewarded with verbal praise and one further pellet. If it left too early, before eating all of the pellets required, no praise was given. Finally, if the rat ate more than the correct number, it was punished with a loud "no" and a hand clap that sent it running back to the start. The results of this experiment are shown in Figure 10.5. As the top graph for each group shows, rats began by always eating too many pellets. Over 200 trials of training, however, the rats in all three groups learned to eat predominantly the number of pellets required for verbal reward before leaving the feeding area.

It should be emphasized that the H. Davis and Bradford (1991) experiment controlled many of the problems that cast doubt on earlier experiments of this nature. Since the size of the food pile varied from trial to trial, rats could not be eating until they were cued by a fixed quantity of remaining food. Were rats perhaps leaving after they had ingested a fixed quantity of food? In a further procedure, H. Davis and Bradford changed the food from uniform reward pellets to sunflower seeds that varied in size from seed to seed. Rats continued to leave the feeding area after eating the correct number of sunflower seeds. Was the experimenter providing "Clever Hans" cues to the rats? In another control procedure, the experimenter left the experimental room and observed subjects from a closed-circuit television monitor. Rats continued to limit their intake to the criterion number of food items.

Learning to Make a Fixed Number of Responses

The question of whether an animal can learn to make a fixed number of responses to gain access to reward was addressed in studies carried out by Mechner (1958). Two response levers were available, A and B. In the *fixed consecutive number* (FCN) procedure, a rat was rewarded half the time for completing a fixed number of presses on lever A. On the other half of the runs of responses on lever A, however, the rat had to complete at least the fixed number on lever A and then press lever B for reward. If it switched to lever B before completing the required number of responses on lever A, it got no reward for pressing lever B and was required to start over on lever A. Rewarded and non-rewarded runs of responses on lever A were randomly intermixed. An optimal strategy for a rat was to press on lever A until either it was rewarded or it was certain it had completed the fixed number on lever A. Excessive nonrewarded

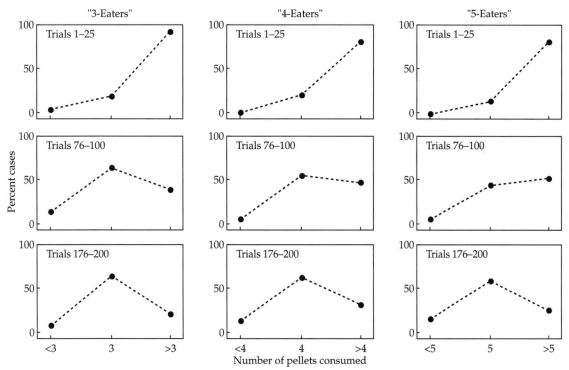

FIGURE 10.5. Curves show the percentage of cases on which rats ate different numbers of food pellets during successive stages of restricted food intake training. From left to right, the curves show data from groups of rats trained to eat three, four, or five pellets.

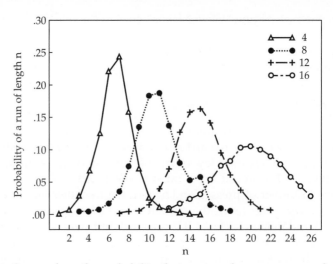

FIGURE 10.6. Curves show the probability that a rat made n responses on lever A before switching to lever B. From left to right, the curves represent performance when the fixed number on lever A was 4, 8, 12, or 16 responses.

responding on lever A delayed the opportunity to obtain reward by responding to lever B. Mechner varied the lever A requirement among 4, 8, 12, and 16 responses.

The question of interest is how accurately rats completed the fixed number when responses on lever A were not rewarded. The curves in Figure 10.6 show the probability of response runs of different lengths for one rat. The curves and their peaks shift to the right as the fixed number was raised from 4 to 16. In each curve, the peak probability falls a few responses beyond the fixed number. Note also that the variability of the number of responses increased as the fixed number increased, much as timing variability increases with the time to be estimated in the peak procedure.

One concern with these findings is that rats could have used time and not number to switch from lever A to lever B. Since number of responses is correlated with time, rats might have switched after a fixed period of time had passed. To control for this possibility, Mechner and Guevrekian (1962) tested FCN performance under varying number of hours of food deprivation. Although rats' rate of response increased with deprivation, thus lowering the time taken to complete a fixed number of responses, the number of responses made on lever A before switching to lever B remained constant. These findings suggest that rats were responding to number and not time.

The fact that rats overestimated the fixed number seems understandable since reward for response to lever B was only earned if the fixed number on lever A was reached or exceeded. It was then most profitable to err on the side of overresponding on lever A. However, could the contingencies of this experiment be adjusted to produce more accurate performance? An experiment by Ferster (1958) suggests they can. Ferster required a chimpanzee to press lever A three times before pressing lever B for reward. Unlike Mechner's (1958) procedure, however, exactly three presses on lever A were necessary to prime reward on lever B. Any number of responses on lever A other than three led to a 10-second time-out when lever B was pressed. The chimpanzee learned to make exactly three responses on lever A on 80 percent of the response runs on lever A, and this level of accuracy rose to 98 percent when multiple sets of responses had to be made on lever B for reward. Although we cannot directly compare a chimpanzee's performance with that of a rat, this finding and others (Hurwitz, 1962; Platt & Johnson, 1971) suggest that number of responses more closely approximates a fixed number as stiffer nonreinforcement contingencies are introduced for making the wrong number of responses.

In an impressive study of number production, a chimpanzee named Lana was trained to move a cursor to a fixed number of targets on a videomonitor (Rumbaugh & Washburn, 1993). Lana was presented with one of the numerals 1 through 4 at the top of the screen and then required to move a cursor successively through a number of boxes to the one that corresponded to the number shown. Each box turned blue when contacted by the cursor. To receive a reward, Lana had to return the cursor to the target number. Although her accuracy dropped as the target number increased from 1 to 4, she responded with the correct number significantly above chance with all four numerals.

RESPONSE-NUMBER JUDGMENTS

After completing a fixed number of responses, can an animal render an accurate judgment concerning its own behavior? Rilling and McDiarmid (1965) addressed this question using a procedure similar to the delayed-matching task discussed in Chapters 3 and 4. On some trials, a pigeon was required to peck a white center key 50 times. After the 50th peck, the center key was darkened, and two side keys were illuminated. If the bird pecked the right key, it was rewarded immediately, while a peck on the left key delayed reward for 60 seconds. On other trials, the number of pecks made on the center key before it went dark was set at a number less than 50. In this case, a peck on the left key led to immediate reward. When the smaller number was 35 pecks, pigeons chose the side keys with about 90 percent accuracy. As the smaller number was moved toward 50, accuracy dropped, but pigeons still chose the correct side key 60 percent of the time when the smaller number was 47.

Were pigeons' judgments in the Rilling and McDiarmid (1965) experiment based on differences in the time to complete different lengths of fixed-ratio schedules on the center key? In a careful analysis of psychophysical data, Rilling (1967) was able to reject this possibility by showing that accuracy of side key choice was little affected by the duration of the center key light. The importance of this work is that it suggests that animals may be able to discriminate large numbers as well as small numbers. Most of the other studies reviewed required animals to discriminate numbers under 10. The findings of Rilling and McDiarmid suggest that animals may be capable of discriminations between closely spaced numbers as high as 50.

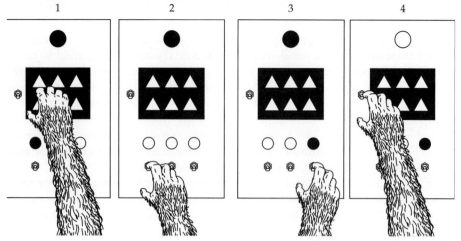

FIGURE 10.7. Drawing of a chimpanzee writing a binary number that matches the number of triangles shown on the screen. After turning on the display in Panel 1, the chimp presses the keys under the display until it judges the pattern of lights is correct. It then presses the upper key in Panel 4, and the reinforcement light above the display comes on if the number is correct.

CAN ANIMALS COUNT?

As pointed out earlier in this chapter, a true counting system must possess the properties of cardinality and ordinality (Gelman & Gallistel, 1978). When these requirements are applied to animals, they suggest that we have to see some evidence that animals associate different number tags with different numbers of items and that these tags are applied in a fixed order (H. Davis & Perusse, 1988).

Associating Symbols with Numbers of Objects

Some evidence is available that suggests that animals can learn to use symbolic number tags to indicate the cardinal number that identifies a set of items. In an early study, Ferster (1964) trained two chimpanzees, Dennis and Margie, over many thousands of trials to "write" the number of objects seen on a screen. A binary counting system was used in which a row of three lights signaled the numbers 1 through 7. Depending on whether it was turned off or on, the right-hand light indicated 0 or 1, the middle light 0 or 2, and the left-hand light 0 or 4. The chimpanzees initially learned to match light patterns to numbers of objects by choosing between correct and incorrect rows of lights. Eventually, the chimpanzees learned to press switches beneath each light to "write" the correct number that matched the number of objects seen (see Figure 10.7). Accuracy was quite high, with less than 1 percent error seen over a block of 1,000 trials. To eliminate the cues that might be correlated with number, the items the chimps counted were constantly varied in size, shape, and pattern.

In a similar experiment, Matsuzawa (1985) presented a chimpanzee named Ai with different numbers of common objects through a display window. There were 14 objects, such as a padlock, a glove, a rope, a spoon, a key, and a pencil.

These objects could be presented in 11 different colors, and the number of objects presented varied from one to six. Keys on a console provided symbols that corresponded to each object and each color, and six keys presented the Arabic numbers 1 through 6. As in other studies of this nature, Ai required a vast number of training trials to reach her final level of competence. She was eventually able to respond to displays accurately along all three dimensions. For example, when shown five blue toothbrushes, she successively pressed the keys for "blue," "toothbrush," and "five." Over a final block of 830 trials, her number-naming accuracy was greater than 98 percent. The items shown were displayed either in a row or in the experimenter's hand, with orientation and angular separation of items varied from trial to trial.

At Ohio State University, chimpanzees were trained over a two-year period to associate Arabic numbers with numbers of objects (Boysen, 1993; Boysen & Berntson, 1989). Stages in this training are shown at the top of Figure 10.8. Initially, chimps were trained to match numbers of objects on a tray to placards containing the same number of items. Then, cards containing Arabic numerals were substituted for the placards until chimps could choose the numbers 1 through 7 that corresponded to the number of objects shown. In receptive number comprehension training, chimps were further trained to perform this task in the opposite direction. After seeing an Arabic number displayed on a videomonitor, chimps learned to select the placard that contained the correct number of markers (see bottom of Figure 10.8).

The use of number symbols to represent quantities has been shown to be useful to chimpanzees in a social food-competition task (Boysen & Berntson, 1995; Boysen, Berntson, Hannan, & Cacioppo, 1996). Two chimpanzees acted as "selector" and "observer" in a food- selection experiment. Both chimpanzees were shown two trays, with one tray containing more food items than the other. The selector was allowed to select one tray by pointing at it; the food on the selected tray was then given to the observer, and the selector received the food on the nonselected tray. It was expected that the selector chimpanzee would soon realize that it should point to the smaller amount of food in order to obtain the larger amount for itself. Quite to the contrary, however, over many trials of testing, the selector continually pointed at the tray containing the larger amount of food most of the time.

The experimenters then switched from showing food to the selector to showing an Arabic numeral on each tray. Thus, the selector might be confronted with the numbers 2 and 4; if it chose 4, then the observer was given four food items, and the selector was given two food items. Almost immediately, the selector now adopted the strategy of pointing at the smaller number on most of the trials, thus giving the observer the smaller amount of food and itself the larger amount. Would the chimpanzees then maintain this strategy when tested again with real food shown on the trays? This was not case, as the selector quickly returned to its strategy of pointing at the larger amount of food when symbols were replaced with actual food items. It appears that although chimpanzees understood the "rules of the game," they could not overcome a natural tendency to choose the largest amount when real food was present. Only with number symbols could they short-circuit this "go for the most" strategy and use their understanding of the contingencies to actually obtain the largest amount.

FIGURE 10.8. The upper drawing shows the stimuli used to train chimpanzees to use Arabic numerals. The top three panels show the initial task on which chimps matched number of items on a tray by choosing a placard with the same number of items. The lower drawing shows a chimpanzee performing the comprehension task by matching a placard to a numeral shown on a videomonitor.

Studies of relative judgments between number symbols have been carried out with a dolphin and two rhesus monkeys. In both studies, animals were taught to associate symbols with number of reward items. In the case of the dolphin (Mitchell, Yao, Sherman, & O'Regan, 1985), it was allowed to choose among objects that floated on the surface of its pool, such as a mixing bowl, an ice-cube tray, and a utensil tray. Choice of each item was consistently followed by a fixed number of food items, zero to six fish. The monkeys were trained to operate a joystick that moved a cursor on a videomonitor until it intersected one of two Arabic numbers that varied from zero to nine (Washburn & Rumbaugh, 1991). A monkey always received a number of food pellets that corresponded to the number chosen on the screen. For example, a monkey might see the numbers 3 and 5 on the screen; if the monkey used the joy stick to move the cursor so that it intersected the number 5, the monkey received five food items from the food cup. Both species of animals learned to consistently choose the symbol that represented the larger number of food items in tests with choice between two symbols and in some tests with as many as five symbols. Although these studies are open to a possible interpretation in terms of differential reinforcement properties conditioned to symbols by differences in amount of reward, the precision of the discriminations between symbols suggests that the animals learned the symbolic relationship between the number symbol and the quantity it indicated.

The studies reviewed thus far suggest that the ability to learn to associate cardinal number symbols with different numbers of objects may be limited to large-brained mammals. An important study of the African gray parrot (Pepperberg, 1987) shows clearly that this is not the case. A parrot named Alex was tested on a number of cognitive tasks, in which he responded to verbal questions from the tester with vocal English words. Alex was initially trained to use the labels "3" and "4"; with months of further training, he learned to use "2," "5," and "6." On a series of tests, Alex was shown displays of two to six objects. The objects were pieces of paper, keys, popsicle sticks (called "wood" by Alex), clothespins (called "peg wood" by Alex), and corks. These objects varied in size and arrangement from one test to another. On a typical test, Alex was shown four popsicle sticks and asked by a trainer, "What's this?" Alex was scored correct if he replied with both the number and the type of object. Thus, to be correct, Alex would have to reply "4 wood." Alex was correct on 79 percent of these tests. However, this percentage may underestimate his numerical ability; about 60 percent of his errors were trials on which he responded with the name of the object but omitted the number. When further asked "How many?", Alex provided the correct number 95 percent of the time. It should be pointed out that reward for correct responses was verbal praise and an opportunity to interact with (take in his beak) the objects shown.

In further tests, Alex was shown different numbers of a variety of objects that were novel and for which he therefore had no name. Such objects as antacid tablets, bottles of typewriter correction fluid, and beads were shown, and Alex responded with the correct number on 80 percent of the tests. Thus, neither familiarity with items nor the ability to provide a generic label for them was necessary for Alex to provide a correct numerical response. Alex also showed some evidence of being able to count subsets of items within a heterogeneous group. For example, Alex might be shown a tray containing three keys and two corks and asked, "How many key?" Alex responded correctly on 7 out of 10 tests of this type, indicating that he may have been able to perceptually partition a collection of items into different subsets for numerical evaluation.

There now appears to be sufficient data to conclude that some animals can reliably respond with different symbols that are associated with different numbers of objects. Does this mean that animals were counting the objects seen? Not necessarily. As mentioned earlier, it is possible that animals were using subitizing or pattern matching. Thus, a collection of objects would be seen as a pattern to which a symbol was associated and not as a number of counted objects. However, to accept such an argument means that we must accept a very broad definition of pattern matching. In most of the studies reviewed, the objects shown varied widely in their type, size, color, and pattern. With sets of items larger than three or four, consistently familiar patterns, such as triangles or rectangles, cannot be seen. Another possibility is that animals became adept at perceptually partitioning larger groups of items into smaller subsets that could be seen as canonical patterns. Thus, the perception of a rectangle and a triangle together might be associated with choice of the "7" symbol. On the other hand, the objects shown to Ai by Matsuzawa (1985) were often presented in a row, with the spacing between them varied. Canonical subpatterns presumably could not be seen in this case. Furthermore, it is not clear how Alex would use such a process to correctly label a subset of objects presented in a heterogeneous array. For the moment, the mechanism used by animals to correctly label numbers of objects remains somewhat controversial.

Evidence of Ordinality

As H. Davis and Perusse (1988) pointed out, the assignment of numerical symbols to numbers of objects is not itself sufficient evidence for the use of a counting system. In addition to the use of cardinal tags, it must be shown that an organism understands that these tags must follow one another in a fixed order. What evidence do we have for the ordinal use of symbols in animals? The material covered in Chapter 9 on serial learning and memory seems somewhat relevant here. We reviewed findings showing that both pigeons and monkeys could learn to choose sets of colors or geometric patterns in a fixed order. However, being able to respond to stimuli in a fixed order is not necessarily evidence of an ordinal representation. For example, Terrace's (1991) analysis of his pigeons' behavior suggested that pigeons used simple rules about first and last items and interitem associations to peck stimuli in a correct sequence. The fact that pigeons could not correctly order interior subsequences was particularly damaging for any notion that pigeons had a complete ordinal understanding of the list. D'Amato and Colombo's (1988, 1989) data from their studies of cebus monkeys, on the other hand, provided a convincing argument for ordinal representation. Their monkeys were able to correctly order adjacent and nonadjacent items involving all combinations of end items and interior items, after learning an ABCDE list. The latency data bolstered this interpretation by showing that reaction time increased linearly with the distance between items on subsequence tests.

With regard to the question of ordinality, some further aspects of the Washburn and Rumbaugh (1991) study should be emphasized. Their monkeys initially learned to respond to the numerals 0 through 5. When the numerals 6 through 9 were introduced, certain pairs of numerals were never presented on the videomonitor; these were 6:4, 6:5, 7:5, 7:6, 8:5, 9:7, and 9:8. Eventually, tests with these novel pairs of numbers were given to the monkeys. One of the monkeys, Abel, chose the larger member of the pair on his first exposure to each of these combinations, and the other monkey, Baker, chose the larger numeral on five out of the seven tests. The important point here is that information about the order of symbols was necessary to correctly choose the larger value. For example, the monkeys previously learned that $7 > 5$ and that $6 > 5$ by responding to tests with these pairs of symbols, but knowing that 7 > 5 and that 6 > 5 does not imply that 7 > 6, unless the symbols have been ordered by the number of reward pellets each yields. The monkeys' success on first tests with novel combinations suggests that they may have already understood that 7 > 6 > 5.

Washburn and Rumbaugh's (1991) final experiment also provided evidence suggestive of ordinal representation of numerical symbols. Both monkeys were tested with pairs of numerals up to this point but were now confronted with five randomly chosen numbers on the videomonitor. Choice of any numeral with the cursor led to delivery of its number of pellets and left the remaining numbers on the screen. The monkey could then choose another numeral and be rewarded until it made four choices. Both Abel and Baker chose the largest numeral at significantly above-chance level on all four choices and showed this high level of performance on their initial introduction to the five-number task. These findings imply that Abel and Baker learned not just the correct choice between two numerals but also the ordinal values of the entire series of numerals.

The Functional Use of Counting

The data reviewed show that animals use symbols to represent the cardinal number of a set of objects and that at least monkeys have an understanding of ordinal relationships between numerical symbols. However, even if we assume that an animal possesses a symbolic scheme that has the properties of cardinality and ordinality, we cannot be certain that the animal is capable of counting unless we have some evidence of its functional use of the system. In other words, the animal has to use the system to count things. As behavioral evidence for counting in an animal, an ideal observation is one in which the animal uses obvious number tags as it enumerates a series of objects. For example, most would agree that a chimpanzee is counting if it places number cards containing 1, 2, 3, 4, and 5 successively on each of five items shown and then turns to a computer console and presses the key containing the "5" symbol to indicate the total. Of course, evidence this good is not available, but some observations tempt some observers to suggest they might represent functional counting.

An often-cited observation made in Koehler's laboratory (H. Davis & Memmott, 1982) concerns a jackdaw that was trained to take five food items from a row of boxes. The first five boxes in the row contained one, two, one, zero, and one food items, with no food items in any of the boxes after the fifth. On a particular trial, the bird visited only the first three boxes and returned to its home cage. When the experimenter recorded an incorrect trial because the bird took only four food items, the bird returned to the boxes and made a bow at the first box it visited, made two bows in front of the second box, one in front of the third, and then opened the lids on the fourth and fifth boxes. After consuming the food in the fifth box, it left the arena and returned to its cage. One interpretation of this description is that the bird was making symbolic counting responses of number of food items consumed by bowing in front of the boxes it had just visited.

In Mechner's (1958) study of FCN, he reported that some rats performed motor activities while pressing lever A that could be interpreted as discriminative stimuli for the switch to lever B. One animal was observed to press the lever with its right paw while moving its left paw through a semicircle on the wall. When it reached the end of the semicircle, it switched to lever B. Another rat pressed lever A with its teeth, lowering its head slowly until its teeth slipped off the bar; at this point, it switched to lever B.

Boysen and Berntson (1989) observed possible motor tagging behavior in a chimpanzee named Sheba as she learned to use Arabic numbers. After about 18 months of number training, during which her trainer consistently tagged items counted by touching them, "She was observed to begin to touch, point to, or move items in an array before making her final decision" (p. 24). Further investigation of these "indicating acts" by Boysen, Berntson, Shreyer and Hannan (1995) showed that the number of acts correlated significantly with the size of the array of items shown. However, Sheba tended to overtag the items in an array, often making as many as twice the number of motor tags as items in the array.

These behaviors of a bird, rats, and a chimpanzee may be seen as intentional movements that represent what Koehler called "inner marks" to "think unnamed numbers" (H. Davis & Memmott, 1982). As tempting as it may be to interpret these behaviors as a behavioral manifestation of an internal counting process, caution is advised. Such behaviors are seen in very few animals and then only on limited occasions. A wide variety of numerical discrimination phenomena have been reported, but motor tagging behavior is seldom found in these reports. Finally, the behaviors described here show no evidence of a cardinal counting chain that is applied consistently in a one-to-one fashion to different sets of items.

Transfer of Training

The absence of behavioral evidence for the use of cardinal number tags does not prove that animals do not count. People often count things by assigning number names to them mentally or subvocally. Animals could be using unobservable number tags, or what Gelman and Gallistel (1978) call *numerons,* to count items. If animals use numerons or cognitive symbols to count, we might find some evidence that their behavior satisfies the abstraction principle of human counting. The abstraction principle suggests that a counting system with cardinal labels that are applied in a fixed order can count items from any domain. In the case of animal counting, we should seek evidence of abstraction in *transfer-of-training* experiments. If an animal developed a counting system to deal with discrimination among different numbers of one type of object or event, it should be able to transfer that counting system to a new type of object or event.

We can find some evidence for limited transfer in the literature. In many of the experiments on relative numerousness and absolute number discrimination, animals were tested with a wide variety of different patterns of stimuli. When visual clusters of simultaneously presented items were used, the items varied in shape, size, color, and distribution. In experiments that involved successive stimulation, the duration of stimulation and the intervals between successive applications of a stimulus were varied. Animals learned these discriminations, which involved some degree of transfer between trials. In H. Davis's (1984) study of absolute number discrimination by a raccoon, Rocky readily transferred discrimination of three grapes to three metal balls. H. Davis and Bradford (1991) found that rats trained to eat a fixed number of food pellets continued to eat the same number when transferred to sunflower seeds. Alex, the African gray parrot, continued to correctly label the number of items presented to him when items never before tested were shown.

These examples all involve transfer within the same sensory and motor domain. Some theorists argue that true counting should show a wider degree of transfer (H. Davis & Perusse, 1988; Salman, 1943; Seibt, 1982). Three types of transfer have been suggested (Seibt, 1982): (1) It should be possible to transfer from counting in one sensory modality to counting in a different sensory modality. For example, a number system used to count things seen should be applicable to counting things heard. (2) Transfer should occur between counting things perceived simultaneously and counting things perceived successively. An organism that can count a set of simultaneously displayed objects should be able to count a sequence of light flashes. (3) True counting should be transferable between passive and active modes. If an animal possesses a symbolic counting system, it should be able to use that system both to count the number of events experienced simultaneously or sequentially and to produce a fixed number of events by its own behavior.

Evidence for these three types of transfer in animals is fairly slim. In a review of the earlier literature, Salman (1943) concluded that "No animal . . . has shown any capacity for the transfer of a number-pattern from one qualitative field to another" (p. 212). In a later experiment, Meck and Church (1982) reported intermodal transfer of a relative numerousness discrimination. They initially trained rats to discriminate between sequences of two sound bursts and four sound bursts, much as Fernandes and Church (1982) did in the experiment previously described. When subjects were clearly discriminating between numbers of sound bursts, they were transferred to a discrimination between two versus four presentations of a light signal. Rats continued to choose the lever indicating "four" after four lights and the lever indicating "two" after two lights, although the level of accuracy dropped somewhat from the level at the end of sound training.

H. Davis and Albert (1987) were prompted to test intermodal transfer of the absolute number discrimination they previously trained in rats (H. Davis & Albert, 1986). After rats learned to respond more in the presence of a three-sound sequence than in the presence of a two- or four-sound sequence, they were tested with sequences of two, three, and four presentations of a light. No transfer of training from the auditory cues to the light cues was found. Why did H. Davis and Albert fail to find intermodal transfer, although Meck and Church found such transfer? H. Davis and Albert suggest the answer may lie in the types of discriminations rats were trained to perform. Rats only had to make a more-or-less judgment in the Meck and Church experiment, and this relatively simple numerical discrimination may be easily transferred to a new modality. The more difficult absolute discrimination required by H. Davis and Albert, of the number three against two and four, may require more sophisticated rules that do not transfer as easily across sensory modes.

In an earlier experiment, Pastore (1961) examined the possibility of transfer from simultaneous to successive numerical discrimination in a canary. The canary was initially trained with five simultaneously presented aspirins that covered food wells. Although the positions of the wells and the spacing among them was varied from trial to trial, the third food well from either end always contained a seed reward. After the bird learned to choose the third aspirin, it was switched to an apparatus in which it had to walk down a runway past 10 cubicles, each containing a food well. Five of the cubicles contained objects that covered the food well, and the third object encountered always had a reward placed under it. As the location of the third object was varied, the canary could not solve the problem by walking a constant distance down the runway. The canary showed complete failure of transfer from the simultaneous presentation procedure to the successive presentation procedure. In the first 100 trials, the bird chose the correct object only nine times, a level of performance far below chance accuracy.

In addition to these observations, there is little evidence that animals can transfer a number discrimination from a passive or perceptual mode to an active or behavioral mode. It would be of considerable interest to see if a chimpanzee that learned to use Arabic number cards to identify numbers of objects could quickly learn to press a bar the number of times shown on a number card. Or, could Alex the parrot rapidly learn to perform some act the correct number of times, when told to do it two, three, four, five, or six times? Perhaps evidence on such questions will become available in the future.

Protocounting

An interesting discrepancy seems to be found in the animal literature on numerical processing. We found ample evidence that animals perform relative numerousness discriminations and more difficult absolute number discriminations. Further, there is evidence that they associate numerical symbols with different numbers of objects and that at least primates have some understanding of ordinality. Yet, when we seek evidence of humanlike counting, little is to be found. Animals have not shown behavioral use of number tags, and little evidence of transfer of training across qualitatively different dimensions has been found.

Faced with this discrepancy, H. Davis and Perusse (1988) concluded that animals show numerical competency but have not yet revealed evidence of counting. In a number of the cases reviewed, animals show numerical discriminations that cannot be easily explained by the use of noncounting processes such as subitizing, estimation, and rhythm. Since animals have not yet shown true counting, as defined by human counting systems, H. Davis and Perusse argue that animals are using *protocounting*. Protocounting "applies to situations in which we are reasonably confident that the counting process occurred, however, in the absence of additional control tests (e.g., for transfer), there is no evidence that subject possesses a sense of number" (p. 569). This position is a conservative one that suggests we assume the absence of true counting in animals until strong evidence convinces us otherwise. In addition, H. Davis and Memmott (1982) take the position that any form of counting process is unnatural for an animal and "may reflect the boundaries of the animal's associative abilities"

(p. 547). They suggest that animals may use counting only as a last resort, when no other solution to a problem avails itself.

An Alternative View of Counting in Animals

Quite in contrast to H. Davis and Perusse's (1988) view of counting in animals, other theorists (Capaldi, 1993; Gallistel, 1990; 1993) hold the position that counting occurs frequently and relatively automatically in animals. These theorists argue that the cardinality, ordinality, and transfer criteria for counting are satisfied in animal counting experiments and that models for animal counting can be readily constructed.

The Capaldi and Miller Experiments

Evidence for flexible counting in rats was reported in a series of experiments performed by Capaldi and Miller (1988). The basic procedure used in these experiments was to give rats repeated trials in a runway consisting of a fixed number of rewarded (R) trials followed by a nonrewarded (N) trial. If rats could count the number of rewarded trials, they should be able to anticipate the nonrewarded trial and show a decline in running speed. In their initial experiments, rats were given six multiple-trial sequences within a day. Trials were separated by 15 seconds, and sequences of trials were separated by 10 to 15 minutes. Two types of sequences occurred in random order—a three-trial RRN sequence and a four-trial NRRN sequence. The question was whether rats could learn to count the two rewards in each sequence. If rats can count the two rewards, then two rewards could act as a signal for the final nonrewarded trial, and rats should slow down on the final trial.

The data shown in Figure 10.9 suggest that rats learned quite accurately to anticipate the final nonrewarded trial of each sequence. Notice that the curves are relatively flat for the first seven days of testing. Thereafter, they show a drop on the final trial, with precipitous declines in running speed appearing on the final days of training. Is this evidence of counting, or did rats use some other

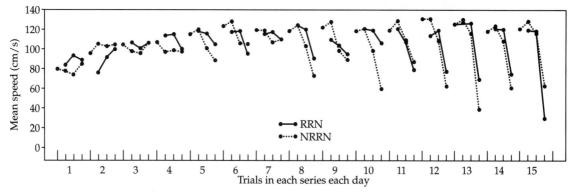

FIGURE 10.9. Running speed in rats trained over 15 days with randomly alternating sequences of trials on which the patterns of reward (R) and nonreward (N) were RRN and NRRN.

cue correlated with the number of reward trials? The experiment was specifically designed to rule out the use of certain alternative cues. For example, rats could not use the total number of trials or the time elapsed since the start of a sequence to determine when the final nonrewarded trial would occur since the final trial was randomly preceded by two or three trials. Other controls for more subtle cuing possibilities were performed, and in all cases the data suggested that rats counted the number of rewards (Capaldi, 1993).

In further experiments designed to examine the flexibility of rat counting, Capaldi and Miller (1988) used different types of rewards. In one experiment, rats were trained with a single sequence, R´RRN, in which R´ represents a piece of a sweetened breakfast cereal and R represents standard reward pellets. After several sessions of training with this series, rats ran rapidly on the first three trials and then slowed down markedly on the fourth trial. Rats were trained with the R´RRN sequence because it introduced an ambiguous counting situation. That is, rats could count these events as one R´ and two R events, or they could disregard the difference in rewards and count the sequence as three reward events. To find out how rats counted this sequence, they were divided into two groups and transferred to new sequences. One group was tested with random alternation of the sequences RRN and NRRN, and the other group was tested with the sequences RRRN and NRRRN. The surprising result was that rats in both groups showed rapid adaptation to these new sequences by running fast on all trials but the final nonrewarded trial. The implication of this finding is that rats were able to count the R´RRN sequence both ways, either as three reward events or as one R´ event and two R events, and then to use whichever counting scheme was appropriate when transferred to the new sequences.

Capaldi and Miller (1988) also provided evidence for the use of abstract number tags and the order irrelevance principle in rat counting. In a true counting system, an animal should be able to assign number tags to events in any order. A group of rats was trained on randomly ordered RRN and R´RRN sequences. Notice that these sequences encourage an animal to count the two R rewards and to discount the initial R´ reward in the R´RRN sequence. After several blocks of sessions with these sequences, rats ran quickly down the runway on all trials but the final one in both the three- and four-trial sequences. On a transfer test, the sequences they encountered were changed to R´R´N and RR´R´N. The subjects continued to show the pattern of fast running on all trials but the final one on these new sequences. The fact that rats could almost immediately transfer the same pattern of behavior to new sequences in which the types of reward were reversed indicates order irrelevance of number tags. In other words, rats counted two R rewards before nonreward in RRN and R´RRN sequences and were able to rapidly switch to counting two R´ rewards before nonreward when transferred to R´R´N and NR´R´N sequences. Rapid transfer occurred because the abstract number tag for two was the critical cue signaling that a nonrewarded trial followed.

These findings and others led Capaldi and Miller (1988) to a position diametrically opposed to that taken by H. Davis and Memmott (1982) and H. Davis and Perusse (1988). They concluded that "rats and, by implication, higher animals in general are highly disposed to counting reinforcing events and do so routinely, perhaps automatically" (p. 15).

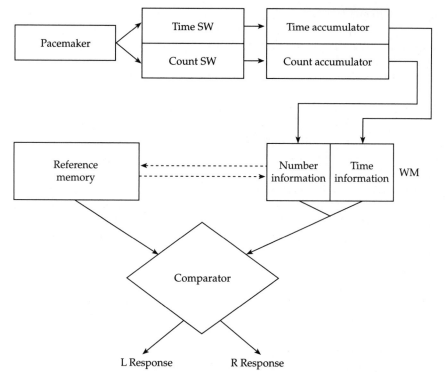

FIGURE 10.10. An information processing model for simultaneous timing and counting. Time and count switches close to allow pulses to enter time and count accumulators. Accumulator totals enter working memory and are compared with reference memory values in a comparator.

A Model for Automatic Counting

Gallistel (1990) and Gallistel and Gelman (1992) advanced the interesting argument that a similar innate and automatic counting system is found in both animals and people. The system evolved because it gave our animal ancestors a survival advantage. They assume that animals both count and perform basic operations on numerical representations, such as addition, subtraction, multiplication, and division. Being able to count and perform operations on numbers made animals sensitive to the rate at which events occurred in their environment. For example, a forager that could compute the rate of prey encounter in different patches by dividing number of occurrences by time could learn to abandon low-rate patches and stay in high-rate patches. Counting in animals is preverbal and is based on numerons, or number representations that correspond to the magnitude of processes in the nervous system. The advance in counting we find in people is that we have mapped verbal and written symbols onto the system of the preverbal numerons we share with animals.

To provide a concrete example of such an automatic preverbal counting system, examine the model shown in Figure 10.10. You should recognize this as a model highly similar to the timing model discussed in Chapter 8 and shown in

Figure 8.9. In fact, it is the model shown in Figure 8.9 with the addition of a count switch and a count accumulator. The advance in this model over the timing model is that it allows an organism to both time and count simultaneously (Meck & Church, 1983; Meck, Church, & Gibbon, 1985). Recall that timing is accomplished by the closing of the time switch to allow pulses from the pacemaker to flow into a time accumulator until the switch is opened. The total pulses in the accumulator are transmitted to working memory, and temporal decisions are made by comparing working and reference memory values in a comparator.

The model shown in Figure 10.10 is called a *mode control model*. Timing is accomplished through the time switch, which operates in a *run mode*, and counting is achieved through the count switch, which operates in an *event mode*. In the run mode, the time switch closes at the beginning of an event or sequence of events to be timed and only opens when the entire sequence is completed. In the event mode, on the other hand, the count switch closes only briefly each time a single event occurs. Each event then adds a fixed number of pulses to the count accumulator. The accumulated number of pulses in the accumulator after each event serves as a magnitude or numeron, which acts as a cardinal number tag, and the total pulses in the accumulator at the end of a sequence of events represents the cardinal number (H. Broadbent, Church, Meck, & Rakitin, 1993). Thus, at the end of a sequence of events that was both timed and counted, different total numbers of pulses reside in the time and count accumulators, and separate comparisons for time and number are made between working and reference memory totals in the comparator.

What evidence do we have for the operation of such a mechanism? Evidence comes from experiments carried out with both rats and pigeons. Meck and Church (1983) trained rats to discriminate between sequences of noise bursts that lasted 0.5 second and occurred once per second. Two levers were made available to rats immediately after a sequence of sound bursts. Subjects learned to press the left lever after two noise bursts that lasted 2 seconds and to press the right lever after eight noise bursts that lasted 8 seconds. In an experiment of very similar design, W. Roberts and Mitchell (1994) trained pigeons to discriminate between sequences of flashes of an overhead red light that illuminated the operant chamber. Each flash lasted 200 milliseconds, and flashes were presented at the rate of one per second. After a sequence of two flashes in 2 seconds, a pigeon was rewarded for pecking an illuminated key on the left side of the front wall of the chamber; after a sequence of eight flashes in 8 seconds, reward was delivered for pecking a key on the right side of the front wall.

Clearly, time and number are confounded in both the rat and pigeon experiments. That is, a rat or pigeon could have learned either discrimination by only using time or only using number; the values on both dimensions indicated the correct response. To find out the degree to which time and/or number controlled the discriminations, probe trials were introduced among the training trials in both experiments. On probe trials, one dimension, either time or number, was held constant while the other dimension was varied. Thus, on probe trials that measured control by time, the number of noise bursts or light flashes was held constant at four, and the length of time taken to present the four events was varied from 2 to 8 seconds. On probe trials that measured control by number, the length of the sequence was held constant at 4 seconds, and the number of noise bursts or light flashes was varied from two to eight.

The findings from these experiments are shown in Figure 10.11. The percentage of choices of the "long" lever or key are plotted as a function of the number of seconds or number of events presented on the probe trials. Although the shapes of the rat curves in the upper graph and the pigeon curves in the lower graph are somewhat different, the important point is that the curves for both species rise as the length or number of the test stimuli increases. Particularly important is the fact that the time control and number control curves are similar, indicating equal degrees of control by time and number in both species. This finding implies that both rats and pigeons keep track of time and number at the same time, and this is exactly what the mode control model predicts.

Evidence of Operations on Numbers

A complete sense of number includes the ability to perform operations upon numbers. As mentioned, Gallistel (1993) argued that since animals are sensitive to the rate at which events occur, they must be able to divide number by time. Is there any more direct evidence for numerical computation in animals? Two studies with chimpanzees suggest that these animals may be able to summate numbers of objects. Rumbaugh, Savage-Rumbaugh, and Hegel (1987) trained two chimpanzees, Sherman and Austin, to discriminate between trays that contained pairs of food wells. Different numbers of pieces of chocolate candy were placed in the wells on each tray so that the sum of the number of pieces in both wells was greater on one tray than on the other. A chimpanzee was allowed to

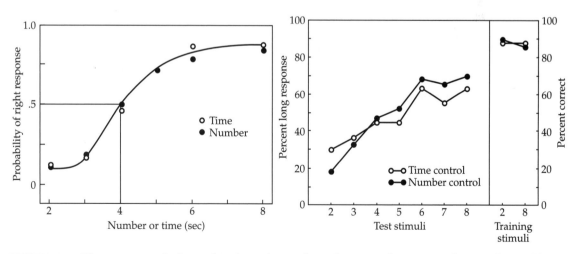

FIGURE 10.11. The upper graph shows data from time and number control tests carried out with rats. The lower graph shows time and number control curves found in a comparable experiment with pigeons.

FIGURE 10.12. Drawing shows a laboratory setting in which the ability to summate was tested in the chimpanzee Sheba. Sheba observed the contents of a tree stump, a food bin, and a dishpan and then returned to a platform to choose among cards containing the Arabic numerals 0 through 4.

choose between the trays and eat all the candy on the tray chosen. From zero to five pieces could be placed in any well, with the maximum total of both wells being 8. A large number of different combinations were tested. On some tests, the totals differed by two or three pieces, as in 4 + 4 versus 5 + 0, or 0 + 4 versus 3 + 3. On other tests, however, the totals differed by only one piece, such as 1 + 4 versus 3 + 3, and 4 + 4 versus 5 + 2. The chimpanzees chose correctly at 90 percent or better when the totals differed by two or three pieces or when small totals differed by one piece (e.g., three versus four). Even when confronted with a choice between totals of seven versus eight, they chose correctly about 80 percent of the time. Rumbaugh et al. concluded that chimpanzees showed summation of numbers of items, possibly by mentally fusing subitized quantities seen in each food well.

Another chimpanzee, Sheba, was tested for her ability to summate pieces of fruit in a study by Boysen and Berntson (1989). Sheba was tested in the laboratory setting shown in Figure 10.12. She was required to make a circuit that entailed a visit to three places: a tree stump, a stainless steel food bin, and a plastic dishpan. Cards containing the Arabic numerals 0 through 4 were placed on a wooden platform where Sheba went after visiting each location. Two of three sites contained from 0 through 4 oranges, with the total number of oranges not exceeding four. Sheba quickly learned to choose the Arabic number that represented the total number of oranges found at the food sites. Thus, if she encountered zero and two oranges, she chose the numeral 2, and, if she found one and three oranges, she chose the numeral 4. In a further demonstration of her ability to sum, Sheba was tested with the Arabic numerals 0 through 4 placed at two of the three locations. Sheba transferred immediately to this task and accurately chose the Arabic numeral that represented the sum of the two numerals encountered on her trip.

Although not a great deal of research on numerical operations in animals has been done, these experiments indicate that summation is found in chimpanzees and suggest that research in the area of numerical operations should be pursued with other animals.

SUMMARY

Numerical processing in animals has been studied since the beginning of the 20th century. A number of early studies led investigators to conclude that animals were capable of responding to number as a discriminative stimulus. These conclusions are supported by contemporary studies that repeated many of the early designs under fully controlled conditions. It is clear that animals show numerical competence. That is, they are capable of forming relative and absolute number discriminations, both among simultaneously presented stimuli and successively presented stimuli. Furthermore, animals are capable of producing a fixed number of responses, which may consist of operating a manipulandum a fixed number of times or eating a fixed number of food items.

The question of whether animals can count remains a controversial one. All theorists agree that a counting organism should show evidence of using a counting system that has the properties of cardinality and ordinality. Several lines of research suggest that animals are capable of associating symbols with different numbers of objects and of some degree of understanding the ordinal relationships within a set of ordered symbols. Nevertheless, H. Davis and Perusse (1988) argue that evidence for abstraction or the transfer of counting between qualitatively different dimensions of perception and performance is weak. Animals show protocounting, a term used to describe numerical competence that falls short of all the properties of human counting.

In stark contrast to H. Davis and Perusse's view, Capaldi (1993) and Gallistel (1993) propose that animals count numerous events routinely and automatically. Capaldi and Miller's (1988) runway studies led them to conclude that rats counted rewards in a flexible manner, being able to transfer counting between different rewards and being able to count an ambiguous sequence in alternate ways. Gallistel (1993) suggests that a basic counting mechanism based on the magnitude of an internal process operates in both animals and people, allowing them not only to count but to perform operations on numerical quantities. The mode control model of Meck, Church, and Gibbon (1985) shows how such a mechanism could work, with time and number represented by the number of pulses gated into accumulators.

The future very likely holds some interesting surprises for those interested in animal numerical processing. The major advances in theory and research methodology we have seen over the past 90 years or so should be matched by equivalent or greater advances in coming years. In particular, our understanding of the counting process in animals may be clarified considerably by future research.

CHAPTER 11

Concept Learning

In human cognition, concepts refer to mental categories into which people place experiences of the world. Such categories are of considerable importance because they allow us to quickly evaluate and label many different events, even though none of those events is identical to any other one. As we encounter a stimulus from one time to another, our perception of that stimulus changes somewhat, either from some physical change in the stimulus itself or from a change in our point of view. Yet, we are able to generalize from one occasion to another and recognize our perception as being that of the same stimulus. We form a concept of that stimulus. Concepts then have an open-ended quality because they often allow us to categorize stimuli we have never encountered before. Human conceptualization also can be very abstract in that people have concepts that incorporate objects, actions, and ideas that have little or no physical resemblance to one another. Some examples are the concepts of "tools," "games," and "beauty." Such abstract concepts are presumably based on complex networks of linguistic associations a person has acquired throughout her lifetime.

Studies of concept learning in animals suggest that analogs of most forms of human conceptualization can be found with other species. One example was already discussed in Chapter 8: chunking. The evidence presented there suggested that both people and animals learn to treat sequences of stimuli that have common properties or form a pattern as a single unit of information. Thus, the members of a chunk may be thought of as a concept. In addition, animals are capable of forming concepts consisting of stimuli that are not presented contiguously or in succession. Such concepts may be based on perceptual similarity, relationships between stimuli, or common associations. In this chapter, we examine both the extent of concept learning and limitations upon concept learning thus far discovered in animal cognition.

PERCEPTUAL CONCEPT LEARNING

In a landmark article by Herrnstein and Loveland (1964), pigeons were trained to peck at a key when slide-projected pictures were presented on an adjacent screen. The pictures presented were photographs that either contained people or from which people were absent. A picture was presented for a period lasting from 10 to 90 seconds. Whenever a picture containing people appeared on the screen, a pigeon earned a food reward by pecking the key on a variable-interval schedule. However, whenever a picture without people in it appeared on the screen, no reward could be earned by key pecking. After several sessions of training under these conditions, pigeons learned to peck at a high rate whenever a picture containing people appeared and to peck at a low rate or withhold pecking whenever a picture without people was shown. It should be emphasized that the pictures used came from a large collection of pictures, and, thus, different pictures with or without people occurred on each picture presentation. Pictures of people contained one person or two or more people, contained people dressed in different clothing, and were shot at varying distances, including long-distance shots and closeups. In subsequent research (Herrnstein, Loveland, & Cable, 1976), the types of pictures of natural objects pigeons could discriminate from pictures without these objects were extended to trees, bodies of water, and pictures of a single person shown while carrying out many different activities. Pigeons appeared to easily form visual discriminations based on natural categories.

More recent research indicates that pigeons can not only discriminate pictures of natural objects from a particular category from pictures without the object but can sort pictures containing several different types of objects into appropriate categories (Bhatt, Wasserman, Reynolds, & Knauss, 1988). Pigeons were tested in an operant chamber containing a screen upon which pictures were projected. As shown in Figure 11.1, four pecking keys were available, one placed at each corner of the screen. The pictures displayed fell into four categories: cats, flowers, cars, and chairs. As in the Herrnstein, et al. (1976) experiments, different pictures from each category were shown on each trial within a session. Each time a picture was presented, the subject was required to make 30 pecks on the picture, thereby ensuring that the picture was clearly observed by the subject. After the final peck on the picture, the four key lights at each corner of the screen were illuminated. Depending on the category of the picture shown, only one of the keys was correct and delivered a food reward when pecked. For example, one subject was rewarded for pecking the upper-left key whenever a flower was shown, the lower-left key whenever a car was shown, the upper-right key whenever a cat was shown, and the lower-right key whenever a chair was shown. Over 30 sessions of training, pigeons' ability to categorize pictures rose from the chance level of 25 percent to about a 75 percent accuracy level. Furthermore, correct responses were significantly above chance for pictures in each category.

One possible explanation for this excellent performance with different pictures is that pigeons simply memorized each picture and the response that was appropriate to it. We know from other research (Vaughan & Greene, 1984) that pigeons can learn and remember the reward status of as many as 160 unrelated pictures. Because pictures are often repeated over sessions in categorization experiments, memorization of each picture and its outcome could have served as the basis for discrimination performance. If this were the case, then categorization would be more apparent than real; similarity among pictures in their appearance and the identity of the assigned categories would be of no importance.

FIGURE 11.1. A drawing of a pigeon performing a conceptual sorting task. Pictures from different categories (cats, cars, flowers, chairs) appear on the screen. The pigeon must peck a different key for each category to be reinforced.
From Wasserman, 1995.

Two important findings indicate that memorization is not the sole basis for picture categorization by pigeons. The first finding involves tests with novel pictures, pictures which a pigeon has not seen before and therefore could not have stored in its memory. When trained pigeons are presented with novel pictures from a particular category, a number of experiments indicate that they responded significantly above a chance level of accuracy to such pictures. A particularly good example of this phenomenon is shown in Figure 11.2. Bhatt et al. (1988) trained a group of pigeons over 96 sessions to discriminate between pictures of people, cars, flowers, and chairs. On odd-numbered sessions, the same set of pictures was repeated for categorization, but, on even-numbered sessions, pigeons were shown novel or nonrepeating pictures in each category. Although pigeons did categorize repeating pictures somewhat better than nonrepeating pictures, Figure 11.2 shows that pigeons learned to categorize new pictures at levels that far exceeded chance. This performance with novel pictures would be impossible if pigeons were only able to respond accurately to previously seen pictures.

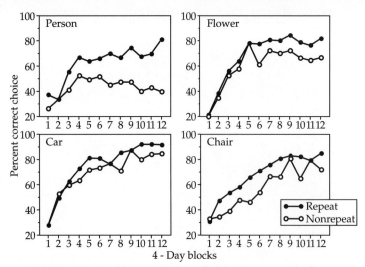

FIGURE 11.2. Curves showing the acquisition of correct sorting responses to pictures in four different categories. Repeat pictures were shown repeatedly on successive sessions. Nonrepeat pictures were shown on only one session. Since the pigeon must choose between four keys, the chance level of accuracy is 25 percent.

Consider another kind of experiment, the *pseudocategory* experiment. In a study carried out by Wasserman, Kiedinger, and Bhatt (1988), one group of pigeons, the category group, was presented with the standard training procedure just described—sets of pictures of 20 cats, 20 cars, 20 chairs, and 20 flowers, each requiring a different key response. In a second group, the pseudocategory group, pigeons also had to respond to the same four different groups of pictures by pecking four different keys. However, the pictures within each group formed combinations of categories. Each set of pictures requiring a response to a particular key contained different subsets of five cars, five flowers, five chairs, and five cats. If pigeons learn to categorize only by memorizing the correct response for each picture, the pseudocategory group should have learned at the same rate as the category group. The findings from this experiment are shown in Figure 11.3 and reveal that pigeons trained to sort on the basis of categories learned substantially faster than pigeons trained to sort on the basis of pseudocategories (see also Herrnstein & de Villiers, 1980). These findings suggest that pigeons see similarities and differences among objects that are very much like those seen by people and that lead to category distinctions in human languages.

THEORIES OF PERCEPTUAL CONCEPT LEARNING

The Genetic Hypothesis

The findings just reviewed raise the question of how animals are able to respond discriminatively to visual categories. One possibility is that a pigeon

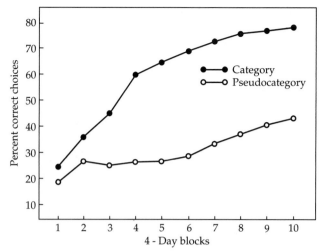

FIGURE 11.3. Acquisition of correct categorization responses when pigeons were required to sort pictures into categories and pseudocategories.

comes into a concept learning experiment with already formed concepts. Perhaps some cognitive representation or neural center is activated whenever a picture of a tree is shown, and this activation forms the basis for discrimination between pictures with and without trees. Herrnstein et al. (1976) raised the possibility that concepts might be genetic. The *genetic hypothesis* might suggest that, over eons of evolution, genes are selected that give rise to neural structures that respond when a tree, body of water, or particular predator appears. The problem with this hypothesis is that pigeons actually can learn to categorize a number of objects that are not present in their evolutionary history. Herrnstein et al. (1976) found that pigeons learned to respond only to pictures of a particular student at Harvard University. How could a pigeon have a genetic concept of a single person living in the 20th century? In research carried out by Herrnstein and de Villiers (1980), pigeons were trained to discriminate between underwater pictures that did and did not contain fish. Since pigeons did not evolve in an aquatic environment, they could not have evolved a concept of fish. Finally, Bhatt et al. (1988) found that pigeons could learn to accurately sort pictures of cars and chairs, manmade objects that did not even exist during the evolution of the contemporary pigeon.

These findings suggest that we must search within the pictorial stimuli used in categorization experiments to understand how pigeons form categories. A popular approach to understanding picture processing is to analyze a picture for its *features*. Unfortunately, the identification of features is a rather subjective enterprise. Features may exist along several different dimensions. Thus, we might describe a picture in terms of selected geometrical structures that occupy different parts of the picture and also in terms of the hue, brightness, and saturation of those parts. In addition, pictures have an emergent property of depicting a whole object or scene, which transcends the individual parts. Both the component parts and the whole scene may be features of a picture, and which of these is a functional stimulus at any given moment may depend on the process of attention discussed in Chapter 2.

Classical Feature Theory

An initial theoretical question that must be considered is the nature of the stimulus requirements for the definition of a concept. Much early research on human concept formation was based on *classical feature theory* (Smith & Medin, 1981). A subject is shown a number of cards containing geometric figures that vary in shape, size, color, and number. The subject guesses that a particular card is or is not a member of the concept the experimenter had in mind and receives feedback from the experimenter as to whether his response is correct or incorrect. Eventually, the subject learns to correctly identify each card as a member or nonmember of the concept. The identification of a particular category is based on learning that the correct concept is identified by a fixed set of features, such as three, large, green triangles. These four features—three, large, green, and triangle—are *necessary* and *sufficient* features for the concept. That is, all four features must be present, and no other features are required to identify the concept.

In numerous studies with animals, discrimination was required between stimuli that contained necessary and sufficient features. A pigeon was rewarded for pecking at a large blue triangle but not for pecking at a small yellow circle. The features that defined the positive and negative stimuli were easily defined and manipulated, and such discriminations were learned readily.

The discovery that animals can learn perceptual concepts based on pictures of natural or artificial objects proves difficult for classical feature theory to explain. The problem is that no feature is necessary or sufficient when pictures of complex objects that form real-world concepts are used. For example, it is agreed that green leaves are one feature of the concept of a tree. Yet, green leaves are not necessary to identify a picture as a tree; deciduous trees may be correctly identified when seen in the fall with red or yellow leaves or in the dead of winter with no leaves. Furthermore, by itself, green leaves may not define a tree; green leaves also appear on flowers, vegetables, and shrubbery. Perceptual concepts are often described as having the property of *polymorphism*, meaning that many different combinations of features may identify the items from the same category (Herrnstein, 1984; Jitsumori, 1993; S. E. G. Lea & Harrison, 1978). Perceptual categories have far more breadth and flexibility than was envisioned by classical feature theory.

Prototype Theory

Although the notion of a genetic representation of a category appears to be ruled out, it may be argued that such a representation is acquired from experience with category items. The term *prototype* refers to an original version of some object, after which later copies are modeled and thus are highly similar to the prototype. This order is reversed in prototype theory, which suggests that a prototype is built from a number of presented members of a category. Thus, a prototypical tree representation is constructed from seeing a number of reinforced tree pictures, or a prototypical bird representation is constructed from seeing a number of reinforced bird pictures. The prototype is an average of the examples shown from a particular category and contains all of the most common features appearing in those examples. New examples are then judged as members of the category to the extent that they resemble or contain the features contained in the prototype.

The strongest evidence for prototypical representations comes from research with human subjects. If people are asked to sort drawings or patterns into different categories, subsequent tests show that subjects respond to an average of the patterns that formed a particular category as being a particularly strong example of the category (Posner & Keele, 1968; Reed, 1972). Attempts to find prototype effects with animals have had limited success with simple patterns, such as sets of rectangles that vary in color and height (Aydin & Pearce, 1994; Pearce, 1989). No experiments have shown a prototype effect with the wide-ranging types of photographs used to demonstrate natural categories in animals. W. Roberts and Mazmanian (1988) demonstrated that squirrel monkeys learned to choose rewarded pictures that contained animals in preference to nonrewarded pictures that did not contain animals. The animals shown included insects, fish, amphibians, reptiles, and mammals, including human and nonhuman primates. It is difficult to conceive of a prototype or average animal that would encompass all of these diverse classes of animals.

Exemplar Theory

Unlike the genetic hypothesis and prototype theory, *exemplar theory* does not assume that categorization is based on the activation of a single representation of a concept. Exemplar theory holds that, over a number of trials, a subject stores in memory each picture exemplar and its response and outcome. If responses to flower pictures are always reinforced, and responses to cat pictures are nonreinforced, a library of reinforced pictures is stored that contains flowers, and a library of nonreinforced pictures is stored that contains cats. Thus far, this account sounds like the memorization explanation previously discredited. However, an important additional assumption made by this theory is that animals show *primary stimulus generalization* from one picture to another (Astley & Wasserman, 1992; Wasserman & Astley, 1994).

The importance of the process of stimulus generalization was originally discovered in experiments that varied stimuli along single physical dimensions, such as wavelength, sound intensity, or the angular orientation of a line (see Chapter 5). A pigeon trained to peck at a key illuminated with light of 555 nm for reward showed stronger response to lights of 545 and 565 nm than to lights of 525 or 585 nm. Generalization was shown by the tendency to respond strongly to stimuli close to the training stimulus, and *generalization decrement* was shown by the decline in response that occurred as the test stimulus was moved further away from the training stimulus.

Stimuli could be quantified easily along single dimensions, and it was assumed that points along a dimension excited neural structures that gave rise to sensations that became more dissimilar as the distance between stimuli increased. With complex pictures, however, dimensions of similarity become difficult to identify. Pictures may be more or less similar to the extent that they contain or do not contain common features, but, as already pointed out, it is often difficult to precisely identify the features of a picture. Nevertheless, people can readily judge pictures along a scale of similarity and typically rate pictures falling into a common linguistic category as more similar to one another than pictures falling into different linguistic categories. If we assume that pictures and the objects they represent vary in similarity for animals as they do for people, exemplar theory then provides a powerful analysis of concept learning experiments in animals.

Consider once again the findings shown in Figure 11.3. It was suggested that it was easier for pigeons to learn to make different responses to pictures that fell into categories than into pseudocategories. An additional factor may have limited pigeons' ability to learn to sort pictures in pseudocategories— errors arising from stimulus generalization. Suppose that a cat picture in one pseudocategory strongly resembles a cat picture in another pseudocategory. Through stimulus generalization, the correct key for response to the first cat may be pecked when the second cat is shown, and this response is registered as an error.

To examine this possibility more directly, Wasserman et al. (1988) carried out the following experiment. Pictures from two categories were shown; for example, a pigeon saw 20 pictures of different flowers and 20 pictures of different chairs. Furthermore, the pictures of flowers and chairs were divided into two sets of 10 pictures each, and different responses had to be made to each set of 10 pictures. Thus, the assignment of correct keys to pictures was first 10 flowers—upper-right key, second 10 flowers—lower-left key, first 10 chairs—upper-left key, and second 10 chairs—lower-right key. Pigeons learned to respond accurately to these four sets of pictures, reaching a level of choice slightly more than 70 percent correct. Of more interest was the analysis of errors that occurred during learning. This analysis showed that pigeons clearly confused pictures from the same perceptual category. For instance, when a picture from the first 10 flowers was shown, and an error was made, the error was far more likely to be choice of the lower-left key than choice of the upper-left or lower-right key. Similarly, when a chair from the second 10 chair pictures was shown, an error was most likely to be choice of the upper-left key. Wasserman et al. labeled these mistakes *conceptual errors.* When an error was made, the probability of making an error by striking any one of the remaining three keys by chance was 33 percent. By contrast, conceptual errors were made at a rate of 55 percent. This rate of conceptual errors was reached after about 40 sessions of training and was maintained throughout the remainder of the experiment, which lasted 112 sessions.

The findings of the pseudocategorization experiment and the conceptual errors experiment can be better understood with the aid of the diagram shown in Figure 11.4. This diagram makes the simplifying assumption that there is a single linear dimension along which pictorial stimuli can be placed, with stimuli close to one another being similar in appearance and stimuli distant from one another being dissimilar. The positions on this dimension of two sets of eight stimuli from two classes, A and B, are shown in the multiple-exemplars line at the top of the figure. The tendency for the response learned to these

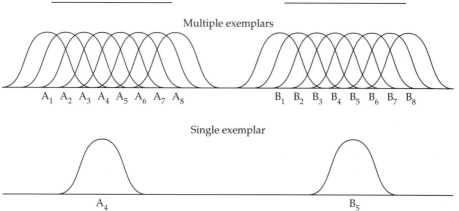

FIGURE 11.4. Curves show stimulus generalization of the tendency to respond to reinforced exemplars from two classes of picture stimuli, Class A and Class B. Notice the greater range along the dimension of similarity encompassed by multiple exemplars from either category than by a single exemplar.

stimuli to generalize to similar stimuli is shown by the Gaussian curves drawn above each stimulus. The generalization curves for stimuli within Classes A and B overlap with one another, but not with those for stimuli in the other class, because within-class similarity is high and between-class similarity is low. Note, however, that the generalization curves for stimuli in each class do not all overlap, showing that there is some dissimilarity among stimuli within classes and that stimuli within classes should be discriminable. The diagram suggests that experimental contingencies that require discrimination between classes leads to rapid learning, as in the category group, because each stimulus within a class benefits by stimulus generalization from adjacent similar stimuli within that class. On the other hand, experimental contingencies that require discrimination within classes promote slower learning, as in the pseudocategory group, because stimulus generalization among class members causes subjects to make conceptualization errors.

Consider tests with novel items. Suppose that a new picture from Class A is shown. It should be located some place along the dimension of stimulus similarity where other Class A stimuli are found. However, it does not reside at exactly the position any of the A_{1-8} stimuli occupy. If it resides between Stimuli A_3 and A_4, then, through stimulus generalization, there should be a tendency to respond to it as the subject learns to respond to A_3 and A_4. There should be little tendency to respond to it as a member of Class B stimuli since stimuli in the Class B region do not generalize that far along the scale. The new item then usually should be responded to as a Class A stimulus. Notice, however, that since the new item does not exactly match a previously trained item, the tendency to respond to it as a Class A stimulus is somewhat weakened through stimulus generalization decrement. As a consequence, novel items should be classified somewhat less well than trained items that have been presented repeatedly. This outcome is exactly what Figure 11.2 shows; although pigeons learned to correctly categorize both repeating and nonrepeating pictures, nonrepeating pictures were responded to somewhat less accurately than repeating pictures.

A further important implication of exemplar theory is that there should be an interaction between stimulus similarity and the number of exemplars learned. Examine the single exemplar line shown at the bottom of Figure 11.4. In this case, a subject was trained to respond to only one stimulus in each of Classes A and B. The subject's ability to correctly classify novel stimuli critically depends on their distance from the A_4 and B_5 training stimuli. Thus, Stimuli A_3 and A_5 and B_4 and B_6 are categorized correctly through stimulus generalization, but other stimuli more distant in similarity from A_4 and B_5 are not. Wasserman and Bhatt (1992) provided evidence that supports this model. Pigeons were trained to peck different keys when pictures of cats, cars, flowers, and chairs were shown, as in the category condition previously described, but the number of different pictures from each category varied among three groups of subjects. Group 1 was trained to categorize with only one picture in each category, Group 4 with four pictures in each category, and Group 12 with 12 pictures in each category. Group 1 learned to discriminate pictures faster than Group 4, which, in turn, learned faster than Group 12. When all three groups reached a criterion of learning, they were tested with 32 novel pictures, eight from each category. The effect of number of training exemplars on ability to generalize to novel pictures was just the opposite of its effect on rate of learning. The percentage of correct responses made to novel items was 27 percent for Group 1, 45 percent for Group 4, and 62 percent for Group 12. Just as the model depicted in Figure 11.4 suggests, the more exemplars along a dimension of similarity that were sampled within a class, the better animals generalized to new items.

Further evidence supports the idea that training with a single exemplar leads to accurate categorization if test stimuli are highly similar to the training stimulus. Cerella (1979) trained pigeons to peck at a picture of a single oak leaf and not to peck at pictures of non-oak leaves (see Figure 11.5). When subjects were tested with 40 novel pictures of oak leaves, they showed perfect generalization to these new pictures. If oak leaves are examined, however, their shapes are found to be highly similar. If stimuli are close to one another in similarity, training with a single exemplar may be sufficient to produce strong within-class generalization.

Let us return to the W. Roberts and Mazmanian (1988) study mentioned earlier. That study showed that squirrel monkeys could learn to discriminate pictures of animals from pictures that did not contain animals, although the animal pictures varied from shots of insects to shots of mammals. Any dimension of similarity that encompassed the entire animal kingdom would have to be very long, with animals at one end bearing little resemblance to animals at the other end. Thus, there are regions of this dimension that show no stimulus generalization to other regions. Nevertheless, exemplar theory can account for the categorization behavior found in this study. First of all, it took considerable training with many exemplars for monkeys to begin to accurately discriminate

FIGURE 11.5. Patterns of oak leaves are shown in the top row, and patterns of non-oak leaves are shown in the bottom row. Pigeons were trained to discriminate the center oak leaf and then were tested with novel oak leaf and non-oak leaf patterns, such as the remaining patterns seen in the figure.

animal from nonanimal pictures. During this period, monkeys may have built mini-libraries of reinforced pictures within different classes of animals. Thus, collections of reinforced pictures were stored for insects, fish, amphibians, reptiles, birds, and mammals. Eventually, enough reinforced pictures were stored within each class to allow novel pictures to be accurately classified by stimulus generalization. Even though a spider may not resemble a buffalo, correct classification of either type of picture can occur if sufficient insect pictures are stored so that one resembles the novel spider picture and sufficient mammal pictures are stored so that one resembles the novel buffalo picture.

In conclusion, it should be emphasized that exemplar theory is based on perceptual similarity. Although future research may eventually find evidence for higher-order category representations in animals, such as labels or prototypes, most of the current evidence on picture classification can be explained by perceptual resemblance and stimulus generalization (Wasserman, 1995). The fact that animals often sort pictorial images into the same categories as people do suggests a high degree of isomorphism or agreement between human and nonhuman primates and pigeons. That this may not always be so, however, was suggested by another finding reported by W. Roberts and Mazmanian (1988). They found that both pigeons and monkeys found it difficult to discriminate between birds and other classes of animals, even though people did so quite easily. This finding suggests that perceived similarity between objects in the world may not always be identical in people and animals. Future investigations of perceived similarity among objects in different species may inform us about differences in the way humans and animals dissect the perceptual world.

RELATIONAL CONCEPT LEARNING

In the perceptual concept learning experiments just discussed, animals were required to respond to the *absolute properties* of stimuli—to judge one stimulus in terms of its similarity to another stimulus. At a more abstract level, animals can be asked to learn about *relational properties* among stimuli. Whereas only stimuli that looked similar or shared common features were placed in the same category in perceptual concept learning, sets of stimuli that have no perceptual features in common but share a common relationship may still be judged to fall into the same category in relational concept learning. One example of a relational concept can be found in the absolute numerical discrimination problems reviewed in Chapter 10. Animals learned to respond to the number of items presented in an array, even though the items presented and their arrangement changed from one trial to the next. The concept of *number* was contained in the relationship among the items.

Human subjects are commonly asked to make same/different judgments in psychology laboratories. A subject may be shown pairs of words or pictures, which are presented either in rapid succession or side-by-side, and the subject must indicate whether the items are the same or different. A typical procedure has the subject press one key for a same response and another key for a different response. Subjects quickly learn to perform this task and typically make few errors. The data of importance are usually the subject's latency to respond, which reflects the time required to make decisions about different pairs of items. Notice that in this task, the items presented on successive trials may have no resemblance to one another. That is, a pair of human faces might appear on one trial and a pair of buildings might appear on the next. Nevertheless, the same relationship may appear on both trials. If the two faces are identical and the two buildings are identical, then the relationship of sameness or identity is the same between the two pair of stimuli. If the two faces are not the same and the two buildings are not the same, then the same relationship of difference exists between the two pair.

A number of investigators studied whether animals can learn a *same/different concept*. D. Premack (1983) argued that many animal species are capable of forming perceptual concepts based on similarity of the absolute properties of stimuli and suggested that this ability arises from the use of an *imaginal code*. The imaginal code is closely tied to the perceptual properties of objects. Beyond the imaginal code, D. Premack suggested that relational judgments, such as same and different, require an *abstract code*. In this case, an organism must be able to abstract the same relationship from a variety of perceptual situations that have no absolute features in common. D. Premack advanced the hypothesis that only humans and other primates possessed an abstract code and that, among primates, use of the abstract code is only manifested in animals that undergo training on a symbolic language system.

One means of testing D. Premack's (1983) hypothesis is to look for evidence of relational concept learning in nonprimate animals. In fact, several types of relational learning studies have been carried out with pigeons. Matching-to-sample with identical sample and comparison stimuli may be used for this purpose. In Chapter 4, it was pointed out that early transfer experiments generally failed to offer much support for the idea that pigeons had learned the rule, "Peck the comparison stimulus that looks like the sample stimulus." Pigeons trained to peck a red key when shown a red sample stimulus and to peck a green key when shown a green sample stimulus showed little ability to match-to-sample when a yellow stimulus was introduced. These findings led to the suggestion that pigeons learned specific "if–then" rules about which response to make after each sample, rather than a general matching rule (Carter & Werner, 1978; Cumming & Berryman, 1965; Farthing & Opuda, 1974).

Other research offered some support for the idea that pigeons could learn a general relational rule. In these experiments, one group of pigeons was trained to match-to-sample and a second group was trained to nonmatch-to-sample. If the sample was red and the comparison stimuli were red and green, the matching group learned to peck red for reward, and the nonmatching group learned to peck green for reward. When birds had learned to match or nonmatch at a high level of accuracy, they were switched to discrimination problems involving new stimuli. In some experiments, these stimuli were new colors, such as yellow and blue, and, in other experiments, these stimuli were from a new dimension, such as a white circle and a plus on a black background. Half the subjects in each group were transferred to problems that required the same relational response as the first problem in order to obtain reward. These subgroups involved matching-matching and nonmatching-nonmatching sequences of problems and were designated *nonshifted* groups. The other half of the subjects in each group learned new problems that required the opposite relational response to the one learned in the original problem. These subgroups learned matching-nonmatching and nonmatching-matching sequences and were called *shifted* groups. The question of interest was whether nonshifted birds would show a higher level of performance than shifted birds.

In general, experiments of this nature showed better performance in non-shifted than in shifted groups (Zentall & Hogan, 1974; 1976; 1978). The findings from one such experiment (Zentall & Hogan, 1974) are shown in Figure 11.6. Pigeons were trained with red and green sample and comparison stimuli and then transferred to new discriminations with yellow and blue stimuli. The non-shifted curve depicts the average performance of matching-matching and non-matching-nonmatching subgroups, and the shifted curve depicts the average performance of matching-nonmatching and nonmatching-matching sub-groups. Performance in Session 1 is particularly important in such experiments because it reveals immediate transfer of learning between problems. Subjects in the shifted condition were slightly below the chance level of 50 percent on Session 1, but subjects in the nonshifted condition made about 60 percent correct responses. This difference was maintained throughout a number of subsequent sessions of learning.

In subsequent research (Zentall & Hogan, 1978), pigeons were trained over three successive discriminations. After initially learning matching and non-matching discriminations with circle and plus stimuli, birds were transferred to shifted and nonshifted discriminations with red and green stimuli. Finally, these birds were transferred to shifted and nonshifted discriminations with yellow and blue cues. By the third problem, nonshifted birds performed at 82 percent accuracy on the first session of acquisition, but shifted birds performed at

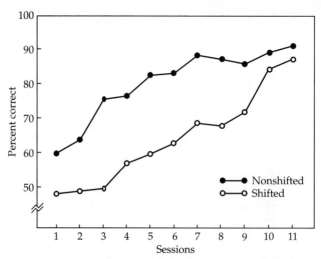

FIGURE 11.6. Acquisition of a transfer discrimination by groups of pigeons that were nonshifted (matching-matching or nonmatching-nonmatching) and by groups of pigeons that were shifted (matching-nonmatching or nonmatching-matching). The initial problem required discrimination between red and green stimuli, and the transfer problem required discrimination between yellow and blue stimuli.

.

only 42 percent accuracy. Training with three sets of stimuli appeared to promote positive transfer of relational concept learning.

The importance of training with multiple stimuli was shown dramatically in a study reported by Wright, Cook, Rivera, Sands, and Delius (1988). In an innovative piece of apparatus, pigeons were shown sample and comparison stimuli on a videomonitor mounted in the floor of an operant chamber. When a pigeon pecked at the correct picture, grain was dispensed from a tube directly onto the stimulus. In this way, birds ate in a natural fashion—off the ground— and they closely associated reward with the correct choice. Two groups of pigeons were trained. One group was trained with 152 different cartoon pictures, like those shown in Figure 11.7. This group received *trial-unique* stimulus presentation because different sample and comparison stimuli were presented on every trial of the 76-trial sessions. The other group was trained with the same two stimuli used on every session, with each stimulus alternating as sample and incorrect comparison stimulus over trials within a session. It took the trial-unique group substantially longer to reach a criterion of 75 percent correct responses than it did the two-stimulus group. Upon reaching criterion, both groups were tested with 20 novel pictures, intermixed among the training pictures. As shown in Figure 11.8, both groups matched at about 80 percent accuracy when tested with the training or baseline stimuli. However, when the novel or transfer stimuli were presented, the trial-unique group was still at 80 percent accurate, whereas the two-stimulus group dropped to only sightly better than the chance level of 50 percent matching. This study clearly shows that pigeons can learn a matching concept if training is carried out with a wide

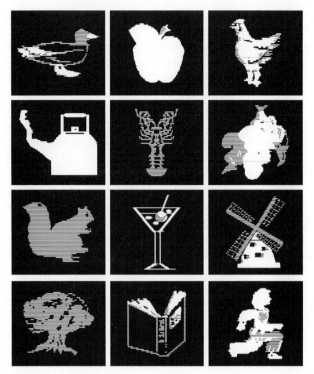

FIGURE 11.7. Examples of the cartoon pictures pigeons saw as sample and comparison stimuli in a matching concept experiment. A different pair of stimuli could be shown on each trial within a session.

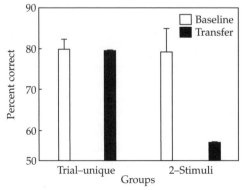

FIGURE 11.8. The percentage of correct matching responses made by pigeons in a group trained with trial-unique stimuli and in a group trained with only two stimuli. Baseline tests refer to performance with training stimuli, and transfer tests refer to performance with novel stimuli.

variety of items. These findings show an interesting parallel to the Wasserman and Bhatt (1992) finding that pigeons learned a perceptual concept better with a large number of category exemplars. In both cases, it appears that pigeons needed to experience a wide variety of examples of a concept before it was learned.

In a somewhat different version of the same/different experiment, pigeons are shown a centrally located key with two stimuli on it, one on the left half of the key and the other on the right half. If the two stimuli are the same (both red or both green), then the correct response is to peck another key located on the right. However, if the two stimuli are different (one side is red and the other is green), then the correct response is to peck a key to the left of the center key. In a procedural variation of this experiment, only the single central key is used, and subjects must learn to peck for reward when either the same or different stimuli appear on it and to inhibit pecking when the opposite relationship is shown. Tests for transfer are then carried out with new stimuli, as in the experiments previously described. Early experiments of this type showed varying degrees of positive transfer with new stimuli (Honig, 1965; R. Malott, K. Malott, Svinicki, Kladder, & Ponicki, 1971; Zentall & Hogan, 1975).

In a later variation, Santiago and Wright (1984) used a pool of 210 different pictures. Pigeons were given 70 trials per session, with no picture repetitions. On each trial, pictures appeared on two screens; the pictures were either identical or different. Pecks to keys on the right and left of the screens yielded reward when same and different pictures were presented, respectively. After training to a criterion of 88 percent accuracy on six sets of 70 different pairs of items, birds were tested with 20 novel items intermixed with training pictures. Both of the pigeons trained and tested in this manner made about 70 percent correct same/different responses on novel pairs of pictures, again indicating that pigeons are capable of learning this relational concept.

A tempting conclusion from the findings just reviewed is that pigeons can learn the same/different concept only after training with many different sets of stimuli. A recent finding suggests that this is not the case. Wright (1997) trained pigeons to match-to-sample using combinations of only three stimuli: cartoon drawings of a duck, an apple, and some grapes. Four groups of pigeons were trained, with each group required to make a different number of peck responses on the sample stimulus picture to turn on the comparison stimuli. The fixed ratio (FR) on the sample was 0, 1, 10, or 20 pecks. Thus, given a duck picture sample stimulus, pigeons in different groups would have to peck at the duck picture 0, 1, 10, or 20 times to attain a choice between duck and apple or duck and grapes comparison stimuli. When each group reached a criterion of 70 percent or better matching accuracy, tests were carried out with 50 novel pairs of stimuli. Pigeons trained with an FR 20 on the sample stimulus matched equally well with training and novel displays of stimuli (about 80 percent correct). Performance with novel stimuli declined as the FR declined to 10, 1, and 0.

Wright's (1997) findings indicate that pigeons do not need to be trained with large numbers of sample and comparison stimuli to learn a same/different relationship. Simply requiring a large number of responses to the sample stimulus leads to relational learning. Wright argued that pigeons trained with a small FR requirement learned only configurational or item-specific responses.

Examples of item-specific learning are learning to go left each time a configuration appeared with duck in the middle, duck on the left side, and apple on the right side and learning to peck right each time the configuration contained duck in the middle, duck on the right, and apple on the left. The effect of higher FRs on the sample stimulus may have been to break up this configurational learning and to force pigeons to learn the relationships between sample and comparison stimuli.

Nonhuman primates learn the same/different concept rapidly. In a study with infant chimpanzees by Oden, Thompson, and Premack (1988), five young chimpanzees were initially trained to match-to-sample with two objects—a lock and a cup. The subject was handed one of these objects as a sample and allowed to put it in a container. A matching object and a nonmatching object were then offered, and choice of the matching object was rewarded with food and social reinforcement. After a chimpanzee mastered this discrimination to better than 80 percent accuracy, it was tested on six more problems with new stimuli on each one; the new stimuli used were two pairs of objects, two pairs of pieces of fabric, and two pairs of food items. There were 12 trials given with each pair of novel items, and, of particular interest, the chimpanzees were not differentially reinforced for their choices on these transfer tests. Overall, the young chimpanzees chose the matching item on 81 percent of the test trials, with choice of the matching item on the first trial with each novel pair being 77 percent. The important aspect of this study is that once the chimpanzees were trained to match with a single pair of items, they could transfer the matching concept to a variety of novel stimuli.

Chimpanzees also show evidence of same/different conceptualization in sorting tasks. In such tasks, chimpanzees are given several objects, such as toys or utensils, that vary in color. Combinations of items of one type, A, and of another type, B, are presented. These combinations might be AAB, AABB, AAAB, AAABB, or AAABBB. Note that there are a number of ways in which these combinations can be divided into subsets. However, several studies report evidence that chimpanzees tend to sort items by identity or similarity (Matsuzawa, 1990; Spinozzi, 1993; Tanaka, 1995). Given two trays, for example, chimpanzees tend to place all of the A items on one tray and the B item(s) on the other tray.

Tanaka (1995) also reported that chimpanzees learned to sort objects on the basis of their complementary relationship. When given two items that complement one another, such as a bottle and cap, and a third odd item, the chimpanzees tended to place the complementary items on one tray and the odd item on another tray. Complementary sorting occurred only after chimpanzees had an opportunity to learn the relationship between the complementary objects. In this case, the relationship that formed the basis for conceptual sorting was not identity but the functional relationship between two objects that fit together or were used together.

Chimpanzees are also capable of understanding second-order same/different relationships (D. Premack, 1983; D. Premack & A. Premack, 1983). Suppose that instead of showing a chimpanzee two objects and asking it to identify the relationship as same or different, we present the chimpanzee with two *pairs* of objects, and ask it to respond "same" or "different" with respect to the first-order relationship. In this case, the animal is asked to make a second-order judgment about the perceptual identity or difference contained in first-order relationships. Although the pairs compared with one another have no similarity to one another, the correct answer may be "same." For example, a chimpanzee is shown two identical books and two identical forks. The correct answer is "same" because the relationship contained within each pair is the same; one book is the same as the other book, and one fork is the same as the other fork. On other tests, the pairs to be compared might be two flowers compared with a pencil and an apple. In this case, the chimpanzee makes a response that indicates "different" since the relationship shown within the flower pair is different from that shown between the pencil and apple.

Tests for the understanding of relationships can be carried to still the third order and beyond. A subject can be asked if the relationships shown between two sets of pairs are the same or different. For example, is the relationship shown between AA and BB the same as or different from the relationship shown between XX and YY? The answer is same, as it would be for the relationship between the pairs AB and CC and the pairs XY and ZZ. On the other hand, the answer would be different if the subject were asked to compare the pairs AA and BB with the pairs XX and YZ. The ability to correctly conceptualize higher-order relationships may be an important way of distinguishing between levels of abstract thought in humans and animals (Gleitman, 1981). Only further research will inform us about higher-order conceptual abilities in animals. Thus far, however, only chimpanzees that have had symbolic language training or that have learned to match symbols to same-different relationships have been shown to correctly respond to second-order conceptual problems (R. Thompson & Oden, 1993; R. Thompson, Oden, & Boysen, 1997).

ASSOCIATIVE CONCEPT LEARNING

Both perceptual concept learning and relational concept learning in animals involve visual discrimination between visual stimuli based on similarity. The perceptual concept learning tasks discussed required animals to categorize pictures based on the similarity of their features. In relational concept learning, decisions about the relationship between two objects had to be made on the basis of their identical or different appearance. In addition to making these kind of conceptual decisions easily, people deal with abstract concepts that have no physical similarity. For example, a number of objects may be conceptualized under terms such as "foods" or "tools" because these objects have common functions, although they do not look alike. Presumably, people have higher-order associations with common uses for these objects, and this ties them together conceptually. In this section, the possibility that animals also might be able to learn higher-order concepts based on associations is explored.

When an animal perceives a stimulus in an operant learning task, two events typically follow: The animal responds to the stimulus, and this response yields an outcome, either some form of reward or nonreward. Some years ago, Tolman (1959) suggested that associations of stimulus-response-outcome (S-R-O) formed the basis for expectancies. Given a stimulus, an animal could anticipate its response and outcome based on the formation of S-S associations through contiguity. Suppose that in some cases, several stimuli enter into association with either a common response and/or a common outcome. These stimuli might become grouped together through a common association. Several findings with animal subjects suggest that, in fact, groups of otherwise unrelated stimuli do come to act as a common unit or concept when associated with common responses or outcomes.

Associative Concepts Based on a Common Response

It is important that, in experiments on associative concepts, stimuli are used that have no greater intraclass similarity than interclass similarity. In this way, any evidence that stimuli are treated as a single category cannot be attributed to perceptual categorization. Assume that two sets of stimuli, A, B, C, D and W, X, Y, Z, have this property. Thus, Stimuli A, B, C, and D are not more similar to one another than they are to Stimuli W, X, Y, and Z. Through training, Stimuli A, B, C, and D are associated with one response, R1, and Stimuli W, X, Y, and Z are associated with a different response, R2. We now ask whether these two sets of stimuli have become separate categories through their association with a common response. One way to test this question is through the use of an *instance-to-category generalization test* (S. E$_1$. G. Lea, 1984). Suppose that two of the stimuli in each set are now trained to be associated with different responses; Stimuli A and B become associated with R3, and Stimuli W and X become associated with R4. If these stimuli are treated as members of a common category, there should be some tendency for Stimuli C and D to elicit response R3 and for stimuli Y and Z to elicit response R4.

Vaughan (1988) presented pigeons with 40 pictures of trees, which were divided randomly but consistently into two sets of 20 each (Set A and Set B). Pecks on a red key adjacent to the screen containing a picture were reinforced when a Set A picture was presented and were nonreinforced when a Set B picture was presented. When pigeons clearly discriminated between Sets A and B by responding to Set A pictures and withholding response to Set B pictures, the reinforcement contingencies were reversed, and pigeons had to learn to peck at presentation of Set B pictures for reinforcement and not to peck at presentation of Set A pictures, which now were nonreinforced. After this reversal was learned, a third and further reversals of the reinforcement contingencies were trained. After a number of reversals, birds began to respond accurately to pictures in each set after only a few pictures with the reversal had been experienced. To be specific, after 30 reversals, pigeons began to respond more to reinforced pictures than to nonreinforced after the 12th slide of a reversal had been shown. In other words, the responses made to the initial pictures of either set within a reversal generalized to the remaining pictures in the same set. Pigeons learned to treat pictures in each set as categories based on the consistency of the responses required during the earlier stages of training.

Notice that in the Vaughan (1988) study, initial instances of a category were reversed in meaning or significance from reinforced to nonreinforced or from nonreinforced to reinforced, leading to a change in response from pecking to nonpecking or from nonpecking to pecking. The instance-to-category generalization

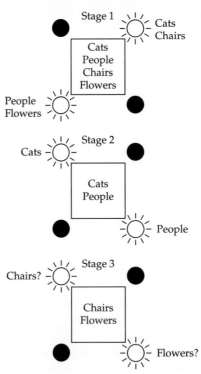

FIGURE 11.9. Diagram shows the three stages of an experiment that revealed associative conceptualization by common response. Stages 2 and 3 involve an instance-to-category transfer test based on the common-response training given in Stage 1.
From Wasserman, Devolder, & Coppage, 1992.

was shown by the change in response to pictures shown later in a reversal session. Vaughan suggested that pigeons had formed *equivalence sets.* Changing the response required to a few members of a category propagated this change throughout all members of the category (Herrnstein, 1990). Category membership had to be based on prior training with common responses because pictures in Set A looked no more similar to one another than they did to pictures in Set B.

Consider an experiment by Wasserman, Devolder, and Coppage (1992) as a second example of categorization by common response. Figure 11.9 depicts an apparatus containing a central screen with a key at each corner. In Stage 1, pigeons viewed 48 slide-projected pictures sequentially on the screen, 12 each from the categories flowers, people, chairs, and cats. The order of the pictures was random and changed from one session to the next. Only the diagonally located keys at the lower-left and upper-right corners of the screen were lit for pecking. Pictures from pairs of perceptual categories required the same response for reward. Thus, whenever a picture of a cat or a chair appeared, only a response to the upper-right key produced reward. Similarly, only a response to the lower-left key yielded reward when a picture of a person or flower was shown. Pigeons acquired this discrimination over a number of training sessions.

The question then addressed was whether new hybrid categories were formed through a common response, one made up of cat and chairs and the other of people and flowers. An instance-to-category generalization test was carried out in Stages 2 and 3. As the middle diagram in Figure 11.9 shows, pigeons in Stage 2 were presented with only the cats and people pictures from Stage 1, and responses could be made only to the upper-left and bottom-right keys. Only responses to the upper-left key were reinforced when cat pictures were shown, and only responses to the lower-right key were reinforced when people pictures were shown. Thus, half the items in each set that required a common response in Stage 1 were now associated with a different response in Stage 2. Note that these instances bore very little similarity to the nontrained members of the category; that is, cats do not look like chairs, and people do not look like flowers.

In Stage 3, chair and flower pictures were presented intermixed with cat and people pictures, and, as in Stage 2, only the upper-left and lower-right keys could be pecked for reward. If the new responses learned to cat and people pictures generalized to chair and cat pictures by virtue of the common response training given in Stage 1, pigeons should have preferred to peck the upper-left key when chair pictures were shown and the lower-right key when flower pictures were shown. These preferences were shown clearly; pigeons responded in agreement with Stage 1 categorization training on 72 percent of the test trials. Apparently, classes of pictures that had low visual similarity to one another could be combined into a new superclass by requiring that they elicit a common response.

Associative Concepts Based on a Common Outcome

Suppose that the members of a set of stimuli each require a different response, but each response yields a common outcome. Would these stimulus-response sequences form a category based on the common outcome? In an experiment carried out by Olthof, Macuda and W. Roberts (1995), rats were trained to run down the arms of a 12-arm radial maze with different outcomes (rewards) placed in food cups at the end of each arm. The arms on the maze were divided randomly into two sets of six arms each, Set A and Set B. On any given session, all of the arms in one set contained a small piece of chocolate, and all of the arms in the other set contained a Noyes pellet, a standard reward pellet for rats. Because each arm presents a different stimulus or location in space and entering each arm is a different response, the experiment provides an opportunity to examine the hypothesis that a common outcome alone can lead to categorization.

During 30 sessions of training, the outcome placed on arms in Sets A and B changed randomly from session to session. Thus, the assignment on one session might be chocolate in Set A arms and Noyes pellets in Set B arms, and the assignment on the next session might be Noyes pellets in Set A arms and chocolate in Set B arms. This procedure is analogous to the picture-response reversal procedure used by Vaughan (1988) with pigeons. It is important to remember that rats have a strong preference for chocolate over Noyes pellets and enter arms containing chocolate before arms containing Noyes pellets if the same arms always contain these rewards (Macuda & W. Roberts, 1995).

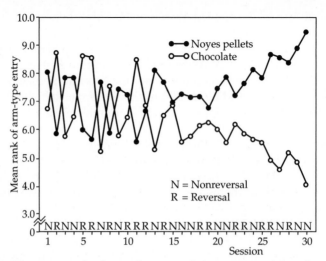

FIGURE 11.10. The mean rank of entry into sets of six arms containing chocolate or Noyes pellets as reward on a 12-arm radial maze. The assignment of chocolate and Noyes pellets to sets of arms was either nonreversed (N) or reversed (R) randomly over 30 sessions of training.
From Olthof, Macuda, & W. Roberts, 1995.

In Figure 11.10, preferences for arms containing chocolate and Noyes pellets are shown by plotting mean rank of entrance into arms containing each type of reward over sessions. A low mean rank means early entrance into arms of that type, and a high mean rank means late entrance. The letters N and R indicate the initial assignment of reward types to sets of arms (nonreversal = N) and the reversal (R) of that initial assignment. Through the first 15 sessions, little difference between the rewards appeared. Over Sessions 16 through 30, however, there emerged a clear preference for entering arms containing chocolate before arms containing Noyes pellets. Importantly, this preference was equally strong on N and R sessions. These data indicate that rats only needed to sample the outcome on an initial arm or two of a session to find out which set contained chocolate, and they then entered the remaining chocolate arms before entering the Noyes pellets arms. Just as in the Vaughan (1988) study, the initial choices of a session served to inform the subject about the change in outcome for a few members of a category, and the subsequent behavior on the radial maze showed instance-to-category generalization.

SUMMARY

A concept or category is said to have been learned when an organism responds to a group of stimuli in the same way because these stimuli have common properties. The properties stimuli have in common may differ. Concepts may be based on common perceptual properties, common relational properties, and common associational properties. Evidence for these types of conceptualization is found in both human and animal cognition.

Animals show evidence of perceptual concepts by learning to discriminate among pictures that fall into the same linguistic classes used by humans. Thus, pigeons shown pictures of cats, cars, flowers, and chairs can accurately discriminate among the classes of pictures by pecking different keys when pictures from different classes are presented. Even when novel pictures never seen before appear, they are accurately categorized. In general, perceptual concepts are learned best when a large number of diverse members of each category are used in training.

The stimuli classified in perceptual concept studies are described as polymorphic because many different combinations of a large set of features make up different members of a class. The ability to classify such stimuli is not easily explained by classical feature theory because no feature appears to be necessary or sufficient to define a class. Perceptual categories do not appear to be innate or carried in the genes because pigeons can learn to select items from categories based on human artifacts that did not exist during the evolution of the pigeon. Since animals can learn a category as broad as animals in general, it seems unlikely that a prototype or average member of the category serves as a representation of the concept. A theory based on the storage of memory of individual exemplars of a class seems to best account for the available findings. An important assumption of this theory is that animals relate members of a perceptual class to one another through stimulus generalization. Thus, classification of novel class members occurs because members of a perceptual class typically generalize strongly to one another and weakly to members of other perceptual classes.

Although perceptual concepts depend on identifying similarities among the absolute properties of stimuli, relational categories depend on identifying common perceptual relationships among different sets of stimuli. In the same/different relationship, two pair of objects that bear no perceptual relationship to one another may be instances of the same concept if the relationships of items within the pairs are both same or both different. Some evidence for relational concept learning has been reported in studies with pigeons. The typical experiment involves training subjects to perform an identity matching-to-sample discrimination or a same/different discrimination and then transferring the subjects to performance of the same relational discrimination with a new set of stimuli. Pigeons show positive transfer to new stimuli, and the degree of transfer is highest when birds are trained either with a large number of examples of same and different stimuli or are required to make a large number of pecking responses on a sample stimulus. Chimpanzees readily mastered the concept of sameness after training with only one pair of objects.

Some recent experiments suggest that animals are able to form conceptual categories among stimuli based only on a common association. Although the stimuli within two sets are no more similar to one another than they are to members of the other set, these sets may form independent categories if members of each set are associated with a different common response. A group of pictures associated with pecking a particular key in an operant chamber become a category different from the category associated with pecking another key in the chamber. Evidence from radial maze studies indicates that collections of maze arms may also become categorized based on common reward outcomes experienced on the arms. Evidence for categorization through common response or outcome associations is found in instance-to-category tests; if a subset of the members of a category becomes associated with a new response or outcome, the other members of the category show evidence that the new association has been propagated to them as well. These examples of associative concepts in animal cognition may be simple analogs of the complex, abstract concepts we find in human cognition.

CHAPTER 12

Primate Cognition

In the preceding chapters, experiments with monkeys and apes were included in the discussion of various topics, including memory, spatial cognition, serial learning, numerical processing, and concept learning. Why, then, is an additional chapter needed on the topic of primate cognition? The answer lies in the unique evolutionary position nonhuman primates occupy relative to human primates and the types of research this relationship has inspired. On the evolutionary tree, monkeys and apes are related most closely to people, with apes being our nearest relatives. It is generally agreed that at some point in our evolutionary history, an ancestor of the modern chimpanzee, *Pan,* and an ancestor of contemporary humans, *homo,* diverged from a common ancestor. There is considerable disagreement as to when this division occurred, with estimates ranging from 3 million to 15 million years ago (Coppens, 1994). As a result of this relatively recent common ancestry of humans and apes (in evolutionary time), humans and apes are estimated to share about 99% DNA in common (Byrne, 1995). DNA, or deoxyribonucleic acid, forms the genetic material that directs the pre- and postnatal development of an organism's structure and behavior. Thus, both recency of common descent and degree of shared genetic makeup suggest that humans and apes share many cognitive and behavioral traits. In addition to this scientific evidence, people have a "natural curiosity" about the abilities of these animals that appear to resemble us.

It is often suggested that psychological studies of nonhuman primate cognition concern advanced or higher cognitive processes. From an evolutionary standpoint, however, one process is not higher than another (Hodos & C. Campbell, 1969; C. Campbell & Hodos, 1991). Many different physical structures and abilities allow different species to adapt to different environments and to survive; these mechanisms differ greatly between species and should not be put on a scale of superiority. Nevertheless, the adaptive characteristics of hominoids have been particularly cognitive, and we may ask to what extent our closest ancestral relatives share these characteristics. Thus, studies of nonhuman primate cognition are often directed at questions about the extent to which monkeys and apes show hominoid abilities. This endeavor has been seen as both frightening and enlightening. For those who fear for human uniqueness, studies of primate intelligence are seen as attempts to demonstrate that all human abilities can be revealed in animals. Others see such studies as a means of illuminating our evolutionary roots and determining which human abilities are genuinely unique.

The topics covered in this chapter include communication and the ape-language controversy, abstract reasoning, theory of mind, the self-concept, social intelligence, imitation, and tool construction and use by primates. A few points about the investigation of these topics should be made. First, examples of humanlike cognition in nonhuman primates often appear only after substantial training and new learning by a subject. This point, of course, is true of most of the research thus far discussed in this book. However, the amount of training given monkeys and apes in laboratory studies often far exceeds that given to rats and pigeons. In some cases, primate subjects spend their entire lives serving as laboratory subjects. Some years ago, Harlow (1949) showed that rhesus monkeys given a large number of discrimination problems in succession between novel stimuli showed marked improvement in their rate of learning. After several hundred such problems, a monkey needed only one informational trial to tell it which stimulus was correct or incorrect, and it could immediately respond correctly on subsequent trials with the same stimuli. Harlow argued that monkeys learned how to learn or formed a *learning set.* Most of the sophisticated cognitive abilities reported in the primate literature are performed by animals with a highly developed learning set. That is, these animals' ability to rapidly acquire a new task and perform it well has been honed by a long history of training in past experiments that usually bear some similarity to the current task. It is often remarked that primate subjects perform cognitive feats that far exceed anything seen in or demanded of members of that species in a natural setting. Although years of laboratory experience may underlie this difference, it should be realized that complex cognitive behavior could not be demonstrated in primates if the neural basis for learning and understanding new tasks was not already present.

Although much of primate cognition research appears to be driven by comparative questions, this research also gives us a deeper understanding of the minds of nonhuman primates. Despite the fact that apes share a common ancestor and considerable genetic material with people, they evolved with different adaptations to environmental demands. Their processing and understanding of information may not always mirror that of humans but may show unique variations that can be revealed by careful research and observation (Cheney & Seyfarth, 1990c). Of course, a better understanding of how a monkey or ape views the world can only help us better answer comparative questions about differences and similarities between human and nonhuman primates.

Finally, as a word of warning, controversy abounds in the field of primate cognition, apparently far more than in other areas of animal cognition. This is understandable because claims of complex humanlike abilities in animals are made far more frequently in primate cognition research than in research with nonprimate species. As described in Chapter 1, the early anecdotal approach to animal cognition was rife with claims of human abilities found in animals. In reaction to the anthropomorphic nature of these claims and the poor science upon which they were based, animal psychology swung toward the study of behavior in highly controlled experiments, with internal processes defined operationally. Within this conservative framework and a concern that history does not repeat itself, claims of the discovery of human cognitive processes in animals often meet with resistance. Critics of reported new discoveries often argue that the data have been overinterpreted with a bias toward anthropomorphism or that the experiments did not adequately control for Clever Hans effects or other sources of artifact. An even-handed approach is taken in this chapter, with both sides of these controversies discussed.

COMMUNICATION IN PRIMATES

Linguist Charles Hockett devised a list of design features or properties that define human languages (Hockett, 1960). Some of these properties, listed in this paragraph, particularly describe the symbolic and flexible nature of language and provide a basis for a comparative analysis of communication. (1) One important property of human language is *semanticity*, which means that the words or signs used stand for other things, such as objects, actions, or concepts. Although this point seems obvious, it became a major concern in studies of ape sign language. (2) Human language has the property of *arbitrariness*, meaning there is no inherent relationship between the thing represented and its sign. A good example of arbitrariness is the fact that different languages throughout the world use different words to describe the same things. (3) Human language frequently shows *displacement*, in that we communicate about things that are distant in time and space from our present location. (4) A hallmark of human language is its *productivity* or *generativity*; each of us can speak unlimited different phrases and sentences by combining the words in our vocabulary in different orders. (5) An important further property of productive communication in human language is *syntax*. Syntax refers to the fact that words fall into certain categories and that a language requires words from these categories to follow one another in a particular order. (6) Humans acquire language through learning or *traditional transmission*. Thus, children learn the particular language of their culture from their parents. In contrast to a language transmitted by learning, other communication systems found in animals may be transmitted genetically. The bee dance language and the stickleback fish mating ritual described in Chapter 9 are examples of stereotyped communication systems transmitted genetically and used for a limited function. (7) A final characteristic of human language that may be particularly unique to humans is *duality of patterning*. All of the thousands of words of a spoken language are formed by recombining a limited number of basic speech sounds or phonemes. For example, the words *tea* and *eat* mean different things but are formed by opposite orderings of two basic sounds.

Signaling in Wild Primates

A particularly good example of vocal communication with discriminative semantic content has been discovered in vervet monkeys. Struhsaker (1967) reported that vervet monkeys living in Amboseli National Park in Kenya emitted distinctly different alarm calls in the presence of different predators. Short, tonal calls were emitted in the presence of a leopard, low-pitched staccato grunts were made when an eagle was seen, and high-pitched chutters were emitted if a snake was detected. Furthermore, Struhsaker reported that when one monkey emitted an alarm call, other monkeys within hearing range of the caller behaved in different and appropriate ways, depending on the nature of the signal. The leopard call caused monkeys to climb trees, where it was difficult for a leopard to capture them. Upon hearing eagle calls, monkeys scanned the skies and often ran into the bush. Snake calls led them to look on the ground around them and to mob a snake once it was located.

Although these observations were fascinating, they were not completely convincing as evidence of semantic communication among vervet monkeys. As alternative explanations, it was argued that other monkeys responded because they also saw the predator or were imitating the defensive behavior of the caller. Or, perhaps the different calls all served the same purpose of being a general alarm call, with the different predator behaviors arising from inferences monkeys drew from the context in which the call was made. To test these possibilities, Seyfarth, Cheney, and Marler (1980) made recordings of the three alarm calls from a number of different monkeys. They then performed a *playback study.* Recordings of each of the three calls were played from a hidden speaker in the presence of different groups of vervet monkeys. Under these conditions, monkeys could respond only to the signal and not to the behavior of other monkeys. The results showed convincingly that monkeys responded to the semantic content of the signals. When the experimenters played the leopard signal, monkeys climbed into trees; similarly, they searched the sky and hid in the bush when an eagle call was played and scanned the ground when the snake call was sounded.

Further evidence indicated that alarm calls and their meanings were acquired by traditional transmission. Although infant monkeys emitted alarm calls, their calls were often made to inappropriate stimuli. For example, the eagle alarm call was made when many nonraptor birds were sighted, and the leopard call was emitted in the presence of a wide variety of other terrestrial mammals. As monkeys became older, they learned to restrict their calls to sightings of the appropriate predator.

Teaching Sign Language to Chimpanzees

Although the vervet monkey study shows semantic content in the communications of wild animals, the number of different signs and their meanings is small compared with the rich productivity of human language. Could a primate be taught to use a more complex language system? In fact, interest in the possibility of establishing a common language between apes and humans can be traced back several hundred years (Hewes, 1977; Ward, 1983). Serious attempts to teach vocal language to chimpanzees were undertaken in the first half of this century. Both the Kelloggs (1933) and the Hayes (1951) raised young chimpanzees in their homes and tutored these animals in spoken English. These attempts to teach spoken language were unsuccessful. After four years of work with a chimpanzee named Vicki, the Hayes taught Vicki only four "words" that vaguely approximated their English pronunciation. One important reason for this failure was the later realization that the chimpanzee's vocal tract was not designed to produce all of the sounds necessary to speak human languages (Lieberman, Crelin, & Klatt, 1972). Although chimpanzees emit food barks and other sounds when excited, they are incapable of closely mimicking a large number of human phonemes.

A number of authors mentioned the possibility of teaching apes a sign or gestural language (Ward, 1983). In fact, the renowned primate psychologist, Robert Mearnes Yerkes, specifically suggested in the 1920s that apes might be taught sign language (Yerkes, 1925). Nevertheless, the first real effort to teach sign language to a chimpanzee was not performed until Beatrice and Allen Gardner (R. Gardner and B. Gardner, 1969) carried out their ground-breaking work in the 1960s. The Gardners raised an infant, female chimpanzee named Washoe in a setting near the University of Nevada. All of the people who worked with Washoe signed to her using the American Sign Language (ASL), a language often used by deaf people to communicate with one another. In ASL, gestures of the arms and hands, along with facial expressions, are used to form phrases and sentences. Many ASL signs are iconic, such as touching a thumb extended from a fist to the mouth to indicate "drink," but others are arbitrary, such as striking the sides of the fisted hands together to sign "shoes." At the beginning of the project, Washoe's trainers decided they would not speak English in her presence to avoid any confusion she might encounter by exposure to two language systems at the same time.

To teach a language to a chimpanzee, a vocabulary must first be established. Washoe was repeatedly shown ASL signs and the referents (objects or actions) they stood for. Washoe learned a number of these signs through imitation. However, she did not always imitate gestures immediately; gestures learned by observation might be imitated at a later time but in an appropriate context. Thus, Washoe was taught the sign for "toothbrush" in one setting and did not imitate it immediately but later made the toothbrush sign in the presence of a different toothbrush. In addition to imitation, Washoe's trainers often helped her to form signs by molding her arms and hands into an appropriate sign. The reward of tickling was frequently used to reinforce her use of signs in appropriate situations.

Over a 21-month period, Washoe showed an accelerated rate of sign acquisition. Four new signs were learned in the first seven months, 9 new signs in the second seven months, and 21 new signs in the third period of seven months. This pattern of sign acquisition is similar to that seen in children, who learn more new words each month than they learned the preceding month. Within 51 months of training, Washoe acquired an active vocabulary of 132 signs, and it was estimated that her receptive vocabulary was substantially larger (B. Gardner & R. Gardner, 1975). Of particular importance was the finding that Washoe often combined signs into phrases containing two, three, or four items. Some examples are "listen dog," signed when a dog was heard barking, and "open food drink," signed in the presence of the refrigerator. In some cases, Washoe appeared to form spontaneous combinations of signs that named an object for which she had not been taught a sign. She signed "water bird" after seeing a swan, "candy fruit" when first given a piece of watermelon, and "cold rock" after handling an ice cube. One interpretation of these observations was that Washoe was showing productivity in the use of sign language; that is, she was combining already learned signs in new combinations to form new meanings.

The use of sign language with apes was particularly popular because it had an open-ended quality that appeared to allow an animal to spontaneously communicate its interests or desires to another individual. Signing was used with other chimpanzees (Fouts, 1973; Terrace, 1979b), with an orangutan (Miles, 1983), and with a gorilla (Patterson & Linden, 1981). However, the 1970s saw an explosion of interest in the possibility of forming an ape-human language bond, and still other forms of communication with apes were invented.

A Chimpanzee Learns a Language of Plastic Symbols

In a different approach to the acquisition of language by an ape, a five-year-old chimpanzee named Sarah was taught to communicate by placing plastic symbols on a magnetic board (D. Premack, 1971; 1976; A. Premack & D. Premack, 1972; D. Premack & A. Premack, 1983). Initially, Sarah was taught to associate symbols with objects by requiring her to place the symbol for that object on the board. Thus, Sarah was shown a banana but was required to place its symbol (a pink rectangle) on the board before she was given the banana. Similarly, she was required to place a blue triangle on the board to obtain an apple. Sarah was then taught to write sentences on the board by placing symbols in a vertical row. To teach Sarah the specific meanings of symbols, she was given several from which to choose. Thus, Sarah was given a piece of apple if she wrote, "give apple," but if she wrote, "cut apple," the trainer cut the apple into pieces but gave none of it to Sarah. Eventually, Sarah had to specify the recipient of these statements. Each member of the laboratory had a specific symbol. If she specified, "Give banana Sarah," Sarah got the banana, but, if she wrote, "Give banana Gussie," another chimpanzee named Gussie received the banana. Sarah quickly learned to use the symbol that specified herself as the recipient.

By arranging objects and symbols in different ways, Sarah was required to answer questions that were designed to teach her new meanings for symbols. As the training proceeded, progressively more abstract meanings for symbols were taught to Sarah. As shown in the top panels of Figure 12.1, Sarah was shown two identical objects or two different objects and required to specify whether their relationship was same or different. She answered these questions by removing a symbol that stood for the interrogative (?) and inserting in its place a symbol that stood for either same or different. The bottom panels in Figure 12.1 show that questions using these symbols can be asked in different ways. Sarah was given an object and asked what it was the same as or different from. In this case, she had to remove the interrogative symbol on the right and replace it with the object that was either the same as or different from the object on the left. Eventually, Sarah was taught a number of concepts concerning properties of objects, such as color, size, and shape, and concepts about quantity, such as some or none. Throughout her training, Sarah's vocabulary of signs grew to about 130 items.

As a further test of Sarah's comprehension of sentences, a complex command was written on her board with plastic symbols. The drawing in Figure 12.2 shows Sarah responding to the sentence, "Sarah insert apple pail

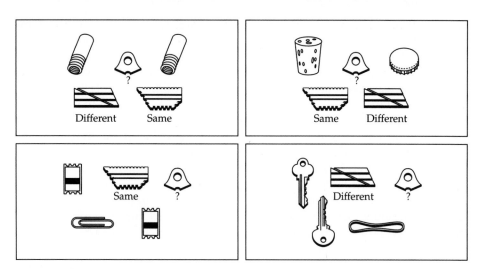

FIGURE 12.1. The top panels show displays presented to Sarah to teach her the concepts same and different. In the bottom panels, Sarah is asked which item is the same or different.

FIGURE 12.2. Drawing shows Sarah responding to the message, "Sarah insert apple pail banana dish."

banana dish." To respond correctly to this message, Sarah had to put the apple in the pail first and then place the banana on the dish. In even more complex messages, Sarah was taught the meaning of "if–then" by making an outcome specified in one sentence dependent upon an activity specified in another. Thus, Sarah was confronted with the sentences, "Sarah take apple," and "Mary give Chocolate Sarah," with the if–then symbol placed between them. If Sarah took the apple, Mary would give her chocolate. On another occasion, however, Sarah was given the sentences, "Sarah take banana," if–then "Mary no give chocolate Sarah." Sarah now had to refrain from taking the banana to receive the chocolate. Sarah learned the meaning of the if–then symbol in these sentences and was able to apply it to new situations.

D. Premack's (1971) procedure for teaching Sarah language is a more closed system of training than the sign language training used by the Gardners (1969). Sarah was constrained to communications about things her trainers wanted to teach her, whereas Washoe could express herself more spontaneously. Nevertheless, both systems agreed in showing that a chimpanzee could develop a vocabulary of more than 100 signs and could use and comprehend sign combinations.

Reading and Sentence Completion by a Chimpanzee

In research carried out at the Yerkes Regional Primate Center in Georgia, Duane Rumbaugh taught a third female chimpanzee, named Lana, a language that captured aspects of both sign language and D. Premack's plastic symbol language (Rumbaugh, 1977; Rumbaugh, Gill, & von Glasersfeld, 1973). Lana learned language by responding to symbols that were presented as keys on a computer. Each symbol consisted of a different geometric pattern of white lines on a colored background. These symbols were called *lexigrams* and could be used in combination to form phrases and sentences in a language called *Yerkish*. Figure 12.3 is a picture of Lana working at her computer console; the diagram on the right shows the various branching sentences Lana could write in Yerkish, with each word in a sentence corresponding to a lexigram. All of the sentences involved requests for objects or activities Lana enjoyed. Thus, she might request edibles in the form of foods, candy, and drinks; entertainment in the form of a filmstrip shown on her console; music; an opportunity to look out an open window; or the entrance of her trainer, Tim, into the room where she operated the computer. Each sentence had to begin with a press on the lexigram for "please" and to end with a press on the lexigram signifying "period" or the end of the sentence.

Initially, Lana only had to press a single lexigram between please and period to obtain the requested reward. Gradually, she was trained to insert more and more of the elements of a complete sentence. Eventually, Lana was tested with sentence stems that she had to complete. Some of these stems were valid, such as, "Please machine give," or "Please Tim come," but others were invalid, such as, "Please make machine," or "Please Tim give." Lana's task was to complete a valid sentence with a correct sequence of lexigrams, for which she received the requested reward, and to terminate invalid sentences immediately by pressing the period lexigram. Lana learned to discriminate accurately between valid and invalid stems and completed valid sentences correctly on more than 90 percent of the trials.

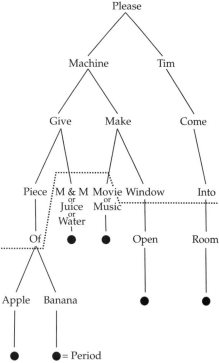

FIGURE 12.3. The photograph on the left shows Lana pressing lexigrams on her computer console. The sentences she could write are shown on the right. *From Rumbaugh, Gill, & von Glasersfeld, 1973.*

The Ape Language Controversy

Although these ape language projects met with mixed reviews from linguists (Seidenberg & Petitto, 1979), they were widely reported in the media and enthusiastically received by the public. Reports of conversations with apes appeared regularly in newspaper and magazine articles and in television documentaries. In the novel *Congo,* written by Michael Crichton (1980), a signing gorilla parachuted into Africa as a member of a scientific team and eventually saved the life of her trainer. It seemed to many that a genuine two-way communication link with other species had been achieved or clearly was in the offing.

Still another chimpanzee was being taught sign language in the late 1970s, but findings with this animal were to have a devastating effect on the ape language movement. Herbert Terrace obtained a young male chimpanzee, whom he named Nim Chimpsky (Terrace, 1979b). Nim's name is an obvious play on the name of the eminent linguist, Noam Chomsky. Chomsky argued that a propensity for the acquisition of human languages was innate and should be found only in modern people and their hominoid ancestors (Pinker, 1994). From this position, it was clearly predicted that apes are not capable of human language. It would have been a grand joke on Chomsky, then, if a chimpanzee named after him could be taught human syntactical abilities. As it turned out, however, the joke was on Terrace.

Nim was taught ASL and, like other language-trained chimpanzees, acquired a large vocabulary of 125 signs. Nim also combined signs and seemed to communicate in phrases or sentences, initially suggesting language mastery to his trainers. However, Terrace was particularly interested in Nim's grammar and in the details of his linguistic interactions with his trainers. Nim's sessions with his trainers were videotaped regularly, providing a detailed record of thousands of interactions. In previous reports of ape signing, only cursory records or outstanding incidents of language were reported. Were these examples of meaningful phrases and sentences infrequent occurrences, or did chimpanzees regularly emit such sequences? Only an analysis of a large corpus of observations could answer this question.

Terrace and his colleagues analyzed these videotapes with several questions in mind (Terrace, Pettito, Sanders, & Bever, 1979). First of all, did Nim show syntax by putting particular types of signs at particular positions within his phrases? He clearly did this. In two-sign combinations, Nim more frequently placed the verb before the object than the object before the verb. Thus, Nim signed "brush me" more often than "me brush" and signed "hug Nim" more frequently than "Nim hug." A further question was to what extent signs added to phrases elaborated on their meaning. When short and long phrases were compared, it was found that the long phrases added little to the meaning of short phrases. For example, if the two-sign combination "eat Nim" was expanded, it became the three-sign combination "eat Nim eat" or the four-sign combination "eat Nim eat Nim." In longer combinations, signs at the end of the sequence were redundant with those at the beginning of the sequence.

Nim's utterances were compared with those of young children over comparable periods of development. One quantitative measure of language is mean length of utterance (MLU), or the mean number of words uttered in a phrase or sentence. Over a 19-month period, Nim's MLU showed no growth, staying between one and two signs. By contrast, hearing and deaf children both showed growth in the MLU from about 1.5 words to around 4.0 words. Nim did occasionally make long utterances, but the signs were largely redundant. For example, Nim emitted the 16-sign utterance, "give orange me give eat orange me eat orange give me eat orange give me you."

In a discourse analysis of Nim's signing, the relationships between Nim's signs and those just made by his trainers were examined. Of considerable interest was the discovery that many of Nim's signs were imitations of signs first given by his trainer. Young children also show imitation, but they come to expand on the meaning of what others have said as they grow older. Nim's utterances showed no signs of expansion over months of training. In addition, the discourse analysis showed that Nim never learned a basic characteristic of human verbal interchange, taking turns. When two people communicate, one talks while the other listens, and then they reverse these roles. Nim, on the other hand, signed just as readily when someone was signing to him as when it was his turn to sign.

Terrace et al. (1979) concluded that there was little evidence that Nim was able to communicate meaningfully in phrases or sentences that even approached human language. Instead, Nim was either imitating his trainers' signs or emitting behaviors he learned would lead to a reward. These conclusions obviously were discrepant with those reached by other ape language researchers, particularly with the reports of the Gardners. Terrace and his colleagues proceeded to resolve this discrepancy by doing a frame-by-frame analysis of films showing communication between Washoe and her trainers. They concluded that, just as with Nim, much of Washoe's signing was imitation of signs previously made by a trainer. Thus, although Terrace set out to demonstrate the sophisticated use of language in a chimpanzee, his careful analysis of Nim's data and that of other researchers led him to the conclusion that language in apes was largely illusory.

The Terrace et al. (1979) article appeared to unleash an avalanche of criticism regarding ape language studies. Accusations against ape language research ranged from fraud to incompetence and naivete (Marx, 1980; Wade, 1980). One shortcoming was that most studies reported only gross statistics and isolated anecdotes about ape signing. It was hard to know whether instances of apparently creative utterances were common or coincidence, without knowing their relative frequency among other utterances. When Washoe signed "water bird," was she creating a new name or just responding to the presence of water and bird independently? If such creative signing occurred frequently among other signs, it might be concluded that she was inventing language; if these unique combinations were infrequent, it might be concluded that they were coincidence.

It was pointed out that psychologists doing language studies with apes want and expect apes to learn language. Anticipation of success may have led them to overinterpret what an ape did and to assign word equivalents to the ape's behavior when the ape may have no understanding of the sign (Savage-Rumbaugh, Rumbaugh, & Boysen, 1980; Seidenberg & Petitto, 1979; Terrace, 1985). The important question raised here is whether ape signing has the property of semanticity. Put another way, are apes' signs referential; that is, do they refer to other objects or events? It should be kept in mind that in all of the articles claiming language in apes, the human tester glossed or interpreted an animal's sign as an English word. But, did the animal intend the behavior to be a sign? Did the chimpanzee understand that the bit of behavior it performed was a symbol that stood for something else? The alternative is that the animal learned only to perform a behavior that it expected to yield a reward. Although the simple act of signing may not provide strong evidence of semanticity, the referential nature of signing can be addressed through transfer experiments in which correct performance can be based only on a representation of a sign's meaning.

In addition to the possibility of precuing and imitation raised by Terrace et al. (1979), the spectre of Clever Hans was raised (Sebeok & Umiker-Sebeok, 1979). Since sign language studies typically involved a close interaction between a trainer and an animal, the potential for the trainer to unintentionally cue the subject was present. Perhaps an ape tried several signs in a particular situation and only stopped when the trainer provided a subtle cue (smile, eyes light up, etc.) that the last one was correct.

Finally, it was suggested that even in cases in which imitation or subtle cuing could not account for language behavior, associative learning processes could explain the results (Terrace, 1979a; C. Thompson & Church, 1980). In the cases in which apes wrote sentences, as Sarah did with plastic symbols and Lana did with lexigrams, it was argued that animals had only learned to make responses in a particular serial order conditional upon contextual cues. We know from the evidence reviewed in Chapter 9 that primates can readily learn to place symbols in a particular order for reward. If an ape could learn to respond to symbols in different orders depending on the reward available, it could give the impression of writing a sentence.

Ape language researchers strove to defend themselves under this withering barrage of criticism. It was argued that Terrace et al. (1979) had not trained and tested Nim under optimal conditions for demonstrating language in an ape and that therefore Nim's behavior was not typical of signing apes (Patterson, 1981). It was suggested that Nim was trained by too many different teachers to form a good communicative relationship with any one person and that most of Nim's trainers were not fluent in ASL. Furthermore, it was pointed out that apes in other studies showed growth in the MLU, uninstructed acquisition of signs, and frequent novel combinations of signs to name new objects (Fouts, 1974; F. Patterson, C. Patterson, & Brentari, 1987). Nevertheless, many of the claims originally made for ape language research were brought into question, and support and enthusiasm for ape language studies began to dwindle during the 1980s.

Subsequent Research on Ape Communication

Interest in ape communication did not completely disappear. Some researchers, notably David Premack, Duane Rumbaugh, and Sue Savage-Rumbaugh, continued to explore ape cognition and communication. Given the setback the earlier claims of language with apes suffered, the Rumbaughs returned to the basic question of referential understanding in chimpanzees. Could a chimpanzee learn that a sign referred to or symbolized something else?

Two young male chimpanzees, Sherman and Austin, were trained with lexigram symbols for objects, but their training differed from that given the older chimpanzee, Lana. Instead of just being asked to name objects by choosing the appropriate lexigram when shown the object, Sherman and Austin were trained to make *functional use* of signs to communicate with human trainers and with one another (Savage-Rumbaugh, 1986; Savage-Rumbaugh, Pate, Lawson, Smith, & Rosenbaum, 1983). Thus, Sherman and Austin were taught to use symbols to request food and to use symbols to request tools to obtain food. In some cases, they learned to give foods or tools to others who symbolically requested them. After learning to use symbols in a variety of functional ways, Sherman and Austin participated in an important categorization experiment (Savage-Rumbaugh, Rumbaugh, Smith, & Lawson, 1980). Initially, the chimpanzees were trained to sort six objects (stick, key, money, beancake, orange, and bread) into the two categories of tools and foods. They were taught lexigrams that stood for the categories of tools and foods and were eventually able to respond with the correct categorical lexigram when shown the objects themselves, photographs of the objects, or lexigrams that stood for the objects. You may recognize this procedure as a version of the associative concept learning experiment discussed in Chapter 11.

Sherman and Austin were then presented with new tools and foods and asked to respond with a lexigram; they both successfully categorized both new objects and photographs of new objects. The final, and most important test, involved presenting the chimpanzees with lexigrams of tools and foods they had never before sorted. Sherman responded with the correct tool or food lexigram on 15 of 16 tests, and Austin was correct on 17 of 17 tests. The important thing to realize about these tests is that the chimpanzees could not respond correctly on the basis of the appearance of the lexigram. Therefore, the object lexigrams had to have elicited a representation of the object the lexigram symbolized.

Lana also was tested in this experiment. Although Lana learned to sort the initial set of six tools and foods and to identify them with categorical lexigrams, she totally failed to be able to assign these lexigrams correctly to new food and tool items. It appeared that Lana did not understand the symbolic categorical meaning of these symbols. Lana's failure on this task is particularly important since she had had extensive prior language training with lexigrams and sentence completion. These findings suggest that her prior training taught her a series of conditional and serial associations that allowed her to behave as if she had language. This experiment is important for two reasons. First, it confirms the idea that much of the simple associative training given in the earlier ape language studies may not have led to symbolic understanding on the part of the animals trained. Second, it shows that apes can learn the symbolic meaning of arbitrary signs if given extensive functional training with those signs.

Communication with a Pygmy Chimpanzee

The chimpanzees thus far discussed, Washoe, Sarah, Lana, Nim, Sherman, and Austin, were all common chimpanzees or *Pan troglodytes.* Much less research has been carried out with a second species of chimpanzee, *Pan paniscus,* often called the pygmy chimpanzee or bonobo. Smaller in stature than the common chimpanzee, bonobos are rare and difficult to obtain. Nevertheless, they hold considerable interest as research subjects because, in several ways, they appear to more closely resemble humans than do common chimpanzees. For example, unlike male common chimpanzees, bonobo males share food and help with child care. Bonobos have been observed to copulate frequently as a form of conflict resolution, and bonobos are the only species of nonhuman primates known to copulate face-to-face. In addition, primatologists suggest that bonobos may be more intelligent than common chimpanzees.

At the Yerkes Regional Primate Center, Savage-Rumbaugh and her colleagues examined the development of language usage in several pygmy chimpanzees (Savage-Rumbaugh, McDonald, Sevcik, Hopkins, & Rubert, 1986). The most noticeable language progress was made by a young male chimpanzee named Kanzi. Interestingly, Kanzi was not formally trained to use lexigrams. His mother, Matata, was given some language training during Kanzi's infancy, but he showed only casual interest in these symbols. At 2½ years of age, Kanzi was separated from Matata for a period of time. He then began to show considerable interest in the keyboard containing lexigrams and began to use it as a means of requesting foods. This behavior was a considerable surprise to the people who cared for Kanzi; they assumed that he had only the most rudimentary understanding of how the keyboard worked as a communication device. Over a period of 17 months, after separation from his mother, Kanzi developed a vocabulary of about 50 lexigrams, which he could use receptively to respond to messages from his trainers or productively to make requests of others.

Kanzi's language skills appeared to differ in several ways from those observed previously in common chimpanzees. As mentioned, he learned lexigram symbols without formal training, apparently initially through observing others' use of the keyboard. Later, he was observed to practice with the keyboard in the absence of human trainers. In the earlier studies with common chimpanzees, an animal appeared to sign predominately to request a food or activity, with itself as the recipient. Kanzi's use of symbols appeared to be more spontaneous and less tied to reward. Only 11 percent of Kanzi's utterances were imitations or responses to a prompt from a trainer. Although Sherman and Austin were able to match lexigrams to objects and photographs of objects, they never were able to respond accurately to spoken English. In addition to matching symbols to objects and photographs, Kanzi accurately matched photographs and symbols to spoken English words. He responded accurately to English words spoken both by a human voice and by computer-synthesized speech.

As other language-trained apes had done, Kanzi combined signs in mostly two- and three-word combinations. Two aspects of these combinations are important when compared with the reported signs emitted by Nim and other signing apes. One of Terrace et al.'s (1979) major findings was that Nim's utterances were highly redundant; later signs in combinations were repetitions of or synonyms for earlier signs in the sequence. Savage-Rumbaugh et al. (1986) reported that when Kanzi extended a sequence beyond two lexigrams, the additional lexigram(s) added new meaning. Thus, Kanzi would say, "ice water go," but not "ice water ice." The second important observation was that many of Kanzi's combinations often requested some activity that involved other individuals. Thus, Kanzi signed messages such as, "Person 1 grab Person 2," or "Person 1 tickle Person 2." By contrast, Nim's combinations always expressed himself as the agent or recipient of objects or actions.

In several ways, the symbolic communication of a bonobo appeared to be more advanced than that of common chimpanzees. Kanzi appeared to understand symbols more broadly, including spoken as well as visual symbols. His use of symbols conveyed more information and was more productive and less tied to his own needs than the use of symbols seen previously in common chimpanzees.

Syntax Revisited

Recall that syntax refers to the fact that human languages place certain classes of words in a particular order within a phrase or sentence. The search for syntax in ape language was originally a major goal of many of the primate language projects. When it was concluded by many that apes were not even capable of understanding the symbolic nature of language, the question of syntax became irrelevant. Since the more recent findings just discussed suggest that animals are capable of symbolic communication with humans, the question of syntax again becomes of interest.

Dolphins Understand Syntax

One important contribution to the study of syntax in animals comes from studies of dolphins. Although dolphins are sea mammals and not primates, these large-brained animals have often been compared with primates in terms of cognitive development. At the University of Hawaii, Louis Herman trained dolphins to respond to an imperative symbolic language (Herman, Kuczaj, & Holder, 1993; Herman, Richards, & Wolz, 1984). Two dolphins were used; one dolphin, Akeakamai, was trained to respond to visual gestures made by a trainer stationed at the side of the pool (see Figure 12.4), and the other dolphin, Phoenix, was trained to respond to auditory signals played through the water. The dolphins were given commands in the form of a sentence, and the experimenters observed whether the command was correctly performed. The sentences contained arbitrary symbols that referred to objects and actions. The objects were fixtures within the dolphins' pool, such as gate, window, panel, speaker, water hose, and net, and moveable items, such as ball, hoop, pipe, fish, person, frisbee, surfboard, and basket. The action words were those that took a direct object—tail touch, pectoral touch, mouth, (go) over, (go) under, (go)

FIGURE 12.4. Examples of the visual gestures that were combined to form commands signaled to the dolphin Akeakamai.

through, toss, and spit—and two words that took either a direct or indirect object—fetch and in. In addition, there were signs for Phoenix and Akeakamai and modifiers for location, such as right, left, surface, and bottom.

Each dolphin was taught a different syntactical rule. Akeakamai was instructed with sentences in which the indirect object always preceded the direct object, and Phoenix was instructed with sentences in which the direct object always preceded the indirect object. The sentences varied in length from two to five words, depending on how detailed the dolphin's instructions were. Thus, given the three-word sentence, "pipe fetch hoop," Akeakamai's task was to take the hoop to the pipe, and Phoenix's task was to take the pipe to the hoop. Similar instructions would be given to each dolphin in the five-word sentence, "surface pipe fetch bottom hoop," in which more detailed information is given about the location of each object.

After the dolphins were trained to respond to a limited set of sentences, they were tested with a large number of novel sentences that instructed them to carry out actions never before performed. In some cases, the sentences contained the same object and action symbols but reversed the object symbols' positions, making the sentences semantically opposite one another. Both dolphins responded to novel sentences by carrying out the instructions at levels that far exceeded chance performance. It appears that Akeakamai and Phoenix understood the syntactical rules conveyed by the order in which direct and indirect object symbols were presented.

Kanzi Shows Syntax

The dolphin data provide evidence that these animals can acquire syntactical rules in a receptive communication system. Other recent findings with the bonobo Kanzi suggest the use of syntax in productive communication (Greenfield & Savage-Rumbaugh, 1990). All of Kanzi's two- and three-symbol productions were recorded over a five-month period and extensively analyzed. These sequences contained all lexigrams in some cases and combinations of lexigrams and gestures in other cases. Gestures were behaviors that clearly indicated reference to a particular object or action. All imitations and productions that were solicited by a trainer were eliminated to obtain a final corpus of 723 two-symbol productions that were spontaneously emitted. Many of Kanzi's combinations involved an action symbol and an object symbol. During the first month of the study, Kanzi showed no preferred order for these types of symbols. Over the next four months, however, Kanzi showed a clear preference for action symbol before object symbol, by saying, "bite tomato," and "hide peanut," instead of "tomato bite," and "peanut hide." This order was the one used by Kanzi's trainers, and his ordering of these symbols may have reflected a learned syntactical rule.

Other observations of symbol order suggest that Kanzi invented his own syntactical rules. Many of Kanzi's productions involved a lexigram combined with a gesture. Kanzi strongly preferred to place the lexigram before the gesture. In some cases, she actually traveled from the location where the gesture was to be made to the keyboard in order to press the lexigram before making the gesture. Kanzi apparently invented the rule that lexigram symbols should precede gesture symbols. As another example, when Kanzi produced combinations that contained two action symbols, he strongly preferred to place the lexigrams for "chase" and "tickle" before the lexigrams for "hide," "slap," and "bite." Greenfield and Savage-Rumbaugh (1990) argue that this order of these two classes of words reflects Kanzi's preferred action order. That is, in interactions with people or other chimpanzees, Kanzi and other bonobos prefer to chase and tickle before they hide, slap, and bite.

These findings from dolphins and a pygmy chimpanzee indicate that animals can understand and utilize syntax in symbolic communication. Rules about the order in which types of symbols occur can be acquired in both receptive and productive language-usage modes. The discovery that a chimpanzee can create its own syntactical rules is very important from an evolutionary point of view. As Greenfield and Savage-Rumbaugh (1990) point out, if the potential for productive language usage is found in both humans and apes, the likelihood that this potential was present in the common ancestor of modern humans and apes is strengthened.

REASONING IN PRIMATES

One of the first thorough examinations of reasoning ability in nonhuman primates was carried out by the gestalt psychologist, Wolfgang Kohler. During a period of internship as a political prisoner during World War I, Kohler studied chimpanzee behavior at the Anthropoid Station on the island of Tenerife. His findings were published in a famous book, *The Mentality of Apes* (Kohler, 1925). Kohler's tactic for studying reasoning in apes was to make food available to animals in a location that was out of their reach. However, a number of objects lay about the animal's enclosure that could be used as tools to obtain the food. Thus, food might be hung from the top of the ape's enclosure, out of the normal reach of the chimpanzee. However, by stacking boxes on top of one another, chimpanzees formed a ladder that allowed them to reach the food. In one case, a chimpanzee led the keeper beneath the food and used the keeper as a ladder to reach the food. On one occasion, the keeper bent down as the chimpanzee climbed on his shoulders. The chimpanzee immediately leapt off the keeper and pushed him into a straight posture before using him again as a ladder. In another problem, food was placed outside the enclosure, beyond the chimpanzee's reach. As a solution to this problem, chimpanzees used sticks available in the enclosure as rakes to rake in the food.

In one particularly well-known observation, the chimpanzee Sultan was placed in the enclosure with food placed outside the reach of either of two bamboo sticks he was given. After several failed attempts to reach the food with these sticks, the ape appeared to give up and abandoned use of the sticks. His keeper observed that he picked up the two sticks and appeared to play with them until he happened to fit the end of one stick into the hollow end of the other. In an instant, he was on his feet and racing to the site of the food, where he now used his extended stick to rake in the food.

This example is often described as an instance of insightful thinking in apes. However, it is unclear whether Sultan actually devised the solution of putting the sticks together or only happened to do so by accident while manipulating them. In either case, apparently he realized instantly the potential use of this longer stick. This account emphasizes Kohler's (1925) theoretical position regarding reasoning in apes. He stressed the importance of perception in problem solving. He observed that problem solving progressed more rapidly when animals could readily see the potential use of an object as a tool. Thus, sticks placed on the ground parallel to one another were seen as tools more easily than crossed sticks. Sticks that were placed across one another appeared to be attached and thus not easily used as a rake. A box was used for a ladder sooner if it was in the open than if it was placed against a wall. When placed against a wall, the box looked as if it was attached to the wall and thus could not be detached and used for another purpose. Chimpanzees often made "good errors" in attempting to solve a problem. When food was placed outside the reach of a single stick, a chimpanzee might push the first stick toward the food with another stick. Although, the food still could not be obtained, the chimpanzee made a *perceptual connection* between itself and the food.

In a technologically updated version of Kohler's experiments, D. Premack and Woodruff (1978a) showed the chimpanzee Sarah videotapes depicting a person confronted with different problems (see the left panel of Figure 12.5). In each tape, the person was attempting to reach bananas that were out of reach. Each 30-second videotape was shown to Sarah and put on hold for the final 5 seconds. Sarah then was given two cards, one of which showed the person using a tool to solve the problem and the other of which showed the person performing behavior that would not solve the problem. She was left alone to choose one of these cards and place it on a paper towel in front of her. Sarah chose the card depicting the correct solution on 21 of 24 trials, showing excellent comprehension of the problems.

In other tests, Sarah was shown videotapes of a person trying to escape from a locked cage, shivering in a cage, trying to wash down a dirty floor when the hose was not connected to the faucet, and trying to play a phonograph record when the machine was not plugged in (see the left panel of Figure 12.6). The correct solutions to these problems were to select pictures that showed a key on a ring to get out of the locked cage, a torch in flames to warm the shivering person, a hose connected to the faucet to wash the floor, and a plug connected to the wall socket to play the phonograph record. Sarah chose correctly on 12 of 12 tests with these problems. These problems are particularly interesting because they required Sarah to use practical knowledge about how things worked in order to solve them.

Imaginal and Abstract Codes

D. Premack's theory of dual codes in primate cognition, discussed in Chapter 11, can be applied to the D. Premack and Woodruff findings. Recall that the *imaginal code* involves mental manipulation of things that can be directly perceived. Kohler's problems and most of the D. Premack and Woodruff problems could have been solved using an imaginal code; rearranging the locations of objects seen in the real world or on videotape would allow the acquisition of food by the ape or the human seen on videotape. Two of the problems shown, however, could not be solved in this way. When shown a person trying to get out of a

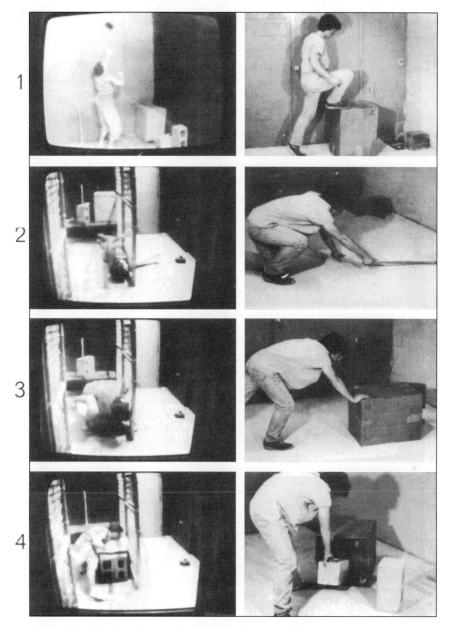

FIGURE 12.5. The photographs on the left are taken from videotaped problems shown to Sarah. They show her trainer attempting (1) to reach a banana suspended by a rope, (2) to reach under a wire mesh partition for bananas, (3) to reach around a box for bananas, and (4) to push aside a box filled with cement blocks to reach bananas. The correct solutions to each problem are shown in the photographs on the right.
From D. Premack & Woodruff, 1978a.

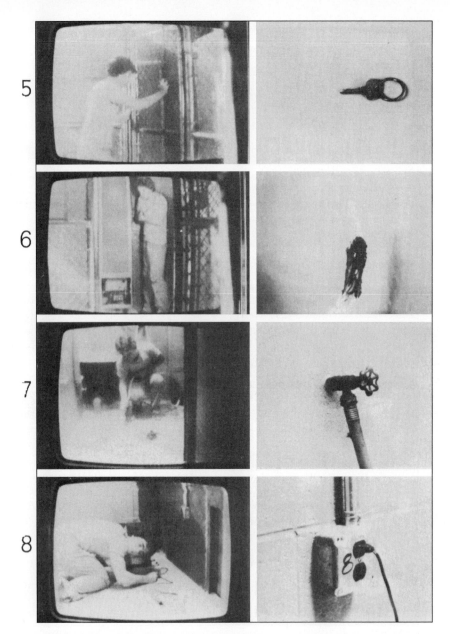

FIGURE 12.6. The photographs on the left show still shots from four more problems shown to Sarah. Her trainer now is (5) attempting to escape from a locked cage, (6) shivering and trying to keep warm, (7) attempting to wash down a dirty floor with a disconnected hose, and (8) attempting to play a phonograph record on an unplugged machine. Photographs of the correct solution to each problem are shown in the right panel.

From D. Premack & Woodruff, 1978a.

locked cage, no key was shown. When shown a person shivering, no fire was shown. To solve these problems, it appears that Sarah had to use an *abstract code.* That is, she had to understand the relationship between a lock and key and reason that a key would open the locked door. Similarly, she would have to understand the relationship among fire, warmth, and shivering to correctly choose the burning torch picture.

D. Premack tested Sarah and other language-trained chimpanzees on several other types of tests that required the understanding of abstract relationships. On one form of an *analogical reasoning test,* Sarah was shown the relationship between two stimuli and asked to complete the same relationship between two other stimuli (Gillan, D. Premack, & Woodruff, 1981). As shown in Figure 12.7, the relationship between the two sawtooth shapes on the left is that the lower one is a smaller version of the one on top. The trapezoidal symbol represents the relationship "same as," and the large triangle with a dot in the center shows half of the relationship to be completed on the right. Sarah had to choose one of the two triangles at the bottom of the figure and place it below the upper triangle to complete the figure. Notice that the correct choice— the small triangle with a dot in its center—bears no visual similarity to the figures shown on the left. The problem can only be solved by understanding the relationship shown between the figures on the left and then transposing that relationship to the figures on the right. A number of problems of this nature were given to Sarah, with the relationship based on changes in three different features of the shapes, size, color, or marking. Overall, Sarah was correct on 45 of 60 tests, far better than the 50 percent level expected by chance.

In the tests with geometric figures, the analogy was seen in the visual relationships among the forms. In another set of tests, Sarah was confronted with analogies based on the functions of common household items. In this case, Sarah had to use her reference memory for the use of these items to infer the relationship shown. Two examples are shown in Figure 12.8. Problem A asks the chimpanzee, "Which of the two items below has the same relationship to a

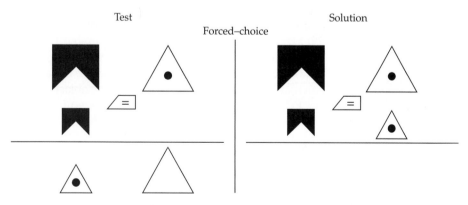

FIGURE 12.7. An example of the analogy problems presented to Sarah. She had to choose the form below the line that made the relationship between the figures on the right the same as that between the figures on the left.

Problem A   Problem B

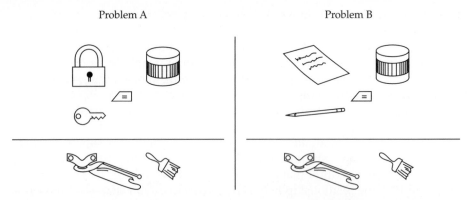

FIGURE 12.8. Examples of practical conceptual analogy problems presented to Sarah. She was required to choose the object below the line that made the relationship between the objects on the right the same as that between the objects on the left.

painted can as the key has to the closed lock?" The subject needs to remember that key opens lock and then see that the can opener has the same relationship to the can. In Problem B, the painted can and the choices between can opener and paint brush are the same as in Problem A, but the relationship shown on the left is between marked paper and a pencil. In this case, the paint brush is the correct choice because it marks the can as pencil marks the paper. Sarah completed the analogy correctly on 15 of 18 tests.

Chimpanzees also were given *action tests* (D. Premack, 1983). To score accurately on these tests, an animal had to understand the operation by which an object had its state or appearance changed. For example, a chimpanzee was shown a whole apple followed by a blank followed by an apple cut in pieces. To fill in the blank, the chimpanzee had to choose between three objects: a knife, a pencil, and a glass of water. The correct choice was the knife, the one instrument that could be used to make the displayed change in the state of the apple. Three language-trained chimpanzees successfully passed action tests of this type. Sarah was also given action tests in which she had to understand that the direction of causality was from left to right. Thus, she was shown paper, blank, marked paper on one occasion and marked paper, blank, paper on another occasion. In both cases, she had to fill the blank with one of three objects: water, pencil, or eraser. The correct choice was pencil when paper changed to marked paper and eraser when marked paper changed to paper. Sarah was given 60 novel tests of this type and chose the correct answer on 45 of these, once again being substantially above the chance level of choice of 33 percent.

D. Premack's findings show a remarkable ability to solve both perceptual and practical analogies in chimpanzees. However, the ability to solve these problems was limited to language-trained apes. D. Premack suggested that somehow language training gave Sarah and other chimpanzees the ability to understand abstract relationships that are not contained directly in a pictorial display (D. Premack, 1983). Non-language-trained primates may possess the abstract code as a latent ability not yet manifested. It is not clear exactly what aspects of the language training given in D. Premack's laboratory would have conferred this ability upon his subjects. The type of language training given Sarah was described earlier and involved a number of choice tests designed to teach her higher-order relationships among objects. It may have been this intense training on a variety of relationships, and not the communicative aspects of language, that allowed Sarah to learn to understand abstract relationships.

Limits on Reasoning in Primates

The Trap-Tube Task

Primates do not always show insightful solutions to problems. Consider the trap-tube task, displayed in Figure 12.9. The apparatus consisted of a transparent cylindrical tube, mounted on a frame, with an opening in the middle of the tube, called the trap. A piece of food was placed randomly on the left or right side of the tube on successive trials. The subject's task was to use a stick tool to push the food along the tube. If the subject pushed the food out of either end of the tube, it was allowed to consume it. However, if the subject pushed the food into the trap, the reward was lost on that trial. An insightful solution to this task would be to assess the position of the food relative to the trap and then insert the stick so that the food never passed over the trap.

Visalberghi and Limongelli (1994) tested four capuchin monkeys on this task. Over 140 trials of testing, only one monkey learned to obtain the food at better than the chance level of 50 percent. Further examination of this monkey's behavior suggested that it did not have a full understanding of the nature of the problem. For example, when the trap tube was inverted so that the trap was on the top of the tube, the monkey continued to perform as if the food could be lost by dropping through the trap. It was concluded that the monkey learned an associative strategy of always inserting the stick into the opening of the tube farthest from the reward.

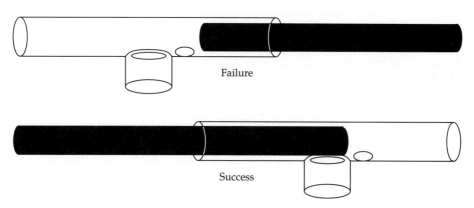

FIGURE 12.9. Diagram of the trap-tube task used to test monkeys and chimpanzees. Insertion of the stick as shown in the top example causes the reward to fall into the trap. Correct insertion of the stick leads to retrieval of the reward as shown in the bottom example.

Would an ape have more insight into this problem than a monkey? In a study performed by Limongelli, Boysen and Visalberghi (1995), five common chimpanzees were tested on the trap-tube problem. After about 70 trials, two of the chimpanzees, Sheba and Darrell, successfully solved the problem, but the other three stayed at chance over 140 trials. Did these successful chimpanzees understand the problem? In a second experiment, a tube was used that had the trap displaced from the middle toward one end of the tube. Food now appeared to be closer to the end containing the trap, regardless of which side of the trap it was placed on. If a subject now inserted the stick from the end farthest from the reward, it would be correct on only half the trials. Both Sheba and Darrell showed immediate solution of this problem, obtaining the food on more than 90 percent of the trials.

The finding that three chimpanzees showed no improvement on the trap-tube problem indicates that this task is difficult for these apes to understand. However, the fact that Darrell and Sheba did solve it and showed understanding of its cause-and-effect nature indicates that the task is not beyond the chimpanzee's ability. Interestingly, children under the age of 36 months fail to learn the trap-tube problem, but older children find the solution in only a few trials (Limongelli et al., 1995). The problem then is sensitive to developmental stage in humans. The further observation that none of the capuchin monkeys were able to show an insightful solution to the problem suggests an interspecies difference in problem-solving ability. Perhaps apes, but not monkeys, can achieve a meaningful representation of the solution to this problem.

Sensitivity to Danger Cues

In the earlier discussion of vervet monkeys' response to alarm calls, it was clear that monkeys learned that different calls signal different predators. This highly intelligent signaling system then allows vervet monkeys to take appropriate defensive or evasive action before a predator comes near. We expect then that these monkeys would be sensitive to other signals of dangerous predators they might encounter. A surprising set of experiments carried out by Cheney and Seyfarth (1990c) suggests this is not always the case. In a series of studies carried out in the vervet monkey's home range, they arranged sets of visual cues they reasoned should be certain signs to monkeys that a particular predator was near. In one experiment, they mimicked the behavior of a leopard by hanging the carcass of a Thompson's gazelle from a tree. They then observed the behavior of groups of vervet monkeys when they encountered the hanging carcass. In another experiment, they observed the behavior of vervet monkeys when they encountered either real or artificial python tracks made on the ground. In both experiments, vervet monkeys showed no alarm response whatsoever to these visual cues. Monkeys did not take cover, search for a predator, or emit alarm calls. In one case, monkeys actually followed a python track into the bush, only to leap back in fear when a snake was encountered.

These findings are puzzling, since one expects selective pressure to favor the survival of monkeys who could learn to associate secondary visual cues with the predators that produce them (Cheney & Seyfarth, 1990c). However, the absence of a reaction to these cues shows that monkeys do not always reason intelligently, even in situations where it may mean life or death. Cheney and Seyfarth suggest that the reason for this inability to recognize visual signs of danger may lie in an inability to understand cause and effect. In this case, vervet monkeys may not be able to reason that the presence of a hanging carcass was caused by a leopard or that python tracks were caused by a python. It is interesting to juxtapose these observations with the trap-tube problem findings. Although vervet monkeys are Old-World monkeys and capuchins are New-World monkeys, could it be that they have in common an inability to easily see correlations between causes and their effects? Since chimpanzees did solve the trap-tube problem, we might expect to find that wild chimpanzees learned to react to secondary danger cues that signal the nearby presence of a threatening animal (Cheney & Seyfarth, 1990c).

THEORY OF MIND

One of the activities Kanzi participated in while acquiring the use of symbols was taking trips through the woods to 17 different food-site locations. Kanzi selected one food from a series of photographs and then led a person to the correct location by riding on the person's shoulders and pointing the way with his hand. Savage-Rumbaugh et al. (1986) reported that after selecting a photograph, Kanzi often made certain that the person had seen the photograph also. While traveling through the woods, Kanzi turned the person's head in the correct direction. One interpretation of these behaviors is that Kanzi wanted the person to have the necessary information in order to get to the food site. If this was the motivation for Kanzi's behavior, we would say that Kanzi had a *theory of mind*. A theory of mind means that an animal or person understands that others have a mind or cognitive apparatus that processes information in the same way he does. A theory-of-mind interpretation of Kanzi's actions implies that Kanzi intended to provide his traveling companion with the necessary information to find the food site.

The concept of a theory of mind was introduced by D. Premack and Woodruff (1978b) and was used to explain Sarah's successful solutions to the videotaped problems already described. They suggested that an ape or a person with a theory of mind is able to impute mental states to itself and others, including intention, belief, knowledge or lack of knowledge, and positive and negative emotions. Sarah's success with videotaped problems of a person placed in a predicament was attributed to her understanding that the person intended to change the situation in a particular way; she then chose the alternative that was in keeping with the person's intention. In more recent years, the notion of a theory of mind in nonhuman primates has been discussed widely, and more direct experimental tests of a theory of mind in animals have been carried out.

The Role-Reversal Experiment

One implication of a theory of mind is that the participants in communication understand that information has been exchanged between them. Thus, if one individual sends a message to a second individual that affects the second individual's behavior, theory of mind holds that both individuals assume that the change in behavior was caused by new knowledge acquired by the second individual. The question of communicative understanding was examined in rhesus monkeys by Povinelli, Parks, and Novak (1992). Based on a procedure originally devised by Mason and Hollis (1962), they used the apparatus shown on the left side of Figure 12.10 to study role reversal. The apparatus consists of a set of two food trays that move in opposite directions. When the operator pulls one tray toward himself, the other tray moves in the opposite direction, toward an informant. The contents of a food tray are blocked from the operator's view by an opaque shield. However, an informant on the other side of the apparatus can see the contents of each tray and signal to the operator the correct one to be pulled in for food reward, either by pointing or orienting toward the correct tray. Two monkeys learned to perform this task with the monkey as the operator and a human as an informant. Two other monkeys took the role of informant, while a human acted as the operator. When the operator pulled the handle on the tray containing food, both the operator and informant were rewarded. Both the operator and informant monkeys learned to perform this task at around 90 percent accuracy.

The critical test now came on trials in which the role of operator and informant were reversed. If monkeys understood that the informant's behavior sent a message to the operator about which handle to pull, they should be able to reverse roles and still maintain a high level of accurate choice. In fact, performance in all four dyads dropped to the chance level on the initial transfer session. Although they eventually learned to perform their new role accurately, informer monkeys initially showed no ability to point at the food tray, and operator monkeys showed no ability to choose the tray pointed at by the

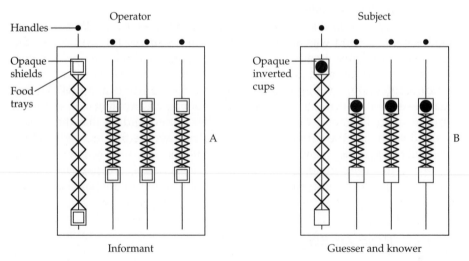

FIGURE 12.10. A drawing of the apparatus used in the role-reversal experiments (left) and in the guesser-knower experiments (right). In each case, the subject or operator pulls a handle that moves a food tray toward him.

human informer. In other words, these monkeys showed no evidence of theory of mind in a role-reversal task.

In another experiment, Povinelli, Nelson, and Boysen (1992) tested four common chimpanzees on the role-reversal task. These animals also learned to perform the initial task quite accurately, but their behavior when transferred to the opposite role was quite different from that of the monkeys. Three of the chimpanzees (two switched from operator to informant and one switched from informant to operator) continued to perform the task with no loss of accuracy. The authors suggested that these successful chimpanzees understood the communicative nature of pointing behavior in this task.

The Guesser-Knower Experiment

An organism that has a theory of mind also should understand the relationship between perceiving and knowing. An observer who sees an event should form a mental representation of that event, but one who does not see the event should have no knowledge of it. A subject who understands the seeing-knowing relationship should prefer to obtain information about the event from the individual who saw the event. As a test of an animal's ability to understand the relationship between seeing and knowing, Povinelli, Nelson, and Boysen (1990) carried out the guesser-knower experiment. The apparatus was essentially the same as that used in the role-reversal experiment and is shown on the right side of Figure 12.10.

In this experiment, a chimpanzee subject always operated the handles of the apparatus after being cued by human informants on the other side of the apparatus. Two people acted as informants on each trial. At the beginning of a trial, one informant—the guesser—announced that he was leaving the room and did so. It is important to understand that the member of the pair who served as the guesser changed randomly from trial to trial. The other informant—the knower—stayed in the room and showed the chimpanzee an item of food, which he then hid under an opaque cup on one of the food trays. A barrier prevented the chimpanzee from seeing which cup the knower baited. The guesser then reentered the room, and the guesser and knower each pointed at a different cup; the cup pointed at by the knower always contained the reward, and the cup pointed at by the guesser was always empty. If the chimpanzee chose the cup pointed out by the knower, it was allowed to consume the reward obtained.

Four common chimpanzees all learned to choose the cup pointed at by the knower in preference to the one pointed at by the guesser. However, the level of preference for the cup pointed at by the knower did not exceed 70 percent. In a further test of the chimpanzees' ability to understand the seeing-knowing relationship, the guesser no longer left the room. The guesser and knower now stood together while a third experimenter baited a cup. However, the guesser now put a paper bag over his head while the cup was baited, effectively preventing himself from seeing which cup was baited. Over 30 trials of testing with this new procedure, all four chimpanzees continued to show the same level of preference for the knower's information as they did at the end of the phase in which the guesser left the room.

How do monkeys fare on the guesser-knower task? Essentially the same experiment was performed with four rhesus monkeys as subjects (Povinelli, Parks, & Novak, 1991). Although a variety of training procedures were used, none of these monkeys was able to learn to follow the knower's directions in preference to those of the guesser. These findings then parallel those found with the role-reversal procedure. Of particular importance, in both experiments, chimpanzees transferred without loss of performance to a new testing situation, whereas monkeys either showed no transfer or failed to learn the original task. These findings led Povinelli (1993) to the hypothesis that apes may be the only animals that share a theory of mind with people.

A Critique of Theory-of-Mind Research

A basic criticism of theory-of-mind research is that most of its findings may be explained by conditional discriminations based on *observed behavioral cues* and not by inferences about the contents of another individual's mind (Heyes, 1993a). In the role-reversal experiment, it could be argued that a chimpanzee learned what to do when the roles were reversed by simply observing what its human partner did during the initial phase of the experiment. For example, a chimpanzee informant could learn that the human pulled on the handle corresponding to the food tray it pointed at, and a chimpanzee operator could learn that the human pointed at the tray containing food before it pulled on the handle. These opposite role behaviors and their consequences could have been acquired just through observational learning, without an animal attributing mental states to its co-worker.

In the case of the guesser-knower experiment, instead of inferring the mental states of the guesser and knower, a chimpanzee could simply have learned to choose the alternative pointed to by the person who stayed in the room and to avoid the alternative pointed to by the person who left the room. The fact that accuracy did not exceed 70 percent could arise from proactive interference or confusion between the individuals who change roles between trials. Povinelli et al. (1991) recognized this problem and carried out the test with the guesser's head covered with a paper bag as a control experiment. The fact that chimpanzees immediately transferred without loss of accuracy to this new situation appears to support their theory-of-mind position. However, there also might have been some rapid transfer of conditional discrimination from the earlier task. A chimpanzee might have rapidly reasoned that it should avoid the directions of the individual who does something odd or unusual, such as leave the room or put a bag over his head, and follow the directions of the individual who does nothing unusual.

In defense of these clever theory-of-mind experiments, it should be acknowledged that it is very difficult to devise an experiment for which the outcome cannot be explained by discrimination between behavioral cues. One important fact that casts some doubt on the behavioral cues account is that monkeys completely failed to show transfer on the role-reversal task and completely failed to learn to discriminate between the guesser and knower. If successful performance on these tasks is caused by nothing more than discrimination learning, we might expect monkeys to do as well as chimpanzees. Either chimpanzees are far more sensitive to behavioral cues than monkeys, or chimpanzees may be inferring the mental states of other participants.

Heyes (1993a) argued that further extension of the transfer procedure used in the guesser-knower experiment provides the best approach to establishing a theory of mind. She suggests that chimpanzees be tested with the guesser and knower facing the apparatus during baiting but with a screen obstructing the guesser's view of the baiting procedure. If chimpanzees continue to choose the cup pointed at by the knower, with no loss in accuracy, it would be very difficult to argue that choice was based simply on behavioral cues because the guesser and knower behaved in exactly the same ways. Heyes refers to this procedure of giving subjects successive transfer tests with behavioral cues varied but the guesser's view of the baiting procedure always obscured as *triangulation*. Future research will undoubtedly use a variety of transfer tests to triangulate on an answer to the theory-of-mind controversy.

SELF-AWARENESS

Closely related to theory of mind is the issue of self-awareness in primates. Most people are self-aware or have a self-concept. A human's state of mind is *bidirectional* in the sense that she can both be aware of events in the external world and also be aware of her own consciousness of those events. Self-awareness is a property of *autonoetic consciousness* and *episodic memory*, as formulated by Tulving (1985) and discussed in Chapter 3. An organism with episodic memory has a personal past or can remember past events as they relate to her as an individual. Without awareness of herself as an individual, however, a person could not have an episodic memory with a personal past, nor could she plan a personal future.

Mirror Experiments

If an ape can form a theory of mind about other organisms, it seems likely that it can also have a theory of mind about itself or be self-conscious. But, without the use of language, how can we establish whether an ape is self-aware? The psychologist Gordon Gallup devised a way of studying this problem by examining animals' reaction to their own image reflected in a mirror (Gallup, 1970; 1977; 1979; 1983). When chimpanzees were first exposed to a mirror, they treated the image as if it were that of a conspecific and reacted with threat gestures and other social responses. However, over a period of 10 days, these other-directed behaviors were replaced by self-directed behaviors. The chimpanzees came to use the mirror to examine parts of their bodies and to groom themselves.

The Mark Test

Although this behavior suggested that a chimpanzee was aware of seeing itself in the mirror, a more formal test of self-awareness was carried out. After this period of mirror exposure, each chimpanzee was anesthetized. While a chimpanzee was unconscious, the experimenter painted a bright red, odorless dye over one eyebrow ridge and the top of the ear on the opposite side of the head. Importantly, the chimpanzee could not detect this red coloring on its face without seeing its image in the mirror. When chimpanzees recovered from the anesthesia, they were exposed to the mirror, and their behavior was recorded. It was reasoned that if the chimpanzee recognized the image as itself, it should direct behavior toward the novel red marks. On the other hand, if the chimpanzee only saw the image as another chimpanzee, it might show unusual interest in the image but not respond to the marks on itself. The results clearly revealed that chimpanzees paid unusual attention to the red marks, frequently touching or rubbing them. Fingers were examined frequently visually or smelled after touching red areas. Animals directed responses to marked areas significantly more often than they had during a pretest when the mirror was not present. In addition, control chimpanzees given no prior exposure to mirrors were anesthetized and marked. These animals showed no interest in the marked areas when exposed to a mirror. Both prior mirror experience and marking were necessary to elicit frequent self-directed behavior to the marked areas.

Gallup (1977; 1979) argued that these findings reveal that chimpanzees recognized themselves in the mirror. Furthermore, he suggested that an animal could recognize itself only if it had self-awareness and bidirectional consciousness. This success with chimpanzees led to investigations with other primates. Somewhat surprisingly, the outcomes of these experiments revealed that chimpanzees and orangutans are the only two species of nonhuman primates in which the mirror self-recognition effect can be found. Numerous attempts to obtain the phenomenon with monkeys failed, and the effect even appears to be absent in gorillas (Gallup, 1977; Gallup, Wallnau, & Suarez, 1980; Suarez & Gallup, 1981). The effect also seems to be limited to chimpanzees that have been raised with conspecifics; chimpanzees raised in isolation fail to show any evidence of self-recognition on the mirror test (Gallup, McClure, Hill, & Bundy, 1971). The capacity for a sense of self, therefore, is only found in chimpanzees and orangutans and requires social stimulation to develop to the point that it can be revealed by self-directed behavior. A recent study by Povinelli, Rulf, Landau, and Bierschwale (1993) indicates that self-recognition emerges during development in chimpanzees between four and eight years of age and declines in later adulthood. The finding that the chimpanzee's ability to recognize itself in a mirror declined with age is puzzling since such an important cognition, once acquired, should be retained throughout the lifetime of an animal (Heyes, 1995).

Alternative Accounts of the Mirror Experiments

It may be argued that showing self-directed behavior toward its image in a mirror and inspecting marked areas does not mean that an animal has a concept of self. Perhaps chimpanzees and orangutans learned to respond to a novel moving image seen in a mirror. The fact that that movement of this image correlated with their own proprioceptive feedback and that reflections showing it touching the image with its hands produced tactile sensations may have made the experience more interesting and motivated self-directed behavior. A dramatic change in the image caused by painting parts of it red led to frequent manual investigation of the novel painted regions. However, if apes were responding to their mirror image at this level of cognition, it would not mean that they had a human understanding of the image as representing themselves as a separate entity from others.

Heyes (1994) offered even a simpler interpretation of the mirror experiments. She suggests that chimpanzees and orangutans naturally have a high level of self-directed behavior. When introduced to a mirror, other-directed behavior toward the image in the mirror dominates the self-directed behavior. As the other-directed behavior becomes habituated, the normal level of self-directed behavior reemerges, giving the impression that the animal is showing progressively more interest in its own reflection. Thus, the appearance of growing interest in its own image may arise from nothing more than habituation of other-directed behavior.

As an account of the findings of the mark test, Heyes (1994) suggested that this may be an artifact of recovery from anesthesia. Animals were typically tested first without the mirror and then with the mirror after recovery from anesthesia. If the animals were still groggy from the anesthesia when tested without the mirror, they could have been too lethargic to show a normal or baseline level of self-directed behavior. By the time they were subsequently tested with the mirror, they may have been sufficiently recovered from the anesthesia to perform self-directed behavior at a normal level. The frequency of self-directed behavior, including face touching, would then go up from the mirror-absent test to the mirror-present test, giving the impression animals had an unusual interest in the painted image.

Several replies can be made to such criticism. With regard to the recovery from anesthesia argument, it is typically reported that animals are recovered from the anesthesia before testing. One assumes that primate researchers are able to determine that animals fully recovered motor function before testing them. Furthermore, the argument requires the unlikely assumption that in every experiment in which chimpanzees and orangutans showed significant mark touching, the short interval between the mirror-absent and mirror-present tests led to an appreciable recovery from the aftereffects of anesthesia. Povinelli et al. (1993) measured the mark-touching behavior of eight chimpanzees during periods of mirror monitoring (looking at the mirror) and nonmirror monitoring (not looking at the mirror). The mean number of mark touches was 11.1 during mirror monitoring but only 1.8 during nonmirror monitoring. If mark touching arose only from normal self-directed behavior, we should expect chimpanzees to touch the marked areas with approximately equal frequency while looking at or not looking at the mirror.

In a recent analysis of the face-touching behavior of one marked chimpanzee (Gallup, Povinelli, Suarez, Anderson, Lethmate, & Menzil, 1995), viewers were asked to score a 30-minute videotape for touches on both the marked eye and ear and the unmarked eye and ear. Viewers scored an average of about 5 touches on the marked eye and about 13 touches on the marked ear but only about 1 touch each on the unmarked eye and ear. The use of touches to the unmarked eye and ear as control observations suggests that the chimpanzee was not simply touching areas of its face indiscriminately.

Although the possibility that apes are just responding to an interesting image whose movement is correlated with their own motor behavior cannot be ruled out, it should be remembered that evidence of self-recognition is not found in any species of nonhuman other than chimpanzees and orangutans. One might well expect that monkeys and gorillas would also find intriguing a novel image that responds to their own movements and yields tactile sensations when seen to be touched. The circumscribed nature of the self-recognition phenomenon suggests that some special cognitive ability yields this effect in chimpanzees and orangutans but not in other nonhuman primates.

SOCIAL COGNITION

Social cognition refers to knowledge a primate may have about its position relative to other members of its group and about the positions other members of the group have relative to one another. In many species of monkeys, natal groups are formed of females, infants, and subadult males and females. Adult males tend to migrate to other groups. Within these groups, social associations are based strongly upon matrilineal kinship. Social interaction within groups is facilitated considerably by knowledge of kinship relationships and dominance relationships. To what extent do monkeys have such knowledge?

Kinship Relations

Cheney and Seyfarth carried out several observational studies of vervet monkeys that suggest that they are acutely aware of kinship relationships. In one playback study, they played the recorded screams of a two-year-old juvenile over a loudspeaker to a group of three female adult monkeys, one of whom was the mother of the infant heard (Cheney & Seyfarth, 1980; 1982). The mother looked at the loudspeaker and often approached it, suggesting that she recognized the voice as that of her offspring. Of particular interest, the remaining two females did not look at the loudspeaker or at one another but both looked at the mother. These females apparently associated the screams with the juvenile and its mother, indicating knowledge of which young monkeys belonged to which mothers.

In another study, Cheney and Seyfarth (1986) examined the frequency with which a monkey that had fought with another monkey engaged in aggression with kin of that monkey. A monkey was significantly more likely to threaten kin of another monkey if he fought with that monkey in the last two hours than if he had not fought with another monkey. Of even more interest was the finding that a monkey who observed a fight between his kin and another monkey was more likely to threaten the other monkey's kin within two hours than it was if no fight had occurred. This latter finding appeared only in monkeys over three years of age, suggesting that complete knowledge of social relationships within the group was acquired over a period of development. Evidence of complex kinship understanding has also been found in reconciliation behavior. Vervet monkeys are more likely to show reconciliation behavior toward another monkey following a fight between their kin and kin of the monkey toward whom the reconciliation is aimed (Cheney & Seyfarth, 1990a; 1990b).

Dasser (1988) carried out an experimental study of knowledge of kin relationships in two long-tailed macaques. The subjects were members of a captive group of 40 monkeys. They were trained and tested in apparatus similar to that described in Chapter 11 for studying concept learning in animals. In one experiment, a monkey was shown two pictures, one a picture of a mother-offspring pair and the other a picture of an unrelated pair of monkeys. The monkey was reinforced for always choosing the mother-offspring pair. After training with several pairs, testing was carried out with 14 novel sets of pictures. The mother-offspring pair was chosen on all 14 tests. The other monkey was tested in a matching-to-sample experiment, in which a picture of a female monkey was shown as a sample and the comparison stimuli were a picture of its offspring and a picture of an unrelated monkey. Out of 22 tests with novel sets of pictures, the monkey correctly matched by choice of the offspring on 20 occasions. In a final discrimination experiment, a monkey was rewarded for choosing pictures of sibling monkeys. The incorrect stimuli were pictures of a mother-offspring pair, a pair of matriline members related in some other way, or a pair of unrelated monkeys. Accuracy was quite high when the negative choice was unrelated monkeys or matriline members. When the negative choice was a mother-offspring pair, accuracy dropped to 70 percent (19 of 27) but was still significantly above chance. Apparently, siblings are more easily confused with mother-offspring pairs than with less closely related pairs.

The Cheney and Seyfarth (1990b) and Dasser (1988) experiments suggest that monkeys within a social group have considerable information not only about their own relationship to others but about numerous relationships among other members of the group. This knowledge may be obtained partly by observing the relative amounts of time different pairs or subgroups of monkeys spend together. Cheney and Seyfarth (1990b) argue that monkeys additionally learn about social relationships by observing the ways in which other monkeys socially interact with one another.

Deception

Based largely on field observations made by cognitive ethologists, it was suggested that primates living in social groups occasionally act to deceive one another to their own advantage (Byrne & Whiten, 1988). Because the act of deception means creating a false belief in someone else, the notion that animals are capable of deception implies a theory of mind. Philosopher Daniel Dennett suggested that beliefs may occur at progressively more complex *orders of intentionality* (Dennett, 1983). If a monkey believes that food is behind a tree, this is a first-order representation and requires no theory of mind. If another monkey is present and frequently glances at the tree, this may lead the first monkey to believe that the other monkey also knows where the food is; this is a second-order representation and clearly involves theory of mind. Suppose the second monkey frequently alternates glances between the tree and the first monkey. The first monkey may be led to believe that the second monkey knows both where the food is hidden and that the first monkey knows where the food is hidden. A third-order representation has been created, and still higher levels of representation can be imagined.

Deception may arise from creating a false belief at one level of representation. For example, suppose the first monkey intentionally looks away from the tree to create a belief in the second monkey that he does not know food is hidden behind it. If the second monkey now relaxes and does not attend to the first monkey, the first monkey may be able to make a dash for the hidden food and make off with it before the second monkey can react. The general implication of this scenario is that primates cunningly deceive one another in order to gain advantage in access to food, mates, social alliances, and other desirable things. It is suggested that these forms of behavior in primates represent *Machiavellian intelligence* (Byrne & Whiten, 1988).

As an example of behavior that suggests deception, Menzel (1978) studied social food finding in chimpanzees by showing one chimpanzee the location of hidden food in an open field while its companions remained in an enclosure. The informed chimpanzee was then returned to the group, and all of the chimpanzees were released together to find the food. The chimpanzees soon learned to track the path of the one who had been shown food and often extrapolated that path by running to a location ahead of the knowledgeable chimpanzee. Some chimpanzees that were shown food came to throw off the other animals by running in the opposite direction from the food and then doubling back to get the food before the others caught on. One interpretation of this behavior is that the chimpanzee who knew where the food was hidden wanted to create a second-order false belief in the other chimpanzees so that she could obtain the food for herself.

A general criticism of the argument for deception in primates is that it is mostly based upon anecdotal reports and thus is susceptible to all of faults discussed with the anecdotal method in Chapter 1. In an experimental study of deception carried out by Woodruff and D. Premack (1979), four common chimpanzees participated individually in a task that involved transmission of information between a chimpanzee subject and a human trainer. Two trainers were used, a cooperative trainer and a competitive trainer. The cooperative trainer wore a green laboratory suit and behaved in a friendly manner toward the chimpanzees. The competitive trainer wore black boots, a white coat, sunglasses, and a cloth mask across his mouth; he behaved in a hostile manner toward the chimpanzees, occasionally swatting them and talking to them in a low, gruff voice.

Chimpanzees participated in both production and comprehension experiments. In the production procedure, the chimpanzee was kept within an enclosure in a test room and was shown which of two containers outside the enclosure contained food. When the trainer then entered the room, it was his task to use the chimpanzee's behavior to determine which container had food. If the cooperative trainer chose the baited container, he shared the food with the chimpanzee. If he chose the unbaited container or could not make a choice, the chimpanzee got nothing. If the competitive trainer chose the baited container, he kept the food and gave the chimpanzee nothing. If he chose the unbaited container or could not make a choice because of lack of information, the chimpanzee received the reward. After a number of sessions of this task, the chimpanzees came to orient toward the food in the presence of the cooperative trainer. In the presence of the competitive trainer, they either oriented toward the empty container or provided no information.

In a comprehension version of this experiment, Woodruff and D. Premack (1979) had the chimpanzee and trainer reverse roles. Now, the trainer oriented or pointed toward the food, and the chimpanzee made the choice. The cooperative trainer always pointed at the baited container, and the competitive trainer always pointed at the empty container. The chimpanzees all came to follow the directions of the cooperative trainer and obtain the reward. In the presence of signals from the competitive trainer, however, three of the four chimpanzees came to avoid the container the trainer pointed at.

Chimpanzees behaved in these two experiments as if they had learned that the cooperative trainer was honest and the competitive trainer was a deceiver. In the comprehension experiment, they chose according to the correct information provided by the cooperative trainer, but treated the information provided by the competitive trainer as if it were a lie. As clever as this experiment is, however, it is susceptible to the same criticism made of some of the earlier theory-of-mind experiments discussed. That is, its findings can be explained as a consequence of conditional discrimination (Heyes, 1993a). Chimpanzees might have learned to choose the container pointed at by the person dressed in green and to avoid the container pointed at by the person dressed in white. In the production task, they may have learned to orient toward the baited container when the person dressed in green was present and to orient toward the nonbaited container or provide no information when the person dressed in white was present. Thus, chimpanzees could have behaved intelligently without inferring the intentions of their trainers.

This form of experiment still seems to hold considerable potential for studying the question of deception in primates. The triangulation method discussed with respect to the guesser-knower experiment might be used here. Is it possible to carry out further transfer tests that cannot be easily explained by conditional discrimination? Suppose that cooperative and competitive trainers the chimpanzees encountered in other contexts now acted as informants or had to base their choices on the chimpanzees' information. Would the chimpanzees deceive or treat as a deceiver the new competitive trainer and trust the new cooperative trainer? If the chimpanzees did behave in this way in the presence of new trainers, the claim that chimpanzees understand deceptive intention would be considerably strengthened.

IMITATION

The possibility that animals could learn to imitate the behavior of conspecifics or members of other species has long interested comparative psychologists. Although Romanes (1884) and others initially concluded that virtually all animals imitate, later investigators were highly skeptical of this conclusion and suggested that a variety of other observational learning processes account for what appeared to be imitation (Galef, 1988). For example, it was suggested that simply the presence of one animal may stimulate the performance of certain behaviors in another animal through *social facilitation.* If the induced behavior of the second animal is similar to that of the first, it may appear that one animal is imitating the other. Still another process that may lead to the appearance of imitation is *stimulus enhancement.* In many experimental studies of imitation, an observer animal observes a demonstrator animal perform an instrumental act, such as key pecking or bar pressing (Zentall, 1988). When tested, the observer often shows better performance of the instrumental behavior than control animals not allowed to observe the demonstrator. This positive transfer may arise not from imitation but from enhanced interest in the stimulus being manipulated (key or bar) from seeing another animal operate it.

Evidence of *true imitation* may be more difficult to find in both nonprimate and primate animals (Visalberghi & Fragaszy, 1990). Several criteria can be specified for imitative behavior. (1) The behavior should be *novel* and *complex.* In this way, we can be sure that the behavior is not already part of the animal's natural repertoire or a simple combination of natural behaviors. (2) The behavior should be based on *observation* and not on prior practice of reinforced activity. (3) Finally, imitative behavior should be *seen repeatedly* and should involve imitation of *different behaviors.* A tendency to repeat the behaviors of another in a variety of contexts suggests true imitation and not an isolated instance of behavior matching that might be attributed to other processes. Furthermore, the requirement for repeated observations rules out evidence based on the one-time anecdote.

A particularly promising design for the demonstration of imitation in animals is one in which different groups of animals observe demonstrators performing different behaviors that lead to the same outcome, usually the acquisition of food. True imitation is revealed if the observer then performed only the behavior it saw its demonstrator perform. In one such study carried out by Whiten, Custance, Gomez, Teixidor, and Bard (1996), common chimpanzees observed a human demonstrator open an "artificial fruit," a box containing food that could only be opened by operating a bolt mechanism. In one experiment, one group of chimpanzees observed a demonstrator opening the mechanism by poking bolts out of their ring holders; another group of chimpanzees observed a demonstrator twist and pull the bolts loose. When the observer chimpanzees were given an opportunity to open the artificial fruit, most of them used the particular poking or twisting technique seen used by their demonstrator. This finding suggests rather precise imitation of an observed behavioral act by chimpanzees and cannot be explained easily by either social facilitation or stimulus enhancement.

In a more natural setting, recent findings reported by Russon and Galdikas (1993) appear to provide surprisingly strong evidence of imitation in orangutans. Thirty orangutans were observed over a two-year period at Camp Leakey in Indonesia. All of these orangutans were ex-captive animals that were reclaimed and were undergoing rehabilitation for reentry into their natural habitat. The orangutans moved about freely in the camp area and observed camp workers involved in cooking, building and repairing buildings, boating, and other forms of camp maintenance. Several observers followed orangutans systematically and recorded 54 instances of reproductions of human behavior that were sufficiently complex to conclude that they could not have arisen from prior trial-and-error learning. As some examples, orangutans were observed to behave in ways that suggested they were attempting to siphon fuel out of a fuel can, to start a fire, to chop weeds and put them in a row, to paint with a brush, to hang hammocks, and to take boats out on the water. Many of these behaviors were performed immediately or shortly after an orangutan had observed a person performing the behavior.

The following passage describes the apparent attempts of the orangutan, Supinah, to replicate the camp cook's fire-making routine (see Figure 12.11):

> On entering the cooking area, Supinah picked up a burning stick, blew on its burning end, and briefly bit gingerly at its hot tip. She next went to the metal container, removed the plastic cup and round metal lid sitting on top (top left panel), scooped fuel from the container with the cup, and plunged the burning

FIGURE 12.11. Photographs of the orangutan Supinah imitating components of the camp cook's fire-making routine.
From Russon & Galdikas, 1993.

end of her stick into the fuel [Russon thought the container contained water, not fuel, and so let Supinah continue.] Plunging the stick into the fuel extinguished it. Supinah removed her stick and looked at it, dipped it back into the fuel, removed it and looked at it again, then got a second burning stick, and touched its burning tip to the extinguished tip of her first stick. Next, she poured the fuel from her cup back into the container (top right panel), placed the cup on the ground, picked up the container, poured new fuel from it into the cup (center left panel), stopped when the cup overflowed, and put the container down. She retrieved her first stick, put it back into the cup of fuel (center right panel), picked up the round metal lid, and fanned it repeatedly over the stick in the cup; in fanning she held the metal lid in one hand, in vertical position, and waved it back and forth horizontally in front of the cup and stick (bottom left panel). After this she removed the stick from the cup and blew at its [still extinguished] tip (bottom right panel). Her activities continued for another 10–15 min (pp. 152–153).

The mechanisms responsible for this imitative behavior in orangutans are not clearly understood. Orangutans imitated the behavior of both humans and other orangutans, and individual animals generally tended to imitate the behaviors of others with whom they had a positive affective relationship (Russon & Galdikas, 1993; 1995). Proponents of theory of mind could argue that these apes imitated positive models because they inferred their mental state and motivational goals (Heyes, 1993b). However, a critic could argue that orangutans most often imitated those they felt positive associations toward simply because these were the individuals they most often observed.

TOOL MAKING

Tool use is reported in several species of animals and particularly in primates (Beck, 1980). Most of the examples of imitative behavior by rehabilitant orangutans just discussed involved the use of a tool, and Kohler's (1925) early experiments revealed the use of sticks and boxes as tools. In more natural settings, common chimpanzees were observed to use a variety of tools (Lawick-Goodall, 1972). Termite fishing was observed in a number of instances; chimpanzees locate a termite hole in a mound and use sticks to probe the hole for termites, which they lick off the stick each time it is retrieved. Leaves were used as tools by chimpanzees for a variety of purposes, including wiping themselves and others, dabbing a bleeding wound, and sopping up water from a hollow in a tree. Chimpanzees were often observed to throw rocks and branches at intruders.

In West Africa, a number of field studies found that chimpanzees use a hammer and anvil to crack varieties of wild nuts (Sakura & Matsuzawa, 1991; Struhsaker & Hunkeler, 1971; Sugiyama & Koman, 1979; Whitesides, 1985). Considerable variability in the materials used was found. Two rocks were often used, but, in other cases, the anvil was a piece of wood or a tree root, and the hammer was a stick. Chimpanzees showed strong hand preferences in nut cracking, typically using one hand to place the nut on the anvil and the other hand to wield the hammer (Sugiyama, Fushimi, Sakura, & Matsuzawa, 1993). Nut-cracking behavior was acquired gradually by young chimpanzees and passed through several stages, starting with simple object manipulation and progressing through more advanced stages of striking at the nut until adultlike nut cracking was achieved after three years of age (Matsuzawa, 1994). In one study, use of a *metatool* was reported; chimpanzees used a second stone as a wedge to place under the anvil to keep its surface level (Matsuzawa, 1994).

Although a variety of animals use tools, it was suggested that the distinguishing characteristic of humans is that they can make tools (Oakley, 1949). Some observations of chimpanzees challenge even this idea. Chimpanzees performed extensive tool preparation and modification while termite fishing. They were observed selecting branches or twigs from trees and stripping them to form a stick that fit into the termite hole. If the end of the stick became too flexible with use, it was bitten off to form a more rigid tool (Lawick-Goodall, 1972). If apes can make tools, then we may ask if they can perform a still more complex form of human tool construction—using a tool to make another tool.

Wynn and McGrew (1989) concluded that tool use observed in contemporary apes is no less advanced than that used in Oldowan stone technology by our hominoid ancestors more than 2 million years ago. However, one of the abilities clearly revealed by investigations of Oldowan artifacts was that of forming stone flakes for cutting by striking stones together. In fact, stone knapping was done in a very precise fashion by striking a hammer against a core at the appropriate angle to produce just the right flake needed as a tool. Could an ape learn to do this? R. Wright (1972) trained an orangutan named Abang to use a hammerstone to strike a flint core and produce a stone flake. Abang then used the sharp flake to cut through a cord and gain access to a box containing food.

More recently, a similar study was pursued with the bonobo Kanzi (Savage-Rumbaugh & Lewin, 1994; Toth, Schick, Savage-Rumbaugh, Sevcik, & Rumbaugh, 1993). Wright (1972) used repeated demonstrations to train Abang to imitate his trainer's use of a stone tool to form a cutting tool. In the study with Kanzi, the investigators asked if he could adopt the same type of behavior through insight and not repeated training trials. Kanzi was shown a container with a transparent lid that contained a food reward and that could be opened only by cutting a length of cord. Kanzi was given some preliminary instruction on how to flake stones by striking one against the other and how a sharp flake could be used to cut the cord. However, beyond these initial demonstrations, he was not required to make a tool and use it. He was simply placed in an environment with the baited box and numerous rocks available. Kanzi initially learned to select sharper flakes made by human demonstrators to use to cut the cord. He then began to strike rocks against one another, initially with little force, but eventually with sufficient force and precision to produce stone flakes he could use for cutting (see Figure 12.12). Eventually, Kanzi produced flakes by rock throwing. He was able to shatter rocks by throwing them at the floor when indoors and against other rocks when outside. Thus, Kanzi developed a stone-flake tool-making method that was sufficient for the purpose at hand, although it did not match the more precise stone-knapping techniques used by early hominoids at Oldowan.

FIGURE 12.12. Photograph of the bonobo Kanzi making a stone flake by striking a quartzite hammerstone against a chert core.
From Toth, Schick, Savage-Rumbaugh, Sevcik, & Rumbaugh, 1993.

Evidence for tool use and tool making in apes is impressive. Although their tool-related activities are not elaborate by human standards, their use of tools is highly functional. They appear to use tools or make tools in the simplest form that gets the job done. If apes are given problems that require more sophisticated tool making in future research, we may find evidence of still more complex tool construction by these animals.

SUMMARY

Most of the work reviewed in this chapter has been performed over the past 25 years. During that period, there was a renewal of interest in primate cognition that led to an unprecedented amount of research on the intelligence of monkeys and apes. Over this period, an initial exuberance for the possibility of developing a language link with apes was extinguished by studies suggesting that much of their signing was imitation or operant behavior intended to gain reward. However, investigators profited from that early work by learning how to devise more refined experiments that addressed basic questions about semanticity and syntax. These studies revealed that chimpanzees are capable of understanding lexigrams as symbols and showing syntactical rules in the order in which they produce symbols. The aim of this more recent work was to learn about the communicative abilities of apes rather than to train them to use a human language.

Partly as an outgrowth of the ape language research, a number of other questions about primates' reasoning abilities were raised. A wide variety of types of research addressed these questions, including field observations, experiments carried out in the field, and more precisely controlled experiments carried out in psychology laboratories and zoos with captive primates. It has long been clear that apes can solve many practical problems, such as using sticks to rake in food or stacking boxes to use as a ladder to reach food. In more recent studies, it was asked whether they can solve more abstract problems, such as understanding analogies and the operations by which objects change state. D. Premack (1983) argued that primates have the capability to solve such problems through use of an abstract code; the abstract code emerges, however, only through the conceptual training required for symbolic communication.

Other investigators raised the issue of theory of mind in nonhuman primates. Is a monkey or ape aware of other minds or of its own mind? Closely related work on self-recognition in mirrors, the ability of animals to reverse roles, and the ability to infer knowledge from observing perception by another organism led Gallup and Povinelli to the hypothesis that only apes have a theory of mind. They suggest that apes, but not monkeys, are capable of attributing mental states to other individuals and of being aware of their own mental states. Critics dispute these claims, arguing that more basic associative processes explain many of the findings used to support the notion of theory of mind in apes. The product of this theory and criticism should be better, more controlled experiments aimed at testing the theory-of-mind hypothesis.

Research in other areas tends to support the impression that there is a substantial gap between ape and monkey cognition (Byrne, 1995). Apes solve complex problems (e.g., the trap-tube problem), show true imitation, and use and make tools, whereas these abilities are rarely seen in monkeys. The cognitive capacities of apes, combined with their close genetic and evolutionary links to humans, make research with chimpanzees, gorillas, and orangutans the focus of questions about human uniqueness. Although the cognitive skills of apes still seem primitive relative to human skills, are these differences only quantitative? Are the same abstract reasoning and inferential abilities found in man found in apes in weaker form? Could the capacity for abstract thought have been passed from a common ancestor to both human and ape? These are exciting and important questions. Their answers will illuminate both our evolutionary history and our relationship to our closest animal relatives. The progress toward answering these questions has been immense in the past 25 years. Continuing research with human and nonhuman primates undoubtedly holds further surprising answers in store for us.

References

ADAMS, D. K. (1929). Experimental studies of adaptive behavior in cats. *Comparative Psychology Monographs, 6*, 1–166.

ADAMS, J. A. (1961). The second facet of forgetting: A review of warm-up decrement. *Psychological Bulletin, 58*, 257–273.

ALDRIDGE, J. W., BERRIDGE, K. C., HERMAN, M., & ZIMMER, L. (1993). Neuronal coding of serial order: Syntax of grooming in the neostriatum. *Psychological Science, 4*, 391–395.

ALLAN, L. G., & GIBBON, J. (1991). Human bisection at the geometric mean. *Learning and Motivation, 22*, 39–58.

ALLOWAY, T. M. (1969). Effects of low temperature upon acquisition and retention in the grain beetle (*Tenebrio molitor*). *Journal of Comparative and Physiological Psychology, 69*, 1–8.

AMMONS, R. B. (1947). Acquisition of motor skill: I. Quantitative analysis and theoretical formulation. *Psychological Review, 54*, 263–281.

AMSEL, A. (1962). Frustrative nonreward in partial reinforcement and discrimination learning. *Psychological Review, 69*, 306–328.

AMSEL, A. (1967). Partial reinforcement effects on vigor and persistence. In K. W. SPENCE & J. T. SPENCE (Eds.), *The psychology of learning and motivation* (Vol. 1, pp. 1–65). San Diego: Academic Press.

ANDERSON, J. R. (1980). *Cognitive psychology and its implications.* San Francisco: W. H. Freeman and Company.

ANISMAN, H. (1975). Time-dependent variations in aversively motivated behaviors: Nonassociative effects of cholinergic and catecholaminergic activity. *Psychological Review, 82*, 359–385.

ARNDT, W. (1939). Abschliebende versuche zur frage des "zahl"—Vermogens der haustaube. *Zeitschrift fur Tierpsychologie, 3*, 88–142.

ASCH, S., HAY, J., & DIAMOND, R. M. (1960). Perceptual organization in serial rote-learning. *American Journal of Psychology, 73*, 177–198.

ASH, M., & ROBERTS, W. A. (1992). Central-place foraging by rats on the radial maze: The effects of patch size, food distribution, and travel time. *Animal Learning & Behavior, 20*, 127–134.

ASTLEY, S. L., & WASSERMAN, E. A. (1992). Categorical discrimination and generalization in pigeons: All negative stimuli are not created equal. *Journal of Experimental Psychology: Animal Behavior Processes, 18*, 193–207.

ATKINSON, R. C., & SHIFFRIN, R. M. (1968). Human memory: A proposed system and its control processes. In K. W. SPENCE & J. T. SPENCE (Eds.), *The psychology of learning and motivation: Advances in research and theory* (pp. 89–195). New York: Academic Press.

ATKINSON, R. C., & SHIFFRIN, R. M. (1971). The control of short-term memory. *Scientific American, 225,* 82–90.

AYDIN, A., & PEARCE, J. M. (1994). Prototype effects in categorization by pigeons. *Journal of Experimental Psychology: Animal Behavior Processes, 20,* 264–277.

BADDELEY, A. D. (1978). The trouble with levels: A reexamination of Craik and Lockhart's framework for memory research. *Psychological Review, 85,* 139–152.

BADDELEY, A. D. (1981). The concept of working memory: A view of its current state and probable future development. *Cognition, 10,* 17–23.

BALAZ, M. A., GUTSIN, P., CACHEIRO, H., & MILLER, R. R. (1982). Blocking as a retrieval failure: Reactivation of associations to a blocked stimulus. *Quarterly Journal of Experimental Psychology, 34B,* 99–113.

BALDA, R. P., & TUREK, R. J. (1984). The cache-recovery system as an example of memory capabilities in Clark's nutcracker. In H. L. ROITBLAT, T. G. BEVER, & H. S. TERRACE (Eds.), *Animal cognition* (pp. 513–532). Hillsdale, NJ: Erlbaum.

BEACH, F. A. (1950). The snark was a boojum. *American Psychologist, 5,* 115–124.

BEATTY, W. W., & SHAVALIA, D. A. (1980a). Spatial memory in rats: Time course of working memory and effect of anesthetics. *Behavioral and Neural Biology, 28,* 454–462.

BEATTY, W. W., & SHAVALIA, D. A. (1980b). Rat spatial memory: Resistance to retroactive interference at long retention intervals. *Animal Learning & Behavior, 8,* 550–552.

BECK, B. B. (1980). *Animal tool behavior.* New York: Garland STPM Press.

BHATT, R. S., WASSERMAN, E. A., REYNOLDS, W. F., & KNAUSS, K. S. (1988). Conceptual behavior in pigeons: Categorization of both familiar and novel examples from four classes of natural and artificial stimuli. *Journal of Experimental Psychology: Animal Behavior Processes, 14,* 219–234.

BIEBACH, H., GORDIJN, M., & KREBS, J. R. (1989). Time-and-place learning by garden warblers, *Sylvia borin. Animal Behaviour, 37,* 353–360.

BIEDERMAN, I. (1987). Recognition-by-components: A theory of human image understanding. *Psychological Review, 94,* 115–147.

BITTERMAN, M. E. (1965a). The evolution of intelligence. *Scientific American, 212,* 92–100.

BITTERMAN, M. E. (1965b). Phyletic differences in learning. *American Psychologist, 20,* 396–410.

BITTERMAN, M. E. (1975). The comparative analysis of learning: Are the laws of learning the same in all animals? *Science, 188,* 699–709.

BITTERMAN, M. E. (1996). Comparative analysis of learning in honeybees. *Animal Learning & Behavior, 24,* 123–141.

BJORK, R. A. (1972). Theoretical implications of directed forgetting. In A. W. MELTON and E. MARTIN (Eds.), *Coding processes in human memory* (pp. 217–235). Washington, D.C.: Winston.

BLODGETT, H. C. (1929). The effect of the introduction of reward upon the maze performance of rats. *University of California Publications in Psychology, 4,* 113–134.

BLOCK, R. A. (1971). Effects of instructions to forget in short-term memory. *Journal of Experimental Psychology, 89,* 1–9.

BLOUGH, D. S. (1956). Dark adaptation in the pigeon. *Journal of Comparative and Physiological Psychology, 49,* 425–430.

BLOUGH, D. S. (1957). Spectral sensitivity in the pigeon. *Journal of the Optical Society of America, 47,* 827–833.

BLOUGH, D. S. (1958). A method for obtaining psychophysical thresholds from the pigeon. *Journal of the Experimental Analysis of Behavior, 1,* 31–43.

BLOUGH, D. S. (1959). Delayed matching in the pigeon. *Journal of the Experimental Analysis of Behavior, 2,* 151–160.

BLOUGH, D. S. (1961). Experiments in animal psychophysics. *Scientific American, 205,* 113–122.

BLOUGH, D. S. (1989). Odd-item search in pigeons: Display size and transfer effects. *Journal of Experimental Psychology: Animal Behavior Processes, 15,* 14–22.

BLOUGH, D. S. (1993). Effects on search speed of the probability of target-distractor combinations. *Journal of Experimental Psychology: Animal Behavior Processes, 19,* 231–243.

BLOUGH, D. S., & FRANKLIN, J. J. (1985). Pigeon discrimination of letters and other forms in texture displays. *Perception & Psychophysics, 38,* 523–532.

BLOUGH, P. M. (1991). Selective attention and search images in pigeons. *Journal of Experimental Psychology: Animal Behavior Processes, 17,* 292–298.

BLOUGH, P. M. (1992). Detectability and choice during visual search: Joint effects of sequential priming and discriminability. *Animal Learning & Behavior, 20,* 293–300.

BLUMBERG, M. S., & WASSERMAN, E. A. (1995). Animal mind and the argument from design. *American Psychologist, 50,* 133–144.

BOLHUIS, J. J., & VAN KAMPEN, H. S. (1988). Serial position curves in spatial memory of rats: Primacy and recency effects. *Quarterly Journal of Experimental Psychology, 40B,* 135–149.

BOLLES, R. C. (1970). Species-specific defense reactions and avoidance learning. *Psychological Review, 71,* 32–48.

BOLLES, R. C. (1975). Learning, motivation, and cognition. In W. K. ESTES (Ed.), *Handbook of learning and cognitive processes: Introduction to concepts and issues* (Vol. 1, pp. 249–280). Hillsdale, NJ: Erlbaum.

BOND, A. B. (1983). Visual search and selection of natural stimuli in the pigeon. The attention threshold hypothesis. *Journal of Experimental Psychology: Animal Behavior Processes, 9,* 292–306.

BORING, E. G. (1950). *A history of experimental psychology.* New York: Appleton-Century-Crofts.

BOUSFIELD, W. A. (1953). The occurrence of clustering in the recall of randomly arranged associates. *Journal of General Psychology, 49,* 229–240.

BOUTON, M. E. (1991). Context and retrieval in extinction and in other examples of interference in simple associative learning. In L. DACHOWSKI & C. F. FLAHERTY (Eds.), *Current topics in animal learning: Brain, emotion, and cognition* (pp. 25–53). Hillsdale, NJ: Erlbaum.

BOUTON, M. E., & KING, D. A. (1983). Contextual control of the extinction of conditioned fear: Tests for the associative value of the context. *Journal of Experimental Psychology: Animal Behavior Processes, 9,* 248–265.

BOWER, G. H. (1967). A multi-component theory of the memory trace. In K. W. SPENCE & J. T. SPENCE (Eds.), *The psychology of learning and motivation: Advances in research and theory* (pp. 230–325). San Diego: Academic Press.

BOYSEN, S. T. (1993). Counting in chimpanzees: Nonhuman principles and emergent properties of number. In S. T. BOYSEN & E. J. CAPALDI (Eds.), *The development of numerical competence: Animal and human models* (pp. 39–59). Hillsdale, NJ: Erlbaum.

BOYSEN, S. T., & BERNTSON, G. G. (1989). Numerical competence in a chimpanzee (*Pan troglodytes*). *Journal of Comparative Psychology, 103,* 23–31.

BOYSEN, S. T., & BERNTSON, G. G. (1995). Responses to quantity: Perceptual versus cognitive mechanisms in chimpanzees (*Pan troglodytes*). *Journal of Experimental Psychology: Animal Behavior Processes, 21,* 82–86.

BOYSEN, S. T., BERNTSON, G. G., HANNAN, M. B., & CACIOPPO, J. T. (1996). Quantity-based interference and symbolic representations in chimpanzees (*Pan troglodytes*). *Journal of Experimental Psychology: Animal Behavior Processes, 22,* 76–86.

BOYSEN, S. T., BERNTSON, G. G., SHREYER, T. A., & HANNAN, M. B. (1995). Indicating acts during counting by a chimpanzee (*Pan troglodytes*). *Journal of Comparative Psychology, 109,* 47–51.

BOYSEN, S. T., BERNTSON, G. G., SHREYER, T. A., & QUIGLEY, K. S. (1993). Processing of ordinality and transivity by chimpanzees (*Pan troglodytes*). *Journal of Comparative Psychology, 107,* 208–215.

BROADBENT, D. E. (1958). *Perception and communication.* London: Pergamon Press.

BROADBENT, H. A., CHURCH, R. M., MECK, W. H., & RAKITIN, B. C. (1993). Quantitative relationships between timing and counting. In S. T. BOYSEN & E. J. CAPALDI (Eds.), *The development of numerical competence: Animal and human models* (pp. 171–187). Hillsdale, NJ: Erlbaum.

BROCKBANK, T. W. (1919). Redintegration in the albino rat: A study in retention. *Behavior Monographs, 4,* 1–66.

BRODIGAN, D. L., & PETERSON, G. B. (1976). Two-choice conditional discrimination performance of pigeons as a function of reward expectancy, prechoice delay, and domesticity. *Animal Learning & Behavior, 4,* 121–124.

BROGDEN, W. J. (1939). Sensory pre-conditioning. *Journal of Experimental Psychology, 25,* 323–332.

BROWN, J. (1958). Some tests of the decay theory of immediate memory. *Quarterly Journal of Experimental Psychology, 10,* 12–24.

BROWN, M. F. (1992). Does a cognitive map guide choices in the radial-arm maze? *Journal of Experimental Psychology: Animal Behavior Processes, 18,* 56–66.

BROWN, M. F., & MORRISON, S. K. (1990). Element and compound matching-to-sample performance in pigeons: The roles of information load and training history. *Journal of Experimental Psychology: Animal Behavior Processes, 16,* 185–192.

BROWN, P. L., & JENKINS, H. M. (1968). Auto-shaping of the pigeon's key-peck. *Journal of the Experimental Analysis of Behavior, 11,* 1–8.

BROWN, S. W., & MELLGREN, R. L. (1994). Distinction between places and paths in rats' spatial representations. *Journal of Experimental Psychology: Animal Behavior Processes, 20,* 20–31.

BUNCH, M. E. (1939). Transfer of training in the mastery of an antagonistic habit after varying intervals of time. *Journal of Comparative Psychology, 28,* 189–200.

BUNCH, M. E. (1941). A comparison of retention and transfer of training from similar material after relatively long intervals of time. *Journal of Comparative Psychology, 32,* 217–231.

BURGHARDT, G. M. (1985). Animal awareness: Current perceptions and historical perspective. *American Psychologist, 40,* 905–919.

BYRNE, R. (1995). *The thinking ape: Evolutionary origins of intelligence.* Oxford: Oxford University Press.

BYRNE, R., & WHITEN, A. (1988). *Machiavellian intelligence.* Oxford: Oxford University Press.

CABE, P. A. (1976). Transfer of discrimination from solid objects to pictures by pigeons: A test of theoretical models of pictorial perception. *Perception & Psychophysics, 19,* 545–550.

CABE, P. A. (1980). Picture perception in nonhuman subjects. In M. A. HAGEN (Ed.), *The perception of pictures* (pp. 305–343). San Diego: Academic Press.

CAMPBELL, B. A., JAYNES, J., & MISANIN, J. R. (1968). Retention of a light-dark discrimination in rats of different ages. *Journal of Comparative and Physiological Psychology, 66,* 467–472.

CAMPBELL, C. B. G., & HODOS, W. (1991). The *Scala naturae* revisited: Evolutionary scales and anagenesis in comparative psychology. *Journal of Comparative Psychology, 105,* 211–221.

CANDLAND, D. K. (1993). *Feral children & clever animals: Reflections on human nature.* New York: Oxford University Press.

CAPALDI, E. J. (1958). The effect of different amounts of training on the resistance to extinction of different patterns of partially reinforced responses. *Journal of Comparative and Physiological Psychology, 51,* 367–371.

CAPALDI, E. J. (1966). Partial reinforcement: A hypothesis of sequential effects. *Psychological Review, 73,* 459–477.

CAPALDI, E. J. (1967). A sequential hypothesis of instrumental learning. In K. W. SPENCE & J. T. SPENCE (Eds.), *The psychology of learning and motivation: Advances in research and theory* (Vol. 1; pp. 67–156). San Diego: Academic Press.

CAPALDI, E. J. (1971). Memory and learning: A sequential viewpoint. In W. K. HONIG & P. H. R. JAMES (Eds.), *Animal memory* (pp. 111–154). San Diego: Academic Press.

CAPALDI, E. J. (1992). Levels of organized behavior in rats. In W. K. HONIG & J. G. FETTERMAN (Eds.), *Cognitive aspects of stimulus control* (pp. 385–404). Hillsdale, NJ: Erlbaum.

CAPALDI, E. J. (1993). Animal number abilities: Implications for a hierarchical approach to instrumental learning. In S. T. BOYSEN & E. J. CAPALDI (Eds.), *The development of numerical competence: Animal and human models* (pp. 191–209). Hillsdale, NJ: Erlbaum.

CAPALDI, E. J., & MILLER, D. J. (1988). Counting in rats: Its functional significance and the independent cognitive processes that constitute it. *Journal of Experimental Psychology: Animal Behavior Processes, 14,* 3–17.

CAPALDI, E. J., MILLER, D. J., ALPTEKIN, S., & BARRY, K. (1990). Organized responding in instrumental learning: Chunks and superchunks. *Learning and Motivation, 21,* 415–433.

CAPALDI, E. J., VERRY, D. R., & DAVIDSON, T. L. (1980). Why rule encoding by animals in serial learning remains to be established. *Animal Learning & Behavior, 8,* 691–692.

CARLSON, N. J., & BLACK, A. H. (1960). Traumatic avoidance learning: The effects of preventing escape responses. *Canadian Journal of Psychology, 14,* 21–28.

CARTER, D. E., & ECKERMAN, D. A. (1975). Symbolic matching by pigeons: Rate of learning complex discriminations predicted from simple discriminations. *Science, 187,* 662–664.

CARTER, D. E., & WERNER, T. J. (1978). Complex learning and information processing by pigeons: A critical analysis. *Journal of the Experimental Analysis of Behavior, 29,* 565–601.

CARTWRIGHT, B. A., & COLLETT, T. S. (1983). Landmark learning in bees. *Journal of Comparative Physiology A, 151,* 521–543.

CASTRO, C. A., & LARSEN, T. (1992). Primacy and recency effects in nonhuman primates. *Journal of Experimental Psychology: Animal Behavior Processes, 18,* 335–340.

CATANIA, A. C. (1970). Reinforcement schedules and psychophysical judgments: A study of some temporal properties of behavior. In W. N. SCHOENFELD (Ed.), *The theory of reinforcement schedules* (pp. 1–42). New York: Appleton-Century-Crofts.

CERELLA, J. (1979). Visual classes and natural categories in the pigeon. *Journal of Experimental Psychology: Human Perception and Performance, 5,* 68–77.

CERELLA, J. (1980). The pigeon's analysis of pictures. *Pattern Recognition, 12,* 1–6.

CERELLA, J. (1982). Mechanisms of concept formation in the pigeon. In D. J. INGLE, M. A. GOODALE, & R. W. MANSFIELD (Eds.), *Analysis of visual behavior* (pp. 241–263). Cambridge, MA: MIT Press.

CHAPUIS, N., & VARLET, C. (1987). Shortcuts by dogs in natural surroundings. *The Quarterly Journal of Experimental Psychology, 39B,* 49–64.

CHENEY, D. L., & SEYFARTH, R. M. (1980). Vocal recognition in vervet monkeys. *Animal Behaviour, 28,* 362–367.

CHENEY, D. L., & SEYFARTH, R. M. (1982). Recognition of individuals within and across groups of free-ranging vervet monkeys. *American Zoology, 22,* 519–529.

CHENEY, D. L., & SEYFARTH, R. M. (1986). The recognition of social alliances by vervet monkeys. *Animal Behaviour, 34,* 1722–1731.

CHENEY, D. L., & SEYFARTH, R. M. (1990a). Reconciliation and redirected aggression in vervet monkeys (*Cercopithecus aethiops*). *Behaviour, 110,* 258–275.

CHENEY, D. L., & SEYFARTH, R. M. (1990b). The representation of social relations by monkeys. *Cognition, 37,* 167–196.

CHENEY, D. L., & SEYFARTH, R. M. (1990c). *How monkeys see the world.* Chicago: University of Chicago Press.

CHENG, K. (1986). A purely geometric module in the rat's spatial representation. *Cognition, 23,* 149–178.

CHENG, K. (1988). Some psychophysics of the pigeon's use of landmarks. *Journal of Comparative Physiology A, 162,* 815–826.

CHENG, K. (1989). The vector sum model of pigeon landmark use. *Journal of Experimental Psychology: Animal Behavior Processes, 15,* 366–375.

CHENG, K. (1990). More psychophysics of the pigeon's use of landmarks. *Journal of Comparative Physiology A, 166,* 857–863.

CHENG, K., COLLETT, T. S., PICKHARD, A, & WEHNER, R. (1987). The use of visual landmarks by honeybees: Bees weight landmarks according to their distance from the goal. *Journal of Comparative Physiology A, 161,* 469–475.

CHENG, K., COLLETT, T. S., & WEHNER, R. (1986). Honeybees learn the colours of landmarks. *Journal of Comparative Physiology A, 159,* 69–73.

CHENG, K., & ROBERTS, W. A. (1991). Three psychophysical principles of timing in pigeons. *Learning and Motivation, 22,* 112–128.

CHENG, K., & SHERRY, D. F. (1992). Landmark-based spatial memory in birds (*Parus atricapillus* and *Columba livia*): The use of edges and distances to represent spatial positions. *Journal of Comparative Psychology, 106,* 331–341.

CHENG, K., & WESTWOOD, R. (1993). Analysis of single trials in pigeons' timing performance. *Journal of Experimental Psychology: Animal Behavior Processes, 19,* 56–67.

CHENG, K., WESTWOOD, R., & CRYSTAL, J. D. (1993). Memory variance in the peak procedure of timing in pigeons. *Journal of Experimental Psychology: Animal Behavior Processes, 19,* 68–76.

CHERRY, E. C. (1953). Some experiments on the recognition of speech with one and with two ears. *Journal of the Acoustical Society of America, 25,* 275–279.

CHURCH, R. M. (1978). The internal clock. In S. H. HULSE, H. FOWLER, & W. K. HONIG (Eds.), *Cognitive processes in animal behavior* (pp. 277–310). Hillsdale, NJ: Erlbaum.

CHURCH, R. M. (1993). Human models of animal behavior. *Psychological Science, 4,* 170–173.

CHURCH, R. M., & DELUTY, M. Z. (1977). Bisection of temporal intervals. *Journal of Experimental Psychology: Animal Behavior Processes, 3,* 216–228.

CHURCH, R. M., & GIBBON, J. (1982). Temporal generalization. *Journal of Experimental Psychology: Animal Behavior Processes, 8,* 165–186.

CHURCH, R. M., MECK, W. H., & GIBBON, J. (1994). Application of scalar timing theory to individual trials. *Journal of Experimental Psychology: Animal Behavior Processes, 20,* 135–155.

COHEN, L. R., LOONEY, T. A., BRADY, J. H., & AUCELLA, A. F. (1976). Differential sample response schedules in acquisition of conditional discriminations by pigeons. *Journal of the Experimental Analysis of Behavior, 26,* 301–314.

COILE, D. C., & MILLER, N. E. (1984). How radical animal activists try to mislead humane people. *American Psychologist, 39,* 700–701.

COLE, P. D., & HONIG, W. K. (1994). Transfer of a discrimination by pigeons (*Columba livia*) between pictured locations and the represented environments. *Journal of Comparative Psychology, 108,* 189–198.

COLLETT, T. S., CARTWRIGHT, B. A., & SMITH, B. A. (1986). Landmark learning and visuo-spatial memories in gerbils. *Journal of Comparative Physiology A, 158,* 835–851.

COLLETT, T. S., & LAND, M. F. (1975). Visual spatial memory in a hoverfly. *Journal of Comparative Physiology A, 100,* 59–84.

COLWILL, R. M., & RESCORLA, R. A. (1990). Evidence for the hierarchical structure of instrumental learning. *Animal Learning & Behavior, 18,* 71–82.

COOK, R. G. (1980). Retroactive interference in pigeon short-term memory by a reduction in ambient illumination. *Journal of Experimental Psychology: Animal Behavior Processes, 6,* 326–338.

COOK, R. G. (1992a). Acquisition and transfer of visual texture discriminations by pigeons. *Journal of Experimental Psychology: Animal Behavior Processes, 18,* 341–353.

COOK, R. G. (1992b). Dimensional organization and texture discrimination in pigeons. *Journal of Experimental Psychology: Animal Behavior Processes, 18,* 354–363.

COOK, R. G. (1993a). The experimental analysis of cognition in animals. *Psychological Science, 4,* 174–178.

COOK, R. G. (1993b). Gestalt contributions to visual texture discriminations by pigeons. In T. R. ZENTALL (Ed.), *Animal cognition: A tribute to Donald A. Riley* (pp. 251–269). Hillsdale, NJ: Erlbaum.

COOK, R. G., BROWN, M. F., & RILEY, D. A. (1985). Flexible memory processing by rats: Use of prospective and retrospective information in the radial maze. *Journal of Experimental Psychology: Animal Behavior Processes, 11,* 453–469.

COOK, R. G., WRIGHT, A. A., & SANDS, S. F. (1991). Interstimulus interval and viewing time effects in monkey list memory. *Animal Learning & Behavior, 19,* 153–163.

COONS, E. E., & MILLER, N. E. (1960). Conflict versus consolidation of memory traces to explain "retrograde amnesia" produced by ECS. *Journal of Comparative and Physiological Psychology, 53,* 524–531.

COPPENS, Y. (1994). East side story: The origin of humankind. *Scientific American, 270,* 88–95.

COWAN, E. A. (1923). An experiment testing the ability of a cat to make delayed response and to maintain a given response toward a varying stimulus. *Journal of Comparative Psychology, 3,* 1–9.

COWIE, R. J., KREBS, J. R., & SHERRY, D. F. (1981). Food storing by marsh tits. *Animal Behaviour, 29,* 1252–1259.

COWLES, J. T. (1940). "Delayed response" as tested by three methods and its relation to other learning situations. *Journal of Psychology, 9,* 103–130.

COWLES, J. T., & FINAN, J. L. (1941). An improved method for establishing temporal discrimination in white rats. *Journal of Psychology, 11,* 335–342.

COX, J. K., & D'AMATO, M. R. (1982). Matching to compound samples by monkeys (*Cebus apella*): Shared attention or generalization decrement? *Journal of Experimental Psychology: Animal Behavior Processes, 8,* 209–225.

CRAIK, F. I. M., & LOCKHART, R. S. (1972). Levels of processing: A framework for memory research. *Journal of Verbal Learning and Verbal Behavior, 11,* 671–684.

CRESPI, L. P. (1942). Quantitative variation in incentive and performance in the white rat. *American Journal of Psychology, 55,* 467–517.

CRICHTON, M. (1980). *Congo.* New York: Random House.

CROWELL, C. R., HINSON, R. E., & SIEGEL, S. (1981). The role of conditional drug responses in tolerance to the hypothermic effects of ethanol. *Psychopharmacology, 73,* 51–54.

CUMMING, W. W., & BERRYMAN, R. (1965). The complex discriminated operant: Studies of matching-to-sample and related problems. In D. I. MOSTOFSKY (Ed.), *Stimulus generalization* (pp. 284–330). Stanford: Stanford University Press.

DALLAL, N. L., & MECK, W. H. (1990). Hierarchical structures: Chunking by food type facilitates spatial memory. *Journal of Experimental Psychology: Animal Behavior Processes, 16,* 69–84.

D'AMATO, M. R. (1973). Delayed matching and short-term memory in monkeys. In G. H. BOWER (Ed.), *The psychology of learning and motivation: Advances in research and theory* (pp. 227–269). New York: Academic Press.

D'AMATO, M. R., & COLOMBO, M. (1988). Representation of serial order in monkeys (*Cebus apella*). *Journal of Experimental Psychology: Animal Behavior Processes, 14,* 131–139.

D'AMATO, M. R., & COLOMBO, M. (1989). Serial learning with wild card items by monkeys (*Cebus apella*): Implications for knowledge of ordinal position. *Journal of Comparative Psychology, 103,* 252–261.

D'AMATO, M. R., & O'NEILL, W. (1971). Effect of delay-interval illumination on matching behavior in the capuchin monkey. *Journal of the Experimental Analysis of Behavior, 15,* 327–333.

D'AMATO, M. R., & WORSHAM, R. W. (1972). Delayed matching in the capuchin monkey with brief sample durations. *Learning and Motivation, 3,* 304–312.

DARWIN, C. (1958). *The origin of species by means of natural selection or the preservation of favoured races in the struggle for life.* New York: Mentor Books. Originally published in 1859.

DARWIN, C. (1871). *The descent of man, and selection in relation to sex.* London: John Murray.

DASSER, V. (1988). A social concept in Java monkeys. *Animal Behaviour, 36,* 225–230.

DAVIS, H. (1984). Discrimination of the number three by a raccoon (*Procyon lotor*). *Animal Learning & Behavior, 12,* 409–413.

DAVIS, H. (1992). Transitive inference in rats (*Rattus norvegicus*). *Journal of Comparative Psychology, 106,* 342–349.

DAVIS, H., & ALBERT, M. (1986). Numerical discrimination by rats using sequential auditory stimuli. *Animal Learning & Behavior, 14,* 57–59.

DAVIS, H., & ALBERT, M. (1987). Failure to transfer or train a numerical discrimination using sequential visual stimuli in rats. *Bulletin of the Psychonomic Society, 25,* 472–474.

DAVIS, H., & BRADFORD, S. A. (1986). Counting behavior by rats in a simulated natural environment. *Ethology, 73,* 265–280.

DAVIS, H., & BRADFORD, S. A. (1987). Simultaneous numerical discriminations by rats. *Bulletin of the Psychonomic Society, 25,* 113–116.

DAVIS, H., & BRADFORD, S. A. (1991). Numerically restricted food intake in the rat in a free-feeding situation. *Animal Learning & Behavior, 19,* 215–222.

DAVIS, H., MACKENZIE, K. A., & MORRISON, S. (1989). Numerical discrimination by rats (*Rattus norvegicus*) using body and vibrissal touch. *Journal of Comparative Psychology, 103,* 45–53.

DAVIS, H., & MEMMOTT, J. (1982). Counting behavior in animals: A critical evaluation. *Psychological Bulletin, 92,* 547–571.

DAVIS, H., & PERUSSE, R. (1988). Numerical competence in animals: Definitional issues, current evidence, and a new research agenda. *Brain and Behavioral Sciences, 11,* 561–579.

DAVIS, R. T., & FITTS, S. S. (1976). Memory and coding processes in discrimination learning. In D. L. MEDIN, W. A. ROBERTS, & R. T. DAVIS (Eds.), *Processes of animal memory* (pp. 167–180). Hillsdale, NJ: Erlbaum.

DAWKINS, R. (1986). *The blind watchmaker,* New York: W. W. Norton.

DEMBER, W. N., & FOWLER, H. (1958). Spontaneous alternation behavior. *Psychological Bulletin, 55,* 412–428.

DENNETT, D. C. (1983). Intentional systems in cognitive ethology: The "Panglossian paradigm" defended. *The Behavioral and Brain Sciences, 6,* 343–355.

DENNY, M. R. (1971). Relaxation theory and experiments. In F. R. BRUSH (Ed.), *Aversive conditioning and learning* (pp. 235–295). San Diego: Academic Press.

DENNY, M. R., & DITCHMAN, R. E. (1962). The locus of maximal "Kamin effect" in rats. *Journal of Comparative and Physiological Psychology, 55,* 1069–1070.

DESOTO, C. B., LONDON, M., & HANDEL, S. (1965). Social reasoning and spatial paralogic. *Journal of Personality and Social Psychology, 2,* 513–521.

DEUTSCH, D. (1970). Tones and numbers: Specificity of interference in immediate memory. *Science, 168,* 1604–1605.

DEWEER, B., SARA, S. J., & HARS, B. (1980). Contextual cues and memory retrieval in rats: Alleviation of forgetting by a pretest exposure to background cues. *Animal Learning & Behavior, 8,* 265–272.

DEWS, P. B. (1970). The theory of fixed-interval responding. In W. N. SCHOENFELD (Ed.), *The theory of reinforcement schedules* (pp. 43–61). New York: Appleton-Century-Crofts.

DIAMOND, L. (1967). The effect of training procedures on the double alternation-behavior of laboratory rats in a temporal maze. *American Journal of Psychology, 80,* 594–601.

DIMATTIA, B. V., & KESNER, R. P. (1984). Searial position curves in rats: Automatic vs. effortful information processing. *Journal of Experimental Psychology: Animal Behavior Processes, 10,* 557–563.

DOMJAN, M. (1983). Biological constraints on instrumental and classical conditioning 10 years later: Implications for general process theory. In G. H. BOWER (Ed.), *The psychology of learning and motivation* (Vol. 17). San Diego: Academic Press.

DOMJAN, M. (1993). *The principles of learning and behavior* (Vol. 3). Pacific Grove, CA: Brooks/Cole Publishing Company.

DOMJAN, M., & GALEF, B. G. (1983). Biological constraints on instrumental and classical conditioning: Retrospect and prospect. *Animal Learning & Behavior, 11,* 151–161.

DUNCAN, C. P. (1949). The retroactive effect of electroshock on learning. *Journal of Comparative and Physiological Psychology, 42,* 32–44.

EBBINGHAUS, H. (1885). *Memory: A contribution to experimental psychology,* H. A. RUGER & C. E. BUSSENIUS (Trans.). New York: Dover.

EDWARDS, C. A., JAGIELO, J. A., ZENTALL, T. R., & HOGAN, D. E. (1982). Acquired equivalence and distinctiveness in delayed matching-to-sample by pigeons. *Journal of Experimental Psychology: Animal Behavior Processes, 8,* 244–259.

EHRENFREUND, D. (1948). An experimental test of the continuity theory of discrimination learning with pattern vision. *Journal of Comparative and Physiological Psychology, 41,* 408–422.

EHRENFREUND, D., & ALLEN, J. (1964). Perfect retention of an instrumental response. *Psychonomic Science, 1,* 347–348.

EIBL-EIBESFELDT, I. (1961). The fighting behavior of animals. *Scientific American, 205,* 112–122.

EICH, J. E. (1977). State-dependent retrieval of information in human episodic memory. In I. M. BIRNBAUM & E. S. PARKER (Eds.), *Alcohol and human memory* (pp. 141–157). Hillsdale, NJ: Erlbaum.

EICH, J. E. (1980). The cue-dependent nature of state-dependent retrieval. *Memory & Cognition, 8,* 157–173.

ELLISON, G. D. (1964). Differential salivary conditioning to traces. *Journal of Comparative and Physiological Psychology, 57,* 373–380.

ELLSON, D. G. (1938). Quantitative studies of the interaction of simple habits. I. Recovery from specific generalized effects of extinction. *Journal of Experimental Psychology, 23,* 339–358.

EMMERTON, J. (1983). Vision. In M. ABS (Ed.), *Physiology and behavior of the pigeon* (pp. 245–266). San Diego: Academic Press.

EPSTEIN, W. (1972). Mechanisms of directed forgetting. In *The psychology of learning and motivation: Advances in research and theory* (pp. 147–191). New York: Academic Press.

EPSTEIN, W., MASSARO, D. W., & WILDER, L. (1972). Selective search in directed forgetting. *Journal of Experimental Psychology, 94,* 18–24.

ERICSSON, K. A., CHASE, W. G., & FALOON, S. (1980). Acquisition of a memory skill. *Science, 208,* 1181–1182.

ETKIN, M. W. (1972). Light produced interference in a delayed matching task with capuchin monkeys. *Learning and Motivation, 3,* 313–324.

ETIENNE, A. S. (1992). Navigation of a small mammal by dead reckoning and local cues. *Current Directions in Psychological Science, 1,* 48–52.

ETIENNE, A. S., LAMBERT, S. J., REVERDIN, B., & TERONI, E. (1993). Learning to recalibrate the role of dead reckoning and visual cues in spatial navigation. *Animal Learning & Behavior, 21,* 266–280.

ETIENNE, A. S., MAURER, R., & SAUCY, F. (1988). Limitations in the assessment of path dependent information. *Behaviour, 106,* 81–111.

ETIENNE, A. S., TERONI, E., HURNI, C., & PORTENIER, V. (1990). The effect of a single light cue on homing behaviour of the golden hamster. *Animal Behaviour, 39,* 17–41.

FARTHING, G. W., & OPUDA, M. J. (1974). Transfer of matching-to-sample in pigeons. *Journal of the Experimental Analysis of Behavior, 21,* 199–213.

FEIGLEY, D. A., & SPEAR, N. E. (1970). Effect of age and punishment condition on long-term retention by the rat of active- and passive-avoidance learning. *Journal of Comparative and Physiological Psychology, 73,* 515–526.

FELDMAN, R. S., & BREMNER, F. J. (1963). A method for rapid conditioning of stable avoidance bar pressing behavior. *Journal of the Experimental Analysis of Behavior, 6,* 393–394.

FERNANDES, D. M., & CHURCH, R. M. (1982). Discrimination of the number of sequential events by rats. *Animal Learning & Behavior, 10,* 171–176.

FERSEN, L. VON, WYNNE, C. D. L., DELIUS, J. D., & STADDON, J. E. R. (1991). Transitive inference formation in pigeons. *Journal of Experimental Psychology: Animal Behavior Processes, 17,* 334–341.

FERSTER, C. B. (1958). Intermittent reinforcement of a complex response in the chimpanzee. *Journal of the Experimental Analysis of Behavior, 1,* 163–165.

FERSTER, C. B. (1964). Arithmetic behavior in chimpanzees. *Scientific American, 210,* 98–106.

FERSTER, C. B., & SKINNER, B. F. (1957). *Schedules of reinforcement.* New York: Appleton-Century-Crofts.

FINGER, F. W. (1942). Retention and subsequent extinction of a running response following varying conditions of reinforcement. *Journal of Experimental Psychology, 31,* 120–133.

FJELD, H. A. (1934). The limits of learning ability in rhesus monkeys. *Genetic Psychology Monographs, 15,* 369–537.

FLETCHER, H. J., & DAVIS, J. K. (1965). Evidence supporting an intratrial interpretation of delayed response performance of monkeys. *Perceptual and Motor Skills, 21,* 735–742.

FORBES, S. M., TAYLOR, M. M., & LINDSAY, P. H. (1967). Cue timing in a multidimensional detection task. *Perceptual and Motor Skills, 25,* 113–120.

FOUNTAIN, S. B., HENNE, D. R., & HULSE, S. H. (1984). Phrasing cues and hierarchical organization in serial pattern learning by rats. *Journal of Experimental Psychology: Animal Behavior Processes, 10,* 30–45.

FOUTS, R. S. (1973). Acquisition and testing of gestural signs in four young chimpanzees. *Science, 180,* 978–980.

FRENCH, J. W. (1942). The effect of temperature on the retention of a maze habit in fish. *Journal of Experimental Psychology, 31,* 79–87.

FRISCH, K. VON. (1962). Dialects in the language of the bees. *Scientific American, 207,* 78–87.

GAFFAN, D. (1977). Recognition memory after short retention intervals in fornix-transected monkeys. *Quarterly Journal of Experimental Psychology, 29,* 577–588.

GAFFAN, E. A. (1992). Primacy, recency, and the variability of data in studies of animals' working memory. *Animal Learning & Behavior, 20,* 240–252.

GAGNE, R. M. (1941). The retention of a conditioned operant response. *Journal of Experimental Psychology, 29,* 296–305.

GALEF, B. G., JR. (1988). Imitation in animals: History, definition, and interpretation of data from the psychological laboratory. In T. R. ZENTALL & B. G. GALEF, JR. (Eds.), *Social learning: Psychological and biological perspectives* (pp. 3–28). Hillsdale, NJ: Erlbaum.

GALLISTEL, C. R. (1980). *The organization of action: A new synthesis.* Hillsdale, NJ: Erlbaum.

GALLISTEL, C. R. (1990). *The organization of learning.* Cambridge, MA: The MIT Press.

GALLISTEL, C. R. (1993). A conceptual framework for the study of numerical estimation and arithmetic reasoning in animals. In S. T. BOYSEN & E. J. CAPALDI (Eds.), *The development of numerical competence: Animal and human models* (pp. 211–223). Hillsdale, NJ: Erlbaum.

GALLISTEL, C. R., & GELMAN, R. (1992). Preverbal and verbal counting and computation. *Cognition, 44,* 43–74.

GALLUP, G. G., JR. (1970). Chimpanzees: Self-recognition. *Science, 167,* 86–87.

GALLUP, G. G., JR. (1977). Self-recognition in primates: A comparative approach to the bidirectional properties of consciousness. *American Psychologist, 32,* 329–337.

GALLUP, G. G., JR. (1979). Self-awareness in primates. *American Scientist, 67,* 417–421.

GALLUP, G. G., Jr. (1983). Toward a comparative psychology of mind. In R. L. MELLGREN (Ed.), *Animal cognition and behavior* (pp. 473–510). Amsterdam: North-Holland Publishing Company.

GALLUP, G. G., JR., McCLURE, M. K., HILL, S. D., & BUNDY, R. A. (1971). Capacity for self-recognition in differentially reared chimpanzees. *Psychological Record, 21,* 69–74.

GALLUP, G. G., Jr., POVINELLI, D. J., SUAREZ, S. D., ANDERSON, J. R., LETHMATE, J., & MENZEL, E. W., JR. (1995). Further reflections on self-recognition in primates. *Animal Behaviour, 50,* 1525–1532.

GALLUP, G. G., JR., WALLNAU, L. B., & SUAREZ, S. D. (1980). Failure to find self-recognition in mother-infant and infant-infant rhesus monkey pairs. *Folia primatologica, 33,* 210–219.

GALLUP, H. F., & DIAMOND, L. (1960). Transfer of double alternation behavior of rats in a temporal maze. *American Journal of Psychology, 73,* 256–261.

GAMZU, E. R., & SCHWARTZ, B. (1973). The maintenance of key pecking by stimulus-contingent and response-independent food presentations. *Journal of the Experimental Analysis of Behavior, 19,* 65–72.

GARCIA, J., KIMELDORF, D. J., & KOELLING, R. A. (1955). Conditioned aversion to saccharin resulting from exposure to gamma radiation. *Science, 122,* 157–158.

GARCIA, J., & KOELLING, R. A. (1966). Relation of cue to consequence in avoidance learning. *Psychonomic Science, 4,* 123–124.

GARDNER, B. T., & GARDNER, R. A. (1975). Evidence for sentence constituents in the early utterances of child and chimpanzee. *Journal of Experimental Psychology: General, 104,* 244–267.

GARDNER, R. A., & GARDNER, B. T. (1969). Teaching sign language to a chimpanzee. *Science, 165,* 664–672.

GELLERMAN, L. W. (1931a). The double alternation problem. I. The behavior of monkeys in a double alternation temporal maze. *Journal of Genetic Psychology, 39,* 50–72.

GELLERMAN, L. W. (1931b). The double alternation problem. II. The behavior of children and human adults in a double alternation temporal maze. *Journal of Genetic Psychology, 39,* 297–336.

GELLERMAN, L. W. (1931c). The double alternation problem. III. The behavior of monkeys in a double alternation box-apparatus. *Journal of Genetic Psychology, 39,* 359–392.

GELMAN, R., & GALLISTEL, C. R. (1978). *The child's understanding of number.* Cambridge, MA: Harvard University Press.

GENDRON, R. P. (1986). Searching for cryptic prey: Evidence for optimal search rates and the formation of search images in quail. *Animal Behaviour, 34,* 898–912.

GENDRON, R. P., & STADDON, J. E. R. (1983). Searching for cryptic prey: The effect of search rate. *American Naturalist, 121,* 172–186.

GIBBON, J. (1972). Timing and discrimination of shock density in avoidance. *Psychological Review, 79,* 68–92.

GIBBON, J. (1977). Scalar expectancy theory and Weber's law in animal timing. *Psychological Review, 84,* 279–325.

GIBBON, J. (1981). On the form and location of the psychometric bisection function for time. *Journal of Mathematical Psychology, 24,* 58–87.

GIBBON, J. (1986). The structure of subjective time: How time flies. In G. H. BOWER (Ed.), *The psychology of learning and motivation* (pp. 105–135). San Diego: Academic Press.

GIBBON, J. (1991). Origins of scalar timing. *Learning and Motivation, 22,* 3–38.

GIBBON, J., & CHURCH, R. M. (1981). Time left: Linear versus logarithmic subjective time. *Journal of Experimental Psychology: Animal Behavior Processes, 7,* 87–108.

GIBBON, J., & CHURCH, R. M. (1984). Sources of variance in an information processing theory of timing. In H. L. ROITBLAT, T. G. BEVER, & H. S. TERRACE (Eds.), *Animal cognition* (pp. 465–488). Hillsdale, NJ: Erlbaum.

GIBBON, J., & CHURCH, R. M. (1990). Representation of time. *Cognition, 37,* 23–54.

GILLAN, D. J. (1981). Reasoning in chimpanzees: II. Transitive inference. *Journal of Experimental Psychology: Animal Behavior Processes, 7,* 150–164.

GILLAN, D. J., PREMACK, D., & WOODRUFF, G. (1981). Reasoning in the chimpanzee: I. Analogical reasoning. *Journal of Experimental Psychology: Animal Behavior Processes, 7,* 1–17.

GIRDEN, E., & CULLER, E. (1937). Conditioned responses in curarized striate muscle in dogs. *Journal of Comparative Psychology, 23,* 261–268.

GLANZER, M., & DOLINSKY, R. (1965). The anchor for the serial position curve. *Journal of Verbal Learning and Verbal Behavior, 4,* 267–273.

GLASERSFELD, E. VON (1982). Subitizing: The role of figural patterns in the development of numerical concepts. *Archives de Psychologie, 50,* 191–218.

GLASERSFELD, E. VON (1993). Reflections on number and counting. In S. T. BOYSEN & E. J. CAPALDI (Eds.), *The development of numerical competence: Animal and human models* (pp. 225–243). Hillsdale, NJ: Erlbaum.

GLEITMAN, H. (1971). Forgetting of long-term memories in animals. In W. K. HONIG & P. H. R. JAMES (Eds.), *Animal memory* (pp. 1–44). San Diego: Academic Press.

GLEITMAN, H. (1981). *Psychology.* New York: W. W. Norton & Company.

GLEITMAN, H., & BERNHEIM, J. W. (1963). Retention of fixed-interval performance in rats. *Journal of Comparative and Physiological Psychology, 56,* 839–841.

GLEITMAN, H., & STEINMAN, F. (1963). Retention of runway performance as a function of proactive interference. *Journal of Comparative and Physiological Psychology, 56,* 834–838.

GLEITMAN, H., & STEINMAN, F. (1964). Depression effect as a function of retention interval before and after shift in reward magnitude. *Journal of Comparative and Physiological Psychology, 57,* 158–160.

GLEITMAN, H., STEINMAN, F., & BERNHEIM, J. W. (1965). Effect of prior interference upon retention of fixed-interval performances in rats. *Journal of Comparative and Physiological Psychology, 59,* 461–462.

GLICKMAN, S. E. (1961). Perseverative neural processes and consolidation of the memory trace. *Psychological Bulletin, 58,* 218–233.

GONZALEZ, R. C., & BITTERMAN, M. E. (1964). Resistance to extinction in the rat as a function of percentage and distribution of reinforcement. *Journal of Comparative and Physiological Psychology, 58,* 258–263.

GONZALEZ, R. C., GENTRY, G. V., & BITTERMAN, M. E. (1954). Relational discrimination of intermediate size in the chimpanzee. *Journal of Comparative and Physiological Psychology, 47,* 385–388.

GRANT, D. S. (1975). Proactive interference in pigeon short-term memory. *Journal of Experimental Psychology: Animal Behavior Processes, 1,* 207–220.

GRANT, D. S. (1976). Effect of sample presentation time on long-delay matching in the pigeon. *Learning and Motivation, 7,* 580–590.

GRANT, D. S. (1981a). Stimulus control of information processing in pigeon short-term memory. *Learning and Motivation, 12,* 19–39.

GRANT, D. S. (1981b). Intertrial interference in rat short-term memory. *Journal of Experimental Psychology: Animal Behavior Processes, 7,* 217–227.

GRANT, D. S. (1981c). Short-term memory in the pigeon. In N. E. SPEAR & R. R. MILLER (Eds.), *Information processing in animals: Memory mechanisms.* Hillsdale, NJ: Erlbaum.

GRANT, D. S. (1982). Stimulus control of information processing in rat short-term memory. *Journal of Experimental Psychology: Animal Behavior Processes, 8,* 154–164.

GRANT, D. S. (1988). Sources of visual interference in delayed matching-to-sample with pigeons. *Journal of Experimental Psychology: Animal Behavior Processes, 14,* 368–375.

GRANT, D. S., & BARNET, R. C. (1991). Irrelevance of sample stimuli and directed forgetting in pigeons. *Journal of the Experimental Analysis of Behavior, 55,* 97–108.

GRANT, D. S., & MACDONALD, S. E. (1986). Matching to element and compound samples in pigeons: The roles of sample coding. *Journal of Experimental Psychology: Animal Behavior Processes, 12,* 160–171.

GRANT, D. S., & ROBERTS, W. A. (1973). Trace interaction in pigeon short-term memory. *Journal of Experimental Psychology, 101,* 21–29.

GRANT, D. S., & ROBERTS, W. A. (1976). Sources of retroactive inhibition in pigeon short-term memory. *Journal of Experimental Psychology: Animal Behavior Processes, 2,* 1–16.

GRANT, D. S., & SPETCH, M. L. (1993). Analogical and nonanalogical coding of samples differing in duration in a choice-matching task in pigeons. *Journal of Experimental Psychology: Animal Behavior Processes, 19,* 15–25.

GRAY, P. (1991). *Psychology.* New York: Worth Publishers, Inc.

GREENFIELD, P. M., & SAVAGE-RUMBAUGH, E. S. (1990). In S. T. PARKER & K. T. GIBSON (Eds.), *"Language" and intelligence in monkeys and apes* (pp. 540–578). Cambridge, UK: Cambridge University Press.

GRICE, G. R. (1948). The relation of secondary reinforcement to delayed reward in visual discrimination learning. *Journal of Experimental Psychology, 38,* 1–16.

GRIFFIN, D. R. (1981). *The question of animal awareness: Evolutionary continuity and mental experience.* New York: Rockefeller University Press.

GRIFFIN, D. R. (1984). *Animal thinking.* Cambridge, MA: Harvard University Press.

GRIFFIN, D. R. (1991). Progress toward a cognitive ethology. In C. A. RISTAU (Ed.), *Cognitive ethology: The minds of other animals* (pp. 3–17). Hillsdale, NJ: Erlbaum.

GRIFFIN, D. R. (1992). *Animal minds.* Chicago: University of Chicago Press.

GUILFORD, T., & DAWKINS, M. S. (1987). Search images not proven: A reappraisal of recent evidence. *Animal Behaviour, 35,* 1838–1845.

GUTHRIE, E. R. (1935). *The psychology of learning.* Gloucester, MA: Peter Smith.

GUTTMAN, N., & KALISH, H. I. (1956). Discriminability and stimulus generalization. *Journal of Experimental Psychology, 51,* 79–88.

HALL, G. (1996). Learning about associatively activated stimulus representations: Implications for acquired equivalence and perceptual learning. *Animal Learning & Behavior, 24,* 233–255.

HANSON, H. M. (1959). Effects of discrimination training on stimulus generalization. *Journal of Experimental Psychology, 58,* 321–334.

HAMBERG, J., & SPEAR, N. E. (1978). Alleviation of forgetting of discrimination learning. *Learning and Motivation, 9,* 466–476.

HARLOW, H. F. (1949). The formation of learning sets. *Psychological Review, 56,* 51–65.

HARLOW, H. F., UEHLING, H., & MASLOW, A. H. (1932). Comparative behavior of primates: I. Delayed reaction tests on primates from the lemur to the orang-outan. *Journal of Comparative Psychology, 13,* 313–343.

HARPER, D. N., McLEAN, A. P., & DALRYMPLE-ALFORD, J. C. (1993). List item memory in rats: Effects of delay and delay task. *Journal of Experimental Psychology: Animal Behavior Processes, 19,* 307–316.

HAYES, K. J., & HAYES, C. (1951). The intellectual development of a home-raised chimpanzee. *Proceedings of the American Philosophical Society, 95,* 105–109.

HEBB, D. O. (1949). *The organization of behavior.* New York: Wiley.

HELLYER, S. (1962). Frequency of stimulus presentation and short-term decrement in recall. *Journal of Experimental Psychology, 64,* 650.

HERMAN, L. M. (1975). Interference and auditory short-term memory in the bottlenosed dolphin. *Animal Learning & Behavior, 3,* 43–48.

HERMAN, L. M., KUCZAJ, S. A. II, & HOLDER, M. D. (1993). Responses to anomalous gestural sequences by a language-trained dolphin: Evidence for processing of semantic relations and syntactic information. *Journal of Experimental Psychology: General, 122,* 184–194.

HERMAN, L. M., RICHARDS, D. G., & WOLZ, J. P. (1984). Comprehension of sentences by bottlenosed dolphins. *Cognition, 16,* 129–219.

HERON, W. T. (1949). Time discrimination in the rat. *Journal of Comparative and Physiological Psychology, 42,* 27–31.

HERRNSTEIN, R. J. (1984). Objects, categories, and discriminative stimuli. In H. L. ROITBLAT, T. G. BEVER, & H. S. TERRACE (Eds.), *Animal cognition* (pp. 233–261). Hillsdale, NJ: Erlbaum.

HERRNSTEIN, R. J. (1990). Levels of stimulus control: A functional approach. *Cognition, 37,* 133–166.

HERRNSTEIN, R. J., & DE VILLIERS, P. A. (1980). Fish as a natural category for people and pigeons. In G. H. BOWER (Ed.), *The psychology of learning and motivation: Advances in research and theory* (Vol. 14, pp. 60–97). San Diego: Academic Press.

HERRNSTEIN, R. J., & LOVELAND, D. H. (1964). Complex visual concept in the pigeon. *Science, 146,* 549–551.

HERRNSTEIN, R. J., LOVELAND, D. H., & CABLE, C. (1976). Natural concepts in pigeons. *Journal of Experimental Psychology: Animal Behavior Processes, 2,* 285–302.

HERZOG, H. A., JR. (1995). Has public interest in animal rights peaked? *American Psychologist, 50,* 945–947.

HERZOG, H. L. GRANT, D. S., & ROBERTS, W. A. (1977). Effects of sample duration and spaced repetition upon delayed matching-to-sample in monkeys (*Macaca arctoides* and *Saimiri sciureus*). *Animal Learning & Behavior, 5,* 347–354.

HEWES, G. W. (1977). Language origin theories. In D. M. RUMBAUGH (Ed.), *Language learning by a chimpanzee: The LANA project* (pp. 3–53). San Diego: Academic Press.

HEYES, C. M. (1993a). Anecdotes, training, trapping and triangulating: Do animals attribute mental states? *Animal Behaviour, 46,* 177–188.

HEYES, C. M. (1993b). Imitation, culture and cognition. *Animal Behaviour, 46,* 999–1010.

HEYES, C. M. (1994). Reflections on self-recognition in primates. *Animal Behaviour, 47,* 909–919.

HEYES, C. M. (1995). Self-recognition in primates: Further reflections create a hall of mirrors. *Animal Behaviour, 50,* 1533–1542.

HICKS, L. H. (1956). An analysis of number-concept formation in the rhesus monkey. *Journal of Comparative and Physiological Psychology, 49,* 212–218.

HILGARD, E. R., & MARQUIS, D. G. (1935). Acquisition, extinction, and retention of conditioned lid responses to light in dogs. *Journal of Comparative Psychology, 19,* 29–58.

HOCKETT, C. D. (1960). The origin of speech. *Scientific American, 203,* 88–96.

HODOS, W., & CAMPBELL, C. B. G. (1969). *Scala naturae:* Why there is no theory in comparative psychology. *Psychological Review, 76,* 337–350.

HOFFMAN, H. S., FLESHLER, M., & CHORNY, H. (1961). Discriminated bar-press avoidance. *Journal of the Experimental Analysis of Behavior, 4,* 309–316.

HOFFMAN, H. S., FLESHLER, M., & JENSEN, P. (1963). Stimulus aspects of aversive control: The retention of conditioned suppression. *Journal of the Experimental Analysis of Behavior, 6,* 575–583.

HOFFMAN, H. S., SELEKMAN, W., & FLESHLER, M. (1966). Stimulus aspects of aversive controls: Long term effects of suppression procedures. *Journal of the Experimental Analysis of Behavior, 9,* 659–662.

HOLLAND, P. C. (1985). The nature of conditioned inhibition in serial and simultaneous feature negative discriminations. In R. R. MILLER & N. E. SPEAR (Eds.), *Information processing in animals: Conditioned inhibition* (pp. 267–297). Hillsdale, NJ: Erlbaum.

HOLLAND, P. C., & LAMARRE, J. (1984). Transfer of inhibition after serial and simultaneous feature negative discrimination training. *Learning and Motivation, 15,* 219–243.

HOLLAND, P. C., & RESCORLA, R. A. (1975a). The effect of two ways of devaluing the unconditioned stimulus after first- and second-order appetitive conditioning. *Journal of Experimental Psychology: Animal Behavior Processes, 1,* 355–363.

HOLLAND, P. C., & RESCORLA, R. A. (1975b). Second-order conditioning with food unconditioned stimulus. *Journal of Comparative and Physiological Psychology, 88,* 459–467.

HOLLOWAY, F. A., & WANSLEY, R. A. (1973a). Multiphasic retention deficits at periodic intervals after passive-avoidance learning. *Science, 180,* 208–210.

HOLLOWAY, F. A., & WANSLEY, R. A. (1973b). Multiple retention deficits at periodic intervals after active and passive avoidance learning. *Behavioral Biology, 9,* 1–14.

HONIG, W. K. (1965). Discrimination, generalization and transfer on the basis of stimulus differences. In D. I. MOSTOFSKY (Ed.), *Stimulus generalization* (pp. 218–254). Stanford, CA: Stanford University Press.

HONIG, W. K. (1978). On the conceptual nature of cognitive terms: An initial essay. In S. H. HULSE, H. FOWLER, & W. K. HONIG (Eds.), *Cognitive processes in animal behavior* (pp. 1–14). Hillsdale, NJ: Erlbaum.

HONIG, W. K. (1981). Working memory and the temporal map. In N. E. SPEAR and R. R. MILLER (Eds.), *Information processing in animals: Memory mechanisms* (pp. 167–197). Hillsdale, NJ: Erlbaum.

HONIG, W. K. (1991). Discrimination by pigeons of mixture and uniformity in arrays of stimulus elements. *Journal of Experimental Psychology: Animal Behavior Processes, 17,* 68–80.

HONIG, W. K. (1993). The stimulus revisited: My, how you've grown. In T. R. ZENTALL (Ed.), *Animal cognition: A tribute to Donald A. Riley* (pp. 19–33). Hillsdale, NJ: Erlbaum.

HONIG, W. K., & DODD, P. W. D. (1986). Anticipation and intention in working memory. In D. F. KENDRICK, M. E. RILLING, & M. R. DENNY (Eds.), *Theories of animal memory* (pp. 77–100). Hillsdale, NJ: Erlbaum.

HONIG, W. K., & JAMES, P. H. R. (1971). *Animal memory.* San Diego: Academic Press.

HONIG, W. K., & STEWART, K. E. (1989). Discrimination of relative numerosity by pigeons. *Animal Learning & Behavior, 17,* 134–146.

HONIG, W. K., & THOMPSON, R. K. R. (1982). Retrospective and prospective processing in animal working memory. In G. H. BOWER (Ed.), *The psychology of learning and motivation: Advances in research and theory* (pp. 239–281). New York: Academic Press.

HONIG, W. K., & WASSERMAN, E. A. (1981). Performance of pigeons on delayed simple and conditional discriminations under equivalent training procedures. *Learning and Motivation, 12,* 149–170.

HONIGMAN, H. (1942). The number conception in animal psychology. *Biological Review, 17,* 315–337.

HULL, C. L. (1943). *Principles of behavior: An introduction to behavior theory.* New York: Appleton-Century-Crofts.

HULSE, S. H. (1978). Cognitive structure and serial pattern learning by animals. In S. H. HULSE, H. FOWLER, & W. K. HONIG (Eds.), *Cognitive processes in animal behavior* (pp. 311–340). Hillsdale, NJ: Erlbaum.

HULSE, S. H. (1980). The case of the missing rule: Memory for reward vs. formal structure in serial-pattern learning by rats. *Animal Learning & Behavior, 8,* 689–690.

HULSE, S. H., & CAMPBELL, C. E. (1975). "Thinking ahead" in rat discrimination learning. *Animal Learning & Behavior, 3,* 305–311.

HULSE, S. H., & DORSKY, N. P. (1977). Structural complexity as a determinant of serial pattern learning. *Learning and Motivation, 8,* 488–506.

HULSE, S. H., FOWLER, H., & HONIG, W. K. (1978). *Cognitive processes in animal behavior.* Hillsdale, NJ: Erlbaum.

HULSE, S. H., & O'LEARY, D. K. (1982). Serial pattern learning: Teaching an alphabet to rats. *Journal of Experimental Psychology: Animal Behavior Processes, 8,* 260–273.

HUNTER, R. R. (1941). Symbolic performance of rats in a delayed alternation problem. *Journal of Genetic Psychology, 59,* 331–357.

HUNTER, W. S. (1913). The delayed reaction in animals and children. *Behavior Monographs, 2,* 1–86.

HUNTER, W. S. (1917). The delayed reaction in a child. *Psychological Review, 24,* 74–87.

HUNTER, W. S. (1918). Kinaesthetic sensory processes in the white rat. *Psychological Bulletin, 15,* 36–37.

HUNTER, W. S. (1920). The temporal maze and kinaesthetic sensory processes in the white rat. *Psychobiology, 2,* 1–17.

HUNTER, W. S. (1928). The behavior of raccoons in a double alternation temporal maze. *Journal of Genetic Psychology, 35,* 374–388.

HUNTER, W. S. (1929). The sensory control of the maze habit in the white rat. *Journal of Genetic Psychology, 36,* 505–537.

HUNTER, W. S., & HALL, B. E. (1941). Double alternation behavior of the white rat in a spatial maze. *Journal of Comparative Psychology, 32,* 253–266.

HUNTER, W. S., & NAGGE, J. W. (1931). The white rat and the double alternation temporal maze. *Journal of Genetic Psychology, 39,* 303–319.

HURSH, S. R. (1977). The conditioned reinforcement of repeated acquisition. *Journal of the Experimental Analysis of Behavior, 27,* 315–326.

HURWITZ, H. M. B. (1962). Some properties of behavior under fixed-ratio and counting schedules. *British Journal of Psychology, 53,* 167–173.

HUTTENLOCHER, J. (1968). Constructing spatial images: A strategy in reasoning. *Psychological Review, 75,* 550–560.

INTRAUB, H. (1980). Presentation rate and the representation of briefly glimpsed pictures in memory. *Journal of Experimental Psychology: Human Learning and Memory, 6,* 1–12.

IRION, A. L. (1948). The relation of "set" to retention. *Psychological Review, 55,* 336–341.

IRION, A. L. (1949). Retention and warming-up effects in paired-associate learning. *Journal of Experimental Psychology, 39,* 669–675.

IRION, A. L., & WHAM, D. S. (1951). Recovery from retention loss as a function of amount of pre-recall warming-up. *Journal of Experimental Psychology, 41,* 242–246.

JARRARD, L. E., & MOISE, S. L. (1971). Short-term memory in the monkey. In L. E. JARRARD (Ed.), *Cognitive processes of nonhuman primates* (pp. 3–24). New York: Academic Press.

JENKINS, H. M., & HARRISON, R. H. (1960). Effects of discrimination training on auditory generalization. *Journal of Experimental Psychology, 59,* 246–253.

JENKINS, H. M., & HARRISON, R. H. (1962). Generalization gradients of inhibition following auditory discrimination learning. *Journal of the Experimental Analysis of Behavior, 5,* 435–441.

JENKINS, H. M., & MOORE, B. R. (1973). The form of the auto-shaped response with food or water reinforcers. *Journal of the Experimental Analysis of Behavior, 20,* 163–181.

JENKINS, T. N. (1927). A standard problem box of multiple complexity for use in comparative studies. *Journal of Comparative Psychology, 7,* 129–144.

JITSUMORI, M. (1993). Category discrimination of artificial polymorphous stimuli based on feature learning. *Journal of Experimental Psychology: Animal Behavior Processes, 19,* 244–254.

JOHNSON, J. I. (1961). Double alternation by raccoons. *Journal of Comparative and Physiological Psychology, 54,* 248–251.

KAMIL, A. C. (1988). A synthetic approach to the study of animal intelligence. In D. W. LEGER (Ed.), *Nebraska symposium on motivation: Vol. 35. Comparative perspectives in modern psychology* (pp. 257–308). Lincoln, NE: University of Nebraska Press.

KAMIL, A. C., & BALDA, R. P. (1983). Cache recovery and spatial memory in Clark's nutcrackers (*Nucifraga columbiana*). *Journal of Experimental Psychology: Animal Behavior Processes, 11,* 95–111.

KAMIL, A. C., & BALDA, R. P. (1990). Differential memory for different cache sites by Clark's nutcrackers. *Journal of Experimental Psychology: Animal Behavior Processes, 16,* 162–168.

KAMIL, A. C., BALDA, R. P., & OLSON, D. J. (1994a). The effects of requiring response strategies following caching in Clark's nutcrackers (*Nucifraga columbiana*). *Animal Learning & Behavior, 22,* 373–378.

KAMIL, A. C., BALDA, R. P., & OLSON, D. J. (1994b). Performance of four seed-caching corvid species in the radial-arm maze analog. *Journal of Comparative Psychology, 108,* 385–393.

KAMIN, L. J. (1957). The retention of an incompletely learned avoidance response. *Journal of Comparative and Physiological Psychology, 50,* 457–460.

KAMIN, L. J. (1968). "Attention-like" processes in classical conditioning. In M. R. JONES (Ed.), *Miami symposium on the prediction of behavior: Aversive stimulation* (pp. 9–31). Miami: University of Miami Press.

KAMIN, L. J. (1969). Predictability, surprise, attention, and conditioning. In B. A. CAMPBELL & R. M. CHURCH (Eds.), *Punishment and aversive behavior* (pp. 279–296). New York: Appleton-Century-Crofts.

KAMIN, L. J., BRIMER, C. J., & BLACK, A. H. (1963). Conditioned suppression as a monitor of fear of the CS in the course of avoidance training. *Journal of Comparative and Physiological Psychology, 56,* 497–501.

KARN, H. W. (1938). The behavior of cats on the double alternation problem in the temporal maze. *Journal of Comparative Psychology, 26,* 201–208.

KARN, H. W., & MALAMUD, H. R. (1939). The behavior of dogs on the double alternation problem in the temporal maze. *Journal of Comparative Psychology, 27,* 461–466.

KARN, H. W., & PATTON, R. A. (1939). The transfer of double alternation behavior acquired in a temporal maze. *Journal of Comparative Psychology, 28,* 55–61.

KASPROW, W. J., CACHEIRO, H., BALAZ, M. A., & MILLER, R. R. (1982). Reminder-induced recovery of associations to an overshadowed stimulus. *Learning and Motivation, 13,* 155–166.

KASPROW, W. J., CATTERSON, D., SCHACHTMAN, T. R., & MILLER, R. R. (1984). Attenuation of latent inhibition by post-acquisition reminder. *Quarterly Journal of Experimental Psychology, 36B,* 53–63.

KAUFMAN, E. C., LORD, M. W., REESE, T. W., & VOLKMANN, J. (1949). The discrimination of visual number. *American Journal of Psychology, 62,* 498–525.

KEEHN, J. D., & WEBSTER, C. D. (1968). Rapid discriminated bar-press avoidance through avoidance shaping. *Psychonomic Science, 10,* 21–22.

KELLOGG, W. N., & KELLOGG, L. A. (1933). *The ape and the child: A study of environmental influence upon early behavior.* New York: Whittlesey House.

KEPPEL, G., & UNDERWOOD, B. J. (1962). Proactive inhibition in short-term retention of single items. *Journal of Verbal Learning and Verbal Behavior, 1,* 153–161.

KESNER, R. P., CHIBA, A. A., & JACKSON-SMITH, P. (1994). Rats do show primacy and recency effects in memory for lists of spatial locations: A reply to Gaffan. *Animal Learning & Behavior, 22,* 214–218.

KESNER, R. P., & NOVAK, J. M. (1982). Serial position curves in the rat: Role of the dorsal hippocampus. *Science, 218,* 173–175.

KILLEEN, P. R., & FETTERMAN, J. G. (1988). A behavioral theory of timing. *Psychological Review, 95,* 274–295.

KILLEEN, P. R., & FETTERMAN, J. G. (1993). The behavioral theory of timing: Transition analyses. *Journal of the Experimental Analysis of Behavior, 59,* 411–422.

KIMBLE, G. A. (1961). *Conditioning and learning.* New York: Appleton-Century-Crofts.

KINNAMAN, A. J. (1902). Mental life of two *Macacus rhesus* monkeys in captivity. II. *American Journal of Psychology, 13,* 173–218.

KIRCHNER, W. H., & TOWNE, W. F. (1994). The sensory basis of the honeybee's dance language. *Scientific American, 270,* 74–80.

KLEIN, S. B. (1972). Adrenal-pituitary influence in reactivation of avoidance-learning memory in the rat after intermediate intervals. *Journal of Comparative and Physiological Psychology, 79,* 341–359.

KLEIN, S. B., & SPEAR, N. E. (1969). Influence of age on short-term retention of active avoidance learning in rats. *Journal of Comparative and Physiological Psychology, 69,* 383–389.

KLEIN, S. B., & SPEAR, N. E. (1970a). Forgetting by the rat after intermediate intervals ("Kamin effect") as retrieval failure. *Journal of Comparative and Physiological Psychology, 71,* 165–170.

KLEIN, S. B., & SPEAR, N. E. (1970b). Reactivation of avoidance-memory in the rat after intermediate intervals. *Journal of Comparative and Physiological Psychology, 72,* 498–504.

KOCH, A. M. (1935). The limits of learning ability in cebus monkeys. *Genetic Psychology Monographs, 17,* 163–234.

KOEHLER, O. (1943). "Zahl"-versuche an einem kolkraben und vergleichsversuche an menschen. *Zeitschrift fur Tierpsychologie, 5,* 575–712.

KOEHLER, O. (1951). The ability of birds to count. *Bulletin of Animal Behaviour, 9,* 41–45.

KOFFKA, K. (1935). *Principles of gestalt psychology.* New York: Harcourt, Brace & World.

KOHLER, W. (1925). *The mentality of apes.* London: Routledge and Kegan Paul.

KOHLER, W. (1947). *Gestalt psychology.* New York: Liveright Publishing Corporation.

KONORSKI, J. A. (1959). A new method of physiological investigation of recent memory in animals. *Bulletin de l'Academie Polanaise des Sciences, Serie des Sciences Biologiques, 7,* 115–119.

KOPPENAAL, R. J., JAGODA, E., & CRUCE, J. A. F. (1967). Recovery from ECS-produced amnesia following a reminder. *Psychonomic Science, 9,* 293–294.

KRAEMER, P. J. (1984). Forgetting of visual discriminations by pigeons. *Journal of Experimental Psychology: Animal Behavior Processes, 10,* 530–542.

KRAEMER, P. J., & ROBERTS, W. A. (1984). The influence of flavor preexposure and test interval on conditioned taste aversions in the rat. *Learning and Motivation, 15,* 259–278.

KRAEMER, P. J., & ROBERTS, W. A. (1985). Short-term memory for simultaneously presented visual and auditory signals in the pigeon. *Journal of Experimental Psychology: Animal Behavior Processes, 11,* 137–152.

KRAEMER, P. J., & ROBERTS, W. A. (1987). Restricted processing of simultaneously presented brightness and pattern stimuli in pigeons. *Animal Learning & Behavior, 15,* 15–24.

KRAEMER, P. J., & SPEAR, N. E. (1992). The effect of nonreinforced stimulus exposure on the strength of a conditioned taste aversion as a function of retention interval: Do latent inhibition and extinction involve a shared process? *Animal Learning & Behavior, 20,* 1–7.

KRAEMER, P. J., & SPEAR, N. E. (1993). Retrieval processes and conditioning. In T. R. ZENTALL (Ed.), *Animal cognition: A tribute to Donald A. Riley* (pp. 87–107). Hillsdale, NJ: Erlbaum.

KRANE, R. V., & WAGNER, A. R. (1975). Taste aversion learning with a delayed shock US: Implications for the "generality of the laws of learning." *Journal of Comparative and Physiological Psychology, 88,* 882–889.

KRECHEVSKY, I. (1932). "Hypotheses" in rats. *Psychological Review, 39,* 516–532.

KRECHEVSKY, I. (1938). A study of the continuity of the problem-solving process. *Psychological Review, 45,* 107–133.

LABARBERA, J. D., & CHURCH, R. M. (1974). Magnitude of fear as a function of expected time to an aversive event. *Animal Learning & Behavior, 2,* 199–202.

LADIEU, G. (1944). The effect of length of delay interval upon delayed alternation in the albino rat. *Journal of Comparative Psychology, 37,* 273–286.

LAMB, M. R. (1988). Selective attention: Effects of cueing on the processing of different types of compound stimuli. *Journal of Experimental Psychology: Animal Behavior Processes, 14,* 96–104.

LANGLEY, C. M. (1996). Search images: Selective attention to specific visual features of prey. *Journal of Experimental Psychology: Animal Behavior Processes, 22,* 152–163.

LANGLEY, C. M., & RILEY, D. A. (1993). Limited capacity information processing and pigeon matching-to-sample: Testing alternative hypotheses. *Animal Learning & Behavior, 21,* 226–232.

LANGLEY, C. M., RILEY, D. A., BOND, A. B., & GOEL, N. (1996). Visual search for natural grains in pigeons (*Columba livia*): Search images and selective attention. *Journal of Experimental Psychology: Animal Behavior Processes, 22,* 139–151.

LASHLEY, K. S. (1942). An examination of the "continuity theory" as applied to discrimination learning. *Journal of General Psychology, 26,* 241–265.

LASHLEY, K. S. (1951). The problem of serial order in behavior. In L. A. JEFFRIES (Ed.), *Cerebral mechanisms in behavior* (pp. 112–136). New York: Wiley.

LASHLEY, K. S., & WADE, M. (1946). The Pavlovian theory of generalization. *Psychological Review, 53,* 72–87.

LAWICK-GOODALL, J. (1972). *In the shadow of man.* New York: Dell.

LAWRENCE, D. H., & DeRIVERA, J. (1954). Evidence of relational transposition. *Journal of Comparative and Physiological Psychology, 47,* 465–471.

LEA, S. E. G. (1984). In what sense do pigeons learn concepts? In H. L. ROITBLAT, T. G. BEVER, & H. S. TERRACE (Eds.), *Animal cognition* (pp. 263–276). Hillsdale, NJ: Erlbaum.

LEA, S. E. G., & HARRISON, S. N. (1978). Discrimination of polymorphous stimulus sets by pigeons. *Quarterly Journal of Experimental Psychology, 30,* 521–527.

LEARY, R. W., HARLOW, H. F., SETTLAGE, P. H., & GREENWOOD, D. D. (1952). Performance on double-alternation problems by normal and brain-injured monkeys. *Journal of Comparative and Physiological Psychology, 45,* 576–584.

LEEPER, R. W. (1935). A study of a neglected portion of the field of learning: The development of sensory organization. *Journal of Genetic Psychology, 46,* 41–75.

LEITH, C. R., & MAKI, W. S. (1975). Attentional shifts during matching-to-sample performance in pigeons. *Animal Learning & Behavior, 3,* 85–89.

LEWIS, D. J. (1969). Sources of experimental amnesia. *Psychological Review, 76,* 461–472.

LEWIS, D. J. (1979). Psychobiology of active and inactive memory. *Psychological Bulletin, 86,* 1054–1083.

LEWIS, D. J., MISANIN, J. R., & MILLER, R. R. (1968). Recovery of memory following amnesia. *Nature, 220,* 704–705.

LIBBY, M. E., & CHURCH, R. M. (1974). Timing of avoidance responses by rats. *Journal of the Experimental Analysis of Behavior, 22,* 513–517.

LIEBERMAN, D. A., McINTOSH, D. C., & THOMAS, G. V. (1979). Learning when reward is delayed: A marking hypothesis. *Journal of Experimental Psychology: Animal Behavior Processes, 5,* 224–242.

LIEBERMAN, D. A., DAVIDSON, F. H., & THOMAS, G. V. (1985). Marking in pigeons: The role of memory in delayed reinforcement. *Journal of Experimental Psychology: Animal Behavior Processes, 11,* 611–624.

LIEBERMAN, P., CRELIN, E. S., & KLATT, D. H. (1972). Phonetic ability and anatomy of the newborn and adult human, Neanderthal man and adult chimp. *American Anthropologist, 74,* 287–307.

LIMA, S., & VALONE, T. J. (1986). Influence of predation risk on diet selection: A simple example in the grey squirrel. *Animal Behaviour, 34,* 536–544.

LIMONGELLI, L., BOYSEN, S. T., & VISALBERGHI, E. (1995). Comprehension of cause-effect relations in a tool-using task by chimpanzees (*Pan troglodytes*). *Journal of Comparative Psychology, 109,* 18–26.

LINDSAY, P. H. (1970). Multichannel processing in perception. In D. I. MOSTOFSKY (Ed.), *Attention: Contemporary theory and analysis* (pp. 149–171). New York: Appleton-Century-Crofts.

LIVESEY, P. J. (1964). A note on double alternation by rabbits. *Journal of Comparative and Physiological Psychology, 57,* 104–107.

LIVESEY, P. J. (1965). Comparisons of double alternation performance of white rats, rabbits, and cats. *Journal of Comparative and Physiological Psychology, 59,* 155–158.

LOCKARD, R. B. (1971). Reflections on the fall of comparative psychology: Is there a message for us all? *American Psychologist, 26,* 168–179.

LOGUE, A. W. (1979). Taste aversion and the generality of the laws of learning. *Psychological Bulletin, 86,* 276–296.

LOOMIS, J. M., KLATSKY, R. L., GOLLEDGE, R. G., CICINELLI, J. G., PELLEGRINO, J. W., & FRY, P. A. (1993). Nonvisual navigation by blind and sighted: Assessment of path integration ability. *Journal of Experimental Psychology: General, 122,* 73–91.

LOUCKS, R. B. (1931). Efficiency of the rat's motor cortex in delayed alternation. *Journal of Comparative Neurology, 53,* 511–567.

LUBOW, R. E. (1973). Latent inhibition. *Psychological Bulletin, 79,* 398–407.

LUBOW, R. E., & MOORE, A. U. (1959). Latent inhibition: The effect of nonreinforced pre-exposure to the conditioned stimulus. *Journal of Comparative and Physiological Psychology, 53,* 415–419.

MACCORQUODALE, K. (1947). An analysis of certain cues in the delayed response. *Journal of Comparative Psychology, 40,* 239–253.

MACDONALD, S. E., & WILKIE, D. M. (1990). Yellow-nosed monkeys' (*Cercopithecus ascanius whitesidei*) spatial memory in a simulated foraging environment. *Journal of Comparative Psychology, 104,* 382–387.

MACKINTOSH, N. J. (1975). A theory of attention: Variations in the associability of stimuli with reinforcement. *Psychological Review, 82,* 276–298.

MACPHAIL, E. M. (1980). Short-term visual recognition memory in pigeons. *Quarterly Journal of Experimental Psychology, 32,* 521–538.

MACUDA, T., & ROBERTS, W. A. (1995). Further evidence for hierarchical chunking in rat spatial memory. *Journal of Experimental Psychology: Animal Behavior Processes, 21,* 20–32.

MAIER, N. R. F. (1929). Delayed reaction and memory in rats. *Comparative Psychology Monographs, 36,* 538–549.

MAIER, N. R. F. (1932). A study of orientation in the rat. *Journal of Comparative Psychology, 14,* 387–399.

MAKI, W. S. (1979). Pigeons' short-term memories for surprising vs. expected reinforcement and nonreinforcement. *Animal Learning & Behavior, 7,* 31–37.

MAKI, W. S., BROKOFSKY, S., & BERG, B. (1979). Spatial memory in rats: Resistance to retroactive interference. *Animal Learning & Behavior, 7,* 25–30.

MAKI, W. S., & HEGVIK, D. K. (1980). Directed forgetting in pigeons. *Animal Learning & Behavior, 8,* 567–574.

MAKI, W. S., & LEITH, C. R. (1973). Shared attention in pigeons. *Journal of the Experimental Analysis of Behavior, 19,* 345–349.

MAKI, W. S., & LEUIN, T. C. (1972). Information processing by pigeons. *Science, 176,* 535–536.

MAKI, W. S., RILEY, D. A., & LEITH, C. R. (1976). The role of test stimuli in matching to compound samples by pigeons. *Animal Learning & Behavior, 4,* 13–21.

MALOTT, R. W., MALOTT, K., SVINICKI, J. G., KLADDER, F., & PONICKI, E. (1971). An analysis of matching and non-matching behavior using a single key, free operant procedure. *Psychological Record, 21,* 545–564.

MANDLER, G., & SHEBO, B. J. (1982). Subitizing: An analysis of its component processes. *Journal of Experimental Psychology: General, 111,* 1–22.

MARX, J. L. (1980). Ape-language controversy flares up. *Science, 207,* 1330–1333.

MASON, M., & WILSON, M. (1974). Temporal differentiation and recognition memory for visual stimuli in rhesus monkeys. *Journal of Experimental Psychology, 103,* 383–390.

MASON, W. A., & HOLLIS, J. H. (1962). Communication between young rhesus monkeys. *Animal Behaviour, 10,* 211–221.

MATSUZAWA, T. (1985). Use of numbers by a chimpanzee. *Nature, 315,* 57–59.

MATSUZAWA, T. (1990). Spontaneous sorting in human and chimpanzee. In S. T. PARKER & K. R. GIBSON (Eds.), *"Language" and intelligence in monkeys and apes* (pp. 451–468). Cambridge, UK: Cambridge University Press.

Matsuzawa, T. (1994). Field experiments on use of stone tools by chimpanzees in the wild. In R. W. Wrangham, W. C. McGrew, F. B. M. de Waal, & P. G. Heltne (Eds.), *Chimpanzee cultures* (pp. 351–370). Cambridge, MA: Harvard University Press.

Mazur, J. E. (1994). *Learning and behavior* (3rd Edition). Englewood Cliffs, NJ: Prentice Hall.

McCord, F. (1939). The delayed reaction and memory in rats: I. Length of delay. *Journal of Comparative Psychology, 27*, 1–37.

McCrary, J. W., & Hunter, W. S. (1953). Serial position curves in verbal learning. *Science, 117*, 131–134.

McGaugh, J. L. (1966). Time-dependent processes in memory storage. *Science, 153*, 1351–1358.

McGeoch, J. A. (1932). Forgetting and the law of disuse. *Psychological Review, 39*, 353–370.

McGonigle, B. O., & Chalmers, M. (1977). Are monkeys logical? *Nature, 267*, 694–696.

McNamara, M. C., & Riedesel, M. L. (1973). Memory and hibernation in *Citellus lateralis. Science, 179*, 92–94.

Mechner, F. (1958). Probability relations within response sequences under ratio reinforcement. *Journal of the Experimental Analysis of Behavior, 1*, 109–121.

Mechner, R., & Guevrekian, L. (1962). Effects of deprivation upon counting and timing in rats. *Journal of the Experimental Analysis of Behavior, 5*, 463–466.

Meck, W. H. (1983). Selective adjustment of the speed of internal clock and memory processes. *Journal of Experimental Psychology: Animal Behavior Processes, 9*, 171–201.

Meck, W. H., & Church, R. M. (1982). Abstraction of temporal attributes. *Journal of Experimental Psychology: Animal Behavior Processes, 8*, 226–243.

Meck, W. H., & Church, R. M. (1983). A mode control model of counting and timing processes. *Journal of Experimental Psychology: Animal Behavior Processes, 9*, 320–334.

Meck, W. H., & Church, R. M. (1987a). Cholinergic modulation of the content of temporal memory. *Behavioral Neuroscience, 101*, 457–464.

Meck, W. H., & Church, R. M. (1987b). Nutrients that modify the speed of internal clock and memory storage processes. *Behavioral Neuroscience, 101*, 465–475.

Meck, W. H., Church, R. M., & Gibbon, J. (1985). Temporal integration in duration and number discrimination. *Journal of Experimental Psychology: Animal Behavior Processes, 11*, 591–597.

Melton, A. W. (1963). Implications of short–term memory for a general theory of memory. *Journal of Verbal Learning and Verbal Behavior, 2*, 1–21.

Menzel, E. W. (1973). Chimpanzee spatial memory organization. *Science, 182*, 943–945.

Menzel, E. W. (1978). Cognitive mapping in chimpanzees. In S. H. Hulse, H. Fowler, & W. K. Honig (Eds.), *Cognitive processes in animal behavior* (pp. 375–422). Hillsdale, NJ: Erlbaum.

Miles, H. L. (1983). Apes and language: The search for communicative competence. In J. de Luce, & H. T. Wilder (Eds.), *Language in primates: Implications for linguistics, anthropology, psychology and philosophy* (pp. 43–61). New York: Springer-Verlag.

Miller, D. J. (1993). Do animals subitize? In S. T. Boysen & E. J. Capaldi (Eds.), *The development of numerical competence: Animal and human models* (pp. 149–169). Hillsdale, NJ: Erlbaum.

Miller, G. A. (1956). The magical number seven, plus or minus two: Some limits on our capacity for processing information. *Psychological Review, 63*, 81–97.

Miller, J. S., Jagielo, J. A., & Spear, N. E. (1991). Differential effectiveness of various prior-cuing treatments in the reactivation and maintenance of memory. *Journal of Experimental Psychology: Animal Behavior Processes, 17*, 249–258.

Miller, N. E. (1948). Studies of fear as an acquirable drive: I. Fear as motivation and fear-reduction as reinforcement in the learning of new responses. *Journal of Experimental Psychology, 38*, 89–101.

MILLER, N. E. (1985). The value of behavioral research on animals. *American Psychologist, 40,* 423–440.

MILLER, R. R. (1982). Effects of intertrial reinstatement of training stimuli on complex maze learning in rats: Evidence that "acquisition" curves reflect more than acquisition. *Journal of Experimental Psychology: Animal Behavior Processes, 8,* 86–109.

MILLER, R. R., & GRAHAME, N. J. (1991). Expression of learning. In L. DACHOWSKI & C. F. FLAHERTY (Eds.), *Current topics in animal learning: Brain, emotion, and cognition* (pp. 95–117). Hillsdale, NJ: Erlbaum.

MILLER, R. R., & MARLIN, N. A. (1979). Amnesia following electroconvulsive shock. In J. F. KIHLSTROM & F. J. EVANS (Eds.), *Functional disorders of memory* (pp. 143–178). Hillsdale, NJ: Erlbaum.

MILLER, R. R., OTT, C. A., BERK, A. M., & SPRINGER, A. D. (1974). Appetitive memory restoration after electroconvulsive shock in the rat. *Journal of Comparative and Physiological Psychology, 87,* 717–723.

MILLER, R. R., & SPRINGER, A. D. (1972). Induced recovery of memory in rats following electroconvulsive shock. *Physiology and Behavior, 8,* 645–651.

MILLER, R. R., & SPRINGER, A. D. (1973). Amnesia, consolidation and retrieval. *Psychological Review, 80,* 69–79.

MISANIN, J. R., MILLER, R. R., & LEWIS, D. J. (1968). Retrograde amnesia produced by electroconvulsive shock after reactivation of a consolidated memory trace. *Science, 160,* 554–555.

MISHKIN, M., & DELACOUR, J. (1975). Analysis of short-term memory in the monkey. *Journal of Experimental Psychology: Animal Behavior Processes, 1,* 326–334.

MITCHELL, R. W., YAO, P., SHERMAN, P. T., & O'REGAN, M. (1985). Discriminative responding of a dolphin (*Tursiops truncatus*) to differentially rewarded stimuli. *Journal of Comparative Psychology, 99,* 218–225.

MORGAN, C. L. (1906). *An introduction to comparative psychology.* London: Walter Scott.

MORRIS, R. G. M. (1981). Spatial localization does not require the presence of local cues. *Learning and Motivation, 12,* 239–260.

MOSCOVITCH, A., & LOLORDO, V. M. (1968). Role of safety in the Pavlovian backward fear conditioning procedure. *Journal of Comparative and Physiological Psychology, 66,* 673–678.

MOWBRAY, G. H. (1953). Simultaneous vision and audition: The comprehension of prose passages with varying levels of difficulty. *Journal of Experimental Psychology, 46,* 365–372.

MOWRER, O. H. (1947). On the dual nature of learning—a reinterpretation of "conditioning" and "problem solving." *Harvard Educational Review, 17,* 102–148.

MUNN, N. L. (1950). *Handbook of psychological research on the rat.* New York: Houghton Mifflin.

MURDOCK, B. B., JR. (1962). The serial position effect in free recall. *Journal of Experimental Psychology, 64,* 482–488.

MURDOCK, B. B., JR. (1968). Modality effects in short-term memory: Storage or retrieval? *Journal of Experimental Psychology, 77,* 79–86.

NAKAMURA, C. Y., & ANDERSON, N. H. (1962). Avoidance behavior differences within and between strains of rats. *Journal of Comparative and Physiological Psychology, 55,* 740–747.

NELSON, K. R., & WASSERMAN, E. A. (1978). Temporal factors influencing the pigeon's successive matching-to-sample performance: Sample duration, intertrial interval, and retention interval. *Journal of the Experimental Analysis of Behavior, 30,* 153–162.

NISBETT, R. E., & WILSON, T. D. (1977). Telling more than we can know: Verbal reports on mental processes. *Psychological review, 84,* 231–259.

OAKLEY, K. P. (1949). *Man the tool-maker.* London: British Museum [Natural History].

ODEN, D. L., THOMPSON, R. K. R., & PREMACK, D. (1988). Spontaneous transfer of matching by infant chimpanzees (*Pan troglodytes*). *Journal of Experimental Psychology: Animal Behavior Processes, 14*, 140–145.

O'KEEFE, J., & NADEL, L. (1978). *The hippocampus as a cognitive map.* Oxford, UK: Clarendon.

OLSON, D. J. (1991). Species differences in spatial memory among Clark's nutcrackers, scrub jays, and pigeons. *Journal of Experimental Psychology: Animal Behavior Processes, 17*, 363–376.

OLSON, D. J., KAMIL, A. C., & BALDA, R. P. (1993). Effects of response strategy and retention interval on performance of Clark's nutcrackers in a radial maze analogue. *Journal of Experimental Psychology: Animal Behavior Processes, 19*, 138–148.

OLSON, D. J., KAMIL, A. C., BALDA, R. P., & NIMS, P. J. (1995). Performance of four seed-caching corvid species in operant tests of nonspatial and spatial memory. *Journal of Comparative Psychology, 109*, 173–181.

OLTHOF, A., MACUDA, T., & ROBERTS, W. A. (1995, June). *Incentive effects on the radial maze and evidence for equivalence sets in rats.* Poster session presented at the annual meeting of the Canadian Society for Brain, Behaviour, and Cognitive Science, Halifax, Nova Scotia.

OLTON, D. S. (1978). Characteristics of spatial memory. In S. H. HULSE, H. FOWLER, & W. K. HONIG (Eds.), *Cognitive processes in animal behavior* (pp. 341–373). Hillsdale, NJ: Erlbaum.

OLTON, D. S. (1979). Mazes, maps, and memory. *American Psychologist, 34*, 583–596.

OLTON, D. S., COLLISON, C., & WERZ, M. A. (1977). Spatial memory and radial arm maze performance of rats. *Learning and Motivation, 8*, 289–314.

OLTON, D. S., & PAPAS, B. C. (1979). Spatial memory and hippocampal function. *Neuropsychologia, 17*, 669–682.

OLTON, D. S., & SAMUELSON, R. J. (1976). Remembrance of places passed: Spatial memory in rats. *Journal of Experimental Psychology: Animal Behavior Processes, 2*, 97–116.

OVERTON, D. A. (1964). State-dependent or "dissociated" learning produced with pentobarbital. *Journal of Comparative and Physiological Psychology, 57*, 3–12.

PASTORE, N. (1961). Number sense and "counting" ability in the canary. *Zietschrift fur Tierpsychologie, 18*, 561–573.

PATTERSON, F. G. (1981). Ape language [Letter to the editor]. *Science, 211*, 86–87.

PATTERSON, F. G., & LINDEN, E. (1981). *The education of Koko.* New York: Holt, Rinehart, & Winston.

PATTERSON, F. G., PATTERSON, C. H., & BRENTARI, D. K. (1987). Language in child, chimp, and gorilla [Comment]. *American Psychologist, 42*, 270–272.

PAVLOV, I. P. (1927). *Conditioned reflexes.* Oxford, UK: Oxford University Press.

PEARCE, J. M. (1989). The acquisition of an artificial category by pigeons. *Quarterly Journal of Experimental Psychology, 41B*, 381–406.

PELLEGRIN, P. (1986). *Aristotle's classification of animals: Biology and the conceptual unity of the aristotelian corpus.* Berkeley, CA: University of California Press.

PEPPERBERG, I. M. (1987). Evidence for conceptual quantitative abilities in the African grey parrot: Labeling of cardinal sets. *Ethology, 75*, 37–61.

PERKINS, C. C., JR., & WEYANT, R. G. (1958). The interval between training and test trials as determiner of the slope of generalization gradients. *Journal of Comparative and Physiological Psychology, 51*, 596–600.

PETERSON, G. B., & TRAPOLD, M. A. (1980). Effects of altering outcome expectancies on pigeons' delayed conditional discrimination performance. *Learning and Motivation, 11*, 267–288.

PETERSON, G. B., WHEELER, R. L., & ARMSTRONG, G. D. (1978). Expectancies as mediators in the differential-reward conditional discrimination performance of pigeons. *Animal Learning & Behavior, 6*, 279–285.

PETERSON, G. B., WHEELER, R. L., & TRAPOLD, M. A. (1980). Enhancement of pigeons' conditional discrimination performance by expectancies of reinforcement and nonreinforcement. *Animal Learning & Behavior, 8*, 22–30.

PETERSON, L. R., & PETERSON, M. J. (1959). Short-term retention of individual verbal items. *Journal of Experimental Psychology, 58*, 193–198.

PFUNGST, O. (1965). *Clever Hans: The horse of Mr. von Osten.* New York: Holt, Rinehart, and Winston.

PHELPS, M. T., & ROBERTS, W. A. (1989). Central-place foraging by *Rattus norvegicus* on a radial maze. *Journal of Comparative Psychology, 103*, 326–338.

PHELPS, M. T., & ROBERTS, W. A. (1991). Pattern tracking on the radial maze: Tracking multiple patterns at different spatial locations. *Journal of Experimental Psychology: Animal Behavior Processes, 17*, 411–422.

PIAGET, J. (1952). *The child's conception of number.* London: Rutledge & Kegan Paul.

PIETREWICZ, A. T., & KAMIL, A. C. (1977). Visual detection of cryptic prey by blue jays (*Cyanocitta cristata*). *Science, 195*, 580–582.

PIETREWICZ, A. T., & KAMIL, A. C. (1979). Search image formation in the blue jay (*Cyanocitta cristata*). *Science, 204*, 1332–1333.

PINKER, S. (1994). *The language instinct: How the mind creates language.* New York: William Morrow and Company.

PLATT, J. R., & DAVIS, E. R. (1983). Bisection of temporal intervals by pigeons. *Journal of Experimental Psychology: Animal Behavior Processes, 9*, 160–170.

PLATT, J. R., & JOHNSON, D. M. (1971). Localization of position within a homogeneous behavior chain: Effects of error contingencies. *Learning and Motivation, 2*, 386–414.

POSNER, M. I., & KEELE, S. W. (1968). On the genesis of abstract ideas. *Journal of Experimental Psychology, 77*, 353–363.

POSNER, M. I., & KONICK, A. F. (1966). On the role of interference in short-term retention. *Journal of Experimental Psychology, 72*, 221–231.

POSNER, M. I., NISSEN, M. J., & KLEIN, R. M. (1976). Visual dominance: An information-processing account of its origins and significance. *Psychological Review, 83*, 157–171.

POSNER, M. I., & ROSSMAN, E. (1965). Effect of size and location of informational transforms upon short-term retention. *Journal of Experimental Psychology, 70*, 496–505.

POSTMAN, L. (1961). Extra-experimental interference and the retention of words. *Journal of Experimental Psychology, 61*, 91–110.

POTTER, M. C., & LEVY, E. I. (1969). Recognition memory for a rapid sequence of pictures. *Journal of Experimental Psychology, 81*, 10–15.

POUCET, B. (1993). Spatial cognitive maps in animals: New hypotheses on their structure and neural mechanisms. *Psychological Review, 100*, 163–182.

POVINELLI, D. J. (1993). Reconstructing the evolution of mind. *American Psychologist, 48*, 493–509.

POVINELLI, D. J., NELSON, K. E., & BOYSEN, S. T. (1990). Inferences about guessing and knowing by chimpanzees (*Pan troglodytes*). *Journal of Comparative Psychology, 104*, 203–210.

POVINELLI, D. J., NELSON, K. E., & BOYSEN, S. T. (1992). Comprehension of role reversal in chimpanzees: Evidence of empathy? *Animal Behaviour, 43*, 633–640.

POVINELLI, D. J., PARKS, K. A., & NOVAK, M. A. (1991). Do rhesus monkeys (*Macaca mulatta*) attribute knowledge and ignorance to others? *Journal of Comparative Psychology, 105*, 318–325.

POVINELLI, D. J., PARKS, K. A., & NOVAK, M. A. (1992). Role reversal by rhesus monkeys, but no evidence of empathy. *Animal Behaviour, 43*, 269–281.

POVINELLI, D. J., RULF, A. B., LANDAU, K. R., & BIERSCHWALE, D. T. (1993). Self-recognition in chimpanzees (*Pan troglodytes*): Distribution, ontogeny, and patterns of emergence. *Journal of Comparative Psychology, 107*, 347–372.

PREMACK, A. J., & PREMACK, D. (1972). Teaching language to an ape. *Scientific American, 227*, 92–99.

PREMACK, D. (1971). Language in a chimpanzee? *Science, 172*, 808–822.

PREMACK, D. (1976). *Intelligence in ape and man.* Hillsdale, NJ: Erlbaum.

PREMACK, D. (1983). The codes of man and beasts. *The Behavioral and Brain Sciences, 6*, 125–167.

PREMACK, D., & PREMACK, A. J. (1983). *The mind of an ape.* New York: W. W. Norton & Company.

PREMACK, D., & WOODRUFF, G. (1978a). Chimpanzee problem-solving: A test for comprehension. *Science, 202*, 532–535.

PREMACK, D., & WOODRUFF, G. (1978b). Does the chimpanzee have a theory of mind? *The Behavioral and Brain Sciences, 4*, 515–526.

RASHOTTE, M. E., GRIFFIN, R. W., & SISK, C. L. (1977). Second-order conditioning of the pigeon's keypeck. *Animal Learning & Behavior, 5*, 25–38.

RASMUSSEN, J. L., RAJECKI, D. W., & CRAFT, H. D. (1993). Humans' perceptions of animal mentality: Ascriptions of thinking. *Journal of Comparative Psychology, 107*, 283–290.

RATNER, S. C. (1980). The comparative method. In M. R. DENNY (Ed.), *Comparative Psychology: An evolutionary analysis of animal behavior* (pp. 153–167). New York: Wiley and Sons.

REED, P. (1994). Less than expected variance in studies of serial position effects is not a sufficient reason for caution. *Animal Learning & Behavior, 22*, 224–230.

REED, S. K. (1972). Pattern recognition and categorization. *Cognitive Psychology, 3*, 382–407.

REID, P. J., & SHETTLEWORTH, S. J. (1992). Detection of cryptic prey: Search image or search rate? *Journal of Experimental Psychology: Animal Behavior Processes, 18*, 273–286.

REITMAN, J. S. (1974). Without surreptitious rehearsal, information in short-term memory decays. *Journal of Verbal Learning and Verbal Behavior, 13*, 365–377.

RENSCH, B. (1957). The intelligence of elephants. *Scientific American, 196*, 44–49.

RESCORLA, R. A. (1966). Predictability and number of pairings in Pavlovian fear conditioning. *Psychonomic Science, 4*, 383–384.

RESCORLA, R. A. (1968). Probability of shock in the presence and absence of CS in fear conditioning. *Journal of Comparative and Physiological Psychology, 66*, 1–5.

RESCORLA, R. A. (1969). Pavlovian conditioned inhibition. *Psychological Bulletin, 72*, 77–94.

RESCORLA, R. A. (1982). Simultaneous second-order conditioning produces S-S learning in conditioned suppression. *Journal of Experimental Psychology: Animal Behavior Processes, 8*, 23–32.

RESCORLA, R. A. (1988). Pavlovian conditioning: It's not what you think it is. *American Psychologist, 43*, 151–160.

RESCORLA, R. A., & SOLOMON, R. L. (1967). Two-process learning theory: Relationships between Pavlovian conditioning and instrumental learning. *Psychological Review, 74*, 151–182.

RESCORLA, R. A., & WAGNER, A. R. (1972). A theory of Pavlovian conditioning: Variations in the effectiveness of reinforcement and non-reinforcement. In A. BLACK & W. F. PROKASY (Eds.), *Classical conditioning II* (pp. 64–99). New York: Appleton-Century-Crofts.

REVUSKY, S. H. (1968). Aversion to sucrose produced by contingent X-irradiation: Temporal and dosage parameters. *Journal of Comparative and Physiological Psychology, 65*, 17–22.

RICCIO, D. C., RABINOWITZ, V. C., & AXELROD, S. (1994). Memory: When less is more. *American Psychologist, 49*, 917–926.

RIESS, B. F. (1934). The limits of learning ability in the white rat and the guinea pig. *Genetic Psychology Monographs, 15,* 303–368.

RILEY, D. A., & LANGLEY, C. M. (1993). The logic of species comparisons. *Psychological Science, 4,* 185–189.

RILEY, D. A., & LEITH, C. R. (1976). Multidimensional psychophysics and selective attention in animals. *Psychological Bulletin, 83,* 138–160.

RILEY, D. A., & ROITBLAT, H. L. (1978). Selective attention and related cognitive processes in pigeons. In S. H. HULSE, H. FOWLER, & W. K. HONIG (Eds.), *Cognitive processes in animal behavior* (pp. 249–276). Hillsdale, NJ: Erlbaum.

RILLING, M. (1967). Number of responses as a stimulus in fixed interval and fixed ratio schedules. *Journal of Comparative and Physiological Psychology, 63,* 60–65.

RILLING, M. (1993). Invisible counting animals: A history of contributions from comparative psychology, ethology, and learning theory. In S. T. BOYSEN & E. J. CAPALDI (Eds.), *The development of numerical competence: Animal and human models* (pp. 3–37). Hillsdale, NJ: Erlbaum.

RILLING, M., KENDRICK, D. F., & STONEBRAKER, T. B. (1984). Directed forgetting in context. In G. H. BOWER (Ed.), *The psychology of learning and motivation: Advances in research and theory* (pp. 175–198). San Diego: Academic Press.

RILLING, M., & McDIARMID, C. (1965). Signal detection in fixed-ratio schedules. *Science, 148,* 526–527.

RIZLEY, R. C., & RESCORLA, R. A. (1972). Associations in second-order conditioning and sensory preconditioning. *Journal of Comparative and Physiological Psychology, 81,* 1–11.

ROBERTS, S. (1981). Isolation of an internal clock. *Journal of Experimental Psychology: Animal Behavior Processes, 7,* 242–268.

ROBERTS, S., & CHURCH, R. M. (1978). Control of an internal clock. *Journal of Experimental Psychology: Animal Behavior Processes, 4,* 318–337.

ROBERTS, W. A. (1969). Resistance to extinction following partial and consistent reinforcement with varying magnitudes of reward. *Journal of Comparative and Physiological Psychology, 67,* 395–400.

ROBERTS, W. A. (1972a). Free recall of word lists varying in length and rate of presentation: A test of total-time hypotheses. *Journal of Experimental Psychology, 92,* 365–372.

ROBERTS, W. A. (1972b). Short-term memory in the pigeon: Effects of repetition and spacing. *Journal of Experimental Psychology, 94,* 74–83.

ROBERTS, W. A. (1972c). Spatial separation and visual differentiation of cues as factors influencing short-term memory in the rat. *Journal of Comparative and Physiological Psychology, 78,* 284–291.

ROBERTS, W. A. (1974). Spaced repetition facilitates short-term retention in the rat. *Journal of Comparative and Physiological Psychology, 86,* 164–171.

ROBERTS, W. A. (1979). Spatial memory in the rat on a hierarchical maze. *Learning and Motivation, 10,* 117–140.

ROBERTS, W. A. (1980). Distribution of trials and intertrial retention in delayed matching to sample with pigeons. *Journal of Experimental Psychology: Animal Behavior Processes, 6,* 217–237.

ROBERTS, W. A. (1981). Retroactive inhibition in rat spatial memory. *Animal Learning & Behavior, 9,* 566–574.

ROBERTS, W. A. (1984). Some issues in animal spatial memory. In H. L. ROITBLAT, T. G. BEVER, & H. S. TERRACE (Eds.), *Animal cognition* (pp. 425–443). Hillsdale, NJ: Erlbaum.

ROBERTS, W. A. (1992). Foraging by rats on a radial maze: Learning, memory, and decision rules. In I. GORMEZANO & E. A. WASSERMAN (Eds.), *Learning and memory: The behavioral and biological substrates* (pp. 7–23). Hillsdale, NJ: Erlbaum.

ROBERTS, W. A., CHENG, K., & COHEN, J. S. (1989). Timing light and tone signals in pigeons. *Journal of Experimental Psychology: Animal Behavior Processes, 15,* 23–35.

ROBERTS, W. A., & DALE, R. H. I. (1981). Remembrance of places lasts: Proactive inhibition and patterns of choice in rat spatial memory. *Learning and Motivation, 12,* 261–281.

ROBERTS, W. A., & GRANT, D. S. (1974). Short-term memory in the pigeon with presentation time precisely controlled. *Learning and Motivation, 5,* 393–408.

ROBERTS, W. A., & GRANT, D. S. (1976). Studies of short-term memory in the pigeon using the delayed matching-to-sample procedure. In D. L. MEDIN, W. A. ROBERTS, & R. T. DAVIS (Eds.), *Processes of animal memory* (pp. 79–112). Hillsdale, NJ: Erlbaum.

ROBERTS, W. A., & GRANT, D. S. (1978a). Interaction of sample and comparison stimuli in delayed matching-to-sample with the pigeon. *Journal of Experimental Psychology: Animal Behavior Processes, 4,* 68–82.

ROBERTS, W. A., & GRANT, D. S. (1978b). An analysis of light-induced retroactive inhibition in pigeon short-term memory. *Journal of Experimental Psychology: Animal Behavior Processes, 4,* 219–236.

ROBERTS, W. A., & KRAEMER, P. J. (1981). Recognition memory for lists of visual stimuli in monkeys and humans. *Animal Learning & Behavior, 9,* 587–594.

ROBERTS, W. A., & KRAEMER, P. J. (1984). Picture memory in monkeys. *Canadian Journal of Psychology, 38,* 218–236.

ROBERTS, W. A., & MAZMANIAN, D. S. (1988). Concept learning at different levels of abstraction by pigeons, monkeys, and people. *Journal of Experimental Psychology: Animal Behavior Processes, 14,* 247–260.

ROBERTS, W. A., MAZMANIAN, D. S., & KRAEMER, P. J. (1984). Directed forgetting in monkeys. *Animal Learning & Behavior, 12,* 29–40.

ROBERTS, W. A., & MITCHELL, S. (1994). Can a pigeon simultaneously process temporal and numerical information? *Journal of Experimental Psychology: Animal Behavior Processes, 20,* 66–78.

ROBERTS, W. A., & PHELPS, M. T. (1994). Transitive inference in rats: A test of the spatial coding hypothesis. *Psychological Science, 5,* 368–374.

ROBERTS, W. A., PHELPS, M. T., & SCHACTER, G. B. (1992). Stimulus control of central place foraging on the radial maze. In W. K. HONIG & J. G. FETTERMAN (Eds.), *Cognitive aspects of stimulus control* (pp. 135–153). Hillsdale, NJ: Erlbaum.

ROBERTS, W. A., & SMYTHE, W. E. (1979). Memory for lists of spatial events in the rat. *Learning and Motivation, 10,* 313–336.

ROITBLAT, H. L. (1982). The meaning of representation in animal memory. *The Behavioral and Brain Sciences, 5,* 353–372.

ROITBLAT, H. L. (1987). *Introduction to comparative cognition.* New York: W. H. Freeman.

ROITBLAT, H. L., BEVER, T. G., & TERRACE, H. S. (1984). *Animal cognition.* Hillsdale, NJ: Erlbaum.

ROITBLAT, H. L. & FERSEN, L. VON (1992). Comparative cognition: Representations and processes in learning and memory. *Annual Review of Psychology, 43,* 671–710.

ROMANES, G. J. (1882). *Animal intelligence.* London: Kegan Paul, Trench, & Co.

ROMANES, G. J. (1884). *Mental evolution in animals.* New York: AMS Press.

ROPER, K. L., KAISER, D. H., & ZENTALL, T. R. (1995). True directed forgetting in pigeons may occur only when alternative working memory is required on forget-cue trials. *Animal Learning & Behavior, 23,* 280–285.

ROPER, K. L., & ZENTALL, T. R. (1993). Directed forgetting in animals. *Psychological Bulletin, 113,* 513–532.

ROVEE-COLLIER, C. K., SULLIVAN, M. W., ENRIGHT, M. K., LUCAS, D., & FAGAN, J. W. (1980). Reactivation of infant memory. *Science, 208,* 1159–1161.

RUMBAUGH, D. M. (Ed.). (1977). *Language learning by a chimpanzee: The LANA project.* San Diego: Academic Press.

RUMBAUGH, D. M., GILL, T. V., & GLASERSFELD, E. C. VON (1973). Reading and sentence completion by a chimpanzee (Pan). *Science, 182,* 731–733.

RUMBAUGH, D. M., SAVAGE-RUMBAUGH, S., & HEGEL, M. T. (1987). Summation in the chimpanzee (*Pan troglodytes*). *Journal of Experimental Psychology: Animal Behavior Processes, 13,* 107–115.

RUMBAUGH, D. M., & WASHBURN, D. A. (1993). Counting by chimpanzees and ordinality judgments by macaques in video-formatted tasks. In S. T. BOYSEN & E. J. CAPALDI (Eds.), *The development of numerical competence: Animal and human models* (pp. 87–106). Hillsdale, NJ: Erlbaum.

RUNDUS, D. (1971). Analysis of rehearsal processes in free recall. *Journal of Experimental Psychology, 89,* 63–77.

RUSSON, A. E., & GALDIKAS, B. M. F. (1993). Imitation in free-ranging rehabilitant orangutans (*Pongo pygmaeus*). *Journal of Comparative Psychology, 107,* 147–161.

RUSSON, A. E., & GALDIKAS, B. M. F. (1995). Constraints on great apes' imitation: Model and action selectivity in rehabilitant orangutan (*Pongo pygmaeus*) imitation. *Journal of Comparative Psychology, 109,* 5–17.

SAKSIDA, L. M., & WILKIE, D. M. (1994). Time-of-day discrimination by pigeons. *Animal Learning & Behavior, 22,* 143–154.

SAKURA, O., & MATSUZAWA, T. (1991). Flexibility of wild chimpanzee nut-cracking behavior using stone hammers and anvils: An experimental analysis. *Ethology, 87,* 237–248.

SALMAN, D. H. (1943). Note on the number conception in animal psychology. *British Journal of Psychology, 33,* 209–219.

SALMON, D. P., & D'AMATO, M. R. (1981). Note on delay-interval illumination effects on retention in monkeys (*Cebus apella*). *Journal of the Experimental Analysis of Behavior, 36,* 381–385.

SANDS, S. F., & WRIGHT, A. A. (1980a). Primate memory: Retention of serial list items by a rhesus monkey. *Science, 209,* 938–939.

SANDS, S. F., & WRIGHT, A. A. (1980b). Serial probe recognition performance by a rhesus monkey and a human with 10- and 20-item lists. *Journal of Experimental Psychology: Animal Behavior Processes, 6,* 386–396.

SANTI, A. (1989). Differential outcome expectancies and directed forgetting effects in pigeons. *Animal Learning & Behavior, 17,* 349–354.

SANTI, A., GROSSI, V., & GIBSON, M. (1982). Differences in matching-to-sample performance with element and compound sample stimuli in pigeons. *Learning and Motivation, 13,* 240–256.

SANTI, A., & SAVICH, J. (1985). Directed forgetting effects in pigeons: Remember cues initiate rehearsal. *Animal Learning & Behavior, 13,* 365–369.

SANTIAGO, H. C., & WRIGHT, A. A. (1984). Pigeon memory: *Same/different* concept learning, serial probe recognition acquisition, and probe delay effects on the serial-position function. *Journal of Experimental Psychology: Animal Behavior Processes, 10,* 498–512.

SAVAGE-RUMBAUGH, E. S. (1986). *Ape language: From conditioned response to symbol.* New York: Columbia University Press.

SAVAGE-RUMBAUGH, E. S., & LEWIN, R. (1994). *Kanzi: The ape at the brink of the human mind.* New York: Wiley & Sons.

SAVAGE-RUMBAUGH, E. S., McDONALD, K., SEVCIK, R. A., HOPKINS, W. D., & RUBERT, E. (1986). Spontaneous symbol acquisition and communicative use by pygmy chimpanzees (*Pan paniscus*). *Journal of Experimental Psychology: General, 115,* 211–235.

SAVAGE-RUMBAUGH, E. S., PATE, J. L., LAWSON, J., SMITH, S. T., & ROSENBAUM, S. (1983). Can a chimpanzee make a statement? *Journal of Experimental Psychology: General, 112,* 457–492.

SAVAGE-RUMBAUGH, E. S., RUMBAUGH, D. M., & BOYSEN, S. (1980). Do apes use language? *American Scientist, 68,* 49–61.

SAVAGE-RUMBAUGH, E. S., RUMBAUGH, D. M., SMITH, S. T., & LAWSON, J. (1980). Reference: The linguistic essential. *Science, 210,* 922–925.

SCHACHTMAN, T. R., GEE, J-L., KASPROW, W. J., & MILLER, R. R. (1983). Reminder-induced recovery from blocking as a function of the number of compound trials. *Learning and Motivation, 14,* 154–164.

SCHIFF, R., SMITH, N., & PROCHASKA, J. (1972). Extinction of avoidance in rats as a function of duration and number of blocked trials. *Journal of Comparative and Physiological Psychology, 81,* 356–359.

SCHLOSBERG, H. (1928). A study of the conditioned patellar reflex. *Journal of Experimental Psychology, 11,* 468–494.

SCHLOSBERG, H. (1934). Conditioned responses in the white rat. *Journal of Genetic Psychology, 45,* 303–335.

SCHLOSBERG, H. (1936). Conditioned responses in the white rat. II. Conditioned responses based upon shock to the foreleg. *Journal of Genetic Psychology, 49,* 107–138.

SCHNEIDER, A. M., & SHERMAN, W. (1968). Amnesia: A function of the temporal relation of footshock to electroconvulsive shock. *Science, 159,* 219–221.

SEBEOK, T. A., & UMIKER-SEBEOK, J. (1979). Performing animals: Secrets of the trade. *Psychology Today, 13,* 78–91.

SEIBT, U. (1982). Zahlbegriff und zahlverhalten bei tieren. Neue versuche und deutungen. *Zeitschrift fur Tierpsychologie, 60,* 325–341.

SEIDENBERG, M. S., & PETITTO, L. A. (1979). Signing behavior in apes: A critical review. *Cognition, 7,* 177–215.

SELIGMAN, M. E. P. (1970). On the generality of the laws of learning. *Psychological Review, 77,* 406–418.

SELIGMAN, M. E. P., & JOHNSTON, J. C. (1973). A cognitive theory of avoidance learning. In F. J. McGUIGAN, & D. B. LUMSDEN (Eds.), *Contemporary approaches to conditioning and learning* (pp. 69–110). Washington, D.C.: Winston.

SEYFARTH, R. M., CHENEY, D. L., & MARLER, P. (1980). Monkey responses to three different alarm calls: Evidence for predator classification and semantic communication. *Science, 210,* 801–803.

SHAFFER, W. O., & SHIFFRIN, R. M. (1972). Rehearsal and storage of visual information. *Journal of Experimental Psychology, 92,* 292–296.

SHERRY, D. F. (1987). Foraging for stored food. In M. L. COMMONS, A. KACELNIK, & S. J. SHETTLEWORTH (Eds.), *Quantitative analyses of behavior: Foraging* (Vol. 6, pp. 209–227). Hillsdale, NJ: Erlbaum.

SHERRY, D. F. (1992). Landmarks, the hippocampus, and spatial search in food-storing birds. In W. K. HONIG & J. G. FETTERMAN (Eds.), *Cognitive aspects of stimulus control* (pp. 185–201). Hillsdale, NJ: Erlbaum.

SHERRY, D. F., & SCHACTER, D. L. (1987). The evolution of multiple memory systems. *Psychological Review, 94,* 439–454.

SHERRY, D. F., & VACCARINO, A. L. (1989). Hippocampus and memory for food caches in black-capped chickadees. *Behavioral Neuroscience, 103,* 308–318.

SHERRY, D. F., VACCARINO, A. L., BUCKENHAM, K., & HERZ, R. S. (1989). The hippocampal complex of food-storing birds. *Brain Behavior & Evolution, 34,* 308–317.

SHETTLEWORTH, S. J. (1983). Memory in food-hoarding birds. *Scientific American, 248,* 102–110.

SHETTLEWORTH, S. J. (1990). Spatial memory in food-storing birds. *Philosophical Transactions of the Royal Society (London) B, 329,* 143–151.

SHETTLEWORTH, S. J. (1992). Spatial memory in hoarding and nonhoarding tits. In I. GORMEZANO & E. A. WASSERMAN (Eds.), *Learning and memory: The behavioral and biological substrates* (pp. 25–44). Hillsdale, NJ: Erlbaum.

SHETTLEWORTH, S. J. (1993). Where is the comparison in comparative cognition? *Psychological Science, 4,* 179–184.

SHETTLEWORTH, S. J., & KREBS, J. R. (1982). How marsh tits find their hoards: The roles of site preference and spatial memory. *Journal of Experimental Psychology: Animal Behavior Processes, 8,* 354–375.

SHETTLEWORTH, S. J., & KREBS, J. R. (1986). Stored and encountered seeds: A comparison of two spatial memory tasks in marsh tits and chickadees. *Journal of Experimental Psychology: Animal Behavior Processes, 12,* 248–257.

SHETTLEWORTH, S. J., KREBS, J. R., HEALY, S. D., & THOMAS, C. M. (1990). Spatial memory of food-storing tits (*Parus alter* and *P. atricapillus*): Comparison of storing and non-storing tasks. *Journal of Comparative Psychology, 104,* 71–81.

SHIMP, C. P. (1976). Short-term memory in the pigeon: Relative recency. *Journal of the Experimental Analysis of Behavior, 25,* 55–61.

SHIMP, C. P., & MOFFITT, M. (1974). Short-term memory in the pigeon: Stimulus-response associations. *Journal of the Experimental Analysis of Behavior, 22,* 507–512.

SHUEY, A. M. (1931). The limits of learning ability in kittens. *Genetic Psychology Monographs, 10,* 287–378.

SKINNER, B. F. (1938). *The behavior of organisms.* New York: Appleton-Century-Crofts.

SKINNER, B. F. (1950). Are theories of learning necessary? *Psychological Review, 57,* 193–216.

SKINNER, B. F. (1953). *Science and human behavior.* New York: Collier-Macmillan.

SKINNER, B. F. (1956). A case history in scientific method. *American Psychologist, 11,* 221–233.

SKINNER, B. F. (1974). *About behaviorism.* New York: Knopf.

SMITH, E. E., & MEDIN, D. L. (1981). *Categories and concepts.* Cambridge, MA: Harvard University Press.

SOLOMON, R. L., KAMIN, L. J., & Wynne, L. C. (1953). Traumatic avoidance learning: The outcomes of several extinction procedures with dogs. *Journal of Abnormal and Social Psychology, 48,* 291–302.

SPEAR, N. E. (1971). Forgetting as retrieval failure. In W. K. HONIG & P. H. R. JAMES (Eds.), *Animal memory* (pp. 45–109). San Diego, Academic Press.

SPEAR, N. E. (1973). Retrieval of memory in animals. *Psychological Review, 80,* 163–194.

SPEAR, N. E. (1976). Retrieval of memory: A psychobiological approach. In W. K. ESTES (Ed.), *Handbook of learning and cognitive processes* (Vol. 4, pp. 17–90). Hillsdale, NJ: Erlbaum.

SPEAR, N. E. (1978). *The processing of memories: Forgetting and retention.* Hillsdale, NJ: Erlbaum.

SPEAR, N. E. (1981). Extending the domain of memory retrieval. In N. E. SPEAR & R. R. MILLER (Eds.), *Information processing in animals: Memory mechanisms* (pp. 341–378). Hillsdale, NJ: Erlbaum.

SPEAR, N. E., GORDON, W. C., & MARTIN, P. A. (1973). Warm-up decrement as failure in memory retrieval in the rat. *Journal of Comparative and Physiological Psychology, 85,* 601–614.

SPEAR, N. E., HAMBERG, J. M., & BRYAN, R. G. (1980). Effect of retention interval on recently acquired or recently activated memories. *Learning and Motivation, 11,* 456–475.

SPEAR, N. E., MILLER, J. S., & JAGIELO, J. A. (1990). Animal memory and learning. *Annual Review of Psychology, 41,* 169–211.

SPEAR, N. E., & PARSONS, P. J. (1976). Analysis of a reactivation treatment: Ontogenetic determinants of alleviated forgetting. In D. L. MEDIN, W. A. ROBERTS, & R. T. DAVIS (Eds.), *Processes of animal memory* (pp. 135–165). Hillsdale, NJ: Erlbaum.

SPEAR, N. E., & RICCIO, D. C. (1994). *Memory: Phenomena and principles.* Boston: Allyn and Bacon.

SPENCE, K. W. (1936). The nature of discrimination learning in animals. *Psychological Review, 43,* 427–449.

SPENCE, K. W. (1937). The differential response in animals to stimuli varying within a single dimension. *Psychological Review, 44,* 430–444.

SPENCE, K. W. (1942). The basis of solution by chimpanzees of the intermediate size problem. *Journal of Experimental Psychology, 31,* 257–271.

SPENCE, K. W. (1945). An experimental test of the continuity and non-continuity theories of discrimination learning. *Journal of Experimental Psychology, 35,* 253–266.

SPETCH, M. L., CHENG, K., & MONDLOCH, M. V. (1992). Landmark use by pigeons in a touch-screen spatial search task. *Animal Learning & Behavior, 20,* 281–292.

SPETCH, M. L., & RUSAK, B. (1989). Pigeons' memory for event duration: Intertrial interval and delay effects. *Animal Learning & Behavior, 17,* 147–156.

SPETCH, M. L., & SINHA, S. S. (1989). Proactive effects in pigeons' memory for event duration: Evidence for analogical retention. *Journal of Experimental Psychology: Animal Behavior Processes, 15,* 347–357.

SPETCH, M. L., & WILKIE, D. M. (1982). A systematic bias in pigeons' memory for food and light durations. *Behaviour Analysis Letters, 2,* 267–274.

SPETCH, M. L., & WILKIE, D. M. (1983). Subjective shortening: A model of pigeons' memory for event duration. *Journal of Experimental Psychology: Animal Behavior Processes, 9,* 14–30.

SPINOZZI, G. (1993). Development of spontaneous classificatory behavior in chimpanzees (*Pan troglodytes*). *Journal of Comparative Psychology, 107,* 193–200.

SPRINGER, A. D., & MILLER, R. R. (1972). Retrieval failure induced by electroconvulsive shock: Reversal with dissimilar training and recovery agents. *Science, 177,* 628–630.

SQUIRE, L. R. (1987). *Memory and brain.* New York: Oxford University Press.

STADDON, J. E. R. (1974). Temporal control, attention, and memory. *Psychological Review, 81,* 375–391.

STADDON, J. E. R., & INNIS, N. K. (1969). Reinforcement omission on fixed-interval schedules. *Journal of the Experimental Analysis of Behavior, 12,* 689–700.

STEINMAN, F. (1967). Retention of alley brightness in the rat. *Journal of Comparative and Physiological Psychology, 64,* 105–109.

STEIRN, J. N., WEAVER, J. E., & ZENTALL, T. R. (1995). Transitive inference in pigeons: Simplified procedures and a test of value transfer theory. *Animal Learning & Behavior, 23,* 76–82.

STERNBERG, R. J. (1980). Representation and process in linear syllogistic reasoning. *Journal of Experimental Psychology: General, 109,* 119–159.

STONEBRAKER, T. B., & RILLING, M. (1981). Control of delayed matching-to-sample performance using directed forgetting techniques. *Animal Learning & Behavior, 9,* 196–201.

STRAUB, R. O., & TERRACE, H. S. (1981). Generalization of serial learning in the pigeon. *Animal Learning & Behavior, 9,* 454–468.

STROEBEL, C. F. (1967). Behavioral aspects of circadian rhythms. In J. ZUBIN & H. F. HUNT (Eds.), *Comparative psychopathology.* New York: Grune and Stratton.

STRONG, P. N. (1959). Memory for object discriminations in the rhesus monkey. *Journal of Comparative and Physiological Psychology, 52,* 333–335.

STRUHSAKER, T. T. (1967). Auditory communication among vervet monkeys (*Cercopithecus aethiops*). In S. A. ALTMANN (Ed.), *Social communication among primates* (pp. 281–324). Chicago: University of Chicago Press.

STRUHSAKER, T. T., & HUNKELER, P. (1971). Evidence of tool-using by chimpanzees in the Ivory Coast. *Folia Primatalogica, 15,* 212–219.

STUBBS, D. A. (1976). Scaling of stimulus duration by pigeons. *Journal of the Experimental Analysis of Behavior, 26,* 15–25.

SUAREZ, S. D., & GALLUP, G. G., JR. (1981). Self-recognition in chimpanzees and orangutans, but not gorillas. *Journal of Human Evolution, 10,* 175–188.

SUGIYAMA, Y., FUSHIMI, T., Sakura, O., & MATSUZAWA, T. (1993). Hand preference and tool use in wild chimpanzees. *Primates, 34,* 151–159.

SUGIYAMA, Y., & KOMAN, J. (1979). Tool-using and -making behavior in wild chimpanzees at Bossou, Guinea. *Primates, 20,* 513–524.

SUTHERLAND, N. S., & MACKINTOSH, N. J. (1971). *Mechanisms of animal discrimination learning.* San Diego: Academic Press.

SUTHERLAND, R. J., CHEW, G. L., BAKER, J. C., & LINGGARD, R. C. (1987). Some limitations on the use of distal cues in place navigation by rats. *Psychobiology, 15,* 48–57.

SUTHERLAND, R. J., & DYCK, R. H. (1984). Place navigation by rats in a swimming pool. *Canadian Journal of Psychology, 38,* 322–347.

SUZUKI, S., AUGERINOS, G., & BLACK, A. H. (1980). Stimulus control of spatial behavior on the eight-arm maze in rats. *Learning and Motivation, 11,* 1–18.

TANAKA, M. (1995). Object sorting in chimpanzees (*Pan troglodytes*): Classification based on physical identity, complementarity, and familiarity. *Journal of Comparative Psychology, 109,* 151–161.

TERRACE, H. S. (1979a). Is problem solving language? *Journal of the Experimental Analysis of Behavior, 31,* 161–175.

TERRACE, H. S. (1979b). *Nim.* New York: Knopf.

TERRACE, H. S. (1983). Simultaneous chaining: The problem it poses for traditional chaining theory. In M. L. COMMONS, R. J. HERRNSTEIN, & A. R. WAGNER (Eds.), *Quantitative analyses of behavior: Discrimination processes* (pp. 115–137). Hillsdale, NJ: Erlbaum.

TERRACE, H. S. (1984). Animal cognition. In H. L. ROITBLAT, T. G. BEVER, & H. S. TERRACE (Eds.), *Animal cognition* (pp. 7–28). Hillsdale, NJ: Erlbaum.

TERRACE, H. S. (1985). In the beginning was the "name." *American Psychologist, 40,* 1011–1028.

TERRACE, H. S. (1987). Chunking by a pigeon in a serial learning task. *Nature, 325,* 149–151.

TERRACE, H. S. (1991). Chunking during serial learning by a pigeon: I. Basic evidence. *Journal of Experimental Psychology: Animal Behavior Processes, 17,* 81–93.

TERRACE, H. S., CHEN, S., & NEWMAN, A. B. (1995). Serial learning with a wild card by pigeons (*Columba livia*): Effect of list length. *Journal of Comparative Psychology, 109,* 162–172.

TERRACE, H. S., PETITTO, L. A., SANDERS, R. J., & BEVER, T. G. (1979). Can an ape create a sentence? *Science, 206,* 891–902.

TERRY, W. S., & WAGNER, A. R. (1975). Short-term memory for "surprising" versus "expected" unconditioned stimuli in Pavlovian conditioning. *Journal of Experimental Psychology: Animal Behavior Processes, 1,* 122–133.

THINUS-BLANC, C. (1988). Animal spatial cognition. In L. WEISKRANTZ (Ed.), *Thought without language* (pp. 371–395). New York: Oxford University Press.

THISTLETHWAITE, D. (1951). A critical review of latent learning and related experiments. *Psychological Bulletin, 48,* 97–129.

THOMAS, G. V., LIEBERMAN, D. A., McINTOSH, D. C., & RONALDSON, P. (1983). The role of marking when reward is delayed. *Journal of Experimental Psychology: Animal Behavior Processes, 9,* 401–411.

THOMAS, R. K., & CHASE, L. (1980). Relative numerousness judgments by squirrel monkeys. *Bulletin of the Psychonomic Society, 16,* 79–82.

THOMAS, R. K., FOWLKES, D., & VICKERY, J. D. (1980). Conceptual numerousness judgments by squirrel monkeys. *American Journal of Psychology, 93,* 247–257.

THOMAS, R. K., & LORDEN, R. B. (1993). Numerical competence in animals: A conservative view. In S. T. BOYSEN & E. J. CAPALDI (Eds.), *The development of numerical competence: Animal and human models* (pp. 127–147). Hillsdale, NJ: Erlbaum.

THOMPSON, C. R., & CHURCH, R. M. (1980). An explanation of the language of a chimpanzee. *Science, 208,* 313–314.

THOMPSON, R. K. R., & HERMAN, L. M. (1977). Memory for lists of sounds by the bottle-nosed dolphin: Convergence of memory processes with humans? *Science, 195,* 501–503.

THOMPSON, R. K. R., & ODEN, D. L. (1993). "Language training" and its role in the expression of tacit propositional knowledge by chimpanzees (*Pan troglodytes*). In H. L. ROITBLAT, L. M. HERMAN, & P. E. NACHTIGALL (Eds.), *Language and communication: Comparative perspectives* (pp. 365–384). Hillsdale, NJ: Erlbaum.

THOMPSON, R. K. R., ODEN, D. L., & BOYSEN, S. T. (1997). Language-naive chimpanzees (*Pan troglodytes*) judge relations between relations in a conceptual matching-to-sample task. *Journal of Experimental Psychology: Animal Behavior Processes, 23,* 31–43.

THORNDIKE, E. L. (1911). *Animal intelligence: Experimental studies.* New York: Macmillan.

TINBERGEN, N. (1951). *The study of instinct.* Oxford, UK: Oxford University Press.

TINBERGEN, N. (1952). The curious behavior of the stickleback. *Scientific American, 187,* 22–26.

TINBERGEN, N. (1960a). *The herring gull's world: A study of the social behavior of birds.* New York: Harper and Row.

TINBERGEN, N. (1960b). The evolution of behavior in gulls. *Scientific American, 203,* 118–130.

TINBERGEN, L. (1960). The natural control of insects in pinewoods. I. Factors influencing the intensity of predation by song birds. *Archives Neerlandaises de Zoologie, 13,* 265–343.

TINKLEPAUGH, O. L. (1928). An experimental study of representative factors in monkeys. *Journal of Comparative Psychology, 8,* 197–236.

TOLMAN, E. C. (1932). *Purposive behavior in animals and men.* New York: Appleton-Century-Crofts.

TOLMAN, E. C. (1938). The determiners of behavior at a choice point. *Psychological review, 45,* 1–41.

TOLMAN, E. C. (1948). Cognitive maps in rats and men. *Psychological Review, 55,* 189–208.

TOLMAN, E. C. (1959). Principles of purposive behavior. In S. KOCH (Ed.), *Psychology: A study of a science* (Vol. 2, pp. 92–157). New York: McGraw-Hill.

TOLMAN, E. C., & HONZIK, C. H. (1930a). "Insight" in rats. *University of California Publications in Psychology, 4,* 215–232.

TOLMAN, E. C., & HONZIK, C. H. (1930b). Introduction and removal of reward and maze performance in rats. *University of California Publications in Psychology, 4,* 257–275.

TOMBACK, D. F. (1980). How nutcrackers find their seed stores. *Condor, 82,* 10–19.

TOTH, N., SCHICK, K. D., SAVAGE-RUMBAUGH, E. S., SEVCIK, R. A., & RUMBAUGH, D. M. (1993). Pan the tool-maker: Investigations into the stone tool-making and tool-using capabilities of a bonobo (*Pan paniscus*). *Journal of Archaeological Science, 20,* 81–91.

TRANBERG, D. K., & RILLING, M. (1980). Delay-interval illumination changes interfere with pigeon short-term memory. *Journal of the Experimental Analysis of Behavior, 33,* 39–49.

TREISMAN, A. (1969). Strategies and models of selective attention. *Psychological Review, 76,* 282–299.

TREISMAN, A., & GELADE, G. (1980). A feature-integration theory of attention. *Cognitive Psychology, 12*, 97–136.

TREISMAN, A., & SCHMIDT, H. (1982). Illusory conjunctions in the perception of objects. *Cognitive Psychology, 14*, 107–141.

TREISMAN, A., SYKES, M., & GELADE, G. (1977). Selective attention and stimulus integration. In S. DORMIC (Ed.), *Attention and performance VI* (pp. 333–361). Hillsdale, NJ: Erlbaum.

TSAI, C. (1924). A comparative study of retention curves for motor habits. *Comparative Psychology Monographs, 2*, 1–29.

TULVING, E. (1968). Theoretical issues in free recall. In T. R. DIXON & D. L. NORTON (Eds.), *Verbal behavior and general behavior theory*. Englewood Cliffs, NJ: Prentice-Hall.

TULVING, E. (1972). Episodic and semantic memory. In E. TULVING & W. DONALDSON (Eds.), *Organization of memory* (pp. 381–403). New York: Academic Press.

TULVING, E. (1983). *Elements of episodic memory*. Oxford, UK: Clarendon Press.

TULVING, E. (1985). How many memory systems are there? *American Psychologist, 40*, 385–398.

TULVING, E. (1989). Remembering and knowing the past. *American Scientist, 77*, 361–367.

TULVING, E. (1993). What is episodic memory? *Current Directions in Psychological Science, 2*, 67–70.

TULVING, E., & PEARLSTONE, Z. (1966). Availability versus accessibility of information in memory for words. *Journal of Verbal Learning and Verbal Behavior, 5*, 381–391.

TULVING, E., & THOMPSON, D. M. (1973). Encoding specificity and retrieval processes in episodic memory. *Psychological Review, 80*, 352–373.

TVERSKY, B., & SHERMAN, T. (1975). Picture memory improves with longer on time and off time. *Journal of Experimental Psychology: Human Learning and Memory, 104*, 114–118.

TYLER, D. W., WORTZ, E. C., & BITTERMAN, M. E. (1953). The effect of random and alternating partial reinforcement on resistance to extinction in the rat. *American Journal of Psychology, 66*, 37–65.

UNDERWOOD, B. J., & POSTMAN, L. (1960). Extra-experimental sources of interference in forgetting. *Psychological Review, 67*, 73–95.

URCUIOLI, P. J., & HONIG, W. K. (1980). Control of choice in conditional discriminations by sample-specific behaviors. *Journal of Experimental Psychology: Animal Behavior Processes, 6*, 251–277.

URCUIOLI, P. J., & ZENTALL, T. R. (1992). Transfer across delayed discriminations: Evidence regarding the nature of prospective memory. *Journal of Experimental Psychology, 18*, 154–173.

URCUIOLI, P. J., ZENTALL, T. R., JACKSON-SMITH, P., & STEIRN, J. N. (1989). Evidence for common coding in many-to-one matching: Retention, intertrial interference, and transfer. *Journal of Experimental Psychology: Animal Behavior Processes, 15*, 264–273.

VANDER WALL, S. B. (1982). An experimental analysis of cache recovery in Clark's nutcracker. *Animal Behaviour, 30*, 84–94.

VAN HAMME, L. J., WASSERMAN, E. A., & BIEDERMAN, I. (1992). Discrimination of contour-deleted images by pigeons. *Journal of Experimental Psychology: Animal Behavior Processes, 18*, 387–399.

VAUGHAN, W., JR. (1988). Formation of equivalence sets in pigeons. *Journal of Experimental Psychology: Animal Behavior Processes, 14*, 36–42.

VAUGHAN, W., Jr., & GREENE, S. L. (1984). Pigeon visual memory capacity. *Journal of Experimental Psychology: Animal Behavior Processes, 10*, 256–271.

VICCHIO, S. J. (1986). From Aristotle to Descartes: Making animals anthropomorphic. In R. J. HOAGE, & L. GOLDMAN (Eds.), *Animal intelligence: Insights into the animal mind* (pp. 187–207). Washington, D.C.: Smithsonian Institution Press.

VISALBERGHI, E., & FRAGASZY, D. M. (1990). Do monkeys ape? In S. T. PARKER & K. R. GIBSON (Eds.), *"Language" and intelligence in monkeys and apes* (pp. 247–273). Cambridge, UK: Cambridge University Press.

VISALBERGHI, E., & LIMONGELLI, L. (1994). Lack of comprehension of cause-effect relations in tool-using capuchin monkeys (*Cebus apella*). *Journal of Comparative Psychology, 108,* 15–22.

WADE, N. (1980). Does man alone have language? Apes reply in riddles, and a horse says neigh. *Science, 208,* 1349–1351.

WAGNER, A. R. (1976). An information-processing mechanism for self-generated or retrieval-generated depression in performance. In T. J. TIGHE & R. N. LEATON (Eds.), *Habituation: Perspectives from child development, animal behavior, and neurophysiology* (pp. 95–128). Hillsdale, NJ: Erlbaum.

WAGNER, A. R. (1978). Expectancies and the priming of STM. In S. H. HULSE, H. FOWLER & W. K. HONIG (Eds.), *Cognitive processes in animal behavior* (pp. 177–209). Hillsdale, NJ: Erlbaum.

WAGNER, A. R. (1981). SOP: A model of automatic memory processing in animal behavior. In N. E. SPEAR & R. R. MILLER (Eds.), *Information processing in animals: Memory mechanisms* (pp. 5–47). Hillsdale, NJ: Erlbaum.

WAGNER, A. R., RUDY, J. W., & WHITLOW, J. W. (1973). Rehearsal in animal conditioning. *Journal of Experimental Psychology, 97,* 407–426.

WALDVOGEL, J. A. (1990). The bird's eye view. *American Scientist, 78,* 342–353.

WALTON, A. C. (1915). The influence of diverting stimuli during delayed reaction in dogs. *Journal of Animal Behavior, 5,* 259–291.

WANSLEY, R. A., & HOLLOWAY, F. A. (1975). Multiple retention deficits following one-trial appetitive training. *Behavioral Biology, 14,* 135–149.

WANSLEY, R. A., & HOLLOWAY, F. A. (1976). Oscillations in retention performance after passive avoidance training. *Learning and Motivation, 7,* 296–302.

WARD, E. F. (1983). Teaching sign language to a chimpanzee: Some historical references. *Journal of the Experimental Analysis of Behavior, 40,* 341–342.

WARDEN, C. J. (1951). Animal intelligence. *Scientific American, 184,* 64–68.

WARREN, J. M. (1967). Double alternation learning by experimentally naive and sophisticated cats. *Journal of Comparative and Physiological Psychology, 64,* 161–163.

WASHBURN, D. A., & RUMBAUGH, D. M. (1991). Ordinal judgments of numerical symbols by macaques (*Macaca mulatta*). *Psychological Science, 2,* 190–193.

WASSERMAN, E. A. (1981). Comparative psychology returns: A review of HULSE, FOWLER, & HONIG's *Cognitive processes in animal behavior. Journal of the Experimental Analysis of Behavior, 35,* 243–257.

WASSERMAN, E. A. (1984). Animal intelligence: Understanding the minds of animals through their behavioral "ambassadors." In H. L. ROITBLAT, T. G. BEVER, & H. S. TERRACE (Eds.). *Animal cognition* (pp. 45–60). Hillsdale, NJ: Erlbaum.

WASSERMAN, E. A. (1995). The conceptual abilities of pigeons. *American Scientist, 83,* 246–255.

WASSERMAN, E. A., & ASTLEY, S. L. (1994). A behavioral analysis of concepts: Its application to pigeons and children. In D. L. MEDIN (Ed.), *The Psychology of Learning and motivation* (Vol. 31, pp. 73–132). San Diego: Academic Press.

WASSERMAN, E. A., & BHATT, R. S. (1992). Conceptualization of natural and artificial stimuli by pigeons. In W. K. HONIG & J. G. FETTERMAN (Eds.), *Cognitive aspects of stimulus control* (pp. 203–223). Hillsdale, NJ: Erlbaum.

WASSERMAN, E. A., DEVOLDER, C. L., & COPPAGE, D. J. (1992). Non-similarity-based conceptualization in pigeons via secondary or mediated generalization. *Psychological Science, 3,* 374–379.

WASSERMAN, E. A., KIEDINGER, R. E., & BHATT, R. S. (1988). Conceptual behavior in pigeons: Categories, subcategories, and pseudocategories. *Journal of Experimental Psychology: Animal Behavior Processes, 14,* 235–246.

WASSERMAN, E. A., KIRKPATRICK-Steger, K., VAN HAMME, L. J., & BIEDERMAN, I. (1993). Pigeons are sensitive to the spatial organization of complex visual stimuli. *Psychological Science, 4,* 336–341.

WATHEN, C. N., & ROBERTS, W. A. (1994). Multiple-pattern learning by rats on an eight-arm radial maze. *Animal Learning & Behavior, 22,* 155–164.

WATSON, J. B. (1913). Psychology as the behaviorist views it. *Psychological Review, 20,* 158–177.

WATSON, J. B. (1914). *Behavior: An introduction to comparative psychology.* New York: Henry Holt and Company.

WAUGH, N. C., & NORMAN, D. A. (1965). Primary memory. *Psychological Review, 72,* 89–104.

WEAVER, G. E. (1974). Effects of poststimulus study time on recognition of pictures. *Journal of Experimental Psychology, 103,* 799–801.

WEAVER, G. E., & STANNY, C.J. (1978). Short-term retention of pictorial stimuli as assessed by a probe recognition technique. *Journal of Experimental Psychology: Human Learning and Memory, 4,* 55–65.

WEAVER, J. E., STEIRN, J. N., & ZENTALL, T. R. (1997). Transitive inference in pigeons: Control for differential value transfer. *Psychonomic Bulletin & Review, 4,* 113–117.

WELLS, H. G., HUXLEY, J. S., & WELLS, G. P. (1934). *The science of life.* Garden City, NY: The Literary Guild, Country Life Press.

WENDT, G. R. (1937). Two and one-half year retention of a conditioned response. *Journal of General Psychology, 17,* 178–180.

WESLEY, F. (1961). The number concept: A phylogenetic review. *Psychological Bulletin, 58,* 420–428.

WHITEN, A., CUSTANCE, D. M., GOMEZ, J.-G., TEIXIDOR, P., & BARD, K. A. (1996). Imitative learning of artificial fruit processing in children (*Homo sapiens*) and chimpanzees (*Pan troglodytes*). *Journal of Comparative Psychology, 110,* 3–14.

WHITESIDES, G. H. (1985). Nut cracking by wild chimpanzees in Sierra Leone, West Africa. *Primates, 26,* 91–94.

WICKELGREN, W. A. (1965). Acoustic similarity and retroactive interference in short-term memory. *Journal of Verbal Learning and Verbal Behavior, 4,* 53–61.

WICKELGREN, W. A. (1972). Trace resistance and the decay of long-term memory. *Journal of Mathematical Psychology, 9,* 418–455.

WICKELGREN, W. A. (1993). Chunking, familiarity, and serial order in counting. In S. T. BOYSEN & E. J. CAPALDI (Eds.), *The development of numerical competence: Animal and human models* (pp. 245–268). Hillsdale, NJ: Erlbaum.

WILCOXON, H. C., DRAGOIN, W. B., & KRAL, P. A. (1971). Illness-induced aversions in rat and quail: Relative salience of visual and gustatory cues. *Science, 171,* 826–828.

WILKIE, D. M., SAKSIDA, L. M., SAMSON, P., & LEE, A. (1994). Properties of time-place learning by pigeons, *Columba livia. Behavioural Processes, 31,* 39–56.

WILKIE, D. M., & WILLSON, R. J. (1990). Discriminal distance analysis supports the hypothesis that pigeons retrospectively encode event duration. *Animal Learning & Behavior, 18,* 124–132.

WILKIE, D. M., & WILLSON, R. J. (1992). Time-place learning by pigeons, *Columba livia. Journal of the Experimental Analysis of Behavior, 57,* 145–158.

WILLIAMS, D. R., & WILLIAMS, H. (1969). Auto-maintenance in the pigeon: Sustained pecking despite contingent non-reinforcement. *Journal of the Experimental Analysis of Behavior, 12,* 511–520.

WINOGRAD, E. (1971). Some issues relating animal memory to human memory. In W. K. HONIG, & P. H. R. JAMES (Eds.), *Animal memory* (pp. 259–278). New York: Academic Press.

WISHNER, J., SHIPLEY, T. E., JR., & HURVICH, M. S. (1957). The serial-position curve as a function of organization. *American Journal of Psychology, 70,* 258–262.

WOODRUFF, G., & PREMACK, D. (1979). Intentional communication in chimpanzees: The development of deception. *Cognition, 7,* 333–362.

WORSHAM, R. W. (1975). Temporal discrimination factors in the delayed matching-to-sample task in monkeys. *Animal Learning & Behavior, 3,* 93–97.

WRIGHT, A. A. (1972). The influence of ultraviolet radiation on the pigeon's color discrimination. *Journal of the Experimental Analysis of Behavior, 17,* 325–337.

WRIGHT, A. A. (1997). Concept learning and learning strategies. *Psychological Science, 8,* 119–123.

WRIGHT, A. A., COOK, R. G., RIVERA, J. J., SANDS, S. F., & DELIUS, J. D. (1988). Concept learning by pigeons: Matching-to-sample with trial-unique video picture stimuli. *Animal Learning & Behavior, 16,* 436–444.

WRIGHT, A. A., COOK, R. G., RIVERA, J. J., SHYAN, M. R., NEIWORTH, J. J., & JITSUMORI, M. (1990). Naming, rehearsal, and interstimulus interval effects in memory processing. *Journal of Experimental Psychology: Learning, Memory, and Cognition, 16,* 1043–1059.

WRIGHT, A. A., SANTIAGO, H. C., SANDS, S. F., KENDRICK, D. F., & COOK, R. G. (1985). Memory processing of serial lists by pigeons, monkeys, and people. *Science, 229,* 287–289.

WRIGHT, R. V. S. (1972). Imitative learning of a flaked stone technology—the case of an orangutan. *Mankind, 8,* 296–306.

WYNN, T., & MCGREW, W. C. (1989). An ape's view of the Oldowan. *Man, 24,* 383–398.

YAMAGUCHI, S.-I., & WARREN, J. M. (1961). Single versus double alternation learning by cats. *Journal of Comparative and Physiological Psychology, 54,* 533–538.

YERKES, R. M. (1925). *Almost human.* New York: Century.

YERKES, R. M. (1927). The mind of a gorilla. II. Mental development. *Genetic Psychology Monographs, 2,* 375–551.

YERKES, R. M., & MORGULIS, S. (1909). The method of Pavlov in animal psychology. *Psychological Bulletin, 6,* 257–273.

YOERG, S. I. (1991). Ecological frames of mind: The role of cognition in behavioral ecology. *Quarterly Review of Biology, 66,* 287–301.

YOERG, S. I., & KAMIL, A. C. (1991). Integrating cognitive ethology with cognitive psychology. In C. A. RISTAU (Ed.), *Cognitive ethology: The minds of other animals* (pp. 273–289). Hillsdale, NJ: Erlbaum.

YOUNG, R. K. (1968). Serial learning. In T. R. DIXON & D. L. HORTON (Eds.), *Verbal behavior and general behavior theory* (pp. 122–148). Englewood Cliffs, NJ: Prentice-Hall.

ZENER, K. (1937). The significance of behavior accompanying conditioned salivary secretion for theories of the conditioned response. *American Journal of Psychology, 50,* 384–403.

ZENTALL, T. (1988). Experimentally manipulated imitative behavior in rats and pigeons. In T. R. ZENTALL, & B. G. GALEF, JR. (Eds.), *Social learning: Psychological and biological perspectives* (pp. 191–206). Hillsdale, NJ: Erlbaum.

ZENTALL, T., & HOGAN, D. (1974). Abstract concept learning in the pigeon. *Journal of Experimental Psychology, 102,* 393–398.

ZENTALL, T. R., & HOGAN, D. E. (1975). Concept learning in the pigeon: Transfer to new matching and nonmatching stimuli. *American Journal of Psychology, 88,* 233–244.

ZENTALL, T. R., & HOGAN, D. E. (1976). Pigeons can learn identity or difference, or both. *Science, 191,* 408–409.

ZENTALL, T. R., & HOGAN, E. (1978). Same/different concept learning in the pigeon: The effect of negative instances and prior adaptation to transfer stimuli. *Journal of the Experimental Analysis of Behavior, 30,* 177–186.

ZENTALL, T. R., HOGAN, D. E., HOWARD, M. M., & MOORE, B. S. (1978). Delayed matching in the pigeon: Effect on performance of sample specific observing responses and differential delay behavior. *Learning and Motivation, 9,* 202–218.

ZENTALL, T. R., & SHERBURNE, L. M. (1994). Transfer of value from S+ to S– in a simultaneous discrimination. *Journal of Experimental Psychology: Animal Behavior Processes, 20,* 176–183.

ZENTALL, T. R., SHERBURNE, L. M., & STEIRN, J. N. (1993). Common coding and stimulus class formation in pigeons. In T. R. ZENTALL (Ed.), *Animal cognition: A tribute to Donald A. Riley* (pp. 217–236). Hillsdale, NJ: Erlbaum.

ZENTALL, T. R., STEIRN, J. N., SHERBURNE, L. M., & URCUIOLI, P. J. (1991). Common coding in pigeons assessed through partial versus total reversals of many-to-one conditional and simple discriminations. *Journal of Experimental Psychology: Animal Behavior Processes, 17,* 194–201.

ZOLADEK, L., & ROBERTS, W. A. (1978). The sensory basis of spatial memory in the rat. *Animal Learning & Behavior, 6,* 77–81.

Index

A

Abs, M., 410
Absolute number discrimination, 303, 304, 310–317
Absolute properties, 161
Absolute threshold, 30, 31
Abstract code, 346, 379
Abstraction principle, 305
Action tests, 380
Adams, D. K., 401
Adams, J. A., 401
Adjunctive behaviors, 257
Alarm calls, 361, 362
Albert, M., 408
Aldridge, J. W., 401
Algorithm, 223
Allan, L. G., 401
Allen, J., 409
Alloway, T. M., 401
Alptekin, S., 405
Altmann, S. A., 433
Ambassador of the mind, 5
Ambient, 60
American Sign Language (ASL), 363
Ammons, R. B., 401
Amsel, A., 401
Analogical reasoning test, 379
Analogous, 23
Analysis of adaptation, 23
Analyzer selection, 51
Anderson, J. R., 401, 411

Anderson, N. H., 423
Anecdotal method, 4
Animal care committees, 25
Animal consciousness, 15–17
Animal Intelligence, 4, 12, 136
Animal psychophysics, 29–32
Animal rights movement, 25
Anisman, H., 401
Anoetic consciousness, 68
Anthropocentric program, 22, 23
Anthropomorphism, 1
Anticipatory errors, 267
Ape language, 367–372
Arbitrariness, 361
Argument from design, 16
Arguments, 126
Aristotle, 2, 122
Armstrong, G. D., 424, 425
Arndt, W., 401
Artificial fruit, 394
Asch, S., 401
Ash, M., 401
Associations, 64, 121
Associative concept learning, 352–356
Associative learning, 121–167
    blocking, 146, 147
    classical conditioning; *see*
        Pavlovian conditioning
    contiguity, 160
    discrimination learning, 143–145, 161–163
    extinction, 145, 146

441

E

I

M

N

Q

Credits

Page 19, Figure 1.4: Hodos, W., & Campbell, C. B. G. (1969). Scala naturae: Why there is no theory in comparative psychology. *Psychological Review, 76,* 337–350. Copyright © 1969 by the American Psychological Association. Reprinted by permission.

Page 32, Figure 2.3: Wright, A. A. (1972). The influence of ultraviolet radiation on the pigeon's color discrimination. *Journal of the Experimental Analysis of Behavior, 17,* 325–337. Reprinted by permission of Indiana University.

Page 35, Figure 2.4: Cook, R. G. (1992). Dimensional organization and texture discrimination in pigeons. *Journal of Experimental Psychology: Animal Behavior Processes, 18,* 354–363. Reprinted by permission. Cook, R. G. (1993). The experimental analysis of cogition in animals. *Psychological Science, 4,* 174–178. Copyright © 1993 by American Psychological Society. Reprinted by permission of Cambridge University Press.

Page 36, Figure 2.5: Blough, D. S. (1989). Odd-item search in pigeons: Display size and transfer effects. *Journal of Experimental Psychology: Animal Behavior Processes, 15,* 14–22. Copyright © 1989 by the American Psychological Association. Reprinted by permission.

Page 39, Figure 2.6: Wasserman, E. A., Kirkpatrick-Steger, K., Van Hamme, L. J., & Biederman, I. (1993). Pigeons are sensitive to the spatial organization of complex visual stimuli. *Psychological Science, 4,* 336–341. Copyright © 1993 by American Psychological Society. Reprinted by permission of Cambridge University Press.

Page 41, Figure 2.7: Van Hamme, L. J., Wasserman, E. A., & Biederman, I. (1992). Discrimination of contour-deleted images by pigeons. *Journal of Experimental Psychology: Animal Behavior Processes, 18,* 387–389. Copyright © 1992 by the American Psychological Association. Reprinted by permission.

Page 44, Figure 2.8: Pietrewicz, A. T., & Kamil, A. C. (1979). Search image formation in the blue jay (*Cyanocitta cristata*). *Science, 204,* 1332–1333. Copyright 1979 by the American Association for the Advancement of Science. Reprinted by permission of Science and authors.

Pages 45–46, Figures 2.9 and 2.10: Reid, P. J., & Shettleworth, S. J. (1992). Detection of cryptic prey: Search image or search rate? *Journal of Experimental Psychology: Animal Behavior Processes, 18,* 273–286. Copyright © 1992 by the American Psychological Association. Reprinted by permission.

Page 48, Figure 2. 11: Blough, D. S. (1993). Effects on search speed of the probability of target-distractor combinations. *Journal of Experimental Psychology: Animal Behavior Processes, 19,* 231–243. Copyright © 1993 by the American Psychological Association. Reprinted by permission.

Page 55, Figure 2.14: Riley, D. A., & Leith, C. R. (1976). Multidimensional psychophysics and selective attention in animals. *Psychological Bulletin, 83,* 138–160. Copyright © 1976 by the American Psychological Association. Reprinted by permission.

Page 59, Figure 2.15: Langley, C. M., & Riley, D. A. (1993). Limited capacity information processing and pigeon matching-to-sample. *Animal Learning & Behavior, 21,* 226–232. Copyright © 1993. Reprinted by permission of the Psychonomic Society, Inc.

Page 61, Figure 2.16: Kraemer, P. J., & Roberts, W. A. (1985). Short-term memory for simultaneously presented visual and auditory signals in the pigeon. *Journal of Experimental Psychology: Animal Behavior Processes, 11,* 137–152. Copyright © 1985 by the American Psychological Association. Reprinted by permission.

Page 74, Figure 3.2: Roberts, W. A (1972). Short-term memory in the pigeon: Effects of repetition and spacing. *Journal of Experimental Psychology, 94,* 74–83. Copyright © 1972 by the American Psychological Association. Reprinted by permission.

Page 76, Figure 3.4: Nelson, K. R., & Wasserman, E. A. (1978). Temporal factors influencing the pigeon's successive matching-to-sample performance: Sample duration, intertrial interval, retention interval. *Journal of the Experimental Analysis of Behavior, 30,* 153–162. Reprinted by permission of Indiana University Press.

Page 78, Figure 3.6: Thompson, R. K. R., & Herman, L. M. (1977). Memory for lists of sounds by the bottle-nosed dolphin: Convergence of memory processes with humans? *Science, 195,* 501–503. Copyright © 1977 by the American Association for the Advancement of Science. Reprinted by permission of *Science* and the authors.

Page 83, Figure 3.8: Grant, D. S., & Roberts, W. A. (1973). Trace interaction in pigeon short-term memory. *Journal of Experimental Psychology, 101,* 21–29. Copyright © 1973 by the American Psychological Association. Reprinted by permission

Page 85, Figure 3.9: Grant, D. S., & Roberts, W. A. (1976). Sources of retroactive inhibition in pigeon short-term memory. *Journal of Experimental Psychology: Animal Behavior Processes, 2,* 1–16. Copyright © 1976 by the American Psychological Association. Reprinted by permission. Roberts, W. A., & Grant, D. S. (1978). An analysis of light-induced retroactive inhibition in pigeon short-term memory. *Journal of Experimental Psychology: Animal Behavior Processes, 4,* 219–236. Copyright © 1978 by the American Psychological Association. Reprinted by permission.

Page 104, Figure 4.4: Sands, S. F., & Wright, A. A. (1980). Serial probe recognition performance by a rhesus monkey and a human with 10- and 20-item lists. *Journal of Experimental Psychology: Animal Behavior Processes, 6,* 386–396. Copyright © 1980 by the American Psychological Association. Reprinted with permission.

Page 108, Figure 4.5: Adapted from Honig, W. K., & Wasserman, E. A. (1981). Performance of pigeons on delayed simple and conditional discriminations under equivalent training procedures. *Learning and Motivation, 12,* 149–170. Copyright © 1981 by Academic Press, Inc. Used with permission.

Page 112, Figure 4.7: Adapted from Urcuioli, P. J., & Zentall, T. R. (1992). Transfer across delayed discriminations: Evidence regarding the nature of prospective working memory. *Journal of Experimental Psychology: Animal Behavior Processes, 18,* 154–173. Copyright © 1992 by the American Psychological Association. Reprinted with permission.

Page 114, Figure 4.8: Spetch, M. L., & Rusak, B. (1989). Pigeons' memory for even duration: Intertrial interval and delay effects. *Animal Learning & Behavior, 17,* 147–156. Copyright 1989 © by Psychonomic Society, Inc. Reprinted with permission.

Page 116, Figure 4.9: Adapted from Grant, D. S., & Spetch, M. L. (1993). Analogical and nonanalogical coding of sample differences in duration in a choice-matching task in pigeons. *Journal of Experimental Psychology: Animal Behavior Processes, 19,* 15–25. Copyright © 1993 by the American Psychological Association. Reprinted with permission.

Page 119, Figure 4.10: Urcuioli, P. J., Zentall, T. R., Jackson-Smith, P., & Steirn, J. N. (1989). Evidence for common coding in many-to-one matching: Retention, intertrial interference, and transfer. *Journal of Experimental Psychology: Animal Behavior Processes, 15,* 264–273. Copyright © 1989 by the American Psychological Association. Reprinted with permission.

Page 139, Figure 5.7: From *The Principles of Learning and Behavior,* by M. Domjan. Copyright © 1998, 1993, 1986, 1982 Brooks/Cole Publishing Company, Pacific Grove, CA 93950, a division of International Thomson Publishing Inc. By permission of the publisher.

Page 151, Figure 5.11: Adapted from Roberts, W. A. (1969). Resistance to extinction following partial and consistent reinforcement with varying magnitudes of reward. *Journal of Comparative and Physiological Psychology, 67,* 395–400. Copyright © 1969 by the American Psychological Association. Reprinted with permission.

Page 164, Figure 5.14: Adapted from Garcia, J., & Koelling, R. A. (1966). Relation of cue to consequence in avoidance learning. *Psychonomic Science, 4,* 123–124. Copyright © 1966 by Psychonomic Society, Inc. Used with permission.

Page 172, Figure 6.1: Adapted from Campbell, B. A., Jaynes, J., & Misanin, J. R. (1968). Retention of a light-dark discrimination in rats of different ages. *Journal of Comparative and Physiological Psychology, 66,* 467–472. Copyright © 1968 by the American Psychological Association. Reprinted with permission.

Page 173, Figure 6.2: Kraemer, P. J. (1984). Forgetting of visual discriminations by pigeons. *Journal of Experimental Psychology: Animal Behavior Processes, 10,* 530–542. Copyright © 1984 by the American Psychological Association. Reprinted with permission.

Page 180, Figure 6.3: Spear, N. E., & Parsons, P. J. (1976). Analysis of a reactivation treatment: Ontogenetic determinants of alleviated forgetting. In D. L. Medin, W. A. Roberts, & R. T. Davis (Eds.), *Processes of animal memory* (pp. 135–165). Reprinted by permission of Lawrence Erlbaum Associates.

Page 183, Figure 6.4: Miller, R. R. (1982). Effects of intertrial reinstatement of training stimuli on complex maze learning in rats: Evidence that "acquisition" curves reflect more than acquisition. *Journal of Experimental Psychology: Animal Behavior Processes, 8,* 86–109. Copyright © 1982 by the American Psychological Association. Reprinted with permission.

Page 185, Figure 6.5: Bouton, M. E., & King, D. A. (1983). Contextual control of the extinction of conditioned fear: Tests for the associative value of the context. *Journal of Experimental Psychology: Animal Behavior Processes, 9,* 248–265. Copyright © 1983 by the American Psychological Association. Reprinted with permission.

Page 187, Figure 6.6: Kraemer, P. J., & Roberts, W. A. (1984). The influence of flavor preexposure and test interval on conditioned taste aversions in the rat. *Learning and Motivation, 15,* 259–278. Copyright © 1984. Reprinted by permission of Academic Press, Inc.

Page 191, Figure 6.7: Adapted from Overton, D. A. (1964). State-dependent or "dissociated" learning produced with pentobarbital. *Journal of Comparative and Physiological Psychology, 57,* 3–12. Copyright © 1964 by the American Psychological Association. Reprinted with permission.

Page 194, Figure 6.9: Wansley, R. A., & Holloway, F. A. (1976). Oscillations in retention performance after passive avoidance learning. *Learning and Motivation, 7,* 296–302. Copyright © 1976. Reprinted by permission of Academic Press.

Page 198, Figure 6.11: Miller, J. S., Jagielo, J. A., & Spear, N. E. (1991). Differential effectiveness of various prior-cuing treatments in the reactivation and maintenance of memory. *Journal of Experimental Psychology: Animal Behavior Processes, 17,* 249–258. Copyright © 1991 by the American Psychological Association. Reprinted with permission.

Pages 202 and 204, Figures 7.1 and 7.2: Etienne, A. S., Maurer, R., & Saucy, F. (1988). Limitations in the assessment of path dependent information. *Behaviour, 106,* 81–111. Copyright © 1988. Reprinted with permission of publisher, E.J. Brill, The Netherlands.

Page 206, Figure 7.3: Collett, T. S., & Land, M. F. (1975). Visual spatial memory in a hoverfly. *Journal of Comparative Physiology A, 158,* 835–851. Copyright © 1975 by Springer-Verlag, Inc. Reprinted by permission of the publisher and author.

Page 207, Figure 7.4: Morris, R. G. M. (1981). Spatial localization does not require the presence of local cues. *Learning and Motivation, 12,* 239–260. Copyright © 1981. Reprinted by permission of Academic Press.

Page 209, Figure 7.5: Cartwright, B. A., & Collett, T. S. (1983). Landmark Learning in Bees. *Journal of Comparative Physiology A, 151,* 521–543. Copyright © 1983. Reprinted by permission of Springer-Verlag, Inc. and the author.

Page 211, Figure 7.6: Collett, T. S., Cartwright, B. A., & Smith, B. A. (1986). Landmark learning and visuo-spatial memories in gerbils. *Journal of Comparative Physiology A, 158,* 835–851. Copyright © 1986. Reprinted by permission of Springer-Verlag, Inc. and the author.

Page 213, Figure 7.7: Adapted from Cheng, K. (1988). Some physophysics of the pigeon's use of landmarks. *Journal of Comparative Physiology A, 162,* 815–826. Copyright © 1988. Reprinted by permission of Springer-Verlag, Inc.

Page 215, Figure 7.8: Adapted from Cheng, K. (1989). The vector sum model of pigeon landmark use. *Journal of Experimental Psychology: Animal Behavior Processes, 15,* 366–375. Copyright © 1989 by the American Psychological Association. Reprinted with permission.

Page 217, Figure 7.9: Poucet, B. (1993). Spatial cognitive maps in animals: New hypotheses on their structure and neural mechanisms. *Psychological Review, 100,* 163–182. Copyright © 1993 by the American Psychological Association. Reprinted with permission.

Page 221, Figure 7.11: Chapuis, N., & Varlet, C. (1987). Short cuts by dogs in natural surroundings. *The Quarterly Journal of Experimental Psychology, 39B,* 49–64. Copyright © 1987. Reprinted by permission of the Experimental Psychology Society.

Page 223, Figure 7.12: Olton, D. S., & Samuelson, R. J. (1976). Remembrance of places passed: Spatial memory in rats. *Journal of Experimental Psychology: Animal Behavior Processes, 2,* 97–116. Copyright © 1976 by the American Psychological Association. Reprinted with permission.

Page 225, Figure 7.13: Olton, D. S., Collison, C., & Werz, M. A. (1977). Spatial memory and radial arm maze performance of rats. *Learning and Motivation, 8,* 289–314. Copyright © 1977. Reprinted by permission of Academic Press.

Page 228, Figure 7.14: Roberts, W. A., & Dale, R. H. I. (1981). Remembrance of places lasts: Proactive inhibition and patterns of choice in rat spatial memory. *Learning and Motivation, 12,* 261–281. Copyright © 1981. Reprinted by permission of Academic Press.

Page 230, Figure 7.15: Suzuki, S., Augerinos, G., & Black, A. H. (1980). Stimulus control of spatial behavior on the eight-arm maze in rats. *Learning and Motivation, 11,* 1–18. Copyright © 1980. Reprinted by permission of Academic Press, Inc.

Page 232, Figure 7.16: Phelps, M. T., & Roberts, W. A. (1989). Central-place foraging by *Rattus norvegicus* on a radial maze. *Journal of Comparative Psychology, 103,* 326–338. Copyright © 1989 by the American Psychological Association. Reprinted with permission.

Page 235, Figure 7.17: Published in Shettleworth, S. J. (1983). Memory in food-hoarding birds. *Scientific American, 248,* 102–110. Reprinted with permission of Tom Prentiss.

Pages 242 and 243, Figure 8.1 and 8.2: Biebach, H., Gordijn, M., & Krebs, J. R. (1989). Time-and-place learning by garden warblers, *Sylvia borin. Animal Behaviour, 37,* 353–360. Copyright © 1989 by Academic Press, U.K. Reprinted with permission.

Page 249, Figure 8.4: Church, R. M. (1978). The internal clock. In S. H. Hulse, H. Fowler, & W. K. Honig (Eds.), *Cognitive processes in animal behavior* (pp. 277–310). Reprinted by permission of Lawrence Erlbaum Associates.

Page 250, Figure 8.5: Dews, P. B. (1970). The theory of fixed-interval responding. In W. N. Schoenfeld (Ed.), *The theory of reinforcement schedules (pp. 43–61).* Copyright © 1970. Reprinted by permission of Prentice-Hall Inc., Upper Saddle River, NJ and the author.

Page 251, Figure 8.6: Roberts, S. (1981). Isolation of an internal clock. *Journal of Experimental Psychology: Animal Behavior Processes, 7,* 242–268. Copyright © 1981 by the American Psychological Association. Reprinted with permission.

Page 251, Figure 8.6: Roberts, W. A., Cheng, K., & Cohen, J. S. (1989). Timing light and tone signals in pigeons. *Journal of Experimental Psychology: Animal Behavior Processes, 15,* 23–35. Copyright © 1989 by the American Psychological Association. Reprinted with permission.

Pages 254–255, Figures 8.7 and 8.8: Roberts, S. (1981). Isolation of an internal clock. *Journal of Experimental Psychology: Animal Behavior Processes, 7,* 242–268. Copyright © 1981 by the American Psychological Association. Reprinted with permission.

Page 259, Figure 8.9: Adapted from Gibbon J., & Church, R. M. (1984). Sources of variance in and information processing theory of timing. In H. L. Roitblat, T. G. Bever, & H. S. Terrace (Eds.), *Animal cognition* (pp. 465–488). Reprinted by permission of Lawrence Erlbaum Associates.

Page 262, Figure 8.10: Cheng, K., & Westwood, R. (1993). Analysis of single trials of pigeons' timing performance. *Journal of Experimental Psychology: Animal Behavior Processes, 19,* 56–67. Copyright © 1993 by the American Psychological Association. Reprinted with permission.

Page 263, Figure 8.11: Adapted from Gibbon, J., & Church, R. M. (1990). Representation of time. *Cognition, 37,* 23–54. Copyright © 1990. Reprinted with kind permission from Elsevier Science—NL, Sara Burgerhartstraat 25, 1055 KV Amsterdam, The Netherlands.

Page 270, Figure 9.1: Roberts, W.A. (1992). Foraging by rats on a radial maze: Learning, memory, and decision rules. In I. Gormezano, & E. A. Wasserman (Eds.), *Learning and memory: The behavioral and biological substrates* (pp. 7–23). Reprinted by permission of Lawrence Erlbaum Associates.

Pages 274 and 276, Figures 9.2 and 9.3: Straub, R. O., & Terrace, H. S. (1981). Generalization of serial learning in the pigeon. *Animal Learning & Behavior, 9,* 454–468. Copyright © by Psychonomic Society, Inc. Reprinted by permission of published and author.

Pages 276 and 277, Figures 9.3 and 9.4: D'Amato, M. R., & Colombo, M. (1988). Representation of serial order in monkeys (*Cebus apella*). *Journal of Experimental Psychology: Animal Behavior Processes, 14,* 131–139. Copyright © 1988 by the American Psychological Association. Reprinted with permission.

Page 282, Figure 9.5: Roberts, W. A., & Phelps, M. T. (1994). Transitive inference in rats: A test of the spatial coding hypothesis. *Psychological Science, 5,* 368–374. Copyright © 1994 by the American Psychological Society. Reprinted by permission of Cambridge University Press.